D1560064

The heart of the commonwealth

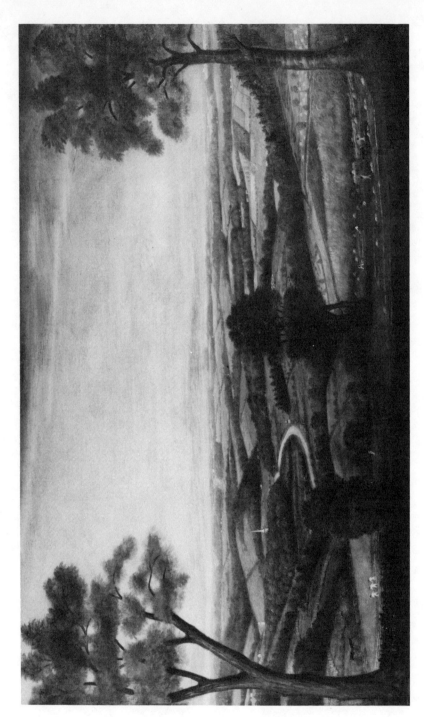

"Looking East from Denny Hill, about 1796," by Ralph Earle.
A view of the town of Worcester as seen from Leicester.
(Courtesy of the Worcester Art Museum, Worcester, Massachusetts)

The heart of the commonwealth
Society and political culture
in Worcester County, Massachusetts
1713–1861

JOHN L. BROOKE
Tufts University

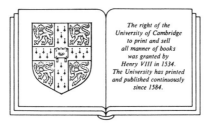

The right of the
University of Cambridge
to print and sell
all manner of books
was granted by
Henry VIII in 1534.
The University has printed
and published continuously
since 1584.

CAMBRIDGE UNIVERSITY PRESS
Cambridge
New York   Port Chester   Melbourne   Sydney

Published by the Press Syndicate of the University of Cambridge
The Pitt Building, Trumpington Street, Cambridge CB2 IRP
40 West 20th Street, New York, NY 10011, USA
10 Stamford Road, Oakleigh, Melbourne 3166, Australia

First published 1989

Printed in the United States of America

Library of Congress Cataloging-in-Publication Data
Brooke, John L.
The Heart of the Commonwealth.
Bibliography: p.
1. Worcester County (Mass.) – History.   2. Worcester
County (Mass.) – Social conditions.   3. Political
culture – Massachusetts – Worcester County.   I. Title.
F72.W9B76   1989   974.4′302   89–9843
ISBN 0-521-37029-9

British Library Cataloguing in Publication Data
Brooke, John L.
The Heart of the Commonwealth: society and political
culture in Worcester County, Massachusetts, 1713–
1861.
1. Massachusetts, Worcester County. Social
conditions, history
I. Title
974.4′3

ISBN 0-521-37029-9 hard covers

For my parents

Contents

Contents

Illustrations and tables

Illustrations

Maps

Figures

Tables

Preface

This is a study of society and public culture in Worcester County, the "Heart of the Commonwealth" of Massachusetts, from the Peace of Utrecht to the Civil War. My purpose is to explore the place of republican and liberal ideology in the experience of this county's people, as they moved from colonial ancien régime through national and industrial revolution to the threshold of modern life. Fundamentally, this is a story of competing visions on a middle landscape of rural neighborhoods, country villages, and growing towns; of how individuals and communities struggled to define their shared social order, after wresting the "wilderness" from the native Algonquin at the end of the seventeenth century, and before being rapidly swallowed up by the "city" in the decades before the Civil War. The debate over republican and liberal ideas has raged for some years in the historiography of early America; I find both sides of the argument powerfully persuasive, and I find ample room for both republican and liberal visions in the narrow confines of Worcester County.[1] In broad overview, this study describes a grand reversal of ideological fortunes, hinging on the triumph of Lockean constitutionalism in revolutionary Massachusetts. A republican vision shaped

---

[1] The debate over the relative significance of republican and liberal ideologies in eighteenth- and early nineteenth-century America is extensive. The republican argument is rooted in Bernard Bailyn, *The Ideological Origins of the American Revolution* (Cambridge, Mass., 1967); Gordon S. Wood, *The Creation of the American Republic* (New York, 1969); and J. G. A. Pocock, *The Machiavellian Moment: Florentine Political Thought and the Atlantic Republican Tradition* (Princeton, 1975). It has been developed for the early national period in Lance Banning, *The Jeffersonian Persuasion: Evolution of a Party Ideology* (Ithaca, 1978); Drew R. McCoy, *The Elusive Republic: Political Economy in Jeffersonian America* (Chapel Hill, 1980); and John Murrin, "The Great Inversion, or Court versus Country: A Comparison of the Revolution Settlements in England (1688–1721) and America (1766–1816)," in J. G. A. Pocock, *Three British Revolutions: 1641, 1688, 1776* (Princeton, 1980), 368–453. The continuing influence of republicanism can be followed in Marvin Meyers, *The Jacksonian Persuasion: Politics and Belief* (Stanford, 1957); Daniel W. Howe, *The Political Culture of the American Whigs* (Chicago, 1979); Michael F. Holt, *The Political Crisis of the 1850s* (New York, 1978); and T. J. Jackson Lears, *No Place of Grace: Antimodernism and the Transformation of American Culture, 1880–1920* (New York, 1981). The liberal thesis has been advanced by Joyce Appleby in "The Social Origins of American Revolutionary Ideology," *JAH* 64 (1978), 935–58; "Commercial Farming and the 'Agrarian Myth' in the Early Republic," *JAH* 68 (1982), 833–949; and *Capitalism and a New Social Order: The Republican Vision of the 1790s* (New

political and social consensus in provincial and revolutionary Massachusetts, while liberal imperatives informed the forces of insurgency. With the ratification of the state constitution in 1780, these positions rapidly shifted; liberal priorities moved to the center of a new consensus, while central republican ideals became the ground for insurgency and protest.

Republican and liberal thought were highly complex; I have found it useful to distill these traditions down to simple visions, summary archetypes that bridge the gap between social experience and intellectual discourse. Thus I find the critical core of republicanism in James Harrington's vision of the independent freeholder acting in defense of an inclusive commonwealth, and the essence of liberalism in John Locke's vision of the rational individual freely entering into association and contract with other such individuals. These Harringtonian and Lockean constructs were not necessarily opposed and antagonistic. Both had been nurtured under the patronage of the Earl of Shaftsbury in his controversy with resurgent absolutism in Restoration England, both were centrally concerned with property and legitimacy, both defended human liberty and equality against arbitrary power. But they did comprise distinct alternatives on a common ideological landscape. Happiness for Harrington lay in the security and stability of the republican commonwealth, maintaining the promise of a historically grounded ancient constitution. A rough equality of condition and the intervention of the political institutions of the commonwealth, the agrarian law and the ballot, were the means to the public virtue necessary for the collective good. In Locke, a theoretical state of nature preempted Harrington's ancient constitution; happiness lay in the security of individual property. Equality and virtue lay in the rational and moral capacities of individuals in the state of nature, rather than in substantive circumstance. Rather than a means to commonwealth, property was an end in itself; the purpose of constituted civil society.

These visions were central elements of a common political discourse shared by Americans throughout this period. In great measure, political worldviews drew

York, 1984); and by Isaac Kramnick, "Republican Revisionism Revisited," *AHR* 87 (1982); and John P. Diggins, *The Lost Soul of American Politics: Virtue, Self-Interest, and the Foundations of Liberalism* (New York, 1985). Jay Fleigelman, *Prodigals and Pilgrims: The American Revolution against Patriarchal Authority, 1750–1800* (New York, 1982), is an important analysis of the influence of Lockean ideas in Revolutionary America. See also Lance Banning, "Jeffersonian Ideology Revisited: Liberal and Classical Ideas in the New American Republic," and Joyce Appleby, "Republicanism in Old and New Contexts," *WMQ* 43 (1986), 3–34; the essays in the special edition on republicanism in *AQ* 37 (1985), and the exchanges in the "Forum" on Wood's *Creation of the American Republic* in *WMQ* 44 (1987), 550–640. For two synthetic views, see Rowland Berthoff, "Peasants and Artisans, Puritans and Republicans: Personal Liberty and Communal Equality in American History," *JAH* 69 (1982), 579–98; and James T. Kloppenberg, "The Virtues of Liberalism: Christianity, Republicanism, and Ethics in Early American Political Discourse," *JAH* 74 (1987), 9–33.

upon a compound of republican and liberal ideals. Certainly the most successful managers of political consensus in Worcester County were able to weave a working synthesis between the two: before 1780, Harringtonian with Lockean undertones; in the decades following, Lockean with Harringtonian undertones. But the status quo was recurrently challenged in episodes of insurgency – episodes when popular mobilization challenged local and metropolitan structures of power and authority – and it was the insurgent coalitions that gravitated to one of the two poles in the common public discourse, insurgencies that were broadly Lockean in form before 1780 and broadly Harringtonian in the decades that followed.

Working from the principle that societies in crisis open views onto fundamental connective tissues linking ideology and experience, this study devotes particular attention to the articulation of ideology in these episodes of insurgency, set in the changing context of economic structures, dominant institutions, and frameworks of legitimacy. My intention is to provide a synthetic view of the social context of ideology and political action over a long period, and thus to suggest patterns of continuity and discontinuity that have been left unexplored by a number of important studies of shorter chronological focus. Though I had hoped to write a "total history" of the public culture of this region, this narrative falls somewhat short of that goal, in that it focuses primarily on the voting or otherwise politically active male population and its relationship with layers of elite authority. To have examined systematically the role of women in the public sphere would have required an entirely different framework of analysis, and a vastly longer text. Thus, unfortunately, in this text women only emerge from the shadows of household production, family reproduction, and church membership onto the public stage in the 1830s.

If it is extensive in its chronology, this study is more limited in its geographic compass, examining a single New England county. Situated on the upland interval between long-settled eastern coast and western valley, Worcester County provides a comprehensive view of Massachusetts society in the eighteenth and early nineteenth centuries, incorporating themes and patterns that characterize very different parts of the state. A central battleground on King Phillip's War of 1675–6, the region that would become Worcester County was settled in the decades following the Peace of Utrecht, by people removing from the old, seventeenth-century towns of the coast and the valley. Areas within this large, sprawling county would take on cultural shadings and economic structures that typified quite different neighboring regions. Most obviously, whereas the north-west uplands shared many qualities with conservative Hampshire County to the west, the Blackstone Valley was an integral part of greater southeastern New England, swept by the formative fires of the Great Awakening. Drawn into the outer edges of the market nets of the port towns of Boston and Providence over the course of the eighteenth century, broad sections of the county would be further interwoven with a capital economy as the processes of industrialization unfolded in the early nineteenth century. And this combination of relatively late settlement followed by rapid economic change spawned a dramatic and unique concentration of political insurgencies between the 1730s and the 1850s. In the 1730s and 1740s Worcester County stood at the forefront of the Popular politics of the Land Bank, followed closely by the Great Awakening and the explosion of dissenting religion. Vigorously involved in the convention politics of the Revolutionary crisis, the county also provided critical support for constitutional demands, economic protest, and armed Regulation in the 1770s and 1780s; in 1788 the county would lead the commonwealth in Antifederalist opposition to the federal Constitution. An intense competition between Federalists and Republicans between 1805 and 1815 was followed in the 1830s by the rise of Antimasonry, and in the decades before the Civil War the county's electorate provided the strc ngest support for political antislavery east of the Burned-Over District. These struggles were patterned in three long cycles, as the relations among electorate, gentry, and metropolis were shaped by differing configurations of conflict and consensus. Roughly speaking, each of these cycles is the subject of one of the parts of the interpretive narrative that follows.

Given its length and detail, I should suggest the outlines of this narrative here. The Prologue discusses the dispossession of the native Nipmucs and the settlement of white households in the late seventeenth century, and the resonances of this process for Harringtonian and Lockean visions of society. Here, my concern is with the emergence of the agrarian middle landscape from the wilderness, a theme that stands as a counterpoint to that of the Epilogue, which discusses the limits that these ideological constructs imposed as the middle landscape gave way to the city in the decades prior to the Civil War. The four chapters of Part I serve a dual role, in part thematic and in part chronological. Chapters 1 and 2 provide an overview of the structure of civil institutions, class, and production that shaped the region until the end of the Revolution, set in the the ideological frameworks of Puritan covenant and monarchical charter. Towns and county courts provided the institutional bulwarks for yeomen and gentry, one overseeing a rough moral economy while the other enforced individual contract. The second half of Chapter 2 introduces the Land Bank, a formative experience for a critically important body of men in the county, and the initial focus of a two-stage process of insurgency in the late provincial era. Although its conception of currency was drastically different from Locke's, the Land Bank is best seen as a Lockean institutional experiment, challenging the corporate institutional order as it offered the possibility of bypassing the gentry's command of credit. Chapter 3 explores the complexities of the Great Awakening in Worcester County. The revivals were critical in drawing the majority of the Land Bankers back into orthodoxy, and situating them permanently on a creative interval between Harringtonian and Lockean visions. The rise of religious dissent, in the form of Separate Baptist societies, introduced an uncompromising and highly successful force for Lockean voluntarism into the county. Having examined institutions, economy, and religion, Chapter 4 takes up political culture, exploring the social dimensions of the county's involvement in provincial politics in thematic fashion, beginning with the Popular Party and the Land Bank insurgency and moving through the remarkable consensus forged by Governor William Shirley in the 1740s and 1750s. Both experiences worked to forge a political tradition that had powerful influences over the next century.

Part II is more simply chronological, resting on the analytical framework established in Part I. Chapter 5 explores the politics of the Revolutionary crisis, particularly the formative role of the Popular party gentry who had their roots in the Land Bank era, and pointing, as have other historians, to the continuities with Shirley's consensus. But if the challenge to British authority lacked the qualities of a local insurgency, it was followed by important episodes that brought insurgent challenges from distinct and opposing quarters. Chapter 6 stresses the role of the Baptists in pressing for a recognition of a Lockean state of nature and for the popular writing and ratification of a constitution. Here I suggest that the principle of voluntary association spread rapidly in the wake of the constitution-making process among strategic groups, marking the emergence of a new social order; Chapter 7 explores another circumstance that was unfolding simultaneously: the economic crisis leading to Shays's Rebellion. Here Harringtonian priorities of independence and commonwealth were primary, and two different social groupings stand out. A perhaps old-fashioned, distinctly orthodox group among the Popular gentry played a central role in the legislative and convention politics of economic protest, and they reemerged to lead the county's staunchly Antifederalist delegation to the Federal ratifying convention. But it was the orthodox yeomen – from regions once dominated by old Court party elites – who stood out among the Regulators who marched to close the courts in the name of the "public good." This Harringtonian extreme was rooted among a people who had no involvement with the Lockean experiments of Land Bank and religious dissent over the previous decades.

Part III, like Part I, serves double duty, combining analysis with narrative. Roughly paralleling Chapters 1 and 2, Chapters 8 and 9 focus on the transformation of public institutions and economic structures that took place between 1790 and 1830. Chapter 8 examines the relationship between voluntary associations and political institutions during the so-called First Party System, and more broadly the first extensive exposure to a competitive political system. Running against the grain of one dominant historiographical school, I suggest that it was the Republicans, with greatest support among the dissenting wing of the old Popular coalition, who articulated a liberal, Lockean vision of the social order, whereas a popular Federalism spoke in Harringtonian terms that would echo far into the nineteenth century. Chapter 9 examines the emergence of the new economic order in some detail – suggesting that there were Federalist and Republican styles of manufacturing, exploring the ways in which the old public institutions of towns and counties were superseded by the new institutions of corporations and banks, and quickly describing the new economy of small-shop networks and factory villages that had emerged by the 1820s. Chapters 10 and 11 turn again to political narrative, and to the grand cycle of political insurgencies running from Anti-masonry through the rise of the Republican Party. Nominally focused on Masonry and the "Slave Power," these insurgencies challenged the Lockean framework of institutional and economic power that had taken hold in Massachusetts since the Revolution. These insurgencies were rooted in the small-shop economy, which, in turn, was grounded in the seedbed of the orthodox wing of the Popular tradition. As was this wing of the provincial Popular experience, Antimasonry and political antislavery were compounded of Lockean and Harringtonian visions. But in the absence of the Harringtonian extreme provided by the Regulators in the 1780s, Antimasonry and Free Soil were the most potent expressions of Harringtonian values of independence and commonwealth in the region's nineteenth-century public culture.

This is a regional study that pays close attention to the relationship between social situation and rhetorical culture. I am concerned with text as rhetoric, as a means by which broad ideological constructs were communicated to peoples in locality, typically by formal and informal speech preserved in print and manuscript, often by the written word in pamphlet and newspaper. I am equally concerned with situation, response, and action. I seek to identify as precisely as possible the circumstances surrounding the production and presentation of a given text: the particular dramas involving particular peoples in which texts articulated ideological constructs and beliefs. Thus I am also concerned with measuring social and political behavior, both in the aggregate, measuring the actions and situations of whole communities across the county in an impressionistic overview, and in individual detail within communities, where the precise dynamic of society, belief, and action can be directly observed.

The analytical narrative that follows is based on several levels of data, each designed to provide a different perspective on the history of the county. First, I have attempted to read as widely as possible in manuscripts, newspapers, pamphlets, and other printed texts to develop a sense of the rhetorical culture deployed in the public arena in Worcester County from its settlement down to the Civil War. In quoting passages from these materials I have tried to preserve the original spelling and grammar as much as possible. Second, I have developed two extensive bodies of quantitative evidence about the aggregate histories of towns as well as personal histories of individuals. At the aggregate, town level, this evidence includes data on population, the economy, debt, the distribution of churches and voluntary associations, and political action recorded in court records, petitions, and voting records. The dominant patterns within this body of data are summarized in the "figures" distributed throughout the text, as determined by logistic regression analyses designed to test the relationships among categorical data. (See Appendix 1 for further discussion.) In addition, I have developed extensive collective biographies of thousands of individuals and families in roughly twelve towns in the county's southwest quadrant, to examine the precise dynamics of society, culture, and politics in a local context. These collective biographies include evidence on kinship, wealth, occupation, debt and credit, neighborhood, gravestone symbolism, religious affiliation, membership in voluntary associations, political action, and service in town government, the militia, as legislative representatives, and as convention delegates. Close attention has been paid to participation in the Land Bank, constitution making, the Regulation, Antimasonry, and antislavery. Participants have been identified from the printed Land Bank mortgage records, towns' archives, the voluminous court records and militia muster rolls relating to the events of 1786–7, and the mass of petitions dating to the 1830s regarding Antimasonry, disestablishment, temperance, the Second Bank of the United States, and antislavery. The families of those individuals politically active during the eighteenth century have been reconstituted from the vital records so as to assess the influence of kinship. Such an effort was simply impossible for the nineteenth century; here only samples of individuals, as well as particularly important or problematical individuals, have been linked to the vital records. The results of these analyses are summarized in tables throughout the text, the notes, and in Appendix 3.

This study had its first manifestations as a seminar paper and a dissertation written under the guidance of Michael Zuckerman at the University of Pennsylvania, from whom I learned to appreciate the complexities and dilemmas inherent in studying past societies. I am similarly indebted to a host of teachers and colleagues from Penn, from my undergraduate days at Cornell, and from my fledgling years as a teacher of history at Tufts, who fostered fruitful environments for learning, research, and writing. I am especially grateful to Robert Ascher, Richard Beeman, Henry Glassie, and Stephen L. Kaplan. Portions of this text have been presented at a number of forums, including meetings of the American Historical Association, the Organization of American Historians, the Society for Historians of the Early American Republic, the Columbia Early American Seminar, the American Antiquarian Society Seminar in Social and Political History, the Boston Area Early American Seminar, and two bicentennial conferences on Shays's Rebellion. In the context of these fellowships, presentations, and a broader scholarly acquaintance, I have learned a great deal from the comments and critiques of fellow scholars; I am especially indebted to Richard D. Brown, Chris Clark, Ronald Formisano, Paul Goodman, Robert Gross, David Jaffee, Kathleen Kutolowski, Lou Mazur, Gregory Nobles, Janet Riesman, Donald Scott, and particularly Robert St. George. Teresa Murphy, Randy Roth, Winifred Rothenberg, Myron Stachiw, and Deborah Van Broekhoven have read all or part of a recent version of the manuscript; their detailed comments have been extremely valuable. I am very grateful to Ned Landsman, who shared his data on early-nineteenth-century Sturbridge and Southbridge at a critically formative stage of my research.

The staffs of a host of libraries and archives have made research on this study both productive and enjoyable: the Historical Society of Pennsylvania; Old Sturbridge Village; the Trask Library at the Andover-Newton Theological School; the Massachusetts Historical Society; the Worcester Historical Museum; the Office of the Clerk of the Supreme Judicial Court; the Worcester County Court House; the Leicester Public Library; the town clerks of Brookfield, Charlton, Leicester, and Sturbridge; and – most importantly – the American Antiquarian Society and the Massachusetts Archives. The staff of the academic computing center at Tufts have been exceptionally helpful in overcoming a range of analytical and technical problems. Carmela Ciampa of Lexington, Massachusetts, transformed a mass of information into the maps and figures. Work on this study has been generously supported over the years by University Fellowships at the University of Pennsylvania, a Samuel Foster Haven Fellowship at the American Antiquarian Society in 1982, a Tufts Faculty Research Award in 1984–5, a National Endowment for the Humanities Junior Fellowship for Research and Writing, and a Charles Warren Fellowship at Harvard University, both in 1986–7. A generous grant from the Tufts/Mellon funds has contributed to the publication costs. Frank Smith, Louise Calabro Gruendel, and Vicki Macintyre – editor, production editor, and copy editor at Cambridge University Press – have, by their expert attention, made this a better book.

I am greatly indebted to Sara C. Balderston for writing a series of sorting and merging programs that allowed me to subdue a host of names in complete freedom from the tyrannies of mainframe computing. My deepest thanks go to Sara, Matthew, and Benjamin for their patience at those times over the last few years when my mind seemed to wander off into another world.

Abbreviations used in the footnotes

AAS	American Antiquarian Society
AHR	*American Historical Review*
AQ	*American Quarterly*
BPAN	Backus Papers, Andover-Newton Theological School
Coll. WSA	*Collections of the Worcester Society of Antiquities*
CSMP	*Colonial Society of Massachusetts Publications*
HWC	*History of Worcester County, Massachusetts*, 2 vols. (Boston, 1879)
JAH	*Journal of American History*
JHRM	*Journal of the House of Representatives of Massachusetts Bay* (Boston, 1919–)
JSH	*Journal of Social History*
MA	Massachusetts Archives
MHS	Massachusetts Historical Society
NEQ	*New England Quarterly*
QHSL	*Quinebaug Historical Society Leaflets*
RTPP	Robert Treat Paine Papers, Massachusetts Historical Society
RWCCP	Records of the Worcester County Court of Common Pleas (at Massachusetts Archives, Columbia Point)
SJC Records	Supreme Judicial Court Records, Suffolk County Court House
SRC	Shays's Rebellion Collection, American Antiquarian Society
WMQ	*William and Mary Quarterly*, 3d series

Prologue: The Nipmuc frontier

On the evening of September 2, 1829, southern Worcester County was struck by a violent thunderstorm, after some days of unseasonable cold. From his farm high on the common at Millbury, the Reverend Joseph Goffe looked out over a landscape lit by an "almost incessant flashing and streaming of lightning" and shaken by the "roar of thunder." Several days later he wrote to his son in Alabama that the lightning "struck in many places, tho' in none very near us. Four barns, with all their contents, were burnt of which we could see the light [of] one in Leicester, one in Paxton, one in Sturbridge, & one in Uxbridge."[1]

In the late twentieth century the broad hills of Worcester County are grown over in a dense cover of deciduous trees, and Goffe's dramatic view of barns burning like matchsticks twenty and thirty miles around would be difficult to replicate. Now a tangle of suburban developments, truck stops, high-speed turnpikes, and scrubby woods, Goffe's view from Millbury Common was of an open landscape of fields, meadows, and dwindling woodlots, ordered by a century of husbandry. In the early years of the new nation such prospects of an agricultural countryside were prized as an emblem of republican virtue and industry. Five miles to the north in Leicester around the turn of the century, Colonel Thomas Denny commissioned Ralph Earle, a noted artist from a local Quaker family, to paint the scene stretching to the east from his father's farm on Denny Hill. In the foreground Earle depicted a group of men cutting hay, with the spires of new churches in the county town of Worcester pointing toward Shrewsbury on the eastern horizon, all set in a mosaic of tilled fields and rolling upland pasture framed in fences and tree lines. Thomas Denny, a prosperous merchant with an interest in sheep raising, moved to the growing central village in Leicester in 1802 to pursue the manufacturing of cards for new wool-carding machines; Earle's painting captured a nostalgic view of the republican countryside for a man responding to the first rumblings of a more complex future.[2]

Passing along the county road from Leicester to Shrewsbury in 1795, Yale president Timothy Dwight was less enthusiastic; he complained of the monotony imposed by "a continued succession of hills and valleys, scarcely distinguishable

[1] Joseph Goffe to Joseph Goffe, Jr., September 8, 1829, Folder 4, Box 3, Joseph Goffe Collection, American Antiquarian Society [hereafter AAS].
[2] Emory Washburn, *Historical Sketches of the Town of Leicester, Massachusetts, during the First Century from Its Settlement* (Boston, 1860), 34, 247–8; Research Files, Worcester Art Museum.

I

from each other in appearance." Worcester County suffered by comparison both with the broad vistas of bleak hilly range and cultivated valley floor along the Connecticut River to the west, and the inherent drama of the indented, sea-struck coast to the east. But Dwight's eye for moral commentary found some virtue in this middle landscape. "In no part of this country," he wrote, was "there a more industrious or thrifty collection of farmers." He admired the "excellent neat cattle" grazing in numbers on the county's high, well-watered hills, and he turned to advantage the inexplicable failure of wheat to thrive in the county. In the absence of local wheat, the customary bread in the region was made from a "dark, glutinous, and heavy" mixture of rye and cornmeal. This rough fare, Dwight wrote, was "preferred by the inhabitants . . . to the best wheaten loaf, and that not by plain people only, but by gentlemen accustomed through life to all that is meant by good living." And, in particular, the material manifestations of agricultural economy drew Dwight's attention. "In no part of this country are the barns universally so large and so good, or the enclosures of stone so general, and everywhere so well formed." Stone walls were, in Dwight's eyes, a central emblem of yeoman virtue. "A farm well surrounded and divided by good stone walls presents to my mind, irresistably, the image of tidy, skillful, profitable agriculture, and promises me within doors the still more agreeable propect of plenty and prosperity."[3]

The open, ordered landscape scoured by lightning in September 1829 was the product of a century of careful husbandry and a symbol of republican order and independence. The property set off by laboriously piled stone walls underwrote a middling plenty; until the constitutional revision of 1821 it also underwrote the right to participate in public affairs, those of both the local community and the state itself, the Commonwealth of Massachusetts. The title of "commonwealth" chosen by the people of Massachusetts in constitutional convention in 1780 evoked a tradition of political economy powerfully persuasive to yeoman freeholders. The seventeenth-century revolutionary upheavals had produced a theory of politics

---

[3] Timothy Dwight, *Travels in New England and New York*, Barbara M. Solomon, ed. (Cambridge, Mass., 1969), 1:265–74. My understanding of the theme of a "middle landscape," situated between wilderness and city, has been shaped by Henry Nash Smith, *Virgin Land: The American West as Symbol and Myth* (Cambridge, Mass., 1950); John William Ward, *Andrew Jackson: Symbol for an Age* (New York, 1953); Leo Marx, *The Machine in the Graden: Technology and the Pastoral Ideal in America* (New York, 1964); Eric Foner, *Free Soil, Free Labor, Free Men: The Ideology of the Republican Party before the Civil War* (New York, 1971); Michael Merrill, "Cash Is Good to Eat: Self-Sufficiency and Exchange in the Rural Economy of the United States," *Radical History Review* 4 (1977); James A. Henretta, "Families and Farms: *Mentalité* in Pre-Industrial America," *WMQ* 35 (1978); and Robert B. St. George, "'Set Thine House in Order': The Domestication of the Yeomanry in Seventeenth Century New England," in J. L. Fairbanks and R. F. Trent, eds., *New England Begins: The Seventeenth Century* (Boston, 1982), 2:159–88.

fundamentally grounded in economy and property. As drawn together in James Harrington's *Oceana*, a name briefly proposed for Massachusetts in 1779, this theory rooted political order in the economic prosperity and independence of a broad spectrum of freeholders, whose liberty from lordships and dependency empowered them to act in the common, public good. Property, independence, and public obligation stood interwoven in the ideal of the Harringtonian republic that the people of revolutionary Massachusetts saw as the model of their condition.[4]

The Harringtonian ideal of the Revolutionary era echoed powerfully in the 1820s, but there were signs that it stood threatened on a number of fronts. New institutional structures were displacing the traditional household as the focus of economic and social action and, similarly, Goffe's open landscape was on the verge of fundamental transformation. Its carefully tended order lay precariously balanced between the inexorable forces of nature and of the city.

If Timothy Dwight saw Worcester County as an agricultural paradise in 1795, the sharp eyes of Jabez Hollingworth, an English immigrant wool machinist employed in the south Leicester mills, caught signs of decline when he wrote his first impressions of the new land to his uncle and aunt in 1827. "Situated near the highest lands in the New England states," the Worcester uplands were, in Hollingworth's view, "not very fit for Agriculture, as it is chiefly barren, stony, and of a sandy soil. . . . Many is going to leave this neighborhood for the Western country to purchase land and settle." Once abandoned, the decline of the countryside could be swift. When James Swan, a profligate gentleman known for his theoretical writings on banking, fled to France to avoid his debtors in the 1790s, the "productive mowing-fields and tillage-lands" on his large estate in Leicester, "after a few years of neglect, were changed into rough and unsavory pastures, covered with brush, and rendered little better than unprofitable wastes." The burdens of debt and costs of production meant that "[l]arge houses half finished and half furnished, and large farms half tilled" were becoming "a striking feature of Massachusetts' scenery."[5]

---

[4] Michael Zuckerman, *Peaceable Kingdoms: New England Towns in the Eighteenth Century* (New York, 1970), 164–5, 190–200; Richard L. Bushman, *King and People in Provincial Massachusetts* (Chapel Hill, 1985), esp. 55–87, 190–206; Chilton Williamson, *American Suffrage: From Property to Democracy, 1760–1860* (Princeton, 1960), 3–19, 190–4; J. G. A. Pocock, *The Ancient Constitution and the Feudal Law: A Study of English Historical Thought in the Seventeenth Century* (New York, 1957), 124–47; J. G. A. Pocock, ed., "Historical Introduction," to *The Political Works of James Harrington* (New York, 1977), 26–7, 42–3, 53–6, 60–8, 144–5; Christopher Hill, *Puritanism and Revolution: Studies in Interpretation of the English Revolution in the 17th Century* (London, 1958), 311.

[5] Thomas W. Leavitt, ed., *The Hollingworth Letters: Technical Change in the Textile Industry, 1826–1837* (Cambridge, Mass., 1969), 14; Washburn, *Leicester*, 166; Emory Washburn, *Address, Delivered before the Worcester Agricultural Society, October 11, 1826: Being Their Eighth Anniversary Cattle Show and Exhibition of Manufactures* (Worcester, 1827), 10–11.

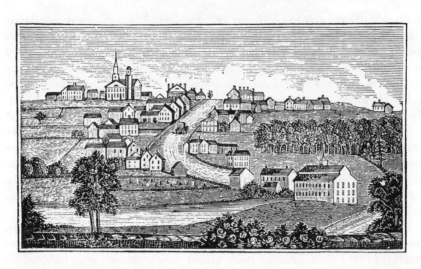

1. Leicester center in the 1830s.
Machine-card shops are located at the outlet of Sargent's Pond in the foreground, and are attached to domestic houses in the village.
From John W. Barber, *Historical Collections ... of Every of Town in Massachusetts* (Worcester, 1839). (Old Sturbridge Village photograph by Henry E. Peach)

2. The Blackstone Canal at the Armory Village, Millbury.
From John W. Barber, *Historical Collections ... of Every Town in Massachusetts* (Worcester, 1839). (Old Sturbridge Village photograph by Henry E. Peach)

Conversely, the celebratory engravings of Massachusetts villages cut in the thirties and published in 1839 in John Barber's *Historical Collections* recorded a second dimension of change on the middle landscape. These pictures depicted orderly villages set in an open countryside, fields bounded by stout stone walls, and streets spotted with ornamental young elms. But here and there a discordant image sticks out in the bucolic scene: the machine-card shop in Leicester at Sargent's Pond; Samuel Slater's long, low cotton mill in Webster; a barge moving smartly along the Blackstone Canal in Millbury; the woolen mills and Hampshire Manufacturer's Bank at Ware Village. If some saw the spread of new productive systems and institutional forms as being compatible with republican virtue and independence, many did not. In 1829 the Jacksonian paper in Worcester attacked the proposal for a western railroad to be built along the old central route through the county from Boston to Springfield. The railroad would introduce a competition that would destroy the farmers' livelihood: "[O]ur territory must therefore become a barren and uncultivated waste, and our people engaged in quarrying marble, mining, or manufacturing." Such employment would surely undermine the rights and liberties of the people. Jabez Hollingworth's brother Joseph made the equation most baldly. "Manufacturing breeds lords and Aristocrats, Poor men and slaves. But the Farmer the American Farmer, he, and he alone can be independent, he can be industrious, Healthy and Happy. I am for Agriculture." Hollingworth may have been "for Agriculture," but his dream of a farm in the west would never be fulfilled; he would spend his life as a textile operative and proprietor of several small shops and mills. The emergence of an urban-industrial order was beginning to undermine the material base of Harringtonian equality and independence. The two were inextricably bound together; the open, middle landscape and the liberties of the people required constant attention and vigilance.[6]

Thick woods and open places

On the verge of decline in the early decades of the nineteenth century, Worcester County's middle landscape was also one of relatively recent origin, in the greater scheme of things. It was shaped by the North Atlantic agricultural traditions of grain and cattle, but it was not ancient and deeply rooted; nature lay waiting in the wings to reclaim its own, as it had done in the recent past.

In 1820 Leicester and Millbury had been settled for only a century. Although scattered attempts at settlement had been attempted since the 1660s, it was only after the Peace of Utrecht in 1713 that the region seemed to be reasonably safe

[6] *Worcester County Republican*, April 1, 1829; *The Hollingworth Letters*, xxv, 23, 75–6, 92–3.

from the Indian attacks that had repeatedly shattered the New England frontier in
the forty years since King Phillip's War. The wave of settlers taking up land in the
decades after 1713 confronted a vast hardwood forest, broken occasionally by
grassy marshes, or "meadows," where the ground was too wet for the trees to take
hold. The material frame of Worcester society would be carved out of these woods,
broken to cultivation, in a process that would continue for the rest of the century.
As late as 1788 a French traveler could with some justice describe Spencer center,
once the west precinct of Leicester, as "a newly built village in the midst of the
woods." As of the 1780s, at best a third of this and the surrounding towns had
been cleared for cultivation and pasturage. By the 1820s, roughly three-fourths of
the land were "improved," the tangled woods giving way to plowland, pasture,
and orchards.[7]

But certainly these woods were not primeval. Rather, they were of recent origin,
indiscriminately covering the carefully tended, open landscape of a prior people.
Native American peoples had inhabited this region for millennia, first as transient
hunter-gatherers, later as relatively dense and sedentary populations of hunter-
horticulturalists, with distinct bands claiming territories of perhaps twenty miles
in diameter, roughly corresponding to the major river drainages. In the seventeenth century the Algonquin-speaking people of future Worcester County were
known as the Nipmucs, or the "Fresh Pond Indians." As did other Algonquin
groups inhabiting the broader hardwood region of southern New England, the
Nipmucs followed a round of subsistence exploiting a variety of ecological zones:
growing corn and squash in village planting fields, fishing in ponds and rivers,
hunting and trapping in dry uplands and wet lowlands. The land bore the mark of
their occupation. Clearing for planting and for winter hearth fires left old village
fields bare; annual burnings cleared brush from abandoned fields and on the drier
upland areas, restoring the low forage for deer and leaving only "a sparse growth of
old timber." In the mid-seventeenth century, the Quaboag Valley was so clear that
lookouts could see from prominent hills; recently burned off, the rise at present
Leicester center was known to the English as "Strawberry Hill." Across the more

[7] Washburn, *Leicester*, 16; William A. Benedict and Hiram A. Tracy, *The History of the Town
of Sutton, Massachusetts, from 1704 to 1876; including Grafton until 1735; Millbury until 1813;
and Parts of Northbridge, Upton and Auburn* (Worcester, 1876, repr. 1970), 12–13; George F.
Daniels, *History of the Town of Oxford, Massachusetts, with Genealogies and Note on Persons and
Estates* (Oxford, 1892), 2–3; Jacques P. Brissot de Warville, *New Travels in the United States of
America, 1788*, trans. by Maria Soceanu Vamos and Durand Echeverria (Cambridge, Mass.,
1964), 108, Improved lands calculated from 1784 Valuation, Microfilm, Massachusetts State
Library, and from statistics in Daniels, *Oxford*, 266; William Lincoln, *History of Worcester,
Massachusetts, from Its Earliest Settlement to September, 1836: with Various Notices Relating to
the History of Worcester County* (Worcester, 1837), 313; Josiah H. Temple, *History of North
Brookfield, Massachusetts. Preceded by an Account of Old Quabaug, Indian and English
Occupation, 1647–1676; Brookfield Records, 1686–1783. With a Genealogical Register* (North
Brookfield, 1887), 374–5.

densely occupied sections of the southern half of the future county, dense forests were only to be found in certain sheltered hardwood groves and swampy bottom lands.[8]

From 1629 to 1675 the Nipmuc and the English found an accommodation of sorts on these open lands. Along a northern and a southern path through this region corn moved from Indian villages to Boston, and Puritan divines and prospectors moved inland in search of souls and precious metals. A gradient of acculturation developed, with praying villages scattered across the southern valleys, most particularly the "hopeful plantation" of Hassanamesit next to the English town of Mendon, standing in contrast to the more traditional Nashaway and Quaboag to the north and west. Even these peoples seemed to be accepting English influences in the 1650s and 1660s, as Puritan outposts were established at Lancaster hard by the Nashaway, at Brookfield in the Quaboag Valley, and just to the east at Worcester. But all of these towns would be swept away in 1675 when the Nipmuc found common cause with other southern Algonquins in King Phillip's War.[9]

By the end of the summer of 1676 the war had run its course, the Nipmucs driven from their hidden encampments in the northwestern uplands, some captured and shot, others sold into slavery. The region lay virtually empty for the next forty years. The Nipmuc populations were decimated, and the English reluctant to move into a dangerous land. Survivors among the praying Indians reestablished small villages in the south, and the English settlements at Lancaster and Mendon were taken up again by 1680. A string of scattered households

---

[8] Temple, *North Brookfield*, 10, 20; Massachusetts Historical Commission, *Historical and Archaeological Resources of Central Massachusetts* (Boston, 1985), 21–49; Washburn, *Leicester*, 21; Henry S. Nourse, *History of the Town of Harvard, Massachusetts, 1743–1893* (Harvard, 1894), 67. More generally, see William Cronon, *Changes in the Land: Indians, Colonists, and the Ecology of New England* (New York, 1983), 24–8, 48–52, Gordon M. Day. "The Indian as an Ecological Factor in the Northeastern Forest," *Ecology* 34 (1953), 329–46; Stanley M. Bromley, "The Original Forest Types of Southern New England," *Ecological Monographs* 5 (1935), 61–89. Stanley W. Bromley, "An Indian Relict Area," *Sci. Monthly* 60 (1945), 153–4, presents evidence that Indians occupying a reservation in Southbridge and Woodstock maintained an open upland forest into the nineteenth century. For a recent critique of the general established thesis of Indian burning, see Emily W. B. Russell, "Indian-set Fires in the Forests of the Northeastern United States," *Ecology* 64 (1983), 78–88. I have benefited from conversations with David Foster and Ernest Gould of the Harvard Forest.

[9] The seventeenth-century history of the Nipmuc lands is detailed in Frederick L. Weis, "The New England Company of 1649 and Its Missionary Enterprises," Publications of the Colonical Society of Massachusetts, *Transactions* 38 (1947–51), 167–70; Daniel Gookin, "Historical Collections of the Indians in New England [1674]," *Collections of the Massachusetts Historical Society*, 1 (1792), 189–95; *History of Worcester County, Massachusetts* (Boston, 1879) [hereafter *HWC*], *passim*; Temple, *North Brookfield*, 20–195; Louis E. Roy, *Quaboag Plantation Alias Brookfield: A Seventeenth Century Massachusetts Town* (West Brookfield, 1965); Lincoln, *Worcester*, 1–39.

8 The heart of the commonwealth

emerged in Worcester and Brookfield in 1684 and 1686, and a tiny group of
Huguenots settled at the meadows in Oxford in 1687; of these, only Brookfield
would survive through the cycle of warfare that began shortly thereafter.[10]

The new settlers at Brookfield were particularly drawn by the tavern trade, their
petition to settle noting that the Quaboag Valley was "a place very commodious for
scittuation in the road to Springfield." By the summer of 1693 three of fourteen
households scattered along the Baypath at Quaboag were licensed as taverns. But
Brookfield was only an isolated outpost in an empty – and changing – landscape.
The renewal of Indian attacks in 1693 provides a view of this inexorable change;
untended by renewing fires, the openings on the land were growing over. In 1675,
when a troop of Brookfield men was ambushed in New Braintree, the survivors
were able to escape by "avoiding any thick woods and riding in open places to
prevent danger." Eighteen years later in 1693 soldiers pursuing Indian raiders had
to fight their way through a trail "most hideous, sometimes swampy, then stony
and horribly brushy, scarce passable for Horses." They found the Indians
encamped in "a most hideous thick woody place." Such "hideous" thick woods
were closing in on the few inhabited places, and provided excellent cover for
Algonquin raiding parties. For the next thirty years attacks on these frontier
settlements invariably came between July and October, high summer and early
fall, when the trees were in full leaf.[11]

Virtually empty of population, either Indian or white, central Massachusetts
in the late seventeenth century became a desolate no-man's-land. Without the
ancient Indian husbandry of annual burning, and not yet broken to the uses of
North Atlantic agriculture, nature reclaimed the land. Open lands, spotted with
old stands of white pine, oak, and chestnut, filled in with weedy trees: ash, birch,
maple. When yeoman householders began to move into the region in numbers
with the Peace of Utrecht in 1713, the unbroken forest they encountered was, in
great part, a recent development obscuring the mark of an earlier people.[12]

[10] Temple, *North Brookfield*, 125ff.; Weis, "The New England Company," 167, 190; Lincoln,
Worcester, 26ff.; Weis, "The New England Company," 167, 190; *HWC*, 2:144; Daniels,
Oxford, 10ff.
[11] Temple, *North Brookfield*, 82, 139–40, 149–51, 166–78; Jonas Reed, *A History of Rutland,
Worcester County, Massachusetts* ... (Worcester, 1838), 97; *HWC*, 1:603, 2:260; Henry M.
Tower, *Historical Sketches Relating to Spencer, Mass.* (Spencer, 1901–9), 1:49–52.
[12] Describing the lower Genessee Valley in 1804, roughly a decade after the land had been
abandoned by the Indians, Timothy Dwight observed that wherever open areas "have been for
a considerable length of time free from fires, the young trees are now springing up in great
numbers, and will soon change these open grounds into forests if left to the course of nature."
Dwight, *Travels*, 4:39. A recent analysis of the forest floor in a "virgin" southwest New
Hampshire forest has demonstrated that there was little disturbance between a fire in 1665 and
a large wind storm in 1897. J. D. Henry and J. M. A. Swan, "Reconstructing Forest History
from Live and Dead Plant Material," *Ecology* 55 (1974), 772–83.

The "inland, vacant places of America"

The regrowth of the forest was only one of a constellation of profound changes marking a more profound transition at the close of the seventeenth century. In the mid-seventeenth century English Puritans had come into the upland interior to save souls and to find exotic minerals. They had acted under divine authority on a grand mission. Eighteenth-century New England yeomen would enter the young wilderness with narrower goals in mind. Their primary concern would be to find a competency for themselves and their families; their religion would have a local, parochial quality. And they would do so within the confines of a dramatically new framework of authority that would place new emphasis on private property, the new charter of government granted to the province by a new constitutional monarchy in 1691.

Settling at a time of great constitutional uncertainty, the Brookfield householders on the Quaboag River were the first to face these new circumstances. While the original settlement had been undertaken in 1665 under the old Winthrop charter, the second began in 1686 under the authority of the government of Sir Edmund Andros, whose entourage rode through the region in October 1688. In June 1692, after Andros had been swept from power and the new charter established, the Quaboag people nervously petitioned the new General Court for the reappointment of a prudential committee of oversight, that they might be "in obedience to their Majs. Royal Charter which of his Royal favour he hath granted to the Province of Massachusetts, former orders now being void." That October, hoping that "the place may go and increase," they petitioned that nonresidents be taxed or give up their holdings, so the petitioners might "in time be better capacitated to serve God and the King & Queen with our persons & Estates." With the 1691 charter, the now-ancient Puritan covenant with God shared equal room with a people's compact with monarchy. Six years later they petitioned for a provincial subsidy to support a minister, but their language suggested as much a concern for things of the world as for those of the spirit.

> [W]e seem called of God, to continue our habitation in this place: We are low in the world, and it would be a breaking thing to our estates to remove to any other plantation; and the Land here is very capable of entertaining a considerable number of people: tho' Inhabitants have been slow to come to us by reason of ye War, yet the land is very Incouraging, capable of affording a comfortable subsistence to many families.

Puritan settlers had long had an eye to their material well-being, but the new framework of government, with political rights extended from the saints to the

freeholders, placed a new premium on property in the political language of the
province of Massachusetts. In a new and closely watched reciprocating compact,
the people would serve the king with their estates, and he would ensure the
circumstances of their "comfortable subsistence."[13]

Life on this frontier outpost was a gamble, but the stakes were high. For the
most part, the heads of these households were men on the leading edge of New
England's third generation, born in the 1660s and married in the 1680s. They were
of a generation for whom life was becoming somewhat confined in the older towns.
Men whose fathers might have had several hundred acres could expect to leave
their sons at best fifty acres, and those worn and used up.[14] Thus the dangers of
Indian attack would have their rewards. Among thirty-three Brookfield men
signing petitions to the General Court between 1698 and 1706, at least three were
killed in Indian attacks, and nine others had died or moved on by the time the
town was incorporated in 1717. But two-thirds of the petitioners survived to be
listed on the new town's first valuation of real property in 1717, and fully one-half
were among the top fifth of the property holders. The rewards for such persistence
could be truly monumental. Joseph Jennings, an innholder and orthodox deacon,
assembled holdings of 1,350 acres; Thomas Barnes, the proprietor of a sawmill,
gathered a total of 1,100 acres. John Hamilton put together a more typical holding
of 556 acres, but far greater than those of his contemporaries in his native
Concord. But not everyone would do this well. John Perry, son of an English
clothworker, settled in 1701 but was only granted 47 acres. He would sell out in
1722, returning to Watertown to die.[15]

Only a third of the early petitioners, a decidedly wealthy group, would have
patrilineal descendants among the taxpayers in 1783, while the patrilineal kin
of most of the poorer households had disappeared. But large landholdings in
1717 did not translate into great wealth in 1783. Rather, the old process of
partible inheritance and land division continued unabated. Although they had
multiplied greatly by 1783, these old families had attained no more than the
"comfortable subsistence" that the early petitioners had hoped for. Few were

[13] Temple, *North Brookfield*, 141, 144–5, 155. For the broader context, see Timothy H. Breen,
The Character of the Good Ruler: Puritan Political Ideas in New England, 1630–1730 (New
Haven, 1970), 180–276.
[14] Philip J. Greven, *Four Generations: Population, Land, and Family in Colonial Andover,
Massachusetts* (Ithaca, 1970), 103–72; Robert Gross, *The Minutemen and Their World* (New
York, 1976), 78ff.; Chistopher M. Jedrey, *The World of John Cleaveland: Family and
Community in Eighteenth Century New England* (New York, 1979), 80–83. This literature is
reviewed in James Henretta, "Wealth and Social Structure," in Greene and Pocock, eds.
Colonial British America, 262–89.
[15] Temple, *North Brookfield*, 505, 650, 703–4.

without property, but few ranked in the top tenth of the taxpaying population.[16]

The surviving families on the early Nipmuc frontier would be joined by thousands of others in the decades after 1713. All pursued the same goal of a "comfortable subsistence," and by the 1790s they collectively had achieved, in Timothy Dwight's turn of phrase, "a tidy, skillful, profitable agriculture." In so doing they had reopened a landscape where nature, over decades of warfare and general abandonment, had obscured the subtle touch of Algonquin lifeway. New England husbandry, in the North Atlantic tradition of grain and cattle, was equally indiscriminate, obliterating nature as it opened the land with unmatched destructive force. The forests were pushed back for cattle grazing, sometimes with wildfires that "greatly injured" the delicate organic soil in upland areas, and in places "destroyed almost the whole growth of timber." Bounties were paid for the extermination of snakes, songbirds, and predators, and the deer were so depleted by the 1730s as to require strict regulation over hunting. And every spring and fall rocky fields were laboriously cleared of the stones that would mark the bounds of private property.[17]

[16] *Wealth and persistence among the Brookfield petitioners, 1698–1783*

| | Petitioning families, 1698–1706, tax decile in 1717 | | | |
| | Family gone by 1783 | | Family present in 1783 | | Descendants of petitioners, tax decile in 1783 | |
Decile[a]						
1	1	*9*	6	*60*	5	*8*
2	3	*27*	2	*20*	8	*13*
3–10	7	*64*	2	*20*	49	*79*
Subtotal	11	*100*	10	*100*	62	*100*
Family gone by 1717	12					
Total	23		10		62	

Note: Figures in italics are percentages.
[a] Decile of tax valuation, 1717 or 1783 (1 = wealthiest tenth).
Among 15 petitioners whose land grant can be accertained, those whose families would persist to 1783 received an average of 518 acres, while those who disappeared received an average of 260 acres. The latter figure is probably too high.
Source: Temple, *North Brookfield*, 194–5, 485ff.; 1783 Valuation of Brookfield, microfilm, Massachusetts State Library, Boston.

[17] Peter Whitney, *The History of the County of Worcester, in the Commonwealth of Massachusetts* ... (Worcester, 1793, repr., nd.), 210, 249; Temple, *North Brookfield*, 201–2; Benjamin Gilbert, *A Citizen Soldier in the American Revolution: The Diary of Benjamin Gilbert in Massachusetts and New York*, ed. by Rebecca D. Symmes, (Cooperstown, 1980), 67.

In this settling on the land, clearing the young wilderness for agriculture in the North Atlantic tradition, one might be tempted to see a social analogue of the political thought of John Locke, the central philosopher in the liberal tradition. The English householders in the Nipmuc country were acting under a new compact with monarchical authority, a contractual relationship that was most notably defined in Locke's *Second Treatise of Government*, establishing the primacy of rational, moral individuals in the state of nature, resisting assertions of arbitrary power, and voluntarily entering into a state of civil society. The Nipmuc settlers seemed to be literally acting out Lockean doctrine, reducing the topographical tabula rasa of the American wilderness, Locke's model of the state of nature, to a civil order. But this Lockean analogue is only of limited value. If Lockean contractualism was enshrined in the 1691 charter, it did not directly inform the shape of local society. Rather, the people's contract with the king acted to reinforce the imperative for corporate unity and unanimity, as a people schooled in Puritan commonwealth confronted the permanent presence of royal authority. Lockean social forms would enter into this local society through insurgent impulses over the decades before the American Revolution and only come to prevail, subject to a continuing contest, after another grand constitutional transformation, that of the 1780s.

The English experience in the Nipmuc lands, and throughout the edge of settlement on the North American coast, lay beyond the limits of Locke's imagination. Locke's state of nature, though filled with references to America, was distant and abstract, not to be directly experienced, and if the New World lay in a state of nature, it was to be shunned. "What would a man value," queried Locke in his essay on property in the *Second Treatise*, "ten thousand, or an hundred thousand acres of excellent *land*, ready cultivated, and well stocked too with cattle, in the middle parts of *America*, where he had no hopes of commerce with other parts of the world, to draw *money* to him by the sale of the product?"[18] For Locke, the focus of legitimate productive endeavor lay at the vortex of established commercial society, not on frontier wild lands.

Contrary to Locke, the settlers on the Nipmuc frontier did indeed value such lands in the "inland, vacant places of America," where as late as 1782 the people of one town could argue that their "distant situation from the metropolis renders the profits of our farms very inconsiderable."[19] Their frontier situation spoke more to

[18] John Locke, *Second Treatise of Government*, ed. by C. B. Macpherson (1690; repr., Indianapolis, 1980), 29. On Locke, see C. B. Macpherson, *The Political Theory of Possessive Individualism* (New York, 1962); John Dunn, *The Political Thought of John Locke* (Cambridge, 1969); John W. Yolton, ed., *John Locke: Problems and Perspectives* (Cambridge, 1969); and Richard Ashcraft, *Revolutionary Politics & Locke's Two Treatises of Government* (Princeton, 1986).
[19] Locke, *Second Treatise*, 23; Spencer Petition. February 11, 1782, Massachusetts Archives [hereafter MA], 187:412.

James Harrington's Oceana than John Locke's state of nature. In choosing to take up land on the frontier, far from "the Maritime and Market Towns," these people were acting out the Harringtonian premise of equality and independence in an expansive agrarian commonwealth. In the 1650s James Harrington had envisioned the conquest of Scotland and Ireland as a means to maintaining the household independence necessary for virtue and stability in his "equal commonwealth." In risking their lives and futures in these "vacant places," these householders were realizing Harrington's military republican utopia, dispossessing Algonquin rather than Irish in their compulsive quest for economic independence.[20] Mitigating the violence of this dispossession was the Harringtonian injunction that private property and personal independence were inextricably tied to public duty and mutual obligation. This equation of independence and commonwealth deeply structured the civil and social fabric of the new towns of the Nipmuc country. And even a century and a half later, after the seeming triumph of Lockean ideals, this Harringtonian equation still echoed powerfully across the old Nipmuc lands, as the young men of Worcester County, as if in atonement for the Algonquin dispossession, marched off in 1861 to save the Union, to the war that destroyed racial slavery and the slave power.

[20] See Pocock, ed., *The Political Works of James Harrington*, 70–2, 181; and *The Machiavellian Moment*, 361–461, 533–45.

PART I

A provincial world, 1713–1763

1

Institutions: Towns, counties, and class

A ritual transfer of civil legitimacy followed the November 1718 incorporation of the settlements on the Quaboag River as the town of Brookfield. Late in the following December Thomas Gilbert, one of the selectmen elected at the first town meeting, rode down to Hatfield in the Connecticut Valley to take the oath of office from Justice Samuel Partridge, whose authority ran to his commission by Governor William Phipps in 1692. Thus anointed, Gilbert returned to the new town and administered the oath to his fellow selectmen. In this manner authority and legitimacy were distributed along a chain descending from the crown to the royally appointed governor, to the governor's justices of the peace and down to the town elders, a chain of legitimation linking the ruled to their rulers in an all-encompassing hierarchy.[1] This chain of authority was inscribed on every warrant for a town meeting, authorized in "his majesties name" by the justices of the peace convened in the County Court of General Sessions. Though functioning as a self-contained and virtually autonomous civil unit, authority and legitimacy within the town in colonial Massachusetts Bay ultimately rested in the king and was overseen by his appointed agents on the county courts. Thus the formal record of each town's proceedings bore the recognition of a power external to the local community, of the fundamental division within early modern Anglo-American society between the ruler and the ruled.[2]

This political language might once have implied the unchecked dominion of king over his people, but by 1718 a century of revolutionary turmoil had undermined whatever claim the British monarchy had to absolute power. The seventeenth century, culminating in the Glorious Revolution, had seen the emergence and legitimation of the mixed polity, with the irreversible establishment of the liberties, rights, and privileges of British subjects. While sover-

---

[1] Francis N. Thorpe, *The Federal and State Constitutions, Colonial Charters, and Other Organic Laws of the States, Territories, and Colonies Now or Heretofor Forming the United States of America* (Washington, D.C., 1909), 3:1882; Louis E. Roy, *History of East Brookfield, Massachusetts, 1686–1970* (Worcester, 1970), 82.

[2] *Town Records of Dudley, Massachusetts*, vol. 1 (Pawtucket, R. I., 1893–4), 73; spelling simplified in places in this quotation.

eignty might ultimately rest in a monarchical figure, the people jealously guarded these rights and privileges against all attempts at arbitrary intervention.[3]

In eighteenth-century Massachusetts Bay, these constitutional antagonisms were manifested most concretely in the public institutions of town governments and county courts. In theory, both fitted into an organic whole, an overarching hierarchy running from crown to subjects. But the towns also derived their functional authority from the consent of the freeholders gathered in town meetings, while the authority of the magistrates of the county courts ran solely from the crown. A subtle but powerful antagonism thus divided town and court, one with firm roots in the seventeenth-century Puritan experience of covenanted collectivity, the other an almost foreign intrusion of a once-renounced monarchy. This antagonism was subtly amplified by its intersection with important divisions within society. The day-to-day workings of towns and courts were taken up with the details of local administration, but they provided an arena in which the relations among social classes were defined and redefined. The most fundamental class division was of course that between the independent householders and the dependent majority. Here the relationship was less one of negotiation than of dictation, as the dependent had only minimal access to institutional power. But access to and control over these public institutions by those of at least minimal propertied independence constituted a central mechanism working to define the relationship among two groupings broadly defined by wealth and influence: the gentry and the yeomen. All independent householders could expect to participate in town government; the town meeting was an arena in which rough yeomen could stand on a level with the local gentry. The social and political personalities of ordinary people were inextricably bound up in the privileges that the towns derived from their corporate status, the frame of a collective moral economy, providing privileges of local empowerment and autonomy that existed in few other places in the early modern world. In contrast, county courts were preeminently the institutions of the gentry: Ruled by leading men, the courts devoted the bulk of their attention to enforcing the private contracts that defined a market economy on the edge of capitalism. Until the emergence of a complex pluralism of private institutions that followed the Revolution, the public institutions of town and court would provide the central arena of class definition and political action in eighteenth-century New England.[4]

---

[3] See Bailyn, *The Ideological Origins*, 22–55, and Wood, *The Creation of the American Republic*, 3–45.

[4] The institutional structure of eighteenth-century Massachusetts has been the subject of some debate. For studies that emphasize the significance of the town, see Zuckerman, *Peaceable Kingdoms*; Gross, *The Minutemen and Their World*; Edmund M. Cook, Jr., *The Fathers of the Towns: Leadership and Community Structure in Eighteenth Century New England* (Baltimore, 1976); Jedrey, *The World of John Cleaveland*; and Christine L. Heyrman, *Commerce and Culture: The Maritime Communities of Colonial Massachusetts, 1690–1750* (New York, 1984). John Murrin has argued persuasively for the increasing importance of the county courts in

The town and the yeomen

The General Court had an overriding purpose in mind when it carefully controlled the incorporation of new towns: the establishment of autonomously functioning communities that would contribute to, rather than draw upon, the public wealth. The province's thirty years of oversight and subsidy of the Brookfield settlement was the exception rather than the rule; in this case the strategic location of the Quaboag Ponds offset the expense of a generally unviable settlement. The settlers of other towns were not so fortunate; a group of Medfield petitioners were repeatedly denied a grant in what was to become Sturbridge because – although it contained an important lead mine – the land was considered too marginal to support a viable community. When the court did grant the "New Medfield" petition in 1729, the stipulated conditions of the grant served as a blueprint for a stable, harmonious, and productive community. The petitioners were to settle

> in seven years time . . . fifty families, each of which to build a house of 18 square feet at least. To break up and bring to, fit for plowing and mowing (and what is not fit for mowing to be well stocked with English grass) seven acres of land. – To settle an orthodox minister, and lay him out a home lot, equal to the other home lots.

Here, then, were the basic elements of what the General Court saw as essential to stability, harmony, and productivity: the exploitation of the land in a "regular way" and the legally mandated material support for the "orthodox Word." From these beginnings each town reproduced a minor variation on the general pattern: a legally structured mesh between the material realities of granted territory and agrarian settlement and the more intangible elements of community unity, moral order, and sacred things. The mechanism tying together the profane and the sacred into an organic bundle was the coercive regulation provided by the town government.[5]

"Anglicizing an American Colony: The Transformation of Provincial Massachusetts," Ph.D. Dissertation, Yale University, 1966, 149–257, and in "The Legal Transformation: The Bench and Bar of Eighteenth Century Massachusetts," in Stanley Katz, ed., *Colonial America: Essays in Politics and Social Development* (Boston, 1971), 415–49. See also John Murrin, "Review Essay," *History and Theory* 9 (1972), 227–75; David T. Konig, *Law and Society in Puritan Massachusetts: Essex County, 1629–1692* (Chapel Hill, 1979); David G. Allen, *In English Ways: The Movement of Societies and the Transferal of English Local Law and Custom to Massachusetts Bay in the Seventeenth Century* (Chapel Hill, 1981), 223–42; Daniel R. Coquillette, "Introduction: The 'Countenance of Authority,'" *Law in Colonial Massachusetts, 1630–1800*, Publications of the Colonial Society of Massachusetts (Boston, 1984); 62:xxi–lxii; and Emory Washburn, *Sketches in the Judicial History of Massachusetts from 1630 to the Revolution in 1775* (Boston, 1840), 151–240.
5 *HWC*, 2:354; Joseph S. Clark, *An Historical Sketch of Sturbridge, Mass. . . .* (Brookfield, Mass., 1838), p. 4.

The issues brought before the town meeting in Dudley in the late 1740s suggest the town government's powers of economic regulation, and the nature of its coerciveness. The people of Dudley considered and passed measures accepting town responsibility for highways, paying for improvements to the meetinghouse, organizing school committees, and building schoolhouses. At the end of every year the town recorded the collection of town, county, and provincial rates and taxes. The minister's salary payment was recorded, as was his provision at town expense of "30 cords of wood for his fires at 30 shillings a cord." Every May the town gathered to choose selectmen and the minor town officials whose job it was to regulate a wide range of economic activities: the clerk of market, the brander of horses, the sealer of leather, the surveyors of shingles, the fence viewers, the tything men, the wardens, and the constables. Occasionally special elections were required, as in March of 1745, when it was "voted that swine shall go at Large being yoked & ringed as ye Law Directs." In keeping with the law requiring that the town monitor aspects of commercial relations, it voted in September 1746 that a "standerd of weights and measures [be] provided for the towns use." In each of these decisions the town intruded into the private autonomy of the individual, requiring him to serve in unpaid menial public positions, to expend time or money for the common good. But behind the town's coercive regulation of the individual stood the seemingly unanimous vote of the town's heads of household; its coerciveness lay not in the threat of external force, but in a shared commitment to a system of corporate oversight that worked to ensure the survival of the community as a legal and social entity.[6]

The people of the town, organized in their respective households, made up a central dimension of a town's calculus of survival. They created the wealth with which the town paid its quota of taxation, and provided the time and energy to serve in unpaid town positions. However, within the context of the town, people were – as the legal verbiage put it – not only "to do duty," but also to "expect privilege." Legal inhabitants of the town could expect support if they fell on hard times. Thus the people of Dudley on several occasions in 1746 and 1747 voted to "grant money to defray the charge of John Rich," who was boarded at various households for one pound a week.[7] On the other hand, these privileges were jealously guarded as the exclusive rights of the legal inhabitants, impoverished noninhabitants being "warned-out." Of equal importance were the efforts of the

---

[6] Temple, *History of North Brookfield*, 226, and Holmes Ammidown, *Historical Collections: Containing . . . the Histories of Seven Towns, Six of Which Are in the South Part of Worcester County, Mass., Namely: Oxford, Dudley, Webster, Sturbridge, Charlton, Southbridge and the Town of Woodstock, now in Connecticut . . .* (New York, 1877), 2:118; *Town Records of Dudley*, 1:136–42. This discussion draws on arguments made by Michael Zuckerman in *Peaceable Kingdoms*, 85ff., and by Oscar and Mary Handlin in *Commonwealth: A Study of the Role of Government in the American Economy, Massachusetts, 1774–1861* (New York, 1947), 53ff.
[7] MA 116:692–3; *Town Records of Dudley*, 1:143–4.

town to prevent viable, prosperous households from separating and joining other towns, thus depleting a finite source of taxes and services.[8] The complementary components in this calculus of survival were the limited resources provided by the land itself. Each town contained within its boundaries a given acreage of improvable land, a finite amount of pasture and mowing meadows, and a certain number of mill sites. Substantial parts of each town were covered with useless cedar bogs, remnants of the postglacial taiga that had covered the area in geologically recent time. The usable features of the land had to be developed as rapidly as possible, and to the best advantage. Mills were a particular problem, requiring a relatively high initial investment; often they were built by the proprietors. In other instances the town offered extra parcels of land in combination with particular mill rights, on the condition that the mill be built within a specified period of time. In one instance, a mill built by the proprietors of the town of Leicester in 1722 had to be abandoned because its pond flooded valuable mowing in the surrounding marshlands.[9]

More often than not, the interests of the proprietors put strain on the limited resources available to the town. Nearly every district or town in southwest Worcester County petitioned at one time or another that the lands of the non-resident proprietors be taxed. The Brookfield householders and tavernkeepers petitioned in 1692 that land claims dating to the earlier settlement be resolved so that taxes could be collected. In Spencer the Reverend Joshua Eaton petitioned the General Court in 1751 for a tax "for the support of your petitioner" on the nonresident proprietors, who owned "above half the land" in the parish. A similar petition from the district of New Braintree, concerning the construction of a meetinghouse in 1756 drew a revealing answer from the proprietors. They claimed that the "Inhabitants" had already sold some of the proprietors' land for taxes, were setting fires and cutting timber on their land, and had chased their cattle "off with their dogs" from the summer grazing on the common lands. In a 1754 petition, the people of the west Oxford lands, soon to be incorporated as the district of Charlton, presented the opposing side of the picture. They complained of "having large herds of cattle brought among us, breaking into our improved lands and destroying our corn and grass, and living so far from the town pound as ten miles, and almost impossible to drive the cattle there; all these things considered, we fear we shall be undone, without the help of the court."[10] Thus the material

[8] Oakham, Mass., Papers, 1770–1867, 1925, AAS. The reverse problem was that of efforts of prosperous outlying households to secede from a town. For a discussion of a typical series of such disputes in Brookfield in the 1750s, see John L. Brooke, "Society, Revolution, and the Symbolic Uses of the Dead: An Historical Ethnography of the Massachusetts Near Frontier, 1730–1820," Ph.D. dissertation, University of Pennsylvania, 1982, 24–8.

[9] *HWC*, 2:355–6; Washburn, *Leicester*, 16, 47; Daniels, *Oxford*, 36–8.

[10] Roy, *East Brookfield*, 46; MA 13:243, 774, 778, 779; MA 116:585–6; quoted in Ammidown, *Historical Collections*, 2:114 with wording regularized.

interests of the inhabitants and of the nonresident proprietors could be distinctly at odds. To the townsmen, the lands held by the proprietors constituted a source of wealth withheld from both private and public use; their grazing of cattle added yet another drain on an already limited set of resources. Private individuals within the town could also threaten common resources. In 1733 the town of Leicester acted against "sum particular persons" who had been "taking in Great Numbers of cattel" for summer feeding, "whereby the feed on the commons in said town is very much diminished." The town voted to levy fines of ten shillings per head, the proceeds to go to the support of the poor. In a near subsistence economy, in a world that faced the reality of a "limited good," private interest was not respected if it interfered with public welfare.[11]

The meetinghouse was the social and physical center of these negotiations, a literal prism of the relationships within town life. Here again, the proprietors had a legal obligation to shape the context of the town's corporate order, an obligation that they generally met, for a completed meetinghouse would attract settlers to their lands. In each case, the meetinghouse would have to be situated at the geographic center of the community, satisfying the centrifugal impulses of out-lying neighborhoods and households. In Oakham, the meetinghouse was to be at the "santer, or next convenient place"; in New Braintree it was to be at "the center of land already laid off." The New Medfield proprietors in 1730 negotiated with the heirs of an early grantee to buy such a location, and set aside the proceeds of seven lots of land to pay for a meetinghouse. This structure, which would serve the people of Sturbridge for fifty years, was to be "fifty foot in Length & fourty foot in Width And Two & Twenty between the sells and plates." Similarly, in 1740 the proprietors of Leicester voted a tax of three pence per acre on their holdings in the western section of the town to assist the people of west Leicester, later Spencer, to build a structure of thirty-five by forty-five feet on land donated "for the accommodation of the meetinghouse, and for a trainingfield, and for such other public uses as the town direct, forever." Slightly smaller meetinghouses built in Leicester and Sutton in 1719 were sheathed in rough clapboards, and the interiors finished with boarding over the post-and-beam framing. The main entry was typically on a long dimension of the building, facing the pulpit, with small doors at each end; small windows of diamond-shaped panes, four below and two above on the long side, framed the minister's pulpit in thin streams of light. With the addition of a long gallery facing the pulpit, an arrangement that called for constant attention and repair, such small buildings would perforce accommodate a burgeoning population until the 1780s, when towns throughout the region built new public structures to carry them into the new century.[12]

[11] Leicester, Mass., General Records [Leicester Town Clerk's Vault], vol. 1 (1720–45), 45, 54.
[12] HWC, 2:120, 159; George H. Haynes, Historical Sketch of the First Congregational Church, Sturbridge, Massachusetts ... (Worcester, 1910), 4; James Draper, History of Spencer, Massachusetts, from Its Earliest Settlement to the Year 1860 ... (Worcester, 1860), 88; Washburn, Leicester, 70–71; Daniels, Oxford, 82–3; Benedict and Tracy, Sutton, 24–5.

These corporate buildings were the arena bringing together the various civil, religious, and military dimensions of the public life of the town. Those involved did not always take these proceedings seriously. Similar to the construction of most structures on this landscape, meetinghouse raisings were notorious for the consumption of alcohol, and for their sexual license; Ebenezer Parkman of Westborough complained at one raising that "the Impudence of Young Men with the Young Women was with them very shameless." Similarly, town-meeting days and weeks could be times of similar frolic. Benjamin Gilbert, a son of a minor gentry family in the North Parish of Brookfield, enumerated in his diary the entertainments of the public days. On March 2, 1778, he spent the afternoon listening to "Complicated Jargon" at the meetinghouse, repaired to Samuel Pickard's tavern, and ended up at a dance until one o'clock in the morning. On the 6th of March, 1780, he attended a town meeting in the West Parish, followed by rum-sling at two taverns on the way home. Three days later he attended a wedding; dancing, drinking, and other festivities continued for the next two and a half days. Late the next May a town meeting in the South Parish was followed by a house raising and "a sort of Militia Training" in the West Parish. A week later the annual "Election at Boston" was marked by three days of dancing and restrained drinking at Moses Hastings's in the South Parish.[13]

But if the town and its corporate life was dominated by a continuing round of negotiation and regulation of limited resources, and made lighter by a round of gregarious festivity, a serious, sacred purpose was always evident as well. Intermingled with work at his father's household and convivial intercourse with his neighbors and others, Benjamin Gilbert regularly attended the funerals of local people, and every Sunday spent morning and afternoon at the orthodox meeting under the eye of the minister. Both brought him to the town's public spaces, indoors and out, where the pews in the meetinghouse and the graves in the burial ground articulated a carefully calibrated hierarchy and geography of family and community honor, unity, and dignity. The legally mandated public support for orthodox religion was a central pillar of the town system. For if the stability of the town depended on the economic regulation of its inhabitants, the purpose of this regulation was, in good part, their spiritual unity and well-being. To ensure the physical unity of its inhabitants, the town laid out a web of roads and tracks to provide each household with "a way to get to mill and meeting."[14] To ensure their spiritual unity, the town assessed these households for the establishment of an orthodox minister of the Word. The relationship between town and minister was

[13] Gilbert, *Diary of a Citizen Soldier*, 26, 65, 69, 73.
[14] Temple, *History of North Brookfield*, 448. See John L. Brooke, "For Civil Worship to Any Worthy Person: Burial, Baptism, and Community on the Massachusetts Near Frontier, 1730–1790," in Robert B. St. George, ed., *Material Life in America, 1600–1860* (Boston, 1988), also published in *Annales: E.S.C.* (1987); and Brooke, "Society, Revolution . . .," 96–110, 361–75.

in theory, and often in practice, one of mutual benefit. This relationship, fusing together profane and sacred categories, was a key social and symbolic buttress of the orthodox moral economy.

In his sermon at the ordination of Brookfield's first regularly established minister in October of 1717, Solomon Stoddard described the relationship rather baldly. "If ministers sow unto them spiritual things, it is not a great thing if they reap their carnal things." This admonition to the congregation against "counting their Ministry a burden" was a part of Stoddard's development of the doctrine that "ministers are by their office to preserve the people from corruption." Beginning from a text from Matthew – "Ye are the Salt of the Earth" – Stoddard built his sermon around the linked metaphors of the preserving qualities of salt and gospel ministers versus the corruptibility of meat and "the inhabitants of the earth." By means of the "constant service" of preaching, instruction (the "sincere milk of the word"), "solemn warnings," "suitable encouragements," and "good government," the minister would "preserve a people from corruption." He would keep them from being "a great affliction one to another," from becoming mired in vice, ignorance, and "formality." What the minister provided was the administration of God's covenant with "his chosen people." Minister and church worked together to create the context where people could "grow in grace" and, in the formulaic words of the pious clause that typically introduced a last will and testament, where they could die "in hope of a Resurrection at the last Day to immortal Glory, thro' Jesus Christ the Resurrection and the Life." The town was a corporate entity to which individuals, as members of patriarchal households, "belonged," where they did "duty" and could "expect privilege." It was not unconsciously that Nathan Fiske, minister of the South Parish in Brookfield, used these terms to describe the sacrament of infant baptism. Baptism brought infants into the covenant, "the promise of the sanctifying influences of the Holy Spirit." The ritual was an important parental duty, for "[t]hrough the channel of the covenant, *salvation come to their house*." This, then, was the spiritual reward for the material support of the Gospel ministry, "the salt of the earth." Their "peculiar privilege" was that they were "God's covenanted people": They enjoyed a special relationship with each other and with their God.[15]

Orthodox townspeople lived in a world defined by a series of interdependent responsibilities and rewards, of "duties" and "privileges." The key to the organic linking of the primary duty of order in household and town and the primary privilege of salvation was the structuring of land, community, and sacred things through the regulation – the moral economy – of the town government. This moral

[15] Solomon Stoddard, *The Duty of Gospel Ministers to Preserve a People from Corruption* (Boston, 1718), 3–4, 20; Nathan Fiske, "The Importance of Baptism," in *Twenty-Two Sermons on Various and Important Subjects; Chiefly Practical* (Worcester, 1794), 131, 133–4 (emphasis in original); Eleazer Ball, Will, 1765, Worcester County Probate Court Records, 2997 (hereafter WCPCR).

economy, and the duties and privileges upon which it was based, derived from the act of incorporation as authorized by the royal charter, but it also rested in a heritage of resistant localism running back to Puritan experiences in late Stuart England. The town was both the locus of legitimacy flowing from the sovereign monarch and a local world controlled and directed by its inhabitants. Beyond the confines of the household this was an open, public world. Its corporate status was the bulwark behind which the ruled were expected to stand united, in order to receive full benefit from its spiritual, political, and material protection. If the 1691 charter had brought a new emphasis on property holding, there survived in the towns a powerful sense of public purpose, of moral oversight and guardianship, firmly rooted in the Puritan tradition of the covenant. The expectation of a minimal well-being, of independence in commonwealth, summarized by the Brookfield petitioners in 1692 as "a comfortable subsistence to many families," was subtly incorporated into this covenant tradition.[16]

The county and the gentry

By the late 1720s, the years following King George's War and the last Algonquin attacks, roughly two-thirds of the old Nipmuc country had been brought under town government. But, just as the settling households were bound in the institutional mesh of town and orthodox church, so too the towns were not isolated polities, but subordinate to county government. The English towns in the Nipmuc country were divided among the counties of Middlesex, Suffolk, and Hampshire, and these early affiliations would color loyalties and affinities for decades to come. In a rough fashion, the geography of the upland extension of these counties into the Nipmuc lands was shaped by the same river drainages that had defined the landscape for the Nipmuc themselves. The towns of the Nashua drainage lay at the outer edge of Middlesex County, those towns in the Blackstone Valley lay in Suffolk County, and Brookfield, situated on the west-flowing Quaboag, were an eastern outpost of Hampshire County. The ease of settling Indian old fields in these river valleys drew the English into the Algonquin settlement pattern in the towns laid out before King Phillip's War: Lancaster, Mendon, Brookfield, Worcester. These older towns centered on broad valley lands would come to dominate the region, with newer towns, situated on the upland interstices, falling within their respective spheres of influence.[17]

[16] On the deeper roots of New England's localism, see Timothy Breen, *Puritans and Adventurers: Change and Persistence in Early America* (New York, 1980), 3–80. For a parallel discussion, see C. J. Calhoun, "Community: toward a variable conceptualization for comparative research," *Social History* 5 (1980), 105ff. The term "moral economy" is adapted from E. P. Thompson, "The Moral Economy o the English Crowd in the Eighteenth Century," *Past and Present* 50 (1971), 76–136.

[17] The definition of the county's regions is discussed in Chapter 4, note 34.

The incorporation of the towns of Rutland, Leicester, and Oxford on the far western fringes of Middlesex and Suffolk counties constituted an important highwater mark. These towns were situated on a low spine of hills running north and south through the region, marking the natural boundary between the broader coastal plain of the Bay and the Connecticut River drainage. The incorporation of these towns in 1713, the year of the Peace of Utrecht, signaled the province's determination to expand its bounds of settlement, confined to a choking point for four decades. But the great distances of these hinterland towns from the courts in Cambridge and Boston would be a source of major grievance. By the late 1720s, with the towns of the Nipmuc country paying only 4 percent of the province tax, elements in the region were emboldened to petition for a new county.[18]

The establishment of a county jurisdiction would do more than simply bring the administration of justice to the center of the old Nipmuc country. The county courts, and the town favored with their location, would be the focal point of the construction of a specific structure of class relations across the county. The towns may have functioned as reasonably autonomous corporate institutions, but they were the legal creatures of the province, which in turn was a royal colony in a widespread empire. Beyond the town stood the urban, mercantile Atlantic world, the centers of education and learning, the sources of political legitimacy and power. The ordinary townsman was aware of his relationship to this wider arena, but typically lacked the cultural and economic resources to engage it on its own terms. To fill this gap a distinct class of legitimators and mediators stood between the townsman and the province, the metropolis, and the empire. If, in Robert Redfield's words, the townsmen were the carriers of the "little tradition," a class of gentry and professionals provided a structural link with the "great tradition" of the Atlantic world. Similarly, county institutions stood at a vitally important point of mediation on this continuum between locality, province, and empire. They would provide the spoils of influence and symbols of ascendancy over which an ambitious gentry would spar for almost a century, until their attention was drawn to new powerful institutional forms.

If the towns were creatures of the covenant, with deep roots in the seventeenth century, the courts were agencies of an intrusive royal power, exclusively rooted in the crown's authority established in the charter of 1691. If Harrington made a prominent place for a ruling gentry – the "horse" in his *Oceana* – there was no monarchical influence in his utopian republic to draw their interests away from the people arrayed in the "foot." But such a monarchical influence intruded upon society in eighteenth-century Massachusetts in the form of the courts. Throughout the century the townsmen would treat these extralocal institutions as a necessary evil. The county courts provided a recourse for justice and a bulwark of

---

[18] *Journals of the House of Representatives of Massachusetts* (Boston, 1919–) [hereafter *JHRM*], 8:70–2, listing of province tax of December, 28, 1727.

order. But their powerful role as an arbiter of economic relationships and contracts and as the focal point of gentry differentiation, aggregation, and predominance would make the county courts the target of hostility and sporadic insurgency, insurgency based upon an inchoate yet distinct politics of household security and corporate solidarity.[19]

The process of county formation began in April 1728, when the young town of Worcester sent a representative to the General Court for only the second time. Captain William Jennison bore with him a petition, which he presented on June 13, 1728, "in behalf of himself and several Inhabitants of the Westerly Towns in the Count[ies] of Suffolk and Middlesex, praying that the several towns enumberated therein may be erected into a separate and distinct County." The petition would move very slowly through committee at the General Court, would not be considered for over a year, and then be only provisionally granted. Another year would ensue before the shire town was established at Worcester, in circumstances that anticipated a central theme in the county's political history.

By size and seniority, Worcester was not the leading town in the Nipmuc country; for decades it would rank behind Lancaster, Mendon, Sutton, and Brookfield in population. But a series of fortuitous advantages worked in its favor, not the least its central location on the Post Road, which would gradually work to reconfigure the political and economic geography shaped by the older counties. The reluctance of Lancaster, and particularly its leading man Joseph Wilder, Esq., to accept even a half-share in the courts, and the turbulence and potential immorality attendant on the court day, played an important role in bringing the courts to Worcester. And it is also highly suggestive that on December 23, 1730, the day of the final vote naming Worcester to be the county town, both William Jennison of Worcester and Maj. John Chandler, the representative from Wood-stock soon to move to Worcester, served on a four-man committee delivering to the governor a bill "for the Relief of, and to Prevent the Oppression of Debtors." This was a continuation of the 1714 legislation that made the paper province bills

[19] Robert Redfield, *The Little Community* (Chicago, 1960), 113–31; *Peasant Society and Culture* (Chicago, 1960), 22–59. My use of the term "mediator" to describe the role of the gentry is influenced by Charles Tilly, *The Vendee* (Cambridge, Mass., 1976), 58–81; and Anton Blok, *The Mafia of a Sicilian Village, 1860–1960: A Study of Violent Peasant Entrepreneurs* (New York, 1974), 25–6. My understanding of the gentry has been influenced by John Clive and Bernard Bailyn, "England's Cultural Provinces: Scotland and America," *WMQ* 11 (1954), 200–13; Murrin, "Anglicizing an American Colony"; Jack P. Greene, "Search for Identity: An Interpretation of the Meaning of Selected Patterns of Social Response in Eighteenth Century America," *JSH* 3 (1970), 189–220; Robert Zemsky, *Merchants, Farmers, and River Gods: An Essay on Eighteenth Century American Politics* (Boston, 1971), 28–98; James Axtell, *School upon a Hill: Education and Society in Colonial New England* (New Haven, 1974), 201–44; and Stephen Innes, *Labor in a New Land: Economy and Society in Seventeenth Century Springfield* (Princeton, 1983). On the "horse" and the "foot," see Pocock, ed., *The Political Works of James Harrington*, 210ff.

legal tender, and was high on the agenda of the Popular Party leadership in the House, specifically house speaker Elisha Cooke, Jr., who would have had the power to accelerate or delay action on the county petition. This early alliance with the Popular leadership would have powerful echoes over the ensuing decades, as the county became a bulwark of the Popular party and its pet project, the Land Bank of 1740.[20]

During the summer of 1731 the courts began to sit in Worcester, first the Probate Court in July, then the Courts of Common Pleas and General Sessions in August, followed in September by a sitting of the traveling high court, the Superior Court of Judicature. The Superior Court would hear the few sensational cases of capital crime, and act upon cases appealed from the lower courts. Most of these cases would come up from the Common Pleas, an endless stream of civil cases of debt and contract, which in turn might have been appealed from the sitting of individual justices of the peace, who heard cases involving value up to forty shillings. The justices would sit in quorum on the General Sessions, overseeing the town governments, laying out the roads, assessing the province and county taxes, and hearing minor criminal cases. In their capacity as county administrators, the General Sessions in September 1731 ordered that a jail be built, to replace the temporary lockup established behind William Jennison's dwelling. The following August they ordered that a courthouse be built on land that Jennison had donated, and asked the advice and financial assistance of "Gent[lemen] at Boston and Elsewhere who have an Interest in Land (in the County and Especially) the Town of Worcester" in building and "adorning" the courthouse.

At the opening of the courthouse in February 1734, Justice John Chandler thanked "Divine Providence," and the benefactions of "sundry worthy gentlemen," for the county's "new and beautiful house, erected purposely for the reception and entertainment of the courts." Chandler's words must have clashed with the circumstances. The surroundings were still primitive; the following May the General Sessions charged a committee to clear the brush around the courthouse and "to make suitable ways to ascend the hill on which it stands." Similarly, the new courthouse measured only thirty-six feet by twenty-six feet, smaller than most meetinghouses, and lacked the height to accommodate galleries. But meetinghouses were designed to hold the entire population of the town in their corporate capacity; the proceedings at the courthouse were the concerns merely of

---

[20] *JHRM* 8:217; 9:134, 149, 173, 364, 365, 376, 381–3; William Pencak, *War, Politics, and Revolution in Provincial Massachusetts* (Boston, 1981), 80–97; Whitney, *County of Worcester*, 9–24; Lincoln, *Worcester*, 58. When the towns were assessed for building the courthouse in 1732, Lancaster was assessed 20% of the total cost, and Worcester only 7%. "Records of the Court of General Sessions," *Collections of the Worcester Society of Antiquity* 5 (1882–3), 59.

those individuals whose cases were being heard, and the attending attorneys and court officers.[21]

The courthouse would not be the sole focus of popular attention on court days. At the opening of the courts in August of 1731 the Reverend John Prentice of Lancaster, echoing the concerns of Squire Joseph Wilder, admonished the people of Worcester to guard against "Sin and Disorder." "Courts held in Country Towns," he stressed, attracted persons "that really have no Business at them," who would "spend their Time unprofitably . . . run[ning] to a great deal of Extravagance of Speech . . . Excess and Intemperance." As Wilder and Prentice feared, the town on court day filled with people looking for amusement, thronging to whippings and occasional hangings. The Sessions Court licensed six taverns in Worcester in 1734 to accommodate the trade of travelers and the court days. The County Road below the courthouse was soon the scene of wrestling matches and horse races; by the 1740s racing on court days became such a problem that it was subjected to a twenty shilling fine to be reserved for the poor of the town of Worcester. Such were the small beginnings of a shire town.[22]

John Prentice's particular concern in his sermon opening the courts that August afternoon was in his charge to the justices. The justices and the county institutions were to act as mediators between a burgeoning population and a covenant-making divinity. "God of his abundant Goodness hath multiplied his People in our Land, & increased them in this Part of the Country, so that it hath been thought needful & convenient, to have an increase in our Counties." The provincial assembly had, in the king's name, established the county and appointed the judges, but they were to act under divine authority and accountability. The judges were "to have the Fear of the Lord upon them, carefully to guard against and avoid all Irregularities, and to do that which is lawful and right." As "Civil Government [was] of God's sovereign *Constitution & Appointment*," the Reverend Prentice charged the judges to "take God for their Pattern."[23]

But, just as revelry and horse racing would violate Prentice's injunctions for order and decorum on the court day, the justices of the Worcester Court were enmeshed in a matrix of worldly concerns that mitigated against the spirit of this divine charge. The court officers appointed in 1731 constituted the nucleus of a gentry class in the new county of Worcester, and their appointments spoke more of

[21] Lincoln, *Worcester*, 58–9, 341–3; D, Hamilton Hurd, *History of Worcester County* (Philadelphia, 1889), 1:xiii–xiv; "Records of the Court of General Sessions," *Coll. WSA* 5 (1882–3), 26–7, 53, 58–9.
[22] John Prentice, *Jehoshaphat's Charge to the Judges Appointed by Him in the Land of Judah, Considered and Applied. A Sermon Preached at Worcester, August 10, 1731, at the Opening of a Court of General Sessions and Inferious Court of Common Pleas, for and within the County of Worcester* . . . (Boston, 1731), 23–4; Lincoln, *Worcester*, 58–9.
[23] Prentice, *Jehoshaphat's Charge*, 6–7, 21–2, and throughout.

a secular pattern of personal ambition than a divine pattern of ultimate judgment. John Chandler, William Jennison, and Joseph Wilder, all involved in the politics of county formation, were appointed justices of the Court of Common Pleas, along with William Ward of Southborough. Chandler was also appointed judge of probate and the first colonel of the county militia. While Judge Chandler remained in the town of Woodstock, where his own father had settled in the 1680s, his son John Chandler, Jr., moved to Worcester in 1731. Appointed clerk of courts and elected registrar of probate, John, Jr., set up in trade on the County Road south of the courthouse, entered town politics as a selectman and representative, and ultimately inherited his father's ranking position in the county. Kinship played a similar role in the appointment of the first county sheriff, Daniel Gookin of Cambridge. Gookin's grandfather had toured the praying Indian towns with John Eliot in 1673, and later received large proprietary land grants in Worcester. Sheriff Gookin also was the son of a former sheriff of Middlesex County, and his experience around the Middlesex jail apparently qualified him for his place in the Worcester County civil list.[24]

The establishment of Gookin and Chandler in Worcester marked the beginning of a long-term process of elite aggregation. The location of the courts at Worcester provided the magnet that would attract generations of aspiring young men of promise from throughout the region. James Putnam, John Adams, and Levi Lincoln would come to learn and to practice law; Stephen Salisbury and Cornelius Waldo would build prosperous merchant houses on the country trade and the traffic moving over the Boston Road from coast and valley. In the long run, the town of Worcester would emerge as a powerful vortex of population, commerce, and public culture, exerting an overwhelming influence on the surrounding region. But the town would not dominate the county until the 1820s. Rather, through the eighteenth century, it competed with a scattering of equally viable central places, shaped by the subtle patterns of river drainage and early county traditions, each with their cluster of leading men. One of the most important attributes of the public culture on this middle landscape, one that would change significantly in the first decades of the nineteenth century, was the widespread distribution of such gentry, broadly educated, with wide-ranging commercial and political contacts, and interrelated in virtual dynasties who acted to define the bounds of legitimacy and to mediate in a multitude of ways between locality and metropolis.

On the county's eastern edge, as with the Wilders at Lancaster and the Wards at Southborough, such leading families had relatively deep roots; to the west they followed the opportunities offered in the opening of the land by a growing population. The towns established along the Boston Road west of Worcester were attractive to professional men looking to establish themselves. Joseph Dwight

---

[24] Hurd, *Worcester County*, 1:vii; Francis Blake, "Some Worcester Matters," *Proceedings of the WSA* 23 (1886), 15–16; Lincoln, *Worcester*, 274–6.

forged a particularly powerful dynasty in Brookfield. Dwight, born into a Hatfield River God family, a Harvard graduate and Springfield merchant, married the granddaughter of John Pynchon, the old Springfield magnate and member of the "prudential committee" appointed to oversee the Quaboag settlements in 1686 and 1691. It was through this connection that Dwight was able to gain title to some of the lands of the original 1665–75 settlement. Moving to Brookfield after his marriage in 1726, Dwight took up land across the road from his uncle, the Reverend Thomas Cheney. With the formation of the county, he was appointed justice of the peace and sworn in as the sole member of the bar. The next year he became county treasurer, in 1734 a special justice, and he sat on the Court of Common Pleas through 1753, when he moved west to Great Barrington to speculate in the new Housatonic lands. All through his years in Brookfield, Dwight dominated the board of selectmen and represented the town for eleven years in the General Court, including one year as speaker. A merchant, his economic and political connections were interwoven with his important role in the affairs of the provincial military establishment. His daughter in turn married Jedediah Foster, another Harvard graduate and a relative of the original settlers from Andover, who had come to Brookfield in 1747. When Dwight moved west to Great Barrington, Foster took over both his lands and his position in the county legal system, and was appointed justice of the peace in 1754 and to the quorum in 1762. Jedediah, and later his son Dwight Foster, were to be the most powerful and influential political figures in southwest Worcester County into the next century.[25]

Men with college educations, legal training, and urban commercial experience could thus move immediately into positions of prominence on the upland frontier. This educated legal elite provided a powerful mode of legitimation. Their application of the common law to the adjudication of civil and criminal cases provided the rough yeoman households striving to "break" the wilderness a slim but important link with the "sacred texts" and deeper traditions of the greater Atlantic World. Their authority in these backcountry towns rested not only in their access to the major intellectual traditions of the Anglo-American world, but in the sets of social relationships, the cultural style, and a broader worldview, developed during a scholarly apprenticeship and reinforced in their continuing links with the metropolis.[26] A sense of the reach that some gentry families might

[25] Clifford K. Shipton, ed., *Sibley's Harvard Graduates* (Boston, 1873–), 7:56–66; D. H. Chamberlain, "Old Brookfield and West Brookfield," *New England Magazine* NS 21 (1899–1900), 498; Zemsky, *Merchants, Farmers, and River Gods*, 55–6; Hurd, *Worcester County*, 1:xviii; Brookfield, Mass. Town Meeting Records, 1719–70 (transcribed by J. Q. Adams, 1875), 6off.

[26] On the growth of the learned professions see Murrin, "Anglicizing an American Colony"; Daniel Calhoun, *Professional Lives in America* (Cambridge, A, 1965); J. William T. Youngs, Jr., *God's Messengers: Religious Leadership in Colonial New England, 1700–1750* (Baltimore, 1976); Donald M. Scott, *From Office to Profession: The New England Ministry, 1750–1800* (Philadelphia, 1978).

attain emerges from a 1768 letter to Jedediah Foster from William Kellogg, a leader among the New England men attempting to establish freeholds on the Livingston manor in the Hudson Valley. Even though the General Court had been dissolved by the governor over the issue of the Circular Letter, Kellogg hoped that Foster would "befriend our cause," as had his father-in-law Joseph Dwight when he moved to Great Barrington. In particular, Kellogg asked Foster to "pay his Honour the Lieut. governor a visit in my behalf and give my duty to him and let him know that my eyes on behalf of the people are still on him and the other gentleman commissioners." Kellogg wanted to know if Foster had agreed to join this commission, established to settle the boundary dispute between New York and Massachusetts, and whether the commissioners would "go over the water" to England to settle the dispute. "We are still a distrest people threatened by tyrants," Kellogg reminded Foster, "and have no medeator but our friends at Boston."[27] Situated on the interval between metropolis and backcountry, the gentry were public men, granted deference in return for mediation with the constitutional framework of the mixed polity.

At least one representative of this legitimating, mediating elite was planted in every town. The development of the professional class began with the sanction of law when, in deeds of incorporation, the provincial government stipulated that the towns must "in seven years time . . . settle an orthodox minister." Despite, or rather to facilitate, his vital role in the organic life of the town as the learned interpreter of Biblical text, the minister was "set apart." Hist effectiveness may have rested in his being "of like mind" with his people, but by law and in theology he was "separated to the work of the Gospel Ministry." Clearly this separateness rested in his education. Ordination sermons rarely neglected to mention that the minister should be of "proper furniture," a "man of knowledge" as well as a "man of religion." The result of both the law and ministerial opinion was that college graduates, typically graduates of Harvard, were settled as established ministers in every town.[28]

The prime characteristic that set the professional apart from his neighbors was thus his education; through his specialized training he had access to the high

[27] William Kellogg to Jedediah Foster, May 31, 1768, Box 33, Folder 8, Foster Family Papers, AAS.

[28] David Hall, *The Vast Importance of Faithfulness in Gospel Ministers. A Sermon Preach'd at the Ordination of Mr Joshua Eaton . . . in Leicester, November 7, 1744* (Boston, 1745), 19–20; Andrew Elliot, *A Sermon Preached at the Ordination of the Reverend Mr. Joseph Roberts . . . in Leicester, October 23, 1754 . . .* (Boston, 1754), 10; Eli Forbes, *The Good Minister. A Sermon Preached at the Ordination of the Reverend Mr. Lemuel Hedge . . . at Roxbury, Canada . . .* (Boston, 1761). The legislation on settling orthodox ministers is summarized in *The Legal Papers of John Adams*, L. K. Wroth and H. B. Zobel, eds. (Cambridge, Mass., 1965), 1:32–47n. Biographical information is from Frederick L. Weis, *The Colonial Clergy and the Colonial Churches of New England* (Lancaster, Mass., 1936).

culture of the Atlantic world. This knowledge of the "sacred texts" of theology and the common law, and their poor cousin, medicine – which bordered on the occult – made him indispensable as a primary legitimator of the social order. But, even including ministers and doctors, the educated professional was a rarity on this upland frontier; such men were only an elite fraction within a broader gentry class. The professional entered these communities from the outside, assuming his station on the merits of his expertise. The greater part of the gentry emerged more slowly, as certain yeoman households accumulated wealth in land, livestock, and improvements, which in turn translated into local prominence and authority. Even more than the professionals, these lesser gentry were caught between two worlds. Their roots lay in particular towns and neighborhoods, yet their prominence and ambition led them into the broader arenas of county and province. There developed, then, in these towns emerging from the wilderness, a gradient of distinction and influence, with gentry families negotiating between two poles of institutional legitimacy: the local covenanted community and the chain of authority running to the charter granted by the crown. This gradient among greater and lesser gentry, each with corresponding degrees of influence among clusters of neighbors and kin, would be of great importance in the articulation of political culture an political action throughout the century.

Entry into gentry position, and the means to further advancement, were the licenses and commissions that fixed a man and his household to the institutional scaffolding of county and province. Appointments of justices of the peace ran from the governor and council, a mark of provincial recognition. These commissions brought with them civil authority, a certain deference, and a modicum of income. Justices collected fees for drafting various writs, summons, recognizances, and warrants, traveling to inquiries, solemnizing marriages, swearing jurors, and attending the courts. But equally importantly, the justices played a powerfully structuring role as members of the Court on General Sessions. The General Sessions heard minor criminal cases and morals cases of fornication and blasphemy, but it also reviewed the operation of town government, assessing taxes and imposing fines. Most importantly, the Sessions Court located and maintained county roads and bridges, the sinews of communication that shaped the economic fate of entire towns. They also licensed innholders and retailers of liquor, after reviewing recommendations of local selectmen. These privileges were thus uniquely suspended between the polities of covenanted corporation and chartered court. The refusal of either body to grant or renew a license, or the delay imposed by the quarterly meetings of the sessions, would have serious consequences for the household seeking such privileges, and required an expensive appeal to the higher authority of the General Court in Boston.[29]

[29] *Acts and Resolves, Public and Private, of the Province of Massachusetts Bay* ... (Boston, 1869–1922), 1:61, 185, 282, 443, 4:291–8, 743–50, 5:240–7; Province Laws (Resolves, etc.) 1767–8, chap. 37, p. 244.

Similarly, officers' commissions in the provincial forces situated aspiring men between locality and province. Their appointments came directly from the governor on the crown's authority, and rested more immediately in the patronage of a more senior officer. Although an officer's appointment was a stepping-stone to gentry rank, his effectiveness rested in his reputation in locality and neighborhood.[30]

The experience of Rufus Putnam of the North Parish of Brookfield in the Lake George campaigns of 1759 and 1760 attests to the raging passions and jealousies attending the distribution of these military honors, to the personal circles of influence around the great gentry figures, and to the relationship between company officers and their neighborhoods. A sergeant in a regiment in 1759 raised by Brig. Timothy Ruggles of neighboring Hardwick, Putnam "wanted to go forward with the army," but – a skilled millwright – he was detailed to build sawmills at the southern outlet of Lake George. Years later Putnam wrote that it was "an arbitrary act ... to compell a Soldier who is a mechanic to work at his trade against his will." Advancement in the world would go to those who distinguished themselves in battle, rather than toiling at a trade behind the lines. He accepted the work only at Ruggles's specific request, whom he had known "for many years," not liking "to offend an officer whome I so highly respected." At the close of the campaign Putnam boarded with a family in New Braintree, a district adjacent to Hardwick, where Ruggles was the leading figure, while clearing some recently purchased land. In the spring of 1760 he was offered recruiting orders by Capt. William Paige of Hardwick, with the expectation of a lieutenant's commission in Ruggles's regiment, which he refused, still smarting from his experiences of the previous summer. But there were also local considerations in New Braintree. "I found that there had been application made in behalf of some older Settlers in town ... whom the Brigadier refused, and some of these appeared very angry, and complained that the Town was insulted by my appointment, therefore I had little reason to expect much success in recruiting among them." When he finally accepted the muster papers, Putnam immediately enlisted a number of experienced soldiers of the neighborhood, but his men were credited to Captain Paige, and he "lost them," and his promise of a commission as well. With Brigadier Ruggles posted to Boston, Putnam was left without a patron, county appointments being put in the hands of Col. Abijah Willard of Lancaster, twenty-five miles away to the northeast. Putnam had no contacts in the Lancaster orbit; Willard "was a total stranger to me and I had no friend to introduce me, and I was too Willfull or too Bashfull to introduce myself." After several weeks in limbo, Putnam was offered an ensign's commission in Willard's regiment. Although he "had expected a Lieutency," Putnam was "really obliged to Colonel Willard for the appointment."

[30] Fred Anderson, *A People's Army: Massachusetts Soldiers and Society in the Seven Years' War* (New York, 1984).

The road to an officer's rank had been a rocky one, but it was an opening into gentry status.[31]

At the end of the 1760 campaign, Putnam's search for advancement took another familiar turn: He married Elizabeth Ayres, the daughter of Squire William Ayres of the North Parish of Brookfield. Buying a mill and privilege in the northeast corner of the parish, Putnam may well have helped Ayres build his own mill in 1762. If so, the marriage was of mutual advantage to this rising young man and to a prominent member of the local gentry. William Ayres also had risen from relatively humble origins. His grandfather had been killed by Nipmuc warriors in Brookfield in 1675, but it was only after the intervention of the General Court in 1713 that his father Joseph had received 132 acres of land in the town. While Joseph had ranked only at the top of the poorest third of the taxpayers on the 1717 valuation (seventh decile), his son William accumulated land and status to become one of the leading men in Brookfield. By the 1750s, when he served several terms as the town's representative to the General Court, Ayres had accumulated 400 acres of land. His rise in the county establishment began in 1744 with an appointment as a coroner, and the year after his election to the General Court in 1753, Ayres was appointed justice of the peace. Reappointed as a justice in 1762, and again by the provisional government in 1775, he ranked among the wealthiest 10 percent when a parish valuation was taken in 1783, and lived to oppose amnesty for the Regulators in the winter of 1786–7.[32]

Receiving his commission at the age of fifty-four, Ayres's rise to prominence typified that of a broad, lesser stratum among the local justices of the provincial period. Among the thirty-one justices appointed in the southwest corner of the county between 1731 and 1774, two paths of recruitment stand out. One was that of the professional men, and those born into families of the judicial elite. Thirteen justices were either college graduates or the sons of other justices. They were quite young, between the ages of twenty-four and fourty-three when commissioned, and on average thirty-one. Although roughly 60 percent of them would serve as representatives, none had been elected at the time of their appointment. Ayres was typical of a second group of eighteen men who lacked the distinction of education or family connections, and whose appointments capped a lifetime of advancement from yeoman status. With one exception, a twenty-seven-year-old son of the Old Light minister in Oxford, they were between the ages of forty-eight and sixty-six in the year of their appointment; on average they were exactly fifty-four years old. Again, roughly 60 percent of them served as representatives, but in this case all

[31] *The Memoirs of Rufus Putnam and Certain Official Papers and Correspondence*, Rowena Buell, comp. (Boston, 1903), 27–33; Temple, *North Brookfield*, 398–410; Putnam's experiences, and the broader context of provincial military experience, are discussed in Anderson, *A People's Army*, 46–8, and *passim*, esp. 26–62.

[32] Temple, *North Brookfield*, 180–1, 496–7; 1783 Brookfield Valuation; Brookfield Protest of 96, MA 190:311–13.

served in the General Court before they became justices. There were thus two paths into the county elite: one through recognized and inherited station, and the other through a gradual process of local emergence and exposure to the legislative process in the provincial capital.[33]

By the early 1760s elective and appointive offices had practically become coterminous; in 1765 over 60 percent of the towns in the county were represented in General Court by justices of the peace.[34] Some of these men would accumulate an even wider range of positions. In the hinterland town of Sturbridge, Moses Marcy parlayed a grant of a mill privilege into holdings of four hundred acres along the Quinebaug River. The only licensed innholder in 1740, he and his son, Jedediah Marcy of Dudley, were both retailers in the early 1770s. In the intervening years Moses Marcy had served as selectman for thirty-one years, and moderator for twenty-four, as well as town clerk and town treasurer for many years and the town's only representative before 1770. Appointed justice in 1754, and serving as a lieutenant colonel in John Chandler's regiment in the French and Indian War, Marcy probably had a hand in his son's lieutenant's commission in Chandler's regiment in 1756, and in his appointment as justice of the peace for Dudley in 1766. An emblematic overmantel picture painted on the woodwork in a front room in the Marcy dwelling around 1760 depicts a figure in an officer's uniform surrounded by the icons of gentry property: a gambrel-roofed house, a full-masted ship, an account book, and the convivial pipe and punch bowl. If this figure is not Marcy himself, it certainly captures the aggrandizing ambitions of the local gentry.[35] At the pinnacle of the county elite, the aggregation of positions could reach epic proportions. In Worcester, the Chandler family and lawyer Timothy Paine – simultaneously and somewhat incestuously a stepson and son-in-

[33] Thirty-one justices appointed in the towns of Worcester, Leicester, Rutland, Hardwick, Brookfield, Spencer, Sturbridge, Oxford, and Sutton between 1731 and 1774. Justices from William H. Whitmore, *The Massachusetts Civil List for the Colonial and Provincial Periods, 1630–1774* (Albany, 1870); college graduates from town histories, and dates of birth from *Vital Records*; see also, Kevin MacWade, "Worcester County, 1750–1774: A Study of a Provincial Patronage Elite," Ph.D. dissertation, Boston University, 1974, 29–31, 36–43.

[34] For discussions of the significance of justices serving as representatives, see Murrin, "Review Essay"; and John L. Brooke, "To the Quiet of the People: Revolutionary Settlements and Civil Unrest in Western Massachusetts, 1774–1789," *WMQ*, 3d. ser., 46 (1989).

[35] Joseph S. Clark, *An Historical Sketch of Sturbridge, Mass., from Its Settlement to the Present Time* (Brookfield, 1838), 8n; *HWC*, 2:355; Nancy S. Voye, ed., *Massachusetts Officers in the French and Indian Wars, 1748–1763* (Boston, 1975); C. D. Paige, "The Marcy Family," *Quinebaug Historical Society Leaflets* [hereafter *QHSL*] 1 (1901–3), 11; Worcester County, Mass., Records of the Court of General Sessions of the Peace [hereafter RCGSP] (County Commissioner's Vault, Worcester County Court House), 2:60, 4:307–8. Kevin Sweeney, "Mansion People: Kinship, Class, and Architecture in Western Massachusetts in the Mid Eighteenth Century," *Winterthur Portfolio* 19 (1984), 248. Old Sturbridge Village research has not definitively determined that the Marcy overmantel is a portrait of Moses Marcy.

3. Overmantel panel, oil on wood, ca. 1760, from a front room in the Col. Moses Marcy house, Sturbridge (now Southbridge), Massachusetts.
(Old Sturbridge Village photograph by Henry E. Peach)

law of John Chandler III – occupied a dizzying array of positions. Paine and six Chandlers received appointments as justices; four ultimately sat on the quorum. They accounted for all the clerks of the courts, and the registrars of probate, for the sheriff after 1751, and for decades of service as judge of probate and – most importantly – justice of the common pleas. Five of them reached the rank of colonel or major of the militia. When they were not representing the town of Worcester in General Court between the 1730s and the 1760s, they were sitting on the governor's council.[36]

The concentration of power and authority among the gentry brought with it a growing social separation from the world of the ordinary households. John Adams's diary of his year as a schoolteacher in Worcester in 1756 records a round of social visits, tea drinking, and dinners with the small group who made up the Worcester elite: Chandlers, Willards, Timothy Paine, Thaddeus McCarty, the orthodox minister who had him hired, and lawyer James Putnam, with whom Adams would clerk over the next few years. The diaries of two ministers in Brookfield, Eli Forbes and Nathan Fiske, suggest less of the stylized detachment of a young Harvard graduate, recording details of household economy and pastoral duty. But these two ministers also recorded a round of visiting, which indicates that exclusive gentry circles were not only to be found in the county town. Fiske visited among a group of families in the Post Road in the South Parish, and was particularly inclined to drink tea at any of three households of the Upham family. Katherine Upham was the widow of Capt. Jabez Upham, a doctor and representative; one son Joshua, a Harvard graduate, was a lawyer and a justice; another son, Phinehas, was in trade and would be a leading Federalist. Forbes's visiting brought him to his brother-in-law's, Capt. Jeduthan Baldwin, to Justice Josiah Converse's, and to merchant Joseph Gilbert's. At an ordination sermon in 1760, Eli Forbes spoke of the "ministerial vow . . . to teach from house to house, by private visits." But neither minister often mentioned religious purposes in their accounts of daily visiting, and they spent a significant amount of time with small cliques of powerful, commercially oriented, gentry families. Bonds of blood, wealth, neighborhood, and shared outlook, authority, and influence separated them from the ordinary householders of the town.[37]

The gentry were similarly separated by the houses that they visited. The typical dwelling on this upland frontier was a single-story or story-and-a-half structure of

[36] MacWade, "Provincial Patronage Elite," 29–43.
[37] *Diary and Autobiography of John Adams*, L. H. Butterfield, ed. (Cambridge, Mass., 1961), 1:1–44; Eli Forbes, "The Diary of Eli Forbes (1762)," *Massachusetts Historical Society Proceedings*, ser. 2 (1892), 7:384–99; Diary of Nathan Fiske (January–July 1771), in "Nathan Fiske Papers, 1750–1799, AAS; Forbes, *The Good Minister*, 20; on tea drinking see Rodris Roth, *Tea Drinking in Eighteenth Century America: Its Etiquette and Equipage* (Contrib. from the Museum of History and Technology, Paper 14, Smithsonian Institution, Washington, D.C., 1961).

700 to 1,000 square feet, usually too small to accommodate the symmetry of the full five-bay Georgian facade. But the leading gentry families – justices and lawyers, merchants, and innholders – built two-story houses with roughly 2,000 feet of floor space and a full Georgian symmetry, certainly by the second half of the eighteenth century. Justice Joseph Dwight built a gambrel-roofed mansion, the mark of the great River God families of the Connecticut Valley; Col. John Murray of Rutland built a hip roofed mansion in the 1750s. As suggested by his overmantel painting, Moses Marcy aspired to the ideal of the two-story mansion, but in reality he could only afford a one and-a-half story saltbox dwelling. Public structures such as the meetinghouses, the taverns, and ultimately the courthouse were two-story, five-bay structures. The two-story form was in itself a symbol of the public role that the gentry assumed, providing space for a range of functions that brought the townsmen into a relationship of deference, while also providing the private spaces of drawing room and office where the gentry families gathered in social circle and business meeting. Such proud structures were few and far between. Looking back on the time of his settlement in the North Parish in 1798, the Reverend Thomas Snell wrote in the 1830 that there had been "not five – if there was one – well-finished and neatly painted house in the town."[38]

If the two-story house was the enduring emblem of gentry aggregation and separation on this middle landscape, the county road stood as an emblem to their primary public role of mediation. As laid out by the General Court and the Court of General Sessions, the roads provided the literal, material link with the outside world, which the gentry attempted to mediate and interpret for the townspeople. The roads brought travelers and soldiers to their taverns, carried their grain and cider to market, brought in the English and West Indian goods that they sold at retail. They were the gentry's conduit to county court and to General Court, where they acted on behalf of individual, familial, and corporate interests.[39] While the ordinary yeoman rarely went more than ten or fifteen miles from his fields and household, and then to court as a debtor or on a military campaign as a common soldier, the gentry were involved in a widespread informal network of peers, which would require at least an annual journey down the Post Road to Boston. The parameters of the yeoman's world were closely defined by the bounds of an almost

---

[38] Sweeney, "Mansion People," 231–55; *Historic Buildings in Massachusetts: Photographs from the Historic Buildings Survey* (New York, 1976), 22, 104, 119, 137; Henry Glassie, *Folk Housing in Middle Virginia: A Structural Analysis of Historic Artifacts* (Knoxville, 1975); Robert B. St. George, "A Retreat from the Wilderness: Pattern in the Domestic Environments of Southeastern New England, 1630–1730," Ph.D. dissertation, University of Pennsylvania, 1982; Brooke, "Society, Revolution . . .," 573–82; "Brookfield Church Council, May 7–8, 1755, in the "Brookfield, Mass., Local Records, 1673–1860," AAS; Thomas Snell, *A Sermon Delivered by the Rev. Dr. Snell on the Last Sabbath in June, 1838 . . . Containing a Brief History of the Town . . .* (Brookfield, 1838), 6–7.

[39] Fiske Diary, May to June, 1771; Gilbert, *A Citizen Soldier*, 67, 71–2.

closed system of local resources, community, and sacred things – a world regulated by the structures and practices of the town. Conversely, the world of the gentry was shaped by repeated crossings of the boundary between isolated locality and cosmopolitan metropolis, linking the concentric circles of town, county, and province that constituted the institutional architecture of social relations in eighteenth-century Massachusetts.

2

Economy: Class, property, credit, and the Land Bank

The aggregation of place by the professional and gentry class suggests that a hierarchy of deferential relations between patron and client might best describe the social order of the provincial Massachusetts upcountry. Great men seem to overshadow this middle landscape, dominating the populace by an accumulation of office, an overbearing display of rank and status, and a manipulation of economic advantage. Such an image leaps from an early nineteenth-century description of Col. John Murray, married to a Chandler, justice of the quorum and representative of the town of Rutland and its associated districts for over twenty years. "[E]nterprising and prosperous he became opulent and popular – being a large land-holder, [he] had some tenants and many debtors. On Representative day all his friends that could ride, walk, creep, or hobble were at the Polls. It was not his fault if they returned dry." Murray thus ruled like an English lord, or a Virginia gentleman, treating his dependents to draughts of rum-sling – and perhaps extensions of credit – on election day. He seems cut from the same cloth as John Pynchon of seventeenth-century Springfield, a landholding entrepreneur whose resources and connections made him the patron, benefactor, and overlord of a broad territory.[1]

Perhaps such lines of dependence were the norm in some places, but one should be careful in equating these upland gentry with the great planters of the Chesapeake. There is also another, very different image of the social order of the provincial Massachusetts countryside, a republican image of relative equals, bound by covenant rather than patronage.[2]

An assessment of the power and authority of the gentry, and of the nature of class relations in this region, requires a shift from impression to proportion. Valuations of property taken at various intervals throughout the eighteenth century provide snapshots of the structure of class and property, and the patterns of debt and credit recorded by the Court of Common Pleas and the Supreme Judicial Court suggest some of the relations between classes. Together, they help

---

[1] Reed, *Rutland*, 157. On Pynchon, see Innes, *Labor in a New Land*.
[2] See Zuckerman, *Peaceable Kingdoms*; Bushman, *King and People*.

to sketch out the connections among class, property, and institutions. The picture that emerges is one of limited and circumscribed gentry power and authority, constrained by a wide distribution of property and by the texture of kinship and exchange in a multidimensional but relatively poor economy. The point at which the gentry had the most leverage on the lives of ordinary householders lay in the supply of credit and in the enforcement of contract through the courts. It was around the flashpoint of credit and debt – and the threat of impoverishment and dependency – that one tradition of popular insurgency would emerge in an episodic challenge to gentry power.

Property and independence

The essential feature of the class structure of eighteenth-century Worcester County was a relatively wide distribution of productive property. Perhaps Colonel Murray owed something of his predominance in Rutland to the loyalty of his tenants, but there is little evidence that farm tenancy was particularly widespread. Compared with the Old World, with other societies in British North America, and with the directions it would take in the early decades of the nineteenth century, society on the Worcester frontier was not marked by extremes of wealth and poverty.

Real and personal property were valued by town, county, and province on legislated valuation years, and the surviving tax valuations provide snapshot views of the distribution of wealth in the region. This distribution suggests a division of the taxpaying population into three broad categories: the gentry, the householding yeomen or husbandmen, and the poorest taxpayers who did not have the property to support a household. Valuations survive for all the towns only for the valuation of 1783, but scattered valuations taken in 1717, 1732, 1740, 1771, 1813, and 1831 suggest the directions of changing patterns of wealth. Overall, the eighteenth-century valuations indicate that wealth was reasonably widely distributed, and that this distribution changed only very slowly. The picture would change rapidly in the first decades of the nineteenth century.[3]

Typically, the absolutely propertyless accounted for less than 20 percent of the taxpayers on each eighteenth-century valuation, and often less than 10 percent. The numbers of the propertyless would increase dramatically after the turn of the century. But those without property accounted for only a part of a larger group who could not have maintained viable, independent households. Between the propertyless and the independent householders lay a number of taxpayers, roughly 20 to 30 percent of the total, paying taxes on small amounts of personal or real property. The upper edge of this group, roughly the seventh poorest decile of the taxpayers, constituted the boundary between independence and dependence.

The town of Leicester provides an example. In 1783, three-quarters of the eighth and ninth poorest deciles held only small amounts of either real or personal property; more that 80 percent of the seventh decile held some of both. The next year, when a much more extensive valuation was taken, almost 70 percent (13/19)

³ *Wealth concentration in Southwest Worcester County, 1717–1860*

	Percentage of total wealth held by top decile	Percentage of taxpayers who were propertyless
Brookfield, 1717	25	n.a.
Leicester, 1732	27	12
Leicester, 1740	34	15
Oakham, 1771	33	21 (real property only)
Worcester, 1771	36	n.a.
Leicester, 1783	35	12
Paxton, 1783	38	6
Oakham, 1783	30	9
New Braintree, 1783	29	24
Spencer, 1783	30	9
Brookfield, 1783		
North Parish	31	16
West Parish	36	12
South Parish	30	2 (adj. to 12)
Charlton, 1783	34	7
Sturbridge, 1783	35	13
Leicester, 1813	51	31
Millbury, 1831	47	47
Ware, 1860	71	over 40
Worcester, 1860	87	over 50
Pelham, 1860	28	over 10

n.a. Not available.

ᵃ After adjustment: the South Parish of Brookfield had very few propertyless taxpayers listed on the 1783 Valuation, which suggests that the parish decided to leave them off. As an adjustment, 17 propertyless "dummies" were added to the original list of 143 total taxpayers, so that the decile ranking of the South Parish taxpayers would be roughly comparable with that of the other parishes and towns.

Source: Brookfield, 1717: Temple, *North Brookfield*, 194–5; Leicester, 1732, 1740: Leicester General Records; Oakham, 1771: Bettye H. Pruit, ed., *The Massachusetts Tax Valuation List of 1771* (Boston, 1978); Worcester, 1771: Cook, *Fathers of the Towns*, 73; 1783 Valuations: microfilms, Massachusetts State Library, Boston; Leicester 1813, Millbury 1831: Leicester Mass., Papers, Millbury, Mass., Papers, AAS; Ware, Worcester, and Pelham, 1860: Robert Doherty, *Society and Power: Five Massachusetts Towns, 1800–1860* (Amherst, 1977), 47. For a review of the literature of economic stratification that emphasizes the changes in relative wealth in the decades following the Revolution, see James Henretta, "Wealth and Social Structure," in Greene and Pole, eds., *Colonial British America*, esp. 275–9.

of the 1783 seventh-decile taxpayers were assessed for a dwelling, as against only 15 percent (3/19) of those in the eighth decile. But the holdings of these seventh-decile taxpayers were clearly insufficient to provide for the needs of a viable farming household. Only a fifth of these taxpayers were assessed for twenty-five acres of improved land including tillage, the bare minimum for household subsistence. Almost half had no tillage at all and less than twenty-five acres of mowing or pasture; this was a group poised on the very knife edge of independence.[4] These seventh-decile households must have rented land to make up the difference, or worked as laborers for others. But most of them paid taxes on a dwelling, and, in general, domestic tenancy must have been a rarity. Out of 125 houses assessed in the town in 1784, only 8 could have been rented out to tenants, these owned by seven men, all in the wealthiest decile, assessed for more than one dwelling. Taxpayers ranking below the seventh decile, then, must have lived as servants and laborers in households belonging to other men; they were thus truly dependent.[5] To a great extent, this boundary between dependence and independence among the taxpayers reflected a hierarchy of age. The vast majority, almost 80 percent, of the Leicester taxpayers ranking below the sixth decile had been born since 1750, whereas 90 percent of those ranking above this line had been born before 1751. In general, then, dependency was a function of age, and the poorer taxpayers might well have expectations of gaining property.[6]

[4] Bettye Hobbs Pruit, "Self-Sufficiency and the Agricultural Economy of Eighteenth Century Massachusetts," *WMQ* 41 (1984), 341; Gross, *Minutemen*, 213–14, n. 35.

[5] *Wealth and ownership of improved land in Leicester, 1783 and 1784*

Decile, 1783 valuation	No improved land, 1784		Improved land, 1784					Total present in 1784
			No tillage, less than 25 acres total		Tillage, less than 25 acres total		Tillage, 25 acres or more total	
high								
1	0		0		0		17 *100*	17
2	1		0		0		17 *94*	18
3	1		0		0		17 *94*	18
4	2		0		2		15 *79*	19
5	3		0		2		14 *74*	19
6	1		2		7 *37*		9 *47*	19
7	2 *10*		6 *32*		7 *37*		4 *21*	19
8	15 *79*		2		2		0	19
9	13 *76*		1		3		0	17
10	12 *100*		0		0		0	12
low								

Note: Figures in italics are percentages.

Source: 1783 and 1784 Valuations of Property, Leicester (State Library).

[6] The relationship of age and wealth in Leicester was very similar to that found elsewhere in eighteenth-century New England. In summary, 88% of the men in the two wealthiest quintiles

If the means of subsistence were quite widely distributed among the taxpayers, this was by no means an egalitarian society. Those without property were the least likely to remain in town, and the least likely to be registered in the vital records. Roughly a third of the propertyless taxpayers in Leicester in 1783 were gone the following year; there was clearly a floating population of young men and women moving from place to place in search of work and a permanent situation. Increasingly, particularly in the war years of the 1760s, these transients would be "warned out" by the town constables: formally notified of their lack of legal residency and threatened with deportation if they failed to show an adequate means of support.[7] Equally importantly, the valuations rarely listed adult women, and these few were widows or occasionally spinsters. Women's lives and productivity were hidden behind a denial of civil status. Lack of civil status was even more of a burden for the relatively few blacks to be found in the region, for the most part slaves before slavery was ruled a violation of the Massachusetts Constitution in 1785. The blacks in the region were a scattered people, less than 1 percent of the population. They lived in lonely isolation in the households of ministers and other gentry, or as servants in taverns, with clusters of fifteen to twenty in some of the leading towns.[8] Their enslavement was an emblem of their owners' gentry status, a faint echo of the absolutist relations structuring the southern colonies. Dependency had its distinctions. Free young men, virtually all white, could expect to rise above the status of laborer in another man's house; women and slaves were locked in their dependent condition by their lack of rights in law and property.

Slavery – the coerced augmentation of household labor – was one marker of the divide that separated the gentry from the ordinary householders of the region. Such divisions were particularly apparent when individuals appeared in court, because they were identified in the records as being a "gentleman" or "esquire," "yeoman," "husbandman," "laborer," or specific type of artisan. These distinctions had a strong but not exclusive relationship with wealth. Among those going to court in 1740 from Leicester, five of six gentlemen ranked in the first decile of

of the 1783 Leicester valuation (46/52) were born between 1701 and 1750; 63% of the third quintile taxpayers (17/27) were born between 1730 and 1750, and 77% of the fourth and fifth quintile taxpayers (34/44) were born between 1751 and 1763. See 1783 Valuation; Washburn, *Leicester*; and Vital Records of Leicester. For comparable evidence from other regions, see Jedrey, *The World of John Cleaveland*, 63–4; Heyrman, *Commerce and Culture*, 48; and Jackson T. Main, *Society and Economy in Colonial Connecticut* (Princeton, 1985), 136–51.

[7] Douglas L. Jones, *Village and Seaport: Migration and Society in Eighteenth Century Massachusetts* (Hanover, N. H., 1981); Francis E. Blake, ed., *Worcester County, Massachusetts, Warnings, 1737–1788* (Worcester, 1899).

[8] Black populations are summarized in the 1764 census published in Josiah H. Benton, comp., *Early Census Making in Massachusetts. 1643–1765* (Boston, 1905); and the *Return of the Whole Number of Persons within the Several Districts of the United States* ... (Philadelphia, 1791), 29–31. A review of "all other free persons" (neither white nor Indian) in the 1790 U.S. Census of Heads of Households shows that they were concentrated in gentry households. See also advertisements for sale of slaves, for example, *Spy*, December 11, 1776.

the 1740 valuation, yeomen were scattered between the second and fourth deciles, and husbandmen between second and eighth deciles. Four and a half decades later, those going to court from six towns in the region showed a similar ranking and grading by wealth, although the pattern was less sharply defined. In a sense there had been a certain rank inflation, perhaps the result of war and upheaval. Few used the label of "husbandman," and those calling themselves "gentleman" were more widely distributed along the spectrum of wealth. But they were distinctly concentrated in the wealthiest tenth of the population, as against yeomen, who made up the better part of the subsequent wealth ranks.[9]

Among a people involved in a basic but diversified agriculture, wealth reflected

[9] *Status and wealth of those in WCCP from Leicester, 1740*

Rank on 1740 valuation Decile	Gentlemen	Innholders	Yeomen	Husbandmen	Artisans	Total
1st Decile	6	1			1	8
2d Decile	1		1	1		3
2d Quintile		1	3	3	1	8
3d Quintile				5		5
4th Quintile				2	1	3
5th Quintile					2	2
Total	7	2	4	11	5	29

Note: For simplicity, esquires, attorneys, sheriffs, and physicians have been included in the "gentlemen" category, and traders and retailers have been included in the "innholders" category in this and the following table.
Source: Worcester County, Mass., Records of the Court of Common Pleas [hereafter RWCCP], 2:191–279; Province Tax List, October 20, 1740, in Leicester General Records, vol. 1 (1722–45).

Status and wealth of those in WCCP from six towns, 1785–6

Rank on 1783 valuation Decile	Gentlemen	Innholders	Yeomen	Husbandmen	Artisans	Total
1st Decile	31	2	7	1	5	46
2d Decile	8	1	18	2	2	31
2d Quintile	10	3	21	5	2	41
3d Quintile	11		11	3	3	28
4th Quintile	2	2	6	1	3	14
5th Quintile	1		3	1	2	7
Total	63	8	66	13	17	167

Note: Plaintiffs and defendants in Court of Common Pleas, December 1785 to June 1786, from the towns of Leicester, Spencer, Oakham, Brookfield, Sturbridge, and Charlton.
Source: RWCCP 13: 1–280; 1783 valuations.

an ability to participate in the wider commercial economy as well as to provide for household needs. The households in the wealthiest fifth of the taxpaying population were able to command labor and resources to strengthen their position on the land. In Leicester in the early 1780s these wealthiest households typically held ten to thirteen cattle and almost as many sheep, while the sixth decile households might have a third as many. These wealthiest households paid tax on between three and five acres under the plow in tillage, while the sixth-decile households had at best one acre. At the yields prevailing in Oakham and New Braintree in 1771, this might make the difference between fifty to sixty bushels of grain and ten to twelve bushels. Given a bare subsistence figure of sixteen bushels per poll, the poorer households would be short by several bushels, while the wealthier households might have a significant surplus. Similarly, the wealthiest households typically produced at least ten barrels of cider, while poorer households might not produce any at all. Cattle, grain, cider – these were commodities that might be traded locally or be sold at market. The wealthier households typically kept a pair of horses in addition to a pair of oxen; thus they had the animal traction necessary to move grain or cider to market in Worcester or Boston. But in the greater scheme of things, these were not overwhelming differences. The distance from market over bad roads limited the commercial opportunities of the wealthier households; and a diversified agriculture, as against a slave-based monocrop, made it even more difficult for a given family or group of families to emerge and tower over their neighbors.[10]

[10] *Assessed tillage, cider production, and pairs of horses and oxen, Leicester, 1784*

Decile, 1783 Valuation	1784 assessment										Two or more oxen	Two or more horses	Total 1783 taxpayers present in 1784
	Acres of tillage				Barrels of cider produced							
	0	1	2	3–5	0	1–5	6–10	11–15	16+				
High													
1	0	0	0	17	0	1	6	3	7	15	14	17
2	1	1	3	13	1	2	4	3	8	15	11	18
3	1	2	10	5	2	4	10	0	2	13	3	18
4	2	2	10	5	5	2	8	1	3	13	4	19
5	3	6	7	3	7	3	7	2	0	10	4	19
6	3	11	2	3	6	6	6	1	0	9	4	19
7	8	10	0	1	9	6	3	1	0	5	1	19
8	17	2	0	0	19	0	0	0	0	0	0	19
9	14	3	0	0	15	1	0	1	0	0	0	17
10	12	0	0	0	12	0	0	0	0	0	0	12
Low												

[a] Includes 5 assessed for half an acre of tillage, 3 in 7th and 1 in both 8th and 9th deciles.
Source: 1783 and 1784 Valuations of Leicester.

Credit, courts, and gentry power

It was the county institutions, specifically the courts, that provided a critical edge
by which the gentry tenuously established a preeminence. The relationship
between class and legal power could be starkly manifested in routine local dramas
such as when Justice William Ayres convicted two transients, John Jones and
Hugh Nisbet, for swearing profane oaths in the early winter of 1758.[11] But it was
played out in a more routine manner before the Court of Common Pleas. Cases of
debt were heard by the court at all four sessions, but the greatest number were
settled at the May and particularly August sessions. The court records provide a
systematic picture of the relationships among individuals of differing ranks and
situations.

Roughly three-quarters of the cases brought before the Court of Common
Pleas involved amounts of less than £35, and, for the most part, plaintiffs and
defendants were from within the local region. These were debts specified
precisely, with interest charged, and occasionally payment in kind provided for.
Thus Aaron Brown of Leominister, a housewright, recovered a £53 debt from
Nathan Dennis, a Dudley husbandman at the August 1755 session. Dennis had
promised to pay off the debt by July 1 in "Lawful money with interest . . . or the
market value thereof in grain or pork at ye Market price or in cattle . . . the price
to be determined by indifferent men."[12] Judging from the cases involving people
from towns in the southwest corner of the county, the court records reflect a
remarkably stable pattern of trade and indebtedness within the county. Involvement with economic partners beyond the county increased very gradually from 9
percent in 1740 to 20 percent in 1786.[13] Only a small minority of the debts were

[11] "Indictments, 1731–1828," Box 1, Folder 3, Worcester County, Mass., Papers.
[12] RWCCP, 4:256
[13] *Residence of plaintiff in cases of debt, Worcester Court of Common Pleas*

	1740		1755		1786	
Same town	33	*29*	33	*37*	49	*25*
Worcester town	16	*14*	16	*18*	35	*18*
All other in county	54	*48*	27	*30*	72	*37*
Other rural Mass.	6		5		10	
"Metropolitan" Mass.	3	*3*	3	*3*	15	*8*
Other states	1		5		15	
Total	113	*100*	89	*100*	196	*100*

Note: Defendants were inhabitants of the following towns: 1740 – Brookfield, Dudley,
Hardwick, Leicester, Oxford, Rutland, Sturbridge, Sutton; 1755 – Brookfield, Charlton,
Dudley, Leicester, New Braintree, Oxford, Spencer, Sturbridge, Sutton; 1786 – as 1755,
plus Oakham. Figures in italics are percentages.
Source: RWCCP, 2: 191–279; 4: 209–308; 13: 1–280.

owed to men in coastal, commercial centers such as Boston, Cambridge, Salem, or Newport, although such debts would increase slightly after the Revolution. Almost all of the cases were decided for the plaintiff in the Common Pleas. An appeal to the Superior Court of Judicature was one avenue of recourse, but always an option constrained by the difficulty and expense of getting to court. For example, more than 80 percent of the cases involving defendants from Leicester heard in the 1740 sessions of the Common Pleas were appealed to the Superior Court, as against less than 10 percent of those involving defendants from the distant towns of Sturbridge and Hardwick. Living within three or four miles of the courthouse, defendants in Leicester could well afford to keep their cases in court; defendants in Hardwick and Sturbridge would have to ride ten to fifteen miles over rocky roads to delay writs of execution.

The proceedings of the court thus reflected the constraints of a relatively limited economy in an underdeveloped region. They also reflected the basic structure of class and wealth, and the flows of credit that constituted the most fundamental and problematic links within that structure. For access to the Common Pleas were not evenly distributed across social space. Rather, the paired appearances of plaintiff and defendant matched the overall differentiation of society among the gentry, the ordinary householders, and the dependent. The decisive advantage of the gentry, in this society of widespread landownership, lay in its command of credit and its use of the courts as a collection agency.

The dependent were most conspicuous in their absence. Women rarely ventured into court, and when they did it usually involved obligations incurred by deceased husbands. Similarly, laborers were almost entirely absent from the proceedings of the Common Pleas. They had no property to be won at suit, and – equally importantly – they lacked the resources to successfully prosecute a case in court. This was the experience of Joseph Hambleton, a Brookfield laborer, when he tried to sue a Worcester husbandman for a debt of £20 in 1755. Not able to afford a lawyer, Hambleton misspelled his opponent's name, probably a recent employer, and lost the case.[14] Occasionally men of lesser stature were successful as plaintiffs against debtors of higher rank but, in aggregate, they were far more often listed among the defendants. In 1740, husbandman from eight towns were sued by gentlemen, attorneys, innholders, traders, or yeomen in forty-one cases, whereas the situation was reversed in only three cases, a ratio of greater than 10 to 1. In 1755, the ratio was roughly the same. By 1786 the label of "husbandman" had

---

[14] RWCCP, 4:255.

fallen into disfavor; yeomen were sued by gentlemen, traders, innholders, and the like three times more often than the reverse.[15]

The court records cut through a mass of smaller and larger transactions, a constant Brownian motion of exchange that characterised the region's economy. But within this dense web of interaction the Court of Common Pleas intervened in situations where one party failed to meet an obligation; in the majority of cases this was a man of relatively low station. The debt often seems to have been incurred as a part of the cost of establishing a farmstead. Thus, the debt that Nathan Dennis owed to the housewright from Leominister may well have been owed for the framing of a house or barn. The ten debts owed in 1740 to innholders Noah Ashley and Israel Richardson and merchants Joseph and Josiah Dwight of Brookfield by husbandmen and carpenters in Hardwick were most likely for supplies provided for establishing households in a newly settled town. The gentry clearly provided a source of working capital for the development of the region. Such capital would be loaned as notes-at-hand or in supplies, brought overland from Boston at a merchant's expense. Thus, if landed property was widely distributed, the capital necessary to improve that land often would have to be borrowed. Therein lay the key to the gentry's position on the social landscape. They had no direct control over the economic fortunes of men in their neighborhoods and towns, but their role as bearers of credit put them at a decided advantage. They risked their money, but they also used the court to ensure that they did not lose the value of their loan. Credit then formed a key source of gentry power, interlocking with their mediating and legitimating roles and their command of county government.

[15] *Status of plaintiffs and defendants, cases heard at WCCP in 1740, 1755, and December 1785–6*

| | | Number and percentage of cases | | | | | |
Plaintiff	Defendant	1740		1755		Dec. 1785–6	
Gentlemen, innholders	Gentlemen, innholders	11	*10*	7	*8*	49	*25*
Gentlemen, innholders	Yeomen, husbandmen	36	*32*	33	*37*	60	*31*
Yeomen, husbandmen	Gentlemen, innholders	5	*4*	4	*4*	22	*11*
Yeomen, husbandmen	Yeomen, husbandmen	40	*35*	21	*24*	26	*13*
Gentlemen, innholders	Artisans	10	*9*	6	*7*	16	*8*
Artisan	Gentlemen, innholders	1	*1*	2	*2*	4	*2*
All others		10	*9*	16	*18*	19	*10*
Total		113	*100*	89	*100*	196	*100*

Note: For categories and samples, see notes 9 and 13 above. Figures in italics are parcentages.
Source: RWCCP, 2: 191–279; 4: 209–308; 13: 1–280.

Exchange, persistence, and yeoman notables

This web of institutional and economic power was not quite as seamless as it might appear. There were significant limits to gentry preeminence, institutional buffers that mitigated against their unchallenged economic and political sway. The gentry were not the only source of working capital and economic assistance. Historians have documented the importance of local exchange networks, rooted in kinship and neighborhood, along which labor, produce, or equipment would move among a series of households, allowing each to maintain a level of subsistence. For example, more than a third of the households in Leicester's middle quintile did not own a pair of oxen in 1784, as well as a half of the seventh-decile households paying taxes on tillage. In order to work their plowland, such households would have had to exchange the service of oxen for labor or produce. Patterns of persistence in Leicester between 1740 and 1783, and in Oakham between 1771 and 1783, suggest that informal exchanges within the bounds of kinship were critical to the survival of families in particular locations. Family names appearing only once in the earlier valuation were far more likely to disappear, particularly if they ranked in the poorer deciles, than names with multiple entries. The latter were generally clans of interrelated households, often a father and several sons, sometimes brothers and cousins. Simple numbers could account for their persistence, but undoubtedly exchanges within such extended families would cushion the impact of economic adversity.[16]

Given the expense of maintaining a pair of oxen, plowing was a particularly important point in such exchange relationships. In Leicester in 1784 all but nine of the thirty-five taxpayers assessed for tillage but not for a pair of oxen had close relations from whom they might borrow plow animals. The two Ebenezer Kents, father and son, were each assessed for one ox in 1784; presumably they worked together in plowing. Among the Green clan, four households lacked oxen, but there were eleven oxen between the twelve Greens paying taxes in 1784. Jonathan

---

[16] Of the 55 surnames that appeared only once on the 1740 Leicester valuation, 50.9% (28/55) survived to 1783 in Leicester or the associated districts of Spencer, Paxton, or Auburn; of the 100 taxpayers whose surnames appeared more than once in 1740, 76 were members of families whose names survived to 1783. The attrition of familial isolates was more extreme in Oakham, where only 29.8% (14/47) of the single surnames persisted between 1771 and 1783, as against 84.4% (38/45) of the multiples. See 1740 Province Tax List, Leicester General Records, 1783 Valuations of Leicester, Paxton, Spencer, and Oakham; 1784 Valuation of Leicester; 1771 Valuation of Oakham, in Bettye H. Pruit, *The Massachusetts Tax Valuation List of 1771* (Boston, 1978), genealogical appendix to Henry B. Wright and Edwin B. Harvey, *The Settlement and History of Oakham, Massachusetts* (New Haven, 1947); Leicester, Auburn, and Oakham *Vital Records.*

Newhall, Jr., had two acres of tillage and no oxen, but his father had two and his childless older uncle had four. Similarly, fathers provided material and supplies to help their sons get established. When Benjamin Gilbert of North Brookfield moved to Otsego County, New York, in 1785, he enumerated the tools he needed to work his frontier farm, hoping that his father would "find your circumstances such as to enable you to give me those articles as an encouragement." A year later Gilbert wrote up an inventory of items that he had "received of my Father for which payment has not been made it being his gift." Kin-based pyramids of peers and family elders, mutually interdependent and supportive, offset the necessity to go into debt to gentry creditors. In general, it may have been the familial isolates who were the most exposed to the unmoderated impact of the credit system and the operations of the court.[17]

Exchange could take on wider connotations of obligation when people did find themselves in court. An appeal to the Superior Court involved posting a bond; typically the sureties were put up by lawyers in Worcester. But on the eve of Shays's Rebellion in 1786, a series of men of local standing stood surety for debtors in the town of Spencer in the place of the usual lawyers. The next year dozens of Regulators would bypass progovernment justices to sign oaths of allegiance with Justices John Bisco of Spencer and Edward Rawson of Leicester; in the summer of 1786 these two men stood surety for six debtors in Spencer, four of whom would be Regulators. One was Oliver Watson, Jr., indebted to Nathaniel Paine of Worcester; Watson's father, Deacon Oliver Watson, Sr., joined Bisco and Rawson in standing surety for two sons of Deacon John Muzzy, for a debt of £53 to trader Samuel Hinckley of Brookfield. Deacon Watson also joined with Elijah Howe of Spencer to stand surety for Thomas Grout in a debt of £18 to gentleman Clark Chandler of Worcester, and Howe joined with Bisco to stand surety for John Lamb, similarly in debt to Chandler.[18]

This web of legal exchanges, strung together to offset the power of creditor and lawyers in the courts, meshed together a series of archetypal yeoman households. Three Muzzy households, including four taxpayers, shared a pair of oxen to work eleven and a half acres of tillage; together they produced twenty-six barrels of cider. Four Watson households shared four oxen to work twelve acres of tillage, and produced twenty barrels of cider. These two families were connected to extended kinship networks as complicated as any among the gentry, if more localized to networks that produced a number of Regulators in 1786. Justices Bisco

[17] Gilbert, *Citizen Soldier*, 77–82. For parallel analyses, see Gross, *Minutemen*, 68–108; and "Culture and Cultivation: Society and Agriculture in Concord," *JAH* 69 (1982), 42–61; Bettye H. Pruit, "Agriculture and Society in the Towns of Massachusetts, 1771: A Statistical Analysis," Ph.D. dissertation, Boston University, 1981; and Susan Geib, " 'Changing Works': Agriculture and Society in Brookfield, Massachusetts, 1785–1820," Ph.D. dissertation, Boston University, 1981.
[18] Supreme Judicial Court Records, Dockets 154968, 155016, 155052, 155076, 155127; RWCCP, 13:268; MA 190:107, 151, 165–6.

and Rawson were recent arrivals in the vicinity, and had been first commissioned justice by the new state government. They were thus marginal to the established gentry class, and this marginality was formalized when Rawson lost his commission in 1788. Bisco retained his commission until just before his death in 1808, but in 1788 he exchanged positions with another man in this little drama. It was a sign that he was accepted as a man of the covenant, rather than the court, when he was elected deacon of the Congregational church in 1788, several months before the death of Deacon John Muzzy.[19]

John Muzzy had been first and foremost a man of the corporate, covenanted locality. He was a man who rose to the edge of gentry status and refused to step over the line. The son of a Lexington innholder, he and his wife Abigail had moved to Rutland in 1739, settling adjacent to the household of Abigail's brother Benjamin Reed, who married Mary Muzzy in the early 1740s. John Muzzy served as selectman and assessor in Rutland before moving to Spencer in 1752, where he was immediately elected a Congregational deacon and, over the next two decades, served almost continuously as selectman, assessor, and town clerk, for many years with Oliver Watson. Muzzy might well have followed the same path into the ranks of the gentry taken by Moses Marcy, William Ayres, or Rufus Putnam. Like others in Spencer, Muzzy had acted as an informal adviser in legal matters, "frequently employed as scribe in writing wills, deeds, and other legal instruments." But when the time came for Muzzy to enter the appointed ranks of the gentry, he stood back. Granted a commission as justice of the peace by Governor Thomas Hutchinson in March of 1772, he refused the appointment on the grounds that he was not "qualified to act in the office." Certainly others had accepted the office with less experience, but Muzzy preferred to remain – as he labeled himself on his last will and testament – a "yeoman" of the town of Spencer in the county of Worcester.[20]

Consensus and insurgencies

Thus gentry power, rooted in access to cosmopolitan culture, mercantile credit, and county institutions, was blunted on a number of fronts. Widespread property holdings, relative to most other contexts in the early modern world, worked with the family and community-based exchange networks to limit their economic control over the population. These exchange networks can be seen as loose, stratified, patriarchal alliances of affiliated households, each bringing together a combination of resources and labor that provided the basis for a mutual sub-

[19] 1784 Valuation of Spencer; JP appointments from *Massachusetts Register*, 1780–1808; deacon appointments from Harold F. Worthley, ed., *An Inventory of the Records of the Particular (Congregational) Churches Gathered 1620–1805* (Cambridge, Mass., 1970), 586.
[20] *Massachusetts Register*, 1781–8; Reed, *Rutland*, 149–51; Draper, *Spencer*, 176–7, 227–8; 1784 Valuation of Spencer.

sistence. Leading each of these pyramids of affiliated families might be one or more men we can call yeoman notables, men like John Muzzy or Oliver Watson, who commanded authority and respect within the local circle of corporation and covenant, but who had no aspirations to move beyond to the horizons defined by the charter and metropolis.

Gentry power was limited by a wide distribution of economic resources and a tenacious tradition of economic cooperation, but it was also limited by explicitly political forces. First, the town system itself placed certain limits on gentry authority. Deference was paid to gentry stature in a political calculus of exchange; deference was exchanged for accountability, for attention to the interests of their constituents in corporate and covenanted association. Leading men would receive the respect of the town when they acted disinterestedly in the common good, perhaps to the detriment of their own aspirations. Town meetings gave the yeomen a direct voice in local government. Their power to elect or reject town officers and representatives was unique in early America, and gave pause to gentry pretensions. No matter what the attractions of the world of the court, the metropolis, and the charter, the gentry were bound to the broader commonalities of corporatism; gentry differentiation was limited and constrained by the same ethic of unity and consensus that ruled their yeoman neighbors. The gentleman selectman or representative would serve the interests and speak the mind of his fellow townsmen, or be replaced.

Beyond the routine politics of the town system lay the real possibility of insurgency. Across the long century-and-a-half from the Peace of Utrecht to the Civil War, popular insurgencies in Worcester County moved in two broad and distinct streams. One of these streams of insurgent tradition flowed from the priorities of independence in commonwealth best articulated by James Harrington. Rooted in the corporate town experience, these Harringtonian impulses would move from the center of a consensus into insurgency with the Revolutionary era. They would be most sharply articulated in the Regulators' attack on the county courts in Shays's Rebellion, and would be a formative subtext in the popular Federalism of 1812. Though conditioned by an overarching Lockean climate, the Harringtonian priorities of independence and commonwealth would be powerfully restated in the Antimasonic response to a new social and economic landscape in the early 1830s, and in the stridently nostalgic appeal of Free Soil and Republicanism in the decades before the Civil War. A second tradition, flowing from Lockean priorities of rational, moral individualism, moved in the opposite direction, from provincial insurgency to early national consensus. Exploding with demands for rights of religious self-determination in the 1750s, this Lockean insurgency would crest with the Constitutionalist movement of the 1770s, only to provide the building blocks of a new Lockean ideological and institutional order worked out between 1780 and the 1820s.

The long cycle of religious revivals running from 1740 to the early 1750s, known broadly as the Great Awakening, would be critical in shaping these two paths of insurgency. But in the late 1730s no such differentiation of the seventeenth-century legacy had occurred, and the first such insurgent movement to sweep the county, the Land Bank of 1740, was a compound of conflicting impulses. Sharing with the Harringtonian insurgencies a direct focus on the structure of the economy, the Land Bank was conceived in institutional terms that anticipated the thrust of voluntary rationalism at the heart of the Lockean agenda. This ideological fusion would shape the enduring place of the Land Bank adherents at the center of the county's political spectrum down to the ratification of the federal Constitution in 1788.

The Land Bank

The conditions of credit were directly related to conditions of exchange, and the problem of a viable currency was a highly charged issue in provincial Massachusetts. With bullion constantly drained off to pay for British imports, the province was perpetually short of silver currency for the purposes of internal trade and governmental finance. One of the legacies of the decades of warfare ending with the Peace of Utrecht was a system of paper money, bills of public credit issued by the province that would serve as legal tender, some redeemable as taxes, others loaned at interest. Initially adopted to pay soldiers and to buy supplies, the bills of credit were so integral to the Massachusetts economy that the people demanded their continued emission in peacetime, first in the postwar year of 1714, and subsequently in 1716, 1721, and 1728. These public bills were a compromise position between the reestablishment of a silver currency, a persistent demand of the merchants in the import trade, and proposals for a private bank, issuing legal tender in exchange for mortgages on landholdings. Such land bank proposals had circulated briefly in the mid-seventeenth century, and reemerged in 1686, 1714, 1720, and finally were realized briefly in the Land Bank or "Manufactory Scheme" of 1739 to 1740. Advocacy of public bills and private banks would divide the province into two political factions, the Court party and the Popular party, until 1749, when silver currency was finally reinstated.[21]

Paper money had a strong appeal for those interested in developing an inland region. Some of the settlers taking up land in the 1720s may well have read *A Word of Comfort to a Melancholy Country*, especially those from Essex County moving into the sprawling towns of Sutton, Mendon, and Uxbridge, all to be centers of Land Bank subscription. This pithy tract on the virtues of the 1720 land bank scheme was written by the Reverend John Wise of Chebacco Parish in Ipswich, under the pseudonym of "Amicus Patriae," and anticipated much of the history of the settlement of the Nipmuc country. Writing in a lively, popular style, Wise

---

[21] The complexities of public finance in provincial Massachusetts are discussed in Andrew M. Davis, *Currency and Banking in the Province of Massachusetts* 2 vols. (New York, 1900; repr. 1970); E. James Ferguson, "Currency Finance: An Interpretation of Colonial Monetary Policies," *WMQ* 10 (1953), 153–80; Theodore Thayer, "The Land-Bank System in the American Colonies," *Journal of Economic History* 13 (1953), 145–59; George A. Billias, *The*

proposed that paper money emitted by a private land bank would stimulate the internal trade of the province, benefiting merchant, manufacturing mechanic, salaried clergy, and farmers and husbandmen, "the great Studd and Strength of our Country." But a land bank would also "be instrumental for the Increase of the Number of our Towns and People." It would facilitate the settling of the inland "Range of Townships, from River to River." Wise proposed a loan of £150 to "every Head of Family" settling these new interior towns: "By these means we may Subdue and Settle those Desolate Lands with very good and Effective Men: and if done each Town would be worth more than *Ten Thousand Pounds* to the Publick, at the Expiration of the Term." Expressing widely shared anxieties, Wise noted that these settlements would destroy "those Woods and Swamps which are now Impregnable Forts and Ramparts for a Naked Skulking Enemy," and form a barrier "like the Wall of *China*" against further Indian attacks. This done, the province could "go on with great Encouragement, Boldness, and Dispatch to fill up such Vacancies as will still remain between the Old and New Settlements, which will add greatly to our Strength." There were people aplenty for such settlements; the province could well "invite our good Brethren out of *North-Britain* and *Ireland*." Similarly, the old towns were crowded beyond capacity: "Many of our People are slow in Marrying for want of Settlements. . . . We have Old Batchelours, with Dames to Match them, to settle several Towns." Paper would ease the growing pressure of population on resources in Massachusetts.[22]

At least some of the early proprietors of the lands in the Nipmuc country shared Wise's enthusiasm for paper money and private bank. William Stoughton and Joseph Dudley reviewed Indian titles in the southwest in 1681, and in 1682 they both received large grants of land. Five years later, as members of the council, Stoughton and Dudley supported a private bank scheme proposed by Capt. John Blackwell, another proprietor of lands that would become Dudley and West Oxford, later Charlton. All three men were listed among the proposed bank's assessors when a constitution was written in 1687, just prior to the arrival of Governor Edmund Andros, who vetoed the project. Popular party men William Taylor and Peter Sargeant would be among those who inherited Stoughton's

Massachusetts Land Bankers of 1740 (Orono, Me., 1959); Pencak, *War, Politics, and Revolution*, 62ff., 101ff.; Herman Belz, "Paper Money in Colonial Massachusetts," *Essex Institute Historical Collections* 101 (1965), 149–63; and Bushman, *King and People*, 144ff. I am particularly indebted to the following unpublished essays: Kathy Mitten, "The New England Paper Money Tradition and the Massachusetts Land Bank of 1740," M.A. thesis, Columbia University, 1979; Joseph A. Ernst, "The Political Economy of Shays's Rebellion in Long Perspective: The Merchants and the Money Question," paper presented at the Colonical Society of Massachusetts Conference on Shays's Rebellion, October 1986; and Janet Riesman, "American Paper Currency," Chapter 4 of "The Origins of American Political Economy, 1690–1781," Ph.D. Dissertation Brown University, 1983.

22 [John Wise], *A Word of Comfort to a Melancholy Country* (Boston, 1721), in Andrew M. Davis, ed., *Colonial Currency Reprints, 1682–1751* (New York, 1911), 2:178–92, esp. 187–9, 197.

shares in the Oxford lands in 1712, and there were also a few Popular men among the Leicester proprietors. But, for the most part, the proprietors who sold land to settlers in the decades following the Peace of Utrecht would be staunch hard-money advocates. After issuing paper to cover wartime expenses, Governor Joseph Dudley turned to silver. He opposed the land bank scheme of 1714, and only reluctantly allowed a peacetime emission of £50,000 to undermine land bank sentiments. The proprietors of the Nipmuc lands were primarily drawn from the Court faction that developed around Dudley, interconnected by marriage and business interest. His son Paul Dudley, attorney general of the province and proprietor of Leicester and Sutton, wrote a pamphlet attacking the 1714 bank proposal. Another Leicester proprietor, Thomas Hutchinson, Sr., was appointed trustee of the 1714 public loan bills, as were Addington Davenport and John White, proprietors of the Leicester and Rutland. Hutchinson and his son were the authors of 1738 proposal to emit public bills to be redeemed in silver in ten years. Samuel Sewell, Jr., another Leicester proprietor, was involved in the silver-based Merchant's Bank of 1734 and a director of the Silver Bank, formed in 1740 in opposition to the Land Bank; in 1714 his father, Judge Samuel Sewell, had been a leading proponent of a public loan, to be controlled by the governor. Vast holdings of unimproved lands were worthless if they could not be translated into hard coin.[23]

If the proprietors were, on balance, hard-money men of the Court party, the people settling the region were decidedly in favor of paper. The late 1730s brought a growing transatlantic economic depression and, just as it would be in the early 1770s and the mid-1780s, currency was drained off to meet the demands of British merchants. At the same time Governor Jonathan Belcher had standing instructions to retire all Massachusetts-issued paper currency by 1741. As a solution to the "great scarcity of bills of credit," the House of Representatives in June 1739, proposed the creation of a private bank, and the following January the Land Bank was established.[24] Lying at the outer edge of the economic network running back to England, Worcester County might not have been directly affected by any currency contraction, but the county had the largest concentration of Land Bank mortgagers, relative to population, of all the counties in the province. The bank was particularly popular in the Blackstone Valley, notably in Worcester, Leicester, and Sutton, but there were also concentrations of Land Bank support to the north in Harvard and Lunenberg. The county also cast an overwhelming vote to up-

[23] Daniels, *Oxford*, 4, 6, 30, 32–3; Benedict and Tracy, *Sutton*, 10–12; Washburn, *Leicester*, 9–14; Reed, *Rutland*, 9–11; Lucius R. Paige, *History of Hardwick, Massachusetts* (Boston, 1883), 16; Davis, "Introduction," *Currency and Banking*, 1:9, 57; Pencak, *War, Politics, and Revolution*, 64, 72–3, 101–2, 267–8; Roy H. Akagi, *The Town Proprietors of the New England Colonies* (Philadelphia, 1924; repr. 1963), 175–88.

[24] On the economy, see John A, Schutz, *William Shirley: King's Governor of Massachusetts* (Chapel Hill, 1961), 29–30; see also John J. McCusker and Russell R. Menard, *The Economy of British America, 1607–1789* (Chapel Hill, 1985), 65, 67. For the Land Bank, see Davis, *Currency and Banking*, 2:130–67, 267–86; Billias, *The Massachusetts Land Bankers*, 1–16.

hold the bank in the 1740 General Court, marking the first of many electoral rebellions.[25]

Concentrated in the Blackstone Valley, the leading Land Bank towns were, relative to the county, settled and prosperous; few in the raw new settlements being carved out to the north and west were drawn into the scheme. But the Land Bank subscribers, those who mortgaged their property in exchange for bank notes, were of ordinary circumstances. There were certainly some prominent men among them, including town proprietors, innholders, and a number of ministers, but in aggregate the Worcester County Land Bankers did not stand out as men of wealth and status. Strikingly, their profile was quite similar to that of defendants appearing in cases of debt in the 1740 Worcester Court of Common Pleas, and quite different from that of the plaintiffs. Both Land Bankers and the 1740 defendants were overwhelmingly yeomen or husbandmen, rarely innholders or gentlemen of various kinds.[26] Just as they had few gentlemen or innholders in their ranks, the Land Bank subscribers were not especially wealthy, if those in

[25] In nine of twenty-one towns in Worcester County with Land Bank subscribers the ratio of Land Bank subscribers to their 1743 assessed tax was higher than the county figure. These nine leading Land Bank towns were, in ranked order, Uxbridge, Grafton, Worcester, Leicester, Lunenberg, Harvard, Sutton, Mendon, and Upton. These towns paid 44% of the county's share of the 1743 province tax, and accounted for 78% of the Land Bank subscribers in the county. Andrew M. Davis, "The Land Bank Mortgagers in Worcester County," *American Antiquarian Society Proceedings* 16 (1903), 85–90; the January 1743 tax assessments are listed in JHRM 20 (1742–4), 152–3. Estimates of the relative strength of Land Bank support in the various counties are based on Stephen Patterson, *Political Parties in Revolutionary Massachusetts* (Medison, 1973), 258–65; Mitten, "Paper Money," appendix on delinquents. See also Billias, *The Massachusetts Land Bankers*, 21.

[26] *Status of Land Bank subscribers, and of adversaries in WCCP, 1740*

| | | | Comm Pleas, 1740 | | | |
			Defendants		Plaintiffs	
Gentlemen	28	*15*	15	*13*	30	*26*
Innholders	16	*8*	2	*2*	27	*24*
Yeomen/husbandmen	133	*70*	77	*68*	45	*40*
Artisans	14	*7*	19	*17*	10	*9*
Widows/spinsters					1	*1*
Total	191	*100*	113	*100*	113	*100*

Note: Figures in italics are percentages.
The status of 191 Land Bank subscribers was noted on lists of mortgagers, MA 102:122, 128, 142, 144. The status of husbandmen was rarely used in these records, so yeomen and husbandmen have been combined. I have used the figures cited in Betz, "Paper Money," 161, adjusting to include an innholder category using the General Sessions Records, Davis, "Land Bankers in Worcester County," and the original lists in the Massachusetts Archives. For CCP cases, see RWCCP 2: 191–279. George Billias, examining the circumstances of 46 of the 89 original subscribers in Worcester County came to quite different conclusions. See *The Massachusetts Land Bankers of 1740*, 21–6.

4. Land Bank or Manufactory Bill, September 9, 1740.
(Courtesy of the Massachusetts Historical Society)

Leicester were typical. There were twenty-two Land Bank subscribers on the 1740 Leicester valuation, broadly distributed across the list, roughly two-thirds in the wealthiest two quintiles, but the selectmen among them were decidedly poorer than those who did not join the bank.[27] These Leicester Land Bankers seem to

[27] *Leicester Land Bankers, selectmen, and the 1740 valuation*

Quintile in 1740	Land Bank subscribers		Selectmen, 1725–45			
			Land Bankers		Others	
1	7	*32*	4	*50*	13	*81*
2	7		2		3	
3	3		1			
4	4		1			
5	1					
Subtotal	22	*100*	8	*100*	16	*100*
Unknown	2		0		3[a]	
Total	24		8		19	

Note: Figures in italics are percentages.
[a] One ranked in the first quintile, two in the second, on the 1732 valuation.
Source: Ministerial Rate List, January 6, 1731/2, Province Tax List, October 20, 1740; in Leicester General Records, vol. 1 (1720–45); Davis, *Currency and Banking*, 2: 295–313; Washburn, *Leicester*, 459–60.

have been a rising group within the town. Half of them had not paid taxes in 1732; they were either newcomers or young men coming of age. Among them were Samuel Brown, elected to a first term as selectman in 1740, seemingly on Land Bank votes, and twenty-two-year-old Oliver Watson, a son of a poor family recently emigrated from Ulster, who had just taken upland in the proprietors' lots, what would become the west precinct, later Spencer.[28]

Although they may not have been particularly prominent or wealthy, the Land Bank subscribers were certainly in debt. Most importantly, their debts were relatively large, and contracted outside of their town of residence, if the cases heard in Worcester court in 1740 are any indication. Where debtors who did not subscribe to the Land Bank typically owed £20 or less, often to men within their own town, Land Bankers typically owed sums of £20 to £100 to men in neighboring towns. Samuel Brown, elected selectman in Leicester in 1740, owed £54 to Antipas Brigham, a Grafton yeoman; and Ichabod Merrit, a shoemaker in Leicester, owed Brigham two large debts of over £200. Samuel Scott, an Oxford husbandman, owed Worcester gentleman Joseph Dyar £22. Thomas Harback, a clothier in Sutton, owed £43 to a shoemaker in Bolton and, with Benjamin Marsh, the pastor of a small Baptist church in Sutton, a large debt of £103 to a Mendon yeoman.[29] It would appear that Land Bankers were men taking significant risks in an uncertain economy, contracting large obligations with relative strangers, beyond the safe limits of familial and communal exchange networks. Venturesome in their economic dealings, Land Bankers were ambitious men on the make,

---

[28] Julia D. Bemis, *History and Genealogy of the Watson Family* ... (Spencer, 1894).

[29] *Debt size and location of Land Bankers and other debtors in court in 1740*

Debt size	Residence of plaintiff						Total	
	Same town		Neighboring town		All other locations			
Land Bankers								
£1–20	1	*4*	4	*17*	3		8	*35*
£21–100	3		9	*39*	0		12	*52*
Over £100	0		3		0		3	*13*
Total	4	*17*	16	*70*	3	*13*	23	*100*
Other debtors								
£1–20	22	*24*	34	*38*	2		58	*64*
£21–100	4		11	*11*	5		20	*22*
Over £100	3		5		4		12	*13*
Total	29	*32*	50	*55*	11	*12*	90	*100*

Note: Figures in italics are percentages. (See notes 13 and 26 above.)
Source: Davis, *Currency and Banking*, 2, 295–313; RWCCP:191–279; Superior Court of Judicature Docket Book, 1740–5, 1740 sessions (six cases appealed from 1739 WCCP).

straining to advance their position against the monetary constraints of the imperial relation.[30]

"Wise and well Regulated Countries" vs. "the ingenious Mr. Lock"

The Land Bank presented a potent challenge to the governor in his constitutional role as the agent of the crown. Condemning the Land Bank as "a fraudulent pernicious scheme," Belcher dissolved the 1741 General Court for its ardent support of the bank, and there was a storm of protest when the British government extended the Bubble Act to Massachusetts, suppressing unchartered private corporations.[31] But, if the bank defied the chain of authority running from the king, it was not derived unambiguously from that contervailing force: the people in their corporate, covenanted capacity. Rather, it occupied an as yet poorly defined hinterland, standing in some tension with the assumptions of a unitary social order that informed both poles of the mixed polity. Most fundamentally, the assumptions of the land bank project pointed to a liberal order of plural, private interests, rather than a corporate order defined by an overarching public interest.

First, the relationship of the Land Bank to town government was weak and indistinct. Land Bank adherents were poorly represented among the selectmen in strong Land Bank towns before the bank scheme began to emerge, and although they often took over the board of selectmen in 1741, they rarely retained a dominant position in subsequent years. Sutton was an important Land Bank center, but there was no surge of subscribers onto the board of selectmen. Where two Land Bankers served in 1735 and 1736, only one, Benjamin Woodbury, served between 1738 and 1743, and the town took no action on the bank bills. There were no Land Bankers among the selectmen in Grafton and only one in Mendon, where the town voted in 1741 to accept the bank bills for town debts in 1741. In Hardwick two Land Bankers were elected in the spring of 1741, and the town also voted to accept the land bank money. Similarly, Brookfield and Leicester voted to accept the bills for town charges, but even in Leicester, with a large number of subscribers, Samuel Brown was the only Land Banker elected in 1740 and 1741, where there had been two future subscribers in the previous two years. In Brookfield a new group of men took over the board of selectmen in 1741, including one Land Bank subscriber, but three of the ousted selectmen were reelected in

---

[30] See the formative discussion of the place of paper money in the eastern counties of Connecticut, just south of Worcester County, settled by similar people at roughly the same time, in Richard L. Bushman, *From Puritan to Yankee: Character and the Social Order in Connecticut, 1690–1765* (New York, 1970), 116–21, 124–6.

[31] *JHRM* 19:9; Billias, *Massachusetts Land Bankers*, 36; Davis, *Currency and Banking*, 2:160.

1742, including Justice Joseph Dwight, who regained his customary post as moderator in 1743. The voters in the northern Land Bank town of Harvard similarly withdrew support from the Land Bankers, electing two in 1739 and 1740, one in 1741, and none in the subsequent two years. In Lunenburg, three Land Bankers dominated the board of selectmen in 1740, but only one was reelected in 1741, and the town took no action on the Land Bank bills. The county seat of Worcester had the most dramatically competitive politics. Here a slate of Land Bank subscribers swept the elections for selectmen in 1741, replacing a group of trustees of the public loan money with whom they had been in competition since the mid-1730s. But when a petition was offered "to see if manufactury bills shall pay all town debts," the matter was postponed, no action was taken, and the Land Bankers were replaced by the public loan trustees in 1742.[32]

A comparison with the Regulation of 1786 is useful. In sharp contrast to this sporadic record in 1741, sitting selectmen played an important role in mobilizing militias to close the courts of 1786. Elected in the spring of that year, they would open town stocks of ammunition, send provisions, and provide "encouragement" for the Regulators; Regulator sympathizers dominated town governments into the early 1790s.[33] There is, however, little to suggest that support for the Land Bank was so well entrenched in the structure of town government. Rather, its center of gravity lay outside of town government, and only sporadically and briefly swept into local office as the crisis was drawing to a close.

There were rumors and suggestions that an uprising like the Regulation of 1786 might take place in the spring of 1741. The governor and council heard testimony about a band of "Dreamers" in rural Suffolk County where men were said to be organizing to demand grain for Land Bank notes. One report from Hingham said that "they had now got the Dream into writing . . . they would come to Boston, & if corn was there & the Merchants would not let them have it they would through them into the dock." An isolated outbreak that ultimately came to nothing, the purported rising of the 'Dreamers' suggests that a tradition of moral economy and just price lay below the surface of the Land Bank agitation. But on balance, this was a dog that did not bark. Considering the extent of Land Bank support, and the

[32] Brookfield, Mass., Town Meeting Records, 1719–70 (Brookfield Town Hall), 90–110. "Worcester Town Records, 1772–1753," in Collections of the Worcester Society of Antiquities [hereafter Coll. WSA] 2 (1880), 11–25; Temple, North Brookfield, 202; Washburn, Leicester, 59; Paige, Hardwick, 46; Benedict and Tracy, Sutton, 57; Frederick C. Pierce, History of Grafton, Worcester County, Massachusetts (Worcester, 1879), 411–13; Nourse, Harvard, 420–1; Walter A. Davis, comp.,The Early Records of the Town of Lunenburg, 1719–1764, 106–10, and John Metcalf, Annals of the Town of Mendon from 1659 to 1880 (Providence, 1880), 235–7. See Clarence W. Bowen, History of Woodstock, Connecticut (Norwood, Mass., 1926), 1:97.
[33] Box 23 [Box on Shays's Rebellion], Robert Treat Paine Papers, Massachusetts Historical Society. See Chapter 7.

vigorous crowd actions in the Boston Market riots of 1737 and the Knowles Riot in 1747, to say nothing of the Regulation of 1786, it is surprising that the march of the 'Dreamers' was more rumor than fact. John Chandler may have complained in January 1741 that he and Sheriff Gookin had "some enemies in this county," envious of their "Posts of Profit," but there was no uprising against the courts, as there would be in 1774 and 1786.[34]

The Land Bank persuasion did bear broad affinities with the commonwealth assumptions of a moral economy. John Wise had written that a brisk circulation of currency characterized "all wise and well Regulated Countries"; it was the duty of governments to take measures to ensure such a regulation for the well-being of the people.[35] Land Bankers were not rustic harbingers of Adam Smith, proposing an independence of government and economy. Most importantly, their theory of money directly violated that of John Locke. In the *Second Treatise*, Locke insulated monetary value from political power, and thus property from government. In his construct, the mutual agreement of men in the state of nature on the intrinsic value of gold and silver had placed the value of a currency beyond the authority of civil governments. Locke realized this philosophy in policy in the recoinage of 1696, which guaranteed an immutable weight of silver in English currency for centuries to come. The Massachusetts Land Bankers drew upon an opposing tradition in English economic thought that had flourished through the seventeenth century. Ignoring Locke's overriding priority of protecting property from arbitrary power, these men nonetheless wrote with a liberal confidence that the action of markets would generate value. They saw gold and silver currency as simple commodities in that marketplace, with monetary values rising and falling with economic conditions. Similarly, they argued that governments could beneficially intervene to regulate the value of currency, and that paper currencies supported by governments would hold their value better than silver.[36] These ideas were circulating in New England by the 1650s, and figured prominently in debates over currency and land banks through the 1740s. While hard-money men like Samuel Mather cited Locke on the intrinsic value of silver, John Colman and

[34] MA 102:159, 163:64; Francis E. Blake, "Some Worcester Matters, 1689–1743," *Corr. WSA* 7 (1886) 16; Gary Nash, *The Urban Crucible: Social Change, Political Consciousness, and the Origins of the American Revolution* (Cambridge, Mass., 1979), 129–36, 221–3; John Lax and William Pencak, "The Knowles Riot and the Crisis of the 1740s in Massachusetts," *Perspectives in American History* 10 (1976), 163–216. Billias comes to similar conclusions in *The Massachusetts Land Bankers*, 34–6.

[35] [Wise], *A Word of Comfort*, in Davis, *Reprints*, 2:186.

[36] Joyce O. Appleby, *Economic Thought and Ideology in Seventeenth-Century England* (Princeton, 1978), 199–241, 252–9, and "Locke, Liberalism, and the Natural Law of Money," *Past and Present*, 71 (1976), 43–69.

Hugh Vance argued from the commodity theory of silver to advance the idea of land banks.[37]

Land Bank views thus were based in an odd compound of liberal and traditional assumptions; markets were fluid and powerful, capable of generating great value, but governments could and ought to regulate currencies to direct this greater good. Here their conception of the relationship of politics and money violated Locke's dictum, and might even sit well in Harrington's regulated commonwealth. But it was in the measures themselves, the means to such a beneficial regulation, were the Land Bankers made their great departure from the corporate tradition. The Land Bank was most fundamentally an institutional innovation. The Land Bank theorists challenged both charter and covenant in proposing that a private corporation, based on particular interests, could assume a primary role in the provincial economy. As the local situation of the Land Bank suggests, it was not firmly rooted in the corporate town experience, but was a creature of provincial political culture. With an eye to this broader field, John Wise had written in 1721 that "there be very good reasons to be given why a particular Company of suitable Gentlemen, should be entrusted with such a Grand Affair." With "Prudence and a Public Spirit," men of great estate could be trusted to run a private bank, to the benefit of both their own and the public good. The same emphasis on reason and voluntary association had been the underpinning of Wise's *Vindication of the Government of New-England Churches*, published in 1717. If Wise arrived at Lockean postulates of voluntarism and rationalism without direct access to Locke, Hugh Vance shamelessly expropriated Locke's writings on money, reversing their meaning to conform to the commodity theory of Locke's opponent John Law. The Land Bankers spoke a language of interest rather than unity, analysis rather than the covenant, a language in which "the ingenious Mr. Lock" was already a name to conjure with.[38]

The Land Bank writers were groping toward a new pluralistic definition of public culture; the hard-money men based their arguments in the common assumptions and framework of unitary corporatism. In 1714 Paul Dudley had

[37] Riesman, "American Political Economy," 81–222; Joyce O. Appleby, "The Social Origins of American Revolutionary Ideology," *Journal of American History* 44 (1978), 950–1; Davis, *Currency and Banking*, 2: 56–101; [Samuel Mather], "A Letter from a Gentleman to His Friend," in Davis, ed., *Reprints*, 3:22; John Colman, *The Distressed State of the Town of Boston Once More Considered* (Boston, 1720), in Davis, ed., *Reprints*, 2:88; [Hugh Vance], *Some Observations in the Scheme projected* . . . (Boston, 1738) and *An Inquiry into the Nature and Uses of Money; More Especially of the Bills of Public Credit, Old Tenor* (Boston, 1740), in Davis, *Reprints*, 3:181–213, 366–453.

[38] [Wise], *A Word of Comfort*, in Davis, *Reprints*, 2:211–19; John Dunn, "The Politics of Locke in England and America in the Eighteenth Century," in Yolton, ed. *John Locke: Problems and Perspectives*, 73 n. 2, and *paissm*; [Vance], *An Inquiry*, in Davis, ed., *Reprints*, 3: 372, 378, 379, 380, 390, 398, 401–4, 412, 434, 436, 470.

argued strenuously that such corporations could only be "Derived from the King"; Land Bankers presumed to violate the order of things by "Erect[ing] themselves a *Body Politick*." It was the hard-money men who invoked the covenant tradition, blaming the people's extravagance for the inflation of prices and the loss of silver to Britain. The virtues of a fixed, immutable value of silver and gold were put in metaphoric relation to the virtues of a people steadfast in their covenant. As it often was, the language of the people's tradition was thus subverted to the uses of a particular interest, in this case that of the import merchants.[39]

Land Bankers ultimately were concerned with the prosperity of the people as a whole; their goal was that of commonwealth. But their means, that of faction and private association, marked a profound departure from the covenanted corporatism through which the townspeople participated in the commonwealth tradition. As an interest-based faction, the Land Bankers stood outside the corporate tradition that still set the fundamental assumptions and parameters of public culture and action in provincial Massachusetts. They were pursuing a liberal experiment in a Harringtonian environment.

The cross-pressuring of these values of the marketplace and the commonwealth may explain the rapid collapse of overt Land Bank sentiment in the 1740s. But these ideological tensions would continue to shape the assumptions of a generation of rising men in Worcester County. The Land Bank experience was indeed formative, but its conditionally liberal thrust would be muted further by subsequent experience. In the main, aggressive young men in the late 1730s, those most attracted to the Land Bank, would be drawn back into corporate orthodoxy in the first stages of the Great Awakening, and into the provincial consensus by a popular wartime governor. The effect of the Great Awakening, over the long term, would be to dramatically differentiate large bodies of people across the county between Lockean and Harringtonian priorities. Situated between these extremes, the men of the Land Bank experience – a Popular gentry – would occupy a strategic middle ground guaranteeing them a leading role in county affairs for a half-century to come.

---

[39] [Paul Dudley], *Objections to the Bank of Credit Lately Projected at Boston* (Boston, 1714), in Davis, *Reprints*, 1:243ff.; Pencak, *War, Politics, and Revolution*, 74, 104; Riesman, "American Political Economy," 192–8; Perry Miller, *The New England Mind: From Colony to Province* (Boston, 1965), 288–324.

3

Awakening: Orthodoxy, dissent, and a new social architecture

The Land Bankers' departure from tradition was only a prologue to more powerful stirrings. In October of 1740, after preaching to thousands for several weeks in and around Boston, the Reverend George Whitefield made a tour west through the county, on his way to visit Jonathan Edwards in Northampton. Whitefield was escorted to Worcester by Governor Belcher, where he was "kindly entertained" by John Chandler. Neither of these men could have imagined the ultimate consequences of Whitefield's visit.[1]

Governor Belcher had sent his son to meet Whitefield on his way north from Philadelphia, and while the evangelist preached in and around Boston during September and early October the governor had given him every consideration. On the afternoon of October 14, Belcher appeared suddenly at the Marlborough meetinghouse, where Whitefield was to preach en route to Northampton. Greatly "affected" by Whitefield's preaching, Belcher rode with him that night to Chandler's in Worcester. On the morning of the 15th, after prayers, the governor took Whitefield aside. In Whitefield's account, Belcher "kissed me, and exhorted me to go on in stirring up the Ministers; 'for,' says he, 'reformation must begin at the house of God.'" As they walked to the Worcester common, the governor urged Whitefield to "not spare Rulers any more than Ministers: no, not the Chief among them." Reflecting on his encounter with the governor, Whitefield wrote that he "had greater power than ordinary whenever the governor has been at public worship."[2]

The Great Awakening came to Worcester County with the approval and patronage of the most powerful men in the county and the province. An event that would ultimately turn society on end began in a harmonious synthesis of civil and religious authority. Governor Belcher may well have found spiritual solace in

---

[1] Joseph Tracy, *The Great Awakening: A History of the Revival of Religion in the Time of Edwards and Whitefield* (Boston, 1842), 96–7; Lincoln, *Worcester*, 168.

[2] Tracy, *Great Awakening*, 98–9; *An Continuation of the Rev. Mr. Whitefield's Journal ...* (London, 1741), 44; Lincoln, *Worcester*, 168; Nash, *Urban Crucible*, 207, 214; William H. Kenney, "George Whitefield: Dissenter Priest of the Great Awakening, 1739–1741," *WMQ* 26 (1969), 86–8.

Whitefield's preaching, but he seems to have had a broader agenda. October 1740 marked the height of the Land Bank crisis, the most powerful challenge to the governor's rule in a decade of controversy over the province currency. Belcher saw Whitefield as a means of diverting the people's attention from the politics of money: Whitefield was to be the agent of the "general reformation" that the hard-money jeremiads had invoked as the solution to the province's troubles.

From Worcester, Whitefield proceeded west on the province road. Preaching at Leicester center on the afternoon of the 15th "with some, though not so much power as in the morning," he spent the night in Brookfield. The next morning he had great misgivings, but standing high on a rock before hundreds gathered on a hilltop on Colonel Joseph Dwight's land, Whitefield "preached, not with extraordinary freedom at first, but at last the word ran, and melted many down." Then he took the north road to Hadley and Northampton, leaving the region to work out the consequences of a charismatic intrusion.[3]

Whitefield's progress through the county marked the onset of a decade of religious turmoil. It would be an episode of fits and starts, long interludes of building tension, breaking in cathartic outburst. Many people would be "melted down," brought to a conviction of personal sin and of the power of saving grace. But not all of them would be brought humbled to the orthodox church, as Belcher and Whitefield hoped, and even that result would in the long term run contrary to Belcher's purposes. The Awakening would generate challenges to New England's institutional and political order of far greater power than the Land Bank.

The Awakening brought a bifurcation in public culture, or more precisely a trifurcation, moving peoples in Worcester County – explicitly and implicitly – toward the poles of the seventeenth-century ideological inheritance, while it defined a mediating middle ground. At one extreme, the explosion of New Light separatism engendered by the Awakening, finding stable institutional form in the Separate Baptist movement, brought the priorities of Lockean voluntary contractualism directly to bear on local society. Breaking away from orthodoxy in a swirling series of local rebellions – moral insurgencies – the Lockean impulses of New Light separatist dissent would reach their most powerful political expression in the Constitutionalist movement of 1776–80. And free of orthodoxy's constraints of commonwealth and moral economy, many among the religious dissenters plunged into priorities of the marketplace, dramatically expressed in a later generation in their enthusiasm for the "cotton mill fever" of 1812. At the other extreme, in those places where the Awakening did little to disrupt the inclusive polity and communion of traditional moderate Calvinism, people remained entrenched in the secular priorities of corporate locality. It was among these places

[3] Tracy, *Great Awakening*, 98–9; *Continuation*, 45; Lincoln, *Worcester*, 168; Temple, *North Brookfield*, 190–3, 202, 224; Shipton, *Sibley's Harvard Graduates*, 7:57.

that Regulator sentiment of 1786 and 1787 brought the sharpest expression of the values of the Harringtonian commonwealth. But between these extremes emerged the broad ranks of New Light orthodoxy. Particularly among those peoples drawn to the promise of the Land Bank, the Great Awakening brought a reemersion in traditional institutions, infused with the transcendent purposes of the evangelical cause. The experiences of New Light orthodoxy, in combination with those of the Land Bank, shaped a Popular center in Worcester County politics, situated between Lockean and Harringtonian extremes, which would endure for a half-century, moving from the consensus forged by Governor William Shirley in the 1740s to a leading role in the Revolutionary crisis, a staunch advocacy of economic justice in the legislative and convention politics of the 1770s and 1780s, and a militant Antifederalism in 1788.[4]

The new light among the orthodox

The most successful – and best documented – of the region's orthodox revivals took place in Sutton, just south of Worcester. The Sutton people had settled David Hall as the orthodox minister in 1729, after dismissing their first minister, John McKinistry, a Scottish Presbyterian. Hall had "discouraging apprehensions" about their state of religion, but he soon had an effect on his charges, bringing numbers into the church in 1731 and 1736. Whitefield's preaching in Worcester had a powerful influence on Hall, and that November he began to write a detailed and introspective diary, chronicling personal and public piety and shortcomings. That December, as sickness spread through the town, he called a day of fasting and prayer, but by the following spring there were so few signs of

---

[4] The interpretations of the causes and consequences of the Great Awakening are numerous and complex. Very briefly, I see the roots of the orthodox Awakening to be connected to an anxiety about commercial striving. Here I draw upon the interpretations of Bushman, *From Puritan to Yankee*, particularly 183–93, and Bumsted, "Religion, Finance and Democracy." On the outcome of the orthodox revivals, I see the Awakening reinforcing orthodox corporate stability, as does Christine Leigh Heyrman, in *Commerce and Culture: The Maritime Communities of Colonial Massachusetts, 1690–1750* (New York, 1984), but also to have an "antientrepreneurial" thrust not unlike that which Gary Nash stresses in *The Urban Crucible*, 216ff. Unlike Bushman and Heyrman, I do not see the Awakening in orthodox communities as reinforcing commercial ambition. Rather, I see the emergence of the Separates and the the Separate Baptists, and particularly their attack on the institutions of corporate unity, as legitimating individual economic behavior with only minimal regard for mutual reciprocity and moral economy. Here I find very useful the analysis of the secularization of ethics and the calling in J. E. Crowley, *This Sheba, SELF: The Conceptualization of Economic Life in Eighteenth Century America* (Baltimore, 1974), esp. 65–75. When his interpretation is applied only to the Separates and Separate Baptists, I find Bushman, *From Puritan to Yankee*, 193–5, especially persuasive.

revival that he spoke of resigning to find a more responsive flock. This threat struck home: Hall later wrote that "Sundry persons came to me under soul-concern soon after." The ensuing months saw the slow, quiet building of a revival that mirrored that developing in Northampton. District religious meetings, held monthly for a few years after the 1735–6 revival, were begun anew, meeting weekly for "reading, praying, singing praises, and speaking one to another of their particular experiences." David Hall invited colleagues to preach. The Sutton people heard Jonathan Edwards as well as Ebenezer Parkman of Westborough, Solomon Prentice of Grafton, and finally – in the summer of 1742 – the itinerant Daniel Rogers. But it was during the previous winter that the people began to come under conviction. Hall wrote an evocative description of the peak of this quiet but powerful season of revival.

> It is observable how, at this remarkable day, a spirit of deep concern would seize upon persons. Some were in the house, and some walking in the highway; some in the woods, and some in the field; some in conversation, and some in retirement; some children, and some adults, and some ancient persons, would sometimes on a sudden be brought under the strongest impressions from a sense of the great realities of the other world and eternal things.[5]

Hall's revived church lay in a broad region within the county, the Blackstone Valley and some surrounding towns, where the orthodox turned to the New Light. In addition to David Hall, Ebenezer Parkman, and Solomon Prentice, Worcester County New Light ministers included Nathan Webb of Uxbridge, Joseph Dorr of Mendon, David Goddard of Leicester, Thomas Weld of Upton, and John Seccomb of Harvard, all but one located in the relatively prosperous, settled towns of the Blackstone Valley in the county's southeast quadrant. Strikingly, these New Lights were united not only by proximity, but also by involvement in the Land Bank. Five of these New Light ministers – Hall, Webb, Weld, Prentice, and Parkman – had mortgaged their property to the Land Bank, and all but seven of the county's nine New Light Congregational churches were in towns with strong contingents of Land Bank mortgagers. Conversely, all but two of the sixteen Old Light churches in the county were located in somewhat less prosperous towns, mostly in the north and west, where the Land Bankers were relatively few in number. The one minister of an Old Light church who took a Land Bank mortgage, Perley Howe of Dudley, was dismissed by his congregation for

[5] Benedict and Tracy, *Sutton*, 58–9; Hall, in *Christian History*, 2:166, quoted in Tracy, *The Great Awakening*, 162–5. See also Shipton, 7:347–9 for a slightly different account. On Northampton, see Patricia J. Tracy, *Jonathan Edwards, Pastor: Religion and Society in Eighteenth Century Northampton* (New York, 1980).

intemperance. Clearly, the connection between Land Bank and Awakening was not coincidental.[6] What, then, was the relationship between the Land Bank insurgency and the orthodox revivals of the Awakening? Certainly, the Land Bank mortgagers were a minority among the awakened, but they seem to have been a minority symptomatic of broader tendencies in the towns swept by the New Light. The evidence suggests that the Awakening was a reaction to the factionalism and "covetousness" that so characterized the conflict-ridden 1730s; people caught up in the quest for worldly goods and possessions were swept into the Awakening by an overpowering sense of guilt an anxiety. Rather than a symptom of rebellion, the early orthodox revivals brought a submission to traditional, deferential, corporate unity and harmony. It seems, in the short run, that Governor Belcher's apparent hopes that Whitefield could cool the Land Bank crisis were realized. The Land Bank was retired without serious opposition, and in subsequent years the energies of young men in rural Massachusetts were turned toward imperial warfare. There would be no further talk of private "bodies politic" issuing legal tender – except perhaps among the growing tribe of counterfeiters – until the post-Revolutionary economic crisis of the 1780s, and the Massachusetts backcountry would be remarkably inert as a source of political opposition until the decade of the Stamp Act.

The experience of Sutton illustrates the connections between the Land Bank and the orthodox Awakening. In the decade between David Hall's settlement in 1729 and the Awakening, the town appointed committees to consider adjustments to his salary, relative to the inflation of the province bills. Gradually, over the course of the 1730s, the committees recommended increases in Hall's salary above his settlement of £100, which the town generally approved. In 1733 they recom-

---

[6] *The Land Bank and the Great Awakening in Worcester County, 1740*

Orthodox minister	Land Bank subscription	
	Strong	Weak
New Light	7 *4*	2 *1*
Old Light	2	14 *1*[a]
Total towns by 1745	9	16

Note: Figures in italics are the number of ministers subscribing to the Land Bank.
[a] Perley Howe of Dudley, dismissed for "intemperance."
Source: For the Land Bank towns, see Chapter 2, note 25. For the attitudes of the ministers toward the revival, see *The Testimony and Advice of an Assembly of Ministers* ... (Boston, 1743); Charles Chauncey, *Seasonable Thoughts on the State of Religion in New England* ... (Boston, 1743); John Prentice, *Testimony of an Association of Ministers* ... (Boston, 1745); Lincoln, *Worcester*, 169; Daniels, *Oxford*, 53–4; Paige, *Hardwick*, 70 183ff., 225ff.; Shipton, *Sibley's Harvard Graduates*, 6: 520–1; 7: 55–7, 351–2, 273–4, 617, 8: 249; 9: 53–4. On the Land Bank and the Awakening, see John C. Miller, "Religious, Finance, and Democracy in Massachusetts" *NEQ* 6 (1931), 29–58; J. M. Bumsted, "Religious, Finance, and Democracy in Massachusetts: The Town of Norton as a Case Study," *JAH* 57 (1971), 817–33; and Harry S. Stout, "The Great Awakening in New England Reconsidered: The New England Clergy," *JSH* 8 (1974), 25–7, 40–1.

mended an increase to £130, which Hall diplomatically refused; in 1735 they recommended £150, in 1737 £163, and in the revival year of 1741 the grand sum of £230.

Two groups stand out among these committeemen. Six would be Land Bankers with Hall in 1740, and six others would be leaders in the movement for a second parish in 1741, a movement that was clearly Old Light in orientation. This division reflected a broader split within the town. The Second Parish, to become Millbury in 1814, was incorporated in November of 1743, but it was not until 1747 that the petitioners established a church and called a minister, the liberal James Wellman. This secon parish church adopted the Half-Way Covenant and allowed persons to enter in full communion without a public statement of their conversion experience, both key Old Light doctrines. The division of the salary committees between New Light Land Bankers and Old Light Second Parish men reflected a broaded division within the town at large; only one of the twenty-two Land Bank subscribers in town joined the Second Parish secession.[7] Similarly, the Land Bank families responded to the Awakening with particular fervor. Members of these families were particularly likely to be admitted to the church during the revival years, especially if they were from families of Land Bankers who had served on the salary committees. There appears to have been a decided sequence of experience and affiliation among the families of a select group of salary committeemen, first to the Land Bank in association with the minister, and then into revival.[8]

[7] Benedict and Tracy, *Sutton*, 37–67, 449–51. One man, Solomon Holman, appeared in both groups. In 1760 he would affiliate with the Leicester Baptists after a bitter dispute in the North Parish of Sutton. See Hiram C. Estes, "Historical Discourse," in *The Greenville Baptist Church in Leicester, Massachusetts: Exercises on the 150th Anniversary of Its Founding . . .* (Worcester, 1887), 26.

[8] *Admissions of males to full communion in the Sutton Congregational church, 1721–50*

Years	Land Bank families		Second Parish families		Other families		Total	
1721–9[a]	7	*19*	9	*25*	20	*55*	36	*100*
1730–9	8	*16*	13	*26*	28	*57*	49	*100*
1740–5	17	*27*	10	*16*	37	*58*	64	*100*
1746–50	1	*8*	0		12	*92*	13	*100*
Total	33	*20*	32	*20*	97	*60*	162	*100*
Families of salary committeemen only								
1721–9[a]	4	*23*	6	*35*	7	*41*	17	*100*
1730–9	4	*22*	8	*44*	6	*33*	18	*100*
1740–5	10	*67*	4	*27*	1	*7*	15	*100*
1746–50	0		0		1		1	
Total	18	*35*	18	*35*	15	*29*	51	*100*

Note: Figures in italics are percentages.
[a] Various covenant lists.
Source: Benedict and Tracy, *Sutton*, 428, 430, and genealogical appendices; Sutton *Vital Records*; Sutton Mass., First Church Record Book [c.1720–c.1825], microfilm copy, AAS.

Thus, clearly defined New Light and Old Light factions emerged in Sutton in the 1740s, one drawn to the Land Bank, the other to territorial secession. However, these factions did not have obvious roots in the previous decade. Paradoxically, the families of the Land Bankers contributed relatively few new members to the church in the 1730s, although they appeared in equal numbers with Second Parish families on the pew list drawn up in 1731. The Land Bankers thus had no history of support for the minister who would join them in subscribing to the Land Bank, at least as measured by religious conversion. Similarly, people from Land Bank families dominated the list of church members who were disciplined by the Sutton church during the 1730s. Five of the seven people admonished and disciplined during the 1730s were from Land Bank families that would contribute numbers of converts in the Awakening. Samuel Dudley, who lost his commission as justice of the peace for his involvement in the Land Bank, drew the church's "General Dissatisfaction" in 1736 because he had never received a letter of dismissal from his original church in Littleton. The next year, after an extended controversy, Dudley joined the Church of England, but two of his sons joined Hall's church at the height of the Awakening in 1742. Another Land Banker and a member of the 1733 salary committee, Perez Rice, was declared an "Intruder" after he failed to obtain a similar letter in 1736. He would join the church in 1740 and his brother in 1745. Three members of the Stockwell family were disciplined by the church in the late 1730s. Lieutenant John Stockwell, appointed by the town to sit on numerous committees regarding the province bills and Hall's salary, and a Land Banker with his brother David, was drawn into an extensive quarrel with the church over his drunkenness at James Leland's tavern in Grafton. He finally confessed in 1739, and his son Ichabod joined the church in 1743. Another Stockwell brother, William, was called before the church in 1739 for "vain language, intemperance," and improper "carriage" with a local widow. His son, too, would be admitted in 1742. And in 1738 Sarah Severy, sister of the Stockwell brothers and wife of Land Banker Joseph Severy, was censured by the church for her civil conviction for "stealing and lying"; her son Joseph would join in 1741.[9]

It is safe to say that there were unruly people among the Land Bank families – proud and disputatious, given to the "common Profaneness" and "vitious Practices," which Hall worked to stamp out among his people; given also to sharp business dealings of the sort that apparently brought Sarah Severy into court. These were not poor people; when the pews were assigned in 1731, Samuel Dudley was the first on the list, reflecting his justice's commission and extensive landholdings, and nine of the eleven Land Bankers were listed in the first floor pews, while six out of ten future Second Parish petitioners sat upstairs in the

[9] Sutton, Mass., First Church Records, pp. 11–13, and membership lists; genealogies in Benedict and Tracy, *Sutton*.

gallery. Contentious and dominant families at odds with the institutions of corporate harmony in the 1730s, clearly conversant with the problems of currency and inflation, they were humbled in the Awakening. Brought under church discipline, they would be trusted more often with town leadership, the town electing Land Bankers as representatives and selectmen far more often in the mid-to-late-1740s than they had in the late 1730s.[10]

David Hall himself seems to have joined the Land Bank in an effort to get out of the personal debt ' ' plagued him for his entire life. Given the town's willingness to adjust his sala., .e may well have agreed with John Wise that the commerce engendered by a land bank would "sustain the whole ministry." Rather than standing with the hard-money men as did many other ministers, Hall and his New Light colleagues may have seen the possibility that an expansive, inflationary economy would solve their problems of maintaining a competency in these new towns.[11]

Apparently, Hall regretted his involvement in the Land Bank. A striking event in the summer of 1743 suggests that the Awakening was a vehicle for Hall's personal retreat from the temptation of paper money. That July Hall was invited by "sundry of the people" to preach to "a great assembly" in the town of Brookfield. But he was turned away as "not orderly" by the established minister, Thomas Cheney, who only grudgingly had allowed George Whitefield to preach three years before. Spurned by the minister, David Hall was entertained by Cheney's nephew, Colonel Joseph Dwight, the governor's friend, who had lost his seat in the General Court for voting against the Land Bank in 1739, and on whose land Whitefield had preached in 1740. David Hall found Colonel Dwight "to be a Godly man" and his family "hopefully the subjects of the Grace of God." Here we come full circle, back to one of the great men who seemingly sponsored Whitefield as an antidote to the fever for paper money, this time sitting down with a reformed paper-money advocate, and a shepherd of many other such men.[12]

Moral insurgency: Itinerants and separations

If Colonel Dwight welcomed David Hall to Brookfield in 1743, he could not have been aware of the long-range implications of his hospitality. However sincere and well-meaning, itinerant preaching was opening a door to a second, more radical phase of the Awakening. It threatened to shatter the fixed and organic relationship between established minister and his people that lay at the center of the orthodox system. By the time that George Whitefield returned to New England in 1745, what had begun with hopes of a general reformation had splintered into controversy and

---

[10] Benedict and Tracy, *Sutton*, 45–6, 795–6; representatives from *JHRM*.

[11] Shipton, *Sibley's Harvard Graduates*, 7:351–2; Wise, *A Word of Comfort*, in Davis, *Reprints*, 2:184ff.; Bushman, *Puritan to Yankee*, 157.

[12] David Hall Diary, July 27, 1743, Massachusetts Historical Society; *HWC* 1:334–5.

faction. Whitefield himself had sounded the alarm against an unconverted ministry, given to reason, logic, and routine, rather than an inspired and unmediated preaching of the word. On his return to Boston in 1745 in 1745, Whitefield complained that such ministers were "raising penny pamphlets" against him. In the years since his grand tour the attractions of itinerant evangelicals had alienated many people from their settled ministers and raised the threat of separatism. In 1743 ministers from throughout New England, including Thomas Cheney of Brookfield, had subscribed to Charles Chauncey's *Seasonable Thoughts on the State of Religion*, an attack on untrained itinerants, and in the same year the orthodox pastor of Oxford, John Campbell, published a *Treatise on Conversion*, in which he "intreat[ed] both Ministers and People of the *New Scheme* to desist from invading the Provinces and Districts of their Fellow Laborers and Brethren." In 1745 the conservative Marlborough Association, which included ministers from across northeast Worcester County in the orbit of the old town of Lancaster, published another condemnation of itineracy, arguing that it threatened to "destroy the Peace and Order of these Churches, and to throw them off the good Foundation upon which they were settled by our wise and pious *Ancestors*."[13] Even New Light ministers began to oppose itinerant preaching. Ebenezer Parkman of Westborough, a friend of Edwards, had welcomed Whitefield and Presbyterian evangelical Gilbert Tennent in the first phases of the Awakening. In July 1743, when the New Lights united in a *Testimony* to the "late happy Revival of Religion," Parkman and his neighbor Joseph Dorr of Mendon with thirteen other ministers signed with a reservation against "ministers and others intruding into other ministers' parishes without their consent." Evangelical "intruders" threatened to divide people from their settled ministers, and often set the stage for institutional separatism. David Hall's "intrusive" preaching played a role in the emergence of separatism in Worcester in 1743, and New Light David Goddard of Leicester was similarly involved in separatism in Framingham.[14] Communities where civil and religious had always been coterminous and mutually reinforcing were now faced with the splintering of moral unity.

In 1748 David Hall himself would be faced with separatists cursing that "the Devil was in [his] heart."[15] The late 1740s saw an explosion of evangelical separations from the orthodox churches, an explosion that eventually would settle into a new institutional structure on the middle landscape. Dissenting societies, typically Separate Baptist churches linked together in affiliation with the widespread Warren Association, would be the most important legacy of the Great

[13] Kinney, "George Whitefield," 90–3; Charles Chauncey, *Seasonable Thoughts on the State of Religion in New England* ... (Boston, 1743); Daniels, *Oxford*, 53–4; John Prentice, *The Testimony of an Association of Ministers Convened at Marlborough* ... (Boston, 1745), 4.
[14] *The Testimony and Advice of an Assembly of Pastors of Churches* ... (Boston, 1743); Shipton, *Sibley's Harvard Graduates*, 5:521–2, 9:43; Lincoln, *Worcester*, 169.
[15] Shipton, *Sibley's Harvard Graduates*, 7:350.

Awakening. Individual conversions were certainly powerful personal events, but in the absence of institutional change their long-term impact was limited; the Awakening served to renew but not to transform religious commitment among the orthodox. But those who began to meet "together separate from the world" made the Awakening a permanent presence on the middle landscape.[16] With the emergence of dissenting institutions, the terms of public culture and action would be dramatically altered. If the Land Bank had failed as a means of introducing pluralistic, Lockean structures, situated outside of the corporate categories of covenant and charter, the dissenting societies were eminently successful. If the categories of independence and dependence, and of gentry and yeoman, were powerful boundaries in this eighteenth-century society, the second phase of the Great Awakening would make the distinctions between orthodoxy and dissent equally powerful.

Institution-building: The dissenting societies and John Locke

The winds of the Awakening swept most powerfully across the southern reaches of Worcester County, across land – once occupied by the Praying Indians – settled immediately after the Peace of Utrecht and emerging from a raw frontier condition by 1740. By 1760 these towns south of the Province Road accounted for all but two of the ten formally constituted dissenting societies in the county, marking a cultural demarcation that would endure for a century to come. The Awakening did not account for all the dissenters in Worcester County. Quaker meetings were established in the lower Blackstone towns of Mendon and Uxbridge by the 1720s and at the upper reaches of the Blackstone drainage at Leicester in 1732. These would be under the authority of the Smithfield, Rhode Island, Monthly Meeting while another meeting in Bolton had ties to the Essex County Quakers. In Sutton and Leicester several families united to join the Boston Baptist church in 1732, forming their own church in 1735 and dividing in 1738. Along the way they gradually distanced themselves from the genteel Arminianism of the urban General Baptists, so that by the time that the Awakening broke out in 1740 they were ready to participate enthusiastically in its evangelical Calvinism, the Leicester Baptists briefly reuniting with the Congregational church under its New Light minister, David Goddard.[17]

[16] Henry Fisk, "The Testimony of a People Inhabiting the Wilderness," Sturbridge, 1753, MS, Isaac Backus Papers, Trask Library, Andover-Newton Theological School [hereafter BPAN].
[17] Estes, "Historical Discourse," 20; McLoughlin, *New England Dissent*, 1:297, 421–2, 466–7; Charles H. Lincoln, "The Antecedents of the Worcester Society of Friends," *Worcester Historical Society Publications* NS 1 (1928), 26ff.; Thyra Jane Foster, *A [Preliminary] Guide to the Records of the Yearly Meetings of the New England Friends with Their Subordinate Meetings* (Rhode Island Historical Society, Providence, 1971).

But this pre-Awakening dissent was only the beginning. During the 1750s Separate Baptist churches began to take shape out of the Separate or Strict Congregationalist movement. In the 1740s, the pietism of the Awakening had impelled certain people "to venture on upon a naked promise"; refusing to remain in communion with the unregenerate who had been admitted under the half-way covenant, they withdrew from the established order into "separate" meetings. In this rejection of orthodoxy lay the roots of an explosive Lockean voluntary individualism.[18]

The experience of the Sturbridge Baptists, originally separating from the Sturbridge Congregational Church in 1747, was typical of the post-Awakening emergence of dissent. In their "Testimony of a People," written in 1753 to document their conflict with the establishment, they claimed to have first objected to the covenant of the Congregational church in 1736, finding it "deficient concerning the order or discipline of the chh." Next, "about the year 1740," following "an extraordinary outpowering of the spirit," they "made frequent applications to the minister of the town that he would receive such as went forth for his name sake who ware instrumental in this day of God . . . [but he] received them not and forbid us that would." With that pronouncement, the Reverend Caleb Rice of the orthodox church barred itinerants such as Whitefield from preaching in Sturbridge. Losing their trust in the established minister, people began to doubt, to ask for signs from God, and to critically read their own Bibles, "attempting to study the Ark by their own wisdom." The next step was separation. A letter written by a Sturbridge Separate justifying her abandoning the establishment cited "being at a Church meeting and seeing so much want of love and faithfulness." Another person suddenly saw the church as

> a dark place Ministers deacon and people lookt Strangely as if they were all going Blindfold to destruction, and tho my body was there, my soul was with the Seperates, praising God as soon as I was dismysed at the meeting house I went to Brother Nevils where my Soul was sweetly refresht, the Lord alone be praised for it was he alone who Brought me out and not any Creature.

In another testimony, a woman wrote that she had been "afraid of the Separate preachers because they had no larning"; she had ceased to worry after she read in Acts 4:13 that the Apostles had been "unlearned and ignorant men."[19] The precedent of a literal-minded interpretation of the Scripture would continue to feed controversy and schism within these new Separate churches, as members

---

[18] C. C. Goen, *Revivalism and Separatism in New England, 1740–1800: Strict Congregationalists and Separate Baptists in the Great Awakening* (New Haven, 1962), 36ff.; McLoughlin, *New England Dissent*, 1:340ff.; Fisk, "Testimony."

[19] Fisk, "Testimony"; The letters of the Sturbridge Separates are located in Congregational Library, Boston, and are printed in part in Ola E. Winslow, *Meetinghouse Hill: 1630–1783* (New York, 1972), 232–6.

searched through their Bibles in an effort to replicate the form of the primitive Christian church. However, although a fear that "formality" would halt the "shower of grace" led to a chaotic unstructured fellowship, a growing countercurrent began to build up, with increasing numbers of people seeking to bring order, conformity, and peace to the dissenting churches, so as to solidify their position against the established order.

Those people in Sturbridge who felt the call came together in a series of meetings between May and November of 1747, gathering themselves into a church, and the next year had an elder and two deacons ordained. In May and June of 1749 a "tryal concerning baptism" came up, and in a pietistic fervor that they "be directed to and in the good old way," thirteen people were "convinced that it be there duty to be Baptized by Immersion." They were then baptized by Ebenezer Moulton of the evangelical South Brimfield Baptist church, and followed by sixty others within a year. One of these was Nathaniel Green of Leicester, who had separated from the Leicester Congregational church with a number of others, not liking the "chh constituty," "the manner of supporting the Gospel," and the "Manner of preaching."[20]

At this stage many of the dissenting meetings followed "open" or "mixed" communion, allowing both the immersed and the "sprinkled" to participate, presumably in the hope that an informal, inclusive polity would encourage the "Gospel spirit." However, this looseness of practice would be challenged both by a continuing insistence on pietistically defined ritual and by demands for a more stable church polity. On a regional level, a meeting of dissenters at Stonington, Connecticut, in 1754 voted to abandon the "open" communion in favor of the closed form, where only those who had been immersed would be allowed into the church. This exclusive, closed communion would gradually work its way into the dissenting churches on the Near Frontier over the following decade.[21]

The very pietistic individualism – not without a quality of personal arrogance – that drove the dissenters to separate created the need for a countervailing order. In Sturbridge, the teaching elder John Blunt recanted his baptism in 1753, having been "persuaded by some of the Separate leaders in Connecticut that the movement was bound to end in all sorts of "errors" and confusion." With the loss of their elder, the Sturbridge Baptists collapsed temporarily, but they renewed their covenant in October of 1757. In 1759 they joined an association of churches in Rhode Island, Connecticut, and Massachusetts that adhered to both the closed communion and to the ritual of the "laying on of the hands" – the "Sixth Principle" – and that seems to have advised them to call a regular minister. They called William Ewing, originally from Scotland, and possibly inclined toward a presbyterian form of church government. This development provoked yet another

[20] Fisk, "Testimony"; "John Davis Ms. 1770–1771," BPAN.
[21] "Davis Ms."; McLoughlin, *New England Dissent*, 1:428, 433–6, 458.

schism, the new separatists claiming that "they were too confined" under the new ordinances. They were led out by Henry and Daniel Fisk, two brothers who had led the original separation from the Congregational church and who "must be put aside ... [if Mr. Ewing] ... came and was settled among them."[22]

In Leicester, Nathaniel Green was having "great difficulties ... in endeavourg to suppress the strange spirit of the Separates." Following the Sturbridge example, he split off from the Leicester Separates in 1762, forming a small, closed-communion, "hands" church with members in Spencer, Leicester, and Charlton, and linking up with the Six Principle Association. This "sixth principle" phase of the Baptist movement proved a failure. Personal egotism and the shaky scriptural grounds for the laying on of hands created more conflict and disunion that it did the unity that had been intended. But the association that the movement established around 1754 was the first of its kind among the Calvinist Separate Baptists, and as such was a harbinger of the transterritorial associations that would define the denominational order of the next century.[23]

The movement toward a common institutionalized form of church polity culminated in 1768–9, when, after a series of meetings beginning in 1765, Separate Baptist leader Isaac Backus persuaded the "hands" churches in Leicester and Sturbridge to give up the divisive Sixth Principle and to join the Warren Association, a growing interprovincial organization of closed-communion Baptist churches. Similarly the Baptist church in Sutton joined the Warren Association in 1768, Monson in 1769, South Brimfield in 1771, and the old Leicester Baptist church in 1774. Thus, by the eve of the Revolution, many of the Baptist groups in the area had weathered the stormy effects of two decades of literal-minded, individualistic pietism and settled on a common form of church government. Uniting behind an interprovincial denominational association that would continue to grow through the rest of the century, providing a model for the proliferation of such associations over the next fifty years, the Baptists had begun to work out the institutional consequences of their moral insurgency.[24]

---

[22] McLoughlin, *New England Dissent*, 1:461, citing Isaac Backus, *A History of New England with Particular Reference to the ... Baptists* (Newton, Mass., 1871), 2:359; "Conference at Sturbridge, May 30, 1768," BPAN; William G. McLoughlin, "The First Calvinistic Baptist Association in New England, 1754?–1767," *Church History* 36 (1967), 410–18; "Davis Ms."
[23] "Davis Ms."; Ammidown, *Historical Collections*, 2:174–5; McLoughlin, "The First Calvinistic," 413, 415, 417; McLoughlin, *New England Dissent*, 2:705.
[24] McLoughlin, *New England Dissent*, 2:506–8; McLoughlin, "The First Calvinistic," p. 417; "Davis Ms."; "Conference at Sturbridge." One group not linked with the Warren Association was a small unincorporated society of Baptists for whom Richard Southgate of Leicester acted as a preacher, using a schoolhouse on the Post Road in western Leicester as a meetinghouse. This group seems to have collapsed by the mid-1770s, some of its members joining the old Leicester Baptist Church. The Southgate group may have been the remainder of the Leicester/Spencer Separates with whom Nathaniel Green had been associated until 1762. Membership lists, Greenville Baptist Church Records, Trask Library, Andover-Newton Theological School; Washburn, *Historical Sketches*, 16, 61, 398.

This process of regularizing and institutionalizing the Baptist movement was also required given the bitter hostility of the established churches. On a series of interrelated levels, the Baptist's voluntarism challenged the corporate structure of spirit and territory that made up such an important element of the ordinary townsman's life experience. On the more intangible level, by separating they destroyed the ideal of a peaceful unity within the town, and by claiming to "touch not the unclean thing" – the federal covenant – they cast a stigma on the religious life of the majority who remained within the orthodox way, disrupting the organic harmony of minister, community, and incorporated locality. On a much more tangible level, the Baptists presented a dire economic threat to the material basis of this corporate system. By organizing themselves into certified dissenting churches, the Baptists could claim exemption from paying rates for the support of the town's established minister, thus raising the costs of religion for the remaining households. Towns with sizable Baptist populations found it difficult to raise the necessary money for the minister's salary, as well as to fulfill their legal commitments made in their deeds of incorporation. Citing the number of Baptists and Quakers in the town, Leicester argued to the General Court in 1744 that if a new district was taken out of the northern part of the town, the remaining inhabitants "would be under an impossibility of maintaining the preaching of the Gospel in the way of the established churches of this province without some special assistance from the Honorable Court." in 1767, the town of Sturbridge requested the remission of a £20 fine for failing to support a grammar school. Among other things they argued that the town had "lately been under charges of settling a minister" (in 1760), and that these expenses had been proportionately greater because "about a quarter part of the inhabitants are drawn off from the Congregationalists to the Baptists so-called." The emergence of dissenters increased the chances that a given town would become a burden to the province, thus threatening its autonomous existence.[25]

Withdrawing from the orthodox parish, the Baptists rejected a learned, salaried ministry. The Baptists condemned the mercenary aspects of the established system and rejected learning as a prerequisite for ministerial status. Preaching was not a skill that could be developed through a "regular course of theological studies" but a "gift" that came, as did grace, from God. Although a man with a "gift" of preaching might be called by a given church, he would be expected to provide for himself. In his diary in 1750, Joshua Eaton, the established minister in Spencer, noted the disdain of even a New Light Congregationalist toward an unlearned exhorter:

> Visiting a sick Person, I heard a lay-Preacher, who delivered some good Truths, but in sich a confused Manner, that tended rather to confuse than edify the Hearer. He delivered some Things also that were not agreeable to the

[25] MA 12:351–2, 339; MA 116–699; MA 118:229; McLoughlin, *New England Dissent*, 1:467.

Word of God: and yet Numbers were pleased therewith. Alas! how are Men carried away at this Day with the empty shew of Religion, and love to be deceived?[26]

In their insistence on a voluntaristic relationship between an unpaid, unlearned preacher and a gathered church, the dissenters threatened to undermine the educated and established minister's role as "the salt of the earth," as the people's sole defense against "corruption." And given the legal relationship between church and state, their lack of subordination to the established church rapidly spilled over into the civil sphere when they were confronted with demands to pay ministerial rates. Refusal to pay these taxes often brought imprisonment in the county jail. In what would be a celebrated case, household goods were taken from the Sturbridge Baptists to pay the orthodox minister's salary in 1750. Itinerancy itself was treated as a crime: Ebenezer Moulton of South Brimfield was arrested and jailed in the same year "as a stroller and a vagabond" for his role in organizing the Baptist church in Sturbridge.[27]

In more subtle yet equally important ways, the emergence of the Baptists constituted a challenge to the chain of mediation between town and province that the gentry had begun to establish under their control. Quite obviously, the town's representative was not going to argue the Baptists' case at the General Court, nor was a legislative body that continued to pass restrictive acts the place for the Baptists to take their plea for toleration. Given the force of these circumstances, the Baptists had to appeal to "the highest place of civil power," to establish a new channel of mediation between the ruled and their ruler. As early as 1750 the Baptists of the Near Frontier were involved in efforts to bypass the entire provincial political process and to appeal directly to the king. In that year John Blunt, Henry Fisk, and David Morse of Sturbridge, Daniel Denny of Leicester, and Ebenezer Moulton of South Brimfield attended a conference in Providence where it was agreed to send an agent to London to present their case. They agreed to request the aid of English dissenters in presenting their

> most humble supplications to the King & in laying before his Majesty in Council of the Illegal & Oppressive measures which for many Years past have been carried on, & still to this very day are coercively extended against our Brethren ... of the Baptist Denomination in this Province, in direct opposition to the Charter ... in open violation of the Act of Toleration ...

---

[26] Forbes, *The Good Minister*, 15; Diary of Joshua Eaton, quoted in Eli Forbes, *Some Short Account of the Life and Character of the Reverend Joshua Eaton, of Spencer* ... (Boston, 1773), xxii; McLoughlin, *New England Dissent*, 1:403–5; Harry S. Stout "Religion, Communications, and the ideological Origins of the American Revolution," *WMQ* 34 (1977), 519–41.
[27] Fisk, "Testimony"; Haynes, *First Congregational Church, Sturbridge, Mass.*, 14; *HWC*, 2:365.

and quite contrary to the Tenor true intent & meaning of the Government at home.[28]

This conference marked an important early step toward both intercolonial and transatlantic denominational cooperation. Beyond these organizational aspects, this Baptist initiative constituted a direct threat to the entire provincial tradition. The Baptists persisted in their appeal to their rights under English law, effectively bypassing the provincial laws that stood against them. In their emphasis on their rights as "his Majesty's dissenters," they were pointing to the flaw in the standing order's position. Under English law the Congregationalists were no more "established" than were the Baptists, though they acted as if the 1692 charter had granted them religious hegemony. In sum, the Baptists' claims exposed the weakness of the Congregationalists' position, adding to fears that the bishops of the real Anglican establishment might soon appear on American shores. These efforts would be intensified when the Warren Association was formed in 1768, providing a unified institution through which the Baptists would pursue their cause in the context of the Revolutionary crisis and the new nation. All of these developments presented a direct threat to the entrenched interests of the orthodox gentry, undermining their control over the means of mediation.[29]

Finally, in a successful lawsuit in 1769, the Baptists were able to begin to put the seal of provincial law on their newly created institutions. At the same time they explicitly invoked John Locke's ideal of voluntary association among rational individuals. The case of Nathaniel Green versus the town of Leicester was a milestone on the road to religious toleration. The legal arguments made during the trial and preserved by John Adams in his case book give a vivid picture of the opinions of both the gentry and the Baptists on the eve of the Revolution. The case grew out of Nathaniel Green's refusal to pay any taxes for the year 1767, claiming exemption as an ordained minister. He had been ordained in 1763, his closed-communion, "hands" church originally meeting in Spencer but probably shifting to Leicester in 1767. The town of Leicester, presumably because there were already two Baptist societies in the town, and because Green's followers lived almost entirely in Spencer and Charlton, would not recognize his ordination, and

---

[28] See Isaac Backus, "Government and Liberty Described; and Ecclesiastical Tyranny Exposed," in William G. McLoughlin, ed., *Isaac Backus of Church, State, and Calvinism: Pamphlets, 1754–1789* (Cambridge, Mass., 1968), 360; McLoughlin, *New England Dissent*, 1:479–80.

[29] For other examples of the Baptists claiming of rights are "His Majesty's dissenters," see Sturbridge petition, MA 13:423–4; and petition of Thomas Green and others, MA 13:496–506. McLoughlin, *New England Dissent*, 1:478–9, 576–7; Bailyn, *The ideological Origins*, 254ff.; Alan Heimert, *Religion and the American Mind: From the Great Awakening to the Revolution* (Cambridge, Mass., 1966), 351ff.

in February of 1769 had him jailed in Worcester. Green paid his rates after six hours in jail and then proceeded to sue the town for overassessment and damages.[30]

The counsel for the town, James Putnam of Worcester, and his former student, John Adams of Braintree, based their argument against Green on the provincial statutes governing the settlement of ministers.[31] In defending Nathaniel Green, attorney John Worthington went directly to John Locke's definition of a church as a voluntary association of individuals. As recorded by John Adams, he argued that "all Ministers are Exempted. By the annual Tax Act. Mr. Locks Defin[ition] of a Ch[urc]h. Ecclesia. A Number of Persons met to worship God. And that Man they choose for their Head shall be their Minister. He thinks himself as orthodox as any." Worthington's argument apparently swayed the jury; the verdict went to Green and was upheld the following September in the Superior Court. The admission of Green's church into the Warren Association in 1769 suggests that the resources of that organization were marshaled for Green's defense. Certainly its leader, Isaac Backus, was clearly pleased by the outcome, writing years later in his *History* that this case indicated "a determination of authority, that the ministers of the Baptist Churches were lawful ministers."[32]

Backus had apparently arrived at his position on religious liberty without reading John Locke,[33] but the year after Green's trial he picked up Worthington's reference. Defending the Baptists of Berwick on the Maine coast, Backus quoted at length from Locke's *Letter on Toleration*:

That great reasoner justly observes that "the business of law is not to provide for the truth of opinions, but for the safety and security of the commonwealth, and of every particular man's goods and person ... [T]o give laws, receive obedience, and compell by the sword belong to none but the civil magistrate; and upon this ground I affirm, that the magistrate's power extends not to the establishing of any articles of faith, or forms of worship, by force of laws ... The care of souls cannot belong to the civil magistrate, because his power consists only in outward force: but the true and saving religion consists in the inward persuasion of the mind; without which nothing can be acceptable to God."

[30] For extended discussions of this case, see L. K. Wroth, "The Rev. Nathaniel Green and the Tax Assessors: Passive Resistance in Eighteenth-Century Massachusetts," *New England Galaxy* 9 (1967), 15–21; Wroth and Zobel, eds., *Legal Papers of John Adams*, 1:32–47; McLoughlin, *New England Dissent*, 1:517–20; for membership in Green's church, see Ammidown, *Historical Collections*, 2:174–5.
[31] Act of 13 Feb. 1760, Act and Laws 386 (1759), quoted in Wroth and Zobel, eds., *Legal Papers of John Adams*, 1:43n, 46–7.
[32] Wroth and Zobel, eds., *Legal Papers of John Adams*, 1:44; Isaac Backus, *The History of New England* ... 2:164, quoted in McLoughlin, *New England Dissent*, 1:165–99.
[33] Goen, *Revivalism and Separatism*, 224, citing Thomas B. Maston, "The Ethical and Social Attitudes of Isaac Backus," Ph.D. dissertation, Yale University, 1939, 239–40.

Locke's language provided the authority for challenging the structure of the corporate established order, and for advancing a doctrine of personal moral autonomy. As the province moved toward revolution and independence, Isaac Backus would develop more extended Lockean proofs for the Baptist's demands for rights of conscience. The Baptists were reaching out from their literal-minded reading of sacred text to find legitimation in the work of one of the high priests of the rational enlightenment. Born in chaos and confusion, the Baptist movement was well on its way toward status as a legitimate institutional alternative on the religious and social landscape of the Near Frontier and of New England as a whole.[34]

"From House to House raising factions"

Thus the mid-eighteenth century saw two institutional challenges to the established order in provincial Massachusetts. Both the Land Bank and religious dissent were framed in a Lockean paradigm of voluntary association that fundamentally challenged the covenanted corporate order of the towns and the royal authority manifested in the county courts. Both the Land Bank and religious dissent were intimately related to the broader processes of the Great Awakening. But the Awakening was a complex series of movements with quite contrary results, too easily conflated and reduced to a single impulse. The orthodox revivals bringing Land Bankers to the New Light blunted – but did not necessarily erase – the Lockean trajectory of the Land Bank experience, as it restored them to the corporate commonwealth. The dissenters, focusing their attention on the achievement of rights of voluntary religion rather than an explicit challenge to the economic order of things, succeeded in framing a new Lockean institutional architecture on the Worcester middle landscape. But religious dissent certainly had an important economic dimension. Ritually separated from the constraints of an inclusive local commonwealth, dissenters were free to pursue the values of the marketplace. Rather than being coterminous, it might be best to see the Land Bank and separatist institution-building as alternative strategies, one directly and one less obviously, to solving the broader problem of achieving a competency, perhaps prosperity, on the middle landscape.

As might be expected, there were a number of future separatists and dissenters scattered among the Land Bank subscribers. Two of the three Land Bankers in

---

[34] Isaac Backus, *A Seasonable Plea for Liberty of Conscience, against Some Late Oppressive Proceedings; Particularly in the Town of Berwick, in the County of York* (Boston, 1770), 11–12. See also William L. McLoughlin, *Isaac Backus and the American Pietistic Tradition* (Boston, 1967), 122. For a discussion of the late-eighteenth-century "marriage" of rationalism and pietism in the fight against the established orthodoxy, see Sidney Mead, "American Protestanism during the Revolutionary Epoch," *Church History* 22 (1953), 279–97.

Hardwick, both deacons, separated from the Congregational church in 1749. One, Samuel Robinson, joined the Hardwick Separates, who ultimately moved to Bennington, Vermont; the other, Christopher Paige, joined the Congregationalists in Petersham. In the east neighborhood of Brookfield, two Land Bank families were linked by marriage and separatist inclinations. Hannah Stephens joined the Sturbridge Baptists in 1749; her brother Nathaniel Woolcott and husband Roger Stephens, both millers on the Five Mile River, had joined the Land Bank in 1740. Although Nathaniel would join the orthodox church in the North Parish, both families would be involved in the Baptist church that was gathered in east Brookfield in the 1790s. In Leicester, Land Bankers John and Nathaniel Potter were Quakers, Joseph Shaw and Joshua Nickols were Baptists, and Ichabod Merrit's brother Henry occupied a pew in the Baptist meetinghouse in 1747. Similarly, the Baptist preacher in Sutton, Benjamin Marsh, joined the Land Bank, as did James Bound, an English Baptist who settled briefly in Sutton. Again, in Oxford, Grafton, and Uxbridge, there was a scattering of Baptist and Quaker names among the Lank Bankers.[35]

But it is also clear that Land Bankers did not move as a bloc into separatism and organized dissent. Although they shared fundamental assumptions, separatism and the Land Bank were not one and the same. Experience in the Land Bank was broadly distributed across the New Light orbit: Most Land Bankers would be drawn into the Awakening, but only a few would move on to build or join dissenting institutions.

Events in Leicester provide a view of the parallel but distinct dynamics of the Land Bank and religious dissent. Dissent came early to Leicester, and its emergence was intimately involved with a heated confrontation with the orthodox minister over his salary. In 1727 Baptist preacher Elisha Callender was invited to Sutton to preach and to baptize among families settling from Salem who had recently been drawn into Baptist teachings. Some of those meeting with the Sutton Baptists were from Leicester, and in June of 1732 the itinerant John Comer baptized eight others in South Leicester. All of those baptized in Sutton and Leicester were admitted to membership in the Baptist church in Boston. The preceding seven years had brought bitter controversy to the town. The Reverend David Parsons had been settled as the orthodox minister in 1721, having been dismissed by Malden after he sued the town for failing to keep up his salary payments. Within three years of his settlement in Leicester, his salary was again in

[35] Davis, *Currency and Banking*, 2:295ff.; Paige, *Hardwick*, 183–5; Fisk, "Testimony"; Temple, *North Brookfield*, 12, 281–2; Estes, "Historical Discourse," 26ff.; Charles H. Lincoln, "The Antecedents of the Worcester Society of Friends," *Worcester Historical Society Publications*, NS 1 (1928), 30–1; Benedict and Tracy, *Sutton*; 461–2; Pierce, *Grafton*, 217–20; Uxbridge *Vital Records*.

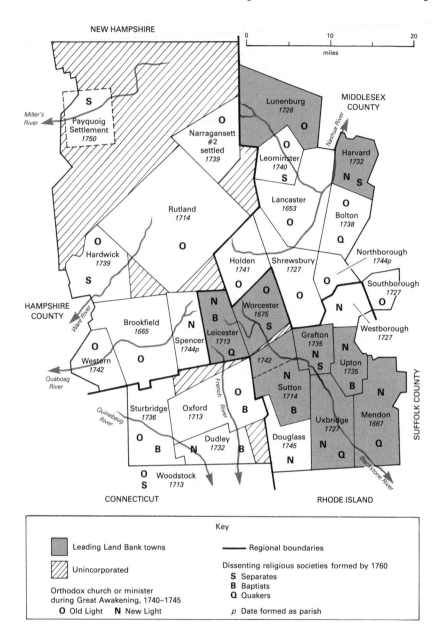

Map 1. Land Bank, awakening, and dissent in provincial Worcester County.
(Drawn by Carmela Ciampa from data by John Brooke)

arrears, diverted to the building of garrisons and undermined by the inflation of the province bills. By 1727 things had deteriorated to the point that the town voted to ask Parsons to "remove and remain out of this town." Finally, after years of petitioning and counter petitioning to the General Court, Parsons brought a suit against the town in the Court of General Sessions, and in May 1732, won a settlement. The selectmen elected in 1731 were fined and the town assessed £75 due under contract. The court case translated directly into Baptist separatism. In every year since 1725 men from what would be dissenter families were a majority on the board of selectmen, and constituted its entirety in 1727 and 1731. Of the five Leicester selectmen fined in 1732, two, Daniel Denny and Thomas Richardson, were baptized that June by John Comers. Five grown children of another selectman, Capt. Samuel Green, long an opponent of the minister, had been baptized in 1727 by Elisha Callendar in Sutton, or were baptized that summer by John Comer. Among them was Thomas Green, who would be the Baptist preacher until his death in 1773. Similarly, the sons of the two other selectmen, Thomas Newhall and Richard Southgate, were already or would soon be Baptists.[36]

The roots of dissent in Leicester were thus entangled in an economic controversy flowing from the expenses of civil and religious government in a frontier town in a period of significant inflation. Such circumstances also provided the context for the wave of support for the Land Bank eight years later. However, although Leicester was a Land Bank stronghold, there were relatively few dissenters among the subscribers. Only one of the selectmen serving between 1725 and 1731 who subsequently joined the Baptists also subscribed to the Land Bank. and he served for only one term. Conversely, other Land Bankers who never were affiliated with the Baptists or the Quakers served a total of fourteen terms between 1725 and 1739. In total, there were only five dissenters among the twenty-two Land Bankers paying taxes in Leicester in 1740, and none of these few dissenting Land Bankers were from the families that had led either the fight with Reverend Parsons or the formation of dissenting groups.[37]

But not all of those who tangled with the minister were drawn into dissent. Prior to his subscription to the Land Bank, Capt. Benjamin Johnson served as selectman in 1725, 1738, and 1739; as one of two "gentlemen" among their number he must have been a leader among the Land Bankers. Johnson also had been a strident

[36] Washburn, *Leicester*, 60, 75ff.; Nathan E. Wood, *The First Baptist Church of Boston* (Boston, 1899), 222–4; McLoughlin, *New England Dissent*, 1:296–8; Estes, "Historical Discourse," 20; Franklin P. Rice, ed., "Records of the Court of General Sessions," *Coll. WSA* 5 (1882–3), 47.
[37] Of 51 selectman's terms served between 1725 and 1739 by dissenters and Land Bankers in Leicester, 36 were served by men only involved in dissent, 16 by men who would be Land Bankers but had no connection to dissent, and only one was served by a man who was both a dissenter and Land Banker. Selectmen from Washburn, *Leicester*, 459–60.

opponent of the minister, and sued Parsons in General Sessions in 1735 for slander. The minister had accused him of having "stolen two years salary from him." In Parsons's words, Captain Johnson was "a tatling man of a Tatler [who] went from House to House raising factions."[38] If Johnson raised factions among the Leicester people, his was not a faction of religious dissenters. Rather than joining the Baptists or Quakers, Johnson was one of at least seven Land Bankers who took up land in the west precinct, later to become Spencer, in the 1740s. Among these Land Bankers were three of the seven founding members of the New Light orthodox church in 1744, including the deacon James Wilson and young Oliver Watson. The early records of the Congregational church in Leicester have not survived, but scattered references suggest a similar connection with this New Light church. And across Worcester County Land Bankers remained within the orthodox orbit. Most of the Land Bankers in Sutton remained affiliated with David Hall's orthodox church. In Worcester, all of the Land Bankers still delinquent in 1763 held pews in the orthodox meetinghouse built that year; in Uxbridge, Congregationalists – including not only the minister Nathan Webb but two deacons – outnumbered Quakers among the Land Bankers by at least nine to one.[39]

Leicester, a town weighed down with the public and private expenses of settling and developing the middle landscape, was overrun with "tatling men" raising factions in the 1730s. But these factions seem to have had different strategies for dealing with these economic problems; some attempted to expand the supply of money on the basis of landed property, others withdrew from the ritual obligations of orthodoxy.

Escaping the expense of supporting the established clergy was clearly an important element in the emergence of dissent. Without a paid minister to maintain, the costs of attending a Baptist meeting were significantly smaller than among the orthodox; here piety meshed with economic advantage. As members of the Boston Baptist church, the Sutton and Leicester Baptists were subject to a province law requiring that all dissenters live within five miles of their meetinghouse to be free of taxation for the established minister. They petitioned the Boston church in 1731 to be allowed to establish their own church, so as to "prevent the [town] officers from Spoiling and abusing" them for ministerial taxes. That December the Boston church refused their request, as they were "not Ripe Enough" and complained that they had been "too Rash" in ordaining Benjamin Marsh, as "the Scripture sais lay hands Suddenly upon no man." The following February they took their case to the Courts of General Sessions,

[38] Rice, ed., "Records of the Court of General Sessions," 119.
[39] Draper, *Spencer*, genealogies; Washburn, *Leicester*, 116n; Worthley, ed., An Inventory, 319; Wall, *Reminiscences of Worcester*, 112–16; Uxbridge *Vital Records*.

petitioning for the right to be exempted from ministerial taxes. The court accepted their lists of members in August 1732, but neither town would forgo their taxes. The Sutton and Leicester Baptists finally formed a church in 1735 – and divided in 1738 – after the five-mile rule was abolished. The onset of the Awakening brought a new climate of opinion; the New Light spirit in both towns brought a functional pluralism. Sutton abated the ministerial rates of Baptists in 1740, and in 1744 voted to choose selectmen and assessors in equal numbers from the two orthodox parishes and the Baptist Society. In 1741 Leicester granted tax-free status to Thomas Green, the preacher in the Leicester Baptist church, and accepted certificates from those attending the meeting. In these towns the Baptists succeeded in avoiding the costs of the established system at a relatively early date, but across the county and the province this issue was far from resolved.[40]

There are other signs that religious dissent constituted something of an economic strategy. Baptist communities were typically closely clustered in distinct neighborhoods, often in valleys where streams provided the opportunity for waterpower. Milling families like the Greens, Nickols, and Richardsons in Leicester or the Woolcotts and Stevens in east Brookfield were often leading families among the Baptists, the ponds powering their mills often serving as baptismal pools. More generally, artisans seem to have been attracted to the Baptist and Quaker communities in disproportionate numbers. In addition to millers there were a number of housewrights, blacksmiths, and tanners among the Leicester Baptists.[41] Similarly, there is good evidence that dissenting communions might constitute reasonably self-contained exchange networks. The account book of Philemon Shepherd, a Baptist farmer in early nineteenth-century Sturbridge, reveals that at least 60 percent of his labor exchanges and 75 percent of his cash exchanges were with fellow Baptists.[42] The accounts of Dr. Robert Craige, a Baptist physician in Leicester who also produced all kinds of wooden implements and tools, suggests a similar concentration of trade with his fellow dissenters. Craige was noted for his spinning wheels and textile looms, and he seems to have sold these widely through the region from Rutland to Sturbridge.

---

[40] Wood, *First Baptist Church of Boston*, 222–3; McLoughlin, *New England Dissent*, 1:297; Benedict and Tracy, *Sutton*, 58, 69; Estes, "Historical Discourse," 22–4.

[41] Artisans and millers from Temple, *North Brookfield*, 11–15, and genealogies; Washburn, *Leicester*, 29–30, and genealogies; Martha Cutting, "Westville and Its Manufactures," *QHSL* 2 (1903–9), 60. An analysis of six samples of Congregationalists, Baptists, and Quakers in Leicester and the North Parish of Brookfield suggests that dissenters were twice as likely to be artisans or the sons of artisans as were the orthodox. See Brooke, "For Honour and Civil Worship," Table 2, and "Society, Revolution ...," 119, 121.

[42] Holly Izard Patterson, "A Small Farmer's World: The Economic and Social Networks of Philemon Shepherd of Sturbridge, Massachusetts," unpublished work, Old Sturbridge Village, Inc.

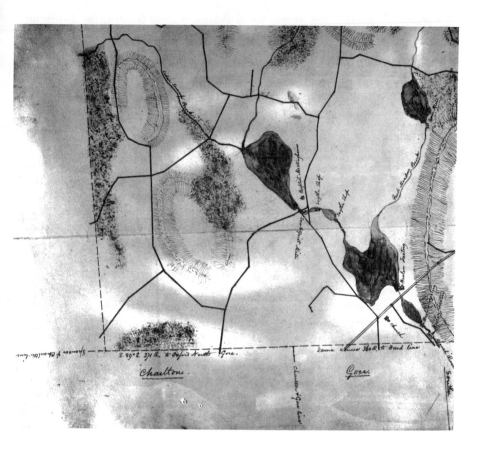

5. The Baptist neighborhood in South Leicester, 1831.
The location of the Green family mill and pond, and the meetinghouse built in 1747, in a hollow between surrounding hills.
Detail of "A Plan of the Town of Leicester, upon a minute and accurate Survey, made in 1831." (Courtesy of the Massachusetts Archives)

Such sales would by necessity often be outside of the Baptist network, but the bulk of his accounts were closer to home. Eighty-five percent of his accounts were with households in Leicester and the adjacent neighborhoods in Oxford, Charlton, and Spencer; within Leicester at least a half of his trade was with fellow Baptists, and much of this trade with his in-laws, the Green family. And, if the experience of Leicester Baptists and Quakers is any guide, such closed exchange networks worked to encourage the persistence of isolated nuclear families, the dissenting community functioning as a buffer against economic uncertainties in the place of wider kin connections.[43]

The rise of the dissenting societies was also a vehicle for the emergence of impatient, ambitious families seeking to carve out arenas of influence and status. The formation of dissenting societies gave institutional form to preexisting networks of kinship – and presumably exchange. Of the eleven original Leicester Baptists, for example, ten were the children of Samuel Green, or their spouses. Clustered in a neighborhood in the south Leicester lowlands near their mill privileges, they may have objected to the costs of building a garrison at the town center as much as to the costs of the minister's salary; none of them signed a request for soldiers during Father Raille's War in 1725. In 1747 Thomas Green built the small Baptist meetinghouse above his millpond in south Leicester, and retained proprietorship for many years; members desiring pews had to pay Green to have them built. The expense of building the meetinghouse apparently had no effect on Green's fortunes; Isaac Backus noted that Thomas Green grew wealthy on land speculation, and died in 1773 with an estate of £4,495, certainly one of the wealthiest men in the county.[44]

Contrary to common assumptions, the dissenters never were an impoverished group. If anything, towns with dissenting groups were located at the higher end of the provincial valuations, and within these towns the assessed wealth of individual dissenters compared favorably with their orthodox neighbors. In 1732 the Leicester Baptists and Quakers were relatively evenly distributed across the rate list drawn up to pay off the Reverend Parsons, with just under 30 percent ranked in the top quintile. By 1740, 40 percent of the Baptists were ranked in the top quintile, a distribution that they would have again four decades later in the 1783 valuation. If the Quakers had not improved their position, they were reasonably well situated; a 1743 petition from Leicester complained that they occupied "several of our most considerable estates." In Sutton, similarly, the Baptists seem to have been well positioned; Capt. William King and Benjamin Marsh, their leading figures, ranked second and third on the meetinghouse list drawn up in

[43] Account Book, Dr. Robert Craig, Leicester, Mass., 1757–81, Research Library, Old Sturbridge Village. Based on a sample of 293 entries drawn from throughout the account book. Craig mixed his records, writing on all the pages in the early years, and filling in entries in blank spaces in later years. Of the 155 taxpayers on the 1740 valuation of Leicester (see Chapter 2, note 16), 27 were Baptists or Quakers. Although the numbers are small, they indicate that the familial isolates among the dissenters were more persistent that among the nondissenters: 60% (6/10) of the single surnames among the dissenters survived to 1783, as against 49% (22/45) of the single surnames among the nondissenters. The rate of persistence among the multiple-entry surnames was exactly the same: 76% (13/17 and 63/83).

[44] Washburn, Leicester, 129; Estes, "Historical Discourse," 27–8; McLoughlin, ed., Backus Diary, 2:432.

1731, immediately following Justice Samuel Dudley.[45] These were, of course, dissenting societies that emerged before the Awakening. The Sturbridge Separate Baptists seem to have been drawn from a somewhat poorer – or at least disadvantaged – group, and this situation may indeed have colored their secession from the orthodox church. Here proprietorship marked an important divide between orthodox and separates. More than 40 percent of the men joining the orthodox church by 1753 were related to the Medfield proprietors, as against only 18 percent of those joining the Baptists by the same year. They may well have been frustrated with the shape of institutional and economic power in the town. Their leading men, Daniel and Henry Fisk, seem to have been particularly prickly about status an position. They were the sons of a proprietor, but came from Watertown rather than Medfield, as did the majority of other proprietary families. Prominent in the establishment of town and church, they led first the separation from the orthodox church in 1749, and later from the "hands" Baptists in 1759, complaining that they would "be put aside" if a minister were settled.[46]

In Charlton, there are suggestions of similar status-seeking ambitions in the restless career of Ebenezer Davis, the son of Justice Edward Davis, a leading Congregationalist in Oxford. Rejecting his father's orthodoxy, Davis joined the Charlton Baptists in 1767; ten years later he was fined for refusing military service in the Revolution, and in 1779 joined a small group of Universalists. Growing rich on the provisions trade, Davis became a "well-known capitalist" and died the richest man in the county.[47]

---

[45] Quotation from MA 12: 359. Sutton pew list in Benedict and Tracy, *Sutton*, 45.

Leicester Baptists and Quakers: Wealth in 1732 and 1740

	Baptists				Quakers			
Quintile	1732		1740		1732		1740	
1st	3	*27*	6	*40*	2	*29*	3	*27*
2d	3		1		1		4	
3d	3		5		2		2	
4th	1		2		0		1	
5th	1		1		2		1	
Total	11	*100*	15	*100*	7	*100*	11	*100*

Note: Figures in italics are percentages.
Source: Estes, "Historical Discourse," 26ff.; Lincoln, "Antecedents," 30–1; Ministerial Rate List, 1732, and Province Tax List, 1740, Leicester General Records, vol. 1.

[46] Proprietor's list in Clark, *Sturbridge*, 4–5; Congregationalists from *Manual for the Use of Members of the Congregational Church, in Sturbridge* ... (West Brookfield, 1843), 26–8; Baptists from Fisk, "Testimony," and "John Davis Ms."

[47] Anson Titus, "Reminiscences of Early American Universalism," *Universalist Quarterly and General Review* (1881), 438–9; Daniels, *Oxford*, 466.

Dramatic signs of economic striving and competition exploded among the Leicester Baptists in 1780s, when a faction of "Dissaffected Brethren" united to stridently oppose paying support for a newly settled minister. Led by Samuel Denny and Deacon Isaac Choate, both men of large property, they complained that the minister "was a Lazy Man ... a Discont [ent] Person, not being easy without [having] two or three Sorts of grain in the House – that [he] wearied out the church with unreasonable complaints." The minister, Isaac Beals, countered that Deacon Choate had asked him "the market price of Pork, that was not well fatted." The 1780s, a time of profound economic turmoil, apparently brought considerable stress to the Leicester Baptist community, for in 1784 the church established a procedure by which members could, after efforts at reconciliation, take another member to court for payment of debts without fear of church action.[48]

By the 1780s, and probably well before, the Baptists in the region were as wealthy as their orthodox neighbors.[49] As a group they did not occupy a distinct class; rather, the dissenting householders increasingly divided into the same broad classes that characterized orthodox society. The leading families of the various Baptist societies were interwoven by marriage; mill proprietors, innholders, doctors, and prosperous artisans and farmers – but never justices of the peace – they presided over a dramatically new institutional architecture on the middle landscape. Among their number can be detected men who showed a strong predisposition toward the aggressive economic individualism that would characterize the century to come.

[48] Greenville Baptist Church Records, vol. 1, minutes, 11, 17–18, letters, 9–27.
[49] *Congregational and Baptist church members on the 1783 valuation*

Quintile	Brookfield		Sturbridge		Spencer		Total	
Congregational								
1st	53	*33*	17	*39*	16	*42*	86	*35*
2d	45		11		11		67	
3d	36		7		7		50	
4th	18		3		3		24	
5th	9		5		1		15	
Total	161	*100*	43	*100*	38	*100*	242	*100*
Baptist								
	Leicester		Sturbridge		Charlton		Total	
1st	9	*41*	8	*32*	10	*31*	27	*34*
2d	5		8		10		23	
3d	5		5		3		13	
4th	2		2		3		7	
5th	1		2		6		9	
Total	22	*100*	25	*100*	32	*100*	79	*100*

Buried in baptism: Ritual practice and the Awakening's legacy

By the mid-1750s the evangelical spirit of the Awakening had long since faded among the orthodox. New membership would come into the churches only slowly, shaped by the gradual succession of family generations rather than by broad impulses sweeping through neighborhoods and regions. With the waning of the revival spirit came the reassertion of the forms of routinized orthodoxy. The New Light church founded in Spencer in 1744 soon abandoned aspirations to a pure covenant of full members. In 1745 they instituted the halfway covenant, voting to "esteem it a duty incumbent on all baptized persons publicly and solemnly to take hold of the Covenant of God." The church reaffirmed this vote in 1756, and in 1766 agreed to lower barriers even further, allowing people to join in full communion without making "a Publick Relation of their Christian Experience." The minister in Spencer, Joshua Eaton, had been censured by the Worcester church in 1743 as "being actuated by an over-heated Brain" for preaching itinerant sermons in Grafton. In the ensuing decades this ardent New Light would amicably cooperate with his fellow orthodox ministers in the Brookfield Association, changing pulpits with Nathan Fiske of the South Parish of Brookfield, a man of decidedly liberal tendencies, and with Eli Forbes of the North Parish, a moderate Calvinist. As the Awakening receded in time, doctrinal differences among the established ministry no longer were the source of bitter controversy. In the long view, the drama of the orthodox Awakening must be balanced against the weight of the popular experience among the orthodox: the ordered interweaving of households into a corporate, territorial community across decades of routine piety.

Note: Figures in italics are percentages.
Source: 1783 Valuations of Brookfield, Charlton, Leicester, Spencer, Sturbridge (Massachusetts State Library); *Catalogue of the Members of the Congregational Church in West Brookfield, From 1758 to 1861 with an Alphabetical Index* (West Brookfield, 1861); *The Confession of Faith and Covenant of the First Congregational Church in North Brookfield, Mass., with a Catalogue of the Members (1752–1878)* (West Brookfield, 1878); *Rules of Order and Discipline . . . of the Evangelical Congregational Church in Brookfield, Mass., with Historical Notes and Names of Officers and Members* (West Brookfield, 1878); *Manual for the Use of Members of the Congregational Church, in Sturbridge, January, 1843* (West Brookfield, 1843); Membership Book, First Congregational Church of Spencer, Mass (MS., Church Collection); records of the Greenville Baptist Church, Leicester Mass., vol. 1 (BPAN); Estes, "Historical Discourse," in *The Greenville Baptist Church . . .* (Worcester, 1887), 26ff.; Fisk, "Testimony"; The Records of the Baptist Church of Christ in Sturbridge (microfilm, research Library, Old Sturbridge Village); Holmes Ammidown, *Historical Collections . . .* (New York, 1877), 2: 176–9.

Ultimately, the orthodox Awakening brought not an overwhelming personal transformation, but a confirmation of collective tradition.[50]

The shape of routine orthodox piety was most suggestively manifested in the public symbolism of death and the dead that came to dominate the town centers. Public burial grounds were laid out by proprietors and selectmen at the incorporation of the towns and districts. Almost invariably, they were immediately adjacent to the meetinghouses in a corner of the ground set aside for a training field; like the meetinghouses, they were to be maintained at public, civil expense. Starting in the 1740s, and with greater and greater frequency in the 1750s and 1760s, burials in these graveyards were marked with headstones carved with images of death's heads and of the soul in flight. Emblazoned with a powerful religious symbolism, these gravestones were also suffused with secular and territorial connotations. Carvings were imported from throughout New England, reflecting the geographic origins of the settlers and the residual influences of early county divisions. Like the town meetinghouses, the face-decorated gravestones evoked the fusion of civil and religious categories that stood as the central pillar of the orthodox town system.[51]

This conflation of civil and religious in the town graveyards was an important reason why the dissenters abandoned them – and their powerful symbolism of souls in flight. The withdrawal of the dissenters from the central meetinghouses was paralleled by the withdrawal from the central graveyards. This process began in Leicester in January 1736, with the death of Capt. Samuel Green, the leading opponent of the orthodox minister and the father of a vast Baptist clan. Rather than being buried at the town graveyard, Green was buried on a knoll overlooking his millpond, adjacent to where his son Thomas would build the Baptist meetinghouse eleven years later. This was the first of four peripheral graveyards established in eighteenth-century Leicester.[52] A similar dispersal of the dead to sectarian and family plots marked all of those towns in which religious unity was shattered in the Awakening and its aftermath. Baptists and Quakers also shunned the carved stones that populated the town center graveyards: Congregationalists were four times as likely to purchase these markers, which allowed the dead to exhort the living from beyond the grave.

The traditional material culture of the dead marked death as a supremely important boundary for the orthodox. Each critical transition in the life cycle was

[50] First Congregational Church of Spencer, Mass., "Church Records, vol. A," 20, and n.p.; Forbes, *The Good Minister*, 17; Forbes *Some Short Account of . . . Joshua Eaton*, iv, v, vi, vii; Eli Forbes, *Christ, The Life, and Death, the Gain of the Godly . . .* (App. to *Some Short Account*), 146; Fiske Diary, April 27–8, 1771; William B. Sprague, *Annals of the American Pulpit* (New York, 1859–65), 1:495, 573. See a broadly similar interpretation in Heyrman, *Commerce and Culture*.
[51] See Brooke, "Society, Revolution . . .," 361–446.
[52] Washburn, *Leicester*, 161–3.

6. Soul effigy carving on the gravestone of Abigail Muzzy of Spencer, 1720–66, wife of Deacon John Muzzy.
Gravestone carved by William Young of Worcester.
Rubbing by Ann Parker and Avon Neal. (Photograph courtesy of the Worcester Art Museum, Worcester, Massachusetts)

marked by a change in religious status for the Congregationalists. At birth they were baptized, given the promise of the national covenant. At parenthood they might join the church in full or half communion, thus transmitting the rights of baptism to a new generation. And at death they were buried with the expectation that they would rise in the new birth at the resurrection, they would "come forth at the dawn of the everlasting day, beautiful and immortal, fashioned like unto Christ's glorious body . . . their faithful monuments will render back their dust." The Baptists explicitly rejected this interpretation. Baptism by immersion, not death and earthly burial, was the true equivalent of Christs' death and resurrection. The Baptists were to be "buried in baptism"; one Baptist preacher in Leicester argued that "plunging . . . signified the immersion of the old and the raising of the new man." Rather than waiting for death, the Baptists would be transformed in life. Their religious life would bear no relation to a personal life cycle: The events distributed in ordered sequence through the earthly existence of the Congregationalist would be telescoped into one cathartic experience of conversion an immersion. The Congregationalist would not be reborn until the general resurrection; the rebirth of the Baptist would come with his emergence from the baptismal pool. Freed by watery immersion from the customary expenses of the orthodox world, dead to sin and no longer of this world, the Baptist could pursue his personal calling without consideration for the obligations of the corporate moral economy that continued to structure the expectations and assumptions of his orthodox neighbors.[53]

The dissenting societies constituted a well-defined social and political orbit by the 1760s. Concentrated in the county's southern valleys, they were stitched together both by a thickening web of kinship and intermarriage and by a series of formal institutions – the Six Principle Baptist Association, the Warren Association, the Smithfield Monthly Meeting – that anticipated the form and process of institutions that would structure the nineteenth-century landscape. And if family ties and traditions drew many into dissent, may others – like Ebenezer Davis in Charlton – defied tradition to associate and disassociate as individuals. In the mideighteenth century both the Land Bank and separatist dissent introduced Lockean concepts of individual autonomy and rationality into the region's political culture. The Land Bank was a spectacular failure, and for many its opening onto the future was buried in a renewed immersion in corporate covenant. But separatist dissent was eminently successful, and established a powerful challenge of voluntary individualism to the prevailing unitary structures of covenant and charter.

[53] Quotes from Daniel Foster, *Consolation in Adversity and Hope in Death. A Sermon Preached on the Death of Jeduthan Baldwin* ... (Worcester, 1789), 15; Benjamin Foster, *The Washing of Regeneration, or the Divine Right of Immersion* ... (Boston, 1779), 29. For a comparative analysis of the symbolism of death in orthodoxy and dissent, see Brooke, "Society, Revolution ...," 96–156; and Brooke, "For Honour and Civil Worship."

4

Politics: From Popular insurgency to Shirley's consensus

Every spring the freeholders of provincial Massachusetts met in town meeting to elect officers for the following year. In a March meeting they chose local officials: selectmen, assessors, constables, surveyors, and fence viewers; in May they met to make the important and problematic choice of a representative, or deputy, to serve in the legislature. In the language of the warrant calling the people of Brookfield to a meeting on May 17, 1738, they were to elect a man to "serve and Represent Sd Town at a Great and Gennerall Court or assembly to be Convened, held and kept for his majesties sarvis at the Cort House in Boston."[1] The representative would serve two masters: his constituents and the king. Meeting at the ornate yet strikingly small State House in Boston, the assembled representatives would consider routine petitions about taxes, schools, and boundaries from throughout the province, and sponsor petitions from their towns and localities. Such was the assembly's role as a "General Court," overseeing the more direct government of the province that took place in the Court of General Sessions and most fundamentally in the towns themselves. But the representatives also considered broader provincial affairs regarding the structure of government, the defense of the province, and the ebb and flow of revenue and expenditure. In these they participated in a structured politics of court and country, confronting the governor, the king's agent, in the interest of their constituencies.

The General Court, comprised of governor, council, and house of representatives, was thus the central arena of a ritualized contest between governor and people, a contest nominally structured within a framework of royal protection of popular rights and popular allegiance to royal authority. The governor, appointed by the king on the advice of the Board of Trade, attempted to rule the province in accordance with instructions that increasingly called for formalizing the imperial system and reducing the autonomy of a colony that had been a virtual republican commonwealth for two generations in the seventeenth century. While they were charged with attending to "his majesty's service," the representatives were also instructed by their towns to defend the interest of their constituents and the people of the province in general. As the king's agent, the governor was constantly held

---

[1] Brookfield, Mass., Town Meeting Records, 1719–70, 70.

97

to the letter of the 1691 charter, the ultimate framework of social order and legitimacy that bound king and people in a mutual compact almost as powerful as that with the Puritan divinity. The members of the house worked to enhance their powers in the government of the province, stretching the language and provisions of the charter at every opportunity.[2]

This broader contest was encapsulated in miniature in the institutional structure of the General Court itself. The House of Representatives resisted the encroachment of royal power, while the governor attempted to contain the assembly's reach and size; each argued that they acted in accordance with king's will in the interest of the common good. Worcester County's introduction to legislative politics centered on this problem of institutional definition.

Soon after settlement, the people of the new and struggling town of Leicester had sought to find a man of influence to represent them in General Court, and they invited Judge John Menzies to settle in the town. A member of the Edinburgh Faculty of Advocates, Menzies had been appointed Judge of the Court of Admiralty in 1715. Settling first in Roxbury, he was induced to remove to Leicester by a grant of 1,600 acres of land from the proprietors, many of whom had been his Roxbury neighbors. Before he actually moved to the Nipmuc frontier, Menzies was elected to represent Leicester. In 1693 the town of Oxford had similarly elected Daniel Allen, a Boston merchant and proprietor Joseph Dudley's half-brother, as a nonresident representative to the General Court. But in 1720, after the rise of the Popular party, which was opposed to the governor, the political climate was drastically different, and the house refused to seat Menzies as a nonresident. Elected four times while living on the frontier, Menzies caused a great controversy in 1726, when he was again elected by Leicester after he had returned to live in Boston. Again he was expelled from the house, but this time his nonresidency was compounded by the publication of a letter he had written in his capacity as judge of the admiralty, complaining "that it is a thing impossible to get a Jury in the Country that will do the King justice" in maritime cases. Led by Speaker Elisha Cooke, the leader of the Popular faction, the house censured

---

[2] This chapter is influenced particularly by Bushman, *King and People*, and also draws upon Jack P. Greene, "Changing Interpretations of Early American Politics," in *The Reinterpretation of Early American History: Essays in Honor of John Ewin Pomfret*, Ray A. Billington, ed. (San Marino, Calif., 1966), 151–84; Bernard Bailyn, *The Origins of American Politics* (New York, 1968); Zuckerman, *Peaceable Kingdoms*; Zemsky, *Merchants, Farmers, and River Gods*; Stephen E. Patterson, *Political Parties in Revolutionary Massachusetts* (Madison, 1973); Pencak, *War, Politics, and Revolution*; John Murrin, "Political Development," in Pole and Greene, eds. *Colonial British America*, 408–47. I borrow the term "arena" from Victor Turner, *Dramas, Field, and Metaphors: Symbolic Action in Human Society* (Ithaca, 1974); and I have found useful Marc J. Swartz, "Introduction," to *Local Level Politics: Social and Cultural Perspectives* (Chicago, 1968), 1–46; Eugene Genovese, "The Political Crisis of Social History: A Marxist Perspective," *JSH* 10 (1976), 205–220; Tony Judt, "A Clown in Regal Purple: Social History and the Historians," *History Workshop* 7 (Spring, 1979), 66–94; Clifford Geertz, *Negara: The*

Menzies for writing "a very Base & injurious Misrepresentation of his Majesty's true & faithful Subjects of this Province."[3]

Menzies's expulsion was laden with factional considerations: As a royal officeholder he was certain to side with the governor against the Popular men. But his expulsion was cast in language of provincial allegiance to the crown: Menzies was a dual threat to the assembly, both as an adherent of the governor and a source of threatening complaints. Twenty-three years later in 1749 the house again drew on this language of allegiance in demanding that the west precinct of Leicester, now firmly in the Popular ranks, be incorporated as a town with rights of representation. In vetoing town incorporation, Lt. Governor Phipps had cited royal instructions stipulating that the house not be enlarged; the house countered that the incorporation of a "Part of Leicester into a distinct Township, will be for the Prosperity of his Majesty's Subjects, in which his Majesty always takes Pleasure." The house continued that the full representation of the people in the assembly was "agreeable to their Majesty's Charter and the Laws of the Province." Phipps's superior, Governor William Shirley, was of a very different mind than the house, and would have revised that charter if given the opportunity. That same year he had drawn up a "Plan of Civil Government" for the new province of Nova Scotia, which repeated much of the Massachusetts charter, except for granting wider patronage powers to the governor, and granting rights of representation to counties rather than towns. Shirley's plan, if imposed on Massachusetts, would have brought a southern system of government to New England. Rather than a host of often unruly town representatives closely monitored by their constituents, a county system would have restricted political power to the same county elite who dominated the courts. The large house, with its annual elections and local representation, provided a degree of popular participation in provincial politics unique in early America and a thorn in the side of successive royal governors. The issue of house size and reduction would emerge repeatedly over the next century, as the people of Massachusetts met in constitutional convention to structure their governmental framework. The tenacious tradition of corporate representation forged in two centuries of colonial experience would only be broken in 1857, as the concentration of population in a few urban places made it a political anachronism.[4]

Theatre State in Nineteenth-Century Bali (Princeton, 1976); Thomas Bender, "Whole and Parts: The Need for Synthesis in American History," *JAH* 73 (1986), 120–36; the exchanges in the subsequent "Round Table," in *JAH* 74 (1987), 107–30; and William E. Leuchtenberg, "The Pertinence of Political History: Reflections on the State in America," *JAH* 73 (1986), 585–600.
[3] Daniels, *Oxford*, 13; Washburn, *Leicester*, 62, 177–8; *JHRM* 7:xiv–xv; 167–8, 194, 191–4, 216–18.
[4] Draper, *Spencer*, 34–9, *JHRM* 26:152–3; on Shirley's plan, see Zemsky, *Merchants, Farmers, and River Gods*, 151–4.

Without direct elections for governor between the granting of the Royal Charter in 1691 and the adoption of a state constitution in 1780, political action in provincial Massachusetts became particularly focused on the assembly and the General Court. Election of a representative was a freeholder's highest political expression. The gentry, men of prominence and standing, were particularly likely to be chosen to represent the town in General Court, but they were not free to act as they pleased; they served at the will of their constituents, subject to instructions and annual election. Conversely, the governor used his patronage powers to build a gentry following that would restrain the demands of popular constituencies and uphold the influence and authority of the prerogative. The representatives were thus poised between governor and people, each independently holding the keys to places of honor and power, each in a position to reward or punish the representative for his action in the assembly. Politics in provincial Massachusetts was built on this matrix of opposing forces, the varying qualities of each determining the shape of political action in the arena of the General Court. The aspirations, temperament, and political skills of successive governors, to say nothing of their instructions from the crown, made up one set of forces; the interests, loyalties, and beliefs of local constituencies made up another. The provincial contest between governor and people, ruler and ruled, forged an enduring political geography in Worcester County that would shape political culture and action through the Revolutionary era and beyond to the first decades of the nineteenth century. Assumptions developed under its formative influence would continue to be felt even after the county's public culture had been reshaped by the early industrial revolution and the new institutions of democratic party politics.

The contest of governor and constituencies in Massachusetts Bay constituted one slice through the concentric layers structuring public culture and institutions in early America. At one extreme lay the imperial – and later the national – government, with primary responsibility for the broadest issues of the collective interest, particularly the defense of the integrity of the empire or union and its legitimating constitutional framework. At the other extreme lay the people and their local institutions of town, church, and militia. Between the empire-nation and the people in locality lay a hierarchy of public arenas, the province or state and the county. The public culture of a given local community was defined by both its internal configuration of class and community and its changing relationships with the arenas of county, province, and empire. Here gentry elites, mediating between locality and metropolis, were particularly critical, engaged in a complex balancing act, steering between provincial prestige and local loyalties. Acting in their role as mediators, the gentry, by turns, acted to cement provincial consensus or to figure in two orders of conflict, either leading the people against the metropolis, or taking the force of a popular insurgency. The political history of Worcester County between the Peace of Utrecht and the Civil War followed a long cyclical pattern, an oscillation between periods of relative quiet, of relative agreement among these concentrically layered public arenas, and recurrent episodes of dramatic confrontation, when popular forces challenged the authority both of the metropolis and of the leading elements of the county gentry. Each would shape and reshape the political landscape, leaving a cumulative legacy of traditions, assumptions, and institutions.

Over the five decades between the region's settlement and the Stamp Act, Worcester County passed through a full cycle of confrontational insurgency and stable, reasonably quiescent, consensus. In the broadest terms, the Land Bank insurgency was the culmination of an era of confrontation falling between the 1720s and 1744, when the people of the Worcester frontier allied themselves with the Popular faction, and was followed by two decades of quiet agreement between the people and the governor – a calm before the storm of the Revolutionary crisis.

During this era of relative calm the moral insurgency of religious dissent remained outside the formal arena of provincial politics. It would have a certain limited influence on popular politics in the late 1750s, but the dissenters' insurgency would enter the political arena decisively only in the 1770s, when the break with Britain threw the province into a Lockean state of nature. At the center of the county's late provincial political experience lay the gradual emergence of a Popular gentry leadership – of strong oppositional principles and responsive to constituency – which would lead the county through the Revolution down to the ratification of the federal Constitution. This Popular leadership negotiated between the ideological poles imposed by the structure of provincial legitimacy. The charter had established a Lockean compact between king and province, but the defense of that compact required a Harringtonian unity and vigilance among the people. The formative experiences of the Popular leadership lay in social circumstances that exposed them to these ideological cross-pressures: the dramatic career of the Land Bank, a Lockean experiment smothered in the corporate imperatives of the orthodox New Light revivals; the practices of political compromise demanded by the new Lockean institutional architecture of religious dissent; the promise of landed independence – so central to the construct of a Harringtonian commonwealth – offered by Governor William Shirley's militant imperialism.

Jonathan Belcher, the Land Bank, and the rise of the Popular tradition in Worcester County

The first suggestion of a county political culture of opposition came in January 1726, when the house grudgingly accepted the Explanatory Charter, which defined precisely the governor's powers to dismiss the General Court and to approve the house's choice lof speaker. Justice John Menzies, perhaps aware of his ambiguous position, refrained from voting, but the other three representatives from the

Nipmuc towns voted two to one in opposition to the revision of the charter, almost exactly the reverse of the vote throughout the rest of the province.[5]

Despite the importance of the institutional framework of the popular contest with the governor, economic issues, particularly the demand for paper money that would culminate in the Land Bank, were far more powerful in drawing the constituents and representatives of the Nipmuc frontier to the Popular party. The county's political culture, in fact its very existence, was interwoven with the Popular faction's battle with the governor over public credit and expenditure.

When Governor Jonathan Belcher arrived to take up his appointment in 1729, he carried royal instructions ordering him to establish a permanent salary for his office, and to bring the Massachusetts bills of credit under control, retiring all of them by 1741. The ensuing battle between governor and the house, under the leadership of Elisha Cooke, reached a peak in December of 1730. On the 17th the governor ordered the house to provide him with a permanent annual salary of £1,000, and condemned the bills of credit as a "common Delusion to Mankind." On December 23, the day that Worcester was voted the county seat, two representatives from the new county joined with the Popular party leadership in challenging the governor. William Jennison and John Chandler, representing Worcester and Woodstock, served on a committee conveying to the governor legislation maintaining the legal tender of the paper bills. On January 1, Chandler was sent to the council to inquire about the bill; he was told that nothing had been done. Within a week Belcher had dissolved the rebellious house, but this served only to further mobilize the people. When a new house was chosen in a special election in February 1731, the towns of the new county doubled their representation to an unprecedented seven members, apparently responding to both the incorporation of the county and the governor's challenge.[6]

The town of Sutton was a leading force in the movement for a county, and their actions between 1730 and 1732 underscore the connections between the politics of county formation and the politics of money. The town elected Samuel Dudley as their first representative to the General Court in August 1730, and that month sent delegates to a convention of towns meeting at James Leland's tavern in east Sutton, now Grafton, charged with considering a "skeam . . . to Procure a new County." After the county was voted and then the house dissolved, Samuel Dudley was reelected Sutton's representative in the February and May elections in 1731. In September 1731, he was instructed by the Sutton town meeting not to "yeald ye Pintt that hath been so long in Debate between his excellency ye governor and ye honourable House of Representatives Relating to ye suply of ye

[5] JHRM 6:458; Bushman, King and People, 77–8; Pencak, War, Politics, and Revolution, 70, 77, 79–81.

[6] Pencak, War, Politics, and Revolution, 95ff.; JHRM 9:338, 341, 364–5, 378; 381–3; Boston Weekly News Letter, December 17, 24, 31, 1730, January 7, February 11, 1731.

treasurry." Sutton had accepted its share of the £60,000 public loan in 1728, but in the spring of 1732 the town refused to appoint trustees for this province money, signaling further its opposition to the governor. An oppositional political culture particularly concerned with public finance was born in the new county.[7]

The province's confrontation with Governor Belcher started afresh in 1739, when – with renewed royal demands that the province retire its public bills – the assembly asked the public to come forward with proposals for "the furnishing of a medium of trade." Two banks were proposed by competing groups of Popular Party men and hard-money Court merchants – the Land Bank and the Silver Bank. Both would be private: the first proposed to exchange paper bills for mortgages of land, to be gradually redeemed in payments of manufactured and agricultural goods, the second proposed to emit bills to be redeemed in silver or gold by 1755. The 1739 house rejected the governor's proposal for public bills of credit that would be retired by the end of 1741, but it also ordered that the directors of both new banks be "strictly forbidden [from] issuing any notes . . . or bills" until the next House had been elected. Only three towns were represented in 1739, and two of these representatives, Joseph Dwight and Ebenezer Wilder from the old towns of Brookfield and Lancaster, had voted for the public bills that would be retired as the royal government had demanded. Roused from their apathy, twelve towns sent representatives in April of 1740; Wilder and Dwight were unseated and six of the new representatives were Land Bank subscribers. All but one of the twelve Worcester County representatives voted to support the Land Bank directors in a roll call vote that June. The bill passed, but Worcester County's greater than 90 percent vote by far surpassed that of the rest of the province. Again, in the following January, the Worcester representatives surpassed the other delegations in voting to appoint a committee to review the governor's proclamations regarding the banks. The surge of representation in 1740, and the opposition vote of the county's delegation marked the first of many electoral rebellions.[8]

The broad support for the Land Bank initiative among the Worcester County representatives indicates that this insurgency was a broad political movement, not simply an uprising of ambitious, poor-to-middling yeomen and husbandmen. Its directors in Boston were men of prominence, if not men of the governor's party, and within the county there were gentlemen and even justices of the peace scattered among the bank's subscribers and supporters. As were many, but not all,

---

[7] Benedict and Tracy, *Sutton*, 41–8.

[8] The June, 1740 house vote supporting the Land Bank was 59 to 37 (61.4%); Worcester County representatives voted 11 to 1 (91.7%), and all other representatives voted 48 to 36 (57.1%). The January 1741 vote was 42 to 28 (60%); the Worcester County representatives voted 7 to 2 (77.7%). *JHRM* 17:257–8, 260–1; 18:47–8, 185–6; Pencak, *War, Politics, and Revolution*, 101–5.

of the political insurgencies that swept across the Worcester middle landscape between the Peace of Utrecht and the Civil War, the Land Bank was a coalition between a broad popular base and elements of the county gentry class. Such coalitions were complex and problematic; their membership often had very different motivations and expectations. Ambitious, rising gentry were often allied with men from yeoman and artisan households deeply concerned about their ability to survive, perhaps to prosper, on the republican middle landscape.

The appointive gentry who sided with the Land Bank were the first to feel the government's wrath, as the governor began to exercise his powers of patronage to stifle support for the bank. Beginning in November of 1740, six months after the Land Bank's victory in the house and the month following George Whitefield's westward progress through the province, Governor Belcher began to publish a series of proclamations declaring that all those holding civil or military commissions found to have signed or encouraged the use of the bank bills would "be removed from office." In December the council asked the county registrars of deeds to return lists of Land Bank mortgagers, and it informed the justices of the various county courts that they were to act to suppress the bills, and to warn in particular the "taverners, retailers, or Common Victualers in your County." These local men were to be held to the larger structure of royal policy: "We desire and expect that in the granting of Licences you carefully Consider of this Affair, and do not give out the Licences to such Persons as may despise Government and disturb peace and good Order."[9]

The governor's assault met with a spirited popular response. Acknowledging that they had accepted Land Bank notes, eight officers from Woodstock resigned their commissions in Col. John Chandler's regiment of militia at the end of December. They declared that in accepting the bills they were "serving the true Interest of our Native Country"; they were "not so mercenary, greedy, or ambitious of Honour as to do that which we apprehend will be hurtful to [that] interest."[10] The following April, Henry Lee, a justice of the peace in Worcester, similarly defied the governor. In response to the governor's inquiry, he wrote that the bank was "well calculated to serve the Interest of the Province" and as its operation was "not contrary to any Lawful authority," it was his "privilege as an Englishman" to encourage and support the bank. Lee, as well as Samuel Dudley of Sutton and Samuel Wright of Rutland, lost his justice's commission in the general purge of Land Bankers. But if these men stood up to the governor, others swallowed their pride in order to hang onto their places. William Jennison and John Chandler, Jr., justices in Worcester, both wrote humble letters to the governor disclaiming any connection with the plan, when inquiries were made into their encouraging the Land Bank. Jennison admitted that he had accepted some of

⁹ *Boston Weekly Newsletter*, November 6, December 18, 1740.
¹⁰ *Boston Weekly Newsletter*, January 8, 1741.

the notes, but that he had not been involved in "that affair for I never liked the Scheme that was Laid about Sd bills." Chandler was rejected by the town as representative after serving for most of the previous decade. The Land Bank crisis thus forced the gentry of the new county to choose between loyalty to the governor or to the people.[11]

The confrontation between the governor and these Land Bank supporters points to the fundamental character of this insurgency; the Land Bank crisis was played out on a provincial stage. Governor Belcher applied pressure through lines of provincial patronage: although it had primary support among a stratum of aspiring but relatively undistinguished yeomen, the Land Bank was a creature of provincial politics, rather than of local corporatism. The Land Bankers were far more successful in the provincial politics of representation than they were in the local arena of town government. Of twenty men elected to the house from the Worcester towns in 1740 and 1741, nine were Land Bank subscribers, and only one, Edmund Morse of Mendon, had served in previous legislatures. But if they were elected to the house in great numbers in 1740, Land Bankers moved only sporadically and briefly into town politics in 1741. In seven leading Land Bank towns, almost three-quarters of the representatives elected in 1740 and 1741 were Land Bankers, but only a quarter of the selectmen. The Land Bank was not rooted in local corporate politics; rather it moved from the provincial arena to the locality.[12]

Popular opposition in Massachusetts had its origins in the struggle of the Puritan commonwealth with the resurgent power of the crown following the Restoration of 1660. John Wise, the theoretician of the 1720 Land Bank, had been a central figure in the Ipswich revolt of 1689. The memory of the autonomous and virtuous seventeenth-century commonwealth would be a powerful symbol in provincial political culture down to the Revolution. But the Popular Party did not simply perpetuate the Puritan tradition. Key figures in the Puritan establishment had come to an accommodation with the crown with the grant of the charter of 1691. For Puritan divines such as the Mathers, allegiance to the king was a bulwark of the Puritan establishment in the early decades of the eighteenth century.[13] And most importantly, the social construct realized in the Land Bank was at odds with both crown prerogative and Puritan corporatism. Certainly a

---

[11] MA 102:132, 133, 153.

[12] In seven leading Land Bank towns, 72% of the representatives' terms served in 1740 and 1741 (8/11) were served by Land Bank subscribers (who cast a total of nine pro–Land Bank votes) as against only 24% of the selectman's terms (17/70). Data for the towns of Sutton, Grafton, Mendon, Lunenburg, Leicester, Worcester, and Harvard. For sources, see Chapter 2, note 32.

[13] Miller, *Colony to Province*, 171ff., 274ff., 310ff.; Breen, *The Character of the Good Ruler*, 182–3; Pencak, *War, Politics, and Revolution*, 9–53; Richard R. Johnson, *Adjustment to Empire: The New England Colonies, 1675–1715* (New Brunswick, 1981), 340, 350–1, 392–3.

powerful undercurrent of sentiment about commonwealth lay behind the Land Bank, but the result was a voluntary association of individuals, resonating more of John Locke than of James Harrington. Strikingly, the Land Bankers were not drawn from the ranks of those of deep experience in the corporate regulation of town life, but from aspiring men who set their sights on the provincial arena. Over the next several decades, in war, in General Court, and in Revolutionary crisis, these men would play an increasingly significant role in the public life of the province.

William Shirley and the end of the Popular insurgency

Governor Belcher's confrontation with the assembly reached a deadlock in May 1741. When the newly elected house chose a Land Bank leader for its speaker, Belcher demanded that it elect another. The house responded by routing a group of Belcher's allies on the governor's council. With this challenge, Belcher dissolved the house, calling for new elections, but his days were numbered. Soon after the house's dissolution, important news arrived from London: Belcher would be replaced by William Shirley, an English lawyer with powerful connections in London who had settled in Massachusetts in 1731, building a private law practice while serving as judge of admiralty and provincial advocate general. In his early years in Massachusetts Shirley had been an associate of Belcher, but over the 1730s he had cultivated ties with elements of the governor's opposition, although avoiding any involvement with the Land Bank. A man with influence in London, extensive experience in Massachusetts politics, and a balanced tactical sense, Shirley would soon transform the political climate in the province.[14]

The same wind that brought the news of Shirley's governorship also brought news of British action against the Land Bank. Parliament had extended the Bubble Act of 1720 to Massachusetts, outlawing both the Land Bank and the Silver Bank as of September 29, 1741. When he entered office that August, Shirley thus had the club of British authority behind him, but he chose a path of reconciliation. Intervening on behalf of the Land Bank subscribers, now deeply in debt to note-holding speculators, Shirley engineered a liquidation of the bank that limited the amount for which each subscriber would be responsible. By January 1743 roughly 85 percent of the Land Bank notes had been retired. Shirley had also succeeded in getting legislation by which old debts would be adjusted for inflation, working to eliminate the effects of inflation, which had long been one of the principal concerns of the hard-money men. Wartime expenditures through 1748 required the

[14] *JHRM* 19:9; John A. Schutz, *William Shirley: King's Governor of Massachusetts* (Chapel Hill, 1961), 3–43; Billias, *The Massachusetts Land Bankers*, 32–7.

continued emission of provincial paper money, but Shirley had laid the ground-work for a return to specie currency.[15]

In pacifying the province, Shirley also pacified Worcester County. Where almost half of the men elected to the house by the county's towns in the three elections in 1740 and 1741 were Land Bankers, in 1742 and the three years following their proportion dropped to less than 15 percent. And the voters also turned to the men who previously had been purged; at least four of the ten of the county's delegation in the 1742 house had been rejected by the voters in 1739 and 1740. Justice Joseph Dwight of Brookfield, who had voted with Belcher in 1739, had already been rehabilitated, being elected to the house in the June 1741 election. This election had taken place after Shirley's appointment was common knowledge, and Brookfield's choice of Dwight may have reflected a calculated effort to gain favor and influence with the new administration. Shirley had had extensive experience in law practice before the Worcester courts, where Dwight was a central fixture. Such connections between Shirley and the Worcester elite would rapidly thicken. Dwight was elected to the governor's council for the first of five terms in 1742, and the next year John Chandler of Worcester also would be elected, to serve continuously until his death in 1762. Under Belcher, the county had been represented on the council only by Joseph Wilder of Lancaster, but with the early years of the Shirley administration, a sizable group of the county's leading men were drawn into the new governor's orbit, and were well positioned to use their influence to benefit themselves, their friends, and their neighbors.[16]

In 1743, Governor Shirley appointed John Chandler to a committee to settle the affairs of the Land Bank, a dramatic turnaround for a man who had written so abjectly to Belcher when he was suspected in dealing in Land Bank notes. The next year Shirley sealed his influence in the county with the beginnings of what would be a flood of patronage, expressly in exchange for the election of allies to the council. Two commissions went to Dwight's Brookfield neighbors Thomas Gilbert and Josiah Converse; Converse had been the town's choice to cast pro–Land Bank votes in 1740 and 1741. Shirley did not regrant commissions to the justices who had openly defied Belcher over the Land Bank, but at least four Land Bankers or representatives voting for the Land Bank were commissioned in 1744 and 1745, and another five were commissioned by 1753. The voters ratified the new distribution of patronage by once again electing justices to the house in large numbers. The Land Bank insurgency had been marked by the towns' refusal to elect justices. After electing at least one justice for every three representatives between 1715 and 1739, the Worcester towns bypassed men tied to Belcher's

[15] Pencak, *War, Politics, and Revolution*, 11–119; Schutz, *Shirley*, 51–7; George A. Wood, *William Shirley, Governor of Massachusetts, 1740–1756: A History* (New York, 1920), 155–80.
[16] On Shirley at Worcester, see Schutz, *Shirley*, 11n; Councilors listed in summary form in McWade, "Provincial Patronage Elite," 36–7.

patronage, electing less than one justice for every five representatives between 1740 and 1743. This was the most marked electoral censure of the civil list in the entire provincial period, a further reflection of the depths of the crisis. However, with the first election following Shirley's distribution of patronage in March 1744, the proportion of justices and court officers returned to its former level of roughly 35 percent. The Land Bank insurrection was over.[17]

Thus the political tug-of-war between governor and people, ongoing for a quarter-century, was diffused in three short years under the skillful hands of a new governor. The early 1740s saw a dramatic turn in the public climate in the county and the province. These were the early years of the Great Awakening; the orthodox revivals moving powerfully through the towns also had a quieting effect on the political environment. Conveniently for Shirley, people's minds were turned from secular affairs to concerns of the soul. Justice Joseph Dwight could entertain the evangelist – and Land Banker – David Hall in the summer of 1743 with no sense of the radical consequences that would unfold from religious itinerancy. After decades of religious indifference, violently factional politics, and intensely competitive striving for economic gain, the orthodox revivals and a new governor's conciliatory initiatives and patronage had brought an unprecedented fusion of Court, piety, and people.

Imperial warfare and personal independence

With the outbreak of King George's War in 1744, Shirley turned this quietist consensus to the mobilization of the province for a decade and a half of intermittent imperial struggle. Shirley's greatest accomplishment was to focus the attention of the province – and the assembly – on the problem of confronting and defeating the French enemy in Canada. The conquest of the fortress of Louisburg on Cape Breton would stand as a powerful symbol of provincial achievement; under Shirley's leadership Massachusetts would take the initiative in defending the empire. In so doing, Shirley unknowingly laid the groundwork for revolution.[18] But in the short run, the triumph at Louisburg was the crowning achievement of the fusion of Court patronage and evangelical piety that characterized the early years of Shirley's administration.

---

[17] Daniels, *Oxford*, 760; Schutz, *Shirley*, 83–4; evidence on justices from an analysis of all justices and representatives in Worcester County before the Revolution based on Whitmore, *Massachusetts Civil List*; and *JHRM*; Davis, *Currency and Banking*, 295–313. On the collapse of the Popular Party outside Boston see Bushman, *King and People*, 263; and Pencak, *War, Politics, and Revolution*, 115ff. For the significance of justices being elected to the General Court, see John Murrin, "Review Essay," 269–70.

[18] This is the central thesis of William Pencak's *War, Politics, and Revolution*.

Imperial warfare could be a profitable business for those with the right connections. Troops would have to be enlisted, transported, and provisioned, and
merchants, shipowners, and regimental officers all stood to gain at each juncture.
Beyond the particularities of military logistics lay the dire economic threat posed
to New England fishermen by the French presence in Cape Breton, in position to
cut them off from the Grand Banks. Men from throughout the Land Bank orbit
were not slow to see the economic significance and opportunities of war with
France. Merchant Benjamin Colman, son of the John Colman who had advocated
land banks in 1714, 1720, and 1739, was granted contracts for furnishing uniforms
for the provincial troops heading for Louisburg and provisions for the army after
the successful assault. Judge Robert Auchmuty, another Land Bank director,
turned his pen to the struggle, writing a series of tracts, one entitled *The
Importance of Cape Breton to the British Nation*, stressing the importance of the
fisheries to the imperial economy. Two other Land Bank Directors, Robert Hale
and John Choate, were commissioned to command regiments serving in the
Louisburg expedition; Choate was also appointed judge advocate for both courts
martial and admiralty cases. In contrast, none of the Silver Bankers had a role in
the expedition, and hard-money man Thomas Hutchinson led the legislative
opposition.[19]

Worcester County was also particularly well represented in the Louisburg
forces. Joseph Dwight was commissioned one of two brigadier generals, with
Samuel Waldo, an old political associate of Governor Shirley who had family
relations among the merchants in Worcester. Dwight was put in command of the
artillery, and after the assault was appointed a judge of the admiralty and
commissioned a colonel of his own regiment. Justice Samuel Willard of Lancaster,
who had cast his town's vote for the Land Bank in the 1740 house, was given
command of the Fourth Massachusetts Regiment, recruited primarily within the
county. Willard commissioned his sons Abijah and Levi in the First Company of
his regiment, but he also gave officers' commissions to Land Bankers Joseph
Whitcomb of Lancaster and Palmer Goulding and John Sterns of Worcester.
There were Land Bankers scattered among the company officers and men
throughout the expedition, and they may well have been encouraged to enlist by
the governor's insistence that soldiers and sailors enlisted on provincial service be
immune from suit of debt in court. Relief from creditors may well have been a
consideration for young Oliver Watson, recently settled in the west parish of

[19] Davis, *Currency and Banking*, 2:130–1; Nash, *The Urban Crucible*, 167; Wood, *Shirley*,
220–1; for commissions see Charles Hudson, "Louisburg Soldiers," *NEGHR* 24 (1870),
367–80, and *NEGHR* 25 (1871), 249–69; also Pepperell Papers, Appendix, Coll MHS, ser. 6,
vol. 10; on Hutchinson, see Schutz, *Shirley*, 90.

Leicester when he enlisted in Choate's Eighth Regiment; Watson's Land Bank account would still be delinquent in the 1760s.[20]

In addition to a temporary escape from creditors, soldiering offered the possibility of actual gain. The volunteers were told that Louisburg was enormously wealthy, and they marched off in expectations of receiving "Bounty Money . . . in taking the famous city's plunder." Imperial war was becoming something of a subsistence strategy for the increasing numbers of poor, young men in New England. It might also be an avenue to a independent competency for those well enough situated. In 1730 Thomas Cheney had removed from Cambridge to Dudley as a young man of twenty-two. In 1745 he was commissioned in John Choate's Eighth Regiment at Louisburg, and his share of the plunder – according to local tradition given to him by a dying French officer – enabled him to buy a large block of land in west Dudley. Land Banker Benjamin Gilbert of Ipswich was commissioned as an ensign under the command of John Dodge, another subscriber from Beverly. He seems to have done almost as well as Cheney, for two years later he bought 120 acres of land in the North Parish of Brookfield and established his family in solid circumstances.[21]

These were, of course, officers, and among those fortunate enough to survive the campaign. For every Benjamin Gilbert there was an Eleazer Haywood, a taverner and Land Bank subscriber from Brookfield who died of disease during the cold autumn following the siege. When disease swept through the Louisburg camps, the failure to provision adequately the troops tempered some of the enthusiasm with which the province had followed Shirley into war. But Massachusetts would be at war for the better part of two decades, and thousands of young soldiers would march off to the frontiers to do battle with the French and their Algonquin allies. For a people with a stable, perhaps stagnant, economy, soldiering worked to absorb the energies of a generation of men coming of age in the aftermath of the Land Bank crisis and the Great Revival. Prospects for these men were limited by the very imperial warfare for which they enlisted. The previous generation, in the "window" between the Peace of Utrecht in 1713 and King George's War in 1744 had had the opportunity to carve out a living on the frontier. This avenue to independence would not open again until after 1763, and would be seriously

[20] Hudson, "Louisburg Soldiers"; Nourse, *Harvard*, 286; the Land Bank delinquencies were published in the Boston Gazette, September 12, 1763, and are transcribed in Mitten, "New England Paper Money Tradition," 88–93.

[21] Myron Stachiw, ed., *Massachusetts Officers and Soldiers, 1723–1743: Dummer's War to the War of Jenkin's Ear* (Boston, 1979), xiii–xxiv; Anderson, *A People's Army, passim;* Nash, *The Urban Crucible*, 170–1; George A. Rawlyk, *Yankees at Louisburg*, (Orono, Me., 1967), 45–7; Hudson, "Louisburg Soldiers," *NEGHR* 25 (1871), 251–2; John M. Cockran, "Sandersdale," *QHSL* 2 (1903–9), 210; Temple, *North Brookfield*, 208; Symmes, "Introduction," to Gilbert, *A Citizen Soldier*, 15. This Benjamin Gilbert was the grandfather of the diarist quoted in Chapter 1.

limited until the close of the Revolutionary War. An intervening generation would integrate military service into an increasingly confined and limited round of subsistence. And it is striking how many of these young soldiers would be led by older men who had placed their earlier aspirations for advancement in the failed Land Bank project.[22]

The course of Popular politics in Shirley's Massachusetts

Massachusetts soldiers sailed for Louisburg with hopes of plunder, but they also sailed under a banner inscribed with the motto of the Reverend George Whitefield: "Nil desperandum Christo duce." Whitefield had preached to the troops before their embarkment on April 2, exhorting them to be assured of Christ's ultimate victory. Earlier he had played a decisive role in convincing William Pepperell to command the expedition. The news of the army's victory was received throughout New England as a sign of providential favor and millennial prediction. But if the triumph at Louisburg was born in the harmonious fusion of Court and Puritan traditions that marked the province in the early 1740s, the surviving soldiers returned to a religious climate splintering in the explosion of separatist dissent.[23]

Already of New Light inclinations, many veterans would join the dissenting societies. Capt. Thomas Cheney of Dudley, flush with his Louisburg money, joined the Sturbridge Baptists in February 1751. Oliver Watson remained with the New Light orthodox church in Spencer after his return, but he had served with men from the Leicester Baptist community. John Brown similarly had kin ties to the Leicester Baptists, and Samuel Call, a Land Bank subscriber and Louisburg soldier who would serve as a sergeant in the New York campaigns of the next decade, joined the Leicester Baptists in 1752. Soldiering had taken these men out of the confines of corporate orthodoxy on a voluntary expedition, and in joining dissenting societies they made this voluntarism a permanent fixture.[24]

Neither the cooling of enthusiasm for Shirley nor the explosion of religious dissent had an immediate impact on the Worcester County's participation in provincial politics. Having been firmly in the opposition under Belcher, the

---

[22] L. E. DeForest, ed., *Louisburg Journals, 1745* (New York, 1932), 160–1; Temple, 208; Anderson, *A People's Army*; Stachiw, ed., *Dummer's War to the War of Jenkins' Ear*, xiii–xxiv. For views of the changing expectations of New England youth, see, Gross, *Minutemen*, 68–108; Jedrey, *John Cleaveland*, 80–3; Henretta, "Wealth and Social Structure," 267–9; 282–3.

[23] Wood, *Shirley*, 275–6; Nash, *Urban Crucible*, 171; see in general Nathan O. Hatch, *The Sacred Cause of Liberty: Republican Thought and the Millennium in Revolutionary New England* (New Haven, 1977).

[24] Washburn, *Leicester*, 211–13; Fisk, "Testimony," BPAN.

county's delegation to the General Court titled toward Shirley for the remainder of his administration. As measured by the roll calls recorded through 1755, the Worcester delegation moved from strident opposition toward lukewarm support, while the remainder of the province remained in moderate opposition.[25] The most striking manifestation of Worcester County's turn toward Court politics came in 1748, with Shirley's efforts to use a British reimbursement of the province's expenses in the Louisburg campaign to retire all paper money and establish a specie currency for the first time since the 1690s. The critical vote on the plan came in January 1749, and three positive votes from Worcester County were decisive in the 40 to 37 total. Strikingly, two of these votes were cast by former Land Bankers, William Richardson of Lancaster and Nathaniel Nelson of Mendon, who followed the leadership of John Choate and Robert Hale – Land Bank directors and Louisburg officers – in supporting the redemption plan. The record of the next several years suggests that Land Bank subscribers elected to the General Court were willing to accept the new currency – perhaps against the wishes of their constituents. The county responded to Shirley's initiative on the currency by more than doubling its representation, sending thirteen representatives to the 1749 house, after sending only five in 1748. Despite the votes for redemption cast by Richardson and Nelson, the towns saw Land Bankers as suitable to represent their interests on the subject of currency, and elected them to the house in 1749 and 1750 in numbers not seen since the July 1741 election.[26]

[25] *House roll calls, 1726–64: Worcester County vs. the province*

Years	Worcester County representatives			All other representatives		
	Court	Opposition	Total	Court	Opposition	Total
1726	1 *33*	2	3	47 *61*	30	77
1740–1	5 *21*	19	24	79 *37*	135	214
1748–53	26 *45*	32	58	206 *39*	325	531
1754–5	22 *47*	25	47	174 *47*	194	368
1757–9	8 *32*	17	25	100 *48*	107	207
1761–64	28 *50*	28	56	184 *49*	190	374
Total	90 *42*	123	213 *100*	790 *45*	981	1771 *100*
Other than excise, 1754–5	22 *63*	13	35	146 *56*	112	258

Source: *JHRM*, and Pencak, *War, Politics, and Revolution*, Table 2, 250.
[26] Vote on Redemption in [James Allen,] *A Letter to the Freeholder* ... (Boston, 1749), 11; Davis, *Currency and Banking*, 2:306, 308; *JHRM* 26:4, 27:4 for representatives. For discussions of the politics of redemption, see Pencak, *War, Politics, and Revolution*, 129–33; Schutz, *Shirley*, 145–6. In 1746 the county elected three Land Bankers, in 1749 four (out of thirteen representatives) in 1750 five (out of eleven), and in 1756 three. Otherwise, the county elected one or two Land Bankers per year between 1742 and 1755.

The house's demands for a grant of town privileges to the west parish of Spencer, defining the king's interest in the upholding of the people's rights and privileges, was a measure of Popular sentiment in the 1749 house. But the voters were mistaken if they expected the former Land Bankers to oppose Shirley's plan; in votes in 1751 and 1753 on currency issues these representatives voted 2 to 1 with the governor. Shirley's careful handling of Land Bank liquidation thus had its dividends, as men whom he saved from ruin in 1741 and 1742 rallied to his side. On the other hand, the electorate was not necessarily pleased with the outcome, and removed three of the four former Land Bankers who voted with the governor in 1751, as Hale and Choate had been rejected by their constituents in 1749.[27]

As the province returned to war with the French in the summer of 1754, Shirley's preeminence in the house reached its peak. Supported, Thomas Hutchinson claimed, by former Louisburg officers sitting in the house, Shirley aggressively advanced his imperial dispute with the French. He induced the province to raise two expeditions for service in Maine and Nova Scotia in the winter and spring of 1754 and 1755, and – promising a second specie reimbursement from the British government – won an overwhelming vote in June 1755 to raise forces for the Crown Point expedition. Despite serious setbacks in the fighting on the New York frontier, the province rallied round Shirley to commit huge sums of taxes for the war. To the end of his tenure as governor and continental commander-in-chief, terminated by the military reverses of 1755 and 1756, Shirley retained the loyalty of the province that had followed him to Louisburg.[28] But Shirley's successes in restoring a hard currency in 1748 and raising men and supplies for the final war with the French in 1754 were clearly the high points; although he had far greater influence in the house than Belcher or his predecessors, the tug-of-war between governor and people continued. The Worcester county representatives supported him on currency issues, they voted unanimously to fund the Crown Point expedition, and they strongly supported raising his salary in 1753 when the province in general was narrowly opposed. But on a series of other votes regarding taxation, fiscal procedure, and provincial autonomy, the county's representatives disproportionately opposed the governor. They unanimously supported the excise proposal that bore heavily on Boston and the seacoast towns, they voted overwhelmingly to hold the treasurer tightly accountable for provincial expenditures, and they opposed Shirley's 1754 Plan of Union, which in its original form would have turned over provincial powers of taxation and military enlistment to an intercolonial congress. In all of these opposition votes, the county's delegation was forging a legislative tradition that

---

[27] Schutz, *Shirley*, 145ff.; Pencak, *War, Politics, and Revolution*, 129–33; *JHRM* 27:4, 28:4.
[28] Pencak, *War, Politics, and Revolution*, *War, Politics, and Revolution*, 136–7; Anderson, *A People's Army*, 8–13; *JHRM* 32:116.

placed a premium on the fiscal obligations of the state to its people. This tradition would be strongly reasserted during and immediately following the Revolution.

Competing gentries

In his final years in office Shirley did not simply rely on former Louisburg officers and Land Bankers for support in the General Court. In January 1754, he published a new list of civil appointments, expanding his base of patronage in the county and the province. His return on this patronage investment came in the house elected the following spring. Three of his new justices of the peace – John Murray, William Ayres, and Timothy Ruggles – cast the only votes from Worcester County favoring the Plan of Union, besides that of Justice John Chandler of Worcester, whom Shirley had appointed a delegate to the Albany Congress. In this exchange, the new justices were following an established pattern. Civil patronage worked. During the entire period between the 1720s and the 1760s justices and other court officers cast 60 percent of their recorded votes with the governor, while the governor could expect at best 30 percent of the votes of representatives without civil appointments.[29]

But there was a reverse side to the support that Shirley and other governors received from their civil appointees. Despite the military enthusiasm that Shirley generated in the colony, militia officers, particularly captains, voted overwhelmingly with the opposition throughout the provincial period. To an important degree, the courts and militia comprised two competing gentry orbits, one generally supporting the governor, the other generally in the opposition. Militia officers were elected to the house in higher numbers toward the end of long periods of warfare: 1747, 1756, and 1760 stand out as years when officers made up more than 40 percent of the county's delegation. The six militia captains serving in the legislature in the wake of the disastrous campaigns that followed Louisburg were particularly hostile, casting fifteen out of eighteen votes against Shirley. Of these six, apparently only Land Banker John Brown of Leicester had served at Louisburg, and as an enlisted man. Brown, as well as others like Jonathan Whitney

---

[29] *House votes and titles among Worcester County representatives, 1726–64*

Title	Court		Opposition	Total	
Civil (esq.)	55	*60*	37	92	*100*
Military	11	*26*	31	42	*100*
None	23	*30*	54	77	*100*
Total	89	*42*	122	211	*100*

Note: Figures in italics are percentages.
Source: JHRM.

of Harvard, who led a company on scout into the hot July woods in 1748, seems to have served as an unsalaried captain of the local militia, rather than in the provincial "marching forces."[30] Similarly, several commanders of militia companies that responded to the emergency alarm to relieve the provincial troops beseiged at Fort William Henry in 1757 were elected to the house in the late 1750s, and cast the bulk of their votes with the opposition. Among them was Doctor Jabez Upham of Brookfield, himself once a Land Bank subscriber, and married to the daughter of a former Land Banker among the Leicester Baptists. Elected to the 1755 house after Justice William Ayres had supported the Plan of Union, Upham served as the town's representative through 1760. With Nathaniel Woolcott, Upham was one of two former Land Bankers commanding Brookfield militia companies that marched to relieve the ill-fated Fort William Henry garrison in August 1757. The following December Upham voted with a majority in the house to oppose drafting militia for frontier duty.[31]

The role of these militia officers in the opposition points to their particular place within the broader framework of patronage and constituency. Company officers in the militia were elected by town companies, and their commissions essentially ratified by the governor; justices' commissions rested solely upon the informal lines of influence between the local gentry and governor and council. And as one historian has recently demonstrated, even officers on provincial service – who owed their commissions to the influence of regimental officers in their locality – had an overwhelming obligation to the men who volunteered to "list" for dangerous service under their command; the contract between a particular officer and his men overrode the priorities of British military policy. Militia officers were even more immersed in locality, the nominal leaders of all able-bodied men in a town, excepting ministers, justices, slaves, and Indians. If Rufus Putnam, the son of a Sutton Land Banker, could make his way into the lower ranks of the gentry on the patronage of Brigadier Ruggles and Colonel Willard, he also could desert the army at Stillwater without a second thought, when his enlistment expired in February 1758. In this desertion Putnam's company was led safely through the wilds of southern Vermont in the dead of winter by their captain, Ebenezer Learned of Oxford. Censured by the army and denied another commission, Learned was chosen selectman by the voters of Oxford for the next six years in a row, and for the better part of the ensuing three decades. He would serve as a general early in the Revolution. Learned's mutiny against the British army had

---

[30] According to Washburn, *Leicester*, 211, Brown was a captain at Louisbug, but he is not listed among the officers in Hudson, "Louisburg Soldiers," or in the Pepperell Papers. None of these six men are listed as having a provincial commission between 1748 and 1753 in Nancy Voye, *Massachusetts Officers, 1748–1763*. For Whitney, see Nourse, *Harvard*, 287. On the distinction between militia and provincial troops, see Anderson, *A People's Army*, 26–7; John Murrin, "Anglicizing an American Colony," 61–137.

[31] Temple, *North Brookfield*, 214, 215.

solid roots in the Popular tradition. His father had been sent to the house in the special election of February 1731, when the new county threw its weight behind Cooke's Popular faction, and his cousin, Lt. Isaac Learned, was one of only four Land Bank subscribers in Oxford.[32]

Military service exposed men to the rough edges of the connection between province and empire, and did much to forge a critical view of the relationships between locality, province, and empire. John Adams remembered hearing vehement attacks on British military procedures and imperial policy from his father on the subject of Louisburg, given back to the French after the New Englanders' great victory, and even at Col. James Putnam's in Worcester in the 1750s.[33] Few company officers would ever reach the field grade ranks that offered possibilities for personal profit. They were elected by their communities, rather than appointed over them, and this relationship with constituency reflected in their solid vote with the provincial opposition.

These company officers were also embedded in two other orbits that intersected with the Popular tradition. There was a special affinity between experience with either the Land Bank or New Light dissent and service as a militia officer. At least thirty-two Worcester County Land Bankers served as officers in the 1740s and 1750s, roughly 14 percent of the total Land Bank subscribers in the county, as opposed to six who were appointed justice of the peace. Often in their mid-twenties in 1740, Land Bankers were situated to take up positions of middling responsibility over the next generation. Similarly, Baptists served as militia officers in all the towns where dissenting societies and families took root; in Leicester and Charlton fully one-half of the officers were Baptist members or attenders.[34] Since dissenters were effectively barred from civil appointments – none served in a county post until after Shays's Rebellion – military service provided an avenue to status and advancement. These men would have found service on campaign suited to their New Light tendencies; the leading historian of the provincial military experience has concluded that the evangelical spirit that informed the Louisburg campaign also flourished in the provincial camps during the French and Indian War. "Warm" evangelical preachers regularly exhorted the troops; a ballad recorded in Paxton in the 1790s celebrated the men and events of "fifty-five" with the millennial evangelism forged in the Louisburg campaign, combined with the dream of riches to be taken on the battlefield.

[32] Anderson, *A People's Army*, 26–7; Putnam, *Memoirs*, 16–22; Daniels, *Oxford*, 580–1, 587–8.
[33] Pencak, *War, Politics, and Revolution*, 125.
[34] There were at least eighteen militia and provincial company officers among the Baptist communities in Leicester, Charlton, Sutton, Dudley, Sturbridge, and Spencer, and a scattering of others–like Jabez Upham, Nathaniel Woolcott, and John Brown – with kin ties to Baptists and Separates. From Voye, *Massachusetts Officers*, and various local histories, vital records, and gravestones.

A frightful noise and hideous yell,
As though it came from the jaws of Hell;
The smoke did as a cloud arise,
While Christian prayers did pierce the skies

And God did hear when they did call
And Antichrist received a fall.
Oh, may she bleed and also die,
That Christ may gain the victory!

They quit the field with shameful flight,
As though they saw it dark as night.
Our men did plunder on the place,
And smiles returnéd to their face.[35]

If the initial influence of the Awakening had been to cool political tensions in the province, evangelical fervor began to color Popular confrontation with the governor in the 1750s. A cluster of orthodox and dissenting New Lights with such militia experience were elected to the house in the late 1750s, as provincial and county acceptance of court politics began to wane. In Sutton, Capt. Henry King, of a Baptist family and the nephew of a Land Bank subscriber, was elected in 1756, and served in every house down to the Revolution. In Sturbridge and Dudley, Baptists Lt. Henry Fisk and Capt. Thomas Cheney were elected in 1756 and 1758, Fisk replacing Moses Marcy, an enemy of the Baptists who was appointed justice by Shirley on the 1754 list. In Leicester, Land Banker Capt. John Brown, a member of the New Light orthodox church and married into a Baptist family, was elected in the same year and would serve for the better part of the next decade, and Jabez Upham, similarly situated on the interval between orthodoxy and Baptist dissent, represented Brookfield. All of these men cast solidly Popular votes. They were part of a general turn toward the politics of opposition in the late 1750s, and marked an important dimension of a Popular coalition that would be a powerful force in the decades to come.

Constituencies and the practice of provincial politics

The county geography of this politics of patronage and opposition, as well as the trajectory toward political resistance in the years following Shirley's departure, underscores the broader affinities among the Land Bank, the New Light, and the Popular party. In the formative middle decades of the eighteenth century a consistent political geography took shape across Worcester County, a geography

---

[35] S. A. Green, "Verses Relating to the Events of 1755," *Mass. Hist. Soc. Proc.* 2d ser., 9 (1894), 2, 4, quoted in Anderson, *A People's Army*, 196–223, esp. 210, 221.

that would shape the county's public culture into the next century. It was articulated very roughly along the county's four broad natural regions, defined by the drainage systems of the Blackstone River in the southeast, the Nashua in the northeast, the Quineboag and French rivers in the southwest, and the Quaboag and the Chicopee on the northwest.[36] These drainages had served as the territories of different bands among the Nipmucs, and they had a subtle shaping force on white settlements in the region, with dominating towns established early at the centers of the different river systems at the outer edges of the old counties, each with strands of dependence running back into the settled regions of the bay and

[36] The four regions used as analytical categories in this chapter and successive chapters were defined on the basis of the river systems, the original county lines, date of town formation, orthodox religious culture, and the distribution of gravestone carving traditions. The southeast, the New Light stronghold, includes the towns of the Blackstone drainage, but Old Light Shrewsbury has been assigned to the northeast. Conversely, the northeast includes all the towns within the Nashua, Assabet, and Sudbury drainages, except for New Light Westborough, assigned to the southeast, and the late-settled upland towns of Ashburnham, Westminister, and Princeton, incorporated in 1765 and 1770, assigned to the northwest. Most of the northeastern towns had once been part of Middlesex County, and most of their Congregational ministers were members of the Marlborough Association, while most of the southeastern towns had once been part of Suffolk County, and most of their Congregational ministers were members of the Mendon Association. The county seat of Worcester, at the head of the Blackstone, was naturally a part of the southeast, but given its Court Party elite, it is treated separately before the Revolution. The northwest had connections with Hampshire County, inasmuch as Brookfield was originally part of Hampshire. The northwest region includes all the towns in the Chicopee and Millers drainages, with the addition of Ashburnham, Westminster, and Princeton, the latter town formed from part of Rutland in 1770. The southwest, essentially the headwaters of the south-flowing Thames River, includes the old Suffolk County towns of Oxford and Woodstock, until the latter seceded to Connecticut in 1747, with the towns of Dudley and Sturbridge, both established in the 1730s, and the district of Charlton, established in 1754. This southwest region can be seen as the upper reaches of the "Quinebaug Country" of eastern Connecticut. The only pre-Revolutionary orthodox ministerial association in the northwest was the Brookfield Association, and in the southwest the Oxford Association. Leicester is a problematical town, lying at the height of the Thames drainage with other streams draining into the Blackstone, it was originally part of Middlesex County. Given its New Light orthodoxy, it is assigned to the northeast. Spencer, once the west precinct of Leicester, and associated with it in the district system after 1753, fell in the Chicopee drainage, and its minister was a member of the increasingly conservative Brookfield Association. Thus, although it is something of a borderline case, Spencer is assigned to the northwest. However arbitrary the boundaries of these regions may seem, they are used consistently in this analysis until the 1820s, when economic change suggests a new configuration of northern towns and southern towns divided by a central corridor. (See Chapter 9.) Sources: maps in Massachusetts Historical Commission, *Historic and Archaeological Resources*; representative lists in *JHRM*; affiliations with the various associations are listed in *Extracts from the Itineraries and Other Miscellanies of Ezra Stiles*, Franklin B. Dexter, ed. (New Haven, 1916), 230–1; Joseph Allen, *The Worcester Association and Its Antecedents: A History of Four Ministerial Associations: the Marlborough, the Worcester (Old), the Lancaster, and the Worcester (New) Associations* ... (Boston, 1868); *HWC*, throughout; Hurd, *Worcester County*, 1:iii–v, and throughout.

valley towns, and strands of influence running forward into growing hinterlands of newer towns and districts in the surrounding locality.

Settlement had begun earlier in the southeast, the Blackstone Valley, in the lands of the dispossessed Praying Indians, and away from the threat of the Algonquin attack that retarded the occupation of the northwest section of the county. With this earlier concentration of population in the southeast, reflected in a greater proportion of incorporated towns and higher valuations by the province, came a vigorous participation in the political and religious dramas of the early 1740s. In aggregate, Worcester County had the largest concentration of Land Bank mortgagers, relative to population, of all the counties in the province, but the bank was particularly popular in southeastern towns in or adjacent to the Blackstone Valley. The Awakening, in both its orthodox and dissenting manifestations, hit the county in a similarly concentrated manner, striking the Blackstone Valley and the Land Bank towns particularly hard. Old Lights occupied the pulpits across the rest of the county, and only in the southwest were they challenged by dissenters.[37]

The result was that the county had a widely varied social and religious texture, reflecting in microcosm much of the variation in the province at large. (See Figure 1.) The most pointed contrast lay between the pluralistic institutional structures of the older and more densely settled Blackstone towns and the unitary corporatism of new townships to the northwest, most just being carved out of wildlands

[37] *Worcester County regions before the Revolution*

	Towns incorporated by 1760	Towns incorporated 1761–74	Districts through 1774	Strong Land Bank towns	New Light Ministers	Old Light Ministers	Towns and districts with	
							Separates and dissenting societies by 1775	Towns ranking in top 1/3 of 1761 val.
Northeast	8	0	2	2	1	8	3	4
Northwest	5	6	7	0	1	5	4	2
Southeast	7	0	2	6	8	0	7	5
Southwest	3	0	1	0	0	3	3	0
Worcester	1	0	0	1	0	1	1[a]	1
Total	24	6	12	9	10	17	18	12
All Land Bank towns	9	0	0	9	7	2	8	7

[a] There was a brief separation in Worcester during the Awakening, Lincoln, *Worcester*, 169.

Note: This table can only give an approximation of the status of the towns and districts established in the northwest in the 1760s and early 1770s.

Source: See Chapter 2, note 25; Chapter 3, note 6; and note 36 above.

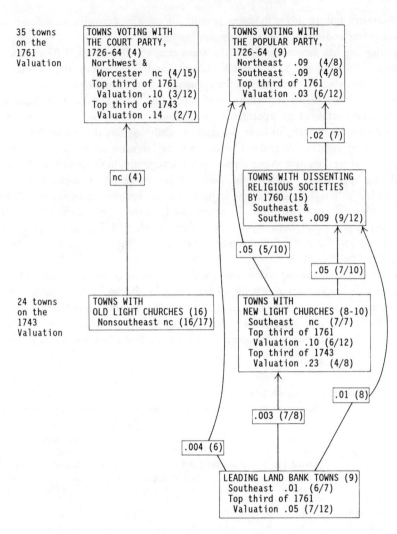

Numbers to the right of decimals are "P-values" measuring the strength
of the relationships between categories. The closer the P-value is to
zero the stronger the relationship is between the two categories.
nc = non-calculable, because all of one category is included in another.

Sources and method: see Appendix 2.

Figure 1. The contours of provincial political culture, 1726–64.

in the 1750s and 1760s, which were articulated around the interlocking institutions of town and orthodox church. This contrast within the county was a microcosm of a larger dichotomy in the province as a whole. The southeastern towns of the Blackstone Valley fell within the broader orbit of southeastern New England, strongly influenced by the religious pluralism deeply rooted in neighboring Rhode Island and the powerful attraction of Providence's bustling commerce. In contrast, the northwest was quite similar to the polar opposite of conservative Hampshire County, noted for its Stoddardean brand of orthodoxy and its economic isolation.[38]

Interwoven with this religious and economic mosaic was a widely varied political culture. The peoples on this middle landscape did not move as one in response to the challenge of provincial politics. Rather, the ebb and flow of Popular opposition and support for the governors' initiatives were strikingly linked with patterns of class and community. Although there were important shifts in regional voting, particularly during Shirley's years, political allegiances varied along the northwest to southeast axis.

The governor's strongest support came from the northwestern towns, and the county town of Worcester, uniformly Old Light in the Awakening. Despite its large number of Land Bankers, Worcester voted strongly with the governor, but its representatives often refrained from voting in the late 1740s and mid-1750s, a sign that they were exposed to considerable challenges within this complex town. The representatives from the towns in the southwest voted most often with the opposition, but they missed a majority of the roll calls throughout the period, suggesting a certain detachment from provincial politics, expressed most concretely in Woodstock's 1747 secession to Connecticut. The strongest Popular votes came from the representatives of the older towns in the eastern half of the county, centering on Lancaster in the northeast and Mendon and Sutton in the southeast. (See Table 1.)

There were very important differences in the political allegiances of these two eastern regions. If the county as a whole moved from opposition to Belcher in the Land Bank era to support for Shirley, and then toward opposition to Governor Thomas Pownall in the late 1750s, it was led by the representatives of the southeastern Blackstone Valley towns. The representatives from this Land Bank and New Light stronghold had a particularly good record of roll call attendance and cast a unanimous vote in favor of the Land Bank in 1740 and 1741, but led the

[38] The distribution of dissenting societies in Massachusetts is summarized in Lester J. Cappon, et al., ed., *Atlas of Early American History: The Revolutionary Era, 1760–1790* (Princeton, 1976), 37 (map), 117 (notes). I have found useful McLoughlin, *New England Dissent; Minutes of the Warren Association;* Goen, *Revivalism and Separatism; HWC;* and Nathaniel B. Sylvester, ed., *History of the Connecticut Valley in Massachusetts,* 2 vols. (Philadelphia, 1879).

Table 1. Worcester County's legislative politics, 1740–64

	1740–1		1748–53		1754–5		1757–9		1761–4		Total		No. of towns
	Court %Crt.	Oppos. Index	Court %Crt.	Oppos. Index	Court %Crt.	Oppos. Index	Court %Crt.	Oppos. Index	Court %Crt.	Oppos. Index	Court %Crt.	Oppos. Index	
Worcester	0 / 0	2 / .66	2 / 100.0	0 / .25	1 / 100.0	0 / .17	2 / 100.0	0 / .66	4 / 100.0	0 / .80	9 / 81.8	2 / .45	1
Northeast	4 / 44.4	5 / .37	7 / 31.8	15 / .34	5 / 31.2	11 / .33	4 / 44.4	5 / .37	8 / 38.1	13 / .52	8 / 36.4	13 / .38	8
Northwest	1 / 50.0	1 / .22	4 / 44.0	5 / .28	9 / 75.0	3 / .50	1 / 50.0	1 / .18	9 / 75.0	3 / .60	24 / 64.8	13 / .34	3/4
Southeast	0 / 0	9 / .43	12 / 57.0	9 / .37	7 / 43.7	9 / .38	0 / 0	8 / .38	5 / 33.3	10 / .43	24 / 34.8	45 / .39	7
Southwest	0 / 0	2 / .17	1 / 25.0	3 / .17	0 / 0	2 / .11	1 / 25.0	3 / .44	2 / 50.0	2 / .27	4 / 25.0	12 / .21	4/3
Total	5 / 20.8	19 / .35	26 / 44.8	32 / .33	22 / 46.8	25 / .34	8 / 32.0	17 / .36	28 / 50.0	28 / .49	89 / 42.4	121 / .36	23
All Land Bank towns except Worcester	0 / 0	11 / .46	14 / 51.8	13 / .42	6 / 31.6	13 / .40	1 / 10.0	9 / .42	5 / 31.2	11 / .40	26 / 31.3	57 / .41	8

	Currency (4)				Salary, crown point (3)				Excise, treasury, plan of union (7)				No. of towns
	Court	%Crt.	Oppos.	Index	Court	%Crt.	Oppos.	Index	Court	%Crt.	Oppos.	Index	
Worcester	0	*0*	0	*0*	1	*100.0*	0	*.33*	2	*100.0*	0	*.29*	1
Northeast	5	*55.5*	4	*.28*	7	*63.6*	4	*.45*	0	*0*	18	*.32*	8
Northwest	1	*33.3*	2	*.25*	5	*100.0*	0	*.55*	7	*53.8*	6	*.62*	3
Southeast	8	*72.7*	3	*.39*	9	*81.8*	2	*.52*	2	*13.3*	13	*.31*	7
Southwest	0	*0*	1	*.08*	1	*100.0*	0	*.11*	0	*0*	4	*.19*	3
Total	14	*58.3*	10	*.27*	23	*79.3*	6	*.44*	11	*21.1*	41	*.34*	22
All Land Bank towns except Worcester	9	*69.2*	4	*.41*	9	*75.0*	3	*.50*	2	*9.5*	19	*.38*	8

Note: Woodstock is included in the southwest until 1747; Petersham is included in the northwest after its incorporation in 1759.

Court = number of roll call votes cast with Court, or governor.

%Crt. = percent of roll call votes cast with Court, or governor.

Oppos. = number of votes cast against the governor.

Index = index of participation, measuring the frequency of voting by region (Index = total recorded votes/towns eligible for representation/number of roll calls).

Number of roll calls: 1739–41: 3; 1748–53: 8; 1754–5: 6; 1757–9: 3; 1761–4: 5; Total: 25.

Percentages are in italics.

Source: JHRM.

county in supporting Shirley between the late 1740s and the mid-1750s, particularly on the issues of revising the currency, improving Shirley's salary, and the defense of Crown Point. The southeastern representatives' shift from the Land Bank in 1740 to specie redemption in 1748 – as well as consistent opposition to currency innovations in the 1760s – indicates that monetary policy was more closely considered here than elsewhere. In aggregate, the nine towns voting predominantly with the opposition between 1726 and 1764 were significantly associated with the Land Bank, dissenting societies, New Light orthodoxy, and, to a lesser extent, the entire eastern region. (See Figure 1.) Opposition voting between 1757 and 1764 was mostly associated with New Light Orthodoxy, closely followed by the southeast, dissent, and the Land Bank. (See Figure 2.) In contrast to the pattern of opposition in the southeast, the northeast region around Lancaster, showing little interest in the Land Bank and largely Old Light in sentiment, followed a trajectory that ran against the overall county pattern, supporting Belcher on the Land Bank, and then swinging against Shirley. (See Table 1.) (The exceptions in the northeast were Harvard and Lunenburg, the two Land Bank towns in the northeast, which voted more consistently with the Popular opposition.) In an important sense, the representatives of the county's southeast and northeast moved in and out of court and country positions as different governors successively ruled the province, each having differing lines of influence during this long period of essential stability and consensus.

Considering the range of public initiatives in this late provincial era – support for the Land Bank, the results of the Awakening, and the votes of representatives in General Court – the most significant regional differences lay between the long-settled Blackstone Valley in the southeast and the new towns and districts of the northwest uplands. The careers of two long-sitting representatives, Timothy Ruggles of Hardwick and Henry King of Sutton, provide a useful view on the very different dynamics of class, community, and political practice that were emerging along the axis between the northwest and the southeast.

Timothy Ruggles was a classical example of the polished professional, assuming high position as a condition of his settlement on the undeveloped frontier. The son of an orthodox minister in Rochester associated with the Hardwick proprietors, Ruggles attended Harvard, was admitted in 1734 to the Plymouth County bar at the age of twenty-two, and two years later was elected representative by the Rochester townspeople. The next year he moved to Sandwich, and by the time he took up his family's land in Hardwick, he had served six times in the General Court, had been appointed a county collector of excise, and in his capacity as the king's attorney had developed an intense rivalry with James Otis, Sr. Moving to Hardwick in the winter of 1753–4, Ruggles was appointed justice of the peace and the quorum in April; he ultimately would be chief justice of the Court of Common Pleas as well as a brigadier general in the militia. Ruggles immediately took control of political affairs in Hardwick. The town had never been represented in General Court, but it elected Ruggles in the spring of 1754; until 1770 he would be their only representative. In his first session at the General Court, Ruggles served the town by having earlier fines remitted, noting with a certain condescension that the people had been in "poor and low circumstances" when they settled the town, that their crops had failed, and that they were burdened with "the support of several poor and indigent persons." In the style of the high gentry common on both sides of the Atlantic, Ruggles made efforts to improve the region's agriculture, and he sponsored a bill in the house in 1762 establishing a county fair that met at Hardwick twice a year down to the Revolution. Developing an elaborate estate in Hardwick, Ruggles sponsored deer hunting on horseback in an enclosed park. In return for his efforts in the house, Ruggles expected and received a measure of deference from the town. He alone was elected to the General Court from 1754 to 1770, and with the sole exception of a vote in favor of the excise in the 1754 house, on which he was specifically instructed by the town, Ruggles cast all his recorded votes with the governor, very much in the style of his neighbor John Murray of Rutland, another brigadier and justice of the quorum.[39]

Without equals in their sphere, Ruggles and Murray, like Joseph Dwight before them, commanded the respect and deference of their neighbors, and enjoyed a literal monopoly over the political mediation between town and province, which was the duty and privilege of the representative. They constituted a bulwark of the governor's – and the monarch's – interest in the county. But it is very suggestive that – unlike Joseph Dwight before them – neither Murray nor Ruggles was often elected to town offices such as assessor, selectman, or moderator.[40] There were limits to the deference of the people in the northwest uplands, who, in holding these men out of town office, erected a barrier between local institutions and their provincial mediators. The ordinary people of the orthodox, Court-dominated northwest towns and districts had a significantly more truncated political development. Settled later, the localities in this region were more likely to have only gained district rather than town privileges, as the royal governors increasingly attempted to contain the size of the house. With the dominant position of men like Timothy Ruggles and John Murray, the lack of town privileges of representation essentially eliminated the opportunity for most men to participate in politics outside the town. Little in their public experience took them outside the seamless web of corporatism and deference; unschooled in the Lockean insurgencies of the Land Bank and religious dissent, the people of the northwest had only the corporate tradition inherited from the Puritan experience – with its suggestions of Harringtonian commonwealth – with which to challenge the Court party men. The result was a building tension between gentry and townspeople. A political tradition of guarded deference, limited popular experience in provincial politics,

[39] Paige, *Hardwick*, 47–50, 481–3; Shipton, *Sibley's Harvard Graduates*, 9, 199–204, 207.
[40] Paige, *Hardwick*, 312ff.; Timothy C. Murphy, *History of Rutland in Massachusetts, 1713–1968* (Rutland, Mass., 1970), 151–3.

and increasing tension between representative and constituency lay behind the Court party voting of the northwest towns. This limited political experience set the stage for a particularly explosive politics at the close of the Revolutionary era.

Henry King represented the town of Sutton in the General Court continuously from 1756 down to the Revolution, but that was the extent of his similarity to Timothy Ruggles. Certainly the King family were well situated, but in a manner very different from the high gentry. Henry's father, William King, had been one of the earliest settlers, taking up land in Sutton in 1718 and serving as selectman and town clerk from 1720; by 1730 he ranked second in the meetinghouse seating, behind Justice Samuel Dudley. But dissenting opinions ran deep in the King family. An ancestor had been whipped for harboring Quakers in Salem in 1659, and in February 1732 William King presented a petition for abatement of rates to the Court of General Sessions on behalf of the Baptists in Sutton and Leicester. William King's brother-in-law, Benjamin Marsh, was the Baptist preacher in Sutton, and a Land Bank subscriber, and his son Henry married into the Baptist Green family of Leicester. Henry King followed his father into town government, serving extensively as assessor and selectman before he was elected representative for the first time in 1756, and with the sole exception of a proposal to monetize gold, King voted uniformly with the popular opposition. Where Ruggles ruled over a vast patronage empire by virtue of his commission as a brigadier of the county militia, King served merely as an elected militia captain.[41] Military service could only be a vehicle of a constituent-based politics if lower-ranking officers had the opportunity to emerge within the towns, translating their direct connections with former soldiers and their families into a local political following. It is striking that only one of the twenty-five men in the county appointed to the rank of colonel or general before the Revolution was from the Blackstone Valley. Men like Henry King stood outside the deep patronage dependencies that flowed through the orbits of men like Ruggles or Murray.[42]

Ruggles and King had very different careers, but they also had very different constituencies. King was rooted in a dissenting family in a New Light town where religious pluralism was accepted without significant turmoil: the town had voted in 1740 to relieve the Baptists from support of the minister, and in 1744 voted to assign a permanent quota of selectmen and assessors to the two orthodox parishes and the Baptist society. Sutton's ecclesiastical order would be further disrupted in the late 1760s with the emergence of a second Baptist society, but through it all Henry King served the town in the General Court and he and other Baptists regularly served in town positions. And contrary to usual Baptist practice, Henry King and his wife were buried in the town burying ground in Sutton center under winged cherubs carved in black slate, a marker of King's leading position in this

[41] Benedict and Tracy, *Sutton*, 670, 680ff.
[42] McWade, "Provincial Patronage Elite," 42–3.

Popular, New Light town.[43] The fluid pluralism of Sutton was inconceivable in the towns north of the county road where the great Court party magnates held sway. In John Murray's Rutland, the orthodox minister was troubled by Scots-Irish Presbyterians until they established themselves into a separate church and district in the town's "West Wing" in 1759; despite their contentious reputation, the Oakham Scots-Irish settled into a corporate pattern that was little different from that of their orthodox neighbors.[44] In Hardwick a group of Separates broke away from the orthodox church in 1749, forming their own church in 1750. According to the sequence typical in the towns across the southern tier of the county, this separation should have led to the formation of a Baptist church. But again, as in Rutland, religious dissent led to geographic division, not a working pluralism. Led by Land Banker Samuel Robinson, recently a captain in the provincial forces serving on Lake George, the Hardwick Separates emigrated as a group to establish the town of Bennington, Vermont, in 1761, leaving Ruggles undisturbed by contrary elements.[45] Interwoven with these different religious cultures was a different experience with the Land Bank: Henry King was embedded in a wide Land Bank connection in Sutton, whereas Samuel Robinson was one of only three Land Bankers in Hardwick.

In sum, two dynamics of political mobilization developed in Worcester County over the middle decades of the eighteenth century, dynamics that had their extreme manifestations along the axis between northwest and southeast. In the northwest, a gentry of grand style dominated a people who had little institutional experience outside the unitary structure of town and orthodox church. The result was a politics of deference regarding provincial matters, with the townspeople regularly electing the great men to the General Court, and stifling any objections that they might have had to their Court party voting. In the southeast, the practices of a constituent-based, oppositional politics were deeply rooted, institutionalized, in a contrasting experience. Here people had been involved in economic and religious initiatives that had taken them outside the confines of the corporate framework toward the beginnings of a Lockean social order. The Land Bank and the various paths of the New Light fueled a popular opposition to the governor's policies, an opposition conditioned during the late 1740s and early 1750s by loyalty to the governor who had charted a safe passage out of the Land Bank crisis.

The combination of influences at work in the southeast towns built a political tradition rooted in a functioning institutional pluralism, shaped by the constant

[43] Benedict and Tracy, *Sutton*, 60–1; "Davis Ms.," BPAN. The Popular leaders in Sturbridge and Dudley, Daniel and Henry Fisk and Thomas Cheney, also Baptists, were similarly buried in the Sturbridge center graveyard.
[44] "Extracts from the Minutes of the Presbytery of Boston: about Rutland, 1747–1755," typescript, Presbyterian Historical society; Wright and Harvey, *Oakham*, 115ff.
[45] Paige, *Hardwick*, 51ff., 225–30.

adjustment of group interests. It was a tradition characterized by the responsiveness of a broad stratum of Popular gentry to the demands and interests of their constituents, a tradition with considerable experience with the problems of currency and a great concern about the fiscal accountability of the government. The royal charter of 1691 brought a complex ideological fusion to Massachusetts Bay; in order to defend their Lockean compact with a distant monarch, the people needed to stand united in corporate unity. Importantly, it was only in the towns moving toward a Lockean, pluralistic order that a Popular gentry emerged to effectively advance the people's interest within the restrictions of the mixed polity. Their experiences in the Land Bank and the Awakening created a productive asymmetry, combining Lockean and Harringtonian dimensions in the Popular tradition.[46]

During the Revolution these tendencies with the Popular tradition would bifurcate, as men of varying inclinations would respond in different ways to the politics of constitutionalism and economic crisis. But by and large the Popular men rooted in the complex experiences of the Land Bank and New Light orthodoxy would provide a center of gravity in the county's revolutionary political culture, perpetuating their role as a loyal opposition forged under Governor Shirley. They would lead the people against the Court Party magnates in the Revolutionary crisis, and they would act in the county's interest and tradition in defending a well-regulated economy and in staunchly opposing the Federal Constitution. The Popular leadership would also stand between two groups newly entering the political arena, each engaged in very different insurgent movements drawing on the extremes within the shared ideological universe. On the one hand, dissenters – the junior partners in the Popular tradition – broke away to demand that a new constitution be written and ratified on Lockean principles. A subsequent generation would form a key Jeffersonian constituency. On the other hand, people across the northwest, poorly integrated into the wider political cultures of the county and the province and firmly rooted in local corporate institutions, entered the political arena in Shays's Rebellion, united in the Regulators' cause, defending a Harringtonian vision of independence in commonwealth.

---

[46] For a useful discussion of "country party" towns (my "Popular" towns), with a somewhat different interpretive focus, see Patterson, *Political Parties in Revolutionary Massachusetts*, 45–8.

PART II

The Revolution, 1763–1789

5

The Popular gentry and
the Revolutionary crisis

As the year 1765 drew to a close, Seth Metcalf, a young veteran of the French wars farming in the district of Paxton, sat down with his journal to review the events of that tumultuous year. His first concern was with the threat of natural disaster to a precarious household economy, and with the evident role of divine intervention. The storms of an "Exceedingly hard winter" were a "frown of Gods providence," but – despite the late frosts – "it pleased God to Crown this year with his goodness and to Give a competency of the Good things of this Life." Only after enumerating these "Remarkable" and "Common providences" did he turn to the year's great public events.

> Also this year Came an act from England Called the Stamp Act that is a Duty Laid on all writings which is thought will be very oppressive to the Inhabitants of North America and occasions Mobbs throughout all the provinces of the Continent The Day comes being the first of November when this Act is to take place But Mobbs keep it Back.

Metcalf worked this course of public affairs into the framework of the divine covenant. "Considering what hath passed over this land this year," the hard snows of December were a sign "that God is angry with us of this land and is now Smiting with his Rod Especially by the hands of our Rulers."[1]

Filled with excitement and a profound unease, Seth Metcalf's language captured the tone of Worcester County's response to the emerging Revolutionary crisis. A new order of things lay just over the horizon, and the Stamp Act crowds were asserting popular volition in a startling manner, but the people of the Worcester middle landscape were still bound by the frameworks of divine covenant and monarchical compact. Over the next quarter of a century, the Revolution would shatter these fundamental assumptions ruling social and political life in the province; the corporate ideology would be wrenched off its foundation in the royal charter and dislodged from its moorings in the orthodox covenant. But in 1765 the corporate language of charter and covenant defined the public world for Seth Metcalf and his peers throughout the county and province.

---

[1] William S. Piper, ed., *Diary and Journal (1755–1807) of Seth Metcalf* (Boston, 1939), 20. .

131

Over the next decade their collective response to the unfolding Revolutionary crisis revealed a powerful allegiance to these traditions.

Across Worcester County resistance to royal authority would emerge from the challenge of exogenous events, to which the county's experience with Popular politics would lend a stabilizing influence. Certainly the Court party magnates like John Murray, Timothy Ruggles, and the Chandlers would be swept away, but the revolutionary leaders would be men with a long experience in political affairs, and they would also be men from the broader gentry class. Certainly they were responsive to the needs and interests of their constituents, but they would not countenance any drastic social dislocation. Leading the county into national revolution, a Whig gentry of Popular origins would maintain order in society by appeals to the traditional framework of royal charter and federal covenant. They would create an effective instrument of provisional government in the county convention; they would not lead the people through a fundamental ideological or constitutional transformation.

"A very great burden of debt"

There was little in the air in the early 1760s that would suggest an imminent upheaval in public affairs. Seth Metcalf's attention in his journal notations was divided between manifestations of divinity in war and nature. In 1760 it "pleased the Almighty God to Give into our hands the Rest of our Enemies Country of Canada," but the following years brought a "scorching drought" and "Great Scarcity for man and Beast." In 1762 he acknowledged "the Great Goodness of God in prospering his Majesties Arms Both by Sea and Land"; in 1763 he thanked divine providence for the "General Peace," which was so "percularly Advantageous to the English Nation." Such patriotism had a central place in orthodox sermons in these years. David Hall exhorted the people of Sutton to celebrate "Israel's Triumph"; Eli Forbes of the North Parish of Brookfield dedicated to Brig. Timothy Ruggles a sermon celebrating "the Success of British ARMS in North America," writing in a millennial vein that "God has given to sing this Day, the downfall of New France, the North-American Babylon."[2]

Revolutionary sentiment was certainly not evident in the county's legislative politics. After shifting toward the opposition between 1757 and 1759, during the administration of Governor Pownall, Worcester County's representatives turned to the court for a last time after 1760, during the early years of Governor Bernard's term. Support for the governor was particularly notable in the county's 9 to 2 vote

---

[2] Diary . . . of Seth Metcalf, 18–19; David Hall, Israel's Triumph . . . A Sermon Preached at Sutton on a Public Thanksgiving, October 9, 1760. For the Entire Reduction of Canada . . . (Boston, 1761); Eli Forbes, God the Strength and Salvation of His People; Illustrated in a Sermon Preached October 9, 1760. Being a Day of Public Thanksgiving Appointed by Authority for the Success of British ARMS in North America . . . (Boston, 1761).

in April 1762, opposing the exclusion of Superior Court justices from sitting in the council or the house, a centerpiece of James Otis's campaign against the writs of assistance. The county's support for the governor on this issue must be attributed to the influence of Brigadier Ruggles, an old enemy of the Otis family, who was elected speaker of the house in 1762 and 1763. The governor's liberal distribution of appointments of justice of the peace in 1762 also must have played a role in moderating opposition sentiment, and over the next three years the towns elected a record number of justices to represent them in the General Court.[3]

From the perspective of the Worcester backcountry, if not the countinghouses and artisan shops of Boston, there was a sense of balance and harmony among locality, metropolis, and empire in the early 1760s, part and parcel of the essential continuity running from 1744, two decades of stability forged by William Shirley. Despite the emergence of an alternative institutional order among the dissenting societies, and periodic opposition to the governor on a narrow but significant range of fiscal issues, the county – like the province as a whole – had been significantly less confrontational in these two decades than it had been between the Peace of Utrecht and the Great Awakening.[4]

Far from the hothouse politics of the depressed seaport towns, the county's response to the Stamp Act was also irregular and uneven. Again Timothy Ruggles would play a central role, with the deferential acquiescence of the town of Hardwick. Ruggles reluctantly accepted his election as a provincial delegate to the Stamp Act Congress meeting in New York in October 1765, where he was elected chair over the aspiration of his old rival, James Otis. Ruggles had resisted house instructions to defend the colonies' exclusive rights to taxation, and as chair he refused to sign the Stamp Act Congress's resolves, and left the meeting before it adjourned. Even though he was formally censured by the Massachusetts house, and his name published on a list of "enemies to their country" who had supported the Stamp Act, Ruggles was reelected to the house in 1766 and in each of the next four years. The only other Worcester County representative whose name was published among the Stamp Act supporters, Ezra Taylor of Southborough, was also reelected in 1766.[5]

Elsewhere the Court Party men trimmed their sails to a rising indignation with

---

[3] *JHRM* 38: Pt. 2, 318–19; Shipton, *Sibley's Harvard Graduates*, 9:207–8; John J. Waters and John A. Shutz, "Patterns of Massachusetts Colonial Politics: The Writs of Assistance and the Rivalry between the Otis and Hutchinson Families," *WMQ* 24 (1967), 543–67. Between 1763 and 1765, 60–70% of the representatives of Worcester County towns were justices of the peace, a record unsurpassed in the provincial era. Based on an analysis of Whitaker, *Civil List*, and the representatives listed in *JHRM*.

[4] Pencak, *War, Politics, and Revolution*, 172–5; Richard D. Brown, *Revolutionary Politics in Massachusetts: the Boston Committee of Correspondence and the Towns, 1772–1774* (New York, 1970), 14–17.

[5] Paige, *Hardwick*, 58–65; Shipton, *Sibley's Harvard Graduates*, 9:208–10; Boston Evening Post, April 28, 1766.

the British measures. John Murray was instructed by the Rutland town meeting "to use his best endeavors . . . to have the Rights and Privileges of this Province, vindicated and preserved to us and our Posterity." The town celebrated the Stamp Act's repeal by raising a Liberty pole, and Murray served as representative through the crisis year of 1774. In Sturbridge, Col. Moses Marcy, a man of Court inclinations, was instructed to "use the utmost of his endeavors *consistent with loyalty*" to have the act repealed. In Worcester, John Chandler, serving simultaneously as representative and councillor, was quietly replaced in the house by another selectman, Capt. Ephraim Doolittle. At an October town meeting that Chandler moderated, Doolittle was simply instructed not to support the Stamp Act in any manner.[6]

The most highly developed response to the Stamp Act was drafted by a committee from the town of Leicester and its associated districts. The October 17, 1765, instructions to representative Capt. John Brown would be the most elaborate political statement to emerge from the region for many years. The committee's primary objections to the new parliamentary duties were constitutional, and were framed in language that revealed a general familiarity with the tenets of Whig political thought. "Esteem[ing] it an essential privilege of Britons to be taxed by their own representatives . . . [the town could] not but think that the said act is contrary to the rights of mankind, and subversive of the English Constitution." In addition to the duties, they complained about "the unparalleled stretch given to admiralty jurisdiction" by the recent strengthening of the Acts of Trade by the Grenville ministry. Pledging their "loyalty to the king" and their "veneration of the Parliament," they based their argument on their natural rights, their rights as Englishmen, and "those granted to us by charter."[7]

Leicester's instructions of 1765 voiced a clear call for the defense of the provincial charter; their tone was distinctly moderated when they considered the destruction of property at the hands of urban rioters. The high point of the Stamp Act crisis in Boston had been the artisan crowd's methodical destruction of the mansions of stamp distributor Andrew Oliver and Lt. Governor Thomas Hutchinson. Noting that the governor had implicated the province at large "in the late tumults in Boston," the people of Leicester hastened to disassociate themselves from those crowd actions of urban laborers. Claiming that they had "an abhorence of such outrages," they instructed their representative to oppose any public payment of the damages "lest it become a bad precedent, and prove an encouragement to such riotous practices in the future." He was to press for payment by the rioters themselves, or by private contribution "as a deed of mercy." Leicester's reaction to the Stamp Act rioters was almost exactly the same as that of the Court faction town of Hardwick, which in August of 1766 notified

---

[6] Reed, *Rutland*, 60–1; Clark, *Sturbridge*, 14; Worcester Town Records, in WSA 4, 128–9; and *JHRM* 43: pt. 2, 4.
[7] Leicester Instructions, October 17, 1765, quoted in Washburn, *Leicester*, 435–7.

Timothy Ruggles of the inhabitants' "utmost abhorence" of the "disorders" and instructed him to ensure that either the rioters or the town of Boston "make good all the damages to the sufferers." In 1767 Andrew Oliver's son Daniel settled in Hardwick, and was accepted by the town to the extent of being elected to the General Court with his patron Timothy Ruggles in 1770. When property was threatened, the Whig householders of Leicester could close ranks with their peers in the governor's orbit.[8]

Leicester would be one of the pivotal towns in the county's revolutionary movement, and the membership of the committee framing the Stamp Act instructions for John Brown reflected the composition of the emerging leadership of resistance in the county. Sixty-two years old, John Brown was himself a veteran of Popular politics. Once a Land Banker and Louisburg soldier, he had occupied Leicester's seat intermittently since 1749. Among the committee members was Capt. Benjamin Johnson, another aged figure, who had "raised factions" against David Parsons in the 1730s and subscribed to the Land Bank in 1740, and served eleven terms as selectman in Leicester and the district of Spencer. Johnson served for Spencer alongside Joshua Lamb, a son-in-law of Land Banker James Wilson. Capt. Jonathan Newhall, a Baptist who was the son-in-law of Josiah Converse, the pro–Land Bank representative in Brookfield in 1740 and 1741, was another committee man with clear roots in the Popular tradition. Thomas Denny, a Baptist who had held a commission in Newhall's company in 1763, and Daniel Henshaw, again the son-in-law of a Land Bank subscriber, also fell within the ranks of the Popular tradition. But these two key figures on the committee had extensive kin connections in Boston, and Leicester's leadership in the resistance movement would derive from such metropolitan connections. Thomas Denny, the author of Leicester's 1765 instructions, was the nephew of Thomas Prince, the liberal minister of the Old South Church. The committee's chairman, Daniel Henshaw, had himself been a prosperous merchant in Boston before moving to Leicester in 1748, and his brother Joshua was an important member of the Boston Whig elite until he fled to Leicester in 1773. Daniel Henshaw's sons William and Joseph were key leaders in the Worcester County Convention in the fall and winter of 1774 and 1775. Joseph chaired most of the meetings of the convention, while William, a lieutenant in the provincial forces at Crown Point in 1759, was particularly involved in military preparations, and was among the first to propose in the fall of 1774 that minute companies be formed to defend the people of the province from British troops. The Boston Henshaws kept their country cousins well informed as to the march of events during the 1760s, and Joseph Allen, a nephew of Boston Whig leader Samuel Adams, reinforced the Boston Whig connection. Allen established himself as a merchant in a house adjacent to the orthodox minister's at

---

[8] Leicester Instructions, October 17, 1765, in Washburn, *Leicester*, 438; Sturbridge Town Records, in Clark, *Sturbridge*, 14; Paige, *Hardwick*, 65; on the Stamp Act riots, see Nash, *Urban Crucible*, 293–6.

Leicester center; he would host the meetings of the Leicester committee of correspondence throughout the Revolutionary crisis.[9]

A similar combination of Land Bank origins and links to Boston characterized the leading Whigs in Worcester. Joshua and Timothy Bigelow, a Land Banker and the son of a Land Banker, respectively, dominated Whig politics in Worcester through the 1770s. Joshua served regularly in the General Court after John Chandler's ejection in 1765, and Timothy – a member of the Boston "Whig Club" – dominated the Worcester Convention with the Henshaws of Leicester, sitting on at least fifteen committees in the fall and winter of 1774 to 1775. More broadly, the Popular tradition provided an important source of Revolutionary leadership throughout the county. Land Bankers and their sons or nephews represented Brookfield, Leicester, Grafton, Mendon, Uxbridge, Sutton, Fitchburg, Petersham, Oxford, Western, and Hardwick variously in the 1768 convention of towns, the 1774–5 county convention, and the provincial congresses. Among them were John Brown of Leicester; Joseph Gilbert, son of Benjamin of the North Parish of Brookfield; Phinehas Upham, son of Dr. Jabez of the South Parish; Henry King of Sutton; and Deacon Oliver Watson of the district of Spencer. In the northeast region, where Land Bank support had been relatively weak, representatives voting against the governor in the 1760s, particularly Artemas Ward of Shrewsbury and John Whitcomb of Bolton, emerged as prominent figures in the Whig cause.[10]

Similarly, the captains of minute companies responding to the Lexington alarm were often drawn from the Land Bank orbit. Timothy Bigelow, son of a Land Banker, led the Worcester Company. Capt. John Putnam of Sutton was the son-in-law of the Reverend David Hall, and Lt. Jonathan Woodbury was the son of Benjamin Woodbury, a Sutton Land Banker and representative. In Brookfield, Capt. Ithamar Wright was the son of Obadiah Wright, briefly elected selectman and town treasurer during the Land Bank crisis, and Capt. John Woolcott was the son of Nathaniel, a Land Banker and the captain of a militia company sent to relieve Fort William Henry in 1757. Capt. Timothy Newell of Sturbridge, who also had served on a number of convention committees, was the son of a Land Banker in Needham. All told, of fifteen officers and sergeants in the three Leicester

[9] Draper, *Spencer*, 146, 215; Washburn, *Leicester*, 231, 235–40, 343 Estes, "Historical Discourse," in *The Greenville Baptist Church*, 20–1; Shipton, *Sibley's Harvard Graduates*, 9:268; 12:268–9; Letters from Joshua Henshaw, of Boston, to William and David Henshaw, of Leicester, in *NEGHR* 22 (1868) 402–3; *NEGHR* 23 (1869) 451–4; *NEGHR* 32 (1878) 168–9. See also "A Sketch of the Life of Hon. Joshua Henshaw, with Brief Notices of Other Members of the Henshaw Family," *NEGHR* 22 (1866), 105–11; John W. Chadwick, "The Town of Leicester, Massachusetts," *New England Magazine* NS 22 (1900) 363.

[10] William Lincoln, ed., *The Journals of Each Provincial Congress of Massachusetts in 1774 and 1775 ... with the Proceedings of the County Conventions* (Boston, 1838), 13–15, 82–3, 276–7, 627–52; Richard D. Brown, "The Massachusetts Convention of Towns, 1768," *WMQ* 26 (1969), 104, Lincoln, *Worcester* 227–9; Davis *Currency and Banking*, 2,: 295–313; and family and town histories and vital records.

companies raised in 1775, six had kin among the Land Bankers, including John
Brown of Leicester, Oliver Watson of Spencer, and Benjamin Marsh of Sutton.
Many more served in the ranks.[11]

Thus a striking number of Whig leaders in Worcester County were drawn from
families involved in the Land Bank three decades before. The nine towns that had
produced significant numbers of Land Bankers in 1740 were also particularly well
represented at the early meetings of the Worcester County Convention in the late
summer of 1774, and among the convention's committee appointments. With the
exception of the town of Worcester, the old Land Bank towns had virtually no
Tory presence, despite the institutional pluralism that had grown up since the
Great Awakening. By contrast, the northern half of the county, where the Land
Bank had little support, was notable for its numbers of Tories; the northwest
section was particularly poorly represented at the early meetings of the county
convention. (See Figure 3, p. 202.)

Reviewing the imperial legislation of the decades before the Revolution, John
Adams noted that "the act to destroy the Land Bank scheme raised a greater
ferment in this province than the Stamp Act did."[12] Adams's insight may have
been particularly true for Worcester County, where the bank subscribers had been
especially numerous and the Stamp Act agitation rather distant. But the two crises
may have been mutually reinforcing, for in September 1763, the Land Bank issue
was reopened with the publication of a list of delinquent Land Bank subscribers.
Worcester County had by far the largest concentration of Land Bank delinquents,
accounting for almost a third of the entire list, and relative to population, three
times the number in the rest of the province. The largest sums on the list are
revealing. Capt. Solomon Wood of Uxbridge, a Popular representative in the early
1760s, led the list with £35, followed by John Hazeltine of Upton, who had
represented his town in the 1740 and 1749 assemblies and served in the provincial
forces before emigrating to Vermont in 1769. Capt. John Brown of Leicester
ranked third with a debt of £20, and John Grout, a small-time lawyer in
Lunenburg whose son Jonathan would emerge as a leading figure during and after
the Revolution, ranked fourth on the list, followed by John Brown's older brother
Samuel, who had recently emigrated to the Berkshire frontier. Other figures owing
lesser amounts in 1763 included Joshua Bigelow of Worcester, Oliver Watson of
Spencer, James Wilson of Leicester, David Hall, Benjamin Marsh, and Benjamin
Woodbury of Sutton, and Jabez Upham and Nathaniel Woolcott of Brookfield. In
the 1760s, the Land Bank was not an experience buried deep in the past; rather it

---

[11] Albert A. Lovell, *Worcester in the War of the Revolution: Embracing the Acts of the Town
from 1765 to 1783 Inclusive* (Worcester, 1876), 119; Benedict and Tracy, *Sutton*, 783; Temple,
North Brookfield 228–30; *Brookfield Town Meeting Records, 1719–1770*; May 18, 1741, p. 100;
Clark, *Sturbridge*, 17; Washburn, *Leicester*, 215–17.

[12] Charles F. Adams, ed., *The Works of John Adams* . . . (Boston, 1851, 4:49); see Bushman,
King and People, 202 n. 59.

reemerged as a powerfully troublesome issue just before the Stamp Act set the stage for revolutionary resistance.[13]

The revival of the issue of the Land Bank came simultaneously with a postwar depression of trade. The threat of his Land Bank delinquency may have been weighing on the Reverend David Hall when, in April 1765, he complained in his diary that he was "in Great affliction in outward regards poor & in Distress by reason of Debt and under hard usage from my People."[14] Similar suggestions of an anxiety about a depressed economy and the problem of debt also began to appear in the instructions and resolves of the towns, marking a renewal of the political language of property and rights, and couched in a fear of impending slavery and lordships. The instructions framed by the Leicester committee of October 1765 were centrally informed by constitutional concerns, but economic language was never far below the surface. Noting that "in carrying on the war" the province had come under "a very great burden of debt," they instructed John Brown to "be very frugal in your grants of the government's money." Repeating their concerns about the province's "grievous burden of debt," the committee argued that the Stamp Act had "a direct tendency to bring us into a state of abject slavery and vassalage." And opposition to the Stamp Act achieved what the Land Bankers had not dared to do; the Courts of Common Pleas were closed from November 1765 until after news of the repeal arrived in April 1766. If the question of the legality of the stamps stopped the meeting of the courts, debtors stood to gain by their closure. To the south in Connecticut there were reports of "riots and tumults" among some who had benefited from "having so long been loose from the curse of the law," anticipating events in Massachusetts in 1774 and 1786. In Worcester the court system came under a new scrutiny after the repeal of the Stamp Act. In 1766 and 1767 the town of Worcester instructed its representatives to act to revise the fee table, particularly with regard to excessive fees granted to the sheriffs, and fines levied on jurymen; reversing the county's position of 1762, they urged their representative to exclude any man holding high places on the civil or military lists from the governor's council. Hostility to the courts and anxiety about debt, resonating with the fears of dependency at the heart of classical republican thought, would emerge again and again throughout the Revolutionary era.[15]

---

[13] The Land Bank delinquents were published in the *Boston Gazette*, September 12, 1763; the list is reproduced in Mitten, "The New England Paper Money Tradition," 88ff.; 1764 population from Evarts N. Greene and Virginia D. Harrington, *American Population before the Federal Census of 1790* (New York, 1932), 21. On John Hazeltine, see *Upton, Massachusetts, 1735–1935* (Upton, 1935), 11. Patterson, *Political Parties in Revolutionary Massachusetts*, 33–62, emphasizes the importance of the Popular tradition in forging the Revolutionary coalition.

[14] Diary of David Hall, MHS, April 18, 1765.

[15] Washburn, *Leicester*, 435; Lincoln, *Worcester*, 69–71; Edmund Morgan, *The Stamp Act Crisis: Prologue to Revolution* (New York, 1963), 218–19, and more broadly 170–2, 181–6, and 215–30. For recent important analyses of the role of debt and dependence in republican

Most immediately, the language of debt and dependency would be invoked in the fall and winter of 1767–8 in the face of the Townshend Acts. A number of towns supported the resolves of the House of Representatives calling for nonconsumption of British goods. A committee in Sutton echoed the language of the house resolves, pointing to "the great Decay of the trade of the Province, the Scarcity of Money, the heavy Debts contracted in the late war, which still remains on the People, and the great Difficulties to which they are by these means reduced." But the house resolves introduced a new theme: Encouragement of domestic manufacturing would eliminate the economic source of dependence and corruption. Sutton, Worcester, and Harvard called for the support of manufacturing in the province; in Brookfield, Dr. Jabez Upham's sons established a short-lived woolen manufactory, housed in a two-story building fifty feet in length, apparently including a fulling mill powered in part by the fall of water at their father's gristmill privilege south of the Quaboag River.[16]

As originally conceived, the Land Bank would have had a similar thrust as the nonimportation and manufacturing plan of 1767–8. Known alternatively as the "Manufactory Scheme," the Land Bank would have accepted a wide variety of agricultural and manufactured goods, including linen, sailcloth, canvas, and bar and cast iron, in payment of the interest and principal on the Land Bank notes. The effect might well have been to stimulate an internal trade and industry at the expense of commerce with Britain – an effective if only implicit nonimportation plan. Gen. Timothy Ruggles was the only representative to oppose the manufacturing proposal in 1768, arguing that domestic industries would draw labor from agriculture and fisheries, and raise the price of labor. His concern may have flown from his experience in Hardwick, where a blast furnace – operated by men who would serve in the Revolutionary conventions – annually hired dozens of young men. The issue of collective economic independence would reemerge in a similar form in the decades following the Revolution. Strikingly, the old Land Bank towns, and the Popular party orbit in general, would develop a thriving small shop economy by 1820, an economy that would profoundly shape the circumstances of these places across the first half of the nineteenth century.[17]

As elsewhere in the colonies, the momentum of oppositional politics sputtered out in the late 1760s. It would rise again in 1772 and 1773, with the royal assumption of judicial salaries and the imposition of the duty on tea, coinciding with another downturn in the Atlantic economy. Again there were strong

ideology, see Bushman, *King and People*, 176–210; and Timothy Breen, *Tobacco Culture: The Mentality of the Great Tidewater Planters on the Eve of the Revolution* (Princeton, 1985), 124–203.

[16] Nourse, *Harvard*, *303*; Lincoln, *Worcester*, 73–4; Benedict and Tracy, *Sutton*, 85–6; Temple, *North Brookfield*, 14. On manufacturing in the 1760s, see Crowley, *This Sheba, Self*, 127–41; Nash, *The Urban Crucible*, 332ff.

[17] Davis, *Currency and Banking*, 2:167–8; Paige, *Hardwick*, 67–8, 307–8; Riesman, "American Political Economy," 192ff.

suggestions of an underlying anxiety about economic relations and the court system, which worked as the mediating institution. The courts negotiated the terms upon which men met in the marketplace, and potentially were the agency by which contract obligations could destroy household economies; the accountability of those courts was thus of great concern, and when the crown announced that the salaries of the justices of the Superior Court would no longer be under the control of the house of representatives, it struck a very sensitive nerve.

Anxiety about control over the court system might have stemmed from purely constitutional grounds, but there may have been a more direct concern. The five sessions of the Court of Common Pleas that met in the fourteen months prior to September 1774, when the courts were closed by convention and militia, had seen a marked increase in the volume of civil actions considered, a roughly 50 percent increase on average over the thirteen sessions between January 1770 and March 1773. Strikingly, a number of cases dating from 1774 were reopened in the mid-1780s, contributing to the massive increase in civil cases that led to the court closings by the Regulators in September 1786. In the context of economic distress and a rising tide of civil actions, some of the language of the Revolutionary resolves suggest a concern about more than political principle. On January 4, 1774, the Whigs in Worcester banded together in the American Political Society; citing "the machinations of some designing persons in this Province, who are grasping at power, and the property of their neighbors," they agreed to "avoid all lawsuits with all men as much as possible." The following April the society voted to notify the county at large that the justices of the Court of General Sessions had failed to make the customary tally of votes for the position of county treasurer, warning the people to "be on their guard against fraud and deception." The town of Leicester voiced more direct concerns about power, property, and the regulation of economic affairs in response to the Boston Port Act. If the crown could assume the "right to dispose of private property" by closing Boston to seaward trade, it might "prohibit . . . any town or husbandman from sowing grain, mowing grass, and feeding his pastures, so long as his majesty thinks proper."[18]

Thus popular resistance was couched in economic language by men whose experience, and that of their fathers, ran back to an earlier struggle with British authority. But this language was distinctly limited. As Richard Bushman has amply demonstrated, behind the nervous references to debt and the inflated rhetoric of slavery lay a fear that the propertied independence of the middle landscape would be swept away, the people reduced to dependent tenancy and "lordships." The political metaphor of slavery could have a transformative effect; as early as 1767 the town of Worcester instructed its representative to demand the legal end of chattel slavery in the province. But slavery was not integral to the province's social and economic structure; the people of Worcester could afford the

---

[18] RWCCP, 8:1–580; 9:1–437; 13:1–280; Lovell, *Worcester in the War of the Revolution*, 21–5; Washburn, *Leicester*, 445; Lincoln, *Worcester*, 76–8.

luxury of such intellectual consistency. Clearly there were important economic undertones to the early Revolutionary movement, but its thrust was distinctly limited by the central priority of conserving the property and independence of middling householders. The region's conservative response to the Stamp Act rioters indicated that there were sharp limits to revolutionary sentiment in the 1760s. The ideal society was a Harringtonian commonwealth, a republic of freeholding yeomen, not an equalitarian democracy.[19]

Equally importantly, the oppositional politics of the 1760s and early 1770s had a broader base than simply the old Land Bank coalition. The Land Bank communities were conspicuous in their growing involvement in the politics of resistance (they were not acting alone) and their response in 1765 had been uneven. Where Leicester, led by a gentry with close connections in Boston, had acted decisively in 1765, Sutton did nothing, although David Hall called a Fast Day in December to ask divine favor on the proceedings of the Stamp Act Congress. In 1768, when Boston called a convention in response to the governor's dismissal of the General Court over the issue of the circular letter on the Townshend Acts, the Land Bank towns responded, but so did the towns in the conservative northeast section of the county. Worcester County's participation in the 1768 convention of the towns divided along geographic lines with the east sending delegates and the western town and districts holding back, much as their neighbors in the court-dominated counties of Hampshire and Berkshire further to the west.[20]

In sum, the Land Bank tradition was a formative dimension of the emerging Revolutionary movement. Sharing with men throughout the colonies a sense that their opportunities were constricted by the imperial connection, the Land Bankers had offered a solution that was rooted in the optimistic view of commerce and marketplace forged by the seventeenth-century liberals, and modeled on the possibility of rational voluntary association. But by itself, the Land Bank heritage was not a sufficient ideological base for the emerging opposition movement. The Land Bank had been a powerful challenge to royal authority, but it also challenged – however briefly and tentatively – the fundamental values of the province. It had been an interest-based faction grounded at least implicitly in Lockean principles, cutting across the grain of the unitary corporate assumptions of Massachusetts orthodoxy. Even if the charter itself had certain connotations of a Lockean contract, the external threat posed by British intervention in colonial affairs required an inclusive, unitary ideology.[21] While Land Bank families and communities would provide an important bloc of Revolutionary leadership, the

[19] Richard Bushman, "Massachusetts Farmers and the Revolution," in Richard M. Jellison, ed., *Society, Freedom, and Conscience: The Coming of the Revolution in Virginia, Massachusetts, and New York* (New York, 1976), esp. 116; Bushman, *King and People*, 190–206; Lincoln, *Worcester*, 71.

[20] Benedict and Tracy, *Sutton*, 84; Diary of David Hall, Nov. 17, 1765; Brown, "The 1768 Convention of the Towns," 104.

[21] On Lockean views of the charter, see Jedrey, *The World of John Cleaveland*, 131–5.

ideological construct that would provide Revolutionary legitimacy stressed a corporate unity and consensus grounded in charter and covenant, the twin pillars framing provincial public culture. To justify their cause, the people needed to remain steadfast and orderly in their allegiance to the charter of 1691, the fundamental compact between the monarch and the people. They needed to adhere to the public values and virtues of the commonwealth, not the private values and virtues of the marketplace. And when the monarch failed to adhere to that compact, the people were asked to turn to their ancient national covenant with the divinity, as interpreted by the orthodox ministers of the Congregational establishment. The Revolutionary crisis, then, would temporarily submerge the pluralistic language of interest and group that Land Bankers and dissenters had forged decades before – and that would reemerge in an explosive and complex politics as soon as the external challenge of British intervention had been turned aside.

The charter

In the early 1770s the Whig leadership in Boston was worried by the province's waning attention to the encroachments of British authority. They feared that a tyrannical, corrupting state power was quietly emerging in the ministry's efforts to regularize and centralize the administration of the royal colonies, and that the populace had grown too apathetic to resist. Their worst fears were confirmed when, in September of 1772, word arrived that the ministry had ordered that the salaries of the governor, the Superior Court justices, and other royally appointed officials would be paid by the crown rather than by the colonial legislatures. Boston's response was the creation of a Committee of Correspondence on November 2, 1772, which was to draw up a statement of "the Rights of the Colonists . . . as Men, as Christians, and as Subjects . . . with the Infringements and Violations thereof," to be sent to the towns for their consideration and reply.[22]

The resulting "Boston pamphlet" reached most of the towns in the province by the end of December. Their response followed the pattern of politicization that had emerged in the mid-1760s, and reflected a very cautious attitude toward the emergent opposition to British authority. By September of the following year roughly two-thirds of the towns in the county had replied to the committee's letter. As usual, Leicester was the first to respond. The town's January resolves reiterated its loyalty to the king but also its devotion to rights under the English constitution; it complained of the infringements by Parliament and the new jurisdiction of the Courts of Admiralty upon those rights. Both Leicester and Sutton instructed their representatives, Thomas Denny and Henry King, to propose that the province raise the judges' salaries in an effort to forestall their

22 Brown, *Revolutionary Politics*, 38–57; Bushman, *King and People*, 171–86.

assumption by the crown. The county seat of Worcester was slow to react, and only after forty-one voters had presented a petition in March 1773 did the town consider the Boston Committee's letter and vote to establish a permanent committee of correspondence. The country towns took a cautious approach typified by Sturbridge's return. "Sensibly affected with the danger of unlimited independent arbitrary government," the town was nonetheless concerned that action be taken in a "lawfull and loyal way . . . at the greatest remove from all unreasonable opposition to Civil Authority." The Tea Act and the Boston Tea Party in December 1773 evoked a concerted response from only a few leading towns. Leicester with its associated districts of Spencer and Paxton formed a Committee of Correspondence and, along with Brookfield, drew up covenants pledging not to drink tea. Brookfield's resolves, declaring that the tax on tea would be "a poison more fatal in its effects to the natural and political rights and privileges of the people of this Country than ratsbane would be to the natural body," dramatically expressed the revolutionary fears about the corrupting influences of imported luxuries.[23]

Despite the opportunity for such high-blown rhetoric, few of the other towns appear to have reacted at this stage of the crisis. In the county town of Worcester, however, the tea controversy set off an intense political confrontation, which, though lasting only six months, suggested the shape of things to come. Here a large group of Loyalists entrenched in the court system and town government managed to forestall any town response to the Tea Act. Worcester's Whigs responded with an extra corporate political organization unique in the region. On December 27, 1773, the same day that Leicester and Brookfield voted their covenants on tea, a group of Whigs in Worcester led by Joshua Bigelow met to form the American Political Society. Worcester would not act on the issue of the duty on tea until the following March, and only after a petition signed by twenty-seven voters was submitted in town meeting. When the meeting approved a committee report opposing the tea tax, a group of twenty-six Loyalists, led by James Putnam and John Chandler, entered a strident protest in the town record. As the county seat, Worcester had had a particularly confrontational town politics, almost urban in quality, as far back as the 1730s and 1740s. Since the 1740s the town had been dominated by a faction entrenched at the top of the court system and linked to the governor's interest. The members of the American Political Society appear to have been a slightly younger and less prosperous group than the Loyalist faction in Worcester, and they had been virtually shut out of town politics; between 1750 and

---

[23] Leicester Resolves and Instructions, Jan. 4, 1773, in Washburn, *Leicester*, 440–1; Letters and Proceedings Received by the Boston Committee of Correspondence, George Bancroft Collection, New York Public Library, photostatic copies at the Massachusetts Historical Society; letter from Leicester to BCC, February 11, 1773, photo. 389, Sturbridge Proceedings sent to BCC January 19, 1773, photo. 807; Brown, *Revolutionary Politics*, 97; Lincoln, *Worcester*, 75–6; Benedict and Tracy, *Sutton*, 89; Extracts, Brookfield Town Records, December 27, 1773.

1763 Loyalists served forty terms as selectmen, while future APS members served a total of five. Between 1764 and 1773 the board of selectmen was evenly divided between the two factions, with the Loyalist Chandler family controlling the town clerkship and the town treasury. Where the country towns were entering the Revolutionary crisis with a traditional, consensual local politics, proto-urban Worcester was divided into clearly defined factions, employing political methods of petition and association anticipating the party politics that would emerge in the first decade of the next century.[24]

Widespread political mobilization would not take place until the full consequences of the Tea Party became known early in the following May. The Coercive Acts imposed by Parliament in the spring of 1774 worked as nothing else had to turn the people against Great Britain. Where the Stamp Act and the Townshend duties had been indirect incursions on the rights of the colonists under the English constitution, the Coercive Acts were direct and conscious efforts to alter the provincial charter, the basic instrument guaranteeing the legitimacy of nearly all local and provincial civil institutions. The new acts of Parliament posed a direct threat to the corporate autonomy of the towns by limiting town meetings to one per year and enhanced the role of the court by taking jury selection out of the control of the towns. Establishing royal control over the council, the courts, and the town meeting, as well as extending protection from local prosecution to crown officials, this shift in British policy provoked a corresponding reaction on the part of the Massachusetts political community. One of the first effects was a perceptible sharpening and alteration of the constitutional arguments with which the Whig gentry defended their opposition to British authority. Paradoxically, this defiant stance was rooted in a loyal deference to monarchical authority under the symbiotic, reciprocating terms of the social contract between the ruler and the ruled.[25]

During May and June Worcester was paralyzed by the Loyalists' continuing efforts to stem the tide of popular Whiggery, so Leicester once again led the county. The earliest and most articulate response to the Coercive Acts from the Near Frontier came in two sets of resolves, the first drawn up by Leicester and associated districts on July 6, 1774, and the second by a convention of towns that met at Worcester on August 9. In both sets of resolves the legitimacy of local institutions and of their defense by the colonists was rooted in a reiterated assertion of loyalty to the crown.

After reviewing the recent acts of Parliament, the people of Leicester saw it as "our duty to take into consideration the constitution of government we are under." Where previous statements had referred rather diffusely to natural rights and to rights under the English constitution, the Leicester resolves focused exclusively on the charter. Noting that the 1629 charter had been "wrongfully wrested from the

[24] Lincoln, *Worcester*, 82–4, 356–7; Lovell, *Worcester in the War of the Revolution*, 27–9.
[25] Brown, *Revolutionary Politics*, 185–90; Zuckerman, *Peaceable Kingdoms*, 220–58.

colony" by James II, Leicester stated that the charter as regranted by "King William and Queen Mary of glorious memory [was] the basis of the civil constitution of government of this Province." As such the charter was a "sacred" compact, which "no power on earth whatsoever hath right or authority to disannul or revoke." Leicester's resolves circulated in the surrounding towns and districts, providing a model for revolutionary language.[26]

Meeting in Worcester a month later, the county convention built on Leicester's arguments, passing resolutions declaring their allegiance to the crown but rejecting the authority of Parliament. Drawing on the argument first made by the House of Representatives in response to Governor Hutchinson's January 1773 attack on the letter of the Boston Committee, these resolves, rejected parliamentary authority and asserted their rights as Americans, rather than Englishmen, on the basis of a particular compact made between the crown and the people of Massachusetts Bay. In the Glorious Revolution they had forcibly stripped sovereignty from the surrogates of James II, and had voluntarily handed it to William and Mary. Thus the colonists had made a particular agreement of protection and allegiance with the crown; since Parliament had had no part in that agreement, that body had no authority in the colonies. With this sacred compact in mind, and in the face of seemingly arbitrary use of power on the part of ministry and Parliament, the Worcester County Convention fell back on the king as the ultimate source of legitimacy and authority in the empire.[27]

Some towns remained hopeful that the king was unaware of the threat to the compact: Rutland wrote that the "fraudulence and Perfidy ... [of] Base and Designing men" had kept the king uninformed of his subjects' plight. But such a presumption of royal innocence was notably absent from the resolves and instructions of other towns, particularly in the summer and fall of 1774. Private fears of royal participation were growing, to become public by the spring of 1775. What concerned the Patriot gentry more was holding up their end of the bargain. As the Worcester convention argued in its August 9 resolves, "an attempt to vacate said charter, by either party, without the consent of the other, has a tendency to dissolve the union between Great Britain and this province, to destroy the allegiance we owe to the king, and to set aside the sacred obligations he is under to his subjects here." The compact was dependent upon the virtue of both parties. By holding strictly to the letter of the charter, the people would demonstrate their innocence in the face of charges of rebellion and place the onus for "vacating" the compact upon the king.[28]

The compact theory informing the province's defense of the charter provided a

[26] Leicester Resolves, July 6, 1774, in Washburn, *Leicester*, 446–8; Rufus B. Dodge, *Historical Sketch of Charlton* ... (Boston, 1899), 73.

[27] Linclon, ed., *Journals*, 630; Bailyn, *Ideological Origins*, 219–24; Wood, *Creation*, 268–73; Brown, *Revolutionary Politics*, 85–91.

[28] Letters and Proceedings Received by BCC, Rutland Proceedings sent to BCC, April, 1773, photo. 689; Lincoln, ed., *Journals*, 630.

powerful rationale for a vigilant attention to social order. If popular tumults could be restrained, the balance of the mixed polity would be disrupted by a tyrannical set of rulers, not by an anarchical democracy. Once tyranny had been proven, it would be the right and duty of the people to redress the balance in justified rebellion. Orderly but forcible action of the ruled against tyrannical rulers was legitimate under the terms of the social contract handed down from the Glorious Revolution: Internal conflict among the ruled was not.[29] The relationship of order in society to the obedience demanded in the social compact was pointedly argued by the town of Brookfield in its covenant against tea of December 27, 1773. Noting that "the Prerogative of the Crown and the rights of the Subjects are by the English Constitution inseparable, so in the maintenance of the one we shall secure the other," the town resolved that it would "not countenance Riots and unlawfull Tumults." Eight months later, noting that "the minds of the people are greatly agitated with the near view of impending ruin," the Worcester County Convention resolved at its August 30 meeting "to use the utmost influence in suppressing all riotous and disorderly proceedings in our respective towns."[30]

A few isolated incidents, such as when the Reverend Eli Forbes of Brookfield's North Parish was stoned while riding in his "chair" in February 1775, indicated the potential for the popular violence that the county gentry feared so much. Ultimately such events were more conspicuous in their absence. For the most part, order prevailed over disorder, an indication of the continuing strength of deference. As the comforting vision of the king's faithfulness to the compact faded into the past, order in society would come to be an important defining quality of the public virtue necessary in a republic. Ultimately the maintaining of local social order would meet two essential goals: the demonstration of virtue to the world, and the continuing dominance of the gentry whatever the outcome.[31]

If local disorder would be a sign of anarchic disobedience, and thus the "vacating" of the compact by the ruled, acquiescence to arbitrary parliamentary "innovations" would have the same effect. The Patriot gentry had to walk a fine line between the threat of disorder and the necessity of opposing these illegitimate measures. Formal resistance began on April 19, 1774, when fifteen grand jurors refused to serve at the Worcester sessions of the Superior Court if Peter Oliver sat

[29] For discussions of crowd action in the early phases of the Revolutionary crisis, see Pauline Maier, *From Resistance to Revolution: Colonial Radicals and the Development of American Opposition to Britain, 1765–1776* (New York, 1974), 3–26; Edward Countryman, "The Problem of the Early American Crowd," *Journal of American Studies*, 7 (1973), esp. 81–2; Patterson, *Political Parties*, 101–2; Taylor, *Western Massachusetts*, 62ff., and Dirk Hoerder, *Crowd Action in Revolutionary Massachusetts, 1765–1780* (New York, 1977).
[30] "Extracts from the Brookfield Town records 1773–1800," in Brookfield, Mass., Local Records, 1673–1860," AAS, December 27, 1773, 7; Lincoln, ed., *Journals*, 633. See also Leicester Instructions, January 9, 1775, in Washburn, *Leicester*, 454; Leicester General Records, 2:173; and Daniels, *Oxford*, 127.
[31] William B. Sprague, *Annals of the American Pulpit* (New York, 1859), 1:494; on order and disorder, see Wood, *Creation*, 65–71.

as chief justice. Oliver had been the sole justice to accept the salary offered by the crown; sitting on his court would have been tantamount to recognizing the annulment of the charter. The grand jurors' position was endorsed later that summer in the resolves of the town of Leicester and of the Worcester convention. Resolving to "maintain and support the king's authority in this Province, according to the charter," Leicester argued that courts set up under the new acts were "unconstitutional and illegal," that verdicts rendered by juries called and appointed by the governor's sheriff should be "null and void," and that the people should resist all judicial officers "who were not appointed according to the charter or the laws of this Province." At its August 30 meeting the convention moved to implement these demands, announcing to the county that it was the "indispensable duty of the inhabitants . . . to prevent the sitting of the respective courts under such regulations as are set forth in a late act of parliament." The people were to attend the September 6 sitting of the Court of Common Pleas en masse and under arms.[32]

Although on the surface it seemed a radical upheaval, the humbling of the Tory officeholders was conducted with a noticeable restraint, a result of both lingering deference toward the old Court faction gentry and efforts of the Whig gentry to contain the "fury" of the crowds of town people. The experience of the mandamus councillors – appointed by the governor – is illustrative. The first of a series of incidents occurred when Timothy Ruggles rode out from his Hardwick estates in mid-August to take up his post. Met at the Furnace Bridge by a militia led by his brother Benjamin, this most obnoxious of the local Tories rode easily through the crowd and on to Boston. On the morning of August 27, two thousand militiamen marched onto the Worcester common and sent a committee to demand that Timothy Paine resign from his council post. Acting in their capacity as gentry, this committee mediated between the demands of "the body of the people" on the common and the proud royal placeholder. After promising him "protection against insult," they finally extracted a satisfactory resignation from Paine, and persuaded him to go out onto the common after receiving "several messages from the Body" that nothing less would be accepted. When Thomas Denny of Leicester attempted to read the resignation to the assembled militia companies, there were further demands that Paine read it himself, with his hat off. After thus obtaining Paine's resignation, the militia marched off to Rutland, where John Murray, another mandamus councillor, had narrowly escaped being caught by sentries posted the previous evening. Again protection from "insult" was offered to his son Daniel, and despite his fears that Murray's property would be the butt of their frustration, the militia "dispersed without doing the least damage to any part of the estate." Of the county's four mandamus councillors, only Col. Abijah Willard of Lancaster was roughly handled. Arrested in Union, Connecticut, Willard was

[32] Lincoln, *Worcester*, 74–9; Leicester Resolves, July 6, 1774, in Washburn, *Leicester*, 448–9; and Lincoln, ed., *Journals*, 632.

taken to Brimfield in Hampshire County, where a crowd demanded that he be jailed. Once inside Worcester County at Strurbridge, however, Willard was released after signing a retraction of his councillor's oath.[33]

This restraint was just as evident when, ten days later, the militia returned to Worcester on the request of the Worcester County Convention that the Court of Common Pleas be closed. Assurances were demanded from the justices that the courts would not sit, and then they were required to walk through a gauntlet of the six thousand assembled militiamen drawn up in two lines, stopping at regular intervals to read and reread these assurances. The next day the convention extracted an apology from a group of fourteen justices who, in an April address, had welcomed General Gage to Boston and promised their support for the implementation of the parliamentary acts. But after these ritual humblings of the established judiciary, the county convention voted to reinstate all of the justices of the peace whose appointments predated June 30, with the sole exceptions of Ruggles, Murray, and James Putnam of Worcester. Similarly, before the militia dispersed on the evening of September 6, their officers resigned their commissions from the governor, only to be reelected to their posts by the assembled men. The lines of county authority were not to be seriously disturbed.[34]

Rather than a radical leveling, the events of late August and early September point to a successful maintenance of the status quo by the Whig gentry. Failing to protect Timothy Paine from "insult," they opted for a strategy of public humiliation, followed by a more quiet reestablishment of the majority of the old judicial elite. Thus they were able to satisfy their own concern that the letter of the charter be upheld as well as the demands of the "body of the people" for a ritual acting out of this political action, while retaining the basic pattern of authority within the county.

The federal covenant

The orthodox ministry stood solidly behind the Popular gentry in their efforts to shepherd the people through the Revolutionary crisis. Although the majority of

[33] Shipton, *Sibley's Harvard Graduates*, 9:213–14; Albert Mathews, "Documents relating to the Massachusetts Royal Council, 1774–1776," *CSMP* 32 (1937), 471, 479; Peter Force, ed., *American Archives* (Washington, D.C., 1837–52), ser. 4, 1:745; Jonathan Smith, "Toryism in Worcester County during the War for Independence," *MHSP* 48 (1914–15), 17–18; Paige, *Hardwick*, 73.

[34] Among these JPs were Joshua Upham of Brookfield and Thomas Steele of Leicester, both of whom continued to express their Tory sentiments. Neither of these prominent members of long-standing legal dynasties were ever physically harassed, most likely because of their kin relations among the Patriot gentry. Steele died of old age two years later, and Upham left the state in 1777, after quietly selling all of his property. Washburn, *Leicester*, 495–501; Shipton, *Sibley's Harvard Graduates*, 8:783–5; 15:495–501; Lincoln, ed., *Journals*, 635–9; Daniels, *Oxford*, 127; Brown, *Revolutionary Politics*, 217.

ministers in the county rarely participated directly in the political proceedings, they prayed and preached at town meetings, at meetings of the convention, at militia musters, and on designated days of "fasting and prayer." On these occasions and in their regular Sunday sermons, the ministers acted in their established capacities as legitimators, translating the political language of the day into the religious metaphors that the people habitually used to characterize their world.

Much of their audience was inclined toward the New Light. If families and communities with experience in the Land Bank and the Popular tradition provided an important bloc of the Revolutionary leadership, so, too, the New Light towns, particularly in the Blackstone Valley, were the most uniformly united in the provincial cause. Loyalists were concentrated in the court town of Worcester and the northern half of the county, particularly in Lancaster, Rutland, and Hardwick, towns that had seen little lasting influence of the Great Awakening. But even given the unanimity of the New Light regions behind the Revolutionary movement, the ministers preached a very conservative religious message, emphasizing the social compact, the national covenant of the federal theology, and the identity of virtue with order and deference in society. With the march of Revolutionary events taken as a backdrop, the ministers focused on the threat of impending chaos. As the king broke his promise of protection under the charter, the ministers seized the opportunity to urge their congregations to turn to God's promise of protection under the federal covenant. However, the assaults on their charter liberties were also indications of failings among the people themselves, afflictions from the Lord to an unworthy and unrepentant generation. Thus the ministers pursued two ends in their sermons: a renewed faith in God's covenant, and the maintenance of order and deference in society.[35]

This message was clearly stated by three orthodox ministers between July 1774 and March 1775. Speaking to an audience in Brookfield on a "day of fasting and prayer" on July 4, 1774, Nathan Fiske discussed the necessity of justice in rulers and righteousness in the people. In the first of two sermons he focused on the "happy effects of a good ruler" and the unhappy effects of a "venal and corrupt"

[35] All 36 proscribed Loyalists listed in MA 154/254 and 154/333 were from Worcester and towns in the northern section of the county. Extracts from Brookfield Town Records, AAS, June 21, 1774; Washburn, *Leicester*, 298; Sturbridge Town Records, 1:267-8; Clark, *Sturbridge*, 16-17; Lincoln, ed., *Journals*, 628, 630, 635, 651. On the role of religion and the clergy in the Revolutionary crisis, I draw upon Alice M. Baldwin, *The New England Clergy and the American Revolution* (New York, 1958); Perry Miller, "From Covenant to Revival," in J. W. Smith and J. J. Jamison, eds., *The Shaping of American Religion* (Princeton, 1961), 1:322-50; Alan Hiemert, *Religion and the American Mind from the Great Awakening to the Revolution* (Cambridge, Mass., 1966); Nathan O. Hatch, *The Sacred Cause of Liberty: Republican Thought and Millenium in Revolutionary New England* (New Haven, 1977); Harry S. Stout, "Religion, Communications, and the Origins of the American Revolution," *WMQ* 34 (1977), 519-41; Philip J. Greven, Jr., *The Protestant Temperament: Patterns of Child-Rearing, Religious Experience, and the Self in Early America* (New York, 1977).

one. His argument rested on the hierarchical diffusion of virtue through society; "pious rulers" spread "a benign influence all around, attracting regard, and inviting imitation." But the consequences of corruption in high places were grave, because "the body of the people" would follow the ruler's example. Provoked at the vast stretches of arbitrary power which they see in their rulers, and not being sufficiently swayed by a principle of justice themselves, they will be in danger of opposing lawful authority; of destroying all distinction and subordination among men."[36] Leaving his audience with this picture of an inherently virtueless people, Fiske took up the problem of what the righteous could do in his second sermon of the day. Granting the right of the "injured" to "complain . . . to be heard and to be relieved," he brought up the difficulty of "determin[ing] exactly where submission ends and resistance may lawfully take place." Under these circumstances, what could they do when, though they "rejoice[d] in being the subjects of King George," all their political efforts at obtaining redress were "deemed mobish and riotous," when they were "reproach'd as rebels" and "traitors"? "There is one course which reason and religion point out as the most effectual, and which, if universally adopted, and persevered in (as God grant it may be) will greatly mitigate, if not wholly remove, the calamities we suffer; and that is, to *live soberly, righteously, and godly in the world.*" At this point Fiske closed his argument with a jeremiad against the people's own "oppressions."

> God does not pour out the vials of his wrath upon a people, unless to punish them for their disobedience. Though we are unwilling to own that we have forfeited our privileges into the hands of men, yet must we not confess, that by our ingratitude and rebellion against heaven, we have forfeited them all into the hands of God?

If the ruler had broken his promise of protection to his people, it was because they sinned against God; to count on God's protection they would have to return to the covenant, to repent their sins and live orderly and righteous lives.[37]

Ten days later Thaddeus McCarty of Worcester drew a more optimistic theme from the federal tradition. As had Fiske, McCarty enjoined the people to reform themselves. But in his formula there would be a reward for the people for their "repentance and reformation." "God will return to them in ways of favor and kindness . . . , he will delight to do them good with all his heart, to smile upon them in all their interests and concerns, and make them a prosperous happy people . . . , and extricate them out of their troubles and perplexities."[38]

In March of 1775, in a sermon to the Worcester County Convention, Elisha

[36] Nathan Fiske, *The Importance of Righteousness to the Happiness and the Tendency of Oppression to the Misery of a People; Illustrated in Two Discourses Delivered at Brookfield, July 4, 1774* (Boston, 1774), 16–17, 20.

[37] Fiske, *The Importance of Righteousness*, 25, 27, 38.

[38] Thaddeus McCarty, *Reformation of Manners, of Absolute Necessity in Order to Conciliate the Divine Favour, in Times of Public Evil and Distress* (Boston, 1774), 24, 26.

Fish, the orthodox minister in the Blackstone Valley town of Upton, finally turned the federal theology to a justification of rebellion. Pursuing Fiske's question of "if the foundations be destroyed, what can the righteous do?" he compared the contract "between a prince and his subjects" to "the covenant between God and his creatures." Where Nathan Fiske had been more hesitant, Fish bluntly stated that "the breach of the covenant is greater on the side of the Prince than the people" and that the prince had clearly broken his promise. However, when these "movable foundations" were destroyed, the people could fall back on the "immovable foundation" of their covenant with the Lord.

> In such a perplexing Day, they can still, by divine grace, give Glory to God,
> by resting on his promises, and faithfulness in keeping with his people . . .
> [a]ccording to his promise unto Abraham, saying *in thee shall all families of the*
> *earth be blessed* . . . . God hath made good his promise to be with and not to
> leave his people in the gospelday, by preserving them under the ten heathen
> persecutions, and long, bloody, and dark reign of Antichrist.[39]

At no point during the Revolutionary era were the established Congregational clergy advocates of a radical populism. Rather, they served as key allies of the Patriot gentry, exerting their influence to provide a religious legitimation for their efforts both to defend the province's charter rights and to maintain social control over a potentially unruly populace. They were actively working to provide an alternative body of theory that might serve as a source of ultimate legitimacy in the face of the king's failure to submit to the conditions of the social compact. In the place of this compact they put the time-honored covenant theorem, which, as under the conditions of the compact between ruler and ruled, made God's promise of protection conditional upon the good behavior of the people. The virtue and "moral reformation" that the ministers urged upon their listeners was the necessary element on which the classical republic depended.[40]

In many towns the people responded readily to the minister's application of the covenant theology. In Spencer, the year 1774 brought the largest number of new members into the church in one year between the founding of the church in 1744 and the revivals of the Second Great Awakening in the second decade of the next century. Twenty-three people joined in 1774, nine joining on July 10 – the largest group in the entire century – six days after Nathan Fiske had delivered his fast-day sermons in Brookfield, and four days after Spencer had joined with Leicester and Paxton in defining their rights and privileges under the charter. All three orthodox

[39] Elisha Fish, *A Discourse Delivered at Worcester, March 28th, 1775, at the Desire of the Convention of Committees for the County of Worcester* (Worcester, 1775), 11–14, 18.
[40] Wood, *Creation*, 65ff., 1143ff.; Hatch, *Sacred Cause*, 97ff. For other sources emphasizing order and the covenant, see Nathan Fiske, *Remarkable Providences to be Gratefully Recollected, Religiously Improved, and Carefully Transmitted* . . . (Boston, 1776), 29–30; Nathan Fiske, *Sermon at Brookfield, March 6, 1778, on the Day of the Interment of Joshua Spooner* . . . (Boston, 1778), 12, 14; Joseph Pope, MSS. Sermon, March 13, 1776, donated to First Congregational Church of Spencer, Massachusetts by Leroy A. Amers.

churches in Brookfield added to their membership in years of the Revolutionary crisis. In the South Parish, twelve people joined in 1774, in the West Parish forty-five joined in 1775 and 1776, the largest group admitted in almost two decades. The Congregational church in the North Parish also had a large in-gathering. Between entries dated July 10, 1774, and October 30, 1776, the clerk records 115 new members' names without dates or manner of entry, suggesting that the church quietly lowered barriers to membership to admit as many as possible in a covenant renewal. David Hall's church in Sutton had no surge in admissions, however, and in January 1777 this church abandoned its New Light principles to adopt the halfway covenant, voting that "the children of the church be considered as members of the church, being baptized," subject to its "watch and care."[41]

Such a return to the inclusive forms of the orthodox establishment were central to the reinvigoration of corporate unity that the Revolutionary crisis brought to the Worcester backcountry and the province as a whole. The religious language of "covenant," with its powerful connotations of a unanimity of consent under divine protection, was applied to resolves of town committees and more illustrious bodies, and to the enlistment agreement drawn up by the minute companies. In its own covenant against the consumption of tea written in December, 1773, the town of Brookfield was particularly concerned that the blanket of unanimous consensus be cast as widely as possible; the resistance spreading across the province was not that of a few malcontents, but of "the whole body of this Great People, a few Placemen and their Dependents only excepted."[42] The townsmen's obsessive concern for collective unity under the covenant rested in a sense that the entire framework underlying provincial social order was in doubt. The legitimacy of town government was threatened by a tyrannical violation of the compact between ruler and people; the people would find a legitimacy only in convenanted and consensus unity.[43]

The county convention

News of the British regulars' disastrous march on Lexington and Concord began to spread into the Worcester backcountry on the afternoon of April 19,

[41] Membership Book, First Congregational Church of Spencer, Mass. The second largest year for church admissions was 1768, with 15 added. *The Confession of Faith and Covenant of the first Congregational Church in North Brookfield, Mass. with a Catalogue of Its Members (1752–1878)* (West Brookfield, 1878), 28–31; Samuel Dunham, *An Historical Discourse Delivered at West Brookfield, Mass.* (Springfield, 1868), 20; Sutton, Mass., First Church Record Book [c. 1720–c. 1825], microfilm copy, AAS, 41.
[42] Extracts from the Brookfield Town Records, AAS, December 27, 1773; Dodge, *Charlton*, 73; Temple, *North Brookfield*, 226–7.
[43] Zuckerman, *Peaceable Kingdoms*, 220–58; Brown, *Revolutionary Politics*, 178–209; and Gross, *Minutemen*, 42–67.

1775. In Sutton, David Hall was up most of the night taking information of new alarms; "a little before day" he prayed with the town's two minute companies before they marched down the south county road toward Boston.[44] The response to the Lexington alarm stands as the ultimate expression of the provincial tradition of corporate unity and vigilance, of the Harringtonian ideal of a yeomanry, independent in their landholdings acting in their corporate capacity to defend the commonwealth. Threatened by fire and sword at the hands of a standing army, the towns acted with uniform dispatch to mobilize their minute companies and protect the province. The Revolution would bring an intensification of the importance of town government and the significance of corporate autonomy. With the charter in doubt and Boston occupied by a hostile standing army, the towns took on even more governing responsibilities than they had had before. Most importantly, until the new state constitution was finally ratified in 1780, the towns – after 1775, including all the old districts – were the only legitimate governmental instruments in the state.[45]

However, this centripetal corporatism was easily offset by countervailing networks of centrifugal forces. The work of the Revolution was not left to the selectmen in their corporate capacity, but was overseen by committees of correspondence, safety, and inspection, created at the behest of the county convention and the Continental Congress, and functioning as a parallel governmental structure. The county convention was a particularly powerful node in this network of provisional Revolutionary government, and as well as facilitating preparations for military and political resistance, it came to fill the governmental vacuum left by the stopping of the royal courts.

Towns that had been involved in the provincial political process were especially well represented at the Worcester County Convention, and their delegates moved swiftly to establish a leading role for the convention early in the crisis. At its August 9 meeting, the convention urged the towns to form committees of correspondence and to send delegates to the next meeting; on August 30 it acted decisively to order that the courts be closed, and to recommend that the "several towns choose proper and suitable officers . . . to regulate the movements of each town, and prevent any disorder." On September 20, the convention next took up the issue of military organization, dividing the county into seven regional regiments, and asking the towns to elect company officers, enlist troops, and outfit one or more artillery pieces. In December and January it attended to further military matters, the growing problem of Loyalist conspiracies, the adoption of nonconsumption covenants, and – particularly significantly – they formed a committee to invite Isaiah Thomas, a printer in Boston, to establish a newspaper in Worcester. The *Massachusetts Spy, or American Oracle of Liberty* began

[44] Diary of David Hall, April 30, 1775, MHS.
[45] Oscar and Mary F. Handlin, *Commonwealth: A Study in the Role of Government in the American Economy: Massachusetts, 1774–1861* (New York, 1974), 2.

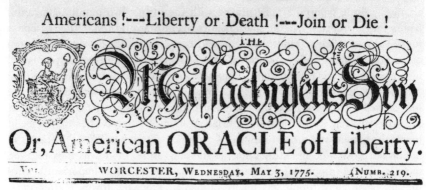

Americans !---Liberty or Death !---Join or Die !

Or, American ORACLE of Liberty.

WORCESTER, WEDNESDAY, MAY 3, 1775.   (NUMB. 219.

7. Masthead of the *Massachusetts Spy*, May 3, 1775.
(Courtesy of the American Antiquarian Society)

publication in a shop near the courthouse on May 3, 1775. Publishing resolves of the county convention, committees of correspondence, and the Provincial and Continental Congresses along with accounts of the battles around Boston, political essays, and European dispatches, the *Spy* was literally the voice of county convention. Of thirty-five agents for subscriptions to the *Spy* in 1775, eighteen had been delegates to the county convention, and another fourteen had represented their towns in the Provincial Congresses; among the remaining three were Joshua Henshaw and Joseph Allen, both critical figures in the Leicester-Boston Whig connection.[46]

But the convention's institutional presence would go beyond political and military affairs. At the September 20 meeting, the convention began to act in the place of the county courts. It directed the sheriff to warn the towns to elect representatives to the Provincial Congress, and formed a committee to instruct the representatives. The sheriff was also advised to hold for trial all those committed on criminal charges, but those held on charges of debt were to be freed. It subsequently addressed many of the issues normally the concern of the court of general sessions: the regulation of innholders, the issuance of warrants for town meetings, the election of the county treasurer, the problems faced by constables failing to return lists of jurors, and the need to avoid civil litigation "as the ordinary course of justice must be stayed." The Revolutionary crisis involved a massive popular mobilization to deal with the external threat of British intervention, but the convention was also concerned with a consolidation of authority over the institutional structure of government.[47]

[46] Lincoln, ed., *Journals*, 632–3; *Massachusetts Spy*, May 3–July 5, 1775; Caleb A. Wall, *Reminiscences of Worcester from the Earliest Period, Historical and Genealogical* (Worcester, 1877), 305–6.
[47] Lincoln, *Journals*, 627–52.

The convention's dominant position in the county was in part a function of the prominence of its members. Delegates to the convention at its first meeting in August were overwhelmingly drawn from the older, larger, and more prosperous towns; the convention was by no means an insurgency against the broader patterns of power and interest in the county. Even two months after the Coercive Acts had arrived, twenty-two of the county's forty-two towns and districts, disproportionately located in the northwest uplands and encompassing roughly 40 percent of the 1776 population, did not send delegates to this meeting. The smaller towns and districts again were poorly represented among the delegates at the January 27, 1775, meeting of the convention. They were especially underrepresented among the men appointed to the committee that actually did the convention's business, which were overwhelmingly made up of men from the larger and middling towns that had been active in provincial politics. The convention institutionalized this centralized influence when it appointed to Worcester and Leicester committees of correspondence to be a permanent standing committee for the county, with the addition of Thomas Denny, Joseph Henshaw, and Joshua Bigelow.[48] Relatively prosperous, and with extensive experience in town government, as company officers in the provincial forces, and in the broader Popular political tradition, the convention delegates were clearly men of rank and position.[49]

As such they could expect to assume positions in county government vacated by the thin layer of departing Loyalists. On September 5, 1775, the provincial council published an initial list of judicial appointments, and a further list on December 25. That December and the following January the Court of Common Pleas met briefly to read the justice's commissions in public, and to transfer the court records from Timothy Paine to the new clerk of courts, Levi Lincoln, a young lawyer recently settled in town. In September 1776, the court met for the first time in full session to consider cases of debt; unlike the courts in the counties to the west, the work of the Worcester County Court of Common Pleas would not be interrupted by crowd action until September of 1786.[50]

The thirty-one justices of the peace reporting to this court were a strikingly familiar group. Fifteen had held commissions under the royal charter; of these, six had cast popular votes in the house in the 1760s, and three had been members of the Worcester County Convention. Twelve other convention members were

[48] Lincoln, *Journals*, 643.
[49] Of 96 known delegates to the Worcester convention, 27 had served as officers in the provincial forces between 1755 and 1763; of 20 who (or their sons) can be identified on the 1783 valuations of the towns south and west of Worcester, 13 (65%) ranked in the top decile, and 16 (80%) ranked in the top quintile. Delegates from Lincoln, ed., *Journals*, 627–52; and "Resolves" of the January 17, 1775, Convention of the Committees for the County of Worcester, untitled broadside (Evans 42987). Military service is from Voye, ed., *Massachusetts Officers in the French and Indian Wars, passim*; 1783 Valuations for Leicester, Spencer, Oakham, New Braintree, Brookfield, Charlton, Dudley, and Sturbridge, Massachusetts State Library. For a more detailed discussion, see Brooke, "Society, Revolution . . .," 177–83.
[50] RWCCP 9:438–48.

appointed to be justices of the peace. Of the remaining four new justices, three had served in the Provincial Congress, and the fourth, William King of Sutton was the son of Henry King, long the Popular representative from this Land Bank town. Similarly, when the council and house appointed county committees for raising troops, inventorying firearms, and exchanging gold and silver currency for Continental notes, they turned to men with experience in the county convention. Convention men were commissioned field officers in the Worcester County militia regiments established in December, 1775. Among seven regiments, only one had no convention members on its staff, but this unit had a strong connection with the Revolutionary leadership. Recruited in Worcester and Leicester, the First Regiment was commanded by Samuel Denny, the younger brother of Thomas Denny, one of the county's leading Whigs who had died in October 1774 while a delegate to the Provincial Congress.[51]

Samuel Denny and William King were important links to the provincial Popular tradition, but they were also the only men of Baptist inclination to be given positions by the Revolutionary government. Such men were strong Revolutionary supporters, yet they were rarely drawn into the new institutional structures. Rather there was a decided bias toward orthodoxy, and toward the rather conservative towns in the northeast corner of the county. This bias was particularly notable in the distribution of new justices of the peace, and also among the highest positions on the county hierarchy: the justices of the Common Pleas and the councilors chosen in the reconvened General Court in 1775 and 1776.[52] Of the four Common Pleas justices and five councillors, only one man was not from the broader northeastern orbit of the old town Lancaster, and he was the exception that proved the rule. Jedediah Foster of Brookfield emerged from the Court tradition to assume a leading position among the Revolutionary provincial elite. By means of a Harvard education and a well-placed marriage, Foster had fallen heir to the lands and influence of Col. Joseph Dwight in the mid-1750s. Appointed justice of the peace by Shirley in 1754 and to quorum by Bernard in 1762, Foster can also be called an orthodox New Light, a member and a deacon of the West Parish church. Moving between these influences, he supported the Court faction in the house through 1765, after which he shifted his influence to the Popular opposition. His support for the Popular party was recognized in May of 1773 when he was elected to the Provincial Committee of Correspondence. His election to the council in 1774 was rejected by General Gage, and, following the Worcester Convention meetings in September, he was sent by his town to the Salem Congress, where he was appointed to its "recess committee of seven." In 1775 he was appointed both justice of the Common Pleas and justice of probate, and was elected to the council;

[51] Council Records, MA, 17:84–5, 95, 106, 114, 147, 153; Commissions of Worcester County Justices, December 25, 1775, Box 3, Folder 6, Worcester Country, MA Papers, AAS; Force, *American Archives* Ser. 4, 4:1271, 1303, 1306, 1317, 1290, 1302–6.
[52] RWCCP, 9:438–9; *JHRM*, 51:6, 13, 15, vol. 52:6–7.

his wife's cousin, Simeon Dwight of Western, was appointed county sheriff. Foster's gradual move toward the Popular party hierarchy ensured that the conservative influence of his well-established family, and of the Brookfield elite in general, would persist through the Revolutionary era and beyond.[53]

In a very important sense, then, the opening phases of the Revolution were continuous with recent provincial experience, rather than making a fundamental break with the past. The resistance to British authority was based in a defense of the charter as a fundamental governing framework against British innovation. The ideological construct driving the Whigs was rooted in this provincial experience of an ongoing contest between rulers and ruled, shaped by assumptions of a symbiotic, reciprocating contract. Other than eliminating a small group of Loyalist placeholders, whose places were soon filled by their Whig equivalents, there was no fundamental challenge to the structures of provincial society. The convention government was indeed a decided innovation, but it was merely provisional in nature, filling a governmental vacuum until traditional institutions could be restored. Ultimately, the Revolutionary crisis was essentially continuous with the long epoch of consensus between 1745 and 1765. As a number of historians have argued, the popular patriotism drilled into the population in the years of warfare with the Catholic French, colored to an extent by New Light energies, forged a sense of collectivity that was simply redirected at the challenge of British imperial innovation.[54] But as soon as the threat posed by British arms receded, a new and transformative politics began to take shape.

[53] Shipton, *Sibley's Harvard Graduates*, 11:396–7; *Catalogue of the Members of the Congregational Church in West Brookfield*, 4.

[54] On the provincial roots of the politics of the Revolutionary crisis see Pencak, *War, Politics, and Revolution*; Patterson, *Political Parties in Revolutionary Massachusetts*; Hatch, *The Sacred Cause of Liberty*; and Heimert, *Religion and the American Mind*.

6

The Baptists and the Constitution

In the summer of 1775 the people of Massachusetts Bay found themselves in rebellion against their former ruler. As the people of the province prepared military forces to oppose "tyrannical oppression," they were faced with a second critical problem: the reestablishment of orderly government among themselves. The first task lay in restoring a legal framework for government and in opening the courts, closed by the action of the county conventions in the previous fall. Upon requesting advice from the Continental Congress in May of 1775, the Second Provincial Congress was counseled to set up a government under the terms of the old charter of 1691. Leaving the posts of governor and lieutenant governor empty, the towns were to elect a House of Representatives, and the house was to select a council that would "exercise the powers of government, until a governor of His Majesty's appointment will consent to govern the colony according to its charter." Many would accept this recommendation; charter rights and privileges had been at the core of the conflict to begin with, and their resumption was seen as natural, and conducive to order, unity, and stability. The charter was resumed that summer, a house and council were elected as a General Court, and new appointments were made to the judicial system. It was these appointments, and the appointment of field-grade militia officers by the council, that brought a resounding protest against the resumption of the charter. The events flowing from this protest would finally result in the popular ratification of a constitution drafted by a specifically elected convention – a seminal event in modern world history.[1]

The Whig gentry had invoked the language of Lockean natural rights in defense of the charter in a mechanical fashion, in no way relinquishing a corporate vision of local society that echoed more of Harrington than of Locke. The Massachusetts Constitutionalists took social compact theory quite literally: The compact between

---

[1] Quotation from John Adams, *Works* (Boston, 1851), 17, as cited in Taylor, *Western Massachusetts in the Revolution*, 78; on the reassumption of the charter, see Taylor, *Western Massachusetts*, 78ff., and Patterson, *Political Parties in Revolutionary Massachusetts*, 117–30; on the significance of the Massachusetts constitution, see Elisha P. Douglas, *Rebels and Democrats: The Struggle for Equal Political Rights and Majority Rule during the American Revolution* (Chicago, 1955), 136; Wood, *The Creation*, 339–41; Ronald Peters, *The Massachusetts Constitution of 1780: A Social Compact* (Amherst, 1978), 13; Willi Paul Adams, *The First American Constitutions: Republican Ideology and the Making of the State Constitutions in the Revolutionary Era*, trans. by R. and R. Kimber (Chapel Hill, 1980), 86–93.

ruler and ruled embodied in the 1691 charter had been "vacated" by the actions of the British government, and thus the people of the province had fallen into a state of nature. To return to a state of civil society they had to assemble to frame a new compact, since the basis for the legitimacy of any new government lay in the sovereignty of the people themselves. However, the process of constitution making would seriously undermine the classical worldview articulated in the Country ideology that had powered the Revolutionary cause since 1765. The framing of an explicit, written constitution would provide the pivot upon which the classical rule of virtue would give way to the practical rule of law.[2] But this crucial political transformation was not achieved in the bloodless realm of intellectual discourse, nor was it uniformly pursued by the people of Massachusetts. Rather, the problem of constitution-making would divide the people along lines of ideological change already well developed in the provincial era.

The organic relationship of incorporated town and established church lay at the center of the implicit constitutional framework governing provincial Massachusetts. The Baptists had challenged the theology of national covenant and the practices of the corporate town during the Great Awakening; during the Revolution they challenged the social contract that underlay this ancient system. In Worcester County, the Baptists spearheaded the attack on the old charter, forcing the popular writing and ratification of a constitution. The constitution-making process brought to fruition the Lockean sensibilities informing religious dissent; if Lockean ideals of a society of reasoning, autonomous individuals had stood at odds with the central ideological constructs in the province, they would form the core framework of the new state.[3]

---

[2] On the "decline of virtue" and the "end of classical politics," see J. R. Pole, *Political Representation in England and America and the Origins of the American Republic* (New York, 1966), 531; Wood, *The Creation of the American Republic*, 606ff.; and J. G. A. Pocock, "Virtue and Commerce in the Eighteenth Century," *Journal of Interdisciplinary History* 3 (1972–3), 119–34.

[3] Such a role for the Baptists is suggested in Douglas, *Rebels and Democrats*, 138–41, 192–4; and in Fliegelman, *Prodigals and Pilgrims*, 123–31, 172–4, 183–8. For the role of the Baptists in constitutional politics in Revolutionary Virginia, see Rhys Isaac, *The Transformation of Virginia, 1740–1790* (Chapel Hill, 1982), 299–321; and Richard R. Beeman, *The Evolution of the Southern Backcountry: A Case Study of Lunenburg County, Virginia,1746–1832* (Philadelphia, 1984), 140–59. It should be noted that the impetus toward a popularly written and ratified constitution did not develop first in Worcester County, but in the towns of central Berkshire County. The Berkshire Constitutionalists emerged from the same social context as those of Worcester County, the religiously pluralistic towns of Pittsfield, Lanesborough, and Lenox, towns where at least two Baptist churches and one Anglican church had been formed before the Revolution. In Pittsfield, where it had been argued as early as August of 1774 that the province had fallen into a state of nature, the two key Constitutionalist leaders were strong supporters of religious voluntarism. Valentine Rathbun was a Baptist preacher and Thomas Allen was one of the few Congregational ministers in Massachusetts who supported the dissenters' rights of conscience. See the town histories in David Dudley Field, *A History of the County of Berkshire,*

While the concerns of the Baptists were not fully satisfied in the constitution written in 1780, they were satisfied in the precedents set in the constitution-making process. The political environment had been redefined: instead of a constant struggle between the ruler, intent on expanding his powers, and the ruled, united in their efforts to defend their granted liberties and privileges, the political process would be characterized by individuals working in groups to advance conflicting private interests, under the umbrella of popular sovereignty. These consequences were by no means fully articulated by the early 1780s, but they were manifested in a growing acceptance of the voluntary principle, and in its first applications beyond the confines of religion. With the transformation from mixed polity to popular sovereignty, the corporate towns implicitly lost their hegemony over the rights of association. With the fading of the sense of the primacy of this corporate union, individuals began to differentiate, to form associations based on interest rather than territory.

"Charters have become bubbles"

If the situation during the summer of 1774 was one of great alarm for the ordinary Massachusetts townsmen, the dissenters faced the Revolutionary crisis with a special unease. Where the majority could call for unity under the federal covenant in the defense of their charter rights, the Baptists were in dissent because they had rejected the "implicit faith" of the covenant theology. It was the charter itself that had been the basis for their oppression by the standing order for more than a century. They could not help but be uneasy when such conspicuous upholders of "infant sprinkling" as Elisha Fish and Nathan Fiske worked to subsume the entire population within the encompassing bounds of the national covenant, and when towns exhorted one another to the "quiet enjoyment of our dearest civil and religious privileges."[4] In fact, it was king and Parliament, now seen as breaking their compact of protection and allegiance with the people of Massachusetts Bay, who had increasingly come to the Baptists' aid under the Act of Toleration in the preceding decade. Thus the Revolutionary crisis saw the Baptists and other dissenting groups on the verge of being hurled onto the less-than-tender mercies of their brethren in the established churches.

Interwoven with a fear for group survival was a pervasive sense of the hypocrisy of an establishment that complained about taxation without representation yet continued to assess dissenters for ministerial rates. Isaac Backus first articulated

Massachusetts (Pittsfield, 1829) and in John H. Lockwood, ed., *Western Massachusetts: A History, 1636–1925* (New York, 1926). On Rathbun and Allen, see Taylor, *Western Massachusetts in the Revolution*, 143ff., and McLoughlin, *New England Dissent*, 1:608–63.
[4] "Extracts from the Brookfield Town Records, 1774–1860," Dec. 27, 1773, in "Brookfield, Mass., Local Records, 1673–1860," AAS.

this argument publicly in 1773 in *An Appeal to the Public for Religious Liberty*, rooting his argument firmly in the pietistic insistence on the differentiation between civil and religious spheres. Where the colonists' objection to British taxation lay in their rights to representation under the English constitution, the Baptists objected to any ecclesiastical taxes or certificates as a violation of a natural right of conscience. Backus argued that since "Christ's kingdom" was "not of this world," obedience to the "blending of church and state" that characterized the New England social order would be disobedience to Christ's command "to *stand fast in the liberty wherewith he has made us free*." Church and state were to be rigidly divided, one armed with "truth and light" to save souls, the other "with the sword to protect the peace and the civil rights of all persons and societies."[5]

This *Appeal to the Public* came in the wake of a renewed persecution of Baptists, especially in newly settled areas. Beginning in Sturbridge in the 1750s and the district of Ashfield in the mid-1760s, the Congregational proprietors and settlers of the frontier fringe had begun a concerted effort to drive out the Baptists, whose refusal to pay ministerial rates made these new towns unattractive to orthodox householders, who would be required to assume the full burden of the minister's settlement. However, where in the Ashfield case the Baptists had successfully petitioned the king in council for relief, the publication of Backus's *Appeal* marked a new turn in the Baptists' quest for their rights of conscience. Avoiding any association with an increasingly suspect monarch, they turned their efforts to persuading those of the standing order with the arguments of the emerging revolutionary rhetoric. The delegates to the September 1773 meeting of the Warren Association voted to pursue a concerted campaign of civil disobedience, specifically by refusing to turn in certificates of Baptist belief and attendance to the various town clerks. At the same meeting they voted to publish Backus's *Appeal* as a means of persuading their Congregational brethren by force of argument.[6]

The most significant attempt to identify the Baptist cause with that of the Revolution was an October 1774 meeting in Philadelphia that brought together the Massachusetts delegation to the Continental Congress, prominent middle colony Baptists and Quakers, and a delegation from the Warren Baptist Association. In the Baptists' view the Continental Congress was replacing the king and parliament as "the highest place of civil power" and thus the most likely place for an oppressed minority to petition. Reviewing the history of ecclesiastical laws and the oppressions at Sturbridge and Ashfield by the Congregational majority, the Baptists' memorial invoked "the great Mr. Locke" to argue that "as the kingdom of Christ is not of this world . . . we claim and expect the liberty of worshipping

[5] Isaac Backus, "An Appeal to the Public of Religious Liberty" (Boston, 1773), in William McLoughlin, ed., *Isaac Backus on Church, State, and Calvinism: Pamphlets, 1754–1789* (Cambridge, Mass., 1968), 315–18, 340.

[6] McLoughlin, *New England Dissent*, 1:531–50, 552–3; Backus, "An Appeal," in McLoughlin, ed., *Pamphlets*, 305.

God according to our own consciences." Whereas the Baptists felt that they were making a legitimate petition to a higher civil power, the Massachusetts delegation saw their effort as merely an attempt to distract attention from the central issue of colonial unity and resistance to British authority.[7]

This was the immediate background to the Baptists' emergence on the revolutionary stage. In addition to a rising tide of anti-Baptist sentiment, particularly in frontier areas, the Baptists were viewed as potential or actual Tories by virtue of their recent appeals to the king and their ill-managed delegation to Philadelphia. This external image, as well as their own qualms about the charter and the federal covenant, meant that they were not to be conspicuously involved in the early phases of the Revolutionary crisis on the local level.

The political marginality of the Baptists at the early stages of the Revolution is clearly evident in the committee appointments in three southwest Worcester County towns. The town of Leicester had both the oldest Baptist church in the region and the most active group of Patriot gentry. Of the nine members of the Revolutionary elite active on town committees between the beginning of 1773 and the fall of 1774, only Thomas Denny had ever been affiliated with the Baptists, and even he had abandoned that affiliation well before the Revolutionary crisis. In Sturbridge, of twenty-three men active in committee assignments in 1773 and 1774, only three were Baptists, and at least sixteen were Congregational members or attenders. In Charlton, of ten men active on Revolutionary committees in these years, two were Baptist attenders. In the three towns together, dissenters constituted between a quarter to a third of the population, but only a seventh of the Revolutionary leadership in its formative stage. Only in Sutton, where in 1743 the town had mandated equal representation in town government for the Baptists by a quota system, were dissenters equally represented on the early Revolutionary committees.[8]

[7] Isaac Backus, "Government and Liberty Described and Ecclesiastical Tyranny Exposed," in McLoughlin, ed., *Pamphlets*, 360; McLoughlin, *New England Dissent*, 1:559, 561; McLoughlin, *Backus*, 131.

[8] Thomas Denny's father Daniel had been one of the founders of the Baptist church at Green's mills in 1732, but, after turning in certificates to the town clerk in 1752 and 1761, Thomas appears to have dropped back into the establishment. He never signed another subscription list for the Baptist church before his death in early November of 1774, and his son would be a prominent member of the Congregational gentry. Estes, "Historical Discourse," in *The Greenville Baptist Church* . . ., 26–67; Greenville (Leicester, Mass.), Baptist Church Records, 1:n.p.; Leicester General Records, 2:338–40; Washburn, *Leicester*, 116. *Manual . . . Congregational Church in Sturbridge* . . ., 26–31; Sturbridge Town Records, 1:233–68, 3:n.p.; Fisk, "Testimony of a People . . .," BPAN; A. R. Leonard, "The Church on Fisk Hill . . .," *QHSL*, 2 (1903–9), 35–46; Dodge, *Charlton*, 60–1; Ammidown, *Historical Collections*, 2:176–8, 157–64. Moses Marcy estimated in 1767 that one-quarter of the inhabitants of Sturbridge were Baptists; in general, the Baptist communities in Leicester and Charlton appear to have been slightly larger than the community in Sturbridge, although an accurate count is impossible without complete lists of members and attenders. See MA 118:229. On Sutton, see Benedict and Tracy, *Sutton*, 69.

This political inactivity was not normal, and would not persist. Baptists long had been involved in town politics, and after the first few months of the Revolutionary crisis had passed, they were able to reassert themselves in the political arena. An important measure of this political reemergence is their share of the seats on the board of selectmen. In Leicester, for example, Baptists filled a third of the selectmen's terms between 1761 and 1773 (21/61), and almost half (17/36) between 1774 and 1780, reaching a peak of four out of five selectmen in 1780, the year of the ratification of the constitution.[9] Temporarily not trusted to pursue Revolutionary affairs in the months of crisis in 1774, the Baptists gradually gained control of the town committees, and as they did so they were able to transform the constitutional arguments expressed in the towns' instructions and resolves. Gradually, between the fall of 1774 and the fall of 1776, references to the charter were eliminated, replaced by strongly worded calls for a new frame of government.

The simultaneous political emergence by the Baptists and fading of rhetoric about charter rights can best be traced in a series of resolves and instructions approved by the town of Leicester. Between January 1773 and October 1776 the town expressed its sentiments on the ideal framework for government on at least nine different occasions. Speaking diffusely about rights and privileges in January 1773 and May 1774, its resolves of July 6, 1774, were a lengthy disquisition on their particular status under the Charter of 1691. Again, on September 29, 1774, the town presented its representative with instructions that he "refuse to be sworn by any person except such as may be appointed agreeable to the charter of this Province." Except for the lapsed Baptist Thomas Denny, all of the members of the committees writing these resolves and instructions were probably affiliated with the standing order.[10]

Leicester's instructions of October 10, 1774, marked a sharp break with the Down's past political rhetoric.

> Charters have become bubbles, – empty shadows, without any certain stability or security: therefore we instruct that you oppose any motions which made for the patching up that under King William and Queen Mary . . . [A]s we are without form, and void, and darkness seems to cover the face of the land, we direct your influence be employed, in the first place, toward establishing some form of government, courts of judicature, &c., as may be best adapted to our present circumstances.

[9] Leicester Baptist sources cited in note 8; for selectmen, see Washburn, *Leicester*, 459–60.
[10] Leicester Instructions, September 29, 1774, in Washburn, *Leicester*, 450. None of these committeemen were Quakers or Baptists, and all who were still in the town in 1783 would purchase pews in the new Congregational meetinghouse in that year. Several others were from the all-Congregational districts of Spencer and Paxton, and no individual information links any of them with the dissenting groups.

Having suddenly given up on the charter, the town ended the instructions by noting that it had "experienced many and great favors from the hand of God, in the course of the year past," and instructed that a day of praise and thanksgiving be set aside by the Salem Congress.[11]

Though written by an all-Congregational committee, this document may reflect a compromise hammered out in town meeting between the standing order and the dissenters: one side giving up on the charter and the other permitting a request for a day of thanksgiving under the precepts of the covenant theology. The social basis for such a compromise was reflected in committee elections late in 1774. The election of a committee to execute the resolves of the Continental Congress in December 1774 saw a radical change in the makeup of the revolutionary elite. Out of a total of nine men elected, five had not been active on committees in the previous two years of politicization, and of these five, four were already or were soon to be Baptist members or attenders. This political reemergence by the Baptists would gradually effect a permanent shift away from support for the resumption of the charter.[12]

This transition was not unopposed. Presumably, Baptist deacon Samuel Green was overruled by four other Congregational members of a Leicester committee that wrote a set of instructions in January 1775 reversing the argument made on the previous October 10. The January instructions noted "the apparent danger" of the province "sinking into anarchy and confusion," and instructed the representative to "urge an immediate assumption of government, as the only means by which we may be reduced to order, and the laws of the Province have their usual and uninterrupted course; remembering in this *to keep as near the charter* as the perplexed state of the Province will admit . . ." Another committee elected the following July had a stronger minority of two Baptists out of five committeemen, and the new instructions limited their constitutional advice to recommend that the General Court be "govern[ed] by [the] resolves and orders of the Continental Congress," advice that all previous instructions had included.[13]

With a committee for the first time dominated by three Baptists, Leicester's May 22, 1776, instructions marked the final break with the past. These instructions, referring to the judicial appointments made by the council the preceding fall, informed the representative, Seth Washburn, that

> your constituents are of the opinion that temporary appointments, sufficient for the peace, order, and defense of the Colony during the present contest, would have answered more valuable; as should the Honourable Congress declare an independence on the kingdom of Great Britain, and form a system of government which may be adopted by the continent, some future court might be under the necessity of undoing most or all the last has done.

[11] Leicester Instructions, October 10, 1774, in Washburn, *Leicester*, 452–4.
[12] Washburn, *Leicester*, 294.
[13] Leicester Instructions, January 9, July 13, 1775, in Washburn, *Leicester*, 454–5; emphasis added.

Under new Baptist leadership, Leicester took the stand that the resumption of the charter was overly hasty, and that the unprecedented condition of independence toward which the colonies were rapidly moving would require a new frame of government under the compact theory. An indication that Baptist priorities were dominant in this set of instructions lay in the town's complaints about a new Test Act, a clause of which, regulating the militia, had caused "universal uneasiness" in the town. Although the people were "willing to believe" that the act was aimed at Tories, the implication was that it might be used against others, perhaps dissenters.[14]

Another issue that Leicester's 1776 instructions addressed was that of the recent Act of Representation. Acting on a petition from Essex County, the General Court had hastily passed an act on May 6, 1776, making representation a function of population, overturning the long-standing rule that had given one representative to each town. This legislation had been intended to protect the property interests of the mercantile gentry who controlled the political life of the large seacoast towns. The act also clearly ran against the corporate interests of the western towns, most of which were very small, and many of which had just emerged from the disenfranchised status of districts in the preceding year. Leicester condemned the new act "as having a manifest tendency to create a jealousy and opposition between the trading and landed interest of the colony," and as an impediment to "unanimity."[15]

With the emergence of political strife over the issue of representation came a growing sense in both east and west that the charter had lost its legitimacy as a frame of government. The General Court came under increasing pressure to begin the process of writing a constitution. After tentatively establishing a number of committees to consider the problem, the House passed a resolution in September 1776, asking the towns to respond on the question of whether the present house and council should join as a single body to frame a constitution.

The Representation Act was very much in mind when the western towns met to consider this resolution. The most systematic response came from Worcester County, where twenty-eight towns met in convention in Worcester on November 26, 1776, under the chairmanship of Joseph Henshaw of Leicester. Although the chairman probably supported the General Court's proposal, the convention narrowly refused to consent, and at least eight of the towns "dissented for unequal representation" or "objected to the present Court." Most importantly, the convention voted that "a State Congress [be] chosen for the sole purpose of forming a Constitution of Government." The county had taken an early stand in

[14] Leicester Instructions, May 22, 1776, in Washburn, *Leicester*, 456–7; see also Hoerder, *Crown Action in Massachusetts, 1765–1780*, 351n.
[15] Leicester Instructions, May 22, 1776; Patterson, *Political Parties*, 143–4, 154–5; Pole, *Political Representation*, 172ff.; and the documents in Oscar and Mary F. Handlin, eds., *The Popular Sources of Political Authority: Documents on the Massachusetts Constitution of 1780* (Cambridge, 1966), 73–87.

favor of a constitutional convention, specially elected for the purpose of erecting a new frame of government.[16]

The towns' votes on the General Court's proposal cannot be explained by the commercial-agrarian model typically used to define the social context of late eighteenth-century politics.[17] Far and away, location in the southern section of the county – swept by the Awakening in the 1740s and 1750s – and the presence of organized dissenting societies were both far more important than the size and commercial complexity of a given town in determining opposition to the General Court's 1776 plan to write its own constitution. Fifty-eight percent of the towns with dissenting meetings (10/17) were opposed to the General Court's plan, as was Leicester, whereas only 26 percent of the towns with only Congregational churches (6/25) were opposed. Large or small, towns without organized dissenters were far more likely to consent to the General Court's plan, or to not even reply to the canvass. (See Figure 2.) Clearly, something was at work besides opposition to the new Representation Act.

The committees formed in Sturbridge and Leicester indicate that the Baptists were indeed behind the rejection of the General Court's request. Of the five men chosen in the Sturbridge town meeting to explain the town's position against the proposal, Daniel and Henry Fisk were leaders of the Baptist church, John Holbrook was in the Baptist orbit, his daughter having married another prominent Baptist in 1773, and Congregationalist Daniel Plympton operated mills just west of the Fisks' land near the Quinebaug River. As Leicester's instructions had done the preceding July, the Sturbridge committee's report presented in November of 1776 placed the basic question of constitutional procedure prior to the problem of representation.

> As the end of Government is the happyness & safety of a people so the sole right and power of forming & Establishing a plan thereof is in the People. Consequently we think it unadviseable & Irrational to consent that any set of men should form & ratify a Constitution of Government for us before we know what it is & allso we look upon the present House of Representatives to be a very unequal representation of this state.[18]

On its part, Leicester rejected the General Court's constitutional proposal as leaving no room "for any amendment, if need be, by any body or bodies of

---

[16] "Resolution of Worcester County Towns, Nov. 26, 1776," from *Massachusetts Spy*, December 4, 1776, in Handlin and Handlin, ed., *Popular Sources*, 165.

[17] Studies that emphasize a division between a commercial east and an agrarian west in Revolutionary and Confederation period Massachusetts include Taylor, *Western Massachusetts*; Patterson, *Political Parties*; Jackson T. Main, *Political Parties before the Constitution* (New York, 1973), 83–119; Van Back Hall, *Politics without Parties: Massachusetts, 1780–1791* (Pittsburgh, 1972); and David P. Szatmary, *Shay's Rebellion: The Making of an Agrarian Insurrection* (Amherst, 1980).

[18] Sturbridge Town Records, 2:293; *Vital Records of Sturbridge*, Martha Cutting, "Westville and Its Industries," *QHSL* 2 (1903–9), 59.

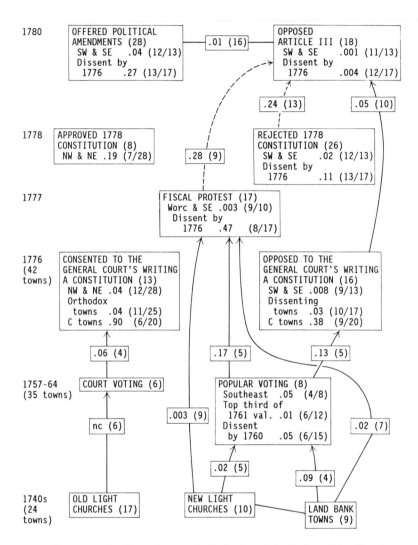

Note: This analysis does not include Ward, formed in 1778, which offered
political amendments in 1780, or Milford, formed in 1780, which opposed
Article III, and offered political amendments.

nc=non-calculable.   Sources: see Appendix 2.

Figure 2. The politics of constitutionalism, 1776–80.

Individuals at their Inspection & perusal," and because the towns were not fully
represented. The committee writing this report was chaired by Baptist deacon
Samuel Green, and included three very obscure men who had not served on any
previous committees. Green apparently cast the town's vote against the plan at the
Worcester County Convention, on the grounds that the town "presum[ed] the
people were excluded the right of approbation or rejection."[19]

The surge of Baptist political activism was formalized the next spring when, for
the first time in the Revolutionary era, Baptists were elected to the General Court
in significant numbers. Reacting to the events of the summer and fall of 1776, the
towns of Worcester County flooded the legislature with representatives in 1777,
increasing the county's representation by 65 percent. Again, small towns with
dissenting societies were particularly notable for increasing their representation,
while small orthodox towns lagged behind. Baptists were elected by Worcester,
Leicester, Sturbridge, Charlton, and Petersham. With the exception of Sturbridge,
where Henry and Daniel Fisk had each served one term respectively in 1758
and 1771, these towns had always been represented by the orthodox gentry.[20]

Observing the new 1777 house, James Warren noted to John Adams that the
members "returned from the County of Worcester . . . came high charged" to
repeal the Represention Act; another commentator wrote that the county had
chosen "men of the *greatest piety* and least *political knowledge*."[21] Despite their
new numbers, the western representatives were unable to achieve their ends. They
failed to overturn the Representation Act, and were mollified by the prospect that
a new constitution would soon be written. However, on this point, the Worcester
County representatives were unable to press the demands of the county
convention for a special constitutional convention. And the following fall they
were unable to block the passage of another set of legislation that would cast a dark
shadow over the next decade. The previous year had been the onset of a staggering
rate of monetary inflation, as the state bills of credit and Continental notes rapidly
lost value. Mercantile interests put forward a series of measures that they thought
would resolve the situation. The representatives of the mercantile centers also
proposed that the state return to the specie currency that had been provincial
policy from 1749 through the beginning of the Revolution, specifically by
exchanging them for treasury notes bearing 6 percent interest to be redeemed
between 1780 and 1782, and they proposed a series of heavy taxes designed to draw

[19] Leicester General Records, 2:207; "Resolution of Worcester County Towns," in Handlin
and Handlin, eds., *Popular Sources*, 164.
[20] Patterson, *Political Parties*, 167ff., representatives from *JRHM* 52: Pt. 1, 5, 53:4–5, 35.
While there was no great difference in the rates of increased representation of orthodox and
dissenting A and B towns, dissenting C towns increased their representation by 57% and
orthodox C towns increased their representation by 30%.
[21] James Warren to John Adams, June 5, 1777, and Thomas Crafts to Benjamin Lincoln, June
16, 1777, both quoted in Patterson, *Political Parties*, 167–8.

in the state and Continental paper money. Both of these were enacted in early October 1777, while many of the western representatives were absent.[22]

Thus the already tangled issues of representation and the writing of a constitution were further complicated by the resurgence of the old conflict between paper and hard currency that had lain dormant since the early 1750s. Although they had supported Governor Shirley's resumption of hard currency in 1749, the Popular men in Worcester County were strident opponents of the hard-money legislation of 1777. Over the next decade they defended paper money as vehemently as they had in 1740.

The old Popular stronghold of Sutton, a center of both the Land Bank and of Baptist dissent, took a leading role in the county on all of the issues: representation, the constitution, and the currency. In November 1776, the town had rejected the General Court's proposal for writing a constitution on the grounds that it would be "irrational" to accept a "Constitution unknown to us," that the Representation Act was not only unjust, but illegal, and that their "Brethren and Neighbors ... gone into the army" must be able to vote on the framing of their rights. The following January Sutton voted to call a county convention to meet in Worcester to consider the Representation Act and other grievances. The town was represented from 1775 through 1781 by Deacon Amos Singletary of the North Parish, a member of the 1774 county convention and a new justice in 1775, and the ranking committee member in the house from the three western counties. The resolves that the town published in the *Spy* on October 30, 1777, seventeen days after the passage of the currency bill, anticipated the powerful language that Singletary would use a decade later to condemn the federal Constitution. Sutton resolved that the new policy was "big with Cruelty, Oppression, and Injustice." In particular, the stipulation that the state would not exchange the old state bills for treasury notes in amounts of less than £10 was "a Point Blank violation of Public Faith, and grossly tends to destroy the common people." Four days later the town called for another convention to meet in Sutton to consider the new economic policy. Attended by six towns from the greater Blackstone Valley, and followed by a burst of petitions of protest from seventeen Worcester County towns, this convention anticipated the structure of political opposition that would emerge in the early 1780s, again with Sutton in a leading role.[23]

If Sutton threw its energies into the complex politics of 1776–7, these initiatives did not spring from a single group within the town. Rather, distinct coalitions emerged around constitutional and economic issues. Most importantly, the focus of dissenters was almost exclusively centered on the question of the constitution, as

---

[22] Patterson, *Political Parties*, 168–9, 177–80; Joseph A. Ernst, "The Political Economy of Shay's Rebellion in Long Perspective: The Merchants and the Money Question," in Robert Gross, ed., *Essays on Shays's Rebellion*, University of Virginia Press, impress.

[23] Benedict and Tracy, *Sutton*, 99–103, 106–9; Patterson, *Political Parties*, 178.

measured by committee service between 1776 and 1780. On the other hand, men affiliated with the orthodox church in the South Parish, the center of the town's support for the Land Bank in 1740, were particularly likely to serve on committees relating to state economic policies, regarding either the issue of the bills of credit and taxation, or the regulation of prices. Men serving on these economic committees were also more likely to have had kin among the Land Bankers than did those who served only on the constitutional committees.[24]

There was a similar division of political labor evident elsewhere in the county. In Leicester, while Baptist Deacon Samuel Green played a key role in the town's redefinition of constitutional issues, Capt. John Brown, now seventy-four years old, was called out of retirement to chair the town's committee that remonstrated against the economic legislation of October 1777. Brown summoned up the powerful cadences of the Popular tradition; the new act "grinds the face of the poor, because it obligeth him to put his money out of his hands that he wants for the support of his family & leave him at the mercy of monopolizers whose tender mercies are cruelty."[25]

Dissenters and Land Bank men, the latter predominantly orthodox New Lights, had made up the core of the provincial Popular coalition. With the explosion of internal politics in Revolutionary Massachusetts, this old coalition began to bifurcate, with men of the Land Bank tradition particularly concerned about the governmental structuring of economic relations, and dissenters concerned about the constitutional framing of governmental powers and individual rights. A comparison of town petitions against the 1776 constitutional plan and the 1777 fiscal legislation across the county indicates that the affiliations of the

[24] *Sutton economic and constitutional committees, 1776–80*

	Economic committees only	Both	Constitutional committees only		Total
North Parish	3	3	5	*45*	11
South Parish	6	2	2	*20*	10
Baptists	1	0	8	*89*	9
Unknown	3	0	0	*0*	3
Total	13	5	15	*45*	33
Land Bank kin	4	3	3	*30*	10

Note: Figures in italics are percentages.
Source: Committee service from Benedict and Tracy, *Sutton*, 96–119; and Handlin and Handlin, eds. *Popular Sources*, 238; South Parish affiliation from Sutton, Mass., First Church Record Book, [c.1720–c.1825], microfilm copy, AAS; North Parish affiliation from *The Confession of Faith and Covenant of the First Congregational Church, in Millbury Mass.* (Worcester, [1866?]); Baptists from *Minutes of the Warren Association*, and Benedict and Tracy, *Sutton*, 461ff.
[25] Leicester, Mass., General Records, vol. 2 (1745–87), 220–1.

committeemen in Sutton, Leicester, and Sturbridge were manifestations of a larger pattern. Both initiatives were rooted in the southern towns, and – to a degree – in towns with a strong Popular voting record in the General Court between 1757 and 1763. (See Figure 2.) The northern towns – lacking experience in the Land Bank, religious dissent, or the broader Popular tradition – rarely spoke out on these economic or constitutional politics. But the constitutionalist and fiscal protests were rooted in the opposing wings of the Popular coalition. The constitutionalist protests of 1776 emerged from towns across the entire southern section of the county and from towns with dissenting societies, but had no significant relationship to the Land Bank experience. The fiscal protest of 1777 was concentrated in the southeast towns of the Blackstone River Valley – now including the county town of Worcester – and in the strong Land Bank towns; it bore no broad-based relationship to dissent. Constitutionalism was rooted in the Lockean moral insurgency flowing from the dissenters' Awakening; it would provide the bridge between the provincial liberal insurgency and the early national liberal status quo. The fiscal protest was rooted in the orthodox center of the Popular tradition, and anticipated the legislative and convention politics of the next decade, as economic issues pushed yet another group in the county toward Harringtonian insurgency.

The most striking departure from established practice came among the four southwestern towns of the Quinebaug and French River drainages. Sturbridge, Oxford, Dudley, and Charlton had been notable for their weak participation in both the provincial legislative process and the convention politics of the Revolutionary crisis. Similarly, these towns had had few Land Bankers, and none reacted to the hard-money initiative of 1777. But all four emerged onto the political stage with the constitutionalist movement, unanimously rejecting the 1776 proposal, and sending two Baptists to the General Court with the enlarged 1777 delegation. Sturbridge, Charlton, and Dudley had Baptist societies dating to the 1750s, and in Oxford and Charlton a movement was brewing that would result in the organization of one of the first Universalist societies in the state. New forces were at work in the southwest that would have a formative influence in the decades to come.

The same pattern of constitutional politics was evident when the legislature submitted its constitution to the towns for ratification in April 1778. This constitution was overwhelmingly rejected, and again in Worcester County the strongest reaction came from the south county towns, and those towns with organized dissenting societies, while the most favorable – and apathetic – response came from the orthodox towns, particularly in the northern half of the county.[26] Again, in the smallest towns where corporate interests were threatened the most by the Representation Act, seven out of eight dissenting towns rejected the constitution, as against only four out of twelve small orthodox towns.

[26] On the ratification vote of 1778, see Patterson, *Political Parties*, 188–96.

Thus, although the reapportionment of representation and control of economic policy were clearly contributing factors, the drive toward a popularly written and ratified constitution appears to have drawn its main strength from dissenters' concerns that the legislature that administered the old corporate system not be allowed to frame the new government. Although the problem of the reapportionment of representation struck at the interests of all the smaller western towns, only where dissenters, and particularly Baptists, made up a significant minority of the population, did the town make a stand against the General Court. Within these towns the Baptist elders provided the leadership for this stand, writing the resolves and instructions that placed a Lockean formulation of the social contract prior to the corporate issue of representation.

The Baptists' exposure to constitutional issues in the extragovernmental forum of the Warren Association seems to have qualified them to lead the struggle with the commercial gentry on this unprecedentedly new issue. Before the Revolution the Baptists had begun to undermine the gentry's monopoly over the means of mediation between the rulers and the ruled by forming such associations and by petitioning the king. Now they were leading a movement that would totally change the rules of the political world. Rather than rulers dispensing corporate privileges to the ruled, the individuals who made up the population of the province would assemble to define the limited powers that they would allow the government to control.

Constitution-making and the Great Baptist Revival

The Baptists were determined to deny to the new government any power over ecclesiastical affairs. Although they had new legislative strength in the 1777–8 session of the General Court, the Baptists were in no position to prevent the Congregational majority from writing an implicit continuation of the standing ecclesiastical laws into the 1778 constitution. This constitutional endorsement of the standing order sparked strong new demands by leading Baptists for a total legal separation of church and state, in an effort that would not reach fruition until 1833.[27] A dissatisfied Baptist leadership would press on for full de jure freedom of religion into the nineteenth century, but more ordinary Baptists – perhaps with a narrower perspective – would be satisfied with a de facto voluntarism accepted by the local establishments. Such a working compromise, a gradual, town-by-town acceptance of the voluntary principle, was hammered out in the early 1780s in the wake of the period of constitution-making, and in the wake of a massive revival that swelled and diversified the ranks of the dissenters throughout Massachusetts. In the towns of the Worcester Near Frontier, at the very least, constitution-making

[27] McLoughlin, *New England Dissent*, 1:595.

was inextricably intertwined with the "organizing process" of a very early phase of the Second Great Awakening.[28]

On learning of the ecclesiastical aspects of the proposed 1778 constitution, Isaac Backus and the Grievance Committee of the Warren Association distributed a petition for Baptist elders to sign, calling for the separation of civil and religious affairs. Since the towns refused to ratify this constitution, the Baptist petition was never presented to the General Court.[29] Not willing to let the matter rest, however, Backus then prepared a new attack on the position of the standing order.

First read to the assembled delegates of the Warren Association at a meeting convened at Green's Mills in south Leicester on September 8, 1778, Backus's *Government and Liberty Described* dwelt upon the inconsistencies in the position of the standing order. In particular, he focused on the conflicting arguments made by Charles Chauncy in his 1768 tract against an American Anglican episcopate and by Philip Payson in his defense of the establishment in May of 1778. Clearly, the Congregationalists were describing themselves as dissenters in one context and as the establishment in another. After dwelling on the hypocrisy of the Congregationalists' shifting position, Backus recounted the details of the Pepperell riot of the preceding spring, where the town selectmen had led a mob that had harassed and driven out a group of Baptists who had gathered "at a small river" for a ritual "of burying in baptism."[30]

This digression was not irrelevant, for the Baptists' rights of conscience were in direct confrontation with the orthodox yeomen's strenuous attempts to maintain a unitary moral economy of town and church. In defense of their pietistic voluntarism, the Baptists drew not only on the Scriptures but on John Locke. Quoting him in passing in *Government and Liberty*, Backus drew on Locke with much more effect in a tract labeled *Policy, as well as Honesty, Forbids the Use of Secular Force in Religious Affairs*, published in August of 1779. In one particularly revealing passage, Backus's application of Locke gave a dramatic illustration of the inherent conflict that lay between the Baptists' demands for constitutional rights of conscience and the standing order's territorial inclusiveness, as summarized in the ritual of infant baptism. Quoting from *On Toleration*, he argued that

> Mr. Locke says, 'A church is a free and voluntary society. Nobody is born a member of any church, otherwise the religion of parents would descend unto children by the same right of inheritance as their temporal estates, and everyone would hold his faith by the same tenure he does his lands, than which nothing can be imagined more absurd.' Yet in reality this imagination lies at the bottom of all this controversy ... [M]en have been brought to

[28] See Donald G. Mathews, "The Second Great Awakening as an Organizing Process, 1780–1830: An Hypothesis," *AQ* 21 (1969), 23–43.

[29] McLoughlin, *New England Dissent*, 1:595.

[30] Isaac Backus, "Government and Liberty Described," in McLoughlin, ed., *Pamphlets*, 352–3, 361–5; Isaac Backus, *History of New England* (Newton, 1871), 221–2.

imagine themselves to be born members of the Christian church and therefore
have had the token of membership put upon them in their infancy, and from
thence hold that the same power which defends their lands should support
their religion.[31]

Clearly, the shape of social and religious life, with pietistic voluntarism pitted
against the "absurd imagination" of the orthodox, was intimately bound up in the
Baptists' drive for constitutional rights of conscience.

The Baptist argument, again with citations from Locke, had been developed by
Samuel Stillman of the First Baptist Church of Boston in an election sermon
before the General Court in May in 1779. Stillman was the first Baptist to deliver
an election sermon, and his invitation by the General Court may have been a
measure of the impact of Backus's *Government and Liberty Described*.[32] He did not
waste this opportunity to lecture the assembled representatives on the necessity of
rights of conscience, taking as his text Christ's injunction to "Render unto Caesar,
the things that are Caesar's, and unto God, the things that are God's" Reiterating
the standard Baptist argument for the separation of "outward" and "inward"
things, he placed his discussion more firmly in the context of constitutional
thought than Backus had. He argued that man set aside the state of nature and
enter into civil society "for their own advantage"; being in complete equality in the
state of nature they "are entitled to *precisely* the same rights and privileges" in civil
society, and among them were "SACRED RIGHTS OF CONSCIENCE."
Discussing the reciprocal duties of the people and the magistrates, he argued that
the civil magistrates derived their authority from "the consent of the people."
However, not having had power over "inward things," the people could not grant
authority over religion to the magistrates. In keeping with the division of things
between God and Caesar, he emphasized that civil affairs were to be resigned to
the civil magistrates, to whom respect and deference were due, a point that would
have particular significance in the following decade, when the Baptists would have
to choose sides in the forceful regulation of the economy and the courts in Shays's
Rebellion. Finally, in a revealing reference to corruption in the British ministry,
Stillman drew a clean line between the political worldviews of the established
order and the dissenters. Five years previously the orthodox clergy had urged the
people back to the national covenant; the virtue engendered by adherence to that
promise would ensure the social stability that the tenets of the Country ideology
demanded. In direct contradiction, Baptist Stillman urged that "we should leave
nothing to human virtue, that cannot be provided for by law or the Constitution."
Where the Congregationalists clung to the classical language of the mixed polity
and the County ideology that underlay the coercion of religious uniformity among
the ruled, the Baptists were moving toward a nineteenth-century world in which

[31] Isaac Backus, "Policy, as well as Honesty, Forbids the Use of Secular Force in Religious
Affairs," in McLoughlin, ed., *Pamphlets*, 376–7.
[32] McLoughlin, *New England Dissent*, 1:599.

the rights of all white Protestants would be equally protected and in which explicit laws would replace implicit virtue as the key to republican stability.[33]

When the 1780 Massachusetts Constitution finally emerged from convention, the Baptists had reason to be both pleased and disappointed. Two articles of the Bill of Rights concerned religion, and parts of one appeared to contradict the other. Article II guaranteed the right of each individual to worship "in manner and season most agreeable to the dictates of his own conscience," and the final clause of Article III guaranteed that "every denomination of Christians . . . shall be equally under the protection of the law: and no subordination of any sect or denomination to another shall ever be established by law." In fact, even the Baptists were to argue that these clauses were far too liberal, in that they did not limit state protection to Protestants. However, these restrictions were amply provided for in the body of Article III, which stipulated that the "several towns, parishes, precincts, and other bodies politic, or religious societies" were "to make suitable provision . . . for the institution of the public worship of GOD, and for the support and maintenance of public Protestant teachers of piety, religion, and morality." Church attendance was to be compulsory.[34] Thus, what the constitution gave with one hand, it took away with the other; if the hiring of ministers was to be in the hands of the "several . . . bodies politic," then minority dissenters would continue to be denied their rights of conscience.

The ambiguous, contradictory nature of these clauses drew a divided response from the Baptist leadership. Isaac Backus, as chairman of the Grievance Committee of the Warren Association, was the most sensitive to these matters. He launched a campaign of newspaper-letter and tract writing aimed at arousing public opinion against Article III, hoping to have it rejected by the towns in the ratifying process. However, Elder Ebenezer Hinds, a prominent if less conspicuous and articulate Baptist preacher, called for an end to this "paper war," arguing that "this is the Best Constitution the Baptists have ever been under." He pointed to the guarantees in the final clause of Article III, to that article's ambiguity in allowing "religious societies" as well as "bodies politic" to call and support public teachers of religion, and to the fact that no certificates of dissent were necessarily required by the constitution's wording. In the early years of the 1780s Isaac Backus himself was to see "*A Door Opened to Christian Liberty*," when a series of court cases interpreted the contradictions in these articles in the Baptists' favor. Later, however, Backus's hopes would be dashed by a 1784 decision that held that dissenting churches would have to be incorporated as "bodies politic" in order to protect their members and attenders from the assessments of the majority church.[35]

---

[33] Samuel Stillman, *A Sermon to the Honourable Council . . ., May 26, 1779* (Boston, 1779), 10–11, 15.
[34] "Massachusetts State Constitution of 1780," in Handlin and Handlin, eds., *Popular Sources*, 442–3.
[35] McLoughlin, *New England Dissent*, 1:604–45.

Where the response of the Baptist leadership to the Massachusetts Constitution of 1780 has been studied at length, that within the local Baptist churches has not. This neglect is unfortunate; the local response was manifested in a sweeping revival. Striking dissenting communities in Massachusetts during the years bracketing the ratification of the constitution, this "New Light Stir" was the most important revival since the First Great Awakening, and marked the opening of the "organizing process" of the Second Great Awakening.[36]

The simplest way to approach the Massachusetts Baptist revival of 1778–82 is through the statistics of baptism and membership reported by churches to the Warren Baptist Association. From a low of 55 baptisms throughout the association in 1777, the revival started in 1778 with 166 baptisms, remained at the same level in 1779 with 197, and then exploded in 1780, the year of the constitution's ratification, with 542 baptisms. Dropping off only slightly in 1781, the revival had faded by 1783, with baptisms finding a new normal level of approximately 150 per year. Between 1777 and 1782 membership in the Warren Association tripled from 1,017 to 3,389 individuals, the average number of members per church jumping from about 50 to more than 80. Thus, in the five years bracketing the ratification of the Massachusetts Constitution, the Warren Association was transformed by a flood of new converts. These figures include only the member churches of the Warren Association; the revival also struck nonaffiliated churches. Far to the west, the Baptist church at New Providence admitted a total of 3 people between 1774 and 1778, but added 64 in 1779, and 14 in each of the two following years.[37]

If this revival struck among Baptists outside Massachusetts, it was in response to the Massachusetts Baptist example. Of the nine churches reporting to the Warren Association from outside of Massachusetts, five were drawn into the revival, but generally in 1781 and 1782, and – with one exception – in towns directly contiguous with the Massachusetts border. The most dramatic evidence as to the specific Massachusetts focus of this revival comes from the minutes of the Philadelphia Baptist Association, whose membership included churches in Pennsylvania, New Jersey, and New York. While the Warren Association tripled membership between 1777 and 1782, the Philadelphia Baptist Association did not even report figures for four years after 1776, and when the churches began reporting again in 1781, the figures show a startling drop in membership per church, on average from 70 down to 55. The explosion of vital piety among the

---

[36] The later phases of the "New Light Stir" are described in Stephen A. Marini, *Radical Sects of Revolutionary New England* (Cambridge, Mass., 1982), but otherwise this very important revival has been ignored in the recent literature.

[37] *Minutes of the Warren Association*, 1771–1807. For a given church to be considered to have had a revival, at least 10% of its reported membership had to have been baptized in the year of the report. For the New Providence Baptists, see Rollins H. Cooke, transc., *Records of the First Baptist Church, Cheshire, Mass., 1769–1841* (Local History collection, Berkshire Athenaeum, Pittsfield, Mass.), 103.

Massachusetts Baptists was not a reflection of a broader, "national" pattern, but an exceptional, specific situation.[38]

Nor does this revival seem to have struck the Congregational churches in Massachusetts with any intensity. In the southwest Worcester County churches for which information is available, the North Parish of Brookfield admitted two by profession in 1778, but no others until 1783, while the Spencer Congregationalists admitted a total of ten between 1778 and 1782. The contrast between admissions to the Spencer Congregational and Charlton Baptist churches probably characterized the ebb and flow of revival in the opposing established and dissenting communities in the Revolutionary era. Spencer's peak year for admissions for the entire century had been in 1774, when 25 people joined; the end of the decade saw only 3 to 4 new members per year. In contrast the Charlton church had baptized only 8 in 1774; between August of 1780 and December of 1781 it baptized 91.[39] Where the Congregationalists felt their call to the covenant at the height of the Revolutionary crisis, the Baptists gained their greatest numbers at the height, or the culmination, of the crisis over the framing of the constitution.

The available evidence for the Baptist churches in southwest Worcester County indicates that they all experienced a revival sometime around the turn of the decade. A small, reconstituted Baptist church in Dudley joined the Warren Association in 1778, with a revival in 1780 and 1781 adding 9 members to the existing 19. The Sturbridge church was a very infrequent correspondent with the Warren Association, but in 1780 the church called a council to overcome "difficulties of several years standing": By 1782 it doubled in size from 24 to 50 members. Where the Charlton Baptist church increased its membership by 70 percent, to 139, in a year and a half, the Leicester church stretched its revival out over four years, adding between 13 and 15 new member annually between 1778 and 1781, as well as 20 new attenders in 1779. The Sutton Baptists added 54 to their rolls between 1780 and 1782, tripling their membership.[40]

Membership lists for the Leicester and Charlton Baptists provide a view of the social makeup of the revival. In both churches, probably 60 percent of the converts were women. For the Charlton church, this proportion was up from 52 percent at the formation of the church in 1762 to 1768, but not yet up to the 75 percent level that women would reach in the first three decades of the nineteenth century. Of the men joining in Charlton, 70 percent were from that town, whereas only a third of the men joining the Leicester church came from within the town. In neither town were these new members particularly poor: Of those who can be

---

[38] Based on an analysis of the records in A. D. Gillette, *Minutes of the Philadelphia Baptist Assoication from A.D. 1707 to A.D. 1807 ...* (Philadelphia, 1851).

[39] Membership Book, First Congregational Church of Spencer, Massachusetts (MSS.); Ammidown, *Historical Collections*, 2:177–8.

[40] *Minutes of the Warren Association, 1778–1781;* Greenville Baptist Church Records, Vol. I; "The Records of the Baptist Church of Christ in Sturbridge," [microfilm, OSV], 2.

linked with the 1783 valuation, approximately 40 percent came from the wealthiest fifth of the population. In the case of the Leicester church, a group of four wealthy (top fifth) men from within the town joined between 1778 and 1779, with the less wealthy and the outsiders joining between 1779 and 1780. In Charlton the bias was one of age and, to a lesser extent, wealth, with older and wealthier men initiating the revival in 1780, followed predominantly by the sons of wealthy and middling men in 1781.[41]

Thus, in each case, the Baptist revival began among a small group within the town elite, and then spread to poorer, younger, and geographically more distant individuals. The evidence also indicates that the elite initiators of the revival had both prior exposure to Baptist belief and active experience in the politics surrounding the writing and ratifying of the state constitution. Dr. Isaac Green joined the Leicester church in 1778; his father had formed the church in the 1730s, and his brother Samuel was a deacon. Both Isaac and Samuel ranked in the top tenth of the 1783 valuation of Leicester. Isaac Green served on the town committee in 1777 and 1778, and was one of the four Baptist selectmen in 1780. Meanwhile his brother, Deacon Samuel, had served on seven different committees between December of 1774 and 1779, three of them directly concerned with constitutional issues. He had also represented the town in 1777, served as selectman four times, and served as messenger to the Warren Association twice between 1773 and 1780. Another brother, Dr. John Green, represented Worcester in the 1777 session of the General Court and joined the Leicester Baptist church in 1778. Isaac Choate, again in the top tenth of the Leicester valuation, joined in 1778; he had served on the board of selectmen in 1774 when the Baptist community established the first of five majorities between that year and 1780. Col. Samuel Denny joined in 1779; he ranked in the top of the second tenth of the 1783 valuation, and his father Daniel had been one of the founding members of the Leicester Baptist church in 1732. With Samuel Green, he was one of the four men from the Baptist orbit to challenge the Congregational Patriot gentry clique by being elected to sit on the executive committee in December of 1774. Appointed to command the First Worcester Militia Regiment in 1775, Samuel Denny served as selectman five times between 1775 and 1780, on the committee of correspondence in 1775 and 1778, and as the church's messenger to the Warren Association in 1780.[42] In short, the evidence strongly suggests that members of the same group that became active in the politics of constitution making in the mid-1770s also played an initiating role in the great Baptist revival of the end of the decade.

Both the political and religious initiatives of this dissenting, constitutionalist

[41] Ammidown, *Historical Collections*, 2:177–8; Greenville Baptist Church Records, Vol. I; 1783 Valuations of Charlton and Leicester.
[42] Greenville [Leicester] Baptist Church Recs., vol. 1; Leicester General Records, Vol. II; Washburn, *Leicester*, 459–60; Force, ed., *American Archives*, Ser. 4, 4:1305. Unfortunately, no systematic list of the female membership of the Leicester Baptist church survives before 1784.

gentry in Leicester began quite early, relative to both the immediate region and the state as a whole. It may well have been because of this leading role that Leicester was chosen for the September 1778 meeting of the Warren Association, when Isaac Backus presented *Government and Liberty Described* for the first time. However, where the Leicester Baptists present a picture of a community in an initiating role, the Charlton Baptists were somewhat less prominent on the political stage, and their revival began a year later.

Although they constituted a significant proportion of the town and, after the disbanding of the Congregational church in 1765, the only religious organization in the town, the Charlton Baptists played a subdued role in the early phases of the Revolution. Between 1773 and 1778, out of fifteen men known of have served on committees, only three were Baptist members or attenders. However, when committees were chosen in May of 1780 to consider amendments to various articles of the constitution, five out of the seven men chosen had or would soon have strong links with the Baptist church in North Charlton. With the exception of Isaiah Blood, none of these men had previously been active in Revolutionary politics. Of the five men who drew up an alternative to Article III, Ebenezer Davis had joined the church in 1767, Isaiah Blood was listed as an attender in 1774, and David Lamb would join at the height of the revival in 1781. When a majority objected to the wording of the article providing for the election of militia officers, Peter Sleeman and Samuel Robinson, messenger to the Warren Association in September, 1780, were on a three-man committee that wrote an amendment stipulating that militia officers should serve for only three years. Sleeman's daughter Eunice Blood and son William joined the church in 1780 and 1781. Samuel Robinson and Stephen Fay, a member of the committee of correspondence in 1774, can be called the initiators of the massive revival that began in August of 1780. They were the first of six to be baptized on August 13, followed eight days later by another six. The largest baptisms to date, these August "plungings" would be surpassed in the church's entire sixty-year history only in the following March and April when, in gradually increasing numbers, thirty-six people were "buried in baptism" on six different days. At least a dozen men and women from the families of four of the five dissenters serving on the constitutionalist committees in Charlton were swept up in the Baptist revivals of 1780 and 1781.[43]

The Baptist revival came as an emotional catharsis after years of growing political tension and agitation. There was no simple, unidirectional relationship between political activism and Baptist affiliation. Of the eighteen Baptists involved in the politics of the mid-to-late-1770s in Leicester and Charlton, exactly half were members or attenders before their entry into the political arena, and the other

---

[43] *Vital Records* of Sturbridge and Charlton; Dodge, *Charlton*, 60–1; Ammidown, *Historical Collections*, 2:157–64, 176–8; Handlin and Handlin, eds., *Popular Sources*, 815–19.

half reversed the sequence. The two movements were intertwoven, each feeding off and supporting the other in a single explosive expression of the Lockean moral insurgency.

From Lockean insurgency to Lockean consensus

Historians long have argued that Article III of the 1780 Massachusetts Bill of Rights was a decided blow to the Baptist cause, delaying full legal separation of church and state until 1833. The force and breadth of the revival of 1778–82 suggests a very different interpretation. The surge of religious commitment by ordinary Baptists throughout Massachusetts at the culmination of the constitution-making process strongly suggests that Elder Ebenezer Hinds's positive assessment was widely accepted. Ultimately, it was "the best Constitution that the Baptists had ever been under," and its ratification marked the beginning of a dramatically new era in the nature of social relations.

By ridding themselves of the king and framing a government based on popular sovereignty, the people of Massachusetts had also undermined the exclusive claim that the corporate towns had on the rights and privileges of association, rights and privileges that had originally rested in royal sovereignty. The Baptists and others oriented toward dissent had worked toward this pluralist goal and, in the great Baptist revival of 1778–81, were the first to reorganize their lives in accordance with it. Among the remainder of the population the realization of this new social order would come only gradually, as specific compromises and agreements were made at the local level by people who perhaps were not totally aware of the wider implications of their actions. Although the constitution and later court decisions reestablished a de jure coercive relationship between state power and spiritual affairs, a de facto voluntarism and pluralism emerged in particular localities, as the dissenters were gradually conceded their rights of free association, and the standing order groped around for a new definition of their own status.

An important indication of the local acceptance of voluntarism was the returns the towns made in ratifying the constitution in May of 1780. Again, the south county towns with dissenters made the strongest objections to the constitution on political grounds alone, and, as might be expected, objected strenuously to Article III of the Bill of Rights. (See Figure 2.) Possibly not wanting to overturn the instrument they had worked so hard to develop, Leicester was the only town in the county with a long-settled group of Baptists not to offer amendments to the political portion of the constitution. However, the town referred Article III to a committee that presented a report pointing out the inconsistencies between that article and Article II. Referring specifically to the clause implying a public, legally enforced support for religion, the report argued that it is against the Principles of a great part of the Community to pay any ministeril Tax at all, other than by a free Contribution by their own hands, we are of the opinion that it is oppressive to the Subjects against whose principle it is [to have the minister's salary] paid by a Tax, and is inconsistent with the 2nd Article of the Bill of Rights.

Charlton and Dudley made other alterations along the same vein. Charlton submitted an amendment to guarantee that "no coercive Measures Shall ever take place within this Commonwealth in any ecclesiastical Matters"; Dudley reworded the passage relating to compulsory church attendance, requiring church going only "if there be any on whose instructions they can conveniently attend, *not other wise*." Although the Congregationalists probably could have mustered a majority in two of these towns, they chose not to, instead giving way to their neighbors' demands for rights of conscience. In nineteen Worcester County towns, objections to the coercive measures outlined in Article III marked a de facto declaration of local acceptance of religious voluntarism.[44]

Things did not go so smoothly in Sturbridge, where the ancient conflict between Congregationalists and Baptists flared up again in 1780. Article III was approved by a vote of 73 to 47, Sturbridge thus becoming the only Worcester County town with an old Baptist community to accept Article III. Henry Fisk wrote an impassioned plea for the Baptist minority in which he condemned "the crying sins of the land Especially for the sin of sitting light by and misimproving our privileges and liberties, while we had them."[45] Apparently, however, the majority opinion in Sturbridge began to change over the next year or two, because in May 1782 a Jonathan Gibbs was repaid for the ministerial rates he had been assessed "since the Constitution took place" and set off for religious purposes to neighboring South Brimfield. At the same meeting the town voted that "those who act from principals of Religion . . . ought of Right to be abated, upon producing proper Certificates as the law directs." A similar vote had been passed in Dudley in March of 1779, and Leicester and Sutton had been accepting certificates from Baptists and Quakers for decades. On the other hand, a December 1778 vote in Leicester to exempt dissenters without certificates was later overruled "after a long debate." While the turning in of certificates to the town clerk did not satisfy Isaac Backus and the Grievance Committee of the Warren Association, it seems to have suited the local Baptists in southwest Worcester County, for there do not appear to have been any more complaints in these towns.[46]

---

[44] Handlin and Handlin, eds., *Popular Sources*, 819, 824, 837 (see 806ff. for all Worcester County returns on the 1780 constitution); *Town Records of Dudley*, 2:210; see also Patterson, *Political Parties*, 272–4.

[45] Handlin and Handlin, eds., *Popular Sources*, 876.

[46] Sturbridge Town Records, 2:375–6; Haynes, *1st Congregational Church, Sturbridge*, 22; *Town Records of Dudley*, 2:198–9, 273, 195; Leicester General Records, 2:261, 263–5.

While these local compromises brought an acceptable level of voluntary freedoms to these Baptist communities, the logic of the situation would soon force the same status upon the Congregationalists themselves. In two cases the catalyst for this change lay in the deteriorating condition of the center meetinghouse. Originally built in the early 1720s, the Sturbridge meetinghouse was in poor repair and too small by the 1760s. The Revolution interrupted an effort to rebuild it in 1773, and when the town voted to build a new one in May 1783, the work was held up by complaints and counterproposals made by people living on the edges of the town. Finally it was agreed to assess "the Inhabitants of the Town belonging to the Revd Mr Paines [Congregational] Society for the purpose of building the New Meetinghouse." The town then took the names of seventy-two subscribers, who thus became a voluntary society in fact if not in name. The seal to the new order was applied when, after disputes arose over the report of the building committee, "a committee from the Baptist Society that were not Interested in the Center Meeting House" was chosen to resolve the problem. A working pluralism was beginning to emerge in Sturbridge.[47]

The handling of a similar situation in Leicester points to the differences that flowed from the degree to which the voluntary principle was accepted in the two towns. When the meetinghouse at Leicester needed to be replaced in 1783, it was decided with little trouble that the cost would be borne by the Congregational Society. However, the most striking contrast came in the mode in which the meetinghouse pews were distributed. The pews in Sturbridge were assigned by a committee that strictly followed the 1783 valuation in descending order, with a number of exceptions made for the dignity of aging, but poorer, church members. Those in the Leicester meetinghouse were sold to the highest bidder, with several wealthy gentry and yeomen buying four, five, or, in one case, as many as nine pews. In Leicester, where a voluntary religious order had been generally accepted for forty years, the erosion of traditional practice by the values of the marketplace was far more advanced than in Sturbridge, where voluntaristic pluralism had been staunchly opposed for as long as possible.[48]

A similar voluntarizing of the Congregationalists was occurring at the same time in Charlton. The Charlton Congregationalists had disbanded before the Revolution from lack of support, the town dismissing Caleb Curtis from his "pastoral relation" in 1776 so that he might involve himself in political affairs. In 1782 the

[47] Haynes, *1st Congregational Church, Sturbridge*, 18–20; W. J. Litchfield, "Southbridge as a Poll Parish," *QHSL*, 1 (1901–3), 1–4; Clark, *Sturbridge*, 38ff.
[48] Leicester General Records, 2:338–40; Sturbridge Town records, 3:n. p.; 1783 Valuation for Sturbridge (Microfilm, Mass. State Library). For discussions of patterns of pew assignments see John Demos, "Old Age in Early New England," in Michael Gordon, ed., *The American Family in Social-Historical Perspective*, 2d ed. (New York, 1978), 244–7; Robert J. Dinkin, "Provincial Massachusetts: A Deferential or a Democratic Society," Ph.D. dissertation, Columbia University, 1968, 179–99; John Coolidge, "Hingham Builds a Meetinghouse," *New England Quarterly* 34 (1961), 435–61.

town met to determine whether they would support a "public teacher, or teachers, of piety, religion, and morality of said town by taxation or by free contribution." Free contribution won a vote of 106 to 55, and the following August those wanting to revive the Congregational Society met at the center meetinghouse and voted to "form our Selves anew into a body Politick." They voted to support the gospel by taxation within the society, sent an invitation to a minister, and assigned a committee to petition the General Court for an act of incorporation. In Dudley the transition was achieved early in the next decade, carrying the town's 1779 decision to exempt declared dissenters to its logical conclusion. Through the 1780s dissenters had announced their convictions in town meeting and had given up their pews in the meetinghouse to the standing order; in 1792 the town voted 51 to 38 to exempt them unconditionally from ministerial taxation – a move that led to the "distinct organization of the Congregational society."[49]

The thrust toward voluntaristic pluralism took on yet another dimension, exemplified by developments based in the neighboring town of Oxford. The religious response to the transformation of the civil order implied in the constitution-making process was not solely a matter of people joining Baptist churches and these churches gaining a de facto acceptance. A significant secondary movement was occurring during the years of the Baptist revival, with people breaking away from the Baptists to form new, non-Calvinist sects.[50] The gradual emergence of a Universalist church in Oxford between 1775 and 1785, a polar opposite to the Baptists in rejecting Calvinist dogma, yet shaped around an equally voluntarist polity, suggests the way in which the turmoil of the Revolution fed the well-established tendencies toward individualistic anticorporatism of those in the dissenting orbit.

This movement began in the winter of 1775–6, when a young Baptist, Caleb Rich, having served briefly in the siege of Boston, took a furlough and sent a substitute to the army so as to work for his brother-in-law and to preach the revolutionary creed of universal salvation "from house to house" in Oxford and the surrounding towns. Calling themselves Friends or Quakers, Rich's brother-in-

---

[49] Ammidown, *Historical Collections*, 2:169–70; Dodge, *Charlton*, 57; "Stone Family Account Books, 1772–1830," vol. 2, AAS; *Town Records of Dudley*, 2:198, 269, 284, 363. A mid-nineteenth-century commentator argued that the 1792 Dudley decision, "though illegal, seems to have been the natural result of the unequal provision for distribution, in the Constitution of 1780, and to have been passed, however injudiciously, in a spirit of liberality. One of the consequences . . . was an immediate distinct organization of the Congregational society." See Joshua Bates, *An Anniversary Discourse Delivered at Dudley, Massachusetts, March 30, 1853 . . .* (Boston, 1853), 55.

[50] See Marini, *Radical Sects of Revolutionary New England*, for a detailed discussion of the emergence of the Universalists, Shakers, and Free Will Baptists in the 1770s and 1780s. More broadly, see Perry Miller, "From Covenant to Revival," in J. W. Smith and A. J. Jamison, ed., *The Shaping of American Religion*, vol. 1 (Princeton, 1961), 322–68; and Daniel W. Howe, "The Decline of Calvinism: An Approach to Its Study," *Comparative Studies in History and Society* 14 (1972), 306–27.

law and seven others unsuccessfully petitioned the town of Oxford of 1777 that
they be exempted from ministerial taxation. The new faith rapidly spread to
receptive households throughout the dissenting orbit in south-central Massachusetts. In Charlton, two families – the MacIntires and the Davises – went
through a parallel transformation, which may have typified the Universalist
experience. Becoming Baptists in the 1750s and 1760s, they were fined for refusing
militia duty and accused of Tory sympathies in 1777 – suggesting a link with the
Oxford Friends. Members of both families were involved in constitutional politics
in 1778 and 1780, and in 1779 and the early 1780s declared themselves
Universalists. The head of one of these families, Ebenezer Davis, "made much of
his wealth . . . in supplying the army about Boston with provisions and beef," and
died the richest landholder in the county. Following Davis's withdrawal from the
Charlton Baptists in 1779 the Warren Association blasted the doctrine of universal
salvation as "a damnable heresy," and the 1780–1 revival among the Charlton
Baptists was stirred up in part to counteract the influence of this "new religion."[51]

In addition to Oxford and Charlton, Universalism was attracting converts from
the Baptist orbit in South Brimfield, Douglas, Sutton, Sturbridge, and Dudley in
these years, and in 1785 "a number of Professors of the Protestant Religion" who
had "for a number of years past assembled upon the Sabbath Day for public
worship" gathered at Oxford in April 1785 to form a Universalist Society. Calling
themselves "a true Independent Church of Christ," these Universalists violated
territorial boundaries at least as much as the Baptists ever had, drawing 70 of their
150 founding members from seven towns to the east, south, and west of Oxford. In
character with their antiterritorial voluntarism, one of their first moves was to call
a convention with the other Universalist societies in Massachusetts and Rhode
Island. At this meeting the Universalists formed an association, making these
societies "cemented in one body, Consequently bound by the ties of love to assist
each other" in maintaining their rights of conscience.[52]

The emergence of these Universalists, and their refusal to pay ministerial rates,
had a devastating effect on the establishment in Oxford. In combination with the
soaring inflation of the late 1770s, the erosion of support for the Congregational
minister brought five years of confrontation between town and minister, ending in
his dismissal in 1784. The town's nineteenth-century historian pointed to the
relationship between religious and social turmoil and the fundamental transformation of civil order in this era. "This was a crisis in the town's history and a new
order of things based on the provisions of the new State constitution ensued.

[51] Anson Titus, "Reminiscences of Early American Universalism," *Universalist Quarterly and
General Review* (October, 1881), 431–4, 438–9; Ammidown, *Historical Collections*, 2:160, 177,
186–7; "Stone Family Account Book," Vol. II, AAS; "The Second Religious Society in
Oxford and the Adjacent Towns (called Universalist). Record Book, 1785–1845," MS,
Andover-Harvard Theological Library, 6–7; Handlin and Handlin, eds., *Popular Sources*, 258,
819; Marini, *Radical Sects*, 71–5, 82–5; McLoughlin, *New England Dissent*, 2:719.
[52] Daniels, *Oxford*, 72ff.; "The Second Religious Society," 8–11.

Socially the results in the community were deplorable. Members of the same family became alienated, heated discussions were common and many personal enmities engendered, which continued many years." Such disunity would become pervasive over the next several decades, as successive waves of people rejected the strict Calvinism of the Baptists, hiving off into a profusion of new faiths – all structured on the voluntary principle forged by the Baptists over the previous half-century. Among them were the Shakers; after the Shaker revival in eastern New York in 1780 Mother Ann Lee's first journey through New England in 1781 attracted Shaker converts throughout Baptist communities in central and western Massachusetts, including Petersham, Harvard, Bolton, and Grafton in Worcester County. The impetus for organization among dissenters spread to the Quakers, those in Worcester County forming a monthly meeting in 1783. However, the theological and denominational shape of the nineteenth century lay with the Methodists, and the formation of an early Methodist class – among former Baptists – in the "Honest Town" section of Charlton in 1790 was an important harbinger of the future. The anticorporate thrust of dissenters in these years is perhaps best exemplified in the 1797 identification in the Sturbridge marriage records of the itinerant Methodist preacher serving this class, not as an inhabitant of any particular town, but as "a Citizen at large."[53]

Thus, within several years of the ratification of the state constitution a variety of circumstances had led to the de facto acceptance of voluntaristic pluralism in a number of towns in southwest Worcester County. Not only were dissenters increasingly accepted and proliferating, but the standing order was itself coming to accept the fact that it also must organize under voluntary principles. In short, the distinction between established and dissenting church was fading with the emergence of the denominational order that would characterize the nineteenth century. However, if changes were evident in the swath of towns lying to the south, they were not in those lying to the north. Across the county, opposition to Article III was concentrated in the dissenting towns in the southern half of the county, while the orthodox towns of the north in the main consented. A small number of Baptists had always lived in Spencer, yet when they tried to swing the town against Article III, they ware defeated 55 to 20. The Baptist revival was stirring some in Brookfield and Hardwick, but in numbers far too small to influence the majority's solid support for Article III. In 1784 the town of Brookfield, arguing that "it has generally been the practice of Christianized protestant Governments to make provision by Law for the support of the Gospel Ministry," instructed its representative to press for a law explaining Article III that would "be couched in terms liable to no misconstruction." Late in the 1790s

[53] Daniels, *Oxford*, 60; Ammidown, *Historical Collections*, 2:186ff.; Sylvester, ed., *The Connecticut Valley in Massachusetts*, 2:1071; Edward D. Andrews, *The People Called Shakers* (New York, 1963), 17ff.; Lincoln, "The Antecedents of the Worcester Society of Friends," 29; *HWC*, 1:377–8; *Vital Records of Sturbridge to the Year 1849*, 156.

Brookfield would make a concerted but unsuccessful effort to have the General Court deny a petition for the incorporation of a Baptist Society in East Brookfield. If denominational voluntarism – a Lockean institutional order – was accepted as a given in most of the towns of southern Worcester County, it was staunchly opposed in the north, where the coercive moral unity of spiritual and material things continued to be enforced.[54]

This differentiation between voluntary and coercive towns was implicitly formalized in the incorporation in 1784 of the first secular voluntary association in the county's southwest quadrant. By the stipulations of its act of incorporation of March 1784, the purpose of the Leicester Academy was both secular and religious; its trustees were bound to "the purpose of promoting true piety and virtue, and the education of youth." The second academy incorporated in the state, the Leicester Academy was an archetypical example of an alliance among the gentry, clergy, and the incorporating power of the commonwealth that would flourish between the 1790s and the 1830s: an alliance whose common goal was the fostering of religion, education, and civil virtue in youth which was seen as crucial to the autonomous survival of the "rising nation."[55]

The impetus for the establishment of this institution came from leading men in the newly voluntaristic Congregational societies of Charlton and Sturbridge, Cols. Jacob Davis and Ebenezer Crafts, each the wealthiest man in his respective town in 1783. They collaborated with Baptist Asa Sprague of Spencer in buying a large house at Leicester center in May 1783. On the following July 4 they sent a petition with a number of others to the General Court asking to be incorporated as a "body politic . . . with such privileges and advantages as are granted to the academy at Andover." Davis had recently had experience with such petitions, having that January sat on the committee that wrote the petition for the Charlton Congregational Society.[56]

[54] Handlin and Handlin, eds., *Popular Sources*, 7871–5; Brookfield Instructions, May 24, 1784, and Brookfield's Answer to the Baptist Petition, May 9, 1799, in "Extracts from Brookfield Town Records, 1773–1800," in "Brookfield, Mass., Local Records, 1673–1860," AAS, 10, 52–3; Roy, *East Brookfield*, 106ff., 145ff. Reviewing the breakup of religious unity in the town from the perspective of the 1850s, the minister of the South Brookfield Evangelical society made the following comment: "As the people of the country adopted new notions of civil and religious liberty, there sprung up a disposition to break away from their accustomed associations for religious worship, and to form new corporations for the purpose." Micah Stone, *Reminiscences of a Half-Century Pastorate* (West Brookfield, 1851), 26.
[55] "History of the Leicester Academy," *American Quarterly Register* 7 (1834), 52. The Leicester Academy was the *county's* third secular voluntary association, after the American Political Society, formed and disbanded in Worcester in 1775, and the Trinity Masonic Lodge, founded in Lancaster in 1778. On the new institutional order, see Handlin and Handlin, *Commonwealth*; Clyde S. Griffen, *Their Brother's Keepers: Moral Stewardship in the United States, 1800–1865* (New Brunswick, 1960); Daniel Calhoun, *The Intelligence of a People* (Princeton, 1973), 47ff.; Peter D. Hall, *The Organization of American Culture, 1700–1900: Private Institutions, Elites, and the Origins of American Nationality* (New York, 1984), 151–77.
[56] Emory Washburn, *Brief Sketch of the History of the Leicester Academy* (Boston, 1855), 9.

The list of twenty-two petitioners and appointed trustees reads like a who's who of the Patriot gentry of Worcester County. Three had served in various capacities in the county convention of 1774, six were orthodox ministers, six had sat as delegates to the constitutional convention in 1779–80, and all except the ministers and the anomalous Asa Sprague – who dropped out of the picture by 1784 – received appointments to the judiciary during the 1780s. But it was a particular section of the Patriot gentry who were the most conspicuous in the formation of the Leicester Academy. Delegates to the county convention of 1774 were outnumbered two-to-one by delegates to the constitutional convention of 1780; the academy plan attracted those most attuned to the new voluntarist, constitutionalist order. Of these twenty-two men, eighteen came from towns that had opposed Article III of the Bill of Rights or that had dissenting societies; nine were leading men from the newly voluntarist Congregational societies in Sturbridge, Leicester, and Charlton. A group of financial contributors from Leicester included Baptist leaders Samuel Green and Samuel Denny, marking the approval of the academy by the constitutionalist dissenter gentry. Similarly, when seven Worcester men formed a joint stock company in 1784 to support another private school, one was a Baptist and three would join the new Unitarian parish established in Worcester in 1787. Constitutionalism and religious denominationalism set the stage for the emergence of private voluntary societies.[57]

The sponsors of the academy were literally the "young men of the revolution"; born on average in 1740, they were a decade younger than the delegates to the 1774 county convention. During the course of the war a new generation of gentry had come to countywide prominence, and their experience brought a new political worldview. The older Patriot gentry had led the county into the Revolution on the basis of the Country ideology, which assumed the stability of the political categories of the mixed polity, the contract between ruler and ruled. By contrast, impelled by both the force of local circumstance and the logic of the constitution-making process, the political worldview of these "young men of the revolution" had found a new set of definitions in the categories of the Lockean contract, voluntarily entered into by autonomous individuals, without regard to immutable territorial allegiances.

The voluntarizing of these "young men of the revolution" should not obscure the fact that it had been the Baptists who were the true initiators in the local movement toward a popularly written and ratified constitution. The Baptists' role in this process indicates an important relationship between the Great Awakening and the Revolution that has not received sufficient attention. The most important legacy of the evangelicalism of the Great Awakening was the seeds of institutional

---

[57] Washburn, Leicester Academy, 8–9, 38–47, 73; Fleet's Register, 1779–87; JHRM, 53: 4–5; A. H. Everett, et al., eds., Journal of the Convention for Framing a Constitution of Government for the State of Massachusetts Bay . . . (1779–1780) (Boston, 1832), 12–13; Lincoln, Worcester, 205, 302. For the Worcester Unitarians, see Chapter 8, Note 15.

pluralism and voluntarism. A pietistic reading of the Scripture had impelled dissenters out of the orthodox churches and toward a form of religious association based on free choice rather than on a territorially defined communal coercion. It was the dissenters' commitment to their rights of conscience – and interest in protecting their growing institutions – that provided the most important impetus for the constitution-making process.

Ultimately the legal stipulations of the state constitution were far less important than the impact of the process itself, wherein a people declared themselves in a state of nature and then voluntarily banded together to create a new framework for government. The process had achieved three particularly important things. First, the mixed polity had been eliminated; talk of the relationship between the rules and the ruled would no longer have a basis in reality. Second, a formative political precedent had been set. Men no longer would participate in political life solely as inhabitants of privileged corporate towns, but as individual citizens of the newly created state. Finally there began to emerge, slowly and raggedly, the perception that the corporate towns had lost their functional hegemony over the rights and privileges of association on the local level.

This brings us to the core of the argument. This broad shift in political worldview led directly to what variously has been called the "organizing process of the Second Great Awakening" or the "urbanization" of rural Massachusetts.[58] The massive growth and spread of voluntary associations in late eighteenth- and early nineteenth-century Massachusetts began with the surge of people into the Baptist churches in the revival of 1778 to 1781, was followed by the formation of a huge number of new churches – many of them of non-Calvinist denominations – in the 1780s, and then moved on to more secular forms. The incorporation of the Leicester Academy marked the first time that Congregationalists in this region formed an organization that crossed town lines, the first violation of the territorial principle among the orthodox. It marked the critical transition from Lockean insurgency to Lockean consensus. Such secular, nonterritorial associations would provide one of the key structural elements of the capitalist, national, middle-class society that would emerge in the coming century. And as Lockean forms of private association moved into the mainstream of public culture, the Harringtonian ideal of independence in commonwealth rapidly became the primary language of insurgency.

[58] Mathews, "The Second Great Awakening as an Organizing Process," and Richard D. Brown, "The Emergence of Urban Society in Rural Massachusetts, 1760–1820," *JAH* 61 (1974), 29–51.

7

Conventions, Regulation, and Antifederalism

On the first Tuesday of September 1786, the day scheduled for the third quarterly sitting of the Courts of Common Pleas and General Sessions, history seemed to repeat itself in the county town of Worcester. The night before, a company of armed Regulators had occupied the courthouse, and on Tuesday morning, reinforced by another two hundred men, they confronted the assembled justices and attorneys of the court, who had gathered at Joseph Allen's house on the main street before proceeding up the hill to the courthouse. Confident that his authority would prevail, Chief Justice Artemas Ward of Shrewsbury, once a Popular partisan in the provincial General Court and recently a general of the Continental line and representative to the Continental Congress, brushed aside an armed sentry and led the justices through the crowd to the steps of the courthouse. Here he was met by Capt. Adam Wheeler of Hubbardston, sword in hand, at the head of a file of men. Attempting to enter the courthouse, Justice Ward was turned back at bayonet point. After a brief confrontation with Wheeler and other officers among the Regulators, Ward drew upon the authority of the Popular tradition. Addressing the crowd from the courthouse steps for two hours, Ward warned the Regulators that they were subverting constitutional government, the legacy of the Revolution. Then, with their dignity reasonably intact, the justices retired to Nathan Patch's United States Arms Tavern, where that afternoon they were presented with a petition from "the body of people now collected for their own good and that of the Commonwealth" that the courts adjourn. The next day, after another two hundred men from neighboring towns sporting sprigs of evergreen had marched into Worcester, the Court of Common Pleas adjourned until the winter term. The Regulation, or Shays's Rebellion, had begun.[1]

As they had almost exactly twelve years before, an armed militia had closed the county courts, halting proceedings of civil litigation. If the impulses of economic insurgency had been veiled and masked in the revolutionary crisis of 1774, they were primary and explicit in the Regulation of 1786. The stresses latent in the provincial structure of class and institutions had been exposed in 1740, 1765, and

---

[1] Lincoln, *Worcester*, 134–8; Paige, *Hardwick*, 127–8; on Artemas Ward see *Dictionary of American Biography*, Dumas Malone, ed. (Boston, 1936), 19:415–16.

1774; in 1786 they exploded. In leading the Regulators against the Courts of
Common Pleas and General Sessions, Adam Wheeler acted on a sense of mutual
obligation and public duty deeply rooted in the corporate experience. "Moved
with the Distress of the People," Wheeler wrote the following November, he had
acted "to prevent Such abuses as have of Late taken place by the Setting of those
Courts." The civil prosecution of "Valueable and Industrous members of
Society" was doing "great Damage not only [to] their families but [to] the
Community at Large." But Wheeler "had no Intention to Destroy the Publick
Government," and his behavior in Worcester suggests that he was as concerned
with order and restraint as had been the patriot gentry of the Worcester
Convention in the fall of 1774. As the Regulators marched off the Worcester
common toward the courthouse, Wheeler was heard to request that "you
gentlemen on Horse Back who are well wishers to our Cause, please to fall in Two
and Two that we may make a more Respectable appearance." Order in the line of
march and the support of at least some gentry would give legitimacy to the
Regulators' forceable actions against the constituted courts. Their concern for
such legitimacy placed the Regulators firmly in the tradition of crowd action
common across the entire early modern north Atlantic world.[2]

   Such continuities were also evident in the heated language used that December
in the upcountry town of New Braintree when Captain Wheeler again asked that
men turn out to stop the courts. James Adams "believed the General Court were
determined to bring us into Slavery," and promised that he would send provisions
for the Regulators; Captain Thomas Whipple "thought that we were in a fair way
to come into Lordships unless something was done to put out the present rulers."[3]
Slavery, lordships, rulers – such language spoke of the classical political tradition
of the mixed polity, and the fear that unaccountable state institutions had been
corrupted to the private interests of powerful men. So, too, the concept of a
"body of people" under arms, acting to regulate the government, bespoke the
provincial confrontation between king and people, not the voluntary politics of the
new constitutional era. Under the terms of the constitution-making process that
Massachusetts had just completed, the people were now the sovereign power, and
they were to choose their own government by election. With the new constitu-

<hr>

[2] Adam Wheeler's Statement, Hubbardstson, November 7, 1786, Folder 1, Shays's Rebellion
Collection [hereafter SRC], AAS; Noah Haven's Testimony, Trial of Aaron Broad [February
1787], Folder 5, SRC, AAS. On the crowd in the early modern north Atlantic, see George
Rude, *The Crowd in History, 1730–1848* (New York, 1964), esp. chaps. 1, 2, 9, 13–15; Charles
Tilly, *The Vendée* (Cambridge, Mass., 1964, repr. 1976), vii–xii, 305ff.; E. P. Thompson, "The
Moral Economy of the English Crowd in the Eighteenth Century," *Past and Present* 50 (1971),
76–136; Maier, *From Resistance to Revolution*, 3–26; Hoerder, *Crowd Action in Revolutionary
Massachusetts*, 40–84. The major studies of Shays's Rebellion, or the Massachusetts Regulation,
include Taylor, *Western Massachusetts in the Revolution*; Robert A. Feer, "Shays's Rebellion,"
Ph.D. dissertation, Harvard University, 1958; Hall, *Politics without Parties*; and David P.
Szatmary, *Shays's Rebellion: The Making of an Agrarian Insurrection* (Amherst, 1980).
[3] New Braintree Evidence, Box 23, Robert Treat Paine Papers [hereafter RTPP], MHS.

tion, the contest between rulers and ruled gave way to interests competing for power in the political arena, but the language of the Regulators was redolent of the older, provincial political culture.

For many staunch patriots throughout the Confederation, the rising of the people in Massachusetts was a dangerous sign that the American states were doomed to collapse in anarchy, that the people lacked the requisite virtue to ensure the survival of a republican form of government. Even the Regulator communities, in the sobering aftermath of the failed rebellion, began to see the contradictions between the traditional beliefs that had informed their actions and the new constitutional framework. "Being persuaded that they have greatly erred and persued measures diametrical opposite to our Constitution," the people of New Braintree petitioned the General Court for a general pardon for the Regulators in February 1787, noting that "every thinking man among the Insurgents are before this, sensible of their wrong steps and are truly sorry for their folly."[4] But if the Regulation itself threatened the collapse of the republic, the causes of the Regulation had indicated the collapse of the commonwealth. Reviewing the growing economic crisis, the jails bulging with debtors, and the rising tide of emigration, the town of Greenwich in Hampshire County asked a fundamental question of the General Court in January 1786: "Honoured Sirs are not these imprisonments and fleeings away of our good inhabitants very injurious to the Credit or honour of the Commonwelth: Will not the people in the neighbouring States say of this state: altho: the [people of] massachusetts Bost of their fine Constitution Their government is Such that itt Devours their inhabitants."[5] Many people across Massachusetts agreed that the new state constitution was allowing private interests to destroy the fundamental basis of society: the independent household economies that should sustain the people in stable communities. Certainly there was much to be celebrated in the achievement of constitutional liberty, but powerful forces seemed to be rapidly undermining decentralized, propertied independence, the bulwark of the Harringtonian commonwealth.

The response to these forces came in a powerful insurgency, a literal civil war exploding across central and western Massachusetts. But viewed against the long-established traditions of political culture in Worcester County, this insurgency would come from a new quarter. In a very important sense, the play of political culture and political action were inverted with the constitution-making process. Until that point, the most powerful insurgent forces on this middle landscape drew upon implied or explicit Lockean critiques of the corporate order and the classical tradition. With the framing of the constitution, people of such Lockean, liberal persuasions were no longer at odds with the dominant ideology; the future lay with the principle of voluntary individual association that they had espoused – to

---

[4] New Braintree Petition, February 5, 1787, Folder 1, SRC, AAS.
[5] Greenwich Petition, January 16, 1786, Folder 1, SRC, AAS.

varying degrees – since the Land Bank and emergence of religious dissent in the Great Awakening. Already in the 1780s the new institutional order that would shape a structural transformation of society and economy was rapidly taking shape. After 1780 insurgent forces would emerge out of those social orbits that were now out of step with a liberal framework, among people who still responded to the corporate categories defining the inclusive, unitary world of provincal orthodoxy. Perhaps conservative, even archaic, the people schooled in these traditions became the political conscience of the new society, carrying the classical republican, Harringtonian synthesis of personal independence and collective obligation far into the nineteenth century.

A disordered economy, conventions of the people, and the Popular tradition

The causes of the Regulation of 1786 lay in a spiraling crisis of the economy that began soon after the opening shots of the Revolutionary War were fired at Lexington and Concord. Both tradition and circumstance would shape the political response to this crisis. When the Second Provincial Congress, facing the same problems of war finance that had confronted the province in its generations of war with France, began to issue paper bills of credit in May 1775, it reopened the deep divisions between the advocates of hard currency and paper money that had smoldered across the province since Shirley had engineered the resumption of specie in 1749. At the same time the circumstances of a society mobilizing for a war of independence with a powerful imperial nation intensified the moral connotations of striving for economic self-interest and personal gain.[6]

The war itself took an enormous toll, both the seige of Boston by provincial and continental troops and the ongoing war at sea contributing to a pervasive shortage of commodities of all kinds. By the time that the British evacuated Boston in March 1776, the increased demand for agricultural goods generated by the military encampments had dried up supplies throughout much of eastern New England, and even as the war moved south the demand for supplies would keep agricultural prices high until 1781. At the same time, the war disrupted the fisheries, coastal commerce, and their allied trades in the seaport towns, and the cessation of commerce with Britain shrank stores of manufactured goods. Despite appeals from such bodies as the Worcester Convention, which in June 1776 condemned exorbitant prices as "of evil example, . . . interrupting that harmony and unity among us which under God, is our strength," merchants and farmers began to run up their prices in a rapid inflationary spiral. As prices rose, the

---

[6] I have benefited from having studied the following two unpublished papers: Ernst, "The Political Economy of Shays's Rebellion in Long Perspective," and Janet A. Riesman, "Shays's Rebellion and Massachusetts Public Finance in the Revolutionary Era," In press in Gross, *Essays on Shays's Rebellion*.

currency depreciated; by February of 1781 the value of paper currency had dropped to a rate of seventy-five dollars to one dollar in coin.[7]

Commodity shortages, price inflation, currency depreciation, and the competing traditions of specie and paper were the variables in a complex economic politics that competed with the politics of constitutionalism between 1776 and 1780. These years of sparring between coastal merchants and inland farmers would end in a draw in 1780, with neither side gaining a clear advantage. The tide would turn in the years immediately following the adoption of the new constitution, with the mercantile interests relentlessly pursuing a program of resumption of hard currency, to bolster their position in international markets, and of high taxation, to quickly pay off public war debts. When these measures were not moderated in the context of a postwar depression and contraction of credit, such as had swept across the north Atlantic in the late 1730s, the mid-1760s, and in 1772–3, they would trigger armed violence across western Massachusetts. But the Regulation was only the final step in a long and tortuous political process beginning in 1777.

Worcester County's response to the growing economic crisis flowed from its long experience with the economic categories of the Popular tradition, modified and directed by the institutional vehicle of the convention. During the 1770s the county threw its weight behind the defense of paper money, the public regulation of prices, and a judicious opposition to heavy taxation. When the General Court began the process of retiring the paper bills of credit in 1777, by replacing them with treasury notes and adopting a high level of taxes to cover the new debt, the county led the state in protesting the new measures. Of thirty-two towns petitioning against the sudden change in financial policy, seventeen were in Worcester County; of these the old Popular party and Land Bank towns of the Blackstone Valley were particularly conspicuous, led by Sutton's call in the *Spy* for a convention to consider the new legislation.[8]

Passions ran high against those who appeared to be hoarding goods, many of whom were themselves prominent in the opening phases of the Revolutionary crisis. In Leicester, retailer Joseph Allen, an important figure on the committee of correspondence, was cleared of a charge of profiteering in December 1775 only at the intervention of a fellow committeeman, Justice of the Peace Joseph Henshaw. Similar accusations may well have been a factor when Benjamin Richardson, again both a retailer and a member of the committee of correspondence, was beaten up by a squad of militia. According to a complaint by Justice Henshaw, their captain,

---

[7] Address of the Worcester County Convention, June 1776, in Force, *American Archives*, ser. 4, 6:1088; in general, see Handlin and Handlin, *Commonwealth*, 1–92; Andrew M. Davis, "On the Limitation of Prices in Massachusetts, 1760–1779," *CSMP* 10 (1905), 119–35; R. V. Harlow "Economic Conditions in Massachusetts during the Revolution," *CSMP* 20 (1918), 163–192, Hall, *Politics without Parties*, 3–130; and Winifred B. Rothenberg, "A Price Index for Rural Massachusetts, 1750–1855," *Journal of Economic History* 39 (1979), 975–1001.

[8] Patterson, *Political Parties*, 178–81; Benedict and Tracy, *Sutton*, 106–9; Paige, *Hardwick*, 112–13. See Chapter 6.

Benjamin Brown, a son of old John Brown the Land Banker, had stood by passively without intervening . In Sturbridge, Ebenezer Crafts, and innholder and captain of a troop of cavalry raised in April 1775, was cursed as a "damned Tory" in 1777, suggesting that he, too, was suspected of profiting from the economic chaos.[9]

After a series of Continental and regional conferences had discussed the growing problems of depreciation and price inflation, the General Court in January 1777 empowered the towns in an "Act to Prevent Monopoly and Oppression" to establish and enforce a fixed list of prices. Although it came under fire from a number of directions, and was repealed the following October, this act set the institutional framework for economic regulation for the rest of the decade. The provisional government's response to the economic crisis was to be channeled through the traditional corporate regulation and oversight of the town governments; local men would intervene in the market in the interests of the public good and in the spirit of a moral economy. In 1777, selectmen and committees of correspondence sat to determine lists of just prices; in the spring of 1779 after a second such act was passed, towns such as Leicester and Sutton established specific committees to look into cases of monopoly and forestalling. Similarly, the Confession Act empowered the towns to elect men to take confessions of debt, thus giving the towns limited authority in an arena that traditionally had been the sole reserve of the justices of the peace and the Court of Common Pleas.[10]

Despite the seeming advantage posed by high agricultural prices, Worcester County took a strong role in the movement to control prices, particularly at the meetings of the Concord Convention in July and October of 1779. In sharp contrast to the two western most counties in Massachusetts, Hampshire and Berkshire, where price regulation was actively opposed, and only a fifth of the towns sent delegates to the convention, every town in Worcester County was represented in the Concord price convention, with the exception of Athol in the county's far northwest corner. That August delegations from the towns also met for ten days in county convention in Worcester to take measures to implement the resolves of the Concord meeting, setting up a list of maximum prices for commodities ranging from Indian corn to raw cotton and German steel, and directing the towns to establish "large committees" to set prices of other non-enumerated goods and to ensure compliance. Towns throughout the county responded by adding members to the committees of safety, correspondence, and inspection.[11]

---

[9] Washburn, *Leicester*, 322; Haynes, *First Congregational Church, Sturbridge*, 43; Shipton, *Sibley's Harvard Graduates*, 12:270; Records of the Court of General Sessions, Vol. 4, 355–6.
[10] Leicester General Records, 2:210, 266; Paige, *Hardwick*, 108–10; Benedict and Tracy, *Sutton*, 112–14; *Town Records of Dudley*, 2:181ff.; Davis, "Limitation"; Handlin and Handlin, *Commonwealth*, 14, Patterson, *Political Parties*, 178–81.
[11] *Proceedings of the Convention Begun and Held at Concord . . . on the 14th Day of July, 1779 . . .* [broadside, Evans 16228]; *Proceedings of the Convention Begun and Held at Concord . . . on*

The recommendations of the Concord convention were clearly a compromise worked out between the advocates of specie and paper money, both in the establishment of price ceilings of commodities and in the prescriptions for economic recovery written into the convention's resolves. Blame for the crisis was laid to the "Set of Jobbers, Harpies, and Forestallers" who mediated between "the fair Merchant and the honest Farmer, especially those situated at a Distance from each other." The address attached to the proceedings of the July convention argued that the crisis lay in "the constant Depreciation of our Currency," and recommended taxation and loans to absorb the excess money, a program that mercantile interests had been advocating since 1777. But the resolves voted by both the July and October meetings stated unequivocally that demands for hard currency were at the root of the crisis, as they set up a spiraling differential between paper and metal; "the buying and selling of Gold or Silver, and the demanding or receiving *either of them*, . . . has been one great Cause of our *present Evils.*" The inhabitants of the state were enjoined against "*such wicked and pernicious practices.*" In the next resolve the General Court was instructed to move slowly and carefully in its measures to reverse depreciation, "as *a gradual*, is far more safe, easy and equitable, *than a rapid Appreciation* of our Currency."[12]

Such recommendations might well have averted crisis in the following decade; they must have appealed to the sensibilities of men of the Popular tradition who sat as delegates for the County of Worcester. Once again, sons of men involved in the Land Bank and Popular politics figured prominently in the Concord and Worcester price conventions, representing Worcester, Leicester, Spencer, Brookfield, Hardwick, Grafton, Sutton, Fitchburg, New Braintree, and perhaps Shrewsbury and Lancaster as well. Among them were Henry King representing Leicester, the son of the leading Popular partisan in provincial Sutton, and David Bigelow of Worcester, the son of a Land Banker and a brother of leading figures in the Worcester convention of 1774. Similarly the chairman and clerk of the 1779 Worcester convention, Joseph Reed and Phinehas Upham, were both sons of Land Bankers. The movement for price fixing was clearly situated at the center of gravity of the county's political culture, firmly rooted in the provincial Popular tradition.[13]

the 6th Day of October, 1779 . . . [broadside, Evans 16229]. (I refer to these two meetings as the "Concord Price-Fixing Convention.") (12668, 12669); *Proceedings of the Convention, Begun and Held at Worcester, in and for the County of Worcester, on the 3rd Day of August, 1779* . . . (Worcester, 1779) [broadside Evans 43736]; Benedict and Tracy, *Sutton*, 114; Leicester General Records, 2:268, 269; Sturbridge Town Records, 326; Lincoln, *Worcester*, 120–2; Daniels, *Oxford*, 130; see also Brookfield Town Meetings, March 3, 1777, Extracts, 19–25, AAS; opposition to price fixing in Hampshire County is discussed in John L. Brooke, "To the Quiet of the People: Revolutionary Settlements and Civil Unrest in Western Massachusetts, 1774–1789," *WMQ*, 3d. ser., 46 (1989).

[12] *Proceedings of the Convention Begun and Held at Concord* . . ., [Evans 12668, 12669].

[13] Based on an analysis of the delegates to the Concord and Worcester Price Conventions, the Land Bankers listed in Davis *Currency and Banking*, 2:295–313; and *Vital Records* and genealogies.

But that tradition was dividing, bifurcating, in the 1770s. Including both New Light Congregationalists and dissenters in its ranks throughout the post-Awakening era, the county Popular tradition had its origins in the Land Bank, an institutional experiment poised on the boundary between Lockean and Harringtonian priorities, a private association formed for the public interest. But those who were particularly attuned to Lockean language, the dissenting Baptists, were concentrating their attention on the constitution-making process. And if their fathers had established an extra corporate institution, the Popular men concerned with revolutionary economic policies made no such proposals. At the same time that a Lockean framework of government was being hammered out, these men were operating within fundamentally corporate assumptions, within a structure of county conventions and town committees that brought public regulation and oversight to the economy. The response to the economic crisis in the 1770s was fundamentally shaped by expectations of corporate oversight. The uncertain circumstances of the provisional government would not permit otherwise, but the new decade – and the new constitution – would bring a decidedly different situation.[14]

Following ratification of the state constitution in the summer of 1780, the mercantile interests in the General Court began to move to reestablish hard money. That spring Congress, in association with the states, had repudiated the old Continental currency and had mandated in exchange for a new tenor issue, which paid 5 percent interest and could be converted into hard coin at the end of 1786. This issue soon began to depreciate as well, and in the fall 1780 session of the General Court the hard-money proponents, holders of large amounts of state debt, pushed through their program, repeating the process that had occurred in 1748–9. On January 24, 1781, after two months of complex legislative politics, the "Consolidation Act" passed by a vote of 75 to 65. The two components of this legislation had drastically different effects. First, the new tenor bills were not to pass at their face value, but at a value determined by the justices of the Supreme Judicial Court, which was to adjust their value downward for depreciation. Seven months later the General Court banned the use of these notes in any private transaction. In effect, the currency that the common people found most easily available was first devalued and then banished from the economy. Second, the state debt was "consolidated," converted into new securities that would not be subject to depreciation, and that would be rapidly repaid in hard currency with interest between 1785 and 1788. The General Court would have to assess the people of the state at very high rates to repay these securities in the time alloted. Rooted in the legislation of 1777, the 1781 Consolidation Act set the stage for a grand political drama.[15]

[14] See Chapter 6; for a parallel analysis, see Eric Foner, *Tom Paine and Revolutionary America* (New York, 1976), 145–83.
[15] Van Beck Hall, *Politics without Parties*, 100–14; Ernst, "The Political Economy of Shays's Rebellion," 44–7; E. James Ferguson, *The Power of the Purse: A Study in American Public Finance, 1776–1790* (Chapel Hill, 1961), 245–50.

The county's response to consolidation was united and consistent. Echoing its overwhelming support for the Land Bank forty years before, the Worcester delegation opposed the new policy by a margin of at least 75 percent on the seven roll calls taken on the issue between November 1780, and January 1781, while the remainder of the state typically cast only 40 percent of its vote against the proposal. On the final vote on January 24, 1781, with almost 59 percent of the county's towns represented, the Worcester representatives opposed consolidation with a vote of 22 to 5, or 82 percent, followed by the delegations from Middlesex and Bristol, which cast 65 percent of their votes against the bill. The county's uniquely united and militant opposition to consolidation would be repeated again and again over the next five years, as the county voted as a bloc against proposals emanating from the mercantile interest. In 1781 the county opposed a new valuation of the state, and supported excise and impost proposals, which were seen as a means of avoiding a heavy direct tax on landed property. In 1782 the county voted to postpone laying a direct tax by a vote of 19 to 1, and supported a measure allowing debts to be paid in personal property by a vote of 12 to 4. In 1783, when the impost was directed to the commutation payments of Continental officers, Worcester County turned against it, and the delegation similarly opposed restoring civil rights to returning Loyalists, measures tightening state authority over tax collectors, levying a stamp tax, and granting supplemental funds requested by Congress in 1785 and 1786. In these votes the county representatives rarely cast less than 70 percent of their votes against the merchant interest, with between 40 and 60 percent of the representatives in attendance; the rest of the state typically supported the measures with between 25 and 40 percent of the representatives voting. On the Evaluation Act and the excise in 1781, the impost in 1783, and the supplemental fund in 1786, the county's representatives voted unanimously with the opposition.[16]

The county's legislative opposition to the centralists' fiscal plans was complemented by a vigorous politics of county convention. Once again, the old Land Bank center of Sutton took the lead, just as it had in 1777 on the issues of representation and the conversion of paper currency into loan notes. On February 23, 1781, the town asked leading men in both orthodox parishes, Deacon Willis Hall and Elder Daniel Greenwood, to issue a circular letter to the county, calling on the towns to send delegates to a convention to meet in Worcester in April to

[16] Hall, *Politics without Parties*, 101–26, 148–61. I am grateful to Professor Van Beck Hall for sharing with me his legislative work sheets, which summarize the votes by county and commercial orientation. The roll call votes are in the manuscript House Journal, Vol. 1; see Hall, *Politics without Parties*, 101–3, 139, 148–9, and 199, for complete citations. Robert A. East, "The Massachusetts Conservatives in the Critical Period," in Richard B. Morris, ed., *The Era of the American Revolution* (New York, 1939), 351, 364–5; and Stephen E. Patterson, "After Newburgh: The Struggle for the Impost in Massachusetts," in James K. Martin, *The Human Dimensions of Nation Making: Essays on Colonial and Revolutionary America* (Madison, 1976), 218–42, both note the near unanimous opposition of the Worcester County representatives to the merchant-supported legislation.

protest the Consolidation Act. Hall was a brother of a Land Banker and had sat in
both the 1777 house and the 1779 price convention; Greenwood was the son of a
Popular party representative of the 1750s. Such continuities were typical in the old
Popular town of Sutton, where at least half of the men serving on committees
relating to the economy between 1777 and 1787 were kin to Land Bank men.[17]
When the convention met in April 1781 it chose two sons of New Light Land
Bankers, William Paige of Hardwick and John Prentice of Ward, as its chairman
and clerk, and voted a set of resolves straight out of the county Popular tradition.
The convention argued that if the new tenor money had been left unmodified, it
"would have continued to appreciate and that so rapidly that in a short time the
difference between paper and silver currency would have been very in considerable." Rather, the legislation encouraged a rapid depreciation by "money-jobbers
& those who have it in their power to make specie either scarce or plenty at their
pleasure," who sought to "amass large quantities of said bills" with the
expectation of redemption with interest in specie. This 1781 convention focused
entirely on the Consolidation Act, and strengthened county opposition; in the next
house the county representatives voted 16 to 1 to repeal the legislation. In March of
1782 the town of Hardwick sent out a circular letter, written by William Paige,
calling for another convention. Meeting in April, May, and August, the convention was particularly concerned with the status of the treasury, demanding
an accounting of "the IMMENSE SUMS of PUBLICK MONEY" assessed in
the previous years, and asked for a settlement of accounts between the state and
the Congress. The convention asked that the 1781 impost then supported by the
county in the General Court be kept under state control; when Sutton called
another convention in 1784, congressional control of the new 1783 impost was a
primary grievance, as was its "making large grants to the Officers of the
Continental Army"; commutation payments were no "more binding on the Good
People of this Commonwealth than that of the Redemption of the Old Money."[18]
     The county conventions meeting in Worcester in the early 1780s thus
articulated the county tradition of close attention to fiscal policy and public
finance, a tradition running back to voting in the provincial house in the 1750s on
issues concerning the treasury and salaries, and back to the Land Bank era.[19] But
if the convention movement articulated the central themes in the county's
provincial political culture and was congruent with the oppositional voting of the
county delegation in the house, its results were mixed. The 1782 convention, in

---

[17] *Spy*, March 22, 1781; Benedict and Tracy, *Sutton*, 119–20, 653, 656. See Chapter 6 herein.
[18] Worcester County Convention Petition, April 4, 1781, MA 142:333–5; Worcester County
Convention Resolves, April 9 and May 14, 1782, Broadside; Worcester County Convention
Petition, April 22, 1784, House Doc. 1320.
[19] The differences between Worcester County and Hampshire and Berkshire to the west,
where Court party traditions predominated before the Revolution, are discussed in Brooke,
"To the Quiet of the People."

particular, was a confused affair, recommending that the towns withdraw their representatives from the General Court if the state did account for its expenditures; the August session broke up in disarray, adjourning without substantive resolves and advising the towns "to come to a new choice" of delegates. The confusion in the 1782 convention may well have contributed to the sole reversal in the county voting in the house, when, in July 1782, the county's representatives voted 10 to 9 to reconsider the direct tax, while the rest of the state narrowly opposed the measure.

More significantly, the conventions came under fire as an illegitimate vehicle of political action; they claimed to be a corporate representation of the county while they advocated what was a private interest, no matter how widely shared. Even before the 1781 convention had met, the *Spy* was printing essays that argued that conventions were illegal. In March, one "Aminadan," who noted that he had sat with Sutton's Willis Hall in the 1779 price-fixing convention, drew a sharp distinction between the provisional institutions of the 1770s and the constituted government that had been established in the summer of 1780. "County conventions, some years hence," he wrote, "when we were without form and void, and darkness covered the face of our land, were beneficial." But it was "truly astonishing" to call a convention "at a time when we are under a new and regular constitution of government, when we are under a new and I hope good set of rulers." In 1784 another writer in the *Spy* targeted Sutton as the lynchpin of the convention movement:

> The town of Sutton, or any other town, or individual person have right to petition the General Court for relief, under any grievance whatever, real or imaginary; but for a town to traverse the county by messengers, or circular letters, and form alliances and combinations with other towns, to make head against the General Court, is ... "direct oppugnation" to the government which the people of this State, have themselves set up.

The chief justice of the Supreme Judicial Court made the same argument, stating that conventions were "repugnant to our constitution, which has parcelled out, in particular channels, all power that is to be exercised under it." Rather than being a lawful mode of protest and petition, the conventions served only "to counteract the General Court" and "to excite treason and insurrection."[20]

To the proponents of conventions, this argument was utter hypocrisy. The conventions justified their existence on the grounds of Article Nineteen of the declaration of rights in the constitution, which granted to the people the right to assemble and "consult upon the common good" and to instruct their representatives. Writing in the *Worcester Magazine*, "Freeman" attacked the argument of a "Citizen" who had written that, since independence, conventions were

---

[20] *Spy*, March 22, 1781; Benedict and Tracy, *Sutton*, 122–3; *Worcester Magazine* II (1786), 406–7.

> unlawful assemblies of men. If he had spoken plain English he would have
> said ... When we had other *Rulers*, Committees and Conventions of the
> people were lawful ... they were then necessary; but since I have *myself*
> become a ruler, they cease to be lawful ... the people have no right to
> examine into my misconduct ... I am sensible it will not bear the test, and
> except I can flatter or frighten people from these odious assemblies, I fear I
> shall lose my place.[21]

The debate over the legitimacy of conventions exposed a rift in perceptions of the new state's constitutional framework. Those writers opposing conventions argued that the constitution-making process had fundamentally altered the structure of power in the state; those supporting them saw a continuing contest between the ever-encroaching powers of the ruler and the fragile liberties and privileges of the people.

Unquestionably, the conventions of the 1780s stood on shaky ground, in a no-man's-land between the mixed polity and constitutional government. Although they claimed to be a corporate institution expressing the will of the people in general, the conventions were acting on behalf of a particular private interest. In an important sense, the convention men of the 1780s were in exactly the opposite position as their forebears in the Lank Bank of 1740. The Land Bank had been a liberal, voluntary institution at odds with a corporate framework; the convention was a corporate institution at odds with a liberal framework. A second generation of leading men in Worcester County were caught on the boundary between corporate and voluntary forms as they attempted to work out the central dilemma of early American political economy: the provision of a circulating medium sufficient for the needs of a growing people.

Despite the attacks on their legitimacy, the conventions expressed a consensus among a broad range of the county gentry, as marked by their votes in the house. The convention men were acting within county traditions running back to the Popular politics of the 1730s, vigilant against the encroachment of arbitrary governmental power, quick to see the collusion of powerful economic interests. But they were not desperate men or a particularly radical group; most had experience in the provincial congresses, legislature, or the price-fixing conventions, and as many would have connections among the government militia as with the Regulators in the winter of 1786 to 1787.[22] And their focused attention on matters of fiscal accountability and public finance addressed only a narrow range of economic stresses raging through the state in the 1780s.

Below the level of the Popular county gentry acting in both legislature and

[21] *Worcester Magazine*, II (1786), 337–8.
[22] Twenty delegates to the Worcester County Conventions of 1781, 1782, and 1784 have been identified from a range of town histories and town records. Service in Provincial Congresses, General Court, and price conventions from Lincoln, ed., *Journals of Each Provincial Congress*; *JHRM*; the *Massachusetts Register*; price convention *Proceedings*. Among these delegates, five would be Regulators (or their kin), and six would be Friends of Government (or their kin).

convention there were contrary currents of political and economic action. If the Popular gentry occupied the political center of gravity in the county, confronting the creditor-mercantile interest from a precarious intersection of voluntary and corporate forms, they stood apart from two patterns of violent mobilization. Direct action would develop within two broad orbits within the county, the two extremes on the continuum between Lockean voluntarism and Harringtonian corporatism, extremes where the Popular tradition had never taken deep root. Riots defending specific private households would break out among the dissenting orbit in the southwestern section of the county, which recently had entered the political arena in the constitution-making era. Conversely, the Regulation, a ritualized stopping of the courts in the name of the public good, would have its primary base among the orthodox communities of the northwest where provincial political experience had been limited, truncated, by the now displaced Court party elite.

Riots and legislative deadlock

The legal alterations of the state's economy passed in the early 1780s rapidly produced pressures on the population that could not be contained within the arenas of convention and legislative politics. The effects of the legislation of 1781, eliminating paper currency and establishing high rates of taxation in hard coin, was compounded by the growing pressure of a postwar depression. At the end of the war an old structure of private debt was quickly reestablished, running in a chain from British merchants to American wholesalers and from there out to backcountry retailers and commercial intermediaries. As British merchants called in their debts, the effect soon rippled through the Massachusetts countryside. Public and private debts seemed to be on the verge of totally consuming the property of households in many of the state's agricultural towns. Towns found it increasingly difficult to raise the required taxes, and in large numbers petitioned the General Court for abatements of their taxes, particularly in 1781 and 1782. The number of private suits for debt surged to roughly four times the pre-war level, and Worcester County was especially hard hit. By late 1785, the county jail at Worcester was jammed with debtors; during the December sitting of the Common Pleas twenty-eight men in the jail signed a petition to the General Sessions, complaining of their "Suffering Condition Occasioned by the Rapid Augmentation of their Number[,] the Smallness of the Gaol, – and the Coldness of the Weather."[23]

The impact of these public and private debts was relatively evenly distributed across the county; towns in the different regions and of different sizes and religious

[23] Feer, "Shays's Rebellion," 530; Szatmary, *Shays's Rebellion*, 19–36, esp. 29; Hall, *Politics without Parties*, 193–5; "Prisoners' Protest, December 7, 1785," Miscellaneous Jail records, 1784–7, Worcester County, MA, Papers, AAS. I am indebted to Lou Mazur for this item.

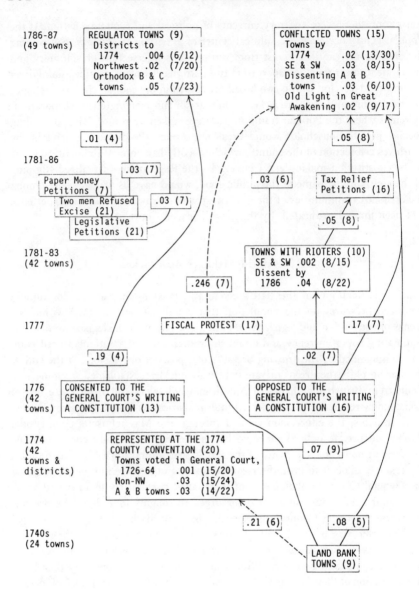

Figure 3. The economic crisis, 1777–87.

composition petitioned for the relief of taxes, and were the residence of imprisoned debtors, at rates roughly comparable to their share of the overall population. The exception was perhaps the smaller dissenting towns, which were particularly likely to send in petitions for tax abatements, and which had relatively few imprisoned debtors in 1785 and 1786. But it was in the south county and dissenting towns and particularly towns in the southwest corner of the county, where scattered small-scale rioting broke out between 1781 and 1783. (See Figure 3.) These riots, usually aimed at stopping "vendue sales" of cattle for failure to pay taxes, were the first sign that the economic crisis was straining the social fabric to the breaking point.[24]

The riot in Dudley in December 1782 was typical. Constable Asa Robinson complained that as he was impounding cattle belonging to Baptist William Wakefield to sell at auction, four men from Dudley and Uxbridge "Came with a Shout, followd by a Large gang, they forced the oxen from us, and Delivered them to their owner."[25] Among sixty such rioters from eight Worcester County towns for which evidence on religious affiliation has been assembled, fully one-half were affiliated with Baptist societies or would join the Universalist society formed in Oxford in 1785. This Universalist connection was quite remarkable, involving rioters from seven different towns, and at least two Universalist notables provided sureties for rioters. Elsewhere, impressionistic evidence suggests the same pattern. Although there was no Baptist society in Paxton, one of ten men rioting against a cattle sale in 1782 had turned in a certificate as a Baptist in neighboring Leicester; in Petersham several of the seven men rioting to prevent the collection of taxes in 1783 were from a Baptist neighborhood, and one, Ebenezer Hammond, was probably a relation of Thomas Hammond, whose house was a gathering point for Shakers in the immediate neighborhood. Overall, of the ten Worcester County towns where inhabitants were charged with riot in these years, eight had dissenting societies.[26]

The center of gravity of the tax riots of 1781 to 1783 lay in the orbit of the dissenting societies, and they bore a strong affinity to the dissenters' confrontations

---

[24] Hall, *Politics without Parties*, 186–8, provides the only discussion of these disturbances in the recent literature. The twelve small ("C") towns with dissenting societies accounted for 23% of the county population in 1790, but they accounted for 42% (14/33) of the county's petitions for tax abatements between 1780 and 1786, but only 12% (15/123) of the men imprisoned for debt between January 1785 and September 1786. The corresponding figures for the small ("C") orthodox towns (29% of 1790 population) were 15% (5/33) and 16% (20/123). Tax abatement petitions from Feer, "Shays's Rebellion," 54–546; imprisonments from jail registers in Folder 1, Box 2, Worcester County, Mass. Papers, AAS.

[25] Dudley Riot Evidence, Box 23, RTPP, MHS.

[26] Rioters listed in Massachusetts Supreme Judicial Court Docket Books, 1783, pp. 212–20, 232, 239–41; 1784, p. 265; 1785, p. 177, Universalist affiliation from the Second Religious Society in Oxford and Adjacent Towns (Called Universalist) Record Book, Andover Harvard Theological Library, on Hammond, see Mabel C. Coolidge, *The History of Petersham, Massachusetts* (Petersham, 1948), 56–7, 234; for a detailed discussion of the social composition of the rioting groups in the early 1780s, see Brooke, "Society, Revolution . . .," 556–62.

with town authorities over the collection of ministerial rates, such as had occurred in Sturbridge in the 1750s. The structure and pattern of the riots of the early 1780s reflects the general circumstance of dissent in its local setting; solidarity within a separatist communion encouraged the assembling of crowds to protect the private property of neighbors and friends. Generally, these were rather poor men, on the edges, rather than the center, of the dissenting communions. Among thirty-three men in Dudley, Sturbridge, and Paxton indicted for rioting, twenty-three (74 percent) either ranked in the bottom half of the valuation or were not on the lists a all. They also showed signs of a deep-running alienation. Oliver Witt of Paxton had been accused of passing counterfeit money and convicted of sedition, having said that "the Congress were designing men and contrived to keep the war along to maintain themselves." Justice Edward Davis had a heated confrontation with Phillip Brown, a Universalist among those rioting in Dudley on behalf of Baptist William Wakefield. "I told him that such conduct was dangerous & if persisted in would brake up the army," Davis testified. "Brown answered, that is the very thing we are after." The tax riots were based on formal agreements of mutual protection, involving cooperation across state lines by a group known as the "reformation men," who had chosen officers and stood "ready to assist at a minutes Warning." In February 1783, a menacing riot in Douglass drew men from seven south county towns, a large band from Gloucester, Rhode Island, and some from Connecticut, as well as at least one deserter from Burgoyne's army. The Worcester Committee of Correspondence, chaired by Joseph Allen, wrote nervously to the governor asking for a suspension of habeas corpus, which was immediately granted.[27]

   With their concentration in the south county towns – particularly the southwest – and in the dissenting societies, the rioters were also immersed in the context of Constitutional voluntarism. The sixteen towns that had opposed the General Court's plan to write a constitution in the fall of 1776, constituting 40 percent of the county's population, produced almost 80 percent of the men indicted for rioting between 1781 and 1783. Even more striking, the rioting was not particularly associated with towns that protested the 1777 currency legislation, which produced rioters roughly in proportion to their population. Importantly, the eight towns that dissented from the General Court's 1776 plan for a constitution but did not petition against the monetary legislation of 1777, produced fully half of the county's rioters, although they accounted for less than 20 percent of the county population. The rioting of the early 1780s, then, exploded in communities that were not particularly involved in the Popular politics of

[27] Jonathan Smith, "Toryism in Worcester County ...," 25–6; Dudley Riot Evidence, Worcester Committee of Correspondence to John Hancock, February 23, 1783, Box 23, RTPP, MHS; Elizabeth A. Perry, *A Brief History of the Town of Glocester, Rhode Island* ... (Providence, 1886), 29–31; Horace A. Keach, *Burrillville; As It Was, and As It Is* (Providence, 1856), 24.

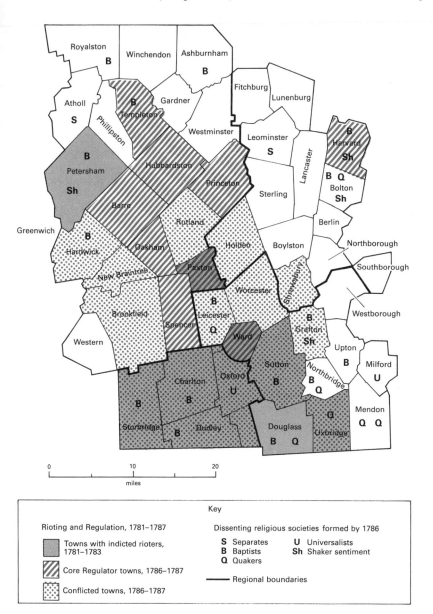

Map 2. Riots, regulation, and dissent in Worcester County: The 1780s.
(Drawn by Carmela Ciampa from data by John Brooke)

money and fiscal policy, with its long tradition of legislative action. Rioting was not part of the Popular tradition of an institutionalized and formal politics of fiscal vigilance, represented by the legistative protest of 1777. Rather, it emerged in communities that had entered the political process in the heady days of the constitution-making process, with its promise of a new individualistic, voluntary order of things. The riots were an indication that traditional rules of social order were eroding rapidly in the newly voluntary towns.[28]

One might expect these small-scale riots to have been a prelude for full-scale rebellion. In aggregate, the rioting towns would number significantly among the towns conflicted in 1786, divided between Regulators and Friends of Government. But among the rioters themselves there was very little continuity between the tax riots of the early 1780s and the court closings of 1786. Of sixty-six Worcester County rioters from towns where complete evidence is available, only five would be Regulators in 1786, and at least six would be affiliated with members of the government militia sent to suppress the insurrection in 1787. Conversely, three of those witnessing against the Paxton and Dudley rioters would be accused of supporting the Regulators in 1786. Two sons of Baptist William Wakefield, for example, whose cattle were the focus of the 1782 Dudley riot, served in Capt. Lemuel Corbin's government militia company in the winter months of 1787, while constable Asa Robinson came under suspicion of "endeavouring to raise an insurrection for the redress of certain pretended public grievances." The discontinuity between riots and regulation suggests that the tax rioters were acting as "private mobs" rather than "public mobs," concerned with private interests,

[28] *Worcester County towns: 1776–86*

Political action	Towns in 1786	Population in 1790	Rioters, 1781–3	Leading Regulators, 1786–87[a]
Opposed 1776 constitution	6	10388	56	13
plan only		*18*	*60*	*19*
All towns protesting	17	21331	41	24
1777 economic legislation		*38*	*37*	*35*
Consent to 1776 plan only	9	11568	10	29
		20	*9*	*43*
All other towns	15	13520	3	2
		24	*2*	*3*
Total	49	56807	110	68
		100	*100*	*100*

Note: Figures in italics are percentages.
Source: Handlin and Handlin, *Popular Sources,* 123, 164–6; *Acts and Resolves,* Vol. 5, 516–18; Rioters: see note 26.
[a] Indicted and imprisoned Regulators: see note 41; population from *Return of the Whole Number of Persons within the ... United States* [1790] (Philadelphia, 1791), 29–32.

rather than what the Regulators would see as the public good. Importantly, Constitutionalist towns producing large numbers of rioters were not particularly notable for their involvement in the Regulation in 1786. Rather, indicted and imprisoned Regulators were especially concentrated in towns that had tacitly supported the provisional government in the 1770s: towns that had actually consented to the General Court's constitutional plan in 1776, and that had not protested the 1777 legislation. Thus the Regulation's center of gravity would lie outside both the Constitutionalist orbit and the old Popular tradition.[29]

The county representatives, in opposing higher taxes and voting for a law that temporarily made personal property legal tender, were indeed acting to alleviate some of the pressures on poor men pressed by both public and private debts. But all their efforts were not greeted with unanimous approval. After the county delegation voted twice in favor of the new excise in the winter of 1781–2, as the lesser evil to a direct tax, their efforts were protested by a number of towns. Spencer objected in particular to the establishment of a post of county collector who might be tempted to "enrich" himself, and to the excise provisions that seemed "to excuse the Rich . . . and Burden the poor." The excise was one of a growing number of issues that drew petitions directly from the towns, bypassing or ignoring the county convention. With its protest against the excise, Spencer also complained about the new valuation law, which, in denying small property holders the right to vote in town meeting, exposed "them to a state of vassalage not to be endured." In November 1785 the town petitioned the General Court to revive the legislation making personal property legal tender or to establish "a Bank of Paper Money to pass in all payments equal to silver and gold." The following winter and spring saw a flood of similar petitions asking that the state set up such a bank. The 1784 county convention had hinted that paper money would be a solution to the state's economic problems, stating that "the people were greatly oppressed and distressed for the want of a balance of a circulating medium," but even the more radical convention of 1786 made only a veiled reference to the need for "a portable representation of property." As the economic crisis became more pressing, towns meeting and petitioning in their corporate capacity emerged as the institutional vehicle for political protest.[30]

In particular, it was the new towns in the northwest uplands that began to bypass the convention in the mid-1780s. The preponderance of town petitions throughout this period came from the small orthodox towns of the northwest, particularly the petitions for a bank of paper money. Similarly, opposition to the

[29] MA 191:175; Testimony against Asa Robinson, Folder 5, SRC, AAS. For a discussion of public and private mobs, see Gordon Wood, *The Creation of the American Republic, 1776–1787* (New York, 1972), 320–1.
[30] Spencer Petition, February 11, 1782, MA 187:412–13; Lincoln *Worcester*, 126–8; Hall, *Politics without Parties*, 117; Taylor, *Western Massachusetts*, 109; Spencer Petition, November 16, 1785, Senate Doc. 525; Feer, "Shays's Rebellion," 117, 540–6; Worcester County Convention Petition, April 22, 1784, House Doc. 1320; "Worcester County Convention Petition, September 28, 1786," printed in *Worcester Magazine* II (1786), 334–5.

excise was concentrated in the northwest, and in midsized Congregational towns. (See Figure 3.) In April 1785 County Collector Caleb Ammidown reported the names of eighty-nine retailers and innholders who had refused to pay the excise; more that half of these men were from the northwest towns, and here they tended to be innholders rather than retailers. In refusing to pay the excise, these men were protesting the transfer of hard currency to the state's creditors, hard currency that they certainly found difficult or impossible to collect from their customers at the bar. All of these developments marked a decidedly new turn in the county's politics; for a half-century political opposition had been centered in the towns in the southern half of the county, particularly in the Blackstone Valley, where the Land Bank and the Great Awakening had struck with the greatest force. The 1780s saw the emergence of the northwest towns as a new focus of political opposition, both to the state and to the county gentry, just as the Constitutionalist politics of the late 1770s had seen the emergence of the southwestern towns.[31]

The emergence of an oppositional political culture in the northwestern towns was also evident within the near unanimity of the county's collective voice in the legislature. There were few significant differences in the voting records of the county's long-established regions on a series of fiscal issues, including status of the new tenor money, the taking of a new valuation, the direct tax, the excise, the 1783 impost, the Stamp Act, and the 1786 supplemental fund. But when the rest of the county had supported the 1781 impost (18 to 4) as the lesser evil to a direct tax, half of the representatives from the northwest opposed the measure (11 to 10) – as well as the direct tax. And in 1783 and 1784 the northwest joined other northern towns to oppose the reinstatement of returning Loyalists by an overwhelming margin (5 to 26), although the rest of the county was divided on the issue (8 to 6). These votes were rooted in a long experience with the old Court party gentry, and most recently in the bitter controversies with the clustering of Tories in the northern towns. The hostility to the Loyalists in the northern towns would take on new significance as the events of 1786 unfolded.[32]

[31] The northwest towns encompassed 40% of the county population in 1790, but they accounted for 54% (48/89) of the men refusing to pay excise in 1785, 71% (22/31) of the petitions for remedial legislation, 85% (6/7) of the petitions for a bank of paper money, and only 37% (45/123) of the men imprisoned for debt in 1785–6. Of the men refusing to pay the excise in the northwest towns, 69% (33/48) were innholders, as against 46% (19/41) of those refusing in the remainder of the county. Petitions from Feer, "Shays's Rebellion," 540–6; imprisonments, see note 24 above; Excise refusals from Caleb Ammidown's Return, April, 1, 1785, Box 1, Folder 9, Worcester County MA Papers, AAS.
[32] The discussion is based on an analysis of nineteen critical roll calls regarding Legal Tender, Evaluation, Excise, Direct Tax, 1781 and 1783 Imposts, Stamp Act, the return of Loyalists, and the 1786 Supplemental Fund; in the Manuscript House Journal, 1:246–7; 2:67–8, 306–8, 432–3, 507, 568, 715–16; 3:140–1, 150–1, 4:121–3, 259–61, 433–4; 5:177–8, 338–9; 6:467–8, 519–20; 7:69–70, 152–5. See Hall, *Politics without Parties*, 102–3; 139, 148–9, 160, 199. On the Tories in the northern towns see above, Chapter 5, and Paige, *Hardwick*, 91–106, which details the extended conflict between the town and Jonathan Danforth, which was still remembered in the 1830s.

The spring of 1786 saw the political situation further deadlocked. James Bowdoin, the leader of the mercantile faction, was elected to a second term as governor in an election that saw a particularly low turnout in Worcester County and across the state. The supplemental fund requested by Congress was voted on in the General Court in March, June, and July; while the Worcester delegation voted against it by a ratio of 20 to 1, their attendance at the roll calls was down from more than half to less than a third. It was in this context that the town of Spencer issued a call for a county convention to meet in mid-June in Leicester. Willis Hall of Sutton was elected chairman, but only seventeen towns attended, and the convention adjourned to August 17. It only issued a fully developed set of resolves after a third meeting in Paxton in late September. The convention's petition to the General Court complained of the "want of a circulating medium" and protested the "amazing expense" of the courts of common pleas and general sessions and the lawyer's fees. But the bulk of the petition was concerned with the fiscal concerns traditional to the county Popular rhetoric: the impost and excise payments to the state's creditors, the commonwealth's accounts with the "Continent," reimbursement of the costs of the failed Penobscot campaign of 1779, the plight of those holding continental paper money, and the grant of the Supplementary Fund. The September convention also exhorted the people to "remain orderly and peaceable," and – in "the hardy spirit of the honest yeomanry of this county" – to patiently wait "the result of the present session of the General Court."[33]

But the honest yeomen of Worcester County had already acted. Following the lead of Regulators in Hampshire County, who closed the courts in Northampton on August 29, Capt. Adam Wheeler of Hubbardston led his men into Worcester to close the courts on September 6. The pressure of debt obligations was clearly the catalyst for direct action. Spencer had petitioned the Common Pleas to adjourn its June session without passing judgment in any suits, but the court did sit, and the June session capped an extremely busy year, although actions were actually down slightly from the previous two years. But the Regulation was not simply a swarming of hard-pressed debtors acting to advance their particular private interests. The Regulation drew upon particular kinds of debtors, from particular kinds of communities. Economic distress certainly triggered the action to close the courts, but this action was conditioned by distinct traditions of political culture that sharply differentiated the peoples on the Worcester middle landscape.[34]

[33] Benedict and Tracy, *Sutton*, 124–5; Lincoln, *Worcester*, 133–4; Draper, *Spencer*, 62–3; *Worcester Magazine*, 2 (1786), 334–6. The August 17, 1786, convention published an abbreviated set of resolves in the *Worcester Magazine*, republished in the *Massachusetts Gazette*, August 25, 1786.

[34] According to the New York *Packet*, August 11, 1786, thousands of people in Worcester County signed subscription papers in late July, promising to assist in closing the courts. See John B. McMaster, *A History of the People of the United States from the Revolution to the Civil War* (New York, 1891–1900), 1:306. If so, those marching in September numbered only about four hundred. Draper, *Spencer*, 63; Hall, *Politics without Parties*, 195.

Debt and the Regulation of 1786

The Regulators' primary target was the sitting of the Court of Common Pleas; the
suits for debt heard here and appealed to the Supreme Judicial Court over the
previous year provide an important window onto this uprising. Six towns lying at
the intersection of the northwest uplands, the southwest, and the upper reaches of
the Blackstone Valley provide a useful sampling. In the three sessions sitting prior
to September 1786, 134 men appeared as debtors at the Common Pleas from the
towns of Oakham, Spencer, Leicester, Charlton, Sturbridge, and Brookfield; 82
appeared as creditors from these six towns. Roughly 60 percent of these men
would take sides in the Regulation, some with the insurgents, and some with
government.[35] Among those taking sides, roughly two-thirds of the creditors
sided with the government, but the debtors were evenly divided between the
support for the Regulation and the government. Simple debt was not sufficient
reason to impel people into the Regulation.

[35] The material identifying the insurgents in southwest Worcester County was produced in
two judicial contexts, and at present is held in four different archives. First, oaths of allegiance
were administered to the rank and file of the movement by the justices of the peace in the towns,
a few as early as December 1786, but the majority in February and March of 1787. Oaths could
be located for all the towns considered here except for Charlton and Sturbridge. The original
lists returned by the local JPs are to be found in Mass. Archives, 190:80, 107, 131, 151,
165–6&3/4, 169, 205, 216, 225B. Second, a body of material produced by the Supreme Judicial
Court sitting in Worcester is located in three archives. Extensive testimony heard against a
small number of insurgents in January, February, and March of 1787 by justices in Worcester is
located in Folder 5, "Arrests and Trials of Several Insurgents, 1787," Shays's Rebellion
Collection, American Antiquarian Society. This material was apparently part of a larger body of
evidence brought before the Supreme Judicial Court at its special April 1787 session in
Worcester. A set of notes and lists taken down by Robert Treat Paine and others at this April
session is located in the "Box on Shays's Reblellion," Robert Treat Paine Papers, Massachusetts Historical Society. The indictments handed down at this session are located in the
Docket Books of the Supreme Judicial Court (Worcester Session), Clerk's Office, Suffolk
County Court House, No. 155325. In addition, Mass. Archives, Vol. 189, contains a considerable amount of useful material from the months following the April session, including a letter
about Josiah Walker of Sturbridge (pp. 163–6) and petitions from Caleb Curtis of Charlton (pp.
200, 237).
   The evidence on the Friends of Government is drawn predominantly from the Mass.
Archives. Muster rolls of the militia and volunteers raised to put down the rebellion are located
in MA 191:113, 113a, 157, 158, 175, 176, 180, 188, 211, 212, 220, 221, 275, 276, 285; and MA
192:1–3, 35, 37, 17, 69, 75–9, 128, 157, 161, 176, and 191. Unlike the insurgents, the militia
men are not identified by town, but each unit was generally drawn from a relatively small area of
between one and four towns. These muster rolls were compared with the 1790 U.S. Census to
link men with towns; names that did not appear in the census were located in the Vital Records.
[In general, the relative short period of settlement (40–50 years) meant that clusters of family

Rather, men with different kinds of debt obligations acted in very different ways. Debtors who sided with the government were more likely to be men owing large debts to creditors in the coastal metropolitan centers: Boston, Cambridge, Newport. Debtors joining the Regulation, like the Land Bankers in 1740, typically owed debts to men in adjacent towns, and these were relatively modest debts.[36] Among these adjacent towns, Worcester, Leicester, and Brookfield – old gentry centers on the Post Road – stand out as points of special negative reference. If a man owed a debt to a creditor in one of these gentry towns, there was better than a fifty-fifty chance that he would support the Regulation. If he owed a debt to a creditor in any of twelve other towns in the immediate area, there was only a one in

names did not predominate, as they did in the eastern towns, and thus the linking of various types of records is quite accurate.] Another important source for identifying Friends of Government is the list of ninety-six inhabitants who signed the Brookfield Protest against a pro-Regulator petition in January 1787, located in MA 190:313. Other sources for the Friends of Government in southwest Worcester County are "Dwight Foster Journal, 1772–1787," January 31–February 3, 1787, Foster Family Papers, vol. 1, AAS; "Ephraim Ward Diary, 1787," January entries, Misc. Mss., Box "W," AAS; Washburn, *Leicester*, 239–329; Emory Washburn, "Topographical and Historical Sketch of the Town of Leicester," *Worcester Magazine and Historical Journal*, 2 (1826), 116–19; Temple, *North Brookfield*, 245–6.

The evidence on debtors and creditors is drawn from the Records of the Worcester County Court of Common Pleas [RWCCP], vol. 13 (1785–6), 1–280, and the Files and Docket Books of the Supreme Judicial Court (Worcester Session), Clerk's Office, Suffolk Country Court House, April and September, 1786 sessions, Files 154708 to 155293.

[36] *Debtors and creditors from six towns, in WCCP and SJC, December 1785 to September 1786*

	Regulator		No evidence		Friend of government		Total	
	Number	%	Number	%	Number	%	Number	%
Total creditors	15	*18*	36	*44*	31	*38*	82	*100*
Total debtors	43	*32*	53	*39*	38	*28*	134	*100*
Debt[a] owed to creditor in								
Metropolitan center	8	*28*	6	*21*	15	*52*	29	*100*
Inland region[b]	6	*27*	9	*41*	7	*32*	22	*100*
Adjacent town	20	*38*	25	*48*	7	*13*	52	*100*
Within same town	9	*29*	13	*42*	9	*29*	31	*100*
x̄ indebtedness	£40.2		£41.9		£77.3		£46.8	
x̄ size of debts	£28.4		£32.2		£36.7		£34.1	

[a] In the cases where an individual debtor owed multiple debts, the largest debt is assumed to be dominant, and the location of that creditor is used in the table.

[b] Towns scattered throughout south-central New England that were neither adjacent nor important coastal "metropolitan" centers.

Source: See note 35.

five chance that he would turn out with the Regulators.[37] The Regulation was a political movement with clearly defined targets; these targets were *not* simply anonymous creditors and speculators living in distant urban centers, but merchants and gentry in the county's leading towns, well known to men who faced them in the county court.

Among these creditors were a few who might evoke memories of an earlier confrontation with the courts. Clark Chandler, son of Loyalist Justice John Chandler, and himself the register of probate under the crown, brought fifteen men into court for debt in the year before the 1786 court closings. Similarly, two of his cousins, Nathaniel and William Paine, sons of Loyalist Timothy Paine, had two other men in court. Nine of these seventeen debtors would join the Regulators. The threat from Loyalist creditors could also come from a distance, and indirectly. Thomas Brattle, acting as the administrator of the estate of William Brattle, a prominent Loyalist merchant formerly of Cambridge, had ten men in court in pursuit of debts that dated to before the Revolution. Thomas Brattle, and Clark Chandler's brother Nathaniel, were specifically named in one of the acts of Tory reinstatement that the northern towns opposed so vehemently. Brattle received writs of execution against Isaac Southgate of Leicester and Samuel Tucker of Spencer for debts dating to 1774 and 1770; both would be Regulators. Brattle was less successful in his case against retailer Samuel Hinckley and two other Brookfield men in a debt of £94 dating to 1771, and appealed his case to the Supreme Judicial Court. Apparently to cover his possible losses, Hinckley brought suits against four men in the Lamb and Muzzy families in neighboring Spencer for two debts totaling £96. Jonas Muzzy and Jonas Lamb would both turn out with the Regulators. There had been hints in 1774 that the economic crisis of 1772 and 1773 had raised the level of tension and anxiety; twelve years later debts that might have been collected in the fall of 1774 if the courts had not been closed added powerful political connotations to a new cycle of economic distress. Rather than being agents of British intrigues, as was argued among the Friends of Govern-

[37] *Men in debt to creditors in adjacent towns*

| | Debtor supported | | | | |
	Regulation		No evidence	Government	Total	
Debt to						
Creditor in Worcester						
Brookfield, Leicester	15	*55*	10	2	27	*100*
Creditor in any of						
twelve other towns	5	*20*	15	5	25	*100*

Note: Figures in italics are percentages.

ment, many Regulators could see themselves in Harringtonian terms, defending the people from the renewed efforts of the old Court party gentry to reduce them to "lordships" and "slavery."[38]

County constituencies and the Regulation

Debt did not translate directly into political mobilization in 1786; the Regulators responded not to simple debt but to particular relationships, to particular types of creditors. Between the impetus of economic stress and action against the courts lay a series of intervening circumstances: traditions and structures of political culture, class, and community.

An aggregate overview suggests how this mobilization was distributed across the county's different regions and cultures. (See Figure 3.) Support for or opposition to the Regulation can be roughly measured by the distribution of men indicted, arrested, and imprisoned by the state, constituting an index of Regulator leadership, and by the distribution of militia captains who turned out men for the government over these fall and winter months.[39] The nine towns in which Regulator leaders were unchallenged had a distinct profile. They were primarily located in the northwest uplands, typically small to middling orthodox towns, mostly districts before the Revolution, with little experience in the provincial General Court or the Revolutionary county convention. These were towns that voted against the 1781 Impost and the return of the Tories who had blanketed the General Court with petitions in recent years and whose citizens were particularly likely to have refused to pay the 1785 excise. These Regulator towns had no strong connections to the provincial Popular tradition or the Constitutionalist movement

---

[38] RWCCP 13: 76, 84, 116, 124, 128, 142, 148, 158, 170, 223–4, 263–8, 271. On Chandler and Paine see Wall, *Reminiscences of Worcester*, 70, 82–3; on the Brattles, see MA 154:48, 253, 332, 335; and Manuscript House Journal, 5:177–8.

[39] On the basis of the evidence on indicted and imprisoned Regulators, who provide a rough index of Regulator leadership, and the identifiable government militia commanders, I have divided the county's towns into four categories of response to the Regulation: Regulator towns with Regulator "leaders" but no militia officers, militia towns with militia officers only, conflicted towns with both, and all others. These categories are used in the analysis in Part III to assess the potential influence of Regulator sentiment in early national politics. By this measure, the nine core Regulator towns were Spencer, Princeton, Paxton, Hubbardston, Oakham, Barre, Ward, Templeton, and Harvard. The militia captains and colonels are from throughout MA 191 and 192. The 68 "Regulator Leaders" include men for whom warrants were issued, who were indicted, or who were imprisoned for activities in support of the Regulation. Sources: Warrants in MA 189:75–6, 81–4, 100–102, 135, 210; indictments in SJC File 155325 (initial list of twenty-one leaders); SJC Docket Book, 1787, 58–60, 63, 77–80, 101–2 (and Sept. session Worc. Co.); prisoners listed in Jail Register, Folder 1, Box 2, Worcester County, Mass., Papers, AAS; SJC File 155296-7.

of the 1770s; they had little background in religious dissent or the Land Bank, which had provided the vehicles, more and less explicitly, of provincial Lockean insurgencies.

There were, of course, exceptions to the rule. In Spencer, Land Banker Deacon Oliver Watson, now sixty-eight years old, represented the town in the 1784 convention and sat on the committee that called the 1786 county convention; two of his sons marched with the Regulators. But such direct links between the Land Bank and the Regulation were few and far between. The towns across the southern half of the county, large and middling towns with dissenting societies, and rioting towns were most likely to be conflicted during the Regulation. The Land Bank towns, the towns in the Blackstone region, and towns protesting the 1777 economic legislation – the broader environment of the old Popular tradition – were particularly likely to produce captains who would lead the government militia against the Regulators. These government men included the sons and grandsons of prominent Land Bankers and Popular partisans of the provincial era: Henry King in Leicester, Timothy Paige in Hardwick, Benjamin Goodrich in Lunenburg, Benjamin Read of Mendon, Timothy Bigelow of Worcester, and Jonathan Holman of Sutton. The old Popular leadership drew men from the neighborhoods to support the government. Men from the old Popular party town of Sutton, for example, served in at least three different government militia companies; roughly a fifth were from the Land Bank families of 1740. Although these men had acted in both convention and legislature to oppose the plans of the merchant interest, they were equally opposed to threats of civil violence by Regulators.[40]

The Regulation's center of gravity lay in the northwestern towns – like Adam Wheeler's Hubbardston – which had experience with neither the Popular tradition nor religious dissent. These were towns where a religious union – and moral economy – of town and orthodox parish remained the central focus of local identity. They were also towns that had been dominated by the great Court party gentry in the late provincial period, men like Timothy Ruggles and John Murray. The political experience of men in these towns was quite limited; they had not been exposed to the give and take of local disputes between the orthodox and dissenting societies, and they had little direct experience with the complex politics of opposition that had characterized other areas of the county, particularly the southeast, in the provincial period. Broadly, their circumstances were quite similar to those in Hampshire county to the west, the epicenter of the rebellion.[41] The Regulation, the armed stopping of the courts, was thus in part the result of a vacuum of political leadership and experience in the old Court party regions; the

[40] Militia commanders from throughout MA 191 and 192; Lincoln *Worcester*, 266–7; Benedict and Tracy, *Sutton*, 785, and genealogies. At least a hundred Sutton men served in the government militia in John Holland's Company (MA 191:269), John Blanchard's Company (MA 191:105), and Sylvanus Town's Company (MA 192:158).
[41] The similarities between Hampshire County in general and Worcester County's northwest towns in particular are discussed in Brooke, "To the Quiet of the People."

relative quiet in the other regions was in no small measure a result of the highly developed relationship between leadership and constituency that had developed over a half-century of experience in the Popular tradition. But the Regulation was also rooted in a strong sense of mutual obligation, of moral economy, fostered within the smaller orthodox communities, in a powerful commitment to the Harringtonian equation of private property and public good that lay at the base of the commonwealth ideal.

Gentry and yeoman; orthodoxy and dissent

The dynamics of class, community, and worldview at work in the Regulation can be most clearly understood through what Charles Tilly calls "a census of the rebellion": a collective biography of hundreds of individuals from a discrete locality participating in the confrontations of 1786 and 1787. This locality is comprised of the six contiguous towns discussed above, at the intersection of the northwest, the southwest, and the upper end of the Blackstone. Two of these, Oakham and Spencer, were among the county's nine core Regulator towns, while the other four, Leicester, Charlton, Sturbridge, and Brookfield, were among the fifteen conflicted towns. Almost six hundred men, more than 20 percent of the ratable polls in these six towns, marched with the Regulators and the government militia in 1786. Paradoxically, in their central tendencies, support for both the Regulators and the government was rooted in interrelated forms of corporate obligation and hierarchical deference that were still powerful among the orthodox, and decidedly absent among the dissenters. Within particular orthodox communities, political action transcended lines of class and interest to unite the people behind local leaders either for or against the court closings. By contrast, the radically simplified dissenting communions were splintered by this political action, with minorities of notables acting to support the government, minorities of hard-pressed debtors joining the Regulation, and the majority withholding support from either side.[42]

Three towns located in the northwest and lacking organized dissenting societies – Oakham, Spencer, and Brookfield – stood out at the two extremes of political action in 1786. Spencer and Oakham, small towns incorporated from subordinate districts in 1775, had neither dissenting societies nor a substantial gentry class; their town selectmen were men of local reputation, at best Congregational deacons or innholders. Well-organized companies of Regulators marched from these towns to close the courts, and none of the local militia captains even attempted to raise companies for the government. With roughly 19 percent of the population in the six towns considered here, Oakham and Spencer accounted for 40 percent of the

---

[42] Charles Tilly, *The Vendee*, 2d ed. (Cambridge, Mass., 1976), 323ff. For sources for the following, see above, note 35.

Regulators and less than 3 percent of the Friends of Government. Brookfield, the second largest town in the county and long a center of gentry influence, mustered no fewer than five companies of government militia and gentleman volunteers. Encompassing 29 percent of the population in these six towns, Brookfield accounted for only 18 percent of the Regulators and 57 percent of the government militia. (See Table 2.)

Behind these sharply different figures lay both the articulation and denial of class interests. The Brookfield gentry, along with a group of Worcester merchants and to a lesser extent the gentry in the pluralist towns, occupied the position of the commercial intermediary. Men with debts to merchants in Cambridge and Boston were overwhelmingly Friends of Government (6/9), as were the creditors of debtors who lived within the town or in adjacent towns (15/24). But Brookfield also stood out as the only location where debtors owing money to creditors within a given town also served with the government militia in significant numbers (7/15); in almost all other contexts such debtors remained neutral or supported the Regulation. Roughly two-thirds of the progovernment militia in Brookfield were church members or their close relations. As would be the case under the Federalists in the following decades, the structures of the orthodox church, supported by an active ministry and a few progovernment deacons, apparently worked to reinforce class relations of deference in this gentry-dominated town.[43]

The smaller orthodox yeoman towns of Spencer and Oakham present a very different picture. Roughly two-thirds of all relations of debt and credit were with men in adjacent towns, rather than with local and metropolitan partners, and 62 percent of the debtors were represented among the Regulators, as against 20–25 percent of the debtors in all other circumstances. In sharp opposition to the gentry town, none of the debtors served with the government militia and – most importantly – five of the ten creditors supported the Regulation.

Among these creditor-Regulators were several who might be called Regulator notables, men who seem to have been acting on altruistic motives, on a sense of obligation to the corporate locality that transcended individual private interest. One of the these was Deacon Oliver Watson of Spencer, who appeared in Supreme Judicial Court as a lay attorney for several of his neighbors when they appealed cases of debt, so that they might avoid an obligation to the court's phalanx of attending lawyers. In June of 1786 he allowed his case against Benjamin Bemiss to be continued, and served on the committee that called the county convention at which Bemiss served as a delegate from Spencer. Two of Watson's householding sons, one a selectman in 1786, would serve in the ranks of the Regulators, as would

[43] On deference in the Federalist era, see James M. Banner, *Toward the Hartford Convention: Federalists and the Origins of Party Politics in Massachusetts, 1789–1815* (New York, 1970); David H. Fischer, *The Revolution of American Conservatism: The Federalist Party in the Era of Jeffersonian Democracy* (New York, 1965), 211ff.; and esp. Ronald P. Formisano, *The Transformation of Political Culture: Massachusetts Parties, 1790–1840s* (New York, 1983), 128ff.

Table 2. *Regulators, Friends of Government, debt, and credit in six Worcester County towns, December, 1785–February, 1787*

	Non-dissenters in an orthodox gentry town	Non-dissenters in plural towns	All dissenters	Non-dissenters in two small orthodox towns	Total
Population, 1790	2,852	2,880	2,339	1,879	9,950
Percentage of total	*29*	*29*	*23*	*19*	*100*
All Regulators	47	56	53	108	264
Percentage of total	*18*	*21*	*20*	*41*	*100*
All Friends of Government	189	89	45	8	331
Percentage of total	*57*	*27*	*14*	*2*	*100*
All debtors	35	32	30	37	134
Percentage of total	*26*	*24*	*22*	*28*	*100*
All creditors	36	21	15	10	82
Percentage of total	*50*	*26*	*18*	*12*	*100*
Regulators from 1st qu. hh[a]	12	12	8	34	66
Percentage of all Regulators	*25*	*21*	*15*	*31*	*25*
Fr govt from 1st qu. hh	65	42	24	3	134
Percentage of all Friends of Govt	*34*	*47*	*53*	*37*	*40*
Regulators among debtors	6	7	7	23	43
Percentage of all debtors	*17*	*22*	*23*	*62*	*32*
Fr govt among debtors	18	14	6	0	38
Percentage of all debtors	*51*	*44*	*20*	*0*	*28*
Regulators among creditors	1	3	6	5	15
Percentage of all creditors	*3*	*14*	*40*	*50*	*18*
Fr govt among creditors	23	5	2	0	30
Percentage of all creditors	*64*	*24*	*13*	*0*	*37*

Categories: Orthodox Gentry town: Brookfield. Pluralist towns: Charlton, Leicester, and Sturbridge. All dissenters: all individuals who can be linked with dissenting societies or by kinship to the broader dissenting orbit. Small orthodox towns: Spencer and Oakham. *Note:* Spencer and Oakham are included in the nine "Regulator" towns in Table 3 and the subsequent tables, having no resident government militia officers. The other four towns all fall into the "conflicted" category, having both resident "Regulator leaders" and government militia officers.
Percentages are in *italics*.
[a] "From 1st qu. hh": individuals from first-quintile households, including heads of households, nontaxpaying sons, and sons in 9th and 10th deciles.
Source: 1783 Tax Valuation and sources listed in Chapter, note 36.

a young son of Benjamin Bemiss. In Oakham there were three selectman in this group of creditor-Regulators. One, innholder Richard Kelly, was in court as a plaintiff in five different cases in the year before the Regulation, but signed an oath of allegiance the next spring. Another Oakham creditor, selectman Ebenezer Nye, "acted in the capacity" of a captain for the Regulator company that marched from Oakham, and his son Timothy signed an oath as well. A third, innholder Joseph Chaddock, the town's delegate to the 1786 convention, was accused of being "very busy in Encouraging" the Regulators, and of giving them the town's store of ammunition. In total, five creditor-Regulators in Spencer and Oakham were owed £176 in ten different debts, and only one of them was a defendant in one case amounting to £14. It would have been in their immediate interest to keep the courts open in September 1786, yet the focus of collective obligation within these communities impelled them into the dangers of the Regulator movement. In sum, eight of the ten sitting selectmen in Oakham and Spencer supported the Regulators. More generally, the Regulation was supported by a large group of men from households in the top quintile of the valuation, the traditional source of town leadership. While the Congregational ministers in both Oakham and Spencer probably opposed the Regulators, five of the seven deacons serving in the 1770s and 1780s were Regulator supporters, and a sixth was moderator of the Oakham town meeting throughout the period, a sign of some popularity in an overwhelmingly Shaysite town. Where, in gentry-dominated Brookfield, orthodoxy seems to have reinforced deference to the interests of the creditor-gentry, such moral unity in the smaller orthodox towns worked to equate the elders' traditional obligation to the corporate community with the interests of the debtors.[44]

The dissenters, and Congregationalists in three pluralist, voluntary towns in the southern half of the county – all three contested by Regulator and progovernment notables – present a quite different pattern. Here there is something of a paradox. The economic interests of debt and credit so evident in the orthodox towns seem to have been of relatively little importance in determining the loyalties of dissenters and their orthodox neighbors in the pluralistic towns of Sturbridge, Charlton, and Leicester, yet support for the government or the Regulation was more sharply divided along class lines. Among both dissenters and the Congregationalists in these voluntary towns only a fifth of the debtors appearing in Common Pleas in the previous year were drawn into the Regulation, as against almost two-thirds of the debtors in the orthodox yeoman towns. Again, only a fifth of the creditors supported the government, as against almost two-thirds of the creditors in the orthodox gentry town of Brookfield. The Regulators' threat to contract apparently was not particularly important to these dissenting creditors, and

[44] Draper, History of Spencer, 62; SJC Files 155016, 155133, 155148; RWCCP, 13:62, 67, 76, 127, 175, 191, 200, 217, 223, 240, 259, 268, 273; Oakham Evidence, RTPP, MHS; MA 190, 107, 165–6; Henry B. Wright and Edwin D. Harvey, The Settlement and History of Oakham, Massachusetts (New Haven, 1947), 285.

conversely, something was working to impede the mobilization of dissenting debtors behind the Regulation. At the same time, there was far less support for Regulation among the wealthiest fifth of the population – the traditional stratum of town leadership – than in the small orthodox towns.[45] Conversely, there was far less support for the government here among the poorer four-fifths of the population than there was in the gentry town of Brookfield. Where the virtual civil war of 1786 united the orthodox towns on one side or the other, the dissenting communities and the orthodox in the pluralistic towns were splintered and divided along class lines.

Whereas support for the Regulation flowed from the core of the small orthodox towns, it was to be found only on the periphery of the dissenting societies. Among the Baptists and Universalists, recruits for the government militia and light horse were drawn from the elite, over half from the top fifth of the valuation. In contrast to the orthodox deacons, none of the six Baptist deacons in Leicester, Charlton, or Sturbridge were linked in any way with the insurrection. Rather, two of them were close kin to members of the government militia raised to put down the Regulation; in Charlton, Deacon Daniel Bacon's son Asa marched with the Oxford militia company in January and February of 1787, and in Sturbridge Deacon Henry Fisk, Jr.'s brother and cousin served in the local troop of Col. Ebenezer Crafts's regiment of cavalry.

If they were not motivated by immediate concerns of debts owed, some of these men may have been drawn to the government simply by a calculation of advantage to be gained in the new government; several Baptists were appointed to positions in the county civil list early in the 1790s, in some cases men who had served in the government militia. Stephen Burroughs left a sarcastic description of one such man, tanner Israel Waters of Charlton. Failing in his "electioneering" to become either captain or lieutenant of the Charlton militia company, Waters joined Ebenezer Crafts's regiment of light horse. "Having been disappointed in all his efforts to become a man of consequence in that society to which his restless ambition had led him, he expected that he had now discovered the only sure road to preferment, viz. by making himself so strong a stickler for government, that he would be taken notice of, and promoted.[46]

Some of the government militia in the pluralist towns were simply ambitious men; others were acting on a sincere commitment to constitutional government. The dissenters had taken the lead in the drive for a popularly written and ratified constitution, and in the voluntary towns they had begun to arrive at mutually

[45] On stratification and town officeholding, see Edward M. Cook, *The Fathers of the Towns: Leadership and Community Structure in Eighteenth Century New England* (Baltimore, 1976), 80–4; Brooke, "Society, Revolution . . .," 554. In four Worcester County towns, first-quintile men served 80% of the selectmen's terms between 1774 and 1783.

[46] Stephen Burroughs, *Memoirs of the Notorious Stephan Burroughs of New Hampshire* (New York, 1924, repr. of 1811 Albany edition), 193. For Waters's militia service, see MA 192:191.

agreeable local compromises with the Congregational gentry, which mitigated the more coercive aspects of the new constitution. In contrast, the orthodox towns in the northwest, where the Regulation was the strongest, had been noticeably backward in their support for the Constitutionalist movement, and the dissenter elite may have seen a parallel between corporatist coercion of ministerial rates and the Regulator's public action against the courts. Of the twelve dissenters in Sturbridge, Charlton, and Leicester who had served on committees expressly concerned with the constitution, six were themselves – or were close kin to – Friends of Government, whereas only two were kin to Regulators. Similarly, the trustees of the Leicester Academy supported the government almost to a man. The academy's founders Timothy Newell and Ebenezer Crafts both raised regiments of government militia in the voluntary towns to suppress the Regulators. And the majority of the selectmen joined the government militia or sent their sons. In Charlton, one selectman elected in 1786 in at least two of these voluntary towns were firmly in the government camp. In Sturbridge, four of five sitting selectmen joined the government militia or sent their sons. In Charlton, one selectman elected in 1786 was a Regulator, and the other four were from progovernment families.[47]

However, unlike the orthodox creditor gentry in Brookfield, these leading men from the voluntary towns, whether Constitutionalists or simply ambitious men on the make, were unable to command the deference of the poorer households in their communities. Similarly, unlike the deacons, selectmen, and innholders in the small, orthodox towns, they felt no particular moral obligation to lead those lesser men against the government. Vertical reciprocal ties of deference and obligation had been dramatically eroded in those places and communities where the new voluntary and pluralistic order had begun to take shape. The result was sharp divisions along class lines within these conflicted communities, and lower rates of participation on either side of the confrontation, as progovernment notables had few followers, and potential Regulators had few leaders.

The few debtors in the Baptist orbit who did join the Regulation seem particularly exposed and isolated. They were distinctly poorer than other dissenting debtors who remained neutral, and although their total indebtedness was equivalent, they were burdened with roughly twice as many individual debts. They were also typically on the periphery of the Baptist communion, having failed to renew subscriptions for society expenses or being affiliated only by family ties. Although a number of Baptist and Universalist notables had stood as sureties for debtors in the Supreme Judicial Court, unlike their counterparts in the smaller orthodox towns they rarely supported the Regulation. For example, innholder Samuel Richardson, Jr., of Leicester, affiliated with the Leicester Baptists in 1779

[47] Leicester General Records, 2:207, 268–9; Washburn, *Leicester*, 239, 351: Sturbridge Town Records, 2:293: Charlton, Mass., Town Records, typed selectmen's list; Handlin and Handlin, eds., *Popular Sources*, 815–20.

but not thereafter, was in court for a total of seven debts totaling £53. Four men had stood as sureties for Richardson over the previous year. Asa Sprague, a debtor from a Baptist orbit family, was the only Regulator in the group. John Brown of Leicester remained neutral, but Charlton Baptist Edward Wheelock served with the light horse, as did several brothers of the prominent Charlton Universalist Ebenezer Davis. Unlike their counterparts in the small orthodox towns, dissenting debtors found that customary intervention and arbitration by community notables was not translated into leadership for the public regulation of the courts.[48]

The "happiness of Individuals," or "Unanimity" in "this Commonwealth"

In one highly suggestive instance, dissenters joining the Regulation drew upon the extracorporate, voluntary tradition as a frame of organization. The only violent incident in the course of the insurgency in Worcester County occurred on February 2, 1787, when Regulators encamped at New Braintree fired on a party

[48] SJC File 155058; RWCCP 13:33, 191, 238, 240, 254, 271; militia lists, Regulator data (see note 35), and Ammidown, *Historical Collections*, 2: 176–9; Records of the Greenville Baptist Church, vol. 1; The Second Religious Society in Oxford . . . (called Universalist), Record Book, 1785–1845.

Values of debts and total indebtedness among all dissenters and the inhabitants of small orthodox towns

	Regulator	No evidence	Friend of Government	Total
Oakham/Spencer (all nondissenters)[a]				
Debtors	23	14	0	37
Percentage in wealthiest quintile	*39*	*29*		*35*
x̄ debt	£22.9	£23.7		£22.8
x̄ indebtedness	£29.9	£36		£31.4
Dissenters				
Debtors	7	16	6	29
Percentage in wealthiest quintile	*0*	*41*	*50*	*34*
x̄ Debt	£20	£42.9	£59	£34.6
x̄ indebtedness	£51	£48.9	£73.7	47.7

[a] There were no dissenting societies in these two towns, but a few Baptists living in Spencer were affiliated with societies in Charlton and Leicester. They are included in the "dissenter" category.

Source: See note 35.

of government men sent from Worcester, wounding two of them. One of the objectives of the government party had been to free Samuel Flagg and John Stanton of Worcester, who had been captured by a party of insurgents, including Asa Sprague, when they had attempted to serve a writ of execution against Isaac Southgate, the son of a Baptist elder in Leicester. The thirteen men connected by subsequent testimony to this affair were drawn broadly from the dissenting orbit and from towns in the southern half of the county that were the scene of rioting between 1781 and 1783. Three were Universalists from Oxford and Ward, at least five were from Baptist families, two were from the Blackstone Valley town of Uxbridge, and two – Reubin Lamb of Oxford and Oliver Witt of Paxton – had been involved in the rioting of the early 1780s. These men appear to have been acting in accordance with an agreement drawn up in Leicester sometime in 1786, pledging to resist writs of execution and urging the "good People of this County" to defend "each individual among the Subscribers who may be injured" in holding to those articles. In effect, the subscribers had established a private debtors' society, based on voluntary principles, in a form and social context that had direct antecedents in the small-scale rioting of 1781–3.[49]

The boundary between these voluntary assumptions and the corporate orthodoxy of the Regulator majority were not totally impermeable. On September 22, 1786, the Leicester articles of agreement were adopted at a public meeting in Hubbardston of people from a number of northwestern towns. Similarly, Adam Wheeler, one of the committeemen at this meeting, wrote the following November of having "Stepped forth in a private Capacity with others to oppose the Setting of the Court of Common Pleas and Gen[era]l Sessions of the Peace." Wheeler's notice of his "private Capacity" suggests a certain uneasiness about the legitimacy of the Regulation. But this was a sole and fleeting reference; the language of the Regulation was otherwise unanimous in its appeal to the corporate tradition. The Regulators led by Wheeler on September 6 were certain that they acted in the "good of the Commonwealth"; on three occasions in a single document they denoted themselves a "Body of People" in the corporate tradition. If the Regulator meeting in Hubbardston on September 22 accepted the Leicester articles, the presiding committee hastened to inform "the People at large" that their aim in the court closings was to "relieve the distresses of their fellow citizens until a redress of grievances could be obtained ... and not as has been injuriously reported to subvert all Government, and throw all things into a state of Anarchy and confusion." The Regulators were acting on a sense of public purpose, not private interest.[50]

[49] Testimony against Asa Sprague, Folder 5, SRC, AAS; New Braintree evidence, Box 23, RTPP, MHS; John Noble, *A Few Notes on the Shays's Rebellion* (Worcester, 1903), 16–25; Leicester Articles of Agreement, MA 318:20 (152 in light pencil).

[50] Hubbardston resolves, MA 318:20 (151 in light pencil); Adam Wheeler's Statement, Hubbardston, November 7, 1786, Folder 1, SRC, AAS; Regulator request to the Court of Common Pleas, September 6, 1786, in Paige, *Hardwick*, 127–8.

Such classical, corporate language suffused a petition sent from Brookfield after a town meeting in late December, controlled by men sympathetic to the Regulation. Noting the threat to "mutual love, peace and good order" posed by the session of the Court of Common Pleas planned for the following January, the town asked that the court be adjourned, habeas corpus be restored, and the imprisoned Regulators be freed. The petition, couched in the traditional form and duly signed by the town clerk, closed with an invocation of the values of the peaceable kingdom, trusting the governor and General Court would act wisely to resolve "the unhappy Divisions among us so that Peace Liberty and Unanimity may be restored Throughout this Commonwealth." In response, a group of ninety-six Friends of Government protested the towns' corporate petition in a form that anticipated those submitted by partisan interests throughout the first half of the next century. Rather than acting as a corporate body, the Brookfield Friends of Government signed as individuals, and they closed their protest with significantly different language. Avoiding an appeal to unanimity and common-wealth, the Brookfield protesters were certain that the General Court was "disposed to adopt every Measure which upon the most serious consideration shall be esteemed salutary to the Government and be promotive of the Peace and happiness of Individuals." While Regulators clung to classical, corporate lan-guage, envisioning the relationship between government and people in terms not unlike that of the mixed polity, the progovernment forces were immersed in – or, as in this case, quickly adopted – the forms and language of Lockean voluntarism.[51]

Hints and suggestions of a political worldview still shaped by the pre-Revolutionary traditions of the mixed polity echoed through subsequent petitions sent from the Regulator towns, as the people attempted to gain a pardon for the Regulators still holding out in the cold midwinter months of 1787. Inverting Capt. Thomas Whipple's exhortation that the people must "put out the present rulers," the town of Ware in the eastern hills of Hampshire County presented a petition in the hope "that Peace & tranquility will be Restored to this commonwealth & that unity and concord will again abound between rulers & ruled and our land become an assilum of Peace." New Braintree wrote in the hope that "you and all our Rulers may be inspired with Heavenly Wisdom," and instructed the court "to mind what the wise man Tells us of a little City and few people therein Beseiged by a great King, but Delivered by a Certain Poor Man." New Braintree, Ward, and Brookfield all spoke of the people as the "subjects" of the state; Ware went so far as to say that "your petitioner do apprehend that the People will Consider themselves as Royal Subjects Peacably Demeaning themselves as such Patiently hoping for a constitutional Relief from the burdens that do subsist."[52]

[51] Brookfield Petition, December 25, 1786, MA 190:298; Brookfield Protest, January, 1787, MA 190:311–13; Zuckerman, *Peaceable Kingdoms*.

[52] Ware Petition January, 15, 1787; New Braintree Petitions, January 1, February 5, 1787; Ward Petition, January 29, 1787; all in Folder 1, SRC, AAS; Brookfield Petition, December 25, 1786, MA 190:298.

These formulas, as much as the limited civil violence of the Regulation, spoke of a former age, of the language and politics of a guarded deference and corporate obligation that had shaped the provincial world. Again, it is critical that such language and action emerged from the northwestern towns in particular, towns whose only previous claim to political drama had been the expulsion of the Court party magnates who had so dominated their lives in the decades before 1774. The lack of continuity between the Constitutionalist agitation of the 1770s and the Regulation of 1786 cannot be overemphasized; the two were based in different regions and among peoples with radically different worldviews, one Lockean and liberal, the other classical and corporate. Unitary, classical assumptions were powerfully persistent in these small, isolated orthodox towns of the northwest. Without commitments to the abstractions of the Lockean constitutional process, local leading men saw the particularities of their neighbors' distress. Without extensive experience in the institutional politics of the Popular tradition, they acted on very traditional assumptions to regulate the relationship between the rulers and the ruled.

"A dread of arbitrary power": Antifederalism and the Popular tradition

If the corporate petitions of the winter of 1787 bore connotations of the mixed polity, the county convention urged a return to constitutional politics. The prescription for a constitutional redress of grievances had been set forth in the "Address to the People" published by the county convention in November 1786: let "every town in future send Representatives to the General Court, and let every voter attend his duty." The results of the state elections in the years just prior to the Regulation clearly indicated that neither towns nor voters had attended their duties. Many towns had regularly neglected to send a representative, and increasingly those that were elected failed to appear at critical legislative roll calls. The vote for governor, open to practically all males over the age of twenty-one, provided a revealing indication of the voters' failure to "attend their duties." After 24 percent of the potential electorate in Worcester County turned out to vote John Hancock into the governor's chair in 1780, participation declined during the 1780s, reaching a low point of about 13 percent in 1785 and 1786. The result of voter apathy was particularly apparent in 1786, when the majority stayed away from the polls and a tiny, commercially oriented minority elected James Bowdoin governor in a lopsided election.[53]

---

[53] "Address of the Convention of the County of Worcester to the People," *Worcester Magazine* 2 (1786), 405. All votes here and below are from "Returns of Votes for Governor," in the Massachusetts Archives. Assuming that J. R. Pole and James L. Banner are correct on the extent of electoral suffrage, the "estimated electorate" was calculated to include most males

But things were dramatically different in the spring of 1787. The Bowdoin government and the General Court had passed highly repressive legislation in February, disenfranchising the hundreds of Regulators, and barring them from public office, even from keeping school or tavern, until 1788. These measures, the march of Lincoln's army, and the suspension of habeas corpus the preceding November, raised fears throughout the state of a tyrannical conspiracy to subvert the constitution and the electoral process. Moderate men throughout the commonwealth saw a far greater threat to the constitution in the government's repression than in the Regulators' limited civil violence, and they surged to the polls in April 1787.[54]

This election has rightly been called "the revolution of 1787." Voter turnout surged to 40 percent at the county level, as Bowdoin was thrown out and Hancock reelected. Even though the Regulators had been disenfranchised by the General Court in February, at least nine Worcester County towns sent accused Regulators as representatives, many others sent known sympathizers, and few if any sent open Friends of Government. The new government that convened in Boston would bring a moderation of the harsh policies of the previous winter, but not a redress of all the grievances protested in the court closings of the previous fall. The General Court did not pardon all the Regulators, nor did it establish paper money or abolish the Court of Common Pleas. But the court did repeal aspects of the Disqualifying Act, and it continued legislation suspending suits of debt, and it failed to pass any new direct taxes. With almost every town represented and every representative voting, the county delegation followed its long tradition of overwhelming opposition, driven by a rising antipathy toward the government's actions. Where the rest of the state voted by more that 60 percent for a modified Disqualifying Act, almost 90 percent of the Worcester representatives held out for a total repeal. Almost as large a majority joined the rest of the state to suspend civil proceedings for debt.[55]

The county's united stance in the summer of 1787 was rooted in the reemergence of the old Popular coalition, which had stood back from the Regulation. In particular, the town of Sutton returned to its leading place, when

over the age of twenty-one by using a total of 80% of the enumerated polls reported in each census. This estimated electorate was calculated for twelve towns and for the county in each census year, and extrapolated for each noncensus year. The results for the county are listed in Appendix 1. See J. R. Pole, "Suffrage and Representation in Massachusetts: A Statistical Note," *WMQ*, 3d ser., 14 (1957), 560–85, and Pole, "Letter to the Editor,' *WMQ*, 3d ser., 15 (1958), 412–16; and James M. Banner, *Toward the Hartford Convention: The Federalists and the Origins of Party Politics in Massachusetts, 1789–1815* (New York, 1970), 10–11, 267–70.

[54] Taylor, *Western Massachusetts*, 164–6; Hall, *Politics without Parties*, 229–32; Richard D. Brown, "Shays's Rebellion and Its Aftermath: A View from Springfield, Massachusetts, 1787," *WMQ*, 3d ser., 40 (1983), 598–615.

[55] Hall, *Politics without Parties*, 227–55, esp. 249–50; Taylor, *Western Massachusetts*, 166; Pole, *Representation*, 240.

Amos Singletary, the towns' representative throughout the 1770s and early 1780s, was elected to sit for the county in the senate for the first of four terms. Sutton had taken a moderate stance during the Regulation. The town contributed few to the Regulators, these mostly from the North Parish, and Sutton men marched in ranks of at least three different government militia companies in the deep winter of 1787. But most importantly, the town threw its weight behind efforts to mediate between the two opposing parties. The town's delegates to the September Paxton convention were instructed to "use their influence to prevent any rising of the people in riotous manner, but to persevere in petitioning" for a redress of grievances. In December and January the town appointed several committees to mediate between the Regulators and both the Court of Common Pleas and Gen. Benjamin Lincoln, who was leading the government's army into the county. Sutton, as well as four other old Land Bank towns that had hung back from the Regulation, also petitioned the governor in January not to send an army against the insurgents. On January 22, Amos Singletary and a number of leading men from Sutton met with the Regulator committeemen and officers at Moses Clark's tavern in Hubbardston in an effort to persuade them to lay down their arms. The following May this committee and others from Sutton who had served with the militia joined in petitioning the governor for a pardon for Henry Gale of Princeton, under sentence of death for treason. So, too, Rufus Putnam's celebrated interview with Daniel Shays was another manifestation of Popular mediation. Putnam was the orphaned son of Elisha Putnam of Sutton, a deacon in David Hall's New Light orthodox church, a Land Banker, and Sutton's representative to the General Court in the tense 1740 and 1741 sessions. And the opening drama of the Regulation in Worcester, Artemas Ward's two-hour address to the assembled Regulators, must also be viewed in the light of the county's political culture. The Regulators' patience with Ward, a stalwart of the provincial Popular party, rested in the long-established relationship between the Popular men and a county constituency.[56]

Their efforts at reconciliation laid the groundwork for the return of Popular men to county leadership. That March, the old Land Bank town of Lunenburg had called a convention to propose a slate of candidates for the state senate, in the manner of the party conventions that emerged in subsequent decades. Even though this meeting was condemned for attempting to exert an "unconstitutional" influence on the election, Amos Singletary of Sutton and Jonathan Grout of Petersham were elected to the senate. Grout, born in Lunenburg, had been active in the conventions and was denied his seat by the governor, but he would be reelected the following year. When Samuel Curtis of Worcester resigned from the senate, his place was taken by John Fessenden of Rutland, another convention

[56] Benedict and Tracy, *Sutton*, 124–7; Feer, *Shays Rebellion*, 342–3n; Petitions for Henry Gale, MA 189:401–2. Putnam's visit with Shays is discussed in Szatmary, *Shays's Rebellion*, 99. For Putnam's family, see Benedict and Tracy, *Sutton*, 706; and Temple, *North Brookfield*, 715.

leader who had attempted to block the marching of Lincoln's army. Sympathetic to their grievances, yet opposed to the Regulators' forceable action, men of the Popular tradition attempted to mediate between the opposing forces, and in 1787 again took up a leading role in county politics.[57]

In the same summer of 1787, a convention of delegates met far to the south in Philadelphia to amend the Articles of Confederation. These gentlemen were very much concerned with what they saw as the specter of anarchy in the Regulator movement in Massachusetts. The product of their deliberations would be a new frame of national government, the federal Constitution, assigning specific powers to particular branches of a national government, on the authority of a sovereign people, whose consent would be determined in state ratifying conventions. The prospect of a battle over ratification had moderated the most hierarchical schemes proposed in the convention in Philadelphia, but many, probably the majority of Americans, were suspicious of the intentions of the constitutional convention. The new constitution faced a stiff fight before it would be ratified.[58]

Nowhere was the ratification of the Federal Constitution more in doubt than in Massachusetts. Support for a stronger central government had been thin and weak before the rebellion; the events of 1786–7 converted many to the cause, afraid of an excess of democracy and hoping for a federal assumption of state debts. But supporters of the new federal Constitution were in a decided minority when the ratifying convention met in Boston on January 9, 1788. By one estimate, the Antifederalists opposing ratification had a lead of roughly 40 delegates out of the total body of 355. Following a half-century-old tradition, the 50 Worcester County delegates were the most united in opposing the new constitution. Edward Bangs, a lawyer recently settled in Worcester who served as a volunteer against the Regulators, wrote to an acquaintance on January 1, 1788, that "most of them entertain such a dread of arbitary power, that they are afraid even of limited authority." Accurately calculating that only 7 or 8 of the 50 would support the constitution, he hastened to add that "some of them are good men – Not all insurgents I assure you." Bangs was right on both counts. The Worcester delegation included at least nine Regulators, but it also numbered members of the various conventions that had met in the previous decade. And as he predicted, it cast forty-three of its fifty votes against the constitution, by far the largest bloc of Antifederalist votes in any county in the state.[59]

[57] *Worcester Magazine*, 2 (1787), 628; Hall, *Politics without Parties*, 224–5, 248–9.
[58] For recent assessments of the origins of the Federal Constitution, see Alfred Young, "Conservatives, the Constitution, and the 'Spirit of Accommodation,'" in Robert A. Goldwin and William A. Schambra, eds., *How Democratic Is the Constitution* (Washington, D.C., 1980), 117–47, and the essays in Richard Beeman, Stephen Botein, and Edward Carter II, eds., *Beyond Confederation: Origins of the Constitution and American National Identity* (Chapel Hill, 1987).
[59] Lincoln, *Worcester*, 148–9; Samuel B. Harding, *The Contest over the Ratification of Federal Constitution in the State of Massachusetts* (New York, 1896), 74.

Some of the most forceful Antifederalist speakers at the convention were members of the Worcester County delegation, including John Taylor of Douglas, Martin Kinsley of Hardwick, and Amos Singletary of Sutton. Taylor rose repeatedly to criticize the lack of annual elections, the small size of the house of representatives, and the federal control of the voting process as means by which men in a new central government would act beyond the control of the people. He also complained about the lack of a bill of rights and the federal government's powers to suspend habeas corpus, issues that were of explosive importance given the events of the spring of 1787. Martin Kinsley, a member of the 1786 county convention, complained of a "power to establish . . . a Federal town of ten miles square, equal to four middling townships," a territorial base from which the "Federal rulers" could despoil the countryside of taxes with standing armies. And in his most famous speech, perhaps the most famous passage in the entire Antifederalist literature, Amos Singletary rose to speak of the issue of taxation as one of "those who had stood forth in 1775." Singletary saw a profound threat to household property in the taxing powers granted by the Constitution. The Federalists were promising that there would be no "dry taxes," but Singletary was sure that the new government would never "be able to raise enough money by impost, and then they will lay it on the land and take all that we have got." From his concern about taxation, Singletary moved directly into the diffuse yet problematic issue of social power that lay behind the Antifederalists' fears.

> These lawyers, and men of learning, and moneyed men that talk so finely, and gloss over matters so smoothly, to make us poor illiterate people, swallow down the pill, expect to get into Congress themselves; they expect to be managers of this Constitution, and get all the power and all the money into their own hands, and then they will swallow up all us little folks, like the great leviathan, Mr. President; yes, just as the whale swallowed Jonah.[60]

Singletary, the quintessential "man of little faith," spoke in language molded by a lifetime in the Worcester Popular tradition. He had lived his life in Sutton, Land Bank center, Popular Party stronghold, and the storm center of convention politic. Singletary had a long experience in the service of his town and county. He represented Sutton in the Revolutionary conventions, and was appointed justice of the peace in 1775. Although he never served as a delegate to the economic conventions, he represented Sutton in the General Court, voting to uphold legal tender and oppose the direct tax. As justice of the peace, he would take confessions of debt without a fee, and he served on a committee that condemned conditions in the county jails in 1785. As an elder of the orthodox church in the North Parish,

[60] Bradford K. Pierce et al., eds. *Debates and Proceedings of the Convention of the Commonwealth of Massachusetts Held in the Year 1788* (Boston, 1856), 118, 134, 147, 149, 151, 161, 189, 202–3, 209, 265; Richard Brown, "Shays's Rebellion and the Ratification of the Federal Constitution in Massachusetts," in Beeman, et all., eds. *Beyond Confederation*.

Singletary stood on the corporate side of the Popular tradition. An anecdote told of him speaks of a stern commitment to the ethic of a moral economy. Sometime in the 1790s Singletary was accosted by Baptist Samuel Waters, a blacksmith in the North Parish, who rushed from his shop, calling out, "O Squire! O Squire! what shall I do to be saved?" Singletary is said to have replied "Put more steel in your hoes."[61]

Such was the experience that shaped Amos Singletary's concerns about the constitution. Singletary's language reflected decades of political struggle between the Court party elite and the Popular men across the county. It also resonated with a deep-running anxiety that powerful institutions – and grasping private men – would absorb property and destroy household independence. Although they stood back from the Regulation, the Worcester County Popular leaders had labored to defend landed household independence through the Land Bank, in votes in the provincial General Court, in the Revolutionary crisis, in the price-fixing conventions, and the county conventions of 1781–4, and again in their skepticism in the ratifying convention. The Popular tradition was literally situated at the "Revolutionary center" of Worcester County politics.[62] It stood in opposition to the Court faction, both in the form of the royal governor's men and the merchant-creditor interest. It also acted as a center of gravity among the broader body of the people, mediating between the cultural extremes in the county: the orthodox yeomen defending a corporate moral economy, and the dissenting societies, the primary advocates of a constitutional voluntarism. The ratifying convention would be the Worcester Popular tradition's most dramatic moment on the political stage, but its influence would continue far into the nineteenth century.

---

[61] Benedict and Tracy, *Sutton*, 106ff., 119, 122–3, 727–8; Lincoln, *Worcester*, 133–4; Cecelia M. Kenyon, "Men of Little Faith: The Anti-Federalists on the Nature of Representative Government," *WMQ* 12 (1955), 3–43.

[62] On the "Revolutionary Center" in Massachusetts, see Formisano, *The Transformation of Political Culture*, 57–83.

PART III

In the new nation, 1789–1861

8

Party spirit

In September 1800, the *Political Repository*, a Federalist paper published in the West Parish of Brookfield, printed a "Political Review" signed by "Union." The writer condemned the notion that society was divided into "two political parties – *Federalists* and *Jacobins*." "Union" was certain that all men of "information, reflection, and sound politics," as well as "the great body of industrious, temperate, honest citizens" were moderate men of no party other than that of the "Constitution." He knew "of no spirit more hostile to reason, than that of political party. We have drank it in to intoxication."[1]

The language used by "Union" captured the fundamental changes that had begun to sweep over the Worcester middle landscape in the decade following the ratification of the federal Constitution. A subtle yet pervasive restructuring of culture and society followed upon this transformation of political framework. This reshaping was accompanied, even driven, by awkward and complex dissonances running through the new nation. Most fundamentally, republican aspirations for order and unanimity in the new nation could not be reconciled with the liberal, Lockean framework established by independence and constitutionalism. New forms of association were clashing with an intensified classical language of political virtue. "Hostile to reason," and to the assumptions of a unitary republic, political parties would be a fundamental feature of the new political order; the vehicles of interest, they were organized by men who sought to define unitary visions of national independence. The tension between the classical tradition and the forms and institutions of partisanship gave the politics of the new nation a fiercely confrontational quality. The dramatic dissonances between corporate ideals and liberal forms made the period powerfully formative for a new generation.

Despite this sound and fury, the three decades following the ratification of the constitution were, in the longer scheme of things, an epoch of consensus. Political strife would center on competing community coalitions ranged behind competing elites, not on economic structures determining the nature of classes. But, as reluctant partisans struggled to define the legacy of the turbulent Revolutionary decades, new institutional forms were taking shape, which would bring the priorities of the provincial Lockean insurgency firmly into the mainstream. This

---

[1] Brookfield *Political Repository: Or, Farmer's Journal*, September 16, 1800.

new institutional architecture would provide the ground for a third cycle of
insurgent politics, shaped by cultural and economic transformations as well as by
deep-rooted Harringtonian assumptions, in the three decades ending with the
Civil War.

The decline of Antifederalism

Worcester County's response to the ratification of the Federal Constitution hinted
at a coming Federalist consensus. Having led a delegation that voted overwhelmingly against the new national framework, John Taylor of Douglas and Josiah
Whitney of Harvard stood up after the convention's final vote on the afternoon of
February 6, 1788, to announce their allegiance to the Constitution. Whitney,
arrested early in 1787 for his sympathy for the Regulation and specifically
instructed to oppose ratification, assured the delegates that he would support the
Constitution "as much as if he had voted for it." Taylor "found himself fairly
beaten," and promised to return to the county "and endeavour to infuse a spirit of
harmony and love among the people." By the end of the month such efforts were
apparently having an effect; it was reported to the Boston newspapers that
Antifederalists throughout the county were accepting the decision of the convention, and coming to the conclusion that the new Constitution would "operate for
the general good." The following October a celebration of the adoption of the
Constitution by eleven states was held at Mr. Brown's English school in
Worcester, featuring a parade by the students dressed in "neat rifle uniforms, and
wearing Federal Caps," and an oration on the "HAPPINESS of UNITED
COLUMBIA."[2]

But when the county's towns assembled to vote for a federal representative that
winter, the old Popular coalition managed to deliver a final victory for the
Antifederalists. Three candidates divided the better part of the county's vote,
requiring three polls to decide a victor. This election saw the reemergence of the
old struggle between the Court tradition and the Popular party that had lain
dormant for a quarter-century. Gen. Artemas Ward of Shrewsbury, the progovernment stalwart of Popular origins who had lectured the Regulators from the
courthouse steps, ended a distant third. Timothy Paine, once a scion of the
Worcester Court elite, Harvard graduate, court officer, and royal councillor,
finished second, with 36 percent of the vote. Paine and Ward did well in towns in
the northeast, five of which had voted for ratification, and in the southwest, where

[2] *Debates and Proceedings . . . 1788*, 281; Harding, *The Contest over the Ratification*, 109, citing
"A Gentleman in Worcester County to His Friend in Suffolk," *Independent Chronicle*, February
21, 1788: Worcester, Mass., *American Herald*, October 16, 1788. For Whitney's arrest, see MA
189:210, Prisoner list, April, 1787, Folder 2, Box 2, Worcester County, Mass., Papers, AAS.

progovernment gentry had entered the political arena in the contest over the framing of the state constitution. But Antifederalist Jonathan Grout of Petersham put together 56 percent of the vote to win on the final ballot in March 1789.[3]

Like Amos Singletary, Jonathan Grout was an archetype of the Worcester Popular tradition. Before his election to the state senate in 1787 he had served in the house, voting with the county majority, and was a leader in the convention movement. In 1788 he cast his town's vote against the Constitution, and in Congress Grout would distinguish himself by being the only Massachusetts representative to vote to restrict the federal government's authority to levy direct taxes. And in electing this Antifederalist to Congress, the county was reaching deep into the Popular tradition, for his father, a small-time lawyer in Lunenburg, had been a Land Banker, had voted for the bank in the 1740 house, and was still listed among the delinquents in 1763.[4]

Grout's vote came from two very different orbits. (See Figure 4.) The orthodox towns of the northwest, the stronghold of the Regulation, joined with the pluralist Popular towns of the Blackstone Valley in the southeast, including two-thirds of the old Land Bank centers and the towns conflicted in the insurgency, to cast strong majorities for Grout. This first national election thus reflected the influence of two insurgencies, the Land Bank and the Regulation: insurgencies separated by four decades and by very different motive forces, one pluralist and one corporate. This coalition would not last long.

Grout's election replicated on the new federal level a broad pattern of Antifederalism expressed in town elections for selectmen, representatives, and convention delegates. Convention men, Regulator sympathizers, and Antifederalists were elected to town and state office throughout the county from 1787 into the early 1790s. But the second federal election, requiring two ballots in October and November of 1790, marked the beginning of the decline of the county's staunch Antifederalism. After again dividing their vote between two candidates, the Federalists united behind by Artemas Ward, who won with 52 percent of the vote. Voter turnout had dropped by a third since the final vote in 1789, and Grout's coalition also had begun to collapse. Although the orthodox, Regulator northwest provided a stronger block of his vote than it had in 1789, Grout lost ground in the large pluralist towns of the Blackstone Valley, particularly in the old Land Bank centers. In the wake of the federal ratification struggle, Antifederalism united orthodox Regulators and men of the plural Popular towns. But within a year and a

[3] In this and the following chapters, all representatives are from the *Massachusetts Register*, and all votes, unless otherwise stated, are from the "Returns of Votes for Governor and Lieutenant Governor," in the Massachusetts Archives.

[4] Abner Morse, *The Genealogy and Descendents of Captain John Grout* (Boston, 1857), 8–10, 41–7; Merril Jensen and Robert A. Becker, eds., *The Documentary History of the First Federal Elections* (Madison, 1975–6), 619, 665–7, 682–3; *JHRM* 18:48; Mitten, "The New England Paper Money Tradition," 90; Hall, *Politics without Parties*, 334.

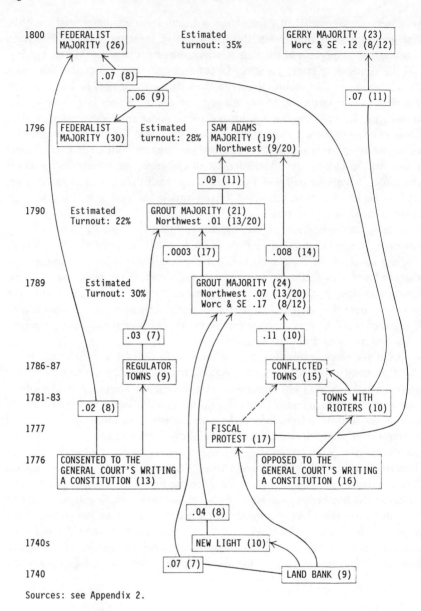

Sources: see Appendix 2.

Figure 4. The politics of the 1790s.

half, the Antifederalist coalition had lost its hold on the core of the county's old Popular tradition.[5]

Grout's defeat as federal representative anticipated the county's gradual movement into the Federalist column. Without true competition for the governor's chair between 1787 and 1795, the county's vote for governor remained nominally Antifederalist. John Hancock and Samuel Adams, old Revolutionary heroes and moderate, trimming Antifederalists who had swayed the convention in favor of the federal Constitution, attracted a broad consensus vote. Only in 1796 – when the popularity of the Jay treaty and his cousin John Adams attracted voters to the Federalist standard – was Sam Adams seriously challenged. Although he held onto the governorship for one more year, Sam Adams's vote in Worcester County declined from 82 percent in 1795 to 35 percent in 1796. By the time that the county turned against Sam Adams, most of the towns had made their peace with Federalist Friends of Government, who were elected to the General Court in increasing numbers in the early 1790s.

In great measure, Worcester County's turn to Federalism – with that of Hampshire to the west as well – flowed from the resolution of the problems of the 1780s. Although the old Regulator towns of the northwest registered a continued – though waning – militance in their 1796 votes for Adams for governor, the county's broad Federalist consensus reflected a certain satisfaction with the results of the revolutionary settlement achieved in 1788. Amos Singletary's fears of direct taxes levied at the point of federal bayonets were allayed in great measure by the adoption of the federal Bill of Rights, and the federal assumption of state war debts immediately alleviated the central issue that had structured Massachusetts politics since the late 1770s and, in the broadest sense, for the entire century since the onset of the wars of empire and the granting of the 1692 charter. Similarly, the volatile issues surrounding debt and the court system were defused by the continuation of legislation suspending civil suits for private debt, for the relief of poor debtors, adding terms to the Court of Common Pleas, and by the decentralization of the probate court, which in the fall of 1787 began to meet on a rotating basis at taverns throughout the county.[6]

At the same time, some of the county's leading men began to speak a new political language, challenging the Popular suspicion of central authority that had characterized political culture in the county from its first encounter with Governor Belcher in 1731. Edward Bangs, who in 1788 had written of the county's "dread of arbitrary power," delivered the July Fourth address in Worcester in 1791. Bangs

[5] Between 1788 and 1793 towns like Leicester, Brookfield, and Spencer stopped sending to the General Court Regulator sympathizers who had opposed the constitution, and began to elect men who would figure in the growing Federalist consensus. For details, see Brooke, "Society, Revolution ...," 468.

[6] Hall, *Politics without Parties*, 335–45; *The Laws of the Commonwealth of Massachusetts*, ... *1780, to ... 1800* (Boston, 1801), 401, 410, 574, 944; *Massachusetts Register* (Boston, 1788), 96.

urged the people to turn from jealousy to confidence in their attitude toward
the new national government. Contrary to the opinion of Amos Singletary at the
ratifying convention, the federal government was not an alien power, but the
servant of the people. "What occasion then have we for jealousy? Why may we not
repose a pleasing confidence in the rulers which we ourselves have chosen?"
"Jealousy" had "been considered a political virtue," but Bangs saw it as an evil;
circumscribing the powers of government would lead to "transgressions" in times
of crisis and open the door to "arbitrary power." "Heaven guard us from it,"
Bangs urged, "and enable us to live, and enjoy our independence, without it." The
door was opening to a postclassical politics.[7]

The voluntary principle in a reordered society

Worcester County's Federalist consensus was interwoven with a broad and deep
restructuring of society and culture. Much of this change lay in a literal reshuffling
of the population. The 1790 census revealed that Worcester County was not as
crowded as the eastern counties, where families outnumbered dwellings and
women outnumbered men, but it was no longer an open frontier. During the
preceding decade and a half the county had grown at twice the rate as the state as a
whole, with much of this growth centered in the undeveloped northwest. This
high rate of population growth added to the instability caused by the elimination of
the Court Party elites in the northwestern towns, presumably playing a role in the
background of the Regulation. In contrast, between 1790 and 1810, the county's
rate of growth slowed to less than the state average, with lower growth rates
particularly notable in the Regulator towns. Emigration to the west had begun in
the 1780s, and clearly expanded significantly in the 1790s. Many of those removing
were from the Regulator orbit, but this emigration also included many Friends of
Government, including Rufus Putnam, who established a military colony in Ohio,
and Ebenezer Crafts of Sturbridge, who became an important figure in northern
Vermont. To a great measure, the turn toward a conservative consensus was
reinforced by this exodus of both farm households anxiously fending off a tumble
into tenancy and dependency and some of the most energetic and ambitious
"young men of the revolution."[8]

[7] Edward Bangs, *An Oration, Delivered at Worcester, on the Fourth of July, 1791* (Worcester,
1791), 7–10.
[8] Greene and Harrington, *American Population before ... 1790*, 36–7; population aggregates
the 1790, 1800, and 1810 federal censuses; Orasmus Turner, *History of the Pioneer Settlement of
Phelps and Gorham's Purchase, and Morris' Reserve* (Rochester, N. Y., 1851) 410–13; Temple,
North Brookfield, 430–31; Buell, comp., *Memoirs of Rufus Putnam*, 102ff., 215ff.; John M.
Cockran, "Col. Ebenezer Crafts, His Ancestry and Some of His Descendents," *QHSL* 1
(1901–3), 183–90. For a discussion of the contrast between dynamic Republican regions and
stable Federalist regions, see David, H. Fischer, *The Revolution of American Conservatism: The
Federalist Party in the Era of Jeffersonian Democracy* (New York, 1965), 211–18.

The slackening of population growth formed the demographic background to the Federalist consensus of the 1790s; a conscious reshaping of society and the landscape itself formed the social and cultural foreground. A key element of the moral economy that shaped the eighteenth-century orthodox world was the inclusive criterion for baptism and membership that prevailed in the churches of the standing order, rooted in turn in their adherence to the federal covenant. Such lax, inclusive standards, institutionalized in the halfway covenant, were typical in the orthodox churches throughout central New England. Late in the eighteenth century, however, the situation began to change dramatically, as the churches suddenly began to reform themselves. Typically, the occasion for this change of polity followed the death of a long-lived minister, but in all cases it came after the Revolution, and predominantly after the ratification of the federal Constitution in 1788. A young generation of clergy of the New Divinity presided over the adoption of strict creed and covenants. Corporate status would no longer be interwoven with the inclusive religious duties and privileges of the federal covenant. A restored discipline in the Congregational churches, and the revived Calvinism, taking hold with the first stirrings of the Second Great Awakening, would provide an important buttress of the new Federalist consensus.[9]

This revival of church discipline was only one element in a broad disciplining of the countryside that began in the 1790s. While reform within the churches worked to control the pious through explicit social means, efforts to transform the sounds and shapes of the countryside worked more subtly to impose order and regularity upon all townspeople. In a post-Revolutionary reshaping of public space, the erection of steeples, bells, and clocks followed a widespread rebuilding of meetinghouses that had begun in the 1780s. Typically, steeples, bells, and clocks were built or purchased by private subscription, indicating towns or parishes as a whole would not agree to invest in time discipline. Just as social discipline was reasserted within the exclusive bounds of church membership, time discipline could only be purchased through private, voluntary investment. Once in place, however, the sound of the bells tolling daily at twelve noon and nine in the evening and the sight of the steeple clock marking out the time at the town center would impose a new predictability and order upon the townspeople as a whole.[10]

[9] In general, see Perry Miller, "From Covenant to Revival," in J. W. Smith and A. J. Jameson, eds., *The Shaping of American Religion* (Princeton, 1961), 322–68, and William Breitenbach, "The Consistent Calvinism of the New Divinity Movement," *WMQ*, 3d ser., 41 (1984), 241–64. For local details see Paige, *Hardwick*, 194–5; Benedict and Tracy, *Sutton*, 438–9; Reed, *Rutland*, 53; Chase *Ware*, 84, 98, 103; Samuel Dunham, *In Historical Discourse Delivered at West Brookfield, Mass.* (Springfield, 1868), 21–2; David Wilder, *The History of Westminster* (Fitchburg, 1853), 230–1; Andrew H. Ward, *History of Shrewsbury, Massachusetts* (Boston, 1847), 181; Samuel C. Damon, *The History of Holden, Massachusetts, 1667–1841* (Worcester, 1841), 100.

[10] Dunham, *Historical Discourse*, 58–60; Benedict and Tracy, *Sutton*, 130–2; Haynes, *First Congregational Church*, Sturbridge, 23–4; Tower, *Spencer*, 1: 141–3; *HWC*, 1:260, 2:120.

This ordering of the physical world was by no means unconscious. In a series of essays on improvement, the Reverend Nathan Fiske of South Brookfield harangued against the "slovenliness" of the Connecticut River towns, and against the yeoman practice of allowing their stock to forage freely in the winter months. Farmers were to "trim and adorn the earth," to drain bogs and swamps, to build "regular and handsome" fencing, and generally to "pay more attention to some things for sake of ornament and sightliness, as well as convenience and advantage."[11] This concern for "ornament and sightliness," for regularity and symmetry was soon expressed in the region's architecture. Presumably financed by initial profits in a reviving commercial trade, members of the mercantile gentry began to build imposing Palladian structures at the otherwise empty town centers. In 1790 lawyer Jabez Upham built a five-bay, hip-roof mansion at West Brookfield center; Gen. Salem Towne built a similar house at Charlton center in 1796, and Col. Jabez Crosby built another at South Brookfield center in 1797. A taste for Georgian symmetry also began to take hold among the younger yeoman households building new dwellings in the 1790s, the five-bay, story-and-half Cape cottage replacing smaller, more asymmetrical house forms.[12]

Like their dwellings, farms, and roadways, the orthodox graveyards were increasingly unsightly to newly refined sensibilities. A physical disorder of unkept graves grazed over by sheep and cattle, tilting gravestones carved with the wild, staring faces of dead elders conflicted with the restoration of an exclusive church polity. In town after town, over the course of the early nineteenth century, the dead were exiled from the village center to rural cemeteries, in many cases long before the founding of the prototype at Mount Auburn in 1831. This segregation of the dead had a long chronology, loosely linked with the emergence of the central village pattern, but within the graveyards the change was immediate. Over the 1790s the effigy carvings that had been such a marker of orthodoxy began to drop out of fashion, to be replaced by the neoclassical urn and willow. By the first decade of the new century the transition was virtually complete. Where the graveyards had once been populated with images of dead elders frozen in flight, silently exhorting the covenanted community, the new imagery depersonalized the dead, and turned attention to the bereaved families, symbolized in the drooping willow – or elm in the central Massachusetts carvings. With the death of

---

[11] Nathan Fiske, *The Moral Monitor, or a Collection of Essays on Various Subjects* (Worcester, 1801), 2:60ff., 155ff.

[12] This discussion is based on an analysis of the Federal Direct Tax of 1798 for the southern half of the town of Spencer, from a 1904 copy of Justice John Bisco's return in the Spencer, Mass., Papers, 1761–1877, AAS, as well as late-nineteenth-century photographs in Tower, *Spencer*, 1:24–5, 52, 89, 156, 2:7, 96. See Brooke, "Society, Revolution . . .," 573–9 for a full analysis. See also *Historic Buildings in Massachusetts: Photographs from the Historic Buildings Survey* (New York, 1976), 22, 104, 119, 137. For an analysis of this transition, see Henry Glassie, *Folk-Housing in Middle Virginia: A Structural Analysis of Historic Artifacts* (Knoxville, 1975.)

Washington and the elaboration of the cult of the "daughters of Columbia," the new funerary symbolism was inextricably bound to the national and republican purposes of a "woman's sphere."[13]

The reshaping of the physical landscape was interwoven with a reshaping of the social landscape. The corporate institutions of town and orthodox church had long been challenged by the dissenting societies, which had introduced the voluntary principle in the drama of the Great Awakening and its aftermath. But in the 1780s, accelerating greatly in 1790s, the voluntary principle of association was taken up by the gentry. The result would be a radical redefinition of the place and purposes of institutions on the middle landscape.

The first of the new institutions, the Leicester Academy, was established in the wake of the constitution-making era by the gentry of the pluralist towns. Importantly, the gentry from the old orthodox town of Brookfield had been conspicuously absent among the Leicester Academy's founding group, a mark perhaps, of their hesitancy to break the ancient unity of corporate institutions. But such inhibitions evaporated in the immediate aftermath of the Regulation. In 1787, "desirous to obtain an habit of accurate thinking, to improve their style of composition and to acquire an ease and pertinence of public speaking," the Brookfield gentry banded together to form the Minervaean Society. Membership lists dating between 1789 and 1793 show that this "fraternal circle" was indeed a select group. Four-fifths came from households in the wealthiest tenth of the 1783 valuation of Brookfield and a third were college graduates; among their number were civil officers, lawyers, doctors, orthodox ministers. Most importantly, four-fifths of the members had supported the government in the Regulation. Their vice-president, Dwight Foster, had been the leading figure in the progovernment protest of January 1787, which had spoken so pointedly of the "happiness of individuals" rather than the good of the commonwealth. The Minervaean Society was typical of a host of such small societies of gentry formed throughout the new nation, bringing together like-minded men and molding a generation of political orators. In the short term, while the ex-Regulator Antifederalists maintained control over town government through 1790, the gentry Friends of Government met under the aegis of Nathan Fiske, the orthodox minister in the South Parish, occupying themselves with performances of Greek tragedy and comedy, reciting "declamations" such as the "Prologue to Cato" and "Pitt's Speech to Parliament,"

[13] In general, see David Stannard, *The Puritan Way of Death: A Study in Religion, Culture, and Social Change* (New York, 1977); and Ann Douglas, "Heaven Our Home: Literature in the Northern United States, 1830–1860," and Stanley French, "The Cemetery as Cultural Institution: The Establishment of Mount Auburn and the 'Rural Cemetery' Movement," both in David Stannard, ed., *Death in America* (Philadelphia, 1975), 49–91. For local details, see *Coll. WSA* 1 (1879), 67; Haynes, *First Congregational Church, Sturbridge*, 17–24; *HWC*, 1:260, 2:259, 359; Paige, *Hardwick*, 116–7; Chase, *Ware*, 194–5; Washburn, *Leicester*, 161; Daniels, *Oxford*, 220–1; Anson Titus, *Charlton Historical Sketches* (Southbridge, 1877), 17–18.

and writing compositions "on churlishness" and "industry." Interspersed with these improving activities they debated a series of political and social issues, ranging from questions of fiscal policy to "whether early Marriages are beneficial to a Society." They would soon return to the political arena.[14]

The institutional pluralism engendered by such voluntary associations was most rapidly developed in the county seat of Worcester, where it was interwoven with a new form of religious separatism. The death of Rev. Thaddeus McCarty in 1784 has set off a dispute within the orthodox church in Worcester that resulted in the secession of a liberal faction, who formed themselves into a voluntary religious society to be presided over by Rev. Aaron Bancroft. Incorporated by state law in November 1787, the second parish in Worcester was the first of many Unitarian separations to occur in the county. Separating from the old parish, the Worcester Unitarians were also conspicuous among the early members of a number of voluntary societies formed in Worcester over the next several years. In 1792, all six men from Worcester joining the new Massachusetts Society for the Promotion of Agriculture were Unitarians, as were twelve of the fourteen founders of the Morning Star Lodge of Freemasons, chartered in 1793. The Worcester Fire Society, also founded in 1793, seems to have been a meeting ground for the elite of both parishs, as the Unitarians accounted for only fifteen of the twenty-six original members; seven of these fifteen were also Masons and five were members of the Agricultural Society. The first components of the interlocking associationalism that would characterize the nineteenth-century urban environment were falling into place in Worcester early in the 1790s.[15]

In June 1793 Aaron Bancroft addressed the Grand Lodge assembled in Worcester to open the Morning Star Lodge. His theme was benevolence, and the qualities of love, beneficence, and "courteous and affable behavior" necessary to its operation in the "smaller circles of society." The Masonic lodge would restore a benevolence and unanimity sorely strained in both town and county in the recent past. Bancroft assured the assembled Grand Lodge that Freemasonry was an institution "calculated to destroy the virulence of national partiality ... to

[14] Nathan Fiske, *The Moral Monitor, or a Collection of Essays on Various Subjects. Accommodated to the State of Society in the United States of America, Displaying and Enforcing the Observance of Individual and Social Virtue* (Worcester, 1801), xi, 62; "Brookfield, Mass., Minervaean Society Records, 1789–1794," AAS; Sprague, *Annals of the American Pulpit*, 1:495. Of the thirteen gentry families in the visitation circles of Rev. Eli Forbes in 1762 and Rev. Nathan Fiske in 1771, nine produced signers of the pro-government protest of January, 1787, and nine produced members of the Minervaean Society.
[15] Lincoln, *Worcester*, 194–6; *Private and Special Statutes of the Commonwealth of Massachusetts* ... (Boston, 1805–), 1;171–2; Joseph Allen, *The Worcester Association and Its Antecedents* ... (Boston, 1868), 123–47; *Laws and Regulations of the Massachusetts Society for Promoting Agriculture* (Boston, 1793), 16–18; Edward S. Nason, *A Centennial History of the Morning Star Lodge, 1793–1893* (Worcester, 1894), 197–209; *Reminiscences of the Original Associates and Past Members of the Worcester Fire Society* ... (Worcester, 1870), 62.

mitigate the calamities of war . . . to still the spirit of party, that still often rages in government and (Must I say?) in religion."[16]

Strikingly, both the Morning Star Lodge and the Massachusetts Agricultural Society drew members from towns that had particularly experienced both "the calamities of war" and "the spirit of party" between 1786 and 1787. Men from all of the county's fifteen towns divided between Regulator and government notables in 1786 joined either the Massachusetts Agricultural Society or the Morning Star Lodge, as against less than half of all the other towns – Regulator, progovernment, or uncommitted. This contrast would persist. As late as 1830 over 70 percent of the conflicted towns of 1786–7 had Masonic lodges, as against a third of the government towns, and only one of the nine Regulator towns. Elite voluntarism followed hard upon civil strife. Like the Minervaean Society in the sorely divided town of Brookfield, these new voluntary societies provided common contexts for likeminded men, typically recent Friends of Government.[17] Eight men from the six-town region discussed in Chapter 7 joined the Agricultural Society in 1792; seven had actively supported the government in 1787. The Morning Star Lodge attracted a slightly more diverse group. Of fifteen joining from these six towns, eight had been Friends of Government – including the ambitious Israel Waters of Charlton and four of his volunteer cavalry men – and three had been convention men or Regulators. Another, Simeon Draper of Spencer, belonged to a family that had straddled the fence; two of Draper's brothers had served respectively in a Regulator company and the government militia.

If there were a few former Regulators and their sympathizers among the new voluntary societies, surely they had made their peace with the more numerous Friends of Government on their opponents' terms; the new voluntary societies were not attractive to the men of corporate orthodox principles who had formed the backbone of the Regulation. Rather, the voluntary societies provided an alternative to the corporate institutions that had nurtured the rebellion, an alternative for ambitious men seeking a more private context or conviviality and improving discourse that would put them in touch with likeminded men throughout the county and the state. This broad reshaping of landscape and institutions was the ground upon which the new Federalist consensus of the 1790s emerged.[18]

Early Federalism and associational politics

Despite its visibility and real permanence, the political realignment of the early 1790s had a miragelike quality: Federalism did not so much rise as Antifederalism

---

[16] Aaron Bancroft, *A Sermon Delivered at Worcester on the Eleventh of June, 1793 . . . before the Grand Lodge of Massachusetts . . .* (Worcester, 1793), 9–13, 18–19.

[17] See Chapter 10, note 29, for sources on the location of Masonic institutions in 1830.

[18] For the Massachusetts Agricultural Society and the Morning Star Lodge, see note 15 above; for Regulators and Friends of Government, see Chapter 7, note 35.

faded away. While one of the basic structures of Massachusetts politics in the 1790s was a growing Federalist hegemony, the other was a consistently low voter turnout. The two decades between the first governor's election in 1780 and the turn of the century saw a broad, fluctuating cycle of political activity, with voter turnout and Federalist support varying inversely. When turnout was low, Federalist candidates received a high proportion of the vote, but a surge in turnout meant that the Federalist proportion plummeted. Roughly, these two decades fell into three periods. (See Appendix 1a.) The years between 1780 and 1786 saw a falling turnout and a rising Federalist proportion of the vote. The pattern was inverted in 1787 and for several years following, as oppositional energies were expressed at the polls. Then, after the residual Antifederalism of the early 1790s had played itself out, the Federalist proportion of the vote again rose to unprecedented heights, while voter turnout dropped to a consistently low level of about 20 to 25 percent. Thus, if some in the new republic were driven to "violence" and "phrenzies," the majority of the Worcester County electorate remained quiescent and apathetic. Even in 1798, at the height of the XYZ affair, the threat of war with France, and the passage of the Alien and Sedition Acts, turnout in the federal election grew only slightly in some of the towns – and declined in others. These excitements were not reflected in the state election at all; the 1798 governor's election had the smallest turnout since 1786. Only when a particular set of grievances demanded redress did large numbers of voters become involved in the political process.[19]

If the wild fluctuations of the Antifederalist vote suggest the persistence of a grievance-oriented politics of opposition, the basic stability in the Federalist vote suggests a core of voters tied together by a web of communication and organization. Long-standing, informal networks of notables and merchants, bound by kinship and interest, provided one vehicle through which the constant level of Federalist voting was maintained. Where the Antifederalists relied on circular letters distributed through the towns, the Federalist gentry communicated in private letters, marshaling influence and wealth to their cause. The legal system, commercial relationships, ministerial associations, common military experience, and ties of kinship all worked to bring the gentry into contact across considerable distances, and their continuing correspondence provided the basis for ad hoc political organization.[20]

Viewed in the context of a uniformly low voter turnout, the strong bias of the new voluntary societies toward the Friends of Government also suggests that they

---

[19] John R. Howe, Jr., "Republican Thought and the Political Violence of the 1790s," *AQ* 19 (1967), 147–65; Marshall Smelser, "The Jacobin Frenzy: Federalism and the Menace of Liberty, Equality, and Fraternity," *Review of Politics* 13 (1951), 457–82.

[20] Jensen and Becker, eds., *The First Federal Elections*, 694–5; Banner, *Toward the Hartford Convention*, 225; Washburn, *Leicester*, 224–5; Theodore Sedgewick to Dwight Foster, December 28, 1802, Feburary 2, 1803, Folder 2, Box 34, "Foster Family Papers," AAS.

may well have played a role as informal political organizations for the emerging and unchallenged Federalism. At the very least, these societies, though formed for overtly cultural purposes served to formalize and thicken relationships among the gentry, providing yet another avenue along which political information and cooperation might flow. At the most, they might have functioned as nominating caucuses, choosing candidates from among their number, and carefully mustering the votes sufficient for their election. The Minervaean Society, for example, seems to have operated as an organizational node for the Brookfield Federalists, as the town government was swept by Antifederalists and Regulators in the wake of the Regulation. If this "fraternal band" was not an explicit political organization, the Minervaean Society's regular "forensic debates" and "ex tempore disputes," where members voted on the arguments of debaters on matters of public policy, were vehicles that helped to forge an explicitly Federalist consensus. In 1791 the society's vice-president, Justice Dwight Foster, was elected the town representative to the General Court, and reelected in 1792, breaking the Antifederalist grip on town politics. The timing of Foster's election to Congress in 1793 and the disbanding of the Minervaean Society in 1794 suggests that the return of at least one of its members to political prominence had been among the group's primary objectives.[21]

Similar circumstances were repeated elsewhere in the county. In Worcester, Federalist until 1800, the two leading representatives, Samuel Flagg and Nathaniel Paine, were both Unitarians, members of the Massachusetts Agricultural Society, and founders of the Morning Star Lodge and the Fire Society. When the Morning Star began to dismiss members to form new lodges, the first to go was the large group from Charlton who formed the Fayette Lodge in 1796, meeting in the second floor ballroom of Gen. Salem Towne's mansion in Charlton center. Towne played a role analogous to that of Dwight Foster: A strong Friend of Government, he replaced men from the Antifederalist orbit as Charlton's representative to the General Court in 1790, serving for four years until he was elected to the state senate in 1794 for the first of many terms. He, too, was a charter member of the Massachusetts Agricultural Society and a justice of the peace. Men in Brookfield would petition for a local lodge in 1797. Their leading figure, Gen. John Cutler, a commander of the government militia in 1787, an early member of the Morning Star Lodge, the Minervaean Society, and the Agricultural Society, would be elected to the General Court for five consecutive terms beginning in 1798. Another former government man among the Morning Star Masons, Sylvanus Town of Federalist Oxford, was elected treasurer of the Olive Branch Lodge when it was formed in Oxford in 1797. The next year Town was elected to the first of four consecutive terms in the General Court, while Jonathan Harris, another early Morning Star Mason with experience in the government militia, was elected town

[21] Temple, *North Brookfield*, 287; "Return of Votes for Members of Congress," MA; "Minervaean Society Records," AAS.

clerk in 1799 for the first of twelve terms. The influence of these voluntary societies could even reach into the former Regulator towns: Justice Benjamin Drury of Spencer – who had not taken sides during the Regulation – joined the Morning Star Lodge in 1793. The next year he was elected to the first of seventeen consecutive terms in the General Court, years when the town voted solidly Federalist. All five towns in the county where Masonic lodges would be in place by 1797 voted for the Federalist candidate for governor in 1796 by a 2-to-1 margin, as against less than half of the other towns in the county. Among the twelve towns lying between Worcester and Sturbridge consistently voting Federalist between 1796 and 1804, Masons and members of the Massachusetts Agricultural Society served in 60 percent of the representatives' terms in the General Court.[22]

In the 1790s, then, voluntary institutional forms spread rapidly among the county gentry, as they had spread among religious dissenters in the decade following the Awakening. Conversation, discourse, and suitable entertainment would bind together the members of these associations, uplifting individuals, neighborhoods, and – by extension – society at large. In Nathan Fiske's words, people was gathering in private societies "for mutual improvement, that they may be qualified and animated to act in their several parts of life, with greater advantage to others, and honour to themselves." Again we come upon the miragelike quality of public culture in the 1790s; here voluntary associations were put to purposes formerly the domain of corporate institutions, purposes of benevolence, unanimity, and public good. These were the stated intentions of the statewide societies, the Masonic lodges, and the social libraries that were being formed throughout the region. Despite their invocations of harmony and unity, these new societies were not public and corporate, but private and voluntary, and they seem to have been the vehicle of the emergent Federalist hegemony. In their 1797 petition, the aspiring Masons in Brookfield had written that "the Spirit of Masonry is kindling fast in this part of the country." Their admission that they were "but little acquainted with the Rules and regulations which are established on Masonry" suggests that the petitioners were more interested in the society as a social form than a system of belief. Rather than "the Spirit of Masonry," they might have said that the spirit of Federalist voluntarism was sweeping the region. While the bulk of the yeoman population remained unorganized and indifferent to the political "phrenzies" of the decade, small groups in each town began to cluster around private organizations, and the towns consistently to return overwhelming Federalist majorities of up to 100 percent with a very low voter turnout. The

[22] See note 15, and table in note 29; and Titus, *Charlton Historical Sketches*, 25; Cheney Reed, et al., to Isaiah Thomas, July 28, 1797, "Isaiah Thomas Papers," AAS; Washburn, *Historical Sketches of Leicester*, 68–9; Paige, *Hardwick*, 252–5; *Centennary of Olive Branch Lodge* ... (Millbury, 1897), 84; Daniels, *Oxford*, 104, 248–9, 272; Whitney, *Worcester County*, 249; Henry P. Wright, ed., *The Fobes Memorial Library, Oakham, Massachusetts* .. (Oakham, 1900), 105–6.

membership of these voluntary associations and the small but effective cadres of Federalist voters must have been very similar. The corporate politics that had characterized the eighteenth century was giving way to organizations. This was not party politics, but rather what can be called associational politics. With a transformation of political framework came the need for new institutional forms; the persistence of classical modes of belief demanded that these institutions not explicitly disrupt the idealized moral unity of the commonwealth.[23]

The Jeffersonian challenge and the First Party System

When "Union" wrote of an "intoxication" with party spirit in 1800, his apprehensions were based upon the turn of events since the fateful year of 1798, when John Adams's policies of quasiwar with the French and absolutism at home – in the form of the Alien and Sedition Acts – had provided those inclined toward opposition in Massachusetts with the first glimmers of controversy and leverage. The quiet stasis of Federalist consensus began to crack in the last years of the century. The stage was set for a real challenge by a Jeffersonian Republican party – as well as the emergence of a popular Federalism. A passionate politics of national independence was sweeping over the region.[24]

From a low point of 18 percent in 1798, voter turnout across the state in the election for governor climbed to 39 percent by 1802, an upward movement that owed its persistence after the presidential year of 1800 to the beginning of grass roots organization. After a lull in 1803, when the Republicans were divided over issues of strategy, the statewide rise in turnout continued, jumping most dramatically from 41 to 51 percent between 1804 and 1805. The returns for the November 1804 federal election, which gave the state's electoral vote to Jefferson for the first time, indicate that the Republicans had made a particularly strong effort in the previous six months. The April 1805 gubernatorial election confirmed the new configuration across the county: Turnout was up from 44 to 60 percent and the Federalist vote down from 70 percent to a new and permanent level of 59 percent.[25] (See Appendix 1a.)

Over the next decade the press of events and the increasingly competitive efforts of the opposing parties fueled an unprecedented political participation. Between 1805 and 1815 voter turnout across the state never fell below 50 percent, reaching a

[23] Nathan Fiske, *The Moral Monitor*, 62; Cheney Reed, et al., to Isaiah Thomas, July 28, 1797, "Isaiah Thomas Papers, AAS. On the broader problem of private and public in the 1790s, see Handlin and Handlin, *Commonwealth*, 93–112; Formisano, *The Transformation*, 24–41, 57ff.

[24] Robert H. Wiebe, *The Opening of American Society: From the Adoption of the Constitution to the Eve of Disunion* (New York, 1984), 66–89.

[25] Paul Goodman, *The Democratic-Republicans of Massachusetts: Politics in a Young Republic* (Cambridge, Mass., 1964), 129; Banner, *Toward the Hartford Convention*, 361.

high of 67 percent in 1812 – a level of participation approached before the Civil War only in the Log Cabin campaign of 1840. These years saw the end of the wild fluctuations in turnout and voter identification that had characterized the preceding twenty-five years; in town after town and across the county and state, voter turnout and party voting suddenly became rock-steady. This broad conjuncture of political action would dominate the first two decades of the new century, rising toward a stable two-party confrontation before 1805, and fading away after 1815. It would have a shaping influence on thousands of young men drawn into the political process; the encounter with competitive party politics during the First Party System was powerfully formative for an entire generation. Those entering the political arena in the first decade of the nineteenth century were the first to experience the organized competition of political parties, and this encounter – mediated by cultural tradition and economic position – would color their attitude toward the political process for decades to come.[26]

The Republicans attempted to use voluntary societies for essentially political purposes, as the Federalists had apparently done in the 1790s. The Morning Star Lodge in Worcester and the Olive Branch Lodge in Oxford came to be dominated by Republicans after 1800 ad 1806, respectively. Similarly, a Royal Arch Chapter – with uniformly Republican officers – was formed in Charlton in 1805. Like the Federalist Masons in Brookfield in 1797, this King Solomon Chapter neglected the formalities of the order. Cited in 1806 by the Grand Chapter as "very reprehensible" for failing to send fees, delegates, and regular return of membership, the Royal Arch Masons almost lost their charter before they began to send representatives to annual meetings in Boston, rotating between prominent Republicans from Sutton and Dudley.[27] But the explosion of partisanship could not be channeled through the cultural voluntary societies. During the years following the explosive emergence of Republican voting in the winter and spring of 1804 to 1805, Charlton's Fayette Lodge of Masons went through considerable turmoil and depletion of its numbers. Meeting at Federalist Salem Towne's mansion at the center through January 1806, the lodge failed to enter minutes in its records until April 1807, when it began to meet at a tavern in a dissenting neighborhood in South Charlton belonging to Moses Dresser, a militia major from a Baptist family. The lodge's numbers were cut from forty-two to twenty-three,

[26] See Chapter 7, note 53, for procedures for estimating turnout. The significance of the competition between Federalists and Republicans is a hotly contested issue, most notably by Fischer in *The Revolution of American Conservatism* and Formisano in *The Transformation of Political Culture*. My position is that politics between 1805 and 1815 was indeed structured by a highly organized two-party system, but that the persisting strength of classical conceptions of commonwealth made the participants highly anxious about their behavior.

[27] Based on an analysis of the officers of the Morning Star and Olive Branch Lodges, in Nason, *Morning Star Lodge*, 165–75, and *Centennary of Olive Branch Lodge* ..., 81–4; and Titus *Charlton*, 25–6; and *Proceedings of the Grand Royal Arch Chapter of Massachusetts, From Its Organization, 1796–1860* (Worcester, 1876), 52, 56, 60.

and prominent men from both the Republicans and the Federalists were missing, although most of the Republicans would return over the next several years.[28] And although nominal Masons dominated the representation from Republican Charlton, filling 78 percent of the terms served in the General Court in the decade between 1805 and 1815, the Masonic presence among the region's representatives was down sharply, from 47 percent between 1796 and 1804 to 23 percent between 1805 and 1815 for twelve towns lying between Worcester and Sturbridge. In the Federalist towns of Oxford and Leicester, Masons were replaced by non-Masons after 1806, in the latter case by men who would be Antimasonic leaders between 1830 and 1834. Similarly, the towns stopped sending members of the Massachusetts Agricultural Society to the General Court. Together, where Masons and Agricultural Society members had been elected to 60 percent of the terms served between 1796 and 1804, during the period of party conflict they were elected to only a quarter of the representatives' terms served. Thus, although specific Masonic lodges had clear partisan affiliations, voluntary associations were no longer able to act as an integrating forum for a now splintered elite.[29]

[28] Analysis of membership lists in the Records of the Fayette Lodge, Charlton, Mass., MSS., Grand Lodge of Masons, Boston.

[29] *Representation and voluntary societies in twelve Worcester County towns, 1796–1830*

	Terms served by				
	Masons	MAS members (not Masons)	Masons and MAS members	Worcester Agricultural Society members (1819)	Total
Federalist representatives 1796–1804	32 *47*	9 *13*	41 *60*	—	68
Federalist representatives 1805–15	15 *15*	5	20 *20*	49 *48*	102
Republican representatives 1805–15[a]	32 *33*	0	32 *33*	68 *72*	95
All representatives 1805–15	47 *24*	5 *2*	52 *26*	117 *66*	197
All representatives 1816–30	47 *24*	—	—	106 *55*	194

— Not calculated.

Note: Data for the towns of Worcester, Paxton, Leicester, Oakham, New Braintree, Spencer, Brookfield, Sutton, Oxford, Charlton, Sturbridge, Dudley. Figures in italics are percentages.

[a] Representatives elected by Worcester between 1800 and 1804 and in Sutton between 1801 and 1804 are included with the Republican group.

Source: For all known Masons, see notes 15, 22, and 27, and returns of lodge openings in *Proceedings of the . . . Grand Lodge of . . . Masons of the Commonwealth of Massachusetts for the Years 1815–1825 Inclusive (Boston, 1928); Proceedings of the . . . Grand Lodge of . . . Masons of the Commonwealth of Massachusetts for the Years 1826–1844 Inclusive (Boston,*

Rather than the implicit understandings of a unitary, associational politics, partisan competition would be built for the first time on organized party structures. Between 1800 and 1804 explicit political organizations spread rapidly across the state, as a hierarchy of committees and caucuses linked the party faithful at town, county, and state levels. Explicitly committed to the advancement of a political interest, the parties could revive an old political form; now divorced from the public connotations that had undermined the convention movement of the 1780s, the convention was revived by both parties as a means of drawing the rank and file into the political process. Ironically, one of the first Federalist caucuses designed to generate popular enthusiasm met in 1808 in Barre where, a generation before, Adam Wheeler and the Regulator leadership had grappled with the conundrum of private and public interests in the political process. But, as elsewhere, the initiative came from the Republicans. Countering the Federalist monopoly over the press, the Republicans founded the Worcester *National Aegis* in October 1801. At least as early as 1803 the Republicans in Worcester began holding partisan public celebrations featuring parades, banquets, and orations. In the critical election year of 1804 the Republicans organized a state central committee, and at the local level, Jefferson's purchase of the Louisiana territory provided a means of generating enthusiasm and party loyalty. In Sturbridge, Gen. Timothy Newell invited "all the true patriots in this and neighboring towns" to a Louisiana celebration in May; a procession from Captain Fairbank's Hall to the meetinghouse was to be followed by an oration by a local Universalist preacher and dinner at two o'clock sharp.[30]

The Federalists responded in kind. In 1800 the *Spy* had printed the names of all candidates for federal representative with the comment that they were all "known to the body of Electors." By 1804 the *Spy* abandoned any pretense of a nonpartisan stance, printing the entire Federalist slate in boldface and urging the voters to attend to "correct principles." As party identification stiffened, the nominating process was regularized. In the 1790s, and even as late as 1801, letters nominating mixed slates for state senator were printed in the *Spy*. Beginning in 1802 the county committees of both parties began to nominate official slates of candidates. Gentry personalism was beginning to give way to party regularity. In 1804 the Republican campaign to control the General Court brought demands for clear party affiliation down to the local level. The Worcester County Republicans worked to have selectmen elected who would not exclude the party faithful from

1828); *Proceedings of the Grand Royal Arch Chapter of Massachusetts, From Its Organization, 1796–1860* (Worcester, 1876). MAS, Massachusetts Agricultural Society members in 1801, from *Papers on Agriculture, Consisting of Communications Made to the Members of the Massachusetts Agricultural Society* ... (Boston, 1801), membership list, 87–93; Worcester Agricultural Society: members at formation in 1819, from Levi Lincoln, *Address, Delivered before the Worcester Agricultural Society, October 7, 1819* (Worcester, 1819), 25–30.

[30] *Aegis*, March 9, 1803; May 2, 1804; *Spy*, June 22, July 6, 1808; see Banner, *Toward the Hartford Convention*, 261ff.; and for a different view, Formisano, *The Transformation*, 110–17.

the polls, and the Federalist county committee printed and distributed a circular letter asking for "systematic exertions" from the local party leaders in the towns. By 1810, the Federalists had developed a highly articulated system for turning out the vote. That spring the Federalist county committee urged upon local leaders in a printed circular

> the necessity of adopting the usual method of dividing your towns in sections, of designating suitable persons in each district, and of urging upon them the duty of seeing every person in their respective districts, of confirming the doubtful, and exerting every well disposed person to a punctual attendance at each of the [town election] meetings, and of sending the constitutional number of representatives.

Nothing was to be left to chance, as local committees were instructed to operate as political machines. The sinews and structures of a competitive two-party system had been established.[31]

Continuities and constituencies

The development of formal party structures set the stage for the emergence of political coalitions that would have great enduring power, their influence stretching far into the new century. Such stable coalitions had not emerged in the fifteen years since the first federal elections. Just as turnout had fluctuated wildly, so, too, the sources of political opposition within the county had changed complexion at several key junctures. (See Figures 4 and 5.) Jonathan Grout had been elected to the U.S. Congress in 1789 with strong support from both the Regulator centers in the northwest upland towns and the old Popular party towns of the southeastern Blackstone Valley. He lost the next election when he lost support in the southeast. In 1796 this pattern took hold in the elections for governor, when Samuel Adams lost in the county for the first time, retaining a measure of support only in small towns in the Regulator northwest. It was with the election of 1800, where moderate Republican Elbridge Gerry cast himself as a friend of John Adams, that the outlines of the new structure of county politics began to emerge. Gerry's support, which gave him just over half of the county's vote, was widely distributed, but weaker in the northwest and stronger in the southeast than the Antifederalist vote of the previous decade. Without a solid organizational structure, the Republicans failed to maintain their advantage, but a new configuration had begun to emerge. The Gerry campaign had turned several large and important towns, including Worcester and Sutton, away from a decade

---

[31] *Spy*, April 2, August 22, 1800, April 1, 1801, October 31, December 12, 1804; Benjamin Heywood, et al., to Dwight Foster, et al., March 1, 1810, Box 34, Folder 6, "Foster Family Papers," AAS; Banner, *To the Hartford Convention*, 227ff., 244, 281ff.; Goodman, *Jeffersonian-Republicans*, 132–4.

of Federalist voting, and a block of such towns would remain permanently in the Republican camp. As measured by the April 1804 returns for governor, the Republicans had captured a preponderance in the old Popular region; this pattern was confirmed and amplified in the elections of the fall of 1804 and the spring of 1805, and would persist for decades to come, as Jeffersonian Republicanism set the stage for Jacksonian democracy.

The aggregate figures for the 1812 election – typical of a pattern prevailing from 1805 through 1824 – indicate a well-defined relationship between this new structure of county politics and previous traditions. Within the broader matrix of a dominant Federalism, the key Republican constituencies were situated within the orbit of the old Popular tradition. Towns in the southeast, with large groups of Land Bankers, with New Light ministers during the Great Awakening, which had espoused Constitutionalist principles in 1776, opposed the turn toward hard currency in 1777, and towns with rioters in the early 1780s as well as dissenting religious societies all stand out as providing the core constituency for the new Republican coalition. Conversely, the towns voting Federalist were concentrated in the northern half of the county, sharing a common experience of undisturbed orthodoxy and anticonstitutionalist sentiment, with no common experience in the various manifestations of the broader Popular tradition. Strikingly, all of the towns in the northeast that voted Republican were towns of the Land Bank tradition: Harvard, Lunenburg, and Fitchburg, set off from Lunenburg in 1764. In short, the aggregate figures suggest that the partisanship of the First Party era restored the division between Court and Popular politics that had so shaped the county's provincial political culture.

These figures also suggest that the Republican emergence bore little relationship to the insurgency of 1786–7, when the northwest – now predominantly Federalist – supported the Regulation, and the southeast – now predominantly Republican – had sided with the government. This is not to say that former Regulators were not to be found in the Republican coalition. Four of the nine Regulator strongholds typically cast Republican majorities between 1805 and 1811. But during these years there was no necessary connection between the Regulation and Jeffersonian Republicanism; the militia towns of 1787 were as likely to vote Republican as were the Regulator towns. And in 1812 and the decade following any tendency among the Regulator towns to vote Republican disappeared altogether. Between 1812 and the final year of First Party competition in 1824 the Republican coalition drew upon a south county constituency shaped by the institutions and politics of the Popular tradition – particularly its dissenting wing. Viewed in the long perspective running from the Peace of Utrecht in 1713 to the Hartford Convention in 1814, oppositional politics was continuous in the southeast with the exception of both its support for the government in 1786 and its acceptance of the Federalist consensus in the 1790s, while "court" politics prevailed in the northwest with the exception of the Regulator and Antifederalist politics of the 1780s and 1790s.

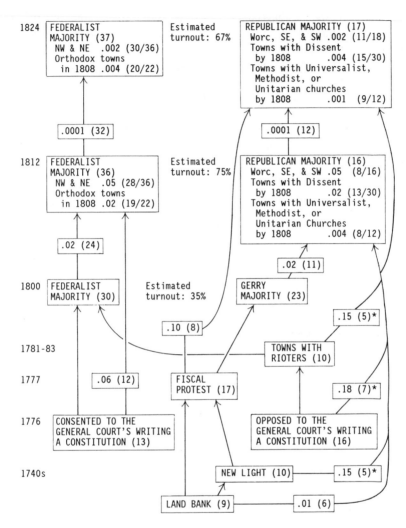

1824 | FEDERALIST MAJORITY (37) NW & NE .002 (30/36) Orthodox towns in 1808 .004 (20/22) | Estimated turnout: 67% | REPUBLICAN MAJORITY (17) Worc, SE, & SW .002 (11/18) Towns with Dissent by 1808 .004 (15/30) Towns with Universalist, Methodist, or Unitarian churches by 1808 .001 (9/12)

.0001 (32) .0001 (12)

1812 | FEDERALIST MAJORITY (36) NW & NE .05 (28/36) Orthodox towns in 1808 .02 (19/22) | Estimated turnout: 75% | REPUBLICAN MAJORITY (16) Worc, SE, & SW .05 (8/16) Towns with Dissent by 1808 .02 (13/30) Towns with Universalist, Methodist, or Unitarian Churches by 1808 .004 (8/12)

.02 (24) .02 (11)

1800 | FEDERALIST MAJORITY (30) | Estimated turnout: 35% | GERRY MAJORITY (23)

.15 (5)*

1781-83 .10 (8) TOWNS WITH RIOTERS (10)

1777 .06 (12) FISCAL PROTEST (17) .18 (7)*

1776 | CONSENTED TO THE GENERAL COURT'S WRITING A CONSTITUTION (13) | OPPOSED TO THE GENERAL COURT'S WRITING A CONSTITUTION (16)

1740s NEW LIGHT (10) .15 (5)*

LAND BANK (9) .01 (6)

Note: All of the initiatives dating between 1740 and the 1780s indicated on this chart had the same relationship with voting in 1824 that they had in 1812, except that those marked (*) showed a stronger relationship with Republican majority in 1824 than 1812 (between .04 and .06).

Sources: see Appendix 2.

Figure 5. The first party system and its antecedents.

The background of the county leadership is a further indication that the emergence of the Republican challenge bore few continuities with either the Regulation or the politics of county convention and constitutional ratification. Very little in their earlier experience distinguished the members of the Republican county committee named in 1808, for example, from their Federalist counterparts. The elites of both parties were drawn from the same stratum of county gentry, strongly supportive of the government in 1787, absent from public affairs during the Antifederalist interlude, and involved in the fluorescence of private societies. At least six of the seventeen Republican county committeemen in 1808 had served in the government militia in 1787, or were the brothers of government men; similarly, they had joined the same voluntary societies that seem to have been such a vehicle of the Federalist consensus of the 1790s. At the head of the list stood Abraham Lincoln and Levi Lincoln, Jr., of Worcester, both members of the Fire Society, the brother and son of Levi Lincoln, Sr., elected lieutenant governor as a Republican in 1807 and 1808. Merrick Rice, an attorney originally from Brookfield, was from a progovernment family that had been involved in the Minervaean Society, as was another Brookfield lawyer, Pliny Merrick, who joined the Morning Star Lodge in 1798. Timothy Newell, the leading Republican in Sturbridge, had been a leading figure in the founding of the Leicester Academy, had raised a regiment in the southern half of the county to suppress the Regulators, and was an early member of both the Minervaean Society and the Massachusetts Agricultural Society. His resignation as a trustee of the Leicester Academy in 1797, increasingly a bastion of Federalism and Congregational orthodoxy, may have been an early sign of the Republican emergence. However, another government stalwart among the Republican committeemen, Thomas Denny of Leicester, had no reservations about remaining an academy trustee until his death in 1814. John Spurr, the leading Republican in Charlton, had served in the government cavalry before joining the Morning Star Lodge early in the 1790s, as did Jonathan Davis, from a progovernment family spread across Oxford, Charlton, and Dudley. Importantly, none of these Republican committeemen had served their towns as delegates to the constitutional convention in the winter of 1788. Among the Republican candidates for state senate in 1801 there was one man drawn from the heart of the county tradition of Antifederalism and Popular politics: Jonathan Grout. But on the same ticket were two men who had staunchly opposed convention politics, the Regulation, and Antifederalism. One was David Henshaw of Leicester who, with Thomas Denny, had attended the 1786 county convention called by Spencer, and with other friends of government had so "effectively clogged" the convention's proceedings that little was accomplished. Henshaw's cousin William, similarly a Friend of Government, would be a staunch Federalist. Another Republican candidate for state senate on Grout's ticket was Edward Bangs of Worcester, who had complained of the county's "dread of arbitrary power" in 1788 and urged confidence rather than jealousy in 1791. With the Lincolns, Bangs was one of the county's leading Republicans, repeatedly nominated for state senate and the U.S. House of Representatives. Like many of the other Republican leaders, Bangs had served with the government militia and was a charter member of the Worcester Fire Society.[32]

Although some might have harbored concerns about the powers of the federal Constitution in the early winter of 1788, the central figures in the Republican Party in Worcester County were not drawn from the ranks of the Regulators, and only symbolically – in the person of Jonathan Grout – from the moderate convention men or the broad group of Antifederalist delegates and representatives. Rather, most of them had stood with the government in 1787 and, although an older generation – whose experience ran back through the Revolution to the last days of provincial politics – spoke for the county's Antifederalism, these future Republican leaders withdrew with other young men into private societies, where they polished their skills in polite discourse, oratory, and institution building.

If the Republican leaders had played no part in the economic or Antifederalist politics of the 1780s, their limited role in the county courts echoed that of the Popular partisans before the Revolution. Levi Lincoln and Edward Bangs had set up as lawyers in Worcester during the Revolution, filling the void left by the departing Tories. Fittingly, Lincoln had served as the first clerk of courts under the provisional government, and he established himself as a champion of the new order in his defense of former slave Quok Walker of Barre in 1781, whose case contributed to the abolition of slavery in Massachusetts under the constitution of 1780.[33] Bangs and four of the Republican county committeemen in 1808 were members of the county bar, arguing cases before both the Supreme Judicial Court and the Common Pleas. But beyond these lawyers there was a sharp line between the leading elements of the two contending parties, for none of the Republican leaders held positions in the courts, while two-thirds of the known Federalist county committeemen sat as justices of the Common Pleas, as clerk of courts, and in positions in the offices of probate and deeds. Among the Republicans, only Timothy Newell of Sturbridge and John Spurr of Charlton had risen as high as justice of the peace and the quorum. To a striking degree, the Federalists replicated the control of the court system which had characterized the pre-

[32] Circular, Worcester County Republican Committee, October 15, 1808, Broadside Collection, AAS; *Reminiscences ... of the Fire Society*, 62; Nason, *Morning Star Lodge*, 197–209; "Records of the Minervaean Society"; Washburn, *Leicester Academy*, 73; on Friends of Government, see Chapter 7, note 35; for David Henshaw, father of the prominent Jacksonian politician, Jonathan Grout, and Edward Bangs, see Goodman, *Democratic-Republicans*, 225, n. 20; *Spy*, April 1, 1801 Jensen and Becker, *First Federal Elections*, 751; and Washburn, *Leicester*, 328; for the Bangs letter, see Harding, *Contest*, 74.

[33] Lincoln, *Worcester*, 228–34; William O'Brien, "Did the Jennison Case Outlaw Slavery in Massachusetts?" *WMQ* 3d ser., 17 (1960), 219–41; Arthur Zilversmit, "Quok Walker, Mumbet, and the Abolition of Slavery in Massachusetts," *WMQ*, 3d ser., 25 (1968), 614–24.

Revolutionary Court Party gentry, while the Republicans stood in the position of the leading Popular men.[34]

Just as the Revolution had loosened the control of the Court party elite, the electoral process brought change to the county judiciary. Beginning tentatively when they won the governorship in 1807 and 1808, and much more strikingly in 1810 and 1811, the Republicans established a system of judicial patronage rewarding the men who worked for the party, entrenching the party's control over the public sphere, and opening a new route in the judicial elite, which had for so long defined the apex of the social order. Local Republicans chaffed at the slow pace of the politicization of the judiciary. Edward D. Bangs, the son of the Republican leader in Worcester, wrote to a friend in Maine after the election of Republican James Sullivan in 1807 that "a pretty thorough removal of the sheriffs throughout the Commonwealth would be no discredit to the governor and a very just retaliation upon the Federalists – I am afraid however Sullivan has not *spunk* enough to do it." Four years later he assured his friend in Maine that Bangs, Sr., was working hard to have him appointed justice of the peace – his town should "be no longer destitute of a Republican Magistrate" – and had "repeatedly spoken to [Lt.] Gov. Lincoln on the subject." Indeed, 1811 was a year of dramatic change. Edward Bangs, Sr., the county attorney since 1807, was appointed an associate justice of the new Circuit Court of Common Pleas in 1811, and the entire bench of the new court of sessions – and the clerk of courts – was drawn from the ranks of the 1808 Republican county committee. In December 1811, Edward D. Bangs wrote proudly and possessively that "our first Circuit Court of Common Pleas" had just finished its session, and "Federal malice was completely subdued." Seen from the perspective of Bangs's ambitions and his letters bearing news of factional fortunes in the hothouse of a county town, the emergence of the Republican party was no insurgency rooted in community and social circumstance. Rather, it seems to have been simply a division within the county elite, ambitious men of essentially similar social position joisting for personal advantage and advancement.[35]

[34] Among seventeen Republican county committeemen in 1808, five were justices and court officers in 1808, and four were attorneys, while among twelve Federalists serving on county committees in 1805, 1808, and 1810, eleven were justices and court officers and two were attorneys. *Massachusetts Register for 1808* (Boston, 1807), 100–102; Republican Circular, October 15, 1808, Broadside Collection, AAS; Federalist Circulars, 1805, 1808, 1810, Box 2, Folder 2, Waldo Papers, Box 34, Folder 6, Foster Family Papers, AAS.

[35] Edward D. Bangs to Nathaniel Howe, November 2, 1807, May 20, 1811, December 16, 1811, in Folder 3, Letters of Edward Dillingham Bangs, 1807–1820, in the Bangs Family Papers, 1760–1866, AAS. Governor Gerry began to appoint justices of the peace and militia officers in 1810 and 1811 who were clearly Republican in loyalty, the JPs having neither professional training or experience in the General Court. Based on an analysis of JPs appointed to eight Worcester County towns, listed in the *Massachusetts Register* for 1800 through 1815, and the militia appointments of 1810–1812, also in the *Massachusetts Register*.

The failure of the Regulator wing of the Antifederalist coalition to shape the oppositional politics of the First Party System more strongly is particularly striking. Ultimately, the political geography of Worcester County in the early republic must be viewed in the light of the profoundly different configurations of public institutions and ideology that the provincial experience had inscribed most vividly on the Regulator northwest uplands and the Popular towns of the Blackstone Valley. The Regulators of the northwest uplands had never escaped the grip of the Court tradition: unitary, corporate institutions and ideology did not provide a fertile ground for a system of competitive politics. But across the southern half of the county the sequence of Land Bank, Awakening, and Popular and Constitutionalist politics had shaped a permanent architecture of plural and competing institutions, most notably the dissenting societies, and it was in this context that the Republican Party thrived.

Here, however, important qualifications are in order. The Popular tradition had been by no means monolithic, nor was the Republican dominance in the old Popular region. The Popular tradition had divided during the Revolution into different camps with distinct priorities, an orthodox New Light wing inclined toward economic issues, and a dissenting wing concerned primarily with the problem of framing the state constitution. Similarly, the Republicans were contested – winning by less than two-thirds of the total vote – in three-quarters (12/16) of the towns that they won at the height of the First Party System in 1812, while 60 percent (22/36) of the Federalist towns voted better than 2 to 1 for the federal candidate. The overwhelmingly Federalist towns were all located in the northern half of the county, whereas contested towns, won by either Federalists or Republicans by less than a two-thirds margin, were concentrated in the south, particularly in the Blackstone Valley. This pattern prevailed throughout the era of competitive party politics, from 1805 through 1824. As much as it built a constituency for the Republicans, the broader Popular experience in the southern towns had built an environment for partisan competition.

Who, then, were the competing groups in the old Popular towns, now voting Republican by a relatively slender margin? It seems reasonable to suggest that these two camps were rooted in the ground laid by the two wings of the old Popular Party. As late as the 1800 election, the presence or absence of dissenting societies bore little relationship to the aggregate votes for oppositional candidates. But by 1804, and throughout the ensuing decade of party strife, the presence of dissenting societies was strongly associated with Republican voting, while their absence was linked with overwhelming Federalist majorities; this aggregate picture is confirmed by local evidence from lists of partisans and church members. The newer denominations of Universalism, Methodism, and Unitarianism were particularly likely to be located in Republican towns. By this measure, Republicanism was built on the ground laid by the Constitutionalist "New Light Stir" of the 1780s. Constitutionalist sentiment of 1776 and experience in the rioting of the early 1780s was associated with the Republican towns of 1812; this relationship would persist through 1824 and far into the century in Democratic towns. Conversely, the Federalists in the old Popular region seem to have been rooted in the tradition of Popular orthodoxy. In Sutton, for example, David Hall's old New Light Congregational Church – the archetype of a Popular orthodox community – was almost uniformly Federalist.[36] The broader Popular tradition

[36] Evidence from reports of contested elections and newspaper subscription lists provides further support for the well-known affinity of dissenters for the Republican Party. In Southbridge, 57% (35/62) of the members of the Congregationalist Society signed a Federalist election remonstrance in 1817, as against only 6% (7/120) of the members of the Baptist Society. In Worcester the Baptist society formed in 1819 included ten known Republicans and no Federalists, and the survivors of the 1787 Unitarian Society (Second Parish) favored the Republicans over the Federalists 9 to 6. Similarly, the Oxford Universalists were dominated by Republican petitioners. In Sutton, dissenting religion was the most significant marker of Republican affiliation. It is important that men from Sutton Land Bank families were not necessarily drawn to the Republicans, but were as often drawn to the Federalists. The relationship between the Land Bank and Jeffersonian Republicanism was thus not direct but indirect, shaped by institutional forms and political styles rather than family traditions. Suggestively, Republicans seem to have been slightly more likely to have come from families involved in Constitutional politics, and Federalists from families involved in the economic politics of the 1770s.

Republicans and Federalists in Sutton, 1799–1820

	Subscribers to the Republican *Aegis*		Federalist petitioners	
Total	27	*100*	137	*100*
Land Bank kin	3	*11*	20	*14*
Congregationalists	7	*26*	80	*58*
Dissenters	10	*37*	2	*1*
Kin of members of town committees dealing with				
Economy, 1777–87	3	*23*	14	*34*
State constitution	4	*31*	11	*27*
Kin of government militiamen	7	*26*	29	*21*

Note: Figures in italics are percentages.
Source: Manuscript Remonstrances of Contested Elections from Oxford, 1809, Sutton, 1810, 1812, Southbridge, 1817, Massachusetts Archives; Subscription lists and committeemen, 1806, "Worcester *National Aegis*, Papers," AAS; "Worcester County, Mass., Washington Benevolent Society, Records," AAS; Ammidown, *Historical Collections*, 2: 480, 490–1; "The Second Religious Society in Oxford and the Adjacent Towns (Called Universalist) Record Book"; *Private and Special Statutes*, 1: 171; *Laws of the Commonwealth*, 5: 233; for other Sutton references see Chapter 6, note 24, and MA 191: 105, 269; and MA 192: 158.

had forged a style of politics in which elites and constituencies were experienced and comfortable with the interplay of competing institutions and interests. In brief, the Popular tradition left a matrix of complex institutions and the beginnings of a liberal, pluralistic ideology in which Jeffersonian Republicanism could compete effectively with Federalism. In the north, a unitary orthodox culture allowed no such foothold for a competitive party system.

Virtue and corruption

The town of Leicester was one of the few old Popular and Land Bank strongholds to cast majority votes with the Federalists across the First Party era. The dominance of the Federalist route out of Popular orthodoxy in this old town was grounded in a changing configuration of institutions, institutions that shaped the rhetorical and cultural underpinnings of early party politics.

Leicester's Baptist church, practically the oldest in the county, fell on hard times in the 1790s, in the wake of the dispute over granting a ministerial salary. By the turn of the century the Leicester Baptists were reduced to two-thirds of the size they had achieved in the New Light Stir of 1779–81. Conversely, the orthodox church at the center prospered as never before. In 1798, with the death of Benjamin Conklin, the church settled Zephaniah Swift Moore as minister, who guided the church through a series of revivals over the ensuing years. Seven years later the church had a revised articles of faith printed in Boston, including Jonathan Edwards's resolutions that "none but visible believers have a right to admission." By 1815 a number of traditionally Baptist families, most notably the Dennys, had gravitated to the revitalized orthodox church.[37] In 1800 Leicester had voted strongly for moderate Republican Elbridge Gerry for governor and for Levi Lincoln for federal representative. But, although the majority of the old Popular towns moved on to a consistent Jeffersonian predominance, Leicester returned permanently to the Federalist fold over the following decade.

On the affinity of dissenters for the Republican Party in Massachusetts in general, see Goodman, *Jeffersonian-Republicans*, 86–96; Banner, *Toward the Hartford Convention*, 197–9, 208–15; and Formisano, *The Transformation*, 153–9. For a more qualified view, see McLoughlin, *New England Dissent*, 2: 1065–1106. Note McLoughlin's comments on the Republicans' "abstract commitment" to a "liberal republicanism." On Methodism in particular, see Paul G. Faler, *Mechanics and Manufacturers in the Early Industrial Revolution: Lynn, Massachusetts, 1780–1860* (Albany, 1981), 40–8.

[37] Greenville Baptist Church Records; *Minutes of the Warren Association*; *Minutes of the Sturbridge Baptist Association* (1805–19); Estes, "Historical Discourse," in *Greenville Baptist Church*, 47; *Manual of the First Congregational Church in Leicester, Mass., with List of Members, 1886* (Worcester, 1886); Washburn, *Leicester*, 96–8; 1815 plan of pews in Leicester meetinghouse, Leicester Local Papers, AAS.

The roots of Leicester's Federalism were bound up in both the collapse of dissent and the revival of orthodoxy, but they were also buttressed by Federalist institution building. Leicester's Congregational meetinghouse shared the height of Strawberry Hill with the Leicester Academy. As his predecessor had been, Zephaniah Moore was very much involved in the academy's affairs, serving as trustee from 1798 and secretary from 1800 until he was appointed a professor at Dartmouth College in 1811. With few exceptions, the trustees and officers of the Leicester Academy were drawn from the ranks of the county's Federalist and orthodox gentry, and these men took with increasing seriousness their charge to promote "true piety and virtue" as well as "the education of youth" in practical and classical studies.[38] A rising generation needed to be guided in the path of virtue, and to be shielded from tumultuous and impious influences. An educational paradigm, made tangible in the work of the academy and most clearly articulated in its context, shaped a central dimension of the rhetorical language through which the Federalist gentry attempted to mold the ideological options of the people at large.

On July 5, 1802, Zephaniah Moore presented the Independence Day oration in Worcester. His presentation touched on the central themes of an embattled Massachusetts Federalism. He invoked the Revolution and "the worthies" who had founded a "wise and judicial system" in Philadelphia in 1787, in contradistinction to the "corrupt, insidious, and designing men" who had recently led the French Revolution – and to the "new order of things" that had been "introduced" into the United States in 1800. Without directly naming the Jeffersonian administration as its source, Moore implied that a corrupting influence was undermining virtue across the new nation, opening the doors to the collapse of the republic, as it had destroyed the prosperity and then independence of the ancient republics. In particular, Moore pointed to knowledge and information as a double-edged sword, the fountain of both virtue and corruption, in language rooted in the revived Calvinism for which he spoke.

> Much is said by utopian projectors in favor of knowledge, as what if universally disseminated, will promote the purity of public opinion, and ensure national prosperity. Great expectations have been raised ... [that] universal good will pervade the earth.... These speculations proceed upon false data. They suppose, that the cause of political corruption ... is ignorance, and not the depravity of man.

Moore's fundamental assumptions were Calvinist: man was limited by his innate evil, and knowledge could thus be put to evil purposes. Speaking as a trustee of the academy, he argued that education "may be made the source of our corruption and final dissolution, or a means of purity and perpetuation of our republic." Similarly, while a free press was a "blessing," a "licentious press [was] a sink of iniquity ...

---

[38] Washburn, *Leicester Academy*, 72–5; *Private and Special Statutes*, 1:72–4.

prostituted to the vile purposes of strengthening foreign influence, of corrupting
public opinion by weakening the ties of religion and morality." Cutting closer to
the political arena, he expressed the Federalist demand for social order, stability,
and deference; corruption was emanating from those "who are under the influence
of restless, unworthy, aspiring ambition," wishing to rise "to places for honor and
authority, to which, from their merit, they can have no claim."³⁹

Four years later Moore's essential points were repeated, though tempered by a
milder Unitarian theology, by Aaron Bancroft of the Second Parish in Worcester
in an address to the Leciester Academy on its twentieth anniversary. Echoing both
Moore's 1802 oration and his own charge to the Morning Star Lodge in 1793,
Bancroft stressed the moral value of education for a young man: education
"disciplines his passions, purifies his temper, and refines his manners ... [; it]
forms the soul to the habits of virtue." He reminded the instructors that "the
essential and primary end of this Academy is the promotion of piety and Christian
virtue," and that "at no period was attention to moral education more necessary
than at the present." The academy's instructors were to guard young minds from
"the contagion of irreligion, ... the impious maxims of the skeptic, and the vain
dogmas of the sophist; amidst the corrupting agitations of political party and the
seductions of vice."⁴⁰

As were Bancroft's remarks before the Worcester Freemasons in 1793, these
proscriptions for a virtuous education were couched in a broader doctrine of
disinterested benevolence, rooted in both the corporate assumptions long traditional in orthodoxy and in new concerns about the order and stability of the
republic. These themes were deeply embedded in the Federalist mentality in the
county and throughout the state. In 1796 the Reverend Nathan Fiske of Brookfield
had warned Harvard students against the influences of that "daring insurgent"
Tom Paine; the next year his son Dr. Oliver Fiske warned the Independence Day
celebration in Worcester that "there are certain limits in human nature" that
threatened the "uninterrupted continuance" of the republic's rising glory.⁴¹

³⁹ Zephaniah S. Moore, *An Oration on the Anniversary of the Independence of the United States
of America ... July 5, 1802 ...* (Worcester, 1802), 5–7, 12, 16, 18–20; it is suggestive that Levi
Lincoln, Sr., served briefly as president of the Leicester Academy between 1800 and 1802,
following Moses Gill and followed by Rev. Joseph Sumner of Shrewsbury, both of whom
served sixteen-year terms. Washburn, *Leicester Academy*, 75. The politics of this brief
presidency – during the fluid period of Republican emergence – may well have informed
Moore's language in this passage.

⁴⁰ Aaron Bancroft, *The Importance of Education, Illustrated in an Oration, Delivered before the
Trustees, Preceptors, and Students of Leicester Academy, on the 4th of July, 1806 ...* (Worcester,
1806), 8, 16, 17.

⁴¹ Nathan Fiske, *A Sermon Preached at the Dudleian Lecture, in the Chapel of Harvard College,
September 7, 1796* (Boston, 1796), 14; Oliver Fiske, *An Oration, Pronounced at Worcester, on the
Anniversary of American Independence, July 4th 1797* (Worcester, 1797), 14–15.

Invocations of the cyclical theory of history were only redoubled after the Jeffersonian victory in 1800. In the midst of the embargo in 1808 Abijah Bigelow, a Federalist leader in the northern section of the county, developed the cyclical theory in a common organic metaphor: "the history of the world is the history of revolutions; ... nations like individuals, have their rise and fall." He warned the party faithful of the multiple threats of their liberties that lay in the Republican allegiance to France, in the embargo policy, and in a "persecuting party spirit." An "alarming crisis" threatened the nation; "a revolution that seems destined to sweep from the face of the Earth, every principle of moral and political rectitude, has already overrun almost all of Europe, and begins to approach these happy shores." He invoked the dead in the name of virtue: "the spirits of your fathers, even the tombs ... [demand] eternal hatred to the enemies of your Independence." When the administration declared war on England in 1812, a convention of Federalists in Worcester warned of the impending "destruction of the rights and liberties of the people," and threatened that "a dissolution of the civil compact" might be "the last and only remedy." Adhering to a strictly classical and cyclical interpretation of the republican ideal, Worcester Federalists stumbled toward paranoia and secessionism.[42]

Fundamentally, Federalist ideology was rooted in the mutual resonances of classical republicanism and the orthodox language of national covenant.[43] Both framed history in grand cycles, hinging on the moral condition of the people, both demanded individual responsibility for the collective welfare, both predicted the collapse of the collectivity with the spread of individual vice, both promised a broad prosperity upon the achievement of individual virtue. In its classical balancing of the individual and the collectivity, Massachusetts Federalism was a particularly hierarchical and organic version of the now ancient Harrington equation of personal independence and public obligation, an equation that had long had a powerful resonance for those who remained committed to orthodox corporatism. Here lay the roots of its obvious yet paradoxical popularity across the broad orthodox majority in Worcester County, the people from whom both moderate convention men and the Regulator militias had been drawn, and who had made up the weight of the county's Antifederalist coalition. Behind the stereotype of an archaic political ideology one can clearly make out continuities that link popular Federalism both back to the Revolution and the economic politics of the 1780s and forward to the third-party insurgencies that would eventually destroy the Second Party System in Massachusetts, feeding the Free Soil–Republican solidarity that would inspire thousands of young men to march off to fight the "slave power" in 1861.

---

[42] Abijah Bigelow, *A Oration, Delivered at Bolton, July 4, 1808* ... (Leominster, 1808), 3, 10–11; *Proceedings of a Convention of Delegates from Forty-One Towns in the County of Worcester, Holden in Worcester, the 12th and 13th of August, 1812* (Worcester, 1812) 5, 18.
[43] This is the central thesis of Banner, *To the Hardford Convention*, esp. 20–83.

Federalism may have been the dominant party within the state, but in the national context it lay in an embattled opposition after 1800, and on the verge of insurgency and secession in 1812. Here, for a long generation culminating in 1812, both gentry and yeomen of the orthodox world found a common ground. Divided in actual civil war in 1786, orthodox gentry and yeomen were fundamentally united in opposition to Madisonian war making. It was during the Republican war with England between 1812 and 1814 that Worcester Federalism reached its zenith. In Hardwick, one Federalist orator urged the people to oppose a "war of honor" with resolutions of "remonstrance." Assembling in Worcester in March 1812, a convention of Federalists complained of the Republican efforts to undermine the traditional structures of the courts and of town government and – echoing Amos Singletary's language in the ratifying convention – warned of the near approach of war and the threats of an oppressive internal tax to support "an immense standing army." Brookfield Federalists writing to the General Court early in 1814 repeated the republican language of slavery that had appeared in 1740, 1774, and 1786: "We cannot, we will not be slaves." "Are the yeomanry of New-England panting for the tug of war?" Francis Blake asked of the Worcester Federalists in July 1812, "Are you eager to beat your plowshares into swords?"[44]

The answer was expressed in the electoral surge toward the Federalists, sweeping through the Regulator northwest and even some of the old Popular strongholds in the Blackstone Valley. When Federalists had proposed policies of war and taxation in 1798 and 1799 they won landslide victories – but had attracted less than a quarter of the potential vote in the county. Only the absence of an organized opposition – and the abstraction of the quasi war with France – had allowed them to prevail uncontested. Between 1802 and 1824 the party typically won more modestly with the support of roughly a third of the potential electorate. But when Republicans pursued similar policies in 1812, the Federalists increased their margin slightly, and attracted between 45 and 48 percent of the potential electorate, a level matched only by Log Cabin Whiggery in the 1840 election. Something besides deference was at work. A popular Federalism, peaking during the war years, triumphed because it played on Harringtonian themes of independence in commonwealth deeply embedded in the political culture of the county's orthodox majority. This popular, Harringtonian Federalism would be powerfully formative in the coming decades.

---

[44] Festus Foster, *An Oration Pronounced at Hardwick, July 4th, 1812* (Brookfield, 1812); *Proceedings of a Convention of Federal Republicans from the South Senatorial District in Worcester, March 11, 1812* (Worcester, 1812), 3–4, 7; Senate Doc. 4820/45, quoted in Banner, *Toward the Hartford Convention*, 317; Francis Blake, *An Oration Pronounced at Worcester (Mass.) on the Thirty-Sixth Anniversary of American Independence, July 4, 1812 . . . Published at the Request of a Numerous Assembly of Citizens . . . and the Washington Benevolent Society . . .* (Worcester, 1812), 26.

"Free natural choice"

Republicans were not immune to the totalistic language that so often characterized Federalist rhetoric. In an 1806 oration in Lancaster, Samuel Brazier of Worcester condemned the "Federal knights of the black cockade" who had imposed the Sedition Act in 1798, and derided Jedediah Morse's fears of the "Illuminati" as a "necromantic spell." The Federalists were merely a "vindictive array of cashiered officers, disbanded judges, disappointed speculators, and party priests ... organized in opposition to the will of the people, drawn up in battle array against their constitutional agents." In 1808 Estes Howe of Sutton spoke of the Federalists' "treacherous baseness" and their "unnatural opposition" to Jefferson's government. Nowhere in the Republican rhetoric was there a direct justification of the dual-party politics that they had inaugurated. In 1815 another Republican orator went to great lengths to disassociate himself from "contracted party politics, the mere paltry disputes of *Ins* and *Outs*." "Think not," he concluded, "that in condemning the one party we necessarily approve all the conduct of the other."[45]

But, on balance, if the Federalists appealed to a cyclical, organic traditionalism, the Republicans spoke in a new language for a new age. Republican rhetoric in Worcester County passed quickly over the problems of corruption and virtue, and it ignored the cyclical fears that so consumed the Federalists. Rather, its central theme was a view of the "rising glory" of the republic, and posed the simultaneously arminian and millennial challenge that "it rests with ourselves to realize brighter destinies."[46] And if Republican orators did not explicitly defend the right of private interests to compete in the public arena, their language was informed by a strong current of Lockean rationalism. Harringtonian and Lockean themes had coexisted within the broader Popular tradition since the 1730s. But, giving voice to their own inclinations and those of a constituency rooted in the pluralist towns, the Republican leadership in Worcester County abandoned Harrington for Locke.

The most formative of the Republican addresses was delivered by Edward Bangs, Sr., at the July 4th celebration in Worcester in 1800. The first Republican to address the celebration, and speaking only two months after the town had cast the first in a continuous sequence of Republican majorities in the gubernatorial election, Bangs's oration stood at a critical turning point in the Jeffersonian emergence. His central themes were the human capacities for civil liberty, and the

[45] Samuel Brazier, Jr., *Oration, Pronounced at Lancaster, July 4, 1806, in Commemoration of American Independence* (Worcester, 1806), 15–18; Estes Howe, *An Oration, Delivered in Worcester, Massachusetts* (Worcester, 1808), 3–4; Peleg Sprague, *An Oration, Pronounced at Worcester, July 4, 1815 ...* (Worcester, 1815), 18.

[46] Samuel Brazier, Jr., *An Oration, Pronounced at Charlton in Commemoration of the Anniversary of American Independence, July 4th, 1811* (Worcester, 1811), 16.

means necessary for preserving such liberty. Reviewing the history of republics and empires, he soon came to his key point: Man would "prefer liberty when left to his free natural choice." Bangs developed this emphasis on human volition in opposition to what he saw as the central premises of Federalist and Calvinist ideology.

> The advocates for what they call efficient government, drawing all their arguments from past history, affirm, that though men individually may pretend to the honor of being rational creatures, they cannot act as such collectively. Self interest, say they, sets them at perpetual war with each other – self interest stronger than reason, and therefore they must be overruled .... What, demand they, has been the never failing fruit of all attempts at reformation, and pretended establishment of equal rights. Corruption and Devastation....[47]

Bangs's Republican answer to Federalist pessimism was stated in terms redolent of Lockean theory. He acknowledged "the imperfections of our natures, the error of our reason, and the madness of our passions" and that "a more perfect future state" awaited in heaven, but he urged his audience that "none can deny that it [heaven] has kindly permitted us to make use of that reason, by which we are distinguished, to improve and ameliorate the present." Given the pace of scientific achievement, Americans had "reason to take courage," to hope to "be able to learn the nature of the human mind and the regulation of its passions." Such ideas directly challenged Calvinist doctrines of innate human depravity, and Bangs's evident deism would cost him support at the polls. Four years later he tangled with a "pratting Federal shopkeeper" who had challenged his "concern for religion."[48]

If Bangs was hinting at the outlines of a system of routinized competition of interests, a science of politics, he did not develop the idea in his closing passages on the means of preserving liberty. Here an "ardent love of liberty" and "a degree of political knowledge" were critical. Bangs touched briefly on the topic of virtue, but he saw no need for new "institutions calculated to inspire the republican virtues and form good citizens." In conclusion, Bangs developed the progressive theme that would shape the nationalist Republican credo for the decades to come. "A new scene of human affairs we believe is approaching – stormy and tempestuous has been night ... but the day has dawned, the mountain tops begin to shine – the sun advances – and though in the European hemisphere the storm is still prevailing – Happy America! Serene is your morning – beautiful and bright are your skies.[49]

[47] Edward Bangs, *An Oration on the Anniversary of American Independence, Pronounced at Worcester July 4, 1800* (Worcester, 1800), 5–6, 9, 10.

[48] Bangs, *Oration ... at Worcester*, 11–12; *National Aegis*, October 17, 1804.

[49] Bangs, *Oration ... at Worcester*, 15–27. On Lockean rationalism, see Fleigelman, *Prodigals and Pilgrims*, 9–35; on Republicans and Locke, see Appleby, *Capitalism and the New Social Order*.

Given the tone and direction of its rhetoric, it is striking that this oration was delivered before Jefferson's election could provide solid grounds for Republican optimism. This optimism would pervade the orations delivered to the party faithful by Bangs's younger associates over the next decade and a half. They challenged the Federalists' hesitant attitude toward education, and avoiding the cyclical theory, developed a language of secular millennialism that bore suggestions of ideas of manifest destiny of a subsequent generation of Democrats. In 1811 Samuel Brazer exhorted the Republicans of Charlton that "it rests with ourselves to realise brighter destinies." Edward Bangs, Jr., told the Sutton Republicans in 1813 that America was "not destined to an early termination of her splendid career.... She is reserved to consumate some higher purpose – 'Westward the star of empire holds its way.'"[50]

It was not until the years immediately following the War of 1812 that the optimistic Republican perspective was combined with an explicit critique of the cyclical theory. Appropriately, the first two orators to make this argument were young men in their twenties who had not been involved in the conflicts of the previous decade. From the first generation to be born in the new nation, it was fitting that they should have been the first to fully articulate the idea of "progress." Pliny Merrick, a young law student in Worcester and the son of a Brookfield lawyer prominent in Republican circles, began the assault on the cyclical theory in a Fourth of July oration in 1817. Merrick maintained that the "theory that assimilated the progress of kingdoms to the life of man," though "fortified ... by the venerable supports of antiquity," had been merely "speculation." He argued that "the analogy had been imperfectly drawn," the appropriate analog for the state was not the physical body, "subject to natural decay," but the mind, which was "susceptible of indefinite improvement." Thus the optimistic Republican vision of education provided a key critique of the cyclical theory; a new reading of history and political science provided another. In considering "the durability of political institutions" in the new nation, people had drawn a second inappropriate analogy too often. Merrick maintained that the institutions and circumstances of the United States had been compared erroneously with the frail republics and despotic empires of ancient and more recent history. Most importantly, the American people had the example of the orderly transfer of executive power before them: "We behold THREE of our fellow citizens [who have] calmly relinquished the highest honours of the nation ... while a FOURTH, just ushered into the office they have left, if cheered by the loud acclamations of his affectionate countrymen." Merrick's argument was elaborated in 1818 by Austin Denny, another young law student from a gentry family in Leicester. Denny saw

[50] Edward D. Bangs, *An Oration, Pronounced at Sutton, Massachusetts, July 5th, 1813* ... (Boston, 1813), 16; see also Zenas L. Leonard, *An Oration, Pronounced at Southbridge, Mass., July 4th, 1816* ... (Worcester, 1816), 17–18; Brazier, *Oration ... at Charlton*, 16.

"increasing evidence of the strength of our free institutions, and of the disposition and ability of the nation to maintain them." He argued that since the shaky beginnings of the late 1780s "thirty years have ... elapsed, and our form of government has been upheld in the midst of the most tremendous commotions which the world ever witnessed."[51]

Just as it brought a public resolution of the ideological debates of the preceding decade, the period following the War of 1812 brought a sudden cooling of party conflict. Voter turnout dropped sharply, to the extent that in November 1818 the *Spy* could complain that "an extreme degree of apathy and indifference to this election seems to have prevailed throughout the state." Edward Bangs, Jr., wrote in 1816 to a friend in Maine that he would be content under the administration of moderate Federalist John Brooks, and that he "had become tired and disgusted with political discussions." Writing again in the summer of 1817, Bangs was confident that the Republicans had prevailed.

> The cause which you and I espoused with such zeal and have defended with such earnestness is now completely triumphant – its purity and excellency are tacitly acknowledged by all – it is forever safe from the attacks of what *was once* federalism (for the party, as a party, is in fact extinct) – and the chief danger of republicanism will now be from the abuses of its own friends.[52]

Party structures and identities had taken shape and hardened quickly at the turn of the century, and they evaporated just as rapidly after 1815; the First Party System was a dramatic but ultimately temporary experiment in a new and alien science of politics.[53]

If Martin Van Buren would object to the collapse of party principles and loyalties, the amalgamation of parties perfectly suited the leading figures in the county of Worcester. Bangs was right; the Worcester Republicans had triumphed, and in 1825 he would go to Boston as secretary to Levi Lincoln, Jr., who would serve seven years as governor of the commonwealth. Lincoln's base would be that fusion of Republicans and Federalists known as the National Republicans, later evolving into the Whig Party. The Lockean assumptions developed by Bangs's father in 1800, building on the Lockean current in the Popular tradition that ran back to the Constitutionalists, to the emergence of religious dissent, and to the institutional frame of the Land Bank, would inform the thinking of both the Nationals and their Jacksonian adversaries in the decades to come. In the years following the end of party strife, however, party adversity would be buried in the resurgence of the inclusive secular voluntarism that had characterized the 1790s.

[51] Pliny Merrick, [Jr.], *An Oration, Delivered in Worcester, July 4, 1817* (Worcester, 1817), 9–10, 14–15; Austin Denny, *An Oration Delivered at Worcester, July 4th, 1818* (Worcester, 1818), 11.
[52] *Spy*, Nov. 11, 1818; Bangs to Howe, May 12, 1816, August 1, 1817.
[53] Formisano, *The Transformation of Political Culture.*

In an attempt to revive the associational politics of the 1790s, the Federalists had turned the forms of voluntary association and organic benevolence to the uses of politics in 1812 and 1814, forming the Washington Benevolent Society and a county Society for the Reformation of Morals. The Washington Benevolent Society was the institutional equivalent of the Federalists' old-fashioned cyclical classicism; The Jeffersonian *Aegis* had written mockingly of initiations and "mysteries" when Oliver Fiske and William Stedman had gone to Northampton to receive a charter for a Worcester society.[54]

But 1812 also saw an effort to restore the framework of a truly unitary associational public culture in Worcester. Isaiah Thomas's American Antiquarian Society balanced Federalists Harrison G. Otis, Timothy Bigelow, and Nathaniel Paine with Republicans Levi Lincoln, Sr. and Jr., and Edward Bangs, Sr., among its leading incorporators. The Worcester Agricultural Society, founded in the spring of 1819, spread the mantle of elite associational culture far more widely across the county. Its officers were divided evenly between the former parties: Levi Lincoln, Sr., was the president, three Federalists served as vice-presidents and treasurer, Levi Lincoln, Jr., and Edward Bangs., Jr., were the secretaries. The society attracted a wide cross section of leading men from throughout the county: Almost 60 percent of the representatives elected to the General Court in May 1819 were already members of the new society, and in the broad region stretching south and west from Worcester the society attracted large groups of men who had served as both Federalist and Republican representatives between 1805 and 1815. The nostalgic purposes of the promotion of agriculture served to unite a body of men divided by politics and religion, and increasingly less involved in farming than in a range of professional, commercial, and manufacturing endeavors. Gathered from throughout the county, the "Gentlemen of the Society" listened to orations on how agricultural improvement might benefit the county's "yeomanry," and sponsored competitions that subtly reinforced a growing stratification of social and economic resources. Like the original voluntary societies in 1790s, the Worcester Agricultural Society provided a context for the reintegration of the county elite, allowing them at least the fiction of a common interest and common purpose, after a long period of intense confrontation.[55]

---

[54] "Worcester County, Mass., Washington Benevolent Society, Records," AAS; "Constitution [and Membership List] of a Branch of the General Society in the County of Worcester, for the Reformation of Morals [1815]," Sutton, Mass., Papers, AAS. *Aegis*, March 25, 1812.
[55] *Private and Special Statutes*, 4:461–2; Lincoln, *Address Delivered before the Worcester Agricultural Society*; for Federalists, Republicans, and the WAS, see note 29.

9

Economic transformation

In March 1812, the president and directors of the Worcester Bank assembled at the bank building on Main Street west of the courthouse to address a petition to the General Court for the renewal of their charter. Their petition proudly recounted the achievements of their institution. The bank's stockholders were not interested in their own "great pecuniary emolument." Rather, they had a "view to the accommodation of the public, and to their own, *but as a part of that public*, in the increase of business, and the facility of its management." And they argued that, in the eight years since its original charter, the Worcester Bank had come to play a pivotal role in the regional economy.

> It has cherished and encouraged the manufactures of the county, it has contributed to improvements in agriculture, it has supported the credit of trade; it has multiplied the resources of business, it has diminished the number of lawsuits. The County of Worcester justly boasts of her mechanics and her artificers; the extent of her workshops, and more especially of the ingenuity of her labors in the fabric of cloths and of paper, and in the greater importance of manufactures in iron. A sum beyond the calculation of your petitioners is constantly employed as a capital in a multiplicity of mechanical engagements. Loans are urgently applied for, and readily granted to those important interests; and your petitioners are authorized in the assurance, that the existence of the bank . . . [is] indispensable to their preservation."[1]

In short, the Worcester Bank petitioners placed their institution at the center of a fundamental transformation of economic structures. The bank's operations were facilitating the rapid emergence of manufacturing and a growing commercialization of agriculture that would characterize a dramatic, seminal break with the eighteenth-century past.[2]

The first decade of the nineteenth century brought two sweeping processes of change to the Worcester middle landscape. On the one hand, a passionate party

[1] Worcester Bank Petition, March 1812, Original Papers, chap. 36, Acts of 1812.
[2] Douglas North, *The Economic Growth of the United States, 1790–1860* (New York, 1966), 156–76; Paul A. David, "The Growth of Real Product in the United States Before 1840: New Evidence, Controlled Conjectures," *Journal of Economic History* 27 (1967), 151–97, esp. 186–8; Henretta, "Wealth and Social Structure," 269–70, 275–9; Gross, "Culture and Agriculture"; Winifred B. Rothenberg, "The Emergence of a Capital Market in Rural Massachusetts, 1730–1838," *Journal of Economic History* 45 (1985), 781–808.

politics was turning political discourse and action from assumptions of organic unity toward those of structured competition. On the other hand, the private corporation, an institution chartered by the state to accumulate and invest capital, was playing an increasingly central role in a powerful reconfiguration of the regional economy. If neither process was complete by 1815, the ground had been laid for their full articulation in the 1830s. Each contradicted and complemented the other in complex ways. Most importantly, political parties and private corporations were key institutional expressions of the Lockean voluntarism that the dissenters had introduced into the county's social landscape with the Great Awakening, and that the gentry had secularized by their own institution building in the decades following the constitutional settlements of the 1780s. The form of insurgency became the framework of status quo.

The connections between party politics and economic change were complex. It has been suggested that the politics of national independence that generated such fire between Federalists and Republicans was often ignored in the pursuit of a local and regional politics of development.[3] But the problems and alternatives of development could just as easily be turned to the rhetoric of national independence. Between 1805 and 1815 Federalists and Republicans in Worcester County moved between conflict and cooperation in economic matters according to a complex calculation of private and public advantage, in a world where the leading focus of enterprise was moving from commerce to manufacturing. Ultimately, however, profit would prevail over political culture, and the amalgamation of Federalist and Republican elites into the National coalition that followed the War of 1812 was rooted in large part in common assumptions about economic purposes.

But the industrial revolution that swept across the county in these years had a far deeper and broader reach than simply the amalgamation of these elite factions. Where the conflict of Federalists and Republicans was rooted in patterns of political culture and political practice running back to county beginnings, the economic transformation well under way in 1812 would dramatically reshape the county's public geography. This new geography would derive from resources and communications, rivers and roads, water power and market access. Political change would not come from the most obvious and conspicuous new development. The spread of textile mills, factory villages, and the emergence of an industrial working class along the banks of the Blackstone and the other rivers running through the southern half of the county would not divert these towns from a political tradition running from the dissenting wing of Popular politics to Jeffersonian and Jacksonian loyalties. Rather, it was along an emergent band of rural "urbanization" running along the Post Road through the center of the county, a social thickening rooted in diversified, small-scale manufacturing, that a

---

[3] Weibe, *The Opening of American Society*, 194ff.

new political tradition would emerge. To some degree, this tradition drew upon the old center of gravity in the county's provincial politics, the orthodox wing of the Popular tradition. But more importantly, the early-nineteenth-century experience along this central corridor – the spread of shopwork along putting-out networks, a heated political environment, and successive waves of orthodox revivalism – powered two cycles of political insurgency. Where textile workers were lost in a Lockean world, moving from mill to mill in search of better wages, with little connection of community, divided and often disenfranchised by their own mobility,[4] the artisan-farmers of the central corridor repeatedly entered the political arena to defend a Harringtonian vision of equal opportunity and personal independence in the context of household and community. The Antimasonic and Free Soil insurgencies would have their center of gravity in this new middle ground between household agriculture and institutionally structured manufacturing, and among people bearing traditions of embattled orthodoxy and popular Federalism. In turn these insurgencies would lay the ground for a broad consensus that the North must not compromise with the southern slave power.

The Jay Treaty

The economic revolution that swept the county – and the nation – in the early nineteenth century had its fundamental origins in the Revolution and the framing of the Federal Constitution. The politics of national independence that began in 1765 were inextricably tied to national economic development; one step behind "Country" language about British subversion of American charters and liberties lay a sense that Americans might develop their economic potential most fully when freed of imperial constraints.[5]

There are hints of a link between politics and a manufacturing economy in pre-Revolutionary Worcester County, particularly during the Townshend crisis of 1768. Thus ironmaster James Woods of New Braintree was the only delegate sent from the Court-dominated northwest uplands to the 1768 Convention of Towns and, in the same year, perhaps working from urban models of workhouse manufactures, the sons of Popular leader Jabez Upham started a small and short-lived woolen factory on their gristmill privilege in south Brookfield.[6] The war

---

[4] This characterization in based in part on the detailed analysis in Jonathan Prude, *The Coming of Industrial Order: Town and Factory Life in Rural Massachusetts, 1810–1860* (New York, 1983), esp. 144–57, 227–35.

[5] Marc Egnal and Joseph A. Ernst, "An Economic Interpretation of the American Revolution," *WMQ* 29 (1972), 3–32; Appleby, "The Social Origins of American Revolutionary Ideology."

[6] Brown, "Convention of Towns," 104; Force, *American Archives*, ser. 5, 3:409–10; Temple, *North Brookfield*, 14; Shipton, ed., *Sibley's Harvard Graduates* 15:496; Nash, *The Urban Crucible*, 332–7.

itself created demands for new industrial ventures. Soon after Isaiah Thomas relocated the Massachusetts *Spy* to Worcester in the spring of 1775, the Worcester County convention resolved that "the erection of a paper-mill in this County would be of great public advantage." By the middle of 1776 Abijah Burbank had established a paper mill in the North Parish of Sutton, later to become Millbury, and the Burbanks would be involved in paper making here and in Worcester until 1830. Other Revolutionary enterprises were also established in Millbury, where a series of well-fed streams ran into the upper reaches of the Blackstone River. The gun-making Waters family had set up a trip-hammer on one of these streams before the Revolution and, with expanded production during the war, Asa Waters, Sr., developed experience and contacts that laid the groundwork for federal armory work between 1808 and 1845. Both the Waters and Burbanks were involved in an oil mill just below the armory site, and adjacent to that was a short-lived powder mill commissioned by the state in 1776.[7] And more importantly, though difficult to measure precisely, the breaking of trade with Britain encouraged the expansion of production of various grades and mixtures of woolen, linen, and cotton yarn and cloth, handspun and handwoven by literally thousands of women in households throughout the region. The production of these women was prodigious; in the spring of 1791 young Elizabeth Fuller of Princeton spun over 40,000 yards of yarn; a year later she spent three months weaving 176 yards of fabric. This cloth was processed by clothiers in relatively primitive fulling mills, such as those established in the 1750s by the Plymptons on the Quinebaug River in what would become the Globe Village district of Southbridge, and in the 1760s by the Waite family in the North Parish of Brookfield.[8]

Economic development between the constitutional settlements of the 1780s and the booming prosperity of the mid-1830s fell into a sequence of movements demarcated by political intervention and economic depression. The unsettled conditions of the 1780s foreclosed any significant industrial developments, and even with the stabilization of the early 1790s, industrial experiments did not prosper. The federal Constitution was a dramatic new departure, easing the economic crisis that had confronted the state since the first years of the Revolution in the assumption of state debts, and laying the framework for Alexander Hamilton's national economic policy regarding finance, trade, and the encouragement of industry. But if Hamilton's Bank of the United States met no significant opposition in Massachusetts, his commercial and manufacturing initiatives were at

[7] Charles G. Washburn, *Industrial Worcester* (Worcester, 1917), 18–19; Benedict and Tracy, *Sutton*, 527–30; 564ff.; *Centennial History of the Town of Millbury, Massachusetts* ... (Millbury, 1915), 462–5.

[8] Rolla M. Tryon, *Household Manufactures in the United States, 1640–1860* (New York, 1966), 104–87; Thomas Dublin, *Women at Work: The Transformation of Work and Community in Lowell, Massachusetts, 1826–1860* (New York, 1979), 14–15; Temple, *North Brookfield*, 13–14; F. W. Rowley, "Globe Village and Its Industries," *QHSL* 2 (1903–9), 92.

cross-purposes. The outbreak of war in Europe in 1793 increased the demand for New England bulk goods, particularly in the West Indies. Despite its humiliating terms, the Jay Treaty stabilized this renewal of the old colonial trade pattern, and it was overwhelmingly popular in Massachusetts. But until Jefferson imposed an embargo on trade in 1807, a relatively free commerce with Britain and the West Indies would stifle the emergence of American industries. The tide would swing in the opposite direction between 1807 and 1815 when, under first the Embargo and then the War of 1812, manufacturing would explode under the hothouse conditions of a virtually autarchic national economy. In the ensuing two decades, a sharp postwar collapse as well as the 1819 depression set the stage for a long, slow process of restructuring, culminating in several years of relative prosperity before the collapse of 1837. Each swing of economic development would resonate powerfully with the county's changing political culture.[9]

The commercial prosperity formalized by the provisions of the Jay Treaty goes a long way toward explaining the unchallenged Federalist consensus that spread over Worcester County over the 1790s. In brief, gentry and yeomen, who clashed so violently in 1786 and 1787, found common cause in the export of local products of farm and shop to the West Indies and the importation of British manufactured goods.[10] The *Moral and Political Telegraph*, published in Brookfield by Elisha Waldo and Samuel B. Rice, first printed the text of the Jay Treaty in July 1795. By February 1796, Waldo and Rice were selling another version in pamphlet form at their printing office in the west village; that March they announced the senate's ratification. The next May, just prior to the governor's election in which the county turned against Samuel Adams, the paper reported that four hundred citizens in the town – roughly two-thirds of the adult male population – had signed a memorial to the General Court declaring that "the material interest of the Farmer, and every other class of citizen will be materially injured" by any further delay in implementing Jay's Treaty.[11]

That spring and summer the Brookfield and Worcester papers were full of advertisements indicating the basis for such a "material interest." In March Cheney Reed and Tilly Rice (Samuel's brother), a merchant partnership in Brookfield, announced that they had a new stock of drugs and medicines, clothier's dyes, paint, English goods, harnessware, and wallpaper for sale, and that "all kinds of Country Produce" would be "received in pay." In May Brazer and Goulding

[9] North, *The Economic Growth of the United States*, 24–74; Rothenberg, "A Price Index for Rural Massachusetts."

[10] M. E. Martin, "Merchants and Trade in the Connecticut River Valley, 1750–1820," *Smith College Studies in History* 24 (Northampton, Mass., 1939); Robert Paynter, *Models of Spacial Inequality* (New York, 1982); Gregory Nobles, "Merchants in the New England Countryside," paper delivered at the Charles Warren Center, 1986.

[11] *Moral and Political Telegraph, or Brookfield Advertizer*, July 8, 1795, February 24, May 4, 1796.

advertised a full line of "European and West Indian goods" in the *Spy*, to be sold for "cash, Ashes, Hoops, Staves, Butter, Bees Wax, Old Rags, Old Pewter and Brass, tow cloth and almost every kind of country produce." John Nazro offered "fresh goods" from Europe, India, and the West Indies and to take "in exchange" a similar list that also included potash salts, wheat, rye, corn, oats, and flax seed. Such ads would continue to appear into the next decade. In 1799 Reed and Rice advertised to purchase cattle, corn, wheat, rye, and "50 pairs of men's socks"; in 1802 they again advertised goods to be sold for cash, credit, or country produce.[12] Merchant entrepreneurs were acting as the distributive agents of a complex network of export that stretched from farm households through coastal ports to the West Indies. Ten years after the explosion of civil strife, farm families who had resisted the growing impulse – or necessity – to emigrate to the west found a modest competency in the sale of grain and cattle as well as the products of household and shop manufacture.

Federalist commerce and domestic manufactures

The merchants' purchases of rough linen cloth mark the first stages of a more extensive domestic manufacturing system that would emerge in the next decades, with merchants and manufacturers putting out yarn and thread to local weavers on a contract basis. But the flourishing trade in imported British goods was not conducive to the development of textile manufacturing on a large scale. The county's clothiers may have been concerned about British competition when they gathered to discuss "matters of importance" in Worcester in the fall of 1795.[13] Similarly, British competition must have played a role in the quick demise of an effort to establish a cotton mill in Worcester as the county was electing its first representative to the new Federal Congress. The Worcester Cotton Manufactury was being planned as early as February 1789, and by that spring a carding machine, spinning jenny, and two hand looms were in operation. The organizers were, almost to a man, members of the new Unitarian society, and virtually all of them would join the Morning Star Lodge or the Fire Society, and their involvement in the cotton factory was apparently another manifestation of the broader early Federalist voluntarism. Certainly, they hoped that national pride would work in their favor; in the summer of 1789 Samuel Brazer advertised cotton cloth from the new mill, noting that it was stronger than imported fabric, "which

---

[12] *Moral and Political Telegraph*, March 2, 1796; Massachusetts *Spy*, May 11, 18, 1796; Brookfield *Political Repository, or Farmer's Journal*, December 2, 1799, March 16, April 20, 1802.
[13] *Moral and Political Telegraph*, September 2, 1795.

circumstance alone, it is presumed, will induce every one to give preference to the Manufactures of their own country." Apparently national pride did not suffice, for by the fall of 1790 the company closed its books, although some of the partners tried to continue to use the machinery in connection with a clothier's mill.[14]

At the same time that the Worcester company was failing, an English immigrant named Samuel Slater began to produce cotton yarn at a small clothier's mill down the Blackstone at Pawtucket, Rhode Island. Rhode Island cotton yarn would sell well in Worcester County, though perhaps not immediately; in 1801 merchant Daniel Waldo, a former associate in the Worcester cotton factory, wrote to Providence merchants Almy and Brown that "the savin[gs] it will make in Private families . . . begins to be generally known in the neighborhood; the consequence is that the demand has increased very sensible." The Slater system of hiring families to produce yarn for domestic weaving, and gradually establishing a formal putting-out network of hand-loom weavers, would be imitated throughout Rhode Island and the Blackstone Valley in the following decades.[15]

In the short run, Slater's success at Pawtucket brought an important new element into the slowly changing economy of Worcester County. One of the critical factors in Slater's rapid development of cotton spinning in Pawtucket was the thick clustering of expert mechanics already established at the falls; the absence of such a group may have doomed the Worcester venture.[16] A body of machine builders would emerge in Worcester by 1812, but Slater's immediate needs spawned a very specialized branch of the trade in neighboring Leicester. Woolen or cotton fibers have to be carded before they can be spun, and hand carding was a slow process and a major bottleneck in textile production. Carding machines were being developed in New England in the 1780s based on English models. These machines required "card clothing": strips of leather set with thousands of wire teeth. Pliny Earle, a Quaker in Leicester, had made such card

[14] Of fifteen Worcester men involved in the 1789 cotton mill, twelve were Unitarians, ten would join the Fire Society, and seven the Morning Star Lodge. Notably, Peter Stowell, a weaver by trade, continued to use the machines, and did not join either of the new societies. Most of the others were merchants or lawyers. David J. Jeremy, *The Transatlantic Industrial Revolution: The Diffusion of Textile Technologies between Britain and America* (Cambridge, Mass., 1981) 18, 178; William R. Bagnall, *The Textile Industries of the United States . . .* (Cambridge, Mass., 1893), 1:127–31; Henry S. Nourse, "Some Notes upon the Genesis of the Power Loom in Worcester County," *Proc. AAS* NS 16 (1903–4), 31–3; Washburn, *Industrial Worcester*, 17.

[15] Daniel Waldo to Almy and Brown, April 27, 1801, Almy and Brown MSS., quoted in Ware, *New England Cotton Manufacture*, 32, and Tucker, *Samuel Slater*, 59.

[16] Jeremy, *Transatlantic Industrial Revolution*, 88; Gary Kulik, "Pawtucket Village and the Strike of 1824: The Origins of Class Conflict in Rhode Island," *Radical History Review* 17 (1978), 7–8; documents in Gary Kulik, Roger Parks, and Theodore Z. Penn, eds., *The New England Mill Village, 1790–1860* (Cambridge, Mass., 1978), 55–97.

clothing for the Worcester cotton mill and, through the Quaker network running down the Blackstone Valley to Almy and Brown in Providence, his work came to the attention of Samuel Slater, who ordered card clothing from Earle for this Pawtucket mill. This connection set the stage for the emergence of machine card manufacturing over the 1790s as a particularly important industry in Leicester. Earle and other Leicester men would patent critical inventions mechanizing the crimping and setting of card wire in the leather backing, and maintained such a monopoly over this technology that as late as 1837, 60 percent of the card clothing produced in Massachusetts was made in Leicester.[17]

The Leicester card manufacturers quickly became a key element in the growing connection between commerce and household manufacture underlying the county's Federalist consensus. Increasingly, this connection would revolve around wool. By 1810 the county would be second only to Hampshire and Berkshire in its per capita household production of textiles, as well as its number of carding machines, hand looms, and fulling mills.[18] Importantly, the county's early textile production would be based on native-grown sheep, not imported cotton. Many of the early Leicester card manufacturers came from a small group of households who were already concentrating on raising sheep in the early 1780s, and Pliny Earle himself was involved both in the importation of Merino sheep and experiments with silkworms.[19] Before it was fully mechanized, the card clothing was produced in part through a putting-out system by women and children throughout the region: Amasa Walker recounted late in life how as a boy in North Brookfield he earned seventy-five cents a week "sticking card teeth" for the Leicester card manufacturers. Such a putting-out system would flow naturally along commercial routes, and it is indicative that five of the seven retailers licensed in Leicester in 1805 and 1812 were also card manufacturers. When card man Jonathan Earle died in 1813, his "card-stock" and "shop goods" were sold together at auction. The demand for card clothing was enormous; in March 1803, Winthrop Earle wrote to John Scholfield, an immigrant English woolworker, that he had orders "to furnish Cards for fifty Machines this Spring." From producing cards, the next step was machine building: both to mechanize card manufacture

---

[17] Washburn, *Industrial Worcester*, 24–30; Washburn, *Leicester*, 32–4; Jeremy, *Transatlantic Industrial Revolution*, 177–8; John P. Bigelow, ed., *Statistical Tables: Exhibiting the Condition and Products of Certain Branches of Industry in Massachusetts* ... (Boston, 1838) 54, 194; Bagnall, *The Textile Industries*, 154–6.

[18] United States Census of Manufactures, 1810, County Aggregates, 4–5.

[19] Among 28 households on the Leicester Valuation of 1783 that had twice as many sheep as cattle, six would be card manufacturers or their relations, three were tanners, one – Baptist Robert Craige – made spinning wheels, and two others were involved in milling. Analysis of 1783 Valuation of Leicester. See also Pliny Earle, *Ralph Earle and His Descendants* (Worcester, 1886), 104–9.

and to build whole carding machines. Pliny Earle and his brothers began machine building in 1802, offering for sale the patent rights to machines for making "regular and complex twilled Cards" in April 1804. They also announced in 1804 that they had set up carding machines, produced by "the united efforts of the best English and American artisans," at mill sites in Grafton, Rutland, and Western as well as in Rhode Island, for the custom work of local farm households.[20]

If the decade of commercial prosperity between Jay's Treaty and the Embargo did not allow the development of full-scale textile production, it did see the beginnings of mechanical adjuncts to household production. Clothiers had been finishing cloth in fulling mills for centuries in England and the colonies, but in the 1790s manuals like Asa Ellis's *Country Dyer's Assistant*, published in Brookfield with a companion manual titled *The Country Trader's Assistant*, began to provide a wider audience with the secrets of cloth finishing.[21] At the same time, this clothier's work was augmented by the spread of carding machines, which relieved women of another arduous and monotonous task. This was not a dramatic transformation; the new carding machines – and improved fulling machines – were integrated into the existing commerce and agricultural production. These new processes would encourage the running of larger and more productive flocks of sheep over the next several decades. And woolen production in particular seems to have fit into the Federalist scheme of things, earlier with the broad improving thrust of the era of the Constitution, and later with the increasingly local, involutionary qualities of an embattled political mentality. The Scholfields had been sponsored by that paragon of Massachusetts Federalism, Jedediah Morse, on their arrival from England in 1793, and Pliny Earle was remembered as a staunch Federalist.[22] If the Earles were mostly Quakers, members and attenders at Zephaniah Moore's New Divinity Congregationalist meeting soon constituted the majority among the Leicester card manufacturers. The new machinery also flowed more easily along Federalist channels, as did the older cloth-finishing technology. The masters of small carding shops and fulling mills, often the same men, were overwhelmingly Congregationalist and Federalist, and carding machines were

[20] James P. Munroe, *The Life of Francis Amasa Walker* (New York, 1923), 8–9; Earle, *Ralph Earle and His Descendants* 104–9; Winthrop Earle to John Scholfield, March 29, 1803, Scholfield Papers, Connecticut State Library, quoted in Jeremy, *Transatlantic Industrial Revolution*, 126; Rita Gottesman, *The Arts and Crafts in New York, 1800–1804*, 422–3; for retailers, see Worcester County General Sessions Records, 7:4, 336; *National Aegis*, November 17, 1813.

[21] Asa Ellis, Jr., *The Country Dyer's Assistant* ... (Brookfield, 1798; William Cobb, *The Country Traders' Assistant* ... (Brookfield, 1799).

[22] Jeremy, *Transatlantic Industrial Revolution*, 119; Earle, *Ralph Earle and His Descendants*, 109.

more commonly located in towns with strong Federalist voting records.[23] This limited protoindustrial development, linking household production with a revived international commerce, thickened rather than transformed the existing social and economic order, and strengthened the Federalist synthesis in post-Revolutionary Worcester County.

Communications, credit, and corporations

At the same time that early industrial processes were emerging out of the broader matrix of Federalist commerce, new institutional forms were taking shape. The economy of the Worcester middle landscape had long been organized around the

[23] *Carding and fulling machines and politics, 1811*

Town, vote, 1805–11	Towns with carding machines in 1811		Towns with fulling machines in 1811		Total towns
Federalist	21	*62*	20	*59*	34
Republican	7	*41*	12	*71*	17

Note: Figures in italics are percentages.
Source: Valuation records, 1801–31, Oversize vol. 2, Worcester County, Mass., Papers, 1665–c.1954, AAS.

Carding, fulling, religion, and politics

	Congregationalist	Baptist	Universalist	Unknown	Total
Carders					
Federalist	6				6
Republican					0
Unknown	3	1		9	13
Total	9	1		9	19
Clothiers					
Federalist	6			1	7
Republican		1	2		3
Unknown	8		1	6	15
Total	14	1	3	7	25

Note: At least five men were both carders and clothiers, and probably many more as well.
Source: Spy, July 9, 1806, June 6, 1813; *Aegis*, June 16, 1813, July 28, 1814, 84; Daniels, Oxford, 14, 207, 213; Temple, *North Brookfield*, 13; Benedict and Tracy, *Sutton*, 535; Ammidown, *Historical Collections*, 2: 360; Rowley, "Globe Village," 92–3; C.D. Paige, "Dresser Manufacturing Company and Central Mills," *QHSL*, 2 (1903–9), 139–41; *HWC*, 1605; Washburn, *Leicester*, 29–30; Washburn, *Industrial Worcester*, 23, 24, 27; Henry P. Wright, *Fobes Memorial Library, Oakham, Massachusetts* (Oakham, 1909), 29.

basic building blocks of household, kin group, and informal gentry alliance. Such organic units and shifting partnerships would persist far into the future, but the leading position in the economy would rapidly be dominated by a new legal creation: the private corporation vested with limited powers by state charter. Where at one time particular bounded localities and their inhabitants had been granted the public duties and privileges of corporate status for the advancement of the general good, now associations of shifting collections of individuals holding only a single private interest in common would be chartered as corporations. The movement of corporations from public to private purposes in Massachusetts was a long and complex process, spanning the entire era from the ratification of the state constitution in 1780 through the establishment of the doctrine of limited liability in the late 1820s.[24] The first tentative steps in building a widely ramified structure of private corporations across Worcester County – fraught with dilemmas for a commonwealth entering a partisan age – began in efforts to solve the ancient economic problems of access to market and access to credit.

The Jay Treaty reopened West Indian ports to American bulk goods. This was a very old trade, traditionally the mainstay of the New England economy, but the circumstances of European warfare made it particularly prosperous. It is unlikely that this trade had operated to a great extent in the Worcester backcountry before the Revolution. Access to markets had long been a problem; in 1782 the people of Spencer had protested that a new valuation had not made "proper allowance" for their "distant situation" from the "maritime and market towns," which rendered "the profits of our farms very inconsiderable." As the conditions of the unratified Jay Treaty were being debated in newspaper and pamphlet, the Federalist gentry began to address the problem of improving communications. Here they brought to bear their recent experience with the principle of voluntary association. In February 1795 taverner Ephraim Mower of Worcester, a Unitarian and a founding member of both the Fire Society and the Morning Star Lodge, joined with stage-operator Levi Pease in petitioning to be allowed to improve the twisting mountain road leading from the Upper Mills in Western to Scott's Tavern in Palmer and to establish a toll. When the First Massachusetts Turnpike Corporation was chartered in June 1796, Mower and Pease were joined by Dwight Foster, Salem Towne, and a number of other men from the newly forming voluntary societies in the area, as well as a large group of gentry from the Connecticut Valley towns.[25]

Although it had a broadly Federalist impetus, the First Massachusetts Turn-pike, and many of those to follow, was not the project of single interest: roads were indeed a common good. Along with a number of Federalist notables, the First Massachusetts incorporators included future Republicans Levi Lincoln and Pliny

---

[24] Handlin and Handlin, *Commonwealth*.
[25] Spencer Petition, February 11, 1782, MA 187:412–3; Josiah H. Temple, *History of the Town of Palmer, Massachusetts*... (Palmer, 1909), 223–4.

Merrick. When the Worcester and Stafford Turnpike was built southwest from Worcester beginning in 1808, Oliver Fiske, a Worcester Federalist, usually sat as president, but the corporate meetings were held at the Northside Tavern in Charlton, owned by the Republican Rider brothers. At least four other turnpike projects had bipartisan support; the opinion seems to have been that the continuing health of the corporation came to require a foot in both political camps.[26]

In their 1795 petition to improve the road through Palmer and Western, Mower and Pease had argued that it was "probably beyond the resources of those towns to make it good travelling in these places."[27] Corporate status traditionally had been associated with the governance of towns or churches; before 1796 only the charters of the Leicester Academy and the Grand Lodge of Freemasons had infringed upon this monopoly of delegated state power in Worcester County. With the turnpikes, the first local application of the voluntary principle being applied to a major economic enterprise, the gentry were beginning to assume functions that had always been the responsibility of the town government, and of a people who seemed unable or unwilling to bear the costs of improvements. The social differentiation achieved in the voluntary societies by the Federalist gentry was beginning to spill over into new spheres. But with bipartisan support, this improving gentry could claim the mantle of the commonwealth tradition, that these new institutions were directly serving the public good while they also hoped for a private profit.

Since 1780 grants of incorporation had been made on the assumption that the enterprise seeking special, state-sanctioned organizational privileges would provide the commonwealth with a unique and indispensable service. But the proliferation of turnpike roads, one competing for traffic with the next, was the first of a series of indications that corporations would have overlapping claims on the public trust, that they would indeed serve different and conflicting interests.[28] A similar situation was taking shape with regard to banking. Under colonial rule, private associations for the concentration of capital like the Land Bank of 1740 were outlawed in the interests of maintaining imperial control over currency and trade. Informal processes of accumulation and investment lay in the hands of prosperous gentry and merchant-entrepreneurs, and the Court of Common Pleas stood as the public arbiter of a complex web of economic transactions between debtors and creditors. Banking would establish a fixed and stable base of capital, a regularized system of mortgages and loans, and currency

[26] *Laws of the Commonwealth of Massachusetts...* (Boston, 1808–38), 1:195; 2:595; *Private and Special Statutes of the Commonwealth of Massachusetts*, 7 vols. (Boston, 1805–37), 3:613; *Spy*, August 28, 1800. For a description of roads, turnpikes, and merchants in an upland town, see Wright, *Fobes Memorial Library*, 24–33.

[27] Turnpike petition, February 5, 1795, in Original Papers, chap. 5, Acts of 1796, MA.

[28] Handlin and Handlin, *Commonwealth*, 93ff., 106–33, 152.

for the needs of the local economy. Banking would also bring into sharp focus the problem of the public control and accountability of private institutions charted by the state.

In Worcester County these issues arose as the dynamic of partisan competition was beginning to develop. Partisan purposes were always at work in the politics of banking, but even here the sense that the bank was an institution founded for public purposes restrained the level of possible confrontation. In an article widely reprinted in Republican papers, the *National Aegis* in early 1802 developed the rationale for what might have been a general incorporation law for banks. "[N]o injury has hitherto arisen from the increase of these institutions," the essayist argued, and the legislature should grant charters to all petitions. If this Republican paper proposed a proliferation of banks, each with their own interest, the petition for a charter of incorporation for a bank in Worcester sent the following year was couched in significantly different language. The petitioners had subscribed to a bank fund of $100,000, taking care "to prevent a monopoly" by any individual or group. Located at the center of the county, the bank would have a pervasive public benefit: "The agricultural, commercial, and mechanical interests of the County, it is believed, will be essentially promoted by such an establishment."[29] For two decades the Worcester Bank would indeed be such a county institution, discouraging or stifling all local competitors who might have been inspired by the *Aegis*'s argument. But in 1803 the petitioners closed their request for a charter with the hope that the legislature would grant them "an equal distribution of . . . the advantages which have hitherto been principally engrossed by a certain portion of the Community." This organic language, directed at the Boston banks, nonetheless reflected the Federalist assumptions of its petitioners. Despite their efforts to avoid a monopoly, the bank's one hundred and thirty-five subscribers were not a perfect cross section of the county's politics or economy. They included nine Federalists prominent in the county committees and as county candidates, and almost a quarter of the bank's subscribers would join the Washington Benevolent Society. In contrast, Republican notables such as the Lincolns or Edward Bangs were conspicuously absent, and only two of the seventeen Republican county committeemen serving in 1808 had signed the petition. The president and directors named in the act of incorporation were also staunchly Federalist; the bank's president, Daniel Waldo, Jr., would be the president of the Worcester branch of the Washington Benevolent Society.[30]

Such was the situation throughout most of the state, and Republicans would have to wait until they had a decisive edge in the General Cour t before they would

[29] Handlin and Handlin, *Commonwealth*, 116; Worcester Bank Petition, March 7, 1804, in Original Papers, chap. 128, Acts of 1803.

[30] Worcester Bank Petition, 1804 and Worcester Bank Charter, in Original Papers, chap. 128, Acts of 1803; Lincoln, *Worcester*, 327; Worcester County Mass., Washington Benevolent Society Records, AAS; for Republicans, see chapter 8, note 30.

gain control over banking. The opportunity came in 1811, when a Republican General Court established a Republican-controlled State Bank and then denied charter renewal to a series of Federalist banks – including the Worcester Bank. Here the importance of a local institution, of whatever political complexion, soon became apparent to ordinary Republicans. In July 1811, the newly chartered State Bank formed county committees to organize subscriptions. Worcester County's committee was drawn from the ranks of the leading Republicans: Levi and Abraham Lincoln, Edward Bangs, and John Spurr.[31] But in January 1812, just three months after the huge new bank went into operation, Republicans joined with Federalists to petition that the Worcester Bank be rechartered. In Worcester James Wilson, the Republican postmaster, joined with local Federalists in supporting the bank; in Leicester and Spencer men of both parties who had recently petitioned for a new turnpike did the same. Two petitions were sent from Sutton, one with leading signatures by the sitting Republican selectmen as well as dozens of other Republicans in the town. Such support may have been in recognition of the fact that county Federalists had failed to oppose the chartering of the State Bank when its charter came up for a roll call vote. But it is much more likely that local economic structures – and the necessity of a local source of credit – weighed more heavily than political considerations. In its 1812 petition to the new, Federalist-controlled legislature, the bank pointed to the petitions of the previous session as evidence of a broad support. "On this subject there are no conflicting claims," their petition stated triumphantly; "men of all parties, classes and situations are satisfied with the present application." Having already appointed Levi Lincoln, Jr., as a director, the Worcester Bank had also begun to make an accommodation with the Republican hierarchy. When local sources of credit were threatened, a basic consensus cut through the fiercest of partisan political struggles.[32]

The people of the Worcester middle landscape had been especially concerned about money and capital for almost a century. Where Land Bankers and convention men had failed in their efforts to increase the availability of currency in the form of paper bills backed by land or state authority, a private institution, chartered by the state and guaranteeing redemption from a specie reserve upon demand, had succeeded. In restructuring the central problem of credit, the bank had alleviated the fundamental flashpoint in the county political economy: As the bank noted in its petition, its operations had "diminished the number of lawsuits." Over the previous century an informal system of debt and credit had brought gentry and yeomen into legal conflict at the Court of Common Pleas, and had

[31] Goodman, *Democratic-Republicans*, 179–80; Amos W. Stetson, *Eighty Years; An Historical Sketch of the State Bank* ... (Boston, 1893), 11–13.

[32] The January 1812 petitions for the Worcester Bank are in Senate Documents, Unpassed Legislation, 4447/1–13, January, 1812. Roll calls on the State Bank are in Manuscript House Journals, vol. 32 (1811–12), appendix.

shaped three powerful political insurgencies. Memories of the troubled 1780s were still relatively fresh in 1812, and no one in Worcester County was willing to let partisan politics stand in the way of a predictable system of local credit.[33]

Jefferson's embargo, Madison's war, and the Republican "cotton mill fever"

In regard to communications and credit, the local politics of development in Worcester County ignored the national politics of independence. But after Jefferson's declaration of the embargo in 1807, the issues of distribution and production rapidly were subsumed by those of national politics. In rhetoric that soon was reflected in reality, Federalists and Republicans became polarized over the advocacy of commerce and manufactures. In the process, the Republicans developed arguments that would leave them in command of the rhetorical field at the end of the War of 1812.

The Federalists entered the 1808 election season with a new intensity. The Republican administration was imposing on the nation "a series of alarming innovations and dangerous experiments": Most importantly, the Embargo was a death threat to the commercial prosperity built up since the ratification of the Jay Treaty. County Federalists meeting at Barre in July were particularly concerned to arouse the farmer to their cause, and their resolutions were studded with pronouncements on the indivisibility of agricultural and commercial interests. "We consider the interests of Agriculture and Commerce as inseparable," the Barre convention resolved. "[E]very attempt to create a belief that the farmer can flourish, while the latter [the merchant] is neglected and depressed" was "an insidious effort to detach from each other different classes of the community, who are united by the strongest ties of reciprocal interest and advantage."[34] The same rhetoric was deployed through the crisis of the War of 1812. Francis Blake urged the Worcester Federalists on the Fourth of July, 1812, to unite "Commerce and Agriculture" in an "indissoluble Union . . . that the the twain may again be one"; the Worcester Peace Convention and Federalist orators throughout the county condemned the Embargo for stifling "American commerce, that great fountain of our national wealth, prosperity, and greatness.[35]

---

[33] Worcester Bank Petition, March, 1812, in Original Papers, chap. 36, Acts of 1812. Also see the language in the Worcester Bank Petition of May 1811, in Senate Unpassed 4447, January 1812. For memories of the 1780s, see Bancroft, *The Importance of Education*, 14.

[34] *Spy*, June 22, July 6, 1808.

[35] Blake, *An Oration Pronounced at Worcester*, 32; *Proceedings of a Convention of Delegates from Forty One Towns . . . 17, 20;* Thomas Snell, *Praying for Rulers and Christian Duty* (Brookfield, 1812), 35; Lewis Bigelow, *An Oration Pronounced at Templeton, July 5th, 1813 . . . Before the Washington Benevolent Societies in the Northern Section of Worcester County and Other Citizens* (Worcester, 1813), 10.

Strikingly, the Federalist orators never spoke of the mechanical or manufacturing interest in their summations of national and regional political economy. If they ignored the brewing of mechanical innovation in their midst, it was for two reasons. First, the spreading carding shops and fulling mills and expansion of household production was as yet bound up in the symbiosis of commerce and agriculture that the Federalists held up as the ideal. But importantly, the Republicans had begun to claim manufacturing as their own, and in so doing forced the Federalists into an ultimately untenable position.

When the Federalists at Barre complained that "attempts" had been made to divide the farmer and the merchant, they had much to be concerned about in the powerful speech delivered by Major Estes Howe of Sutton that same July Fourth at the Republican celebration at Worcester. Howe, recently converted to Republicanism, presented a powerful defense of the embargo in terms that tied manufacturing directly to the cause of national independence. After reviewing threats to the nation from Aaron Burr's conspiracy and from British attacks on shipping, he asked of those who would allow the British to structure American trade, "[d]oes this look like National Independence or has it the appearance of Colonial servility?" Faced with the prospect of war to defend that commerce, he cited the nation's foremost Republican; it was far more preferable to "turn seriously to that policy, which plants the manufacturer and the husbandman side by side, and establish at the door of every one, that exchange of mutual labors and comforts, which we have hitherto sought in distant regions and under perpetual risque" of war.[36]

Such sentiments were repeated over the following cycle of political confrontation. In 1811 Republican Samuel Brazer, Jr., told the people of Charlton that "the extension of and patronage of American Manufactures" were "among the most important means of perpetuating Independence." In 1816 Zenas Leonard similarly reviewed for the Republicans of Southbridge Britain's "artful dissemination of her contaminating principles through . . . the vending of her politics by wholesale and retail in her merchandize." Leonard was certain that "the agriculturalists, manufacturers, and mechanics of America will cautiously guard their rights, and safely preserve the palladium of their country." Republicans were ready to abandon a dangerous international commerce, and to forge a new union between agriculture and manufacturing that would develop the nation's vast internal resources.[37]

Massachusetts's Republican governor James Sullivan played an important role in translating Republican rhetoric about manufacturing into reality. Fully aware that Jefferson's embargo policy would seriously disrupt the state's economy, he

---

[36] Howe, *An Oration, Delivered in Worcester*, 6–11.

[37] Brazier, *An Oration Pronounced in Charlton*, 11; Leonard, *An Oration Pronounced at Southbridge*, 8, 19. See also Sprague, *An Oration Pronounced at Worcester*, 4–5.

proposed and had passed a general law for the incorporation of manufacturing companies, with the hope of stimulating interest in domestic industry. Under the new law, passed in March 1809, a manufacturing concern could assume the same corporate structure as turnpikes and banks; a series of elected officers would direct the affairs of the company, and have the authority to compel cooperation from the shareholders. Despite the lack of liability protection for the individual share-holders, the corporation form proved spectacularly popular. Almost 130 com-panies were incorporated across the state by the end of the War of 1812 in an explosion of enthusiasm for manufacturing. Even more than the turnpikes and the banks, the new manufacturing companies sat in an oddly liminal position between public and private purposes. Cloaked in the patriotic purposes of national independence, the new companies were also competitive entities operating in the market for a private profit, and their multiplication further eroded the corporation's ancient connotation of monopoly privileges granted in the public good. By 1820, as the Handlins put it forty years ago, the spread of manufacturing corporations across the state "had turned a governmental agency into a business form."[38]

The "cotton mill fever" had already infected some Republicans in Worcester County. The first cotton textile company to be incorporated, its works powered by the Nashua River, was organized by a group of Fitchburg men in early 1807. Led by Dr. Peter Snow, a strident opponent of the town's small group of New Divinity Congregationalists, the incorporators of the Fitchburg Cotton Manufacturing Company were typically men of extensive experience in local government in this Republican town.[39] Farther to the south on the same Nashua drainage, Eleazer Rider and his sons, apparently cousins of the Republican Riders in Charlton, began spinning cotton yarn in West Boylston before moving to Holden in 1809. In June 1811 they would be incorporated as the Holden Cotton and Woolen Manufacturing Company, with the leading incorporator being James Estabrook, a member of the 1808 Republican county committee.[40] By December, the Riders had moved on to the Quinebaug Valley in Sturbridge, soon to be set off as Southbridge, where they were joined in the formation of the Sturbridge Manufacturing Company. Over the next year, five textile manufacturing com-panies would be formed in the Quinebaug and adjacent French River drainages in Sturbridge and Dudley, illustrating in microcosm both the new Republican enthusiasm for textile manufacturing and the particular niche where Federalists also could participate.

[38] Handlin and Handlin, *Commonwealth*, 126–8, 180; *The General Laws of Massachusetts* ... (Boston, 1823), 2:201–3 [chap. 65, Acts of 1808].
[39] *Private and Special Statutes*, 4:116; Walter A. Davis, comp., *The Old Records of the Town of Fitchburg, Massachusetts*, vol. 4 (Fitchburg, 1901), 207–8, 322, 349, 361, 370, 377–9.
[40] *Private and Special Statutes*, 4:341; David F. Estes, *The History of Holden, Massachusetts, 1684–1894* (Worcester, 1894), 171, 203.

The Riders provided important technical knowledge for the Sturbridge Manufacturing Company; Nathaniel Rider was hired to build cotton-spinning machinery of a total of 128 spindles, and outside opinions were required when questions about its quality were raised. But for the most part, those involved in this short-lived company were local men, inexperienced in the textile trade but drawn to the possibilities for profit in a protected market. The company was deeply rooted in the Baptist community. The company's three-story factory was built at the site of a gristmill recently purchased by Baptist Moses Fisk; Zenas Leonard, the Baptist minister and Sturbridge's Republican representative to the General Court between 1808 and 1812, was appointed the company's agent, charged with presenting the company's petition for incorporation as "a body politic." Baptist accounts with the company, for everything from materials for the buildings, work in the mills, and various quantities of cotton yarn and twist, were on average more than twice the value of the company's accounts with Congregationalists. Cotton, dissent, and Republicanism were deeply intermingled in this enterprise. Leonard's brother Linus wrote approvingly from North Carolina in July 1814: "I think highly of your stock in a cotton factory. I have no doubt of its being the best of property during the continuance of the war." Discussing options in the southern trade, and commenting that the Baptists were gaining ground in the Carolina tidewater, Linus Leonard's letter points to some of the connections between dissenter Republicans in the Massachusetts interior and the wider world of Jeffersonianism.[41]

Two other companies established in Sturbridge and Dudley similarly combined Republicanism, Baptist dissent, and cotton manufacturing. The Globe Manufacturing Company, incorporated in 1814, had its origins in 1812, when cotton machinery was put into Gershom Plympton's oil mill just downstream from the Sturbridge Manufacturing site. Plympton, whose son Moses ran the machinery until a new factory was built and the Globe company incorporated, was the only wool clothier in the region to turn to the Republicans; he had married into the Baptist Fisk family and had been the leading figure in the forming of the Royal Arch Chapter of Freemasons in Charlton before serving with Zenas Leonard as Republican representative from Sturbridge between 1809 and 1812. Five of the six Globe incorporators were Baptists, and one, James Wolcott, would be a Republican leader in Southbridge. On the French River in east Dudley the Village Manufacturing Company, incorporated in 1812 to spin cotton, and to work wool and linen as well, was similarly grounded in dissent and Republicanism. Baptist revival meetings, led by a black preacher from Boston, were held in the loft of the Village Factory in the winter of 1813–14, and at least seven of the twenty

[41] Ledger belonging to the Sturbridge Manufacturing Company, 1812–14, Linus Leonard to Zenas L. Leonard, July 20, 1814, Leonard Family Papers, Old Sturbridge Village; Cutting, "Westville and Its Manufactures," 59–64; Ammidown, *Historical Collections*, 2:54.

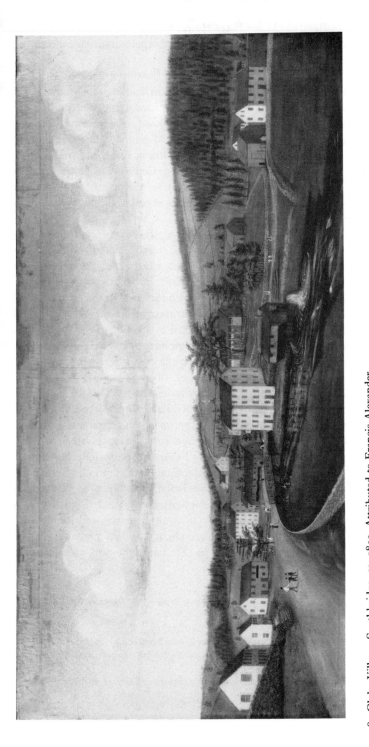

8. Globe Village, Southbridge, ca. 1822. Attributed to Francis Alexander.
In the foreground to the left of the road are two tenement houses and a store. Across the Quinebaug River, moving from left to right, is the four-story mill built by the Globe Manufacturing Company in 1814 and later occupied by the Wolcotts, followed by Gershom Plympton's oil mill and a four-story mill built by the Columbian Manufacturing Company, which was formed by Moses Plympton and others in 1821. The low, dark structure to the right is an eighteenth-century sawmill. Dyed cloth is drying in the fields to the left of the Globe mill. Courtesy of the Jacob Edwards Memorial Library, Southbridge, Massachusetts. (Old Sturbridge Village photograph)

incorporators were Baptists. Major Estes Howe, the voice of Republican manu-facturing in Worcester County, was one of eight incorporators from Sutton who invested in this company.[42]

The Republican organizers of the Village Factory stood in sharp contrast to the men behind another textile company formed in 1812 in Dudley. The Merino Wool Factory Company was rooted in a solidly Congregational and Federalist orbit; their leading figure, Aaron Tufts, was repeatedly elected representative from this Federalist town. Similarly, another company formed on the Quinebaug in 1814 and devoted primarily to wool manufacture, had strong Federalist connections. The Charlton, later Southbridge, Manufacturing Company was set up at a clothier's stand at the old Marcy mill site; when it was incorporated in 1816, three of the five incorporators were Congregationalists and one would be the leader of the Federalist minority in Southbridge.[43]

Thus Federalists could participate in the general enthusiasm for textile manufacture; but their efforts evolved out of their previous experience in woolworking, dating back to the 1790s. Such was clearly the case with a small woolen works incorporated in North Brookfield in 1816, building on the experience of the Waite family as clothiers, which ran back to the 1750s. Daniel Waite probably best captured the Federalist attitude in the introduction to his manual titled *The New American Dier*, published in 1815 to provide the public with the best methods of dying woolen cloth. Beginning with the commentary that "the present is in some respects a time of unhappy change, it is also in many things a time of valuable improvements and discoveries," Waite's manual was endorsed by a list of Brookfield's Federalist notables, including Justice Dwight Foster, the local orthodox minister, and merchants Tilly Rice and Cheny Reed.[44]

This differentiation between Republican experiments in cotton and Federalist continuities in wool was of course not perfect; opportunities for private profit often overrode priorities of political culture. In 1811 Federalist Aaron Tufts had already joined with Republicans Estes Howe and John Spurr in forming the Sutton and Charlton Cotton, Woollen, and Linen Association, possibly a consortium for organizing handloom weavers on a putting-out basis. In 1814 and 1815 two groups of Congregationalists in Oxford, with a leavening of dissenters and Republicans from Charlton, Sutton, and Leicester, received charters and attempted to start up cotton works on the French River.[45] And in 1814 ten of the card-manufacturing

[42] Ammidown, *Historical Collections*, 1:437, 503–5; 2:364–5, 368–9; Rowley, "Globe Village and Its Industries," 93–5.
[43] Ammidown, *Historical Collections*, 1:435, 442; 2:361.
[44] Temple, *North Brookfield*, 13–14; *Private and Special Statutes*, 4:87–8; Daniel Waite & Co., *The New American Dier or, an Entirely New and Superior Method of Dying Woolen Cloths* (Brookfield, 1815), iv–v.
[45] Ammidown, *Historical Collections*, 1:210–11; 2:165; Daniels, *Oxford*, 192, 205; *Private and Special Statutes*, 4:336.

proprietors in Leicester moved directly into textile production, incorporating with other men – including both Levi Lincoln and Daniel Waldo – in three different companies located in West Boylston and Northbridge.[46] But, in aggregate, a consistent picture does emerge. Among representatives elected in the partisan years between 1805 and 1815 from Worcester and eleven other towns to the south and west, Republicans were more likely to be involved in the textile enthusiasm of the Embargo and war years, particularly in cotton, while the Federalists were less so, and they inclined toward the now traditional woolen trade.[47] Strikingly, the

[46] *Laws of the Commonwealth of Massachusetts* ... 6:490, 529; *Private and Special Statutes*, 4:509–11; Thomas R. Navin, *The Whitin Machine Works since 1831* (Cambridge, Mass., 1950), 15–20. The associational affiliations of the Leicester card manufacturers in 1812 suggests that by this juncture they were literally poised on a knife edge between the Federalist and Republican orbits, and other evidence suggests that this ambivalence was rooted in their circumstances as machinemakers. They relied on card wire imported from England, and in January 1812, eight Leicester card manfacturers sent a petition to Congress, asking for a variance from the nonimportation act. Although they were attempting to gain "an independence [from] a precarious Commerce" by experimenting with "drawing Wire from the Bar," they did not expect enough to be "drawn down to make one fourth the quantity needed for the ensuing Spring." The answer to this petition may well have been negative, for in the spring and summer of 1812 four of these petitioners joined the Washington Benevolent Society, along with four other Leicester card men and seventeen others from the town. The membership of the WBS was almost entirely distinct from the Republican-dominated Morning Star Lodge; only 35 of 378 WBS members joined the lodge, and only eleven between 1800 and 1815. Thus it is striking that between the late summer of 1812 and the winter of 1813 eight men from Leicester joined the MSL, of whom seven were card manufacturers, four had been petitioners, and five had joined the WBS. Apparently the card men were pulled in opposite directions in this critical year, first toward the Federalist orbit, and then toward the Republicans. It may be significant that in 1812 an Elliot Prouty began drawing wire in a mill in what would become "Wire Village," about two miles from the card shops in Leicester center. See "Jonathan Earle and Others, Asking Permission to Import Wire for Their Manufactures, January 12, 1812," *New American State Papers: Manufactures, 1789–1860* (Wilmington, Del., 1972), 1:151–2; Washburn, *Leicester*, 31–8; "Worcester County, Mass., Washington Benevolent Society Records," AAS; Nason, *Morning Star Lodge*, 197–209; HWC, 2:333.

[47] *Federalist and Republican representatives and incorporated textile companies, 1805–15*

	Wool		Cotton and mixed		All textiles		Total
Representatives	6	*15*	1	*2*	7	*17*	41
Terms	17	*17*	1	*1*	18	*18*	102
Republicans							
Representatives	1[a]	*3*	5	*18*	6	*22*	27
Terms	4[a]	*4*	21	*22*	25	*26*	95

Note: Figures in italics are percentages.
[a] Gershom Plympton, clothier, Sturbridge.
Source: Massachusetts Register; Private and Public Statutes.

small, less capitalized corporations established between 1807 and 1816 – like the North Brookfield Woolen Manufactury incorporated in 1816 – were concentrated in staunchly Federalist towns, apparently an extension of small woolen works gradually emerging since the turn of the century. But the more highly capitalized textile corporations tended to be located in towns voting Republican across the First Party era down to 1824, the last year of formal competition between Federalists and Republican candidates in Massachusetts.

Both Jeffersonian allegiances and incorporated manufacturing brought institutional change to the Worcester middle landscape. The challenge of the emergent Republican Party had brought the structures of a two-party system, while the multiplication of manufacturing corporations was rapidly draining the connotations of commonwealth and public purpose from this old institution. If the new corporations were contributing to an institutional pluralism, it is striking that the most substantial of them were concentrated in towns that had had a long history of Lockean politics. If these companies were located in Republican towns, these were also towns that had a large number of dissenters, and that had been particularly opposed to the General Court's plan to write the state's constitution in 1776. These were also towns that had seen extensive rioting by "private mobs" in the early 1780s, a pattern that was associated with both dissenting religion and political constitutionalism. Most simply speaking, the more highly capitalized corporations were concentrated in the southern sections of the county, particularly the southwest, where institutional pluralism and Lockean individualism had been brewing since the decade of the Great Awakening, rooted in the Constitutionalist, dissenting wing of the old Popular coalition. (Compare Figures 6a and 6c.)

Perhaps this connection was a fortuitous coincidence of unrelated initiatives; perhaps there was no causal link between the manufacturing experiments of the embargo and war years and the Lockean wing of the old Popular coalition. But scattered among the manufacturing Republicans there were strong echoes of the earlier liberal politics. The Sturbridge Manufacturing Company, for example, brought together men whose fathers and grandfathers had acted together in the cause of constitutional transformation. The Sturbridge committee that had rejected the General Court's 1776 proposal that it write a constitution was led by the old Baptist leaders, brothers Daniel and Henry Fisk, who in 1780 had lamented "the sin of sitting light by and misimproving our liberties and privileges, while we had them." But the committee also included Congregationalist Daniel Plympton, who operated a series of mills on the Quinebaug above the Fisks' privilege. In 1811 sons and grandsons of both Fisks and of Daniel Plympton acted to improve their private circumstances in forming the Sturbridge Manufacturing Company. In submitting one of the earliest petitions for incorporation in the entire state, they give their mutual contract the force of law. Here the Lockean rationalism informing Constitutionalist demands anticipated those of the Republican enthusiasm for manufacturing corporations. And occasionally one finds personal and familial manifestations of this Lockean rationalism. Thus Zenas Leonard, Baptist minister, Republican representative, and the agent of the Sturbridge Manufacturing Company, wrote to his wife from Boston in February 1812 that he had "got the children some small books, entirely new."[48]

The textile men along the Quinebaug also had interesting connections with the rioting of the early 1780s. Franklin Rider served as the clerk of the Sturbridge Manufacturing Company, and his brother William was involved in the Oxford Cotton Manufacturing Company in 1814. Their father, Isaiah Rider, had served in the government forces to suppress the Regulators in 1787 with the Fisks, Plymptons, and others from the new textile families. But in 1783 Isaiah Rider also stood as surety, almost as a prominent sponsor, for Benjamin Albe of Charlton, who was accused of participating in the riot in Douglass that brought a temporary suspension of habeas corpus. Samuel Waters, Baptist iron-tool maker and cider distiller in Sutton (whom Amos Singletary had once confronted over the quality of his hoes), was a prominent investor in the Village Factory in east Dudley in 1812; when the company collapsed he was arrested as a debtor, and preached to his fellow prisoners in the Worcester jail. Thirty years before, as a young blacksmith, Waters had stood as a surety for Nathan Holloway of Oxford, accused of joining the Douglass riot. In jail in 1817 Waters was contrite: he had engaged in "imprudent conduct . . .; men ought never to extend their business beyond the resources of their capital." But his surety for Holloway suggests that Waters had once been sympathetic to the private efforts of others who had been similarly "imprudent."[49]

The emergence of the central corridor

Samuel Waters's "imprudent conduct" can stand in summation of the Republican "cotton mill fever." Protected from British textiles by national policy, these fledgling companies crumbled as soon as commerce was reopened across the Atlantic. Echoing the postwar collapse of 1783–6, the failure of the new cotton mills sent men like Waters to debtor's prison and others fleeing across state lines to avoid prosecution. The postwar trade glut was compounded by the credit crisis that began in 1819; in 1820 manufacturers in Southbridge, North Brookfield, and Western reported their "sales dull" and trade "depressed."[50] In the long run, the

---

[48] Cutting, "Westville and Its Manufactures," 47, 59; Sturbridge Town Records, Vol. II, 293; Handlin and Handlin, eds., *Popular Sources*, 876; Zenas Leonard to Sally Fisk Leonard, February 10, 1812, Leonard Family Papers, 1796–1888 and Undated, Research Library, Old Sturbridge Village. On Locke, Republicanism, and education, see Appleby, *Capitalism and a New Social Order*; and Fleigelman, *Prodigals and Pilgrims*.

[49] SJC Docket Book for 1783, 214–15; for Waters, see Benedict and Tracy, *Sutton*, 186, 324–5, 463–4, 469–70.

[50] Daniels, *Oxford*, 205; Washburn, *Industrial Worcester*, 29; MSS., 1820 U.S. Census of Manufacturing, Worcester County, Mass.

textile experiments of this first phase of rapid expansion would bear fruit. By the 1830s the same south county towns along the Blackstone, the French, and Quinebaug rivers would account for the greater part of the county's textile production, and the towns with the larger early textile corporation saw dramatic increases in population between 1810 and 1830. But when the U.S. Census recorded the number of persons employed in manufactures as of 1820, the institutional innovations of the war years had had no measurable influence on the broader structures of employment in the county; there was no disproportionate concentration of manufacturing employment in the south county textile towns. The "cotton mill fever" was a fast-moving Lockean enthusiasm; despite its dramatic departure, it could not maintain high levels of manufacturing employment during the years of postwar depression.

The industrial development of the embargo and war years did have an immediate and permanent impact on another region. Strikingly, it was the towns with no large-scale incorporated companies that had a slight edge in the level of manufacturing employment in 1820, an edge that points to a particularly important economic transformation taking place during these years. The bulk of the employment in manufacturing was located in a diversity of small shops rather than in larger textile mills. Fourteen towns, which ranked in the county's top third for manufacturing employment but in which no corporations capitalized at over $100,000 had been established by 1820, appear to have been the focal point of this small shop economy. They had a distinctly different profile from the textile towns.[51] (Compare Figures 6b and 6c.)

These fourteen towns were concentrated along a central corridor running east to west through the county, including Worcester and adjacent towns, and the towns bisected by the Boston to Springfield Post Road. This was a newly emerging region, a band of thickening population and economic activity along the major

[51] The manufacturing corporations are listed in the *Report of the Secretary of State, of the Articles Manfactured in the United States ... with a Schedule of Factories Incorporated by State Laws, from 1800 to 1820, Inclusive* (Washington, D. C., 1824), Doc. 45, pp. 25–6; *Massachusetts Register for 1815*, 105–7; and in *Private and Special Statues*, vols. 3–5. Manufacturing employment is recorded in the *Census for 1820. Published by Authority of an Act of Congress, under the direction of the Secretary of State* (Washington, D. C., 1821), returns of Worcester County towns. (A third of the towns in the county (18/54), fourteen of them the "small-shop towns," reported numbers of "Persons engaged in manufacturing" equaling between 28% and 50% of the total of "Persons engaged in Agriculture, Commerce, and Maunfacturing.") The "central corridor" towns are arbitrarily defined as Worcester and immediately adjacent towns, and those towns that were located directly on the Springfield to Boston Road. For the location of this road, see *Archaeological Resources of Central Massachusetts*, map 6; and Frederick J. Wood, *The Turnpikes of New England* (Boston, 1919), map facing p. 57. Several other nearby towns with similar characteristics of good communications, small-shop manufacturing, and a volatile political culture, such as Milford and Upton, might have been included in the "central corridor," but they were not for the sake of consistency and simplicity.

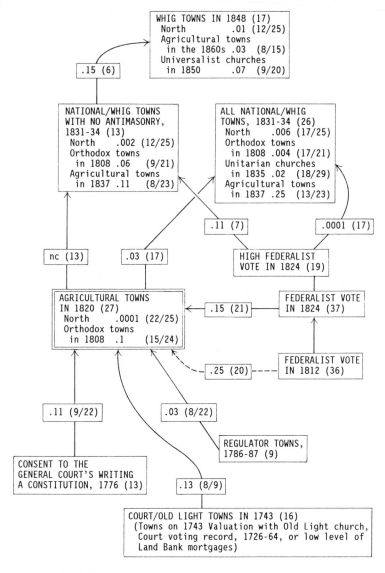

WHIG TOWNS IN 1848 (17)
North   .01 (12/25)
Agricultural towns
  in the 1860s .03 (8/15)
Universalist churches
  in 1850   .07 (9/20)

.15 (6)

NATIONAL/WHIG TOWNS
WITH NO ANTIMASONRY,
1831-34 (13)
North   .002 (12/25)
Orthodox towns
  in 1808 .06   (9/21)
Agricultural towns
  in 1837 .11   (8/23)

ALL NATIONAL/WHIG
TOWNS, 1831-34 (26)
North   .006 (17/25)
Orthodox towns
  in 1808 .004 (17/21)
Unitarian churches
  in 1835 .02 (18/29)
Agricultural towns
  in 1837 .25 (13/23)

.11 (7)   .0001 (17)

nc (13)   .03 (17)   HIGH FEDERALIST
                         VOTE IN 1824 (19)

AGRICULTURAL TOWNS
IN 1820 (27)
North   .0001 (22/25)
Orthodox towns
  in 1808   .1   (15/24)

.15 (21)   FEDERALIST VOTE
            IN 1824 (37)

.25 (20)   FEDERALIST VOTE
            IN 1812 (36)

.11 (9/22)   .03 (8/22)

REGULATOR TOWNS,
1786-87 (9)

CONSENT TO THE
GENERAL COURT'S WRITING
A CONSTITUTION, 1776 (13)

.13 (8/9)

COURT/OLD LIGHT TOWNS IN 1743 (16)
(Towns on 1743 Valuation with Old Light church,
Court voting record, 1726-64, or low level of
Land Bank mortgages)

nc=non-calculable.   Sources: see Appendix 2.

Figure 6a. The Court tradition, the agricultural towns of 1820, North County Federalism, and Whiggery.

communications route, cutting through the old quadrants that had shaped the county's political culture since the turn of the eighteenth century, when the earliest frontier towns had established their regional dominance by taking up the remnants of the Nipmuc's open fields. This new central corridor rapidly came to occupy a distinct place in the growing economy. Where the south county towns turned almost monolithically toward textile production, the towns of the central corridor had a more varied economy, combining textiles, machinery production, paper manufacture, and boot and shoe making. Lacking large-scale corporations, this region had a proliferation of smaller shops, fueled by the commerce flowing along the Boston-to-Springfield road.

The components of the central corridor economy were precisely measured in state and federal surveys taken in the 1830s.[52] When Massachusetts inventoried its industries just before the depression of 1837, the county's most valuable products were woolen and cotton textiles, boots and shoes, chairs, palm-leaf hats, textile machinery, and machine cards. The last four totaled $1.2 million in annual production, and were relatively localized. Machinery and card manufacturing employed about 325 men in the central corridor towns of Worcester, Leicester, and Millbury; chair work employed over 700 men in small shops in the northern towns of Ashburnham, Sterling, and Gardner; and hat making was done by women in hundreds of households scattered across the northern towns. But these industries were far overshadowed by textile and shoe production, which totaled $8.5 million, employing over 12,000 men and women. Cotton and woolen textiles, employing 2,708 men and 3,125 women, and annually producing $5.7 million worth of cloth, dominated the economics of eleven towns, eight of them in the southern valleys, in towns where most of the better capitalized corporations had been established between 1811 and 1816. In sharp contrast, the boot and shoe industry was disproportionately located in the towns of the central corridor, and in towns where there had been no corporations – but a high level of manufacturing employment – by 1820. In only three towns, Grafton, Millbury, and Northbridge, all adjacent in the upper Blackstone Valley on the southern edge of the central corridor, was employment in both shoes and textiles above the county average. (See Figure 6b.)

The boot and shoe industry had a distinctly different economic structure than textile manufacturing. Rather than the increasingly integrated water-powered mills owned by the corporations that dominated textile production by the 1830s, shoework was organized around work put out to households from central shops, and by small-scale family partnerships. Its location in the central corridor was

[52] Louis McLane, ed., *Report of the Secretary of the Treasury, 1832. Documents Relative to the Manufactures in the United States. House Executive Documents*, 22d Cong. 1st Sess., Doc. No. 308 (Washington, D.C., 1833), 1:474–577; Bigelow, *Industry in Massachusetts . . . 1837*, 42–73, 169ff. I have used the figures for 1837 because they capture the Massachusetts economy at the peak of the prosperity of the mid-1830s.

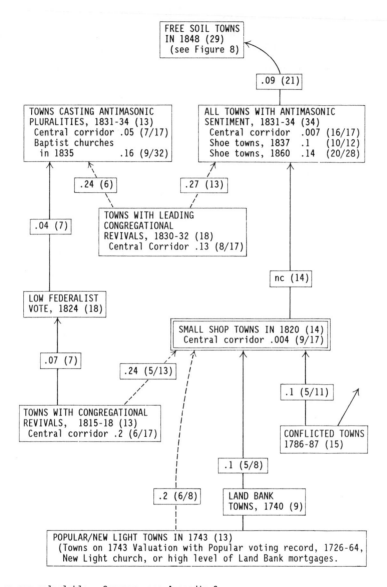

nc=non-calculable. Sources: see Appendix 2.

Figure 6b. Popular orthodoxy, the shop towns of 1820, and the antebellum insurgencies.

simply a function of transportation; work done by hand on a putting-out basis required access to good roads, just as textile manufacturing required reliable water power.[53] The labor in boot and shoework was significantly different from textiles: employing 4,305 men and only 2,142 women in 1837. And the aggregate value of boot and shoe production was significantly lower. The textile mills produced $974 worth of cloth per worker, while the production value per worker in the shoe industry was only $433. This may simply reflect a more occasional and seasonal work routine, with shoework done as a by-employment to farming. Shoework allowed people to preserve the outlines of the traditional household structure of production, but it was not particularly remunerative. As measured by assessed taxes per poll, the people in the shoe towns were significantly poorer than those in the agricultural towns, while the textile towns fell in between.[54] Nonetheless, shoemaking appears to have allowed a higher level of persistence than the textile towns, as measured by the ratio of registered voters to adult males, suggesting that shoeworkers received more of the value of their labor than did textile workers. Agricultural towns had the highest ratio of voters to adult males, textile towns the lowest, while the shoe towns fell in a middle range. Similarly, agricultural and shoe

[53] For my understanding of the textile industry, I have drawn upon Prude, *The Coming of Industrial Order*, and Barbara M. Tucker, *Samuel Slater and the Origins of the American Textile Industry, 179–1860* (Ithaca, 1984). For my understanding of shoemaking, I have drawn upon Blanche E, Hazard, *The Organization of the Boot and Shoe in Massachusetts before 1875* (Cambridge, Mass., 1921); Alan Dawley, *Class and Community: The Industrial Revolution in Lynn* (Cambridge, Mass., 1976); and Faler, *Mechanics and Manufacturers*.

[54] *Valuation per poll in Worcester County towns, 1832*

	Low ($625–835)		Middling ($856–942)		High ($943–1915)		Total ($969)	
Total towns	18	*100*	18	*100*	18	*100*	54	*100*
Town economy in 1837								
Agricultural	6	*33*	7	*30*	10	*55*	23	*43*
Chairs	2		1		0		3	*5*
Shoes	5	*28*	6	*33*	1		12	*22*
Textile/agricultural	0		2	*33*	3	*17*	5	*9*
Textile/Worcester	5	*28*	2		4	*22*	11	*20*

Note: Figures in italics are percentages. For economic categories, see Appendix 1. Webster was incorporated after the 1832 valuation was taken.
Source: State Valuation, *Resolves of the General Court, 1832*, 116–18. See Chapter 2, note 3, for summary of evidence of increasing stratification in early-nineteenth-century Worcester, Leicester, and Millbury. See comparable evidence in Doherty, *Power and Society*, 46–81; Richard Holmes, *Communities in Transition: Bedford and Lincoln, Massachusetts, 1729–1850* (Ann Arbor, Mich., 1980), 88–89, 191; and more generally, Henretta, "Wealth and Social Structure," 275–9.

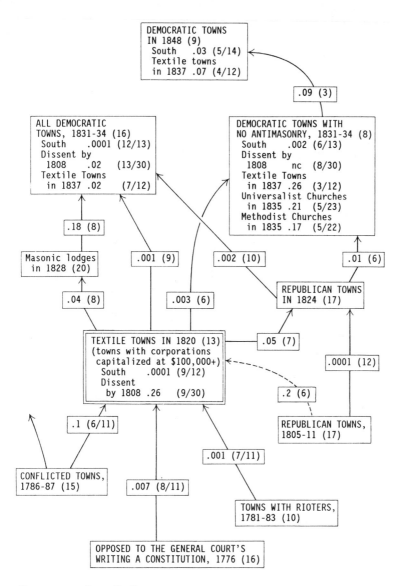

Sources: see Appendix 2.

Figure 6c. Republicanism, the textile towns of 1820, and democracy.

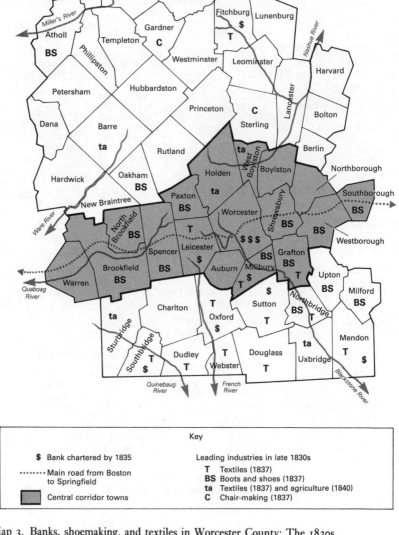

Map 3. Banks, shoemaking, and textiles in Worcester County: The 1830s.
(Drawn by Carmel Ciampa from data by John Brooke)

towns, such as New Braintree and Brookfield, had significantly fewer young men than did dynamic industrial centers like Worcester and Millbury. In sum, textile towns attracted young, poor, and mobile populations, whereas agricultural towns had older, wealthier, and more persistent populations, and shoe towns had older, poorer, but relatively persistent populations. Shoework can be characterized as an adaptive traditionalism, preserving the outlines of the eighteenth-century pattern of production in networks of affiliated households, for a people unwilling to enter the mills and unable to emigrate to better lands in the west.[55]

The growth of manufacturing employment along the central corridor was built upon the networks of trade and local production established by Federalist merchant-entrepreneurs over the previous decades. But it also seems to have involved a certain accommodation between established merchants, predominantly Federalist, and emerging small-shop masters, often Republican. The Worcester machine makers, building a range of machines for the textile trade, seem to have avoided partisan politics; the scythe makers in Sutton and Millbury seem to have been Republican to a man. Shoemaking, a critical feature of the economy of the central corridor by the 1830s, began to emerge during the years of the embargo and the war, and the early shoe entrepreneurs in several cases seem to have been rooted in the Republican orbit. In Leicester, two young brothers from the Baptist Green family were the first to begin making shoes to sell on a peddling route, and they were soon joined by others from the Baptist orbit. The Republican towns of

[55] *A measure of persistence: Legal voters in 42 Worcester County towns per males over 20 in 1840*

	Low (65–75/100)		Middling (76–80/100)		High (81–96/100)		Total	
Total towns	14	*100*	14	*100*	14	*100*	42	*100*
Town economy in 1837								
Agricultural	3	*21*	6	*43*	6	*43*	15	*36*
Chairs	0		0		3	*21*	3	*7*
Shoes	3	*21*	5	*36*	3	*21*	11	*26*
Textile/agricultural	1		1		1		3	*7*
Textile/Worcester	7	*50*	2		1		10	*24*

Note: Figures in italics are percentages. The fourth question on this Whig questionnaire was "No. of legal voters borne on the lists in November, 1839." The completed questionnaires, filled out by local Whig committeemen, survive for only 42 towns. For a useful discussion of the strength of traditional views of the household among shoeworkers, see Mary H. Blewett, "Work, Gender, and the Artisan Tradition in New England Shoemaking, 1780–1860," *Journal of Social History* 17 (1983), 221–48.
Source: See notes on Sources for Tables for economic variables; 1840 U.S. Census of Population, "Whig Party Questionnaires, May 1, 1840," Folder 4, Box 6, Worcester County, Mass., Papers, AAS.

Milford and Grafton were major early centers of shoemaking in the county; from Grafton shoework spread to the North Parish of Brookfield, when Oliver Ward set up shop at a tannery in 1810. Among his many apprentices were Tyler and Ezra Batchellor, sons of a cooper of Baptist connections who had moved from Sutton in 1802 and who briefly led the Republican faction in North Brookfield.[56]

But there were countervailing forces that limited the influence of this early artisanal Republicanism. The national tax imposed by the Republican national government drew an angry response from the county's shoemakers. A broadside circulating in the spring of 1815, focusing on the requirement to post bonds with a federal tax collector, asked whether their situation was "better than that of Virginia negroes," and warned "ye mechanics and manufacturers of all articles and commodities of whatever name and nature" to beware the fines imposed by the new legislation.[57] Religious revival could also turn the shoe orbits from their original Republicanism. In North Brookfield, the revival of 1816–17 brought an end to a generation of conflict between the town's warring political factions. Beginning among the Baptists, the revival spread to the Congregational church. Tyler Batchellor was among those joining the orthodox church in 1817; the next year he started a Sunday School and in 1820 he was chosen deacon. At the same time, he was establishing his own shoe business, setting up his own shop in 1819, and building a new shop on an open farm in 1822. Batchellor may well have been instrumental in having the Congregationalists rebuild their meetinghouse near his shop in 1823; his property soon became the site of the new North Brookfield village. In becoming a major figure in the Congregational church, Batchellor had overcome the former "discord" between his family and the town's Federalist majority; dozens of other Congregationalists had signed a remonstrance against Ezra Batchellor, Sr.'s, election to the General Court in 1812.[58]

North Brookfield's revival was part of a wider revival cycle surging through the northeast between 1816 and 1820, part of a second phase of the Second Great Awakening that had begun around the turn of the century. The churches of the central corridor and the small shop towns responded far more frequently to this phase of the revival than did the agricultural and textile towns to the north and

[56] Washburn, *Industrial Worcester*, 24–30; Benedict and Tracy, *Sutton*, 526–7, 589; *HWC*, 1:541, 2:334; Washburn, *Leicester*, 349; Temple, *North Brookfield*, 226, 267–70, 515–7; North Brookfield Remonstrance, 1812, Contested Elections, Mass. Archives; Ernest A. Bragg, *The Origin and Growth of the Boot and Shoe Industry in Holliston . . . and Milford, Massachusetts* (Milford, 1950).

[57] Washburn, *Industrial Worcester*, 27.

[58] Thomas Snell, *A Sermon Delivered by the Rev. Dr. Snell, on the Last Sabbath in June, 1838 . . .* (Brookfield, 1838), 17–19, 22–3; Joseph Hodges, *Historical Sketch of the Baptist Church in Brookfield* (Brookfield, 1850), 16; Temple, *North Brookfield*, 273–7.

south. This pattern would persist, and the central corridor would be the focal point of Congregational revivalism again in the early 1830s.[59]

Visiting North Brookfield in 1823, Amasa Walker, himself an 1817 convert and later a shoe merchant in business with Batchellor, wrote to his brother that the new "meetinghouse is beautiful beyond description." "I never saw the North Brookfield people in so good spirits, I never saw them so united and happy, and I do hope that the dark days of discord are past."[60] The aggregate figures indicate that North Brookfield's experience was typical; the postwar revivals anticipated the cooling of a particularly contested political climate throughout the central corridor. The politics of the small-shop towns and the central corridor stood in sharp contrast to an opposing uniformity elsewhere in the county. Where the agricultural north and the textile south fell into consistent commitments to Federalism and Republicanism, coupled in the south county towns with a consistently low voter turnout, the towns of the central corridor divided their votes at the height of the First Party competition between 1805 and 1812, and had the highest rates of voter turnout in 1805 and 1812. Here communications may have played a role in these higher turnout levels, with political excitement, and newspaper subscriptions, flowing more easily along the main thoroughfare through the county, to be discussed and read aloud in the region's workshops. In the 1824 election, after the wave of orthodox revivalism, the region inclined toward the Federalists, and turnout was relatively low.[61]

The contested political climate of the central corridor anticipated the emergence of a highly volatile, insurrectionary political culture over the following decades. However, the circumstances of the small-shop towns that dominated the central corridor in 1820 suggest important continuities with the past.

Economically and politically, these towns stood between two extremes. (See Figures 6a–c.) On the one hand, the agricultural towns of 1820 were overwhelmingly located in the conservative northern half of the county, including the core of the Court Party coalition in the provincial General Court, the towns consenting

---

[59] Congregational revivalism is based on the towns listed as having revivals between 1815 and 1818 in Joshua Bradley, *Accounts of Religious Movements in Many Parts of the United States from 1815 to 1818* (Albany, 1819), 46, 49, 63, 162; and the added membership (relative to total population) reported in the "Abstracts of Statistical Reports," in *Minutes of the General Association of Massachusetts*, published annually between 1829 and 1861. The years 1830–2, 1842, 1852, and 1858 were years of significant increases in membership across most of the Congregational associations in Worcester County.

[60] Amasa Walker to Freeman Walker, January 15, 1823, Amasa Walker Papers, 1823–92, MHS.

[61] In 1805, eight of the fourteen central corridor towns were among seventeen towns with voter turnout of 65% or better (P-value of .04), and in 1812, eight of sixteen central corridor towns were among seventeen towns with voter turnout of 78% or better (P-value of .08). Turnout estimate based on estimate of electorate as 80% of polls. (See Chapter 7, note 53.) Source Returns for Governor, MA; U. S. Census of Population.

to the General Court's constitutional plan of 1776, as well as the Regulator strongholds. The north was, in sum, unmoved by the provincial forces of Lockean insurgency, and then passed over by the new forces of economic change. The Harringtonian legacy of the Regulation was undercut by defeat and outmigration; its insurgent defense of moral economy left no permanent mark on the region's political culture. Overwhelmingly Federalist in the First Party competition, the north would be equally solid for the Whigs. On the other hand, the large-scale textile corporations were situated in the south, particularly the southwest, in towns swept by religious dissent, constitutionalism, and "private mobs" between the 1750s and the 1780s: broadly the Lockean wing of the old Popular tradition. Republican from 1805 through 1824, the textile corporation towns would be solidly Democratic in the decades to come.

Between north and south lay the small-shop towns; intermediate in their geography, politics, and their economic adaptation, they were also rooted in the center of the old provincial political culture: the orthodox wing of the Popular tradition. (See Figure 6b.) Strikingly, the networks of small shops were most developed in many towns where the adherence of rising men to "The Manufactory Scheme" of 1740 had been most pronounced three generations earlier; they were the inheritors of the Land Bank tradition. In North Brookfield, Oliver Ward and the Batchellors had relations among the Land Bankers, as did the Keiths, leading shoe entrepreneurs in Grafton.[62] Similarly, the shop towns of 1820 were the most likely to have been swept by the orthodox revivals of the 1740s and to have contributed to the Popular partisanship of the late provincial house. Unlike the textile towns, they were not particularly inclined toward the markers of the Lockean wing of the Popular tradition: dissenting religion, constitutional politics, or the rioting of the early 1780s. Unlike some of the agricultural towns in the northwest, the shop towns of 1820 had not been united behind the Regulation but – like the textile towns – had been divided between competing leaders raising militias for the Regulators and for the government. This background in central tendencies of Popular orthodoxy lay behind the small-shop economy, the competitive First Party politics, and the postwar wave of New Divinity revivals that characterized the central corridor in the first decades of the nineteenth century.

Thus, by a range of measures, the small-shop towns of 1820 were centered between long-standing extremes in the county's political culture. The adaptive traditionalism of shopwork – shoemaking in particular – and the New Divinity revivals gave new form to the old accommodation between corporate commonwealth and voluntary individualism that had characterized the orthodox wing of the Popular tradition. But their circumstances would no longer place them in

[62] Temple, *North Brookfield*, 515–16, 773; Benedict and Tracy, *Sutton*, 587–8; Davis, *Currency and Banking*, 2:296, 304.

the center of political culture, but on the insurgent periphery, manifested in Antimasonry, Free Soil, and Radical Republicanism. Here, the Harringtonian imperative of independence in commonwealth would be the driving force in their critique of the structure of economic and legal institutions within the state and across the nation. But the short term, specifically the 1820s, would see the triumph of that institutional order.

Corporations and limited liability

In June 1825, lawyer Christopher C. Baldwin wrote from the hill town of Barre to his friend Isaac Davis in Worcester that he had "been highly entertained" by the local reception of Governor Levi Lincoln's address to the General Court. "The Yeomanry here read it with their eyes stretched as wide open as an augur hole. They have the most excellent views of the speech and its unprecedently popular author."[63] Lincoln's election had restored political peace to a recently divided state. After almost a decade of political calm, 1823 and 1824 had brought the final explosion of party strife, with the issues of Unitarian control of Harvard College, the denial of a charter for Amherst College, and the renewal of accusations of treason at Hartford in 1814 turning key blocks of orthodox voters away from the Federalists toward the Republicans. In May 1825, three months after native son John Quincy Adams had secured the presidency, Levi Lincoln swept a field of scattered candidates for governor. With Edward Bangs, Jr., at his side as his private secretary, Lincoln settled into the first of eight consecutive terms in the governor's chair. Elected with the nomination of both the Federalists and the Republicans, Lincoln received broad support from a complacent electorate. Turnout in the late 1820s fell to its lowest level since the 1790s, and would not rise to the levels of the height of the First Party system until a competitive two-party competition returned in the late 1830s.[64]

In the meantime, Lincoln's ascendancy brought the triumph of Worcester Republicanism, now transmuted into a broad consensus by the amalgamation of political elites. Within the county the institutional vehicle of this fusion was the Worcester Agricultural Society, over which Lincoln's father had presided in 1819. If the Agricultural Society spanned the partisan divisions of the previous decade, restoring the elite associational politics of the 1790s, its purposes and rhetoric reflected the Republican definition of political economy. Levi Lincoln, Sr., spoke of these purposes in no uncertain terms in the first address delivered to the

---

[63] C. C. Baldwin to Isaac Davis, June 7, 1815, Isaac Davis Papers, vol. 2, AAS.
[64] Formisano, *The Transformation of Political Culture*, 120–7; Arthur B. Darling, *Political Changes in Massachusetts, 1824–1848: A Study of Liberal Movements in Politics* (New Haven, 1925), 40–1.

assembled society in October, 1819. "If Agriculture be the life's blood of the people, the Arts of *Manufacture* constitute the real independence of the nation. We rejoice that the spirit of our citizens has risen superior to a reliance on foreign supply for the most necessary fabricks for personal use, and household consumption." Such sentiments were voiced repeatedly before the society over the next decade, with early concerns that infant industries were not receiving "the fostering care of the general government" giving way to expectations of boundless prosperity after the passage of the woolen tariff of 1826.[65]

At the agricultural society's first "Cattle Show and Exhibition of Manufactures" in October 1819, along with prizes for winning ox teams and prime cattle and swine, awards were presented for Merino sheep and for woolen cloth. But the judges found that none of the woven cotton was "sufficiently good to be entitled to a Premium."[66] This was a judgment on the state of manufacturing in the county, which would be seriously affected by British competition for much of the decade. James Wolcott, Jr., of the Globe Village, was among a group of Southbridge textile men who moved beyond the consensus-building vehicle of the agricultural society to form a local Society for the Encouragement of American Industry in 1824. In their first set of resolves, the Southbridge society pointed to "an undue influence of the mercantile, and through that, the British interest" and called for the protection of American industries as proposed by Matthew Carey. Two years later Wolcott would be a leading figure at a meeting of the county's woolen manufacturers that framed a memorial to Congress protesting the "depressed condition" of their trade.[67]

By the end of the decade, with the woolen tariff, growing efficiencies from twenty years of experience, and an increasingly sophisticated machine-building industry in Worcester, Millbury, and Leicester, the textile industry began to prosper. In many cases the factories working in the thirties were established during the 1820s on the same power privileges as the wartime factories; increasingly they would be controlled by investors from outside the region. In Dudley, Samuel Slater bought up the Merino and Village Factory properties, combining them with his own lands in south Oxford to build the manufacturing complex around which the town of Webster would be formed in 1832. In Leicester, a group of Boston investors bought up a small woolen works and

[65] Levi Lincoln, *Address, Delivered before the Worcester Agricultural Society, October 7, 1819* (Worcester, 1819), 13; Nathaniel P. Denny, *Address Delivered before the Worcester Agricultural Society, September 22, 1822, Being the Anniversary Cattle Show and Exhibition of Manufactures* ... (Worcester, 1822), 7; George A. Tufts, *Address, Delivered before the Worcester Agricultural Society, October 12, 1825* ... (Worcester, 1827), 12–13; Waldo Flint, *An Address Delivered before the Worcester Agricultural Society, October 10, 1832* ... (Worcester, 1832), 14.
[66] Lincoln, *Address*, 19–23.
[67] *Aegis*, April 28, 1824; *Niles Register* 31, November 11, 1826, Washburn, *Industrial Worcester*, 64.

established the Leicester Manufacturing Company. Another Boston group established the Ware Manufacturing Company at an isolated falls where Col. Thomas Denny of Leicester had attempted to set up a machine shop in 1813. As successive depressions struck the industry, the county's textile mills would increasingly fall into the hands of wealthy outsiders, usually from Boston, while the original owners often stayed on to work as the agents of these absentee capitalists.[68]

Textile manufacturing comprised one institutional bulwark of the new National synthesis; banking comprised the second. The monopoly of the Worcester Bank was broken in 1823, with the incorporation of the Oxford Bank. Ebenezer Davis, the Universalist cattle dealer in Charlton, with his younger brother Jonathan of Oxford, long had acted as "private bankers," making small loans to hundreds of local people. Jonathan Davis, once a member of the Republican county committee and subsequently a presidential elector in 1825 and 1829 voting for John Quincy Adams, would serve through 1833 as the new bank's first president.[69]

The spread of banking was inextricably bound up with the new manufacturing order. The Oxford Bank petition, with Jonathan Davis's leading signature next to those of textile men Aaron Tufts and Samuel Slater, stated flatly that the petitioners had "property to a large amount in manufacturing establishments which manufacture goods to one half million dollars annually." Two years later the petitioners for a bank in Leicester, "all businessmen," cited the extensive "manufacturing of cloths and cards" in that town, and "the great inconvenience . . . felt from a want of facility in obtaining a ready supply of money." And in 1828, the Southbridge bank petitioners argued that the "manufacturing business is done more conveniently by means of bank negotiations, and custom has made it almost impossible to do it in any other manner." Yet the established banks in Worcester, Leicester, and Oxford could not be trusted to handle their business in a reliable fashion: "Under the circumstances we are obliged to remain in a state of dependence, or make other arrangements." Across the county, textile manufacturers were unwilling to endure such a dependency, and rapidly established sources of credit subject to their immediate influence and control. By 1830 banks had been established in Oxford, Mendon, Leicester, Uxbridge, Millbury, Southbridge, Sutton, as well as a second bank in Worcester and another in neighboring Ware in Hampshire County. Five of the county's eight new banks

[68] Tucker, *Samuel Slater*, 126ff.; Prude, *The Coming of Industrial Order*, 175–80; Arthur Chase, *History of Ware, Massachusetts* (Cambridge, Mass., 1911), 219; John Gregson, "Fiskdale and Its Industries, *QHSL* 2 (1903–9), 21; Daniels, *Oxford*, 188–219; Original Papers, Incorporation of Leicester Manufacturing Company, June 12, 1823, chap. 6, Acts of 1823; and Incorporation of the Saxon and Leicester Factory, February 8, 1825, chap. 55, Acts of 1825, Mass. Archives.
[69] Daniels, *Oxford*, 232–3; Mary De Witt Freeland, *The Records of Oxford, Massachusetts* (Albany, 1894), 229; *Centennial of the Olive Branch Lodge* (Millbury, 1897), 33–4.

9. Ware Factory Village in the 1830s.
The columned building at the center is the Ware Manufacturers' Bank, and the long building to the right is the Ware Manufacturing Company's mill, built in 1824.
From John W. Barber, *Historical Collections . . . of Every Town in Massachusetts* (Worcester, 1839). (Old Sturbridge Village photograph by Henry E. Peach)

were established in the southern tier of towns, and – except for the Central Bank in Worcester – all were established in towns with large-scale textile mills.[70]

The 1820s thus saw the dramatic extension of the institutional economic order that had fitfully emerged since the ratification of the constitution. This institutional order was on Levi Lincoln's mind when he addressed the General Court in June, 1826. As a good National Republican, Lincoln was interested in education and he called for "the establishment of a Seminary of practical Arts and Sciences." Lincoln was also concerned that the state take an active role in planning the course of canal and railroad development. The Blackstone Canal, first proposed in 1796

[70] For convenience, this note includes all significant sources for banks discussed here and in Chapter 10. Petitions and acts of incorporation in Original Papers, Massachusetts Archives: Oxford Bank, chap. 68, Acts of 1822; Millbury Bank, chap. 42, Acts of 1825; Leicester Bank, chap. 178, Acts of 1825; Southbridge Bank, chap. 130, Acts of 1828; Ammidown, *Historical Collections*, 2:401–2; Sutton Bank, chap. 122, Acts of 1827 chap. 66, Acts of 1828, chap. 132, Acts of 1830, Senate Unpassed, 1836, 9953/1; Central Bank, chap. 131, Acts of 1827; Quinsigamond Bank, chap. 168, Acts of 1833; Citizen's Bank, chap. 172, Acts of 1836. For the incorporation of banks in Mendon (1824), Uxbridge (1825), Fitchburg (1832), and Lancaster (1836), see *Private and Special Statutes*, 6:139, 329, 7:201, 671–2. For the directors of the Worcester, Leicester, Central, Oxford, Millbury, Central, and Quinsigamond Banks in various years, see *Worcester County Republican*, April 22, 29, May 13, 20, 1829; October 13, 1830; October 5, 1831; October 3, 1832; October 8, 1834. Also the *National Aegis*, October 3, 1838.

and begun in 1822, would threaten to siphon off trade to Rhode Island. While Lincoln was hesitant about the feasibility of railroads in 1826, he would soon aggressively advocate the building of the Western Railroad – through Worcester – to better compete with other states, particularly New York. By the late 1840s the middle landscape would be powerfully reshaped by the forces unleashed by the railroad.[71]

But Lincoln's strongest language was reserved for the issue of limiting the liability of stockholders of corporations. The general incorporation act of 1809 had explicitly stipulated that the stockholders would be personally liable in the event of the bankruptcy of a corporation, and the 1825 house considered but failed to act upon a proposal to limit personal liability. In his address to the General Court in 1826, Lincoln hailed the transformative power of the new corporations.

> The surprising influence of these institutions, in promoting the general Improvement of the Country, may be witnessed wherever they are situated. Look but to the villages of Lowell and Ware, places where the very wastes of nature, as if by the magic of machinery, have suddenly converted into scenes of busy population, of useful industry, and of wealth.

But the problem of personal liability was a hindrance to further development: "Provident, and discerning, and enterprizing capitalists" were "deterred from participating in the manufacturing business of the Commonwealth, solely, by the provisions of the Statute." Just as the state's trade was being siphoned off by the Erie Canal and the Blackstone Canal, so too the liability law was diverting capital to neighboring states.[72] That year the legislature began to move on the issue, and by 1830 stockholders of corporations in Massachusetts were freed from any liability and responsibility regarding their investments. The establishment of limited liability stood as the capstone of an era of profound institutional and structural change, as the center of public life in Massachusetts shifted from Harringtonian commonwealth toward Lockean private interest.

Capitalism

The entire configuration of class, credit, institutions, and production on the Worcester middle landscape had been drastically reshaped over the forty years since the county and the commonwealth had been divided by civil war and the politics of ratification. The fall and winter of 1786 and 1787 had seen the crisis of the old order. Under the eighteenth-century regime, relations of credit and debt were interwoven with the face-to-face workings of informal pyramids of influence

---

[71] Levi Lincoln, *Speech of His Excellency Levi Lincoln, Delivered before the Legislature, June 6, 1826* (Boston, 1826), 8–19; Lincoln, *Worcester*, 339–40.
[72] Lincoln, *Speech*, 10–13.

and authority, and they were mediated by the proceedings of public institutions, most obviously the Court of Common Pleas. Economic power was rooted in and limited by personal holdings, perhaps amplified by access to public authority. Credit was a pivotal dimension in the definition of the gentry as a class, but even here their leverage was limited by the strategies of survival and independence employed within the kinship networks of veritable clans of yeoman households, pooling resources and support to avoid as much as possible the threat of debt, and standing together when ruin seemed imminent.

Between 1787 and 1830 the rules and structure of economic intercourse were changed fundamentally. The public institutions of town and county receded in importance, out of the center stage that they had occupied over the entire eighteenth century. Their central place was taken by private institutions. Incorporated by the state, they had the same basis in statute as the old towns and counties, but they were private and exclusive, and inaccessible to public accountability within the locality. The towns, as gentry representatives often had learned to their dismay, were subject to majority rule, and the courts were a public forum that twice during the eighteenth century were halted by militia companies raised in those towns. The new corporations, increasingly stripped of remnant connotations of public purpose, were far more flexible instruments of economic power than the courts ever could have been, bearing legal privileges of association with minimal public responsibilities.

These new private institutions were instruments of capital accumulation and investment that far exceeded anything possible in the eighteenth century. They established a wholly new context of production and labor, superceding the limited capacities of even the wealthiest gentry households. Certainly the households in this backcountry were not self-sufficient isolates; they produced for both household consumption and for sale in a series of local and regional markets. But it would be difficult to argue that full-scale capitalism was operating in the Worcester backcountry during the eighteenth century. If these households were producing for the market, their involvement was restrained by the limits of transportation; the forces of the market were in turn restrained by the limits of capital accumulation and by the persisting assumptions of moral economy and commonwealth in the public culture of the orthodox majority. But between 1790 and 1830 the instruments of a capital economy were distributed across the county. Turnpikes, the canal, and then the proposed railroad brought the county into an increasingly integrated transportation network. Manufacturing corporations and banks were selectively located in towns with good waterpower, creating a mosaic of economic transformation and concentration. Work began to move out of the control of households, once critical units of the public corporate order, and into the control of private institutions operating at the whim of distant capitalists. The spread of local banking in particular accelerated the process of economic development, and it fundamentally shaped the redefinition of social class. Access to capital would remain critical as a new alignment of middle class and working class began to displace the old categories of gentleman, yeoman, and laborer. This redefinition would become the ground for renewed political insurgencies, as some of the county's people, like many throughout the country, attempted to reconcile nineteenth-century realities of growing concentration and stratification with the Revolutionary heritage of equal rights. Not far below the Lockean surface lay the deeply rooted traditions of Harringtonian independence and obligation.[73]

[73] I have found Fernand Braudel, *The Wheels of Commerce*, Vol. II of *Civilization and Capitalism: 15th–18th Century*, trans, by Siân Reynolds (New York, 1982), 25–58, 231–49, particularly useful in thinking about the development of capitalism in early-nineteenth-century Massachusetts. See also Rothenberg, "The Emergence of a Capital Market"; and Morton J. Horwitz, *The Transformation of American Law, 1780–1860* (Cambridge, Mass., 1977).

10

Insurgencies

On March 30, 1831, Emory Washburn, an attorney who had recently moved from Leicester into the thriving village of Worcester, rose to address the Worcester Lyceum. A close associate of Governor Levi Lincoln, Washburn would himself occupy the governorship in the decades to come. He had chosen the topic of the "jealousies which exist in our country, and complaints which are made of an arbitrary classification of society, whereby it is alleged that rights and privileges are unequally distributed and enjoyed." Washburn could not be persuaded "that there are any grounds for the distinctions which are assumed to exist between ranks and classes of men" in the American republic, and "that a candid examination of the true condition of the social relations under our government, would allay these jealousies effectively." The constitution guaranteed equality of men before the law, and rather than the arbitrary classifications of men that had pertained in Europe under the "Feudal system," the only classification in America was the natural and mutable "division of labor" that "must exist in every civilized country where the arts of life are cultivated." But, Washburn complained to the Lyceum members, "self-styled reformers" were "laboring in some of our cities to create jealousies among different classes of citizens."[1]

These reformers were the Workingmen, and their advocacy of universal education as a means to equal rights and opportunities was a challenge to the moral stewardship espoused by the Lyceum. Founded in the late 1820s as a means of improving education and a context for learning and debate, the Lyceum was firmly rooted in the National Republican consensus that had taken hold over the course of the decade. The county Lyceum in particular had taken it upon itself to reform the county's common schools, and to distribute books and "apparatus." Their efforts made those of the Workingmen unnecessary; the established "institutions" were "eminently republican, and equalizing in their nature and tendency," while the Workingmen were "striking at the very foundations of civil society."[2]

Rooted in the National vision of a harmonious, progressive society where leading men gathered in association to advance their conception of the public interest – whether in agricultural societies, corporations, or the Lyceum – Emory

---

[1] Emory Washburn, *A Lecture, Read before the Worcester Lyceum, March 31, 1831* (Worcester, 1831), 3–4, 7–8, 14–15, 20; Levi Lincoln to Emory Washburn, June 18, 1831, Emory Washburn Papers (Box, 1820–5), MHS.

[2] Washburn, *A Lecture*, 18–20; "Worcester County Lyceum Records, 1827–1843, 1869–1874," Worcester County, Mass., Papers, AAS.

Washburn's address had a direct antecedent in Edward Bangs's 1791 critique of "jealousy" in politics. Both assumed the capacity of the constitution to mitigate against unjust usurpation and concentration of power. Bangs had urged confidence in the new national government; Washburn urged confidence in benevolent institutions.[3] But if political jealousies did subside in the 1790s, social and economic jealousies were rising in the late 1820s. The Jacksonian Worcester County *Republican* criticized Washburn's address on April 6, declaring that he had failed to demonstrate that there was no aristocracy in America and that he had misrepresented the Workingmen. The *Republican* had printed complaints about the structure of Worcester society since it began publication in 1829, denouncing the local "oligarchy, the "nobility of this village" for whom Washburn spoke. The paper took on the most revered institution of the National Republican synthesis, printing a letter in 1831 complaining that lawyers, doctors, merchants, and ministers were "admitted without much ceremony" to the Worcester Agricultural Society's "Cattle Show Ball," while "a farmer or mechanic . . . would stand a poor chance against the body aristocratic in Worcester." More fundamentally, the paper complained of a "monied aristocracy" controlling "a system of corporations . . . calculated to deprive the people of their power and rightful influence in government." While the new manufacturing villages were "justly the pride and ornament of the state," abuses in corporate charters subjected "their populations to the will and control of a few capitalists."[4]

This new institutional order was foremost in his mind when Amasa Walker, a leading Antimason, addressed the people of Stoughton on July 4, 1830. He told his audience that the legacy of the Revolution was threatened: "The grim genius of tyranny still haunts our land, and stalks abroad in many a plausible and dangerous form." Tyranny had taken on a new form, more suitable to "the spirit of the age."

> Once, he who could command the most numerous and well-disciplined military force, was the fairest candidate for power; now he who can control and manage the most extended and best organized association, or combination of men, is the most certain of accomplishing his purposes . . . . Voluntary associations have become the great instruments of power in the 19th century; they move and direct the world, though often with an unseen and mysterious hand.

Although he granted that many associations were "productive of great good," Walker argued that, given their "immense power . . . all combinations or associations of men, for what ever ostensible object, are just subjects of jealousy and suspicion."[5]

Despite the hopes and efforts of men like Bangs and Washburn, jealousy – and

[3] Bangs, *An Oration . . . 1791.*

[4] Worcester County *Republican*, November 18, 1829; October 19, 1831; October 31, 1832.

[5] Amasa Walker, *An Oration Delivered at Stoughton, Mass, July 5, 1830. In Commemoration of the 54th Anniversary of American Independence* (Boston, 1830), 5–7.

a broader classical republicanism – was not dead in 1830. Concerns about the subversion of the rights of the people would ring out across the county and the state over the years to come. After four decades during which class-based conflict had been muted in both the presence and absence of two-party confrontation, the early 1830s saw the reemergence of insurgent impulses. Certainly the synthesis of polity, society, and economy forged by the Nationals and inherited by the Whigs, was powerful and persuasive, and its adversarial position in national politics gave it a limited insurgent quality of its own. For the better part of the 1830s and 1840s a majority of the county's voters would support this leading party. But the challenges of Workingmen and Antimasons to the established political order allow an examination of the points of stress and avenues of dissent in this changing society. If these challenges were episodic and short-lived, truncated by the thrust of national politics, they provided the ground for a second and broader upheaval in the late 1840s, as Free Soil swept the county and paved the way for the Free Democratic and Republican assaults on Whiggery and slavery.

All of these political challenges would be rooted in the reconfiguration of society and economy that had unfolded since 1789. But they also resonated with political traditions running deep into the county's past. The ground upon which these insurgencies were forged was drastically different from what generated the Regulator insurgency of the 1780s. Regulators had marched as communities to defend the public good from private-minded individuals; Antimasonry and Free Soil worked as political parties to defend equality of opportunity for private-minded individuals. But it is also clear that – within the restricted range of ideological options available – the antebellum insurgencies couched their primary appeal within the rubric of the ancient Harringtonian formula: personal independence – eroded by economic transformation and negated by the simple existence of slavery – was fundamental to the health and stability of the national collectivity. Slowly but inexorably, the county's political culture would be informed by a certainty that the enslavement of black Americans compromised the viability of the union.[6]

[6] For an understanding of the role of insurgencies in antebellum Massachusetts politics. I am indebted to Formisano, *The Transformation of Political Culture*; and Paul Goodman, "The Politics of Industrialism: Massachusetts, 1830–1870," in Richard Bushman, et al., eds., *Uprooted Americans: Essays to Honor Oscar Handlin* (Boston, 1979), 161–207. The survival of classical politics and republicanism has become a central issue in the political history of the early nineteenth century. See Murrin, "The Great Inversion"; McCoy, *The Elusive Republic*; Meyers, *The Jacksonian Persuasion*; Sean Wilentz, *Chants Democratic: New York City and the Rise of the American Working Class* (New York, 1984); Howe, *The Political Culture of the American Whigs*; Holt, *The Political Crisis of the 1850s*; Lears, *No Place of Grace*; and Joyce Appleby, "Republicanism and Ideology," and the essays following edited by Appleby in *AQ* 37 (1985). On jealousy, see James H. Hutson, "The Origins of 'The Paranoid Style in American Politics': Public Jealousy from the Age of Walpole to the Age of Jackson," in David D. Hall, John M. Murrin, and Thad W. Tate, eds., *Saints and Revolutionaries: Essays on Early American History* (New York, 1984), 332–72.

"Our most distinguished Democrats"

On the national stage the most obvious challenge to Nationals and Whigs came from Jacksonian democracy. But the broader Jacksonian success was one of several factors circumscribing its viability as a focus of opposition in Worcester County. Herein lay a deep irony, for in its rhetoric and constituency the county's Democratic Party bore the evidence of structured continuities with a central strain of oppositional political culture: the provincial Popular coalition and its Constitutionalist and Jeffersonian offspring. But here, as perhaps nowhere else in the state, the liberal strain of the Popular tradition was a well run dry. No longer fundamentally at odds with a unitary, corporate political order, its explosive Lockeanism gave way in the antebellum decades to a cranky and reactionary conservatism.

The origins of the county's Democratic Party lay in an "Old Democratic School," a faction of Jeffersonians who resisted "amalgamation," refusing to follow Lincoln into the National coalition. The *Republican* was the party's voice in the early 1830s, established in March 1829 to support Andrew Jackson, and it advanced a straightforward and traditional platform: economy and simplicity in government. Its attacks on aristocracy were linked with a drumbeat of rhetoric about the costs of state government. Lincoln was the target of their most vehement attacks; he "set the example of luxury – of expensive living – of show – of splendid extravagance"; he lived "in a princely style upon his office." The voters had a clear choice "between economy and reckless profligacy." Rising taxation to support state expenditures for roads and canals would benefit the few at the expense of the many." The salaries of public officials were exorbitant and should be drastically curtailed.[7]

This language had been a staple of the Popular tradition in its close watch on governmental expenditure, expressed in votes from the 1740s through the 1780s and in the language of the county conventions between 1777 and 1786, and of the Republicans over the decade of partisan confrontation between 1805 and 1815. This traditional rhetoric drew a constituency from a well-defined region. Down into the 1850s the Democratic Party drew its voting strength from the old Popular, Constitutionalist, and Republican towns of the southern section of the county. Conversely, the Nationals and the Whigs were most solidly rooted in the towns of orthodox and Court traditions in the northern section of the county, including most of the towns that had given their undivided support to the Regulator movement in 1786. Strikingly, the Nationals and the Whigs, the party of progress and economic development, did best in towns where institutional pluralism – and industrial change – were the least advanced. (See Figures 6a–c.) As had the Republicans, Democratic candidates drew strongly in towns with a strong

---

[7] *Republican* March 17, 24, 1830; March 16, April 30, 1831; October 31, 1832; October 7, 1835.

dissenting tradition, particularly towns where the new non-Calvinist denominations – Universalism and Methodism – had taken root. The *Republican*
complained of the "ODIOUS UNION OF CHURCH AND STATE" per-
petuated by the Nationals, another plank drawn from the Jeffersonian platform.
The impetus for the total disestablishment of religion certainly was a central theme
in Democratic rhetoric, but when the final push came in 1832–3, support for the
measure was broad-based and nonpartisan.[8]

With the surge of organization and participation between 1838 and 1844, when
voter turnout again reached the level typical during the partisan decade of 1805 to
1815, the Democrats began to attract votes outside the old Popular region, most
notably in the northern half of the county. But – as throughout the state – the
Democrats could never surpass the record of the Jeffersonian voting in Worcester
County, which between 1805 and 1824 only once fell below 35 percent, and
between 1805 and 1812 stood between 40 and 45 percent. When Marcus Morton,
the perennial Democratic candidate for governor, first ran as a Jacksonian in 1828,
he received 20 percent of the vote, surging to 36 percent in the next year. But only
between 1838 and 1844 did the Democrats win 40 to 45 percent of the county's
vote, peaking at 49 percent in 1839, when the state finally elected Morton to the
governorship in the wake of the Five-Gallon temperance movement. Given their
lack of experience, the Republicans' challenge to the Federalists was more striking
and sustained than that of the Democrats to the Nationals and then the Whigs.[9]
(See Appendixes 1b and c.)

Down to the Civil War strong support for the Democrats at the polls was
overwhelmingly concentrated in the southern valley towns, and thus in towns
where textile work was coming to play an especially important role in local
economies. It is clear, however, that the Democratic vote in these south county
towns was not rooted in the textile mills. Rather, the two were parallel but hostile
products of the broader Republican coalition of 1805–15, with those succeeding in
manufacturing moving toward the Nationals and then the Whigs, and others
toward Jacksonianism.

This division of the old Republican coalition was not necessarily complete by
the 1830s. Alexander DeWitt, for example, a leading figure in the Oxford Woolen
Company formed in 1826, was elected representative from the now Democratic
town of Oxford between 1830 and 1834, and between 1834 and 1836 stood as a

[8] *Republican* November 7, 1832. The distributions of petitions for disestablishment of religion
submitted in 1830 and 1832 show no particular bias toward Democratic towns, nor away from
towns with only Congregational churches. The county representatives favored disestablishment
by 49 to 14 in the final vote in the house (Universalist *Trumpet*, February 18, 1832). For the
disestablishment petitions, see the Original Papers, Chap. 56, Resolves, March 18, 1833, Senate
Documents, Unpassed Legislation, 1830, 9038, and House Documents, Unpassed Legislation,
1832, 11783–11805, MA.
[9] "Returns of Votes for Governor," MA; Formisano, *The Transformation of Political Culture*,
Appendix II, 349, 351.

Democratic candidate for the state senate. There were others among the early Jacksonian leadership who were involved in textile manufacturing, and the Waters family, operating the Millbury armory on a federal contract, were also strong Democrats.[10] But, for the most part, the local Democratic leadership in these southern towns was drawn from farmers and small-shop proprietors, with a scattering of men who had failed in the first wave of manufacturing. When the Jacksonians in Southbridge gathered to celebrate their hero's election in the spring of 1829, the only manufacturers among them were Jedediah Marcy, who had recently sold his interest in the old woolen works on his land once run by the Southbridge Manufacturing Company, and Larkin Ammidown, who in 1832 would be involved in producing cotton batting. When the Southbridge Nationals assembled in September 1832 to organize against Jackson they were led by Moses Plympton, once a firm Republican, with six other cotton mill proprietors. In the late 1830s Southbridge would elect, among other Democratic representatives, Bela Tiffany, who had been a supervisor, agent, and part owner of Slater's cotton works before turning to farming in 1816 and then living in New York City. Similarly, Oxford in the late 1830s would elect harness maker Sylvanus Harris and millwright Francis Sibley. Sibley had been involved in the Village Factory fiasco in 1812, and made a living running a small thread and match mill during the mid-1830s.[11]

[10] Daniels, *Oxford*, 198–9. Also *Republican*, October 8, 1834, October 14, 1835, September 28, 1836. And Jonas L. Sibley to Joseph S. Cabbot, Esq., March 28, 1834, Box 1, Folder 2, Waters Family Papers, AAS.

[11] I am indebted to Ned Landsman for sharing with me his research files on early-nineteenth-century Southbridge. Occupations from Ammidown, *Historical Collections*, 2: 262; McLane, *Report ... Relative to the Manufactures*, 1: 536–7; and newspaper advertisements in the Southbridge *Village Courier*; Southbridge *Register*; and Southbridge *Reformer and Moralist*. Democrats from Southbridge *Register*, March 10, 1829; Worcester *Palladium*, September 25, 1839, with several representatives added; Nationals from Southbridge *Village Courier*, September 25, October 2, 1832; Antimasons from Southbridge Antimasonic Petition, 1833, House Docs., Unpassed Leg., 12324, MA; for Plympton as a Republican see account of 1821 Republican Celebration, appended to John Bisbe, Jr., *An Oration Pronounced July 4, 1821 in the Baptist Meeting House in Southbridge, Mass* ... (Worcester, 1821), 27; on Tiffany, see Daniels, *Oxford*, 193, 214, 215, 717.

Selected occupations of Southbridge political activists

	Democrat		National		Antimason
Wool	1	*4*	2	*3*	2
Cotton	1	*4*	7	*12*	0
Leather	0		0		1
Merchant	3	*11*	6	*10*	
Total known	26		59		50

Note: Figures in italics are percentages.

Most importantly, the operatives in the larger textile mills did not make up an important element of the Democratic constituency. First, given their high rate of mobility, they were the least likely to have established a residency and thus be qualified to vote; the textile towns had disproportionately low levels of voter registration. Both Whigs and Democrats were certain that the workers in the larger mills voted solidly Whig, either subtly coerced by their employers or motivated by a perception of a common interest in the protection of American manufacturing. After the 1840 election the Democratic Worcester *Palladium* claimed that the party had done well, considering the efforts of "numerous manufacturing corporations, employing no operatives but such as would pledge themselves to vote the Whig ticket." Four years later the Whig committee in Dudley almost admitted such coercion when they noted that their ranks were depleted since the failure of the Dudley Woolen Manufacturing Company, "where a few years ago every voter but one or two (say from 20 to 25 voters) were Whigs." "[S]ince the suspension of business in that village," the committee continued, "the tenements have been rented low, and consequently many of them to our political opponents." Linus Child, once a National in Southbridge, would become the focus of controversy in the close 1851 election when he admitted that, as an agent of one of the Lowell mills, he avoided hiring Democrats.[12]

Democratic voters, then, were concentrated in the southern towns that had been the base of the Popular tradition and of Constitutionalist and Republican politics; they seem to have been affiliated with the newer denominations, and to have stood outside the main channels of textile development. Living in towns with sizable groups of transient mill workers, the Democratic voters may have been more stable and persistent than the textile workers, with some affiliations running back to the earlier political traditions in these towns. In Sutton, for example, leading Democrats Jonas L. Sibley and Reubin Waters were both sons of Jeffersonian notables. But among ordinary Democratic voters it is unlikely that direct family continuities in the region were as important as the broader institutional framework in the south county towns. In Sutton at least, although they were not transients, Democratic voters were often from recently settled families, seemingly drawn to the area by the combination of a diverse economy and a long tradition of religious pluralism and popular politics forged in the eighteenth century.[13]

[12] Worcester *Palladium*, November 18, 1840; William Hancock to John W. Lincoln, July 31, 1844, Box 7, Folder 6, Whig Party Papers, 1844 Campaign, Massachusetts Collections, AAS; for Linus Child, see the Southbridge *Village Courier*, September 25, 1832, and Formisano, *The Transformation*, 286; on this subject in general, see Formisano, 283–8; and Prude, *The Coming of Industrial Order*, 218–19.
[13] A fragmentary poll list of roughly one hundred Sutton Whigs and Democrats in 1839 has survived. Comparing this list with the 1838, 1840, and 1849 tax valuations, Ronald Formisano found Democrats to be only slightly poorer than Whigs. (*Transformation*, 293, 296, 469.) More strikingly, however, only 4% of the Democrats (3/67) were the sons of men signing petitions in the First Party era, as against 37% of the Whigs (13/35). This lack of continuity is particularly

If the electoral base of the Democratic Party in Worcester County was generally restricted to the old Popular region, and never moved beyond the aggregate level of Jeffersonian voting, the reason may lie with the county leadership. Though always a minority party in Massachusetts, the Democrats were able to dominate the politics in some regions of the state and to achieve a record of dynamic opposition, particularly after the party began to absorb more discontented groups after 1835. Their lack of appeal across the county rested in great part in the failure of the county leadership to swing behind the more progressive elements in the party.

Ironically, the Democratic Party in Massachusetts was divided into two factions led by sons of Worcester County. The radical wing was led by George Bancroft, the son of Worcester Unitarian Aaron Bancroft, drawn into Democratic Party politics by the same romantic nationalism that led him to write the first major history of the country. Although he had refused to run when nominated a candidate to the state senate by the Hampshire County Workingmen in 1830, Bancroft had strong ties with the Workingmen, and in 1834 and 1835 drew the bulk of them with him into the Democratic Party. Despite his gentry origins, Bancroft introduced a dramatic – if short-lived – burst of economic analysis to the party platform, writing in a 1835 address to the voters "that pure democracy inculcates equal rights – equal laws – equal means to education – and *equal means of wealth* also, as incidental to the other blessings."[14]

Arrayed against Bancroft was David Henshaw and the *Statesman* faction. From a leading Popular family in Leicester with strong connections among the Boston revolutionary leadership, Henshaw was the son of a justice of the peace in Leicester who had served with the government forces in 1786 and who had run on a Republican ticket in 1801. He had gone to Boston and by 1826 had made his fortune in the druggist's trade, insurance, and banking, but his family's name gave him no entry into polite society. Gravitating to politics, Henshaw had maneuvered among the splintering Republican factions of the late 1820s, supporting first Crawford and then Jackson. In 1829 he was rewarded with the collectorship of the port of Boston, and with the patronage connected with the post he began to build a powerful political machine. Involved in banking, railroad development, and a

striking given the Republican orientation of the 1812 petitions supporting the Worcester Bank Petition. Most of the Whig links (10/13) were with Federalist petitioners, rather than the Worcester Bank petitions. Similarly, 35% of the Sutton Antimasonic petitioners were sons of men active in the First Party era (21/60), again mostly Federalists (15/21). See 1839 Poll List, Box 3, Folder 1, Sutton, Mass., Papers, AAS; Sutton (Federalist) Remonstrances, 1810, 1812, Contested Elections, MA; Sutton Petitions for the Worcester Bank, Senate Docs., Unpassed Leg., 4447/9 and 12; Sutton Antimasonic Petition, 1834, House Unpassed, 13904B. On Sibley and Waters, see Bendict and Tracy, *Sutton*, 724, 743, 810–11.
[14] Formisano, *The Transformation*, 255–7; quotation from Worcester *Republican*, September 30, 1835, emphasis in original, quoted in Formisano, 257; see also Russel B. Nye, *George Bancroft: Brahmin Rebel* (New York, 1944), 90ff.

range of business enterprises, the men of the Henshaw faction were classic examples of Jacksonians who aspired to the same "aristocracy" of wealth that their party condemned.[15]

The Worcester County Democratic leadership had strong connections with the opportunistic Henshaw faction. Jonas L. Sibley, an attorney and leading Democrat in Sutton, was appointed marshall of the port of Boston by Jackson, presumably at David Henshaw's recommendation. Henshaw and Sibley were both Masons, as was Alexander DeWitt of Oxford and at least six of the Democratic leaders in Worcester. And although the radical faction decried banks and corporations, Worcester County Democrats were deeply involved in banking. Sibley was involved in banks in Sutton, Millbury, and Oxford, and DeWitt's brother Sterns DeWitt was an Oxford Bank director in the early 1830s. the Democratic Waters family controlled the Millbury Bank, three Democrats – including Bela Tiffany – were directors of the Southbridge Bank in 1836, and at least ten Democratic activists in Worcester were involved in the Central, Citizen's, and Quinsigamond Banks.[16]

The involvement of the county leadership with banking was so notorious that Robert Rantoul, Jr., an ardent foe of circulating bank currency, moderated his comments on banking in his July Fourth address to the county "Democratic Citizens" in 1837, after making inquiries with Isaac Davis, the leading Democrat in Worcester. Later that day, when the county Democrats convened for dinner at the Worcester House, Rantoul was noticed as "a rising star," but another leading Democrat was the center of attention. A series of toasts were raised to David Henshaw: "an able man of business and a powerful writer" whose "superior talents and sound political integrity . . . placed him in the front rank of our most distinguished Democrats"; "a democrat of the old school . . . well entitled to the support of the present administration and its party notwithstanding the opposition of the Locofocos." Henshaw was at that moment being challenged by Bancroft for control of the Boston port collectorship that he had tried to hand over to a trusted confederate; by "Locofoco," the toast had referred to the radical Bancroft wing of the party. Another toast was more directed. Larkin Ammidown of Southbridge condemned the "Loco Focos of Massachusetts" as the "demagogues and disorganizers of the Democratic Party, worshippers of the golden calf" of patronage. Six months later, when George Bancroft was appointed to the

[15] Washburn *Leicester*, 205–6, 378; Formisano, *Transformation*, 247–8; Darling, *Political Changes*, 43, 48–52, 54, 56, 71–2, 83.
[16] On Sibley's appointment, see Benedict and Tracy, *Sutton*, 263; on Masons, see *Yeoman*, July 16, 1831; Nason, *Morning Star Lodge*, 197–209; *Olive Branch Lodge*, 81; Daniels, *Oxford*, 256; Darling *Political Changes*, 90–5; for banks, see Chapter 9, note 70. The sources for Democratic activists in the town of Worcester include lists in *Republican*, August 28, 1833; September 2, 1835; September 19, 1838; September 2, 1840. Also Worcester *Palladium* and Worcester County *Republican*, October 2, 1839.

collectorship, letters of congratulations flooded into his office from across the state, but none came from any Democrat in the town or the county where he had been born. The lines were sharply drawn between "conservative" and "radical" in the Massachusetts Democratic Party, and the former were firmly in control in Worcester County.[17]

Although its rhetoric sounded the alarm of "aristocracy" and "equal rights," the lines dividing the Democratic Party from the Nationals and then the Whigs in Worcester County were not fundamentally those of class and economy, but of culture and tradition. The core constituencies of each party were predominantly rural people in the southern and the northern sections of the county, respectively, living in communities profoundly shaped by the eighteenth-century mosaic of political culture and religious institutions. If the Democratic leadership in Worcester did not cut quite the same figure as the National and Whig elite, it was not for lack of trying. Jacksonian rhetoric did little to restrain the appetites of this group of rising men.[18]

"Rise up ye Anti-masons"

When Robert Rantoul addressed the Worcester Democrats in 1837, he attacked the Workingmen as "anarchists" and "destructives" in the same breath that he condemned the Whigs as "aristocrats" and "consolidationists." Rantoul could have saved his rhetoric; although the Workingman's movement had attempted to organize in Worcester County in 1831, it never gained more than a meager foothold. A short-lived *Plebian and Millbury Workingmen's Advocate* began publication in the spring of 1831 on a decidedly defensive note. Announcing its advocacy of "that numerous and respectable class of the community" known as "workingmen," the paper disavowed any alliance to "the licentious doctrines of Fanny Wright and Robert Owen." Several weeks later the paper disassociated itself from a more local radicalism, declaring that the Workingmen were not "a species of Jack Cade's faction – a counterpart to the famous Shay[s] insurrection, got up by some ambitious demogogues as a hobby to ride into office."[19]

[17] Robert D. Bulkley, Jr., "Robert Rantoul, Jr., 1805–1852: Politics and Reform in Antebellum Massachusetts," Ph.D. dissertation, Princeton University, 1971, 201, quoted in Formisano, *Transformation*, 319; toasts from MSS., Worcester Democratic Celebration, July 4, 1837, Worcester Historical Museum; Bancroft Papers, MHS; On the significance of the letters to Bancroft, see Formisano, 261, 456 n. 62.

[18] For a different view on the economic politics of the Democratic Party, see John Ashworth, *"Agrarians" and "Aristocrats": Party Political Ideology in the United States, 1837–1846* (New York, 1987).

[19] Robert Rantoul, Jr., *An Oration Delivered before the Democratic Citizens of the County of Worcester, July 4, 1837* (Worcester, 1837), 13; Bulkely, "Robert Rantoul, Jr.," 201; *Plebian and Millbury Workingmen's Advocate*, January 12, Feburary 2, 1831.

That April there was a Workingmen's meeting at the Old Common in Millbury, where attention was directed to the "subjects of great abuse which must be corrected before equal laws will give equal rights to all classes." The Workingmen never took root in Millbury, but in 1833 and 1834 Samuel Allen, the party's candidate for governor drew small blocks of between twenty and sixty-five votes in a scattering of south county towns, including Mendon, Milford, Dudley, Uxbridge, and Webster – where Allen won a narrow plurality in 1834 – and in Hardwick on the Hampshire County line. In aggregate, however, the Workingmen only received 2 percent of the county's vote, less than half of the party's 5 percent across the state as a whole. Democratic radicalism was not welcome in Worcester County. The weakness of the Workingmen left the field open to another insurgent force.[20]

In September 1829, in the same letter in which he described the scene of lightning-struck barns burning across the county, the Reverend Joseph Goffe, the orthodox minister at the Old Common in Millbury, informed his son of the rising political storm regarding the institution of Freemasonry.

> Light upon this ancient & noble subject is increasing daily ... The excitement awakened by the murder of Capt. Morgan is rapidly increasing, even in Massachusetts & the other N. E. States. Public meetings on the subject are mul[t]iplying, & you must not think it strange if you should soon hear that the whole of the grand lodges in these parts are hung for the murders they have masonically committed.

Over the three years since William Morgan had mysteriously disappeared far to the west in Canandaigua, New York, rumors had been spreading into New England. Masonic power in the courts of Genessee and Ontario counties was protecting Morgan's suspected murderers from the consequences of their deed. Oaths sworn in secret ceremonies were elevating a particular set of men above public scrutiny; membership in an exclusive order was establishing a privileged aristocracy unaccountable to the laws of the republic.[21]

In 1829 the New York Antimasons were nearing their goal of destroying the Masonic institution, but the movement was just emerging in Massachusetts. The Antimasonic initiatives in Worcester County were inspired by a committee of inquiry formed that August in Boston, a committee established at the urging of Amasa Walker, a native son of North Brookfield who had recently established

---

[20] *Plebian and Millbury Workingmen's Advocate*, April, 20, 1831.
[21] Joseph Goffe to Joseph Goffe [Jr.], September 8, 1829, Rev. Joseph Goffe Papers, AAS. For the best account of the formative stages of the movement, see Ronald P. Formisano and Kathleen S. Kutolowski, "Antimasonry and Masonry: The Genesis of Protest, 1826–1827," *AQ* 29 (1977), 139–65. For rumors (and counter-rumors), see the Southbridge *Moralist and General Intelligencer*, June 26, July 3, August 7, Sept. 11, and Nov. 13, 1828. I am indebted to Ronald Formisano for sharing biographical information on Joseph Goffe.

himself as a wholesale shoe dealer in Boston. Beginning in November, editorials and letters mildly critical of Freemasonry began to appear in the Massachusetts *Yeoman*, a Worcester paper generally supportive of the ruling National faction. This commentary was part of an effort to set the stage for a county convention of Antimasons that met in Worcester in early December, featuring an address by Pliny Merrick, a Worcester lawyer and Royal Arch Mason whose secession from the order had a galvanizing influence on the development of Antimasonry throughout the region.[22]

After three years of rumors and "intelligences," these local initiatives all brought to the surface a brewing unease among a significant cross section of the population. Masonry was invoked increasingly as the agency behind disturbing changes in society. With Pliny Merrick, the Reverend Joseph Goffe led the county delegates to the Antimasonic convention that met that December; the following May he wrote to his son that the Presbyterians in a neighboring village, a society with "domineering purposes," had hired for a minister "a mason, or cable-towed man of high & obstinate standing." In the same month English immigrant and woolworker Joseph Hollingworth complained to his uncle that his family's recent loss of employment was rooted in "the effects produced by Masonic power and Yankeeism." He wrote that "when we quit I left the following lines within a few rods of the Tavern, in South Leicester."

1st   Come all ye Anti-masons, where ever you do dwell,
        Come, unite all your efforts to break the Mason's spell,
        Destroy all their Lodges, their "mystic knot" untie,
        Then sink them in oblivion, and there let them lie.

2nd   Rise up ye Anti-masons, and all united be,
        Against this Hell-born Monster, I mean Freemasonry;
        O spurn all its precepts – its principles despise,
        For 'tis all imposition, Hypocrisy, and Lies.

3rd   Hark 'tis the blood of Morgan, that calls you to the field,
        To fight the Monster boldly, untill you make yield;
        And when you have subdu'd him, which certainly must be,
        O then erect the Standard of Truth and Liberty.[23]

---

[22] Formisano, *The Transformation*, 202; Temple, *North Brookfield*, 385–6; Massachusetts *Yeoman*, November 7, 14, December 5, 12, 19, 26, 1829, and January 2, 16, 23, 30, 1830; Folders 1 and 2, Pliny Merrick Correspondence, AAS; Pliny Merrick, *A Letter on Speculative Freemasonry* (Worcester, 1829).

[23] Delegates are listed in *An Abstract of the Proceedings of the Anti-Masonic State Convention of Massachusetts, Held in Faneuil Hall, Boston, Dec. 30 and 31, 1829, and Jan. 1, 1830* (Boston, 1830), 26–7. Joseph Goffe to Joseph and Eliza Goffe, September 8, 1829, Goffe to Joseph Goffe [Jr.], May 17, 1830, Rev. Joseph Goffe Papers, AAS; Joseph Hollingworth to William Rawcliff, May 23, 1830, in Leavitt, ed., *The Hollingworth Letters*, 74–6.

Who were the Antimasons in Worcester County? What drew such disparate individuals as an orthodox minister of an old New England family and a poor English woolworker (of Chartist sentiments) into the same movement against the Masonic establishment? As across Massachusetts, Antimasonry in Worcester County was an insurrection within the ranks of the National Republicans against an entrenched establishment that would not listen to demands for the proscription of Masonry. Pride in native son John Quincy Adams, and a greater dislike for Andrew Jackson, may explain the delay in the emergence of Antimasonry in Massachusetts; certainly the destruction of the Second Bank brought many – but not all – Massachusetts Antimasons into the fold of the Whig Party. But for a brief period the Antimasonic movement opened a window onto the stress points within Massachusetts society and within the National–Whig coalition. The Antimasonic insurgency was rooted both in the rapidly changing economic structure of an industrializing society and the ancient Harringtonian ethic of independence in a moral commonwealth. It was fundamentally a movement of proprietors and aspiring proprietors whose assumptions were shaped by the household basis of the early national economy. These men saw Masonry as merely the prime example of the new institutions that were just beginning to undermine their understanding of equal opportunity and personal independence in a republican society.[24]

Antimasonic circumstances and constituencies

Scattered hints suggest that the Popular tradition had some echoes in the Antimasonic insurgency, conditioned by a passage through progovernment sentiment in 1786 and popular Federalism in the first decades of the nineteenth century. Austin Flint, once a Federalist and a leading Antimason in Leicester and a state senate candidate, had marched as a young man in the government's surprise assault on the Regulators encamped at Petersham in February 1787; his father had

[24] The literature on Antimasonry is primarily focused on New York state. See Whitney R. Cross, *The Burned Over District: The Social and Intellectual History of Enthusiastic Religion in Western New York, 1800–1850* (Ithaca, 1950); Lee Benson, *The Concept of Jacksonian Democracy: New York as a Test Case* (Princeton, 1960); Paul Johnson, *A Shopkeeper's Millennium: Society and Revivals in Rochester, New York, 1815–1837* (New York, 1978); Ronald P. Formisano, *The Birth of Mass Political Parties: Michigan, 1828–1861* (Princeton, 1971), 60–80; Anthony F. C. Wallace, *Rockdale: The Growth of an American Village in the Industrial Revolution* (New York, 1978); Kathleen S. Kutolowski, "Antimasonry Reexamined: Social Bases of the Grass-Roots Party," *JAH* 71 (1984), 269–93; and Kutolowski, "Freemasonry and Community in the Early Republic: The Case for Antimasonic Anxieties," *AQ* 34 (1982), 543–61. Formisano's *Transformation of Political Culture* presents an excellent reassessment of Massachusetts politics for this period, to which I owe a considerable debt. I am obliged to Ronald Formisano, Kathleen Kutolowski, and Paul Goodman for useful comments on this chapter.

represented Shrewsbury in the Concord Price Convention of 1779. Similarly, Tyler Batchellor, a leading Antimason in North Brookfield, had relations who had served in the 1779 Concord price-fixing convention and who mortgaged their land to the Land Bank. And Amasa Walker of North Brookfield and Boston came from an orthodox family deeply divided by the Popular politics of the 1780s. Walker's lifelong fascination with the nature of money may have had its roots in his grandfather's experience. Phinehas Walker of Woodstock had lost $1,000 in silver in a government loan during the Revolution, and his relations in Sturbridge had taken widely varying stands during the 1780s. Amasa's great uncle Josiah Walker had led a group of rioters in 1781, and in 1787 admitted to providing provisions to the Regulators and proudly called himself a "convention man." From 1789 through 1798 Josiah Walker served as representative from a staunchly Federalist Sturbridge. Josiah's brother Asa was a Regulator, and his sons were Federalists and Antimasons. Another brother, Nathaniel, served in the government militia company raised by his sister Lucy's father-in-law, Colonel Benjamin Freeman. Such a stew of familial politics might well have laid the ground for Amasa Walker's complex and unique political career, which carried him from orthodox Federalist roots to Antimasonry, to hard-money Jacksonianism, to an interest in the peace movement, and from there to Free Soil and the Republican coalition. Walker was equally eclectic as an intellectual, invoking Harringtonian themes of independence and commonwealth at the same time that he was the nation's leading theorist of laissez-faire. It might not be unreasonable to suggest that Antimasonry had certain affinities with the bubbling of economic controversy that had long characterized the New Light Congregational wing of the old Worcester County Popular coalition, deeply concerned about economic policy but opposed to the Regulation, and then passing into the ranks of popular Federalism.[25]

More immediately and more certainly, Antimasonic voters had been National Republicans in the years before 1831, and Federalists before 1825. In the spring elections of 1831, when the emerging Antimasonic coalition ran candidates for the state senate but not for the governor's seat, the National vote for governor was split

---

[25] Davis, *Currency and Banking*, 2:296, 300: *Proceedings of the Convention Begun and Held at Concord ... 1779* [Evans 16228-9]; Washburn, *Leicester*, 191–2; J. Lawrence Bass, *The Flint Genealogy* (Philadelphia, 1910), 8–9; Frederick C. Pierce, *Batchelder, Batcheller Genealogy* (Chicago, 1898), 359–60; Benedict and Tracy, *Sutton*, 588–9; Temple, *North Brookfield*, 381–90; SJC File #153657; Sturbridge and Charlton Testimony, Box on Shays's Rebellion, RTPP, MHS; MA 119/220–1; Amasa Walker, *The Nature and Uses of Money and Currency, with a History of the Wickaboag Bank* (Boston, 1857); Amasa Walker, *The Science of Wealth; and Manual of Political Economy* (Boston, 1866); Sibney Fine, *Laissez-Faire and the General-Welfare State* (Ann Arbor, 1956), 47; Bernard Newton, *The Economics of Francis Amasa Walker: American Economic Thought in Transition* (New York, 1923), 3–22; Francis A. Walker, "The Hon. Amasa Walker, LL. D.," *New England Historic and Genealogical Register* 42 (1888), 133–41.

between National and Antimasonic senate candidates in towns throughout the county, while Democratic vote totals for governor and senators were virtually the same.[26] Within the National Republican coalition of Republicans and Federalists, Antimasons had clearly been Federalists. Antimasons had signed Federalist election remonstrances in Sutton and Southbridge, and in Worcester at least six had been members of the Washington Benevolent Society. Antimasonic leaders were particularly likely to have responded to the call of popular Federalism. Three of the six Antimasonic State Senate candidates in 1832, including Austin Flint of Leicester, had been members of the Washington Benevolent Society, as had been at least nine Antimasonic representatives and convention delegates from Leicester, Millbury, and Brookfield. There were, of course, some exceptions to the rule of Federalist origins. Tyler Batchellor of North Brookfield, the son of a Republican activist, was a leading Antimason, but Batchellor had made his peace with the Federalist majority in the revival of 1817. The most notable exception was Pliny Merrick, the son of a Republican county committeeman, and the most artful of opportunistic political chameleons. In 1817 Merrick had delivered the address that proposed an end to the classical politics of cycles and corruption, but thirteen years later he was not averse to leading a political movement that saw the demise of the republic in Masonic corruption. After abandoning the Masons for Antimasonry, Merrick would join the Whigs in 1834 and then the Democrats in 1839. Although he was the leading Antimason in the county, Merrick's political career was literally the opposite of the majority of his followers.[27]

Federalism was clearly an important aspect in the formative experience of Worcester County Antimasons, but there were significant modulations in this

[26] *Yeoman*, April 16, 1831; Returns of Votes for Governor, MA.

[27] For the 1832 senate nominations, see Massachusetts *Yeoman*, November 10, 1832; on Merrick, see Pliny Merrick Correspondence, AAS, and *Palladium* August 13, 1834, November 6, 1839. Merrick was the only connection with Republicanism among the Worcester Antimasons, while non-Antimasonic Second Bank petitioners, temperance men, and National activists with experience in the First Party system were equally divided between members of the WBS (15) and subscribers to the Republican *Aegis* (13). In Sutton and Millbury (North Parish of Sutton to 1814), 124 men signed remonstrances against Republican representatives in 1810 and 1812. A petition for the rechartering of the Worcester Bank sent from Sutton in 1812 had 88 signatures. Sutton was a strongly Republican town after 1800 and the large numbers of selectmen signing the Bank petition suggest that it was a Republican initiative. Twenty-two signers of the Federalist Remonstrances (18%) and eight signers of the Bank petition (9%) were later Antimasons. In Southbridge, ten Antimasons had signed an 1817 Federalist remonstrance, while only five signed the 1835 temperance petition. Sutton and Southbridge Remonstrances in "Records of Contested Elections," "MA; Sutton Petitions for Worcester Bank, 1812, Senate Unpassed 4447/9 and 12, MA. See also Octavo Vol. 2, "Worcester County, Mass., Washington Benevolent Society Records," AAS; *Proceedings of a Convention of Delegates from Forty One Towns in the County of Worcester* (Worcester, 1812); and "Worcester *National Aegis*, Papers, AAS.

Federalist background. (See Figures 6a and 6b.) The thirteen towns casting Antimasonic pluralities between 1831 and 1834 had not been overwhelmingly Federalist, nor did they even approximate the institutional unity and stability that had structured both the Regulator insurgency of the 1780s and the popular Federalism of the First Party era. Rather, Antimasonry took root in communities wracked by partisan conflict beginning in the 1780s. Including four towns incorporated after 1790, seven of the thirteen Antimasonic towns had been divided between Regulator and government leaders during Shays's Rebellion, and they were notably divided during the First Party era. Nine of the thirteen Antimasonic towns (or their parent towns) had been contested in 1812, casting less than two-thirds majorities for either the Federalists or the Republicans, and six had been among the towns with the highest turnout in 1812; in 1824 these towns typically cast contested Federalist majorities. In contrast, the National towns of the early 1830s most often had voted better than 2 to 1 for the Federalists in both 1812 and 1824. Close results in these elections often led to bitter disputes and formal petitions to the General Court: The contested elections in Oxford (the Federalist South Gore was included in Webster in 1832), Sutton (the North Parish became Millbury in 1814), North Brookfield, and Southbridge (set off from Sturbridge in 1816) all had Antimasonic echoes in the early 1830s.[28]

Thus Antimasonry blossomed in those Federalist towns that had had the most competitive politics throughout the years of the First Party system. Such a competitive political environment worked in the Antimasons' favor, allowing them to win in these towns over National and Democratic candidates with a plurality of votes, while in noncompetitive towns Antimasons remained a dissident minority. This recent electoral history was of critical importance, because voter turnout rose only modestly during the years of the Antimasonic insurgency. Across the state, turnout did not rise above 45 percent – in the county the peak was 53 percent – and even in strongly Antimasonic towns it never rose much higher. This level of voter turnout was a decided improvement over the doldrums of 1825 to 1828,

---

[28] Towns identified as voting Democratic (16) or Antimasonic (13) between 1831 and 1834 were those towns that cast at least one Democratic or Antimasonic majority or plurality in gubernatorial elections during these years. In the one case (Petersham) where a town cast both Antimasonic and Democratic votes in different elections, the town is assigned to the Antimasonic group. Millbury, Leicester, and Brookfield, analyzed in detail below, were among seven towns that cast two or more majorities or pluralities for the Antimasons in these years. A more inclusive group of thirty-four towns where there was evidence of Antimasonic sentiment (see Figures 6b and 7) includes the thirteen towns with pluralities or majorities, as well as twenty-one towns that cast second-place minorities votes for the Antimasons, which were at least half the majority vote, or towns where groups signed petitions against Freemasonry. Votes are all from the "Returns of Votes for Governor, MA; for the citations for the Antimasonic petitions, see note 35 below.

when under the one-party rule of the Nationals turnout sank to roughly 25 percent, the level that had pertained during the late 1790s. But turnout in the early 1830s only matched that of the postwar era between 1816 and 1822; it never approached the mass political participation evident in both 1812 and 1840, when at least 75 percent of the adult male population turned out to vote. Antimasonry thus seems to have mobilized older, established voters, many of whom may well have dropped out in the late 1820s, rather than a new group of voters.

Behind a competitive political culture lay an institutional pluralism. Antimasonic towns had a significantly greater religious diversity than towns that remained in the National Republican ranks. As of 1825 less than 10 percent of the future Antimasonic towns in Worcester County (1/12) still had only a Congregational church, as against at least a quarter of the future National towns (7/26). This religious pluralism was even more evident in 1808, when future Antimasonic towns were twice as likely as future National towns to have had dissenting societies (61 vs. 34 percent), although less likely than Democratic towns (84 percent). By the mid-1830s the spread of newer denominations practically had overwhelmed the last remnants of orthodox hegemony, but in both decades Antimasonic towns were more likely to have Baptist churches, and Democratic towns Universalist or Methodist churches, while National towns led with Unitarian and evangelical Congregational separations.

For the Antimason the most significant element of institutional pluralism was secular: the fraternal order of Freemasonry. There were roughly two thousand Masons in Worcester County in 1829, and the institutional structure of Freemasonry had been growing rapidly; one-third of the county's nineteen lodges, all five Royal Arch Chapters, and a Masonic Encampment had been chartered since 1820. Masonic institutions were another element contributing to the competitive pluralism in the Antimasonic towns: Masonic Lodges were located in five of the thirteen leading Antimasonic towns and in the parent towns of four others. Here there may have been an indirect relationship with the Regulation. During the 1790s Masonic Lodges were disproportionately established in the recently conflicted towns, typically by the leading Friends of government, setting the stage for the Antimasonic reaction a generation later. But the significance of local Masonry should not be overestimated; Masonry was far more strongly entrenched in the south county towns where Antimasonry never challenged the Democrats, and by 1830 eleven of the county's nineteen lodges were delinquent in their returns to the Grand Lodge. The intransigence of local Masons could not have been of paramount importance when the movement went political in the spring of 1831. In addition to Freemasonry, Antimasons stood outside of and at odds with another important secular association in Worcester County. Although the Democratic papers could condemn the Worcester Agricultural Society as a " body aristocratic," Democratic activists from Worcester and five surrounding towns sat as members beside National and Whig party men as well as Masons; Antimasons were poorly represented. (See Appendix 3, Table 1a.) Local Masonic lodges were only one component of a wider complex of circumstances that drew voters into the Antimasonic insurgency in the early 1830s.[29]

"Wealth is power"

If Antimasonry was rooted in a cultural hostility toward the deistic and perhaps occult rituals of an oath-bound Masonry, the movement soon became a political party, and in the process it took on political themes. If the Democratic Party in Worcester County was essentially a cultural party speaking in economic language, Antimasonry was essentially an economic party speaking in cultural language. Starting with a concern about the threat to equal rights posed by a secret fraternity, Antimasonic rhetoric moved toward a wider critique of the new institutional order in Massachusetts. The avenue for this development revolved around the problem of voluntary association.

Antimasons were not opposed to voluntary association itself, but to un-controllable, unaccountable associations of men operating with the legal sanction of the government. The state charter, the secrecy of the order, and the sworn oaths of fraternal allegiance and aid were the focus of Antimasonic attacks on Masonry as an institution that flaunted the laws of the republic. The 1829 convention concluded that the "Masonic fraternity have erected for themselves a distinct and independent government, within the jurisdiction of the United States."[30] Antimasonry's initial focus on the relationship between Masonry and the state rapidly spilled over into other channels, channels that remind us that Antimasonry was as much a revolt against the National establishment as it was an attack on Masonry. Their examination of the lodges brought to light the funds being raised to build a new Grand Lodge building in Boston. This inspired the Antimasonic convention of 1829 to issue a sweeping statement with implications that transcended their concern with Masonry: "Wealth is power. It is of vast importance therefore that funds in the hands of corporate bodies be limited and restricted by civil law. Otherwise, they may, at the control of ambitious and unprincipled men, prove a most powerful engine against the state, or be devoted to purposes subversive of the public good.[31] Here, then, was a direct opening onto the political language of monopoly and equal rights. It was the Antimasonic

[29] Merrick *Letter*, 8; *Proceedings of the Grand Royal Arch Chapter of Massachusetts, from Its Organization, 1798–1860* (Worcester, 1876); *Proceedings of the Most Worshipful Grand Lodge of Ancient, Free and Accepted Masons of the Commonwealth of Massachusetts for the Years 1815–1825 Inclusive, ... for the Years 1826–1844 Inclusive* (Boston, 1928). On the failure to make lodge returns in 1830, see *Proceedings of the ... Grand Lodge, ... 1826–1844*, 57, 115, 146, 170, 206, 207. On Masonic lodges in the towns conflicted in 1786–7, see Chapter 8.
[30] *Proceedings of the Anti-Masonic State Convention* (Boston, 1830), 10; *Anti-Masonic Republican Convention ...* (Boston, 1832), 29–40.
[31] *Anti-Masonic State Convention* (Boston, 1830), 14.

leadership in Suffolk County that pursued this opening, and forged a real link between Jacksonian ideology and Massachusetts Antimasonry.

Amasa Walker, once of North Brookfield and now one of the leading Suffolk County Antimasons, began developing these themes in his 1830 address at Stoughton, when he warned that the "immense power" of voluntary associations in general made them "just subjects of jealousy and suspicion." Having established this thesis, Walker moved to the subject of Freemasonry, but placed it "among the various associations of the age." Masonry "tower[ed] above all others," he argued, its "potent influence . . . felt from the center to the remotest extremities of the republic." Whereas in 1830 Walker focused his attacks on Masonry as a voluntary association, he and other Antimasons soon introduced the Jacksonian language of class, privilege, and equal rights. The *Yeoman* appealed to "honest yeomen, the bone and muscle of the nation"; the 1831 senate candidates were for "pure republicanism" and "equal rights," and were "opposed to aristocracy and usurpation of every kind."[32] Walker's associate, Benjamin F. Halett, repeated this language at the 1834 convention. Again, the Antimasonic candidates came "not from the exclusive circle of aristocracy, but from the people." They were "substantial, intelligent yeomanry, mechanics, and workingmen." Halett's concluding exhortation was suffused with the classical republican language of virtue and corruption. "'A bold yeomanry's a nation's pride,' who are not so encumbered and tied down by wealth and luxury and love of ease, and social influence, and party discipline, that they dare not express their free opinions against Freemasonry, for fear of losing office and official friends." Both Halett and Walker were involved in the efforts of the Suffolk County Antimasons to move the party into an economic politics. The platform of the Suffolk County Committee for 1834, which nominated Amasa Walker as a candidate for Congress, urged the voters to elect "yeomen" and not "aristocrats" to the house. The Antimasonic platform declared that "the extent to which monopolies have been carried in our Legislature by unnecessary acts of incorporation and other exclusive measures, and the manifest preference of the interests of capital over labor, are alarming to the rights of the people, and ought to be checked." And with language rooted in the Harringtonian tradition, the Suffolk Antimasons reminded the voters that "the object of legislation ought not to be to make the *few* rich, but to make the *many* happy and independent."[33]

Amasa Walker had extensive contacts and influence in his native Worcester County, and the constituency drawn to Antimasonry would have responded readily to an attack on monopoly and a celebration of independence. If Whigs and Democrats were fundamentally divided by culture and tradition, Antimasons were set apart by economic situation. Antimasonic candidates never received more than

[32] Walker, *An Oration Delivered at Stoughton*, 5–7.
[33] *Antimasonic Republican Convention* . . . (Boston, 1834), 11; Antimasonic Republican Resolves, Nov. 3, 1834, Extra to the Boston *Daily Advocate*, Broadsides, MHS. (Emphasis in original.) See more broadly, Benson, *The Concept of Jacksonian Democracy*, 37.

20 percent of the county's vote, but the concentrations of Antimasonic support underscores the importance of economic context and ideology. Antimasonic candidates did poorly in the south county towns and the wider textile region: neither the Jeffersonian tradition nor the growing factory system provided an opening for this third-party insurgency. Similarly, Antimasonry fared poorly in the mainly agricultural north county towns, with the exception of several along the county's western border, where the influence of a strong Antimasonic movement in Hampshire and Franklin counties was evident. But the heart of Worcester County Antimasonry lay in the central corridor. Over half of the towns casting Antimasonic majorities lay in the central corridor towns around Worcester and along the Post Road, and all but one of the corridor towns registered at least a minimal manifestation of Antimasonic support, whether by electoral pluralities, strong minorities, or petitions. (See Figure 6b.) The central corridor towns of Millbury, Auburn, Leicester, Brookfield, and North Brookfield stand out as centers of Antimasonic sentiment, with majorities and pluralities in elections between 1831 and 1834 ranging from 45 to 55 percent of the vote. Similarly, Antimasonic sentiment can be detected in all fourteen of the small-shop towns of 1820 as well as in ten of the twelve towns that had high levels of employment in the boot and shoe industry in the 1830s. Antimasonry's popularity in the shop towns again suggests a distant continuity between the antebellum insurgencies and the orthodox wing of the provincial Popular tradition.

A region of middling persistence and relatively low per capita wealth, hopes for personal independence in the central corridor lay in a complex economy where there were as yet few dominating corporations. Here, in a region with good roads but relatively little waterpower, the Federalist synthesis of commerce, agriculture, and shop production laid the groundwork for the webs of outwork structuring shoemaking. In this economic hothouse the preconditions for a volatile political culture had been brewing for decades. In 1805 and 1812, though not in 1824 – when religious issues dominated the political arena – the towns of the central corridor had the highest rate of voter turnout, and had increasingly close elections. In 1826 its political volatility was registered in relatively weak majorities and losses for Lincoln's National coalition, as votes were given to a scattering of former Federalists, while Lincoln did well in both north and south county. Against this background of political competition and instability, Antimasonry would be followed by an even stronger adherence to political insurgency in the decades to come.

"The continued hard pressure of the times"

Economic instability was a formative precondition to the emergence of Antimasonry in the central corridor towns. In his September 1829 letter in which he first noted the growth of Antimasonic "excitement" in the region, Joseph Goffe indicated that economic affairs in Millbury were very unsettled. "The numerous failures in the town last spring seem to have set everything afloat & confidence in the solvency of each other is much diminished among the people & such is the continued hard pressure of the times that it is feared there will be more failures among us yet." The following May he reported that two storekeepers in the Old Common neighborhood, "Dr. Benedict and Dana Braman[,] were both put in Worcester jail for debt sometime in March, where they both served an apprenticeship of 30 days." Four years later he wrote that General Caleb Burbank, a paper manufacturer on the Singletary stream, had "entirely failed"; Goffe further noted that "it is expected that he has not property enough in the world to pay his debts & meet his other responsibilities[;] his brother Elijah at Worcester has gone done with him, & the prospect now is that after living in prosperity and abounding in wealth they will both die poor men." Millbury would be a strong center of Antimasonry through 1835, and Braman, Benedict, Caleb Burbank, and Elijah Burbank's son Gardner all signed Antimasonic petitions between 1831 and 1834. Failure, or the threat of failure, was clearly an important factor in the lives of these men at roughly the time when they made a commitment to Antimasonry.[34]

Goffe's letters provide hints as to the economic context of Antimasonry in central Massachusetts; an analysis of the occupations and institutional links of Antimasons, Masons, and Nationals in six towns adds more weight to these hints. Worcester, Southbridge, Brookfield, North Brookfield, Leicester, and Millbury provide us with six examples of economically dynamic towns where the survival of petitions supporting Antimasonry, temperance, and the Second Bank of the United States, as well as minimal information on Democratic activists, allow such a comparative exploration.[35] Occupational data are notoriously incomplete for the

[34] Goffe to Joseph, Jr., and Eliza Goffe, September 8, 1829, February 8, 1834, AAS.

[35] The manuscripts of petitions for Antimasonry, disestablishment, and temperance are located in the Massachusetts Archives in the files of passed and unpassed legislation. See discussion in Appendix 3.

Petitions for Antimasonry, Disestablishment, and Temperance

Town	Year	Document	Signers
For Antimasonry[a]			
Leicester	1831	House unpassed 11397	19
Millbury	1831	House unpassed 11425	51
Brookfield	1833	House unpassed 12324	83
North Brookfield	1833	House unpassed 12324	91
Southbridge	1833	House unpassed 12324	48
Worcester	1833	House unpassed 12324	132
Brookfield	1834	House unpassed 13904A	101
Leicester	1834	House unpassed 13904A	60
Millbury	1834	House unpassed 13904A	125
Leicester	1835	House unpassed 13045	65
Millbury	1835	House unpassed 13016	56

1830s: directories and town histories for the most part identify only the proprietors of shops and small mills, and the owners and managers of larger enterprises; only occasionally records have survived that identify laborers. Similarly, lists of bank petitioners and officers, although they suggest patterns of interest and control, do not necessarily reveal the credit practices of individual banks. Given these limitations, however, a consistent pattern emerges, suggesting that the economic circumstances of individuals were quite significant in determining whether they would support Antimasonry or remain with the Nationals in the early 1830s. In

Petitions for Antimasonry, Disestablishment, and Temperance (cont.)

Town	Year	Document	Signers
For Disestablishment[b]			
Brookfield	1830	Senate unpassed 9038/9	58
North Brookfield	1832	House unpassed 11805	70
Brookfield (3 petitions)	1832	Original Papers, Chapter 56,	105
Southbridge	1832	Resolves, March, 18, 1833	61
For Temperance[c]			
Worcester	1835	House unpassed 12946	444
Leicester	1835	House unpassed 12947	120
Millbury	1835	House unpassed 12966	144
Southbridge	1835	House unpassed 12970	45
North Brookfield	1836	House unpassed 1	146

[a] House Documents, Unpassed Legislation: 1831: 11378–11425B, 1833: 12324 (bundle), 1834: 13904A and B (two bundles), 1835: 13010–13046.
[b] See note 8 above.
[c] For 1835–6 only.

Another important source for names of individuals associated with Antimasonry and temperance are the reports and records of various conventions meeting between 1829 and 1834. The reports of the Antimasonic conventions of 1829–30, 1831, 1832, 1833, and 1834 are variously titled (see notes 23, 30–4). Delegates to the 1833 temperance convention in Worcester are recorded in Folder 2, "Massachusetts Society for the Suppression of Intemperance, Papers, 1833," AAS. For the town of Worcester, other sources for temperance men include the members of the Worcester Young Men's Temperance Association, listed in *Republican*, October 9, 1833; and the opponents of liquor licensing, listed in *Spy*, April 8, 1835. Both lists are reproduced in Ian R. Tyrell, *Sobering Up: From Temperance to Prohibition in Antebellum America: 1800–1860* (Westport, Conn., 1979), 326–7.

The petition for the Second Bank of the United States is titled "Proceedings of Citizens of the County of Worcester, Massachusetts, In Relation to the currency." It includes a series of resolutions adopted at a meeting in Worcester on February 19, 1834, and bears a list of roughly 6,180 names of "memorialists." It is printed in United States Congress, *House Documents, 1833–1834*, 23d Cong., 1st sess. vol. 3, 176, pp. 1–43.

Unless otherwise indicated, a reference to "Antimasons" in the text refers to all Antimasonic delegates and petitioners, and "Nationals" or "Whigs" to those signers of the Second Bank petition who were not "Antimasons." See also the discussion in Appendix 2.

each of these six towns, men attracted to the Antimasonic insurrection, while participating vigorously in an expansive entrepreneurial economy, were at a significant occupational and institutional disadvantage to those who remained with the Nationals in the early 1830s. Antimasons were often men who were on the edge of economic failure in the early 1830s, and often had every right to complain that they were losing ground to privileged interests in a highly competitive economy.

The county seat of Worcester provides a useful entry point. In the 1820s and 1830s Worcester was in the process of evolving from a dusty commercial village into the industrial city it would become by the eve of the Civil War. By 1830, two banks, three newspapers, four churches, and a variety of voluntary associations competed for the attention of the town's citizens. The increasing diversity of the town was recorded in village directories published for the first time in 1828 and 1829. While lawyers, merchants, and tavernkeepers – the dominant elements of the old county town – continued to make up the three largest occupations, a variety of machinists and manufacturers were already well established, particularly in the emerging neighborhoods of South Worcester and New Worcester.[36]

Antimasonic candidates were never able to attract more than 20 percent of the vote in Worcester's proto-urban environment; the Antimasons were only a small group in a town where the Nationals and Democrats had well-organized cadres and the support of newspapers whose influence stretched well out into the countryside. However, if the Worcester Antimasons remained a minority, they were a very distinct one. Of the members of six major political and associational groups among the citizens of Worcester in the 1830s, Antimasons were those most likely to be machinists or to be involved in the leather and shoe industries (49 percent), and least likely to be lawyers and merchants (24 percent). Merchants and lawyers accounted for two-fifths to three-quarters of the known occupations of National and Democratic committeemen, members and trustees of voluntary associations including the Masons and the Worcester Agricultural Society, and the non-Antimasonic signers of the Second Bank petition, while less than a fifth of any of these groups were machinists and shoe and leather dealers. Only the non-Antimasonic temperance signers straddled the line, with equal proportions of lawyers and merchants (38 percent) and machinists and shoe or leather dealers (34 percent). Similarly, as occupational groups, shoe dealers and machinists were far

[36] The 1829 register provides a valuable source for occupations in Worcester, while the 1829 directory provides residences, but no occupations. Both are to be found in the collections of the Worcester Historical Museum. *Worcester Village Register, April, 1828* (Worcester, 1828), and *The Worcester Village Directory* ... (Worcester, 1929).

less often members of the town's elite voluntary associations than were merchants or lawyers.[37]

Thus, with the exception of the temperance men, public affairs in Worcester were characterized by a well-defined division. On one side stood Worcester's old legal and commercial establishment, the major party elites, and the community's voluntary associations. On the other stood the proprietors of small shops, often supplying materials to new industries in the surrounding towns, and the Antimasonic insurgency. Machinists and shoe and leather dealers were clearly set off from the rest of Worcester society. They very well may have been a source of complaints about the "aristocracy" of the town; they probably were readers of the *Yeoman.* Their location in the county seat and the structure of their industries

[37] *Worcester petitions, associations, and occupations*

	Machinists		Shoe leather		Merchants		Lawyers		Occupations known
Democrats	3	*15*	2	*10*	5	*25*	5	*25*	20
Antimasons	17	*36*	6	*13*	5	*11*	6	*13*	47
Others[a]									
Second Bank petitions	13	*14*	6	*6*	21	*23*	15	*16*	92
Temperance	15	*26*	5	*9*	12	*21*	10	*18*	58
Masons	3	*10*	0		8	*26*	7	*23*	31
Worcester Agricultural Society	5	*5*	5	*5*	27	*28*	12	*13*	95

Note: Figures in italics are percentages.
[a] "Others": All non-Antimasons in category; these are overlapping categories.

Worcester: Association membership among selected occupations

	Total of each occupational group	Member of Worcester Agricultural Society, Worcester Fire Society, or the Morning Star Lodge	
Lawyer	47	34	*72*
Merchant	69	39	*56*
Stage/tavern/hotel	25	13	*52*
Shoe/leather	20	7	*35*
Machinist	35	10	*28*

Note: Figures in italics are percentages.
Source: Petitions; Washburn, *Industrial Worcester; Worcester Village Register, April, 1828;* Charles B. Nutt, *History of Worcester and Its People* (New York, 1919), 1097–1104; McLane, *Report . . . Relative to the Manufactures,* 1:568–75; *HWC,* 2:657–66; *Reminiscences of the . . . Worcester Fire Society,* 62–8; Nason, *Morning Star Lodge,* 197–209; *Catelogue of the Officers and Members of the Worcester Agricultural Society* (Worcester, 1840), 25–7; for Democrats, see above, note 16.

suggest that they occupied strategic points in an Antimasonic network spreading through the surrounding towns. Although the evidence is fragmentary, it suggests that Antimasonic support moved along channels of communication within the shoe industry and the weaker elements of the woolen textile industry.

Leatherworkers of all kinds appear on the lists of Antimasons in a number of towns throughout the region, including shoemakers, tanners, and curriers in Leicester, Paxton, North Brookfield, Brookfield, Hardwick, Southbridge, Auburn, and Millbury, and these leatherworking proprietors often ranked among the Antimasonic leadership. The connections between Antimasonry and the shoe-making networks are particularly clear in North Brookfield and Brookfield, towns that cast Antimasonic majorities ranging from 45 to 70 percent of the vote and where shoeworkers accounted for 34 and 23 percent of the estimated adult male population in 1832, respectively (and over 100 percent in 1837!). Tyler Batcheller and Freeman Walker, repeatedly serving as Antimasonic delegate and senatorial candidate, were in a shoe partnership between 1830 and 1834. This partnership bought leather from the Antimasonic shop of Francis Merrick and Levi A. Dowley in Worcester, bought supplies from Antimason Allen Newell's store in West Brookfield, and sold shoes to Freeman's brother Amasa in Boston, all of which suggests the natural channels along which Antimasonic information might spread.[38]

In aggregate, North Brookfield shoemakers were more likely to sign the Antimasonic petition than farmers, who tended to avoid the Antimasonic petition and to support the Second Bank petition.[39] No occupational information has survived for the town of Brookfield other than the 1840 U.S. Census, which merely indicates the number of persons in a household engaged in agriculture, manufactures, and commerce. Among 251 Brookfield petitioners and association members identified as heads of households on the 1840 census (see Appendix 3,

[38] Delegate lists in *Abstracts* of Antimasonic conventions; occupations and figures from McLane, *Report ... Relative to the Manufactures* [1832] and Bigelow, *Industries in Massachusetts ... 1837*; Temple, *North Brookfield*, 268–76; and Hazard, *Boot and Shoe Industry*, 202–4.

[39] *North Brookfield: Occupation and the Antimasonic and Second Bank petitions*

	Shoemaking		Woolworking		Farming		Total known occupations	
Antimasons	18	*37*	6	*12*	4	*8*	48	*100*
Non-Antimasonic Second Bank Petitioners	8	*28*	0		8	*28*	28	*100*

Note: Figures in italics are percentages.
Source: Petitions and Temple, *North Brookfield*, 268–76, 485–799.

Tables 4d–f), the Antimasons who neglected to sign the petition in support of the Second Bank of the United States were particularly likely to have households that reported persons engaged in both agriculture and manufacturing. In a town where shoemaking was the only significant industry, this has to indicate that Antimasonry was especially attractive in households struggling to maintain an independent competency by adding shoemaking to an increasingly vulnerable farm economy.[40]

Men in the woolen industry also were drawn to the Antimasonic cause. Here a cyclical economy, technological obsolescence, and concerns about monopoly may have shaped the context of Antimasonic sentiments. After beginning to recover from the postwar depression, the woolen industry was bit by a second slump in 1826, when the depressed conditions of the British industry led to an overwhelming dumping of woolen exports on the American market. Conditions in the industry had begun to improve by 1830, but not as a result of the tariff of 1828. Rather, a continuing "fierce" competition drove out the weaker firms, and forced the survivors into a stepped-up program of mechanization and cost cutting, which brought the woolen industry into stable circumstances by the early 1830s.[41]

One of the consequences of the turmoil in the woolen industry seems to have been a political division between the proprietors of newly mechanized, large-scale mills, often with charters of incorporation, and those involved in marginal, small-scale woolenworks, often having origins in the synthesis of Federalism, wool, and commerce dating to the turn of the century. In North Brookfield, Daniel Waite – the author of the 1815 *New American Dier* – and five other men associated at various times with his small woolen mill were all Antimasons. In 1832, Waite's mill employed six men and five women, did $1,000 worth of wool carding and cloth dressing for local households, and produced 8,000 yards of low-quality kerseymere, "much of it disposed of in the vicinity, the remainder in Boston." By 1855 they had failed completely.[42] Waite's mill was the archetype of the old-style woolenworks, an integral part of the rural economy, and significantly threatened by the broader pattern of change in the industry. Similarly, a few clothiers and

---

[40] This analysis is based on an analysis of the manuscript of the United States Census for 1840. For a similar agrument about palm-leaf hatmaking, an important source of employment for women in northern Worcester county, see Thomas Dublin, "Women and Outwork in a Nineteenth Century New England Town: Fitzwilliam, New Hampshire, 1830–1850," in Steven Hahn and Jonathan Prude, eds., *The Countryside in the Age of Capitalist Transformation: Essays in the Social History of Rural America* (Chapel Hill, 1985), 51–70.

[41] Chester W. Wright, *Wool Growing and the Tariff: A Study in the Economic History of the United States* (Cambridge, Mass., 1910), 44–57; Jeremy, *Transatlantic Industrial Revolution*, 218–39, and throughout.

[42] McLane, *Report ... Relative to the Manufactures* [1832], 1:525; Francis Dewitt, ed., *Statistical Information Relating to Certain Branches of Industry in Massachusetts, for the Year Ending June 1, 1855* (Boston, 1856), 519. See also Chapter 9, note 44.

small woolen proprietors in Millbury and Southbridge signed the Antimasonic petitions, and in north Leicester Antimasonry spread along Kettle Brook, where the proprietors of four small woolen mills and two sawmills all signed the Antimasonic petitions. In sharp contrast with the small wool proprietors, not one man involved in large-scale, incorporated woolen or cotton production sided with Antimasonry, and at least ten Masons were located in strategic positions in seven textile corporations in Southbridge, Sturbridge, Dudley, Oxford, and Leicester, as well as in the Brookfield and Worcester Iron Foundry, incorporated in 1826.[43]

One extremely successful textile manufacturing family did throw their influence to the Antimasons, and this was the exception that proves the rule. Samuel Slater was unique among the large-scale textile manufacturers to avoid incorporating his business concerns under a state charter, and made a persistent effort to maintain family control, training his sons to take over the management of his mills in the new town of Webster and elsewhere in southeast New England. Webster would be the only town in the south county textile region to cast a majority for the Antimasons, and in 1831 and 1834 Slater's son George signed Antimasonic petitions. His affiliation was probably more toward cultural than political Antimasonry, as George Slater organized the Nationals in Webster in 1832. But it is striking that the Slaters, so opposed to incorporation, would be the only major manufacturers in the regions to give their names to the Antimasonic cause.[44]

The link between the woolen industry and Antimasonry was most apparent and problematic among the Worcester machinists. The largest single occupational group among these machinists, and among the Worcester Antimasons as a whole, were those men building machines for the woolen textile mills in the surrounding towns. Given the increasing mechanization of the woolen industry in the late 1820s and early 1830s, one might assume that these woolen textile machinists were prospering and might have remained with the Nationals. However, the woolen machinists were a very unstable group in a highly competitive business, and their position in the economy was a disadvantaged one. Economic historians have argued that textile machinists earned significantly lower wages than skilled industrial labor during the 1820s, the result of a significantly higher rate of immigration for skilled English machinists, particularly through the port of Boston. At the same time, it appears that the small machine shops in Worcester were generally building machinery that was in the public domain, "which had never been patented or for which the patent rights had expired," whereas shops

[43] Washburn, *Industrial Worcester*, 36ff.; *Hollingworth Letters*, 92–3; McLane, *Report ... Relative to the Manufactures* [1832], 1:484, 536–41; Ammidown, *Historical Collections*, 1:435; Daniels, *Oxford*, 189–9; Washburn, *Leicester*, 30–2; *Private and Special Statutes*, for the Worcester and Brookfield Iron Foundry.
[44] Tucker, *Samuel Slater*, 102, 193; Antimasonic petition from Oxford and Dudley, 1831, and from Webster, 1834 (see above, note 35); Southbridge *Village Courier*, October 9, 1832.

affiliated with the larger textile corporations closely guarded new improvements in technology. At the same time, wood was being replaced rapidly by brass and steel in textile machine making, putting certain older and less skilled machinists out of work. Thus it would appear that both masters and laborers in the Worcester shops were subject to intense competitive pressures. According to one authority, these pressures were sufficient to make textile machinery extremely cheap in the United States, facilitating the rapid mechanization of the mills in the late 1820s.[45]

The result for the machine makers was an unstable volatility, which was particularly evident among those who signed the Antimasonic petitions. Of the eleven Antimasons making woolen machinery in Worcester in the late 1820s and early 1830s, only one (9 percent) was still in the business in 1842. The years between 1831 and 1834 appear to have been a period of particularly high turnover, with at least five proprietors selling out or being forced out of the machine-making business. By contrast, six out of thirteen woolen machinists who signed the Second Bank or Temperance petitions but were *not* Antimasons (42 percent) survived until 1842. At least two of these Whig machinists, the partnership of Phelps and Bickford, made power looms under a series of licenses from patent holders, thus ensuring a monopoly on their products.[46]

Monopoly also characterized the dominant industries in neighboring Leicester and Millbury, two of the strongest centers of the Antimasonic insurgency in the county, casting three and four Antimasonic majorities, respectively. The patents obtained by Pliny Earle and John Woodcock for the production of card clothing for textile machinery worked to restrict card manufacturing to that town, and in 1837 the Leicester shops were producing 60 percent of the machine-card output in Massachusetts. Not surprisingly, of thirty-two card manufacturers signing the petitions of the early 1830s, only six were Antimasons. Like their counterparts among the Worcester wool machinists, these six Antimasonic card manufacturers were having serious problems. Four of them had dropped out of the card business by 1834, three between 1831 and 1833 alone. In contrast, only three of the sixteen National card manufacturers in business by 1830 dropped out before 1834;

[45] Jeremy, *Transatlantic Industrial Revolution*, 144–75, esp. 149, 151, 158–9, 232, 256; Nathan Rosenberg, "Anglo-American Wage Differences in the 1820s," *Journal of Economic History* 27 (1967), 221–9; in 1827 Jabez Hollingworth, who was working in the machine shop at the Leicester Manufacturing Company, was characterized as one of two in the family "who may be getting the least wages," Leavitt, ed., *The Hollingworth Letters*, 7. Quotation from Arthur H. Cole, *The American Wool Manufacture*, Vol. I (Cambridge, Mass., 1926), 365; on the corporation machine shops, see the discussion of the Ware Manufacturing Company shop in Jeremy, *Transatlantic Industrial Revolution*, 231; on materials, see Leavitt, ed., *The Hollingworth Letters*, xxi.

[46] Washburn, *Industrial Worcester*, 66–7, 88. Woolen machinists identified in Washburn, *Industrial Worcester*, 31–47, 62ff.; *Worcester Village Directory, April, 1828*; *Worcester Business Directory and Advertizer for 1842–1843*; all in the collections of the Worcester Historical Museum.

another seven entered partnerships after 1834.[47] The professional men of Leicester joined these successful card manufacturers in supporting the Nationals; four ministers, three lawyers, another doctor, and at least two merchants signed the Second Bank or Temperance petitions while avoiding the Antimasonic initiatives. One professional, Dr. Austin Flint, a Congregationalist and an Old School Federalist, led the Leicester Antimasons, signing all three petitions and standing as an Antimasonic candidate for the state senate in 1832 and 1833. But Leicester's second most important Antimasonic leader, Baptist John Hobart, was a blacksmith and tavernkeeper. With the exception of Dr. Flint, Leicester's Antimasons were located in the weaker side of the town's economy, proprietors of and perhaps laborers in smaller woolen mills, failing card shops, a scythe shop, and an old tannery, and probably including some shoemakers.[48]

In the neighboring town of Millbury, the Waters Armory was the centerpiece of the economy, operating between 1808 and 1845 under a federal contract. The armory used machinery for welding gun barrels and lathing the irregular shapes of gunstocks invented and patented by Asa Waters and Thomas Blanchard, inventions that significantly reduced labor costs by replacing skilled labor.[49] In

[47] *Leicester card maufacturers and petitions*

	Began before 1830: Out of business			Began after 1834	Unknown	Total card manufacturers		Total petitioners
	Before 1834		After 1834					
Antimasons	4	*67*[a]	2	0	0	6	*5*[b]	108
Second Bank and Temperance	1	*8*	9	2	0	12	*23*	52
Second Bank only	2	*18*	3	3	3	11	*8*	132
Temperance only	0		1	2	0	3	*7*	43
Total	7	*22*	15	7	3	32	*9*	335

[a] Percentage of total card manufacturers.
[b] Percentage of total petitioners.
Source: Petitions; Washburn, *Leicester*, 32–8. Pliny Earle defended his patents against five card manufacturers in Leicester and Worcester in 1814 and 1815, but the continuing spread of shops in Leicester suggests that patent licenses must have been sold to Leicester men on a preferential basis. The 1832 McLane *Report* listed 52 men employed in the Leicester card shops. See Jeremy, *Transatlantic Industrial Revolution*, 178, 323N9; McLane, *Report*, 502–3; and Bigelow, *Industry in Massachusetts . . . 1837*, 54, 194.

[48] Leicester occupations from Washburn, *Leicester*, throughout.

[49] An eyewitness reported that when Blanchard demonstrated a lathe for turning gun breeches at the Waters Armory in 1819, a gunstocker said "Blanchard has robbed you of your job, but cannot rob us of ours, for he cannot turn a gunstock," A year later Blanchard returned to install his "eccentric lathe," which robbed the skilled gunstockers of their jobs. *Centennial History of Millbury, Massachusetts . . .* (Millbury, 1915), 412–13, 466–7.

Insurgencies 339

addition to the armory, Millbury was noted for its proliferation of machine shops, whose proprietors often had worked in the armory and were often renting space from Asa Waters, and for its large prospering woolen mills, industries that would attract a branch of the Western Railroad in the late 1830s. These industries constituted the advanced component of the town's economy, with its leading element insulated from economic disruption by its federally insured contracts and patents. Again, Antimasons were far less likely to have been involved in these leading industries or in the Branch Railroad than either Masons or the Whig petitioners. In particular, the armory employed two and half times as many Masons as Antimasons. Antimasons were more often proprietors of country stores, among them Goffe's neighbors Benedict and Braman, or shoe entrepreneurs. All of those associated with the old Burbank paper mill were Antimasons. The precarious position of the Burbanks, who failed so spectacularly in 1834, may have been connected with their extensive investments in the Blackstone Canal, a project that was not prospering and that would be completely undermined by the new railroad.[50]

But if Millbury Antimasons were not involved in the town's dominant industries, they were not poor; they ranked higher than the Whig petitioners on the 1831 valuation, and the persistent Antimasons who signed the 1835 petition ranked higher than the Masons. Most importantly, they were distinguished in having a very high ratio of real to personal property, as recorded on the 1831 valuation; again, this was particularly the case among the 1835 petitioners. In combination with a weak occupational profile, the evidence from the valuation

[50] *Millbury occupations and petitions*

	Leading industries[a]		Shoes	Store	Paper manuf.	Total occupations known	
All Antimasons	14	*32*	6	10	3	43	*100*
1835 Antimasonic petition signers	2	*23*	1	3	2	9	*100*
Masons	13	*72*	1	1	0	18	*100*
Whig petitioners[b]	45	*66*	3	6	0	68	*100*

Note: Figures in italics are percentages.
[a] Waters Armory (owners, master workmen, and laborers), woolen mills, machinists, or role in the Millbury Branch Railroad.
[b] Non-Antimasonic signers of Second Bank and Temperance petitions.
Source: Petitions; Armory Workmen, 1833–7, listed Asa H. Waters Diary, octavo vol. 5, Waters Family Papers, AAS; Papers concerning the Millbury Branch Railroad, 1837–9, William Jackson Papers, 1809–53, Baker Library, Harvard Business School; *Centennial History of Millbury*; "Dead Members List," Grand Lodge of Masons, Boston.

strongly suggests that Antimasons were often older men who were heads of farm households. And Antimasons were distinguished from both Masons and Whig petitioners by their allegiance to the old Congregational church, as against the new Presbyterian society located in the Armory Village, a church established by the all-powerful Waters family. The Millbury Antimasons, thus, stood rooted in an older, increasingly outmoded economy and in the remnants of the corporate institutional order, whereas Masons and consistent Nationals were firmly in control of powerful new institutions and economic structures.[51]

The circumstances of rapidly changing local and regional economies played a very important role in shaping the contours of this political insurrection. The precarious position of Antimasonic proprietors – particularly the distribution of corporate charters, exclusive contracts, and patents – suggests that the broader questions of monopoly, equal rights, and independence articulated by Amasa Walker and the Suffolk County Committee played an important part in generating Antimasonic sentiment in this part of Worcester County. The vulnerable economic position of Antimasons, and the appeal of the antimonopoly ideology, is even more obvious when the establishment and subsequent control of local banks is considered. Men attracted to Antimasonry in the early 1830s had not been indifferent to the promise of local banking and credit in the previous decade. Future Antimasons were a strong minority among the petitioners for banks in Worcester, Leicester, Millbury, and Southbridge, and were well represented among the incorporators. But future Antimasons rarely served as directors or officers of these banks after they were incorporated, and the banks fell into the hands of the National Republican elites, and in many cases of men who had not been involved in the original petitioning. In several instances, though not all, the directorships of the local banks came to be dominated by Freemasons. Typically, then, after striving eagerly to establish banks in their towns, men who would become leading Antimasons were pushed out of positions of influence in these new institutions.[52]

[51] *Millbury petitioners, Masons and the 1831 valuation*

	Top quintile of total on 1831 valuation		Top two quintiles with less than 20 percent personal property	
All Antimasons	32/102	*31*	42/54	*78*
1835 Antimasonic petition signers	16/35	*46*	20/21	*95*
Masons	8/20	*40*	9/15	*60*
Whig petitioners	21/96	*22*	21/32	*66*

Note: Figures in italics are percentages.
Source: Petitions; 1831 Valuation in Millbury, Mass., Papers, AAS; for religious affiliation, see note 69 below.

The emerging pattern of control of local banking replicated the economic differentiation between Antimasons and Nationals, and probably heightened this differentiation. Again Worcester provides a useful point of entry. The directorship of the Worcester Bank was originally controlled by Federalists, and in the 1820s and 1830s was a mirror of the city's ruling National establishment, consisting almost exclusively of lawyers, merchants (7/8), and members of the Agricultural and Fire societies (10/10). The petition for the Central Bank, incorporated in 1828, apparently reflected the requirements of artisans and manufacturers for credit, because they made up a majority of the petitioners. Yet lawyers, merchants, and Fire Society members soon dominated the directorship, just as Antimasons were outnumbered by Nationals. A similar process marked the establishment of the Quinsigamond and Citizen's Banks in 1833 and 1836. The Worcester County Institution for Savings, established to provide long-term mortgaging, was also controlled by the National–Whig establishment in Worcester.[53]

[52] *Bank petitioners, incorporators, and directors and their political affiliation in Worcester, Millbury, Leicester, and Southbridge*

	Antimasons		Nationals/ Whigs[a]		Democratic committeemen	
Only signed petition	33	*65*	68	*52*	7	*44*
Only named as incorporator[b]	13	*25*	17	*13*	0	
Director, 1826–36	5	*10*	46	*35*	9	*56*
Total	51	*100*	131	*100*	16	*100*

Note: Figures in italics are percentages.
[a] Non-Antimasonic signers of Second Bank Petition.
[b] Includes six men named as directors or clerk of Millbury Bank in 1825 who appear on no subsequent lists (5 AM, 1 Nat). This row includes men who were both petitioners and incorporators.
Source: For banks see Chapter 9, note 70. Democratic activists identified in *Republican*, August 28, 1833; September 2, 1835; September 19, October 3, 1838. Also *Palladium*, October 24, 1838; September 21, October 2, 1839; September 2, 9, 1840. And in the Whig Questionnaires of 1840, Folder 4, Box 6, Worcester County, Mass., Papers, AAS.

[53] *Occupation and Worcester city banks: 1820–36[a]*

	Lawyers		Merchants		Wool/textile machinists	Boot/shoe/ leather	Other occupations	Total known	
Petitioners and/or incorporators only	14	*18*	15	*19*	5	6	40	78	*100*
Bank directors	10	*37*	10	*37*	0	3	4	27	*100*

[a] Worcester Bank, Central Bank, Quinsigamond Bank, Citizen's Bank.
Source: see Chapter 9, note 70; for the Worcester County Institute for Savings, see the Southbridge *Village Courier*, May 8, 1832.

This economic differentiation extended out into the country towns surrounding Worcester in varying degrees. No banks were incorporated in either Brookfield or North Brookfield, towns noted for their staunch Antimasonry and shoemaking economy. In Southbridge, lawyers, merchants, and agents of the Columbian and Wolcott Manufacturing Companies dominated both the bank petition and the board of directors in 1836. The Millbury Bank was established by Asa Waters, who became its first president, and Armory men and other metal machinists dominated both the petition and the directorship. In Leicester, card manufacturers made up only 20 percent (7/35) of the petitioners but, with the owner of the Leicester Manufacturing Company, 55 percent (10/18) of the bank's early directors.[54]

Masonic "influence" in banking varied from town to town. Freemasons had a relatively insignificant role in the banks in Worcester and Millbury and were a small but probably important minority among those interested in the Southbridge Bank. The banks in Oxford and Sutton were clearly controlled by Freemasons of the Olive Branch Lodge, led by Royal Arch Masons Jonathan Davis and Jonas L. Sibley, one a National and one a Democrat. Here there is another angle on the Antimasonic sentiments of the Slater family, for they were leading figures in an 1830 remonstrance against the rechartering of the Oxford Bank.[55]

But it was in Leicester that the bank appears to have been truly central to a confrontation between Masons and Antimasons, a confrontation that also spilled unambiguously into local politics. Between 1821 and 1828 Masons accounted for 65 percent of the town's selectmen, and in 1824 and 1825 they occupied four out of five seats. These were very important years in Leicester's institutional history, with the establishment of a local Masonic lodge in May 1824 and the submission of a bank petition in May 1825. Eight Masons were among the thirty-five petitioners, four of these men would become directors, joined later by four other Masons who had not signed the petition. In sharp contrast, none of the twelve bank petitioners who later signed Antimasonic initiatives were ever named director of the bank. John A. Smith, a card manufacturer, was named cashier in 1826, only to be replaced two years later by Horatio Henshaw, a merchant, notary public, and Freemason, who would serve for the next twelve years. Smith would become an ardent Antimason, signing all three petitions sent from the town. A similar pattern marked town politics. Masons lost their majority among the selectmen in 1828, and no Mason was elected between 1831 and 1833. Again in sharp contrast, every non-Masonic selectman who had served since 1810 and was still alive in the town

[54] *Centennial History of Millbury*; Asa H. Waters Diary: Washburn, *Leicester*, 31–8; McLane, *Report*, 1:536–7; lawyers from the *Massachusetts Register*; merchants from Southbridge newspapers.

[55] 1830 remonstrance against the rechartering of the Oxford Bank in Original Papers, chap. 73, Acts of 1830. See Prude, *The Coming of Industrial Order*, 161–5, for the broader circumstances of the Slater's ongoing quarrels with both the Oxford and Dudley manufacturing elites.

signed the Antimasonic petitions. Quite clearly, Masonic power was highly visible in Leicester, and apparent both to a generation of town selectmen and to those "businessmen" who had enthusiastically petitioned for local credit facilities in 1825, only to find themselves shut out by the end of the decade. Both groups found the Antimasonic insurrection a convenient and appropriate vehicle of protest.[56]

Masons were only a small minority of the directors of the Millbury Bank; here it was Presbyterians in the Armory Village who controlled the directorship. As in Leicester, there was a striking succession of cashiers at the Millbury Bank. Stephan Blanchard, an undistinguished brother of the inventor Thomas, a blacksmith and Congregational tithingman in traditionalist west Millbury, was appointed cashier in 1825, only to be replaced in the same year by Presbyterian Lewis Mills, who served for the next fifteen years.[57] Like John A. Smith in Leicester, Stephen Blanchard became an important Antimasonic leader, serving as a convention delegate and signing three different Antimasonic petitions. But the most dramatic confrontation with the Millbury Bank involved the Reverend Joseph Goffe of the Old Common. When the bank's charter was being reviewed in 1830, Goffe had submitted a vigorous remonstrance. In particular, his concern was that the vote to request rechartering had been taken by less than half of the stockholders. Goffe wanted to withdraw his investment in the bank; private motives played some role in his protest. Yet his letter to the review committee contained language reminiscent of the eighteenth-century concern for the corporate public good. In the minister's words, the bank in Millbury "after several years experiment, was of no public utility, but rather a damage to the inhabitants . . .," it was "now little more than a family concern." Joseph Goffe was referring to the Waters family, who so dominated the Armory Village, the new Presbyterian church, and the bank itself. In 1829 Goffe had written pointedly to his children of the enormous cost of the "palace" – a Palladian mansion – that the Waters family was building in the Armory Village, and complained of the "domineering purposes" of the Presbyterian Society that Asa Waters had founded. At the 1831 Antimasonic convention Goffe chaired a committee on religion, and urged that Antimasons withdraw from church fellowship with Masons. In making this crusade, he must have had in mind the Armory Village Presbyterian, which included Freemasons in its membership and whose pastor Goffe derided as a "cable-towed man of high & obstinate standing." Masons, Presbyterians, the

[56] Selectmen from Leicester Selectmen's records, Leicester Town Hall; Leicester Bank Petition, Original Papers, chap. 178, Acts of 1825; Nason, *Morning Star Lodge*, 40; *Proceedings of the . . . Grand Lodge, 1797–1815*, 587. Leicester also had been bitterly divided between 1809 and 1812 over a petition to build a turnpike from Worcester to Leicester center. The petition was dominated by card manufacturers, while the protesters seem to have been ordinary farmers and artisans. Original Papers, chap. 159, Acts of 1812. See Chapter 9, note 46, for a discussion of the card manufacturers joining the Morning Star Lodge in 1812–13.

[57] *Centennial History of Millbury*, 296–7.

powerful owners of the armory, and manipulators of the bank – all of these were, in the eyes of Joseph Goffe, "a damage to the inhabitants" of Millbury.[58]

"Sum good things goin on among us"

Commitment to Antimasonry thus was differentiated from allegiance to the Nationals by economic situation. Nationals were characterized by a comfortable agricultural independence (the majority in the northern towns) or involvement in the advanced sectors of the textile industry (the minority in the southern towns). Antimasons seem to have been the men in the middle, scraping out a living on that interphase between traditional household independence and the new industrial economy of shop production that had emerged out of the Federalist commercial networks in the old orbit of Popular orthodoxy.

If they were divided along economic lines, the Antimasons and the bulk of the Nationals did share a broad cultural affinity. The Antimasons shared with the Nationals of the northern towns a common religious background in orthodox Congregationalism, just as they shared a common Federalist tradition. (See Figures 6a and 6b.) But just as there were the modulations in the political climate of this Federalism, challenged in the Antimasonic towns as it had been monolithic in the National towns, there were modulations in the religious climate. Antimasonic and central corridor towns tended to be places where Congregational revivalism was more pronounced, both during the New Divinity revivals of the era following the War of 1812 and the immediatist Finneyite revivals of the early 1830s. Evangelical religion has long been seen as a formative influence on Antimasonry, and these aggregates would seem to bear out this thesis.[59] But the evidence from the petitions qualifies this picture significantly. Rather than being uniformly disposed toward the powerful currents of evangelical religion and moral reform, Antimasons in Worcester County seem to have been divided into two wings, one religious and the other secular – wings that would move in quite different directions over the next decade.

Religious affiliations can be traced for over four hundred Antimasons, Freemasons, and Second Bank and temperance petitioners, in the towns of North

[58] Remonstrance, Original Papers, chap. 132, Acts of 1830; Joseph Goffe to Joseph and Eliza Goffe, September 8, 1829, Goffe to Joseph Goffe, May 17, 1830, Rev. Joseph Goffe Papers, AAS.

[59] Cross, *The Burned-Over District*, 113–25; Benson, *The Concept*, 192–7; Ronald Formisano, "Political Character, Antipartyism, and the Second Party system," *AQ* 21 (1969), 682–709; Kutolowski, "Antimasonry Reexamined," 278–9, 289; Wallace, *Rockdale*, 337–49. Johnson, *A Shopkeeper's Millennium*, has a detailed description of the Finneyite revivals, but downplays an association between them and Antimasonry.

Brookfield, Brookfield, Leicester, and Millbury.[60] Overall, the variation among the first three of these four groups was relatively slight. Antimasons were not especially drawn to the revivals of 1827 to 1834; just over a third of all Antimasons, Freemasons, and Second Bank signers joined Congregational churches in these final years of the Second Great Awakening. Rather, Antimasons were biased toward Congregational membership *before* 1827 and toward the Baptist societies, whereas Masons and Second Bank signers were biased toward the Unitarians. It was among the Congregationalists joining before 1827 that there was a certain differentiation between Antimasons and Masons: 23 versus 9 percent. Thus, just as Antimasonry seems to have mobilized older voters, it drew in particular on converts in the earlier New Divinity revivals, but not those joining churches during the immediatist revivals of the early 1830s. These figures match the county aggregates: Antimasonic towns were less likely to have Unitarian societies and more likely to have Baptist churches. In short, if religion played a role in

[60] *Religious affiliation of Antimasons, Second Bank and temperance petitioners, and Freemasons in Leicester, Millbury, Brookfield, and North Brookfield*

| | Antimasons | | | All non-Antimasons | | | |
	Signed Second Bank petition		Others	Signed Second Bank petition	Signed only temperance petitions	Free masons	
Congregational, before 1827	30	*24*	17	*23*	34	*20*	16	*17*	4	*9*
Congregational, 1827–34	48	*38*	31	*41*	62	*37*	53	*57*	17	*39*
Baptist	18	*14*	9	*9*	15	*9*	6	*6*	4	*9*
Quaker	0		0		1		2		0	
Methodist	6		3		4		3		3	
Episcopal	3		2		7		1		2	
Universalist	3		4		3		1		1	
Unitarian	19	*15*	9	*12*	41	*24*	11	*12*	12	*28*
Total known	127	*100*	75	*100*	167	*100*	93	*100*	43	*100*
Total petitions	244		273		683		282		70	
Known/petitions		*52*		*27*		*23*		*33*		*61*

Note: Figures in italics are percentages.
Source: For petitions, see note 35; church affiliation listed in the following: *Manual of the First Congregational Church in Leicester* ...; Greenville Baptist Church Records; Records of Certificates, Leicester Town Records, Vol. "D" (1830–7); *Catelogue of the Members of the Congregational Church in West Brookfield* ...; *The Confession ... of the First Congregational Church in North Brookfield* ...; *Rules of Order ... Evangelical Congregational Church in Brookfield* ...; East brookfield Baptists listed in Leonard, "The Church on Fish Hill," 44; Records of Certificates, Brookfield records (see note 67); for Millbury Congregationalists, see note 69 below; Hoyt, *Millbury Baptist Church,* 3ff.; Millbury Methodists, Senate Unpassed, 1841, 10959.

Antimasonic motivations, it was an older, austere Calvinism rather then the optimistic new revivalism. Joseph Goffe, the only orthodox minister in the region to participate actively in the politics of Antimasonry, was a staunch adherent of the increasingly unfashionable Calvinist doctrines of the New Divinity. In his letters to his children he complained that "a smooth & easy system & manner," a "refined, sublimated, & metaphysical Arminianism," popular among the younger ministers recently trained under Nathaniel Taylor of Yale, had replaced the "plain, pointed & rousing sentiment & preaching which used to be heard." The revivals of 1831 and 1832, which to his mind "very much resembled Methodist meetings," he termed "almost complete failures" despite the numbers of new converts. Many ordinary Antimasons would have agreed with Goffe's assessment.[61]

Just as it coincided with a flood tide of immediatist revivalism, Antimasonry was closely followed by the movement of temperance into the public arena. Town and county temperance societies began to form between 1829 and 1831, and by 1833 the Worcester South District Temperance Society could claim as members roughly half the adult population of at least ten different towns. Temperance orators urged a "moral" remedy and "total abstinence" for the "self-pollution" of drunkenness. A statewide temperance convention met in Worcester in September of 1833, and in January and February of 1835 a flood of petitions to the General Court demanded the "interposition of the Legislative arm" for the repeal of the law licensing the retail sale of liquor. Swept up in the romantic and millennial perfectionism of the Finneyite revivals, the temperance forces took their cause into the political arena and inaugurated the long history of coercive temperance legislation in Massachusetts.[62]

Again, however, just as they were not particularly likely to respond to Finneyite revivalism, Antimasons as a whole were not disproportionately attracted to the cause of temperance. Antimasonic support for temperance varied from town to town; in some places it was higher than that of Nationals and Freemasons, in others it was lower. It was in the urban context of Worcester, where they were a small minority, that Antimasons were particularly associated with temperance, signing at twice the rate of the Nationals. In North Brookfield Antimasons were also more inclined toward temperance than were Nationals. But in Southbridge, Leicester, and Millbury, Nationals outdid Antimasons in signing the temperance petition, in Leicester by 2 to 1, and in Brookfield, another strongly Antimasonic

[61] Joseph Goffe to Eliza Goffe, Feburary 4 and August 13, 1833, Goffe papers, AAS.
[62] Worcester County *Republican*, October 2, 1833; Waldo Flint, *An Address Delivered before the Leicester Temperance Society at Their Annual Meeting, April 9, 1829* (Worcester, 1829), 3, 10, 18; Worcester Temperance Petition, House Documents, Unpassed Legislation, 1835, 12946; Massachusetts Society for the Suppression of Intemperance, Papers, AAS. Temperance Petitions, MA; Record of 1838–9 legislation, and petitions, Folders 3 and 4, Box 2, "Massachusetts Collection," AAS. Ian Tyrell, *Sobering Up*, 87ff.

town, interest in temperance was so low that no petition was ever sent and the 1838 petition attracted very few signers.[63] Overall, across these five towns, the support of Antimasons as a whole for temperance cannot be distinguished from that of signers of the Second Bank petition. (See Appendix 3, Table 1c.) In short, the evidence from these Worcester County towns cannot be used to argue that that Antimasonry bore a particularly significant relationship to the moral immediatism and coercive perfectionism that exploded out of this final phase of the revival cycle. Similarly, Antimasons were poorly represented among the trustees and officers of benevolent voluntary associations such as the Bible Society, the Religious Charitable Society, the American Colonization Society, and Worcester County Lyceum. Especially in the town of Worcester, these agencies of gradualist post-millennialism were firmly in the hands of the National elite.[64]

But temperance did mark an important divide within Antimasonry. If Antimasons in general were not disproportionately drawn to temperance, one group among them certainly was. Antimasonic petitioners who also signed a massive petition supporting the Second Bank of the United States were particularly likely to join the ranks of temperance, signing the temperance petitions of 1835–6 and attending the Worcester temperance convention. Conversely, it was the failure of the other Antimasons – those avoiding the Second Bank petition – to support temperance that accounts for the relatively weak overall relationship between Antimasonic and temperance activism. The Antimasonic Second Bank petitioners, effectively Antimasonic Whigs, were also more likely to be affiliated with churches. Thus is seems useful to divide Antimasons into two groups, one that responded to the reforming impulses flowing from the churches, and the other – a somewhat larger group – that responded primarily to the republican language of privilege, aristocracy, and monopoly.

Antimasonry in Massachusetts also coincided with another great moral crusade, the disestablishment of religion. An issue among dissenters since before the Revolution, the cause of disestablishment had taken a new turn in the early 1820s, with the takeover of old orthodox parishes by Unitarian groups. Influential

---

[63] For the involvement of the Antimasonic state leadership in temperance, see Formisano, *The Transformation*, 198, 218.

[64] Religious Charitable Society in the County of Worcester, 1814, *Private and Special Statutes*, 4:516; *The Rise and Operations of the Religious Charitable Society* ... (Leicester, 1816); Thomas Snell, *Signs of the Times. A Sermon Preached at the Formation of a Missionary Society, Auxiliary to the American Board of Commissioners for Foreign Missions* ... (Brookfield, 1824); David Damon, *Sermon Preached at Charlton, Mass. ... Sept. 14, 1826, at the Annual Meeting of the Auxiliary Bible Society in the County of Worcester* (Worcester, 1826); see also *Republican*, October 9, 1833; Worcester County Lyceum Records, 1827–31, Worcester County, Mass., Papers, AAS; see also *Yeoman*, January 16, 1830; Formation of the Worcester South Auxiliary of the American Education Society, *Spy*, May 5, 1830; *Report of the Managers of the Worcester County Auxiliary Colonization Society* ... (Worcester, 1832), 7; Worcester County Convention for Improving Public Schools, *Republican*, October 18, 1838.

interpretations of Antimasonry have stressed the alienation of evangelical Trinitarian Congregationalists in building the Antimasonic coalition. But again, there was no particularly strong link between petitioners supporting disestablishment and opposing Freemasonry. On the contrary, local circumstances suggest that those attracted to Antimasonry may well have had ambivalent feelings about the establishment, hostile to the Unitarians who had taken it over, yet nostalgic for the moral commonwealth to which the old orthodox churches had aspired.

After a long and complex legislative and judicial history, the final resolution of the disestablishment issue came in the summer of 1831 and winter of 1832, coinciding with Antimasonry's entry onto the political stage. Leading Antimasons at the state level were involved in the initiative, and in the weeks before the spring 1831 election, the *Yeoman*, recently converted to Antimasonry, trumpeted the formulas of "religious liberty" and "Unitarian conspiracy."[65] Petitions submitted to the General Court demanded that the alteration of Article III of the Constitution allow a close examination of the relationship between Antimasonry and disestablishment at the grass roots level. Between June 1830 and January 1832, forty-two petitions for disestablishment were sent from thirty-one Worcester County towns, but only nine of these towns also sent Antimasonic petitions. In three towns – Brookfield, North Brookfield, and Southbridge – Antimasonic petitioners signed the disestablishment petitions at a slightly higher rate than Second Bank petitioners, but again this difference was entirely due to the disproportionate support of Antimasons who also signed the Second Bank petition; just as they avoided the temperance petitions, other Antimasons were unlikely to support disestablishment. (See Appendix 3, Table 1b.) Strikingly, Masons were more likely than these non-Whig Antimasons to support the end of the old orthodox system.[66]

Rather than favoring disestablishment, Antimasons in some places may have opposed it, as is suggested by the circumstances in Brookfield and Millbury. In Brookfield a bitter division between Evangelicals and Unitarians in 1827, and a landmark case heard before the Supreme Judicial Court in 1830, left the property of the South Parish in the hands of the Unitarians, with the orthodox Calvinists separating as an evangelical society. A Royal Arch Chapter of Masons had been formed in Brookfield in 1825, and several Masons were among the key figures in the Unitarian takeover of the South Parish. But even under these dramatic circumstances, the Calvinists and the Antimasons in Brookfield were roughly half

---

[65] *Yeoman*, March 19, 26, April 2, 1831; McLoughlin, *New England Dissent*, 2:1221–3; Formisano, *The Transformation*, 218–9.

[66] In some instances, disestablishment may have been particularly associated with the Antimasonic leadership; in North Brookfield more than three-quarters (7/9) of the Antimasonic convention delegates signed the disestablishment petition, as against only 23.6% (22/93) of the Antimasonic signers in general.

as likely as Unitarians and Masons to sign one of the two disestablishment petitions forwarded by the town in 1830 and 1832.[67]

The reluctance of the South Brookfield Antimasons to support disestablishment suggests that opposition to Masonry resonated with the ancient ideal of a local moral unity, institutionalized in the old Congregational establishment. Any exclusive societies, whether religious or secular, subtracted from the moral union of the community, just as they seemed to threaten equal rights. Such concerns were made clear in two letters from a "congrigashuner" in Millbury published in the Massachusetts *Spy* in 1830. Millbury's religious unity had been broken up in the late 1820s with the formation of a Presbyterian society, which formalized its break with the inclusive corporate tradition by stipulating that members would be admitted by vote, and that votes would be apportioned by the value of pew space. By the mid-1830s Millbury's new religious pluralism was reinforced with the formation of Baptist and Methodist societies. Written in a protest against the evangelical itinerancies of Baptist ministers from neighboring towns, the first letter to the *Spy* lumped Masons with these new religious denominations.

> We now have sum good things goin on among us and we dont want your medling with the mattur. a few yers ago we had a good tim among us and you and other baptess prechers and the methdists cume in pon us lik a flud and spoilt it all.... We wish you ... and all other baptess and methdists and fremasons wood stay away, and mind thare own bisnes and let us alone.

[67] *Religion, Antimasonry, and disestablishment in Brookfield*

	Signed petitions			
	Disestablishment		Antimasonry	Total
Unitarians	44	*42*	23 *22*	105
Calvinists	14	*21*	24 *37*	65
Masons	7	*37*	0	19
Antimasons	39	*27*	145 *100*	145

Note: Figures in italics are percentages.
Source: Disestablishment and Antimasonic Petitions (see note 35); *Proceedings of the Grand Royal Arch Chapter*, 297; *Proceedings of the ... Grand Lodge ... 1826–44*, 70, 73, 126; Unitarians and Certificates to Evangelical Society: Records of the First Congregational Church and Society in Brookfield from January 15, 1755 to April 1, 1830 (Brookfield Town Hall), 280ff., 306; Records of the First Congregational or Unitarian Society, Brookfield, Mass., from April 1, 1830, to March 1st, 1869 (Brookfield Town Hall) 15–17, 23; Evangelical members: *Rules of Order ... Evangelical Congregational Church in Brookfield*, 28–30. Compare with analysis in McLoughlin, *New England Dissent*, 2:1214.

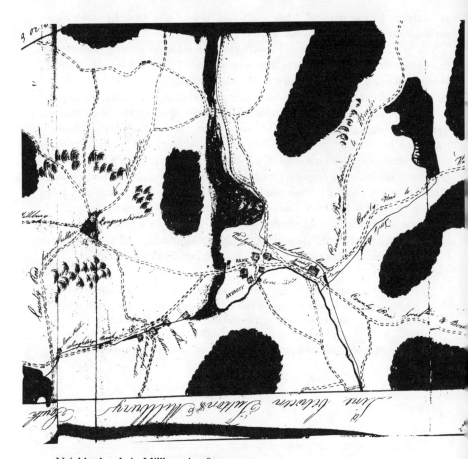

10. Neighborhoods in Millbury in 1831.
Above to the left is the Congregational Church at the old common, below are the mills on the Singletary stream, known to Joseph Goffe as "Squabble Hollow," and to the right is the Armory village.
Detail from "A Plan of the Town of Millbury, ... January 1831." (Courtesy of the Massachusetts Archives)

The same themes we repeated in a second letter, which included "the presbterens" among those interlopers who would "dis track the minds of the pepel."[68] The editor of the *Spy* had "strong evidence that these letters were written by a person holding a very important office in Millbury." Although the illiterate diction of these letters seems to rule out Joseph Goffe, their sentiments were not alien to him; three years later he warned his daughter not to trust Baptists and Methodists, for

---

[68] Hurd, *Worcester County*, 2: 1104; letters in *Spy*, March 10, 1830.

"they are *sectarians* & like others of the kind they seek their own, & not the things of Jesus Christ." The letters in the *Spy* targeted Masons and Presbyterians among others as offenders against the moral unity of old Millbury; the Presbyterians, although an evangelical society, had numbers of Masons in their midst, whereas the old Congregational church was heavily Antimasonic.[69]

The old church was further divided when various factions first asked Joseph Goffe to resign as minister after thirty-six years of service and then moved the church from the Old Common to the industrial village of Bramanville, which Goffe derisively spoke of as "Squabble Hollow." In the wake of these disputes traditionalists objecting to this further erosion of the old parish, including Joseph Goffe, his son, and a number of other staunch Antimasons, seceded to form their own society. When this West Millbury Congregational Society drew up a subscription list in 1836, they again drew upon language echoing the corporatism of the eighteenth century, "believing that the public good and the happiness of ourselves and our families requires that there should be a house built for a place of public worship on Grass Hill."[70]

[69] Joseph Goffe to Eliza Goffe, February 4, 1833, Rev. Joseph Goffe Papers, AAS.

Millbury petitions, religion, and antislavery societies

	Total	Presbyterian church		Congrega-tional church		West Millbury Congrega-tional Society	West Millbury Antislavery Society		Millbury Antislavery Society
All Antimasons	171	19	*11*	46	*27*	7	15	*9*	4
1835 Antimasonic petitioners	56	2	*4*	24	*44*	3	9	*16*	2
Masons	27	11	*41*	3	*11*	0	1	*4*	1
Whig petitioners	239	48	*16*	14	*5*	3	2	*1*	9

Note: Figures in italics are percentages. The Presbyterians are included in the Congregational total in note 60.
Source: Petitions (see note 35); Dead Members List, Grand Lodge; *The Confession of Faith, Covenant, and List of Members of the First Congregational Church in Millbury, Mass.* (Worcester, 1836); *The Confession of Faith and Covenant of the First Congregational Church, in Millbury, Mass.* (Worcester, 1860?); *A Catalogue and Manual, of the Second Congregational Church in Millbury, Mass., 1850* (Worcester, 1850). The membership lists for the West Millbury Congregationalists have not survived; the individuals listed here are a building committee and a pew committee cited in *Centennial History of Millbury*, 322–3, and "Record of a Pew sale to Ebenezer W. Goffe in West Millbury Congregational Meetinghouse, July 20, 1837," Box 1, Folder 1a, Waters Family Papers, AAS. The figures for the two antislavery societies in the town suggest Antimasonic strength in West Millbury. *Proceedings of the Massachusetts Anti-Slavery Society, 1840*, 1x.
[70] *Millbury Centennial History*, 322–3.

In this anxiety about the effects of voluntary religion on the old churches we can see one dimension of the "antiparty" impulse emerging from Congregational corporatism to inform Antimasonry. Antiparty sentiments lay at the heart of Antimasonry, rooted in a persistent, if archaic and perhaps reactionary sense of corporate unity that had its roots in the traditional relationship between church and state. The moral origins of the antiparty sentiments of Antimasons in Massachusetts were not the intense pietism of the revival convert. Rather, they were the diffuse and deeply rooted objections of those of orthodox and nongentry background to "sectarians" of all kinds, whether they be religious societies of dissenters or secular associations of gentlemen. These corporate conceptions of society had been bound up in a sense of moral economy in the eighteenth century; and by the 1830s they were seriously at odds with a rapidly changing institutional order.

Antimasonry brought a powerful resurgence of the Harringtonian formula. Consciously echoing the Revolutionary tradition, Antimasons rose up against a conspiracy of designing men who seemed to be undermining the rights of the people at large, denying their legitimate role in public affairs, and threatening their independence. If the Antimasons, as men of the new century, subscribed to the liberal ethic of individual opportunity – and organized themselves as a political party – they also drew upon the surviving asumptions of the corporate framework and the ancient assumptions of moral unity, commonwealth, and collective responsibility. But they were by no means direct descendants of the Regulators, and if the Workingmen had to deny any association with "the famous Shay insurrection," the Antimasons cloaked their class politics behind a cultural antagonism. Many Antimasons, perhaps most, were from families that had supported the government in 1787; certainly many had responded to the Harringtonian language of popular Federalism in 1812. More distantly, their situation in Congregationalism and the small-shop economy suggests connections running back to the orthodox, Land Bank wing of the provincial Popular coalition. But more than distant – though formative – political traditions, it was the increasingly stressful and divisive circumstances of economic and political life in the central corridor towns that set the stage for an organized party of protest, providing both the sense of grievance against powerful forces in society and the networks of communication among a host of households and small shops. It was the friction between the ancient expectations of commonwealth and the new realities of the growing industrial order, a combination absent for the most part in the north and south county towns, that led men into the Antimasonic insurgency.

11

Antislavery

In their 1834 resolves, Amasa Walker and the Antimasons of Suffolk County warned that "the present ruling party in this state ... dwell entirely upon the politics at Washington, and seem to forget that there is such a government to be administered as the ancient commonwealth of Massachusetts." They declared that the laws to be revised in the next session were "of more consequence to us and our children than all the noise about the Bank question."[1] But the Bank War was only one of a series of new issues that would divert the people's attention from the structure of Massachusetts society and economy over the next several decades. The battle with the monopolists that Amasa Walker hoped to wage within the state would be overshadowed by the destruction of the Bank of the United States, by perfectionist crusades for temperance, and increasingly by the powerful moral and political dilemmas involving the existence of slavery. The questions of the bank and temperance, national and millennial in their frame of reference, would act to restore two-party competition, which had never truly asserted itself since the collapse of Federalist organization in 1825. The slavery question would provide a countervailing force, breaking down allegiances to the two national parties, until, by a process of convergence, it shaped a new consensus across the Worcester middle landscape. But Amasa Walker's – and Joseph Goffe's – controversy with the monied interests in Massachusetts never disappeared in the small shops, mills, and farms of the central corridor, and it would powerfully shape the emergence of the Republican consensus that the slave power must be contained and slavery doomed.

Whiggery: The Second Bank, temperance, and the Log Cabin

The origins of the Whig Party in Worcester County can be dated to February 19, 1834, when a mass meeting convened at the Worcester Town Hall to frame a petition to Congress protesting Jackson's removal of the federal deposits from the Bank of the United States. The petition drawn up at this meeting sounded a theme that would carry the party down to the end of the decade. Four months previously,

---

[1] Antimasonic Resolves, November 3, 1834, Extra to the *Boston Daily Advocate*, Broadsides, MHS.

the county's prosperity had been disrupted by a "pecuniary pressure which commenced upon the sea-board" and spread into "the interior," threatening the livelihoods of businessman, the "industrious mechanic," the manufacturer, the trader, and "the great *mass* of labor." The cause lay in "the late measures of the Executive ... toward the Bank of the United States."[2]

For most of the next decade, reaching a climax in the Log Cabin campaign of 1840, the Whig Party would command the allegiance of a majority of voters in the county and the state with exactly this formula: Democratic action against the national financial system was bringing economic ruin. Signed by over six thousand men, the county's petition to Congress was the equivalent of a founding document for the party. Just as Massachusetts Federalists had deployed a classical republican rhetoric in their confrontation with Jeffersonian innovations, the Whigs similarly invoked the classical tradition in forging a broad interclass coalition. These echoes of the Harringtonian opposition would make a certain contribution to the reshaping of political culture in the decades to come.[3]

The bank crisis brought the rapid demise of both Masonry and Antimasonry. In August 1834, the Antimasonic leadership in Worcester County, led by Pliny Merrick, closed ranks with the old Nationals in opposing Jackson's "strides of executive assumption" against the Second Bank of the United States. Merrick had addressed an open letter to Governor John Davis, asking his opinion on divisions within the ranks of the state's anti-Jacksonians. When Davis recommended "a voluntary surrender of the Masonic institution," a convention of Masonic Nationals met in Worcester to renounce their lodge charters; that November only 7 percent of the county's electorate cast ballots for Antimason John Bailey. The next year all of the towns that had returned Antimasonic majorities since 1831 voted for Edward Everett, the new Whig candidate for governor.[4]

But many Antimasons refused to join the new Whig coalition. With the breakup of the Antimasonic organization, Amasa Walker and Benjamin F. Halett led the Suffolk County Antimasons into the Democratic Party, while George Bancroft was instrumental in recruiting Antimasons in the Connecticut Valley for the Democrats.[5] And if the Worcester leadership urged Antimasons to join the Whigs, the radical leaders were not without influence. In the six towns discussed in Chapter 10, 45 percent of the petitioning Antimasons signed the Second Bank petition, but another 55 percent did not. When Pliny Merrick met with 200

[2] Worcester County Petition, U. S. Congress, *House Documents, 1833–34*, 23d Cong. 1st Sess. vol. 3. no. 176, 2–3.
[3] See broadly, Banner, *Toward the Hartford Convention*; Howe, *The Political Culture of the American Whigs*; Holt, *The Political Crisis of the 1850s*; Formisano, Transformation.
[4] Returns of Votes for Governor, MA; *Palladium*, August 13, 20, 27, September 2, 1834.
[5] Temple, *North Brookfield*, 384–9; Benjamin F. Hallett, *An Oration Delivered July 4th, 1836, at Palmer* ... (Boston, 1836); Nye, *Bancroft*, 109–12; Arthur B. Darling, *Political Changes in Massachusetts, 1824–1848* (New Haven, 1925), 121–6, 172; Formisano, *Transformation*, 215–17.

Antimasons in Millbury in October of 1834 to request their support for the Whigs, a letter to the Democratic Worcester County *Republican* reported that only forty-five would sign the Whig resolves, and declared that "the Antimasons in this town are a subborn set of fellows – they are not to be led captive at the will of any mere man." Vote totals for 1835 and 1836 in Millbury, Brookfield, North Brookfield, and Worcester suggest that a significant block of Antimasons probably were voting Democratic in those years, and Antimasonic representatives from three of these towns cooperated with Democrats in voting to reduce the salaries of state officers in 1835. Similarly, there were at least a few former Antimasons among the Democratic activists later in the 1830s, particularly in Brookfield and North Brookfield, Amasa Walker's hometown.[6] There are also scattered suggestions of a cooperation between Antimasons and the county's very weak Workingman's Party organization. The editor of the briefly published *Plebian and Workingmen's Advocate* signed an Antimasonic petition in Millbury, as did his two agents in Brookfield. Francis Howe, another Brookfield Antimason, participated in a Workingman's convention in Springfield in the fall of 1834. These connections between the Antimasons and the Workingmen were underscored in the fall of 1840, when George Bancroft addressed Democrats in Brookfield, and party man David Henshaw addressed Democrats in "conservative" Sutton. When the Reverend Joseph Goffe complained to his daughter in Alabama in January of 1838 that "the old tories under the modern title of whigs still bear sway, & rule with a high hand in Massachusetts," he was voicing an opinion shared by other former Antimasons, many of whom expressed their grievances by following Bancroft into the Democratic Party.[7]

Ultimately, however, Jacksonian Democracy could only serve as an unstable halfway house for those of antiparty instincts. The Democratic presidential nomination of Martin Van Buren in 1836 was particularly unpopular among Massachusetts Antimasons, and limited the emerging cooperation between Antimasons and Democrats.[8] Increasingly, after 1836, new issues, and a new

[6] *Republican*, October 29, 1834; October 7, 1835. Also Votes for Governor, MA. In Worcester, Millbury, Leicester, and Southbridge there were eleven former Antimasons among eighty-five identifiable Democratic leaders in the 1830s, whereas in Brookfield and North Brookfield eight out of thirteen were former Antimasons, including Amasa Walker and his brother Freeman. Democratic committemen listed in *Palladium*, September 25, 1839, local officials in Whig questionnaires, Folder 4, Box 6, Worcester County, Mass., Papers, AAS, and representatives elected in years of Democratic majorities are also included. See also Chapter 10,note 16, for Democrats in Worcester.

[7] Millbury *Plebian* and Worcester County *Workingmen's Advoate*, March 23, April 20, 1831; *Republican*, October 22, 1834; *Palladium*, October 21, 1840; Joseph Goffe to Eliza Goffe, January 11, 1838, Rev. Joseph Goffe Papers, AAS.

[8] *Resolutions and Address Adopted by the Antimasonic Members of the Legislature of Massachusetts, and Other Citizens of Boston and the Vicinity, Opposed to the Nomination of Martin Van Buren and Richard M. Johnson* ... (Boston, 1836); Darling, *Political Changes*, 172, 186–92, 201, 266.

generation, would begin to occupy the political center of gravity. The late 1830s would see the politicization of a vast new reservoir of young voters, a surge into the public arena equivalent in its formative influence to the militia service of young men in the French and Indian War and the Revolution, and to the explosion of popular participation in the First Party System. As with these earlier episodes, the height of the Second Party system between 1838 and 1844 brought thousands of young men into the political arena under the aegis of established institutions and structures. Again, as with these earlier episodes, the structured surge of the Second Party system would be followed by a powerful insurgency.

Over the longer term, culminating in the Log Cabin campaign of 1840, the competition between Whigs and Democrats would be fundamentally shaped as a referendum on assumptions about Jackson's and Van Buren's responsibility for the economic hard times that began in 1837. But in the intervening years the question of temperance would occupy center stage in Massachusetts. A new and uncompromising element within the Whig coalition began to press for the adoption of the Fifteen Gallon Law, which would outlaw the sale of liquor in small quantities. The result would be an intensification of political partisanship in 1838 and 1839, as the temperance question brought great additions to the ranks of both the Whigs and the Democrats in the years before the definitive emergence of mass party politics.[9]

Both Whigs and Democrats made direct appeals to the rising generation in these years. Both parties formed Young Men's associations; Benjamin F. Hallett in his 1839 address to the Democrats in Millbury decried the burden of special laws of incorporation on "the young men, who have nothing but their hands and heads for capital."[10] But it was among the Whigs, and particularly the advocates of temperance, that the appeal to the new generation had its roots. When a Young Men's Temperance Association was formed in Worcester in the fall of 1833, it was drawing on a well-defined constituency, distinctly younger than the Antimasonic voters, and influenced by the new moral order established in the Finneyite revivals of the early 1830s.[11]

If there were no significant differences among Antimasons, Second Bank petitioners, and Masons in their response to the immediatist revivals of the early 1830s, non-Antimasonic temperance advocates were quite different. In Leicester, Millbury, Brookfield, and North Brookfield, 57 percent of the men responding to

[9] Tyrell, *Sobering Up*, 87–115; Formisano, *Transformation*, 245–67, 275–7.
[10] Worcester *Palladium*, August 19, 1840; *Address of the Whig Young Men's Convention to the People of Massachusetts*; Benjamin F. Hallett, *Oration before the Democratic Citizens of Worcester County, Massachusetts, at Millbury, July 4, 1839* (Worcester, 1839), 39–40.
[11] Worcester Young Men's Temperance Association in *Republican*, October 9, 1833; on generational conflicts, see also William J. Rorabaugh, *The Alcoholic Republic: An American Tradition* (New York, 1979), 181–3; Lois W. Banner, "Religion and Reform in the Early Republic: The Role of Youth," *AQ* 28 (1971), 677–95; Nancy Cott, "Young Women in the Second Great Awakening in New England," *Feminist Studies* 3 (1975), 15–29.

temperance but not to Antimasonry – delegates to the 1833 convention and signers of the 1835 and 1836 petitions – joined Congregational churches between 1827 and 1834 as against roughly 39 percent of Antimasons, Masons, or Second Bank petitioners. In addition, temperance seems to have drawn upon a significantly younger constituency than Antimasonry. One temperance address delivered in Leicester explicitly posed the temperance issue in generational terms, cautioning that the "veneration of elders" might lead to an "imitation of defects as well as virtues."[12] The temperance petition had significant support among the leading manufacturers in Millbury, including even Democrat Asa H. Waters. As elsewhere in the 1830s, it seems likely that joining in the evangelical revival and the forces of temperance was part of a broader strategy of survival and persistence by the young and transient workers of the larger mills and shops, as they began to adapt to the time and work discipline of the early industrial order.[13]

The new moral code of self-discipline and immediatist activism flowing out of the Finneyite revivals would shape a host of initiatives for the reform of society, as well as the dynamism of the Whig campaign in 1840. But in 1838 and 1839 the success of temperance in the passage of the Fifteen Gallon Law provoked a massive backlash. A meeting in Democratic Sutton in September 1838 announced that they were "gratified with the rapid progress of temperance," but vehemently denounced the law as "an act of tyranny and fitted for arbitrary abuse," a violation

[12] Waldo Flint, *An Address Delivered before the Leicester Temperance Society at Their Annual Meeting, April 9, 1829* (Worcester, 1829), 16. Waldo Flint was the son of Austin Flint, but he was a Unitarian, and a consistent National and Whig, spurning his father's orthodox religion and Antimasonic politics.

[13] On temperance and manufacturing, see Johnson, *Shopkeeper's Millennium*; Tucker, *Samuel Slater*, 178–81. The evidence from the Millbury valuation of 1831 indicates that temperance petitioners who avoided signing one of the three Antimasonic petitions were a distinctly young group. The fact that Antimasonic signers were more that three times as likely as exclusively temperance men to appear on this valuation suggests that they were far more rooted in the community. And among those listed in 1831, roughly half of the Antimasons ranked in the top quintile, as against less than a tenth of those signing only the 1835 temperance petition.

Millbury: Antimasonic and temperance petitions and 1831 valuation

	All Antimasonic petitioners		1835 Antimasonic petitioners		1835 temperance petition only	
1st quintile	32	*19*	16	*29*	1	*1*
Valuation total	102	*60*	35	*64*	11	*17*
Total petitioners	171	*100*	55	*100*	65	*100*

Note: Figures in italics are percentages.
Source: Petitions (see Chapter 10, note 35); 1831 Valuation in Millbury, Mass., Papers, AAS.

of "the rights of poor and middling interests."[14] Such sentiments swept the county and the state. That fall the county vote for the Democrats jumped from 33 to 41 percent and the next year, when Democrat Marcus Morton was finally elected governor, 48 percent of the county's electorate voted Democratic. Similarly, voter turnout surged upward, moving toward its record level in 1840.

The results of these two elections were dramatic. (See Figure 7b.) The Democrats carried seventeen new towns, concentrated in the northern half of the county. In November 1839, the Democratic papers targeted the electorate in these northern towns in an "appeal to old Federalists" that played on the classical tradition. Reviewing the partisan politics of the War of 1812, the *Palladium* noted that whereas the Republicans had had "more faith in man's capacities for self-government," the Federalists had been justified in their concern that "all preceding republics had been short-lived." In the present contest, such "old school Federalists" had nothing in common with the Whigs, who were driven by "self-interest." The paper hailed "the sturdy yeomen of old *Templton*" when that northern town recorded the highest Democratic increase in the county.[15] But the Democratic surge in the northern towns was short-lived, episodic, not unlike the Regulation of a half-century before. The next year all but two of these towns would return to the Whig fold; over the longer term seven would vote Democrat later in the 1840s, contributing to only a minor erosion of the Whig dominance of the north.

These surging Democratic votes rarely occurred in towns that had been significantly affected by the Finneyite revivals of the early 1830s. Rather, it was the towns that elected representatives pledged to support strict temperance legislation that had been swept by this awakening.[16] Temperance towns were also likely to have been located in the central corridor, including some shoe towns and some textile towns. But if location and revival differentiated the temperance towns from the formerly Whig, anti–Fifteen Gallon towns, both groups were likely to have had competitive political climates throughout the First Party period, while other Whig towns had voted overwhelmingly for Federalists. And despite their fundamental differences, the opposing forces of temperance and anti–Fifteen Gallon sentiment shared a common enemy: both were insurgencies against the Whig establishment. Anti–Fifteen Gallon voters held the Whig power structure responsible for the obnoxious law, and the temperance forces were equally rebellious in their refusal to abandon the same law in the name of party stability.

---

[14] *Republican*, September 12, 1838.

[15] *Palladium*, November 6, 20, 1839. Towns denominated "Democratic of Whig Origin" are those towns that had voted consistently for the Whigs since 1834, but that cast Democratic majorities in 1838 or 1839.

[16] The temperance representatives and the size of petitions for and against the Fifteen Gallon Law are recorded on printed roll call sheets filed in Box 2, Folder 3, Massachusetts Collection, AAS; see also list of petitions in Box 2, Folder 4.

The Whig mainstream fielded slates of anti–Fifteen Gallon "Liberal Whig" candidates in a concerted effort to stem the Democratic onslaught, and when the Whig county committee distributed questionnaires to party men throughout the county in May 1840, they were consistently told that hostility to the temperance legislation had drawn off voters to the Democrats.[17] The temperance insurgency was rooted in evangelical certainties; the countervailing surge to the Democrats was rooted in a Harringtonian defense of independence. The Whig Party would be doomed when a coalition combined these two appeals in the late 1840s.

In 1840 the Whigs of Worcester County pinned their hopes for a restoration of prosperity on the national candidacy of William Henry Harrison, and with this unique and transformative campaign, national politics finally superceded state politics. For the next two decades, with the exception of the early 1850s, participation in governor's elections would sag between presidential election years, where previously turnout in these national elections had followed the ebb and flow of state politics. But despite its nationalizing effect, the Log Cabin campaign had an undercurrent of insurgency against the Whig establishment. Mass demonstrations and marches would bring thousands of Whigs to the streets of Worcester; one working delegation from Leicester carried a banner inscribed "We need relief/We demand reform/No reduction in wages."[18] Such slogans were two-edged, condemning the Van Buren administration but also challenging the manufacturing elite.

The surge of participation in the late 1830s thus brought new forces into the political arena; most importantly, an evangelical middle class began to challenge gradualist gentry dominance of the Whig Party. While the Democrats increased their vote in the north county agricultural towns, the Whigs gained in the south county textile towns, though rarely reaching sufficient numbers to shift these towns permanently into the Whig camp. The association of temperance and manufacturing must have played a key role in building these Whig constituencies in the southern towns, and temperance seems to have been a pivotal factor in the emergence of a new strata of Whig activists in Worcester. The Whig demonstrations of the summer and fall of 1840 required organization and money, which were provided in great part by a Log Cabin committee in Worcester. Among the subscribers to the Worcester Log Cabin committee who were new to Whig politics, temperance advocates outnumbered proliquor advocates by 7 to 1, whereas among those who had entered Whig politics in 1837 the ratio was only 2 to 1, and among the National activists and elite of the early 1830s the ratio was 3 to 2. Rooted in the temperance movement, the Log Cabin Whigs in Worcester were

[17] *Republican*, October 10, 1838; *Palladium*, October 2, 1839; Whig Party Questionnaires, Box 6, Folder 4, Worcester County, Mass., Papers, AAS. See Formisano, *Transformation*, 298–9; 239–44.
[18] Formisano, *Tranformation*, 265.

also drawn in good measure from Antimasonry, notably from its Whiggish wing of Second Bank and Temperance petitioners. The new Whigs of 1840 might agree with the old elite on broad matters of national economic policy, but they came from a different orbit in Worcester society, attuned to recent insurgent forces and new moral imperatives.[19] (See Appendix 3, Tables 2b–d, 5a–d.)

Although the late 1830s brought a surge in participation and a revival of two-party competition, there were strongly countervailing tides. Among the Whigs in particular, there were signs of dissatisfaction and hints of insurgency against an entrenched Whig leadership. The Whig coalition in Massachusetts was enduring and broad-based, but ultimately unstable. As a new controversy – national in scope and universal in nature – came to dominate the political arena, the fissures in the Whig coalition would again crack open.

Abolition and "the new Antislavery Party"

The year 1840 brought actors very different from Log Cabin Whiggery and William Henry Harrison onto the public stage. That spring Abigail Kelley of Worcester was seated on the business committee of the American Antislavery Society, precipitating a dramatic schism in the abolitionist movement. Abigail Kelley's assumption of public authority was only one symptom of important new forces emerging in Massachusetts and Worcester County since the explosion of immediatist revivalism early in the 1830s. Since 1835 thousands of women from across the county had entered the political arena in petitioning the United States Congress and the state legislature for the abolition of slavery and the slave trade in Washington D.C., against the admission of Texas and Florida as slave states, and for a repeal of the congressional gag on such antislavery petitions. The critical force in the most powerful moral insurgency since the evangelical separatism of

[19] On the insurgent strain in the Massachusetts Log Cabin campaign, see Formisano, *Transformation*, 264–7. The sources for names of Worcester town National Republican and Whig activists include the 1832 committee in *Spy*, October 17, 1832; committee listed in Miscellaneous Papers, "National Republican Committee [probably 1833], Papers," Worcester Historical Museum; 1834 Whig committee in *Palladium*, October 1, 1834; and District Committees, *Spy*, October 11, 1837. Also see Delegates to the State Convention of the Whig Young Men. September 11, 1839, Folder 1, Box 6; Delegates to the Worcester County Whig Convention, October 8, 1839, Folder 3, Box 6; Members of the Worcester Whig Association, 1840, Folder 4, Box 6; Delegates to the Whig State Convention, June 17, 1840, Folder 5, Box 7–all in Whig Party Papers, Massachusetts Collection, 1629–c. 1869, 1898. AAS, Also Log Cabin Committee Papers and Bills, Subscription Book, Whig Committee, June 17, 1840, Kinnicut Family Papers, Worcester Historical Museum. The proliquor men (prolicense) are from *Palladium*, April 8, 1835; and *Aegis*, October 3, 1838, reproduced in Tyrell, *Sobering Up*, 325–6. For temperance, see Chapter 10, note 35.

a century before, their movement would profoundly shape political culture in Worcester County, as it did across the antebellum North.[20]

This new female voice for abolition worked in tandem – if not in harmony – with the traditional, male-defined political insurgency. Over the next decade, as division, chauvinism, and weak finances blunted the impact and impetus of abolitionism, antislavery politics became the catalyst for a second and overwhelming cycle in antebellum insurgency. Driven by the issues of slavery in the District of Columbia, the Gag-Rule, Texas, the Mexican War, the Compromise of 1850, and finally the Kansas–Nebraska controversy, Worcester County became, as it was to be celebrated by George Frisbie Hoar, "the stronghold of the new Antislavery Party." Without the persistence of a solid bloc of the county's people, the growth of political antislavery in Massachusetts – from the petition drives through the Liberty Party to the Free Soil–Republican coalition – would have been meager and weak. Leading the assault on the Whig Party in Massachusetts, this antislavery constituency played a critical role in bringing to power what would be one of the most radical groups in the Republican Party, including the 'martyr' Charles Sumner, one-time shoemaker Henry Wilson, and the Bird Club, against the power and concerted efforts of entrenched manufacturing interests committed to a stable relationship with the cotton south.[21]

In the rise of antislavery politics there were distant and not-so-distant echoes of the regional insurgencies that had swept over Worcester County in the previous century. Like the Land Bank, the economic politics of the 1780s, and Antimasonry, political antislavery was very much an assault on the economic and political power of metropolitan elites within the state, and it also had local targets. At the same time, its national focus on a conspiracy by a "slave power" resonated with the consensual militance that had informed the Revolutionary generation, popular

---

[20] Richards, *John Quincy Adams*, 94–5, 126–7; James E. Mooney, "Antislavery in Worcester County, Massachusetts: A Case Study," Ph.D. dissertation, Clark University, 1971, 82. Aileen S. Kraditor, *Means and Ends in American Abolitionism: Garrison and His Critics on Strategy and Tactics, 1834–1850* (New York, 1969), 39–77; Mary P. Ryan, *Cradle of the Middle Class: The Family in Oneida County, New York, 1780–1865* (New York, 1981), 108–16; Lawrence Friedman, *Gregarious Saints: Self and Community in American Abolitionism, 1830–1870* (New York, 1982), 129–59; John R. McKivigan, "Vote as You Pray and Pray as You Vote: Church-Oriented Abolitionism and Antislavery Politics," and Nancy Hewitt, "The Social Origins of Women's Antislavery Politics in Western New York," in Alan M. Kraut, ed., *Crusaders and Compromisers: Essays on the Relationship of the Antislavery Struggle to the Antebellum Party System* (Westport, Conn., 1983), 179–234. A Maternal Society and a Dorcas Society, were well established in two of the the strongest abolitionist communities, Millbury and West Brookfield. Millbury Maternal Society, Millbury, Mass., Papers, AAS; *HWC*, 2:336–72.

[21] George Frisbie Hoar, *Autobiography of Seventy Years* (Boston, 1903), 1:158. See Formisano, *Transformation*, 329–43; Goodman, "The Politics of Industrialism"; Darling, *Political Changes*, 281, 286–92; Dale Baum, *The Civil War Party System: The Case of Massachusetts, 1848–1876* (Chapel Hill, 1984); and Kinley J. Brauer, *Cotton vs. Conscience: Massachusetts Whig Politics and Southwestern Expansion, 1843–1848* (Lexington, Ky., 1967).

Federalism, and Log Cabin Whiggery. As in the movement of Popular politics
from Land Bank insurgency to the revolutionary consensus, the militancy of the
Civil War consensus was rooted in an insurgency that had begun to unfold decades
earlier. And antislavery politics was also rooted in a social orbit that bore distant
continuities with the Popular tradition: that interval in the county's political
geography lying between Whig and Democratic extremes constituting the central
corridor, defined in the first decades of the century by a small-shop economy,
Congregational revivalism, and a competitive political climate. Most immediately,
antislavery activism and politics were situated within the same wider social orbit
as the Antimasonic insurgency of the early 1830s. What follows is centrally
concerned with charting the paths taken as insurgent energies in Worcester
County moved from Antimasonry to antislavery.

   Abolitionist sentiment emerged in different parts of the county in 1832 and
1833, as scattered individuals began to correspond with William Lloyd Garrison,
and to challenge the complacent and racist gradualism of the American Colonization Society, which had established an auxiliary in Worcester in 1830. Abolitionism early attracted the hostility of the National elite in Worcester; in the summer
of 1835 Levi Lincoln III – the governor's son – had assaulted the Reverend
Orange Scott as he addressed an antislavery rally at the Worcester Town Hall.
Similarly, the Colonization Society was squarely situated at the center of the
National establishment, and included prominent Congregational ministers in its
ranks, whereas early abolitionists were drawn eclectically from odd corners across
the county's mosaic of culture and community, including dissident Congregationalists and particularly Quakers, who had never played a significant role in
public affairs. The first local antislavery society was founded in the strongly
Quaker town of Uxbridge in early 1834, and their leader, Quaker Effingham L.
Capron, was immediately elected vice-president of the New England Anti-Slavery
Society.[22] In December 1837 the combined clergy of the county met in
convention in Worcester to decide upon a "Declaration of Sentiments" on the
subject of slavery. Carefully avoiding provocative language, the convention
endorsed the position that slavery could only be abolished "by the Masters
themselves." At the same time, abolitionist societies spread to communities across
the county. When Joseph Goffe reported to his daughter that "the cause of antislavery appears to be fast gaining ground" in January 1838, there were thirty
societies affiliated with the Massachusetts Anti-Slavery Society scattered across

[22] Mooney, "Antislavery," 7–11, 14, 21; *Republican*, October 13, 1830; *Report of the Managers
of the Worcester County Auxiliary Colonization Society, at the Annual Meeting Held in Worcester,
December 14, 1831* (Worcester, 1832). *Vital Records of Uxbridge, Mass., to the Year 1850*
(Boston, 1916), 223; Friedman, *Gregarious Saints*, 45ff. On the opposition of the Worcester
Unitarian elite to antislavery, see Mooney, 222–3.

Antislavery

363

twenty-one towns in the county, as well as two regional societies encompassing the northern and southern halves of the county.[23]

Not content with the county ministers' timid approach, antislavery activists plunged into the campaigns to petition Congress on the subject of slavery. The first petitions from the county protesting slavery in the District of Columbia sent to Congress were from Millbury, one signed by 138 men in the winter of 1834 to 1835, and a second signed by 153 men roughly a year later. This petition was introduced by John Quincy Adams, representing the Plymouth district, and Adams orchestrated the avalanche of petitions that streamed from the county and elsewhere across the north to the Twenty-Fifth Congress between 1837 and 1839. All told, the Twenty-Fifth Congress received 128 petitions from Worcester County protesting the existence of slavery and the slave trade in the District of Columbia, fifty-four petitions protesting the tabling of antislavery petitions by Congress, and thirty-seven petitions opposing the annexation of Texas, as well as others concerned with the admission of Florida as a slave state and the establishment of diplomatic relations with Haiti.[24]

Antislavery sentiment, judging from the distribution of antislavery societies, the petition campaign, and the numbers of subscriptions to Garrison's *Liberator*,[25] touched all corners of the county. Although there were important pockets of support in the lower Blackstone Valley and in a string of towns running north from Worcester to the New Hampshire border, the core of the county's antislavery

[23] *Proceedings of a Convention of Ministers of Worcester County, on the Subject of Slavery; Held at Worcester, December 5 & 6, 1837 and January 16, 1838* (Worcester, 1838); Joseph to Eliza Goffe, January 11, 1838, Box 3, Folder 4, Joseph Goffe Papers, AAS; *Proceedings of the Massachusetts Antislavery Society, Sixth Annual Meeting, Boston, January 24, 1838*; Mooney, "Antislavery," 33–40.

[24] On Adams's role, see Richards, *John Quincy Adams*, 89–145. The petitions discussed here are located in the Records of the United States House of Representatives (Record Group 233) and the Library of Congress Collection on the House of Representatives, both located in the National Archives. I have attempted to establish a count of all the petitions from Worcester County submitted to the 23d, 24th, and 25th Congresses. The petitions are located in boxed files with either legislative record numbers (HR25 means House of Representatives, 25th Congress) or a Library of Congress, House of Representatives Collection box number (LC/HR Col.). They are also listed in two books recording petitions received by the the 2d and 3d Sessions of the 25th Congress, one listing petitions on the subject of slavery and the other listing petitions against the annexation of Texas, located in Box 122, LC/HR Col. The petitions for the abolition of slavery and the slave trade in the District of Columbia are in HR24A-H1.3 and HR25A-H1.8, and in LC/HR Col. Boxes 48, 49, 122 (not examined), 131, and 133. The petitions protesting the annexation of Texas are in HR25A-H1.1, and LC/HR Col. Box 126. The petitions against the Gag-Rule are located in HR25A-H1.7 and in LC/HR Col. Boxes 131 and 133. I am grateful to Deborah B. Van Broekhoven for sharing critical information about these National Archives holdings.

[25] *Liberator* subscriptions from Mooney, "Antislavery," 280–1.

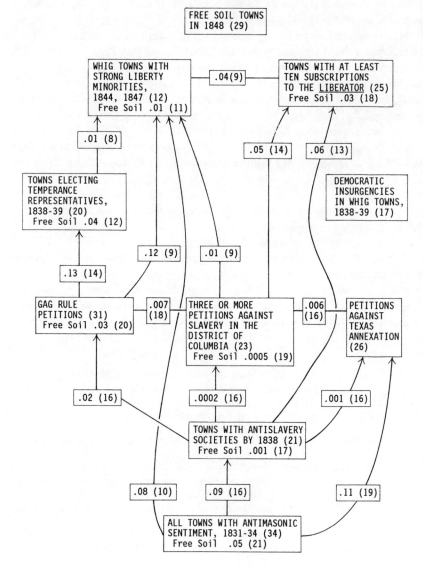

Figure 7a. Antimasonry, temperance, antislavery, and Free Soil.

```
                    ┌─────────────────┐
                    │ FREE SOIL TOWNS │
                    │  IN 1848 (29)   │
                    └─────────────────┘
```

```
┌──────────────────────────────────┐   ┌──────────────────────────────────┐
│WHIG TOWNS WITH STRONG LIBERTY      │   │TOWNS WITH AT LEAST TEN           │
│MINORITIES, 1844 & 1847 ((12)       │   │SUBSCRIPTIONS                     │
│Central corridor .006 (8/18)        │   │TO THE LIBERATOR (25)             │
│Leading Cong. Revivals,             │   │ Central corridor .19 (10/17)     │
│ 1830-32          .13  (6/18)       │   │ Shoe towns                       │
│ 1852             .13  (6/18)       │   │  in 1860s         .07 (16/28)    │
│Baptist churches                    │   └──────────────────────────────────┘
│ in 1835          .06 (10/33)       │
│ in 1850          .07 (10/34)       │
│Textile towns                       │
│ in 1860s         .18  (4/11)       │
└──────────────────────────────────┘
```

```
┌──────────────────────────────────┐   ┌──────────────────────────────────┐
│TOWNS ELECTING TEMPERANCE           │   │DEMOCRATIC INSURGENCIES           │
│REPRESENTATIVES, 1838-39 (20)       │   │IN WHIG TOWNS, 1838-39 (17)       │
│Central corridor .09 (9/17)         │   │North    .06 (11/25)              │
│Leading Cong. Revivals:             │   │Agricultural towns in             │
│ 1830-32          .15 (9/18)        │   │ in 1837 .27  (9/23)              │
│ 1842             .11 (8/15)        │   └──────────────────────────────────┘
└──────────────────────────────────┘
```

Towns sending antislavery petitions to Congress, 1835-1839:

```
┌────────────────┐  ┌──────────────────────────┐  ┌──────────────────────────┐
│GAG RULE         │  │THREE OR MORE PETITIONS    │  │PETITIONS AGAINST         │
│PETITIONS (31)   │  │AGAINST SLAVERY IN THE     │  │TEXAS ANNEXATION (26)     │
│Methodist ch.    │  │DISTRICT OF COLUMBIA (23)  │  │ Central                  │
│ in 1835 .15     │  │ Central                   │  │  corridor .03 (12/17)    │
│       (15/22)   │  │  corridor  .006 (12/17)   │  │ Shop towns               │
└────────────────┘  │ Shop towns                │  │  in 1820  .01 (11/14)    │
                    │  in 1820    .01  (10/14)  │  │ Agricultural towns:      │
                    │ Churches in 1835:         │  │  in 1837  .09 (14/23)    │
                    │  Methodist .02  (18/33)   │  │  in 1860s .08 (10/15)    │
                    │  Baptist   .04  (13/22)   │  │ Leading Cong. rev.:      │
                    │  Unitarian .12  (15/29)   │  │  1815-18  .02 (10/13)    │
                    │ Leading Cong. revivals,   │  │  1830-32  .16 (11/18)    │
                    │  1815-18    .11   (8/13)  │  └──────────────────────────┘
                    └──────────────────────────┘
```

```
┌──────────────────────────────────────────────────────┐
│TOWNS WITH ANTISLAVERY SOCIETIES BY 1838 (21)           │
│ Central corridor       .04   (10/17)                   │
│ Shop towns in 1820     .001  (11/14)                   │
│ Leading Cong. Revivals,                                │
│  1815-18               .19   (7/13)                    │
│ Methodist ch.in 1835 .14   (11/22)                     │
└──────────────────────────────────────────────────────┘
```

```
                ┌──────────────────────────────────┐
                │ ALL TOWNS WITH ANTIMASONIC         │
                │ SENTIMENT, 1831-34 (34)            │
                └──────────────────────────────────┘
```

Sources: see Appendix 2.

Figure 7b. Antimasonry, temperance, antislavery, and Free Soil.

movement lay in the center corridor: Worcester and the surrounding towns and the towns along the turnpikes and railroad leading to Boston and Springfield. (See Figure 7b.) The only exception was the distribution of Gag-Rule petitions, which had no particular geographic focus. On the other hand, although they were particularly linked with the central corridor, the antislavery towns were not necessarily centered on the small-shop and shoemaking economy or the wider orbit of Antimasonic sentiment. Towns with Antimasonic sentiment, as measured by voting pluralities, strong minorities, and petitions, and the towns joining the Free Soil–Republican coalition between 1848 and 1855 were all associated with the small-shop towns of 1820, the shoe towns of 1837, and the shoe towns of the 1860s. But the antislavery towns of the late 1830s – those towns where activists formed societies, circulated petitions, or made at least ten subscriptions to the *Liberator* – showed no particular orientation toward any economic variable in 1837 or the 1860s, although they did bear a strong relationship to the shop towns of 1820. Similarly, they were not necessarily associated with Antimasonry; Antimasonic sentiment anticipated the formation of antislavery societies, petitions against the annexation of Texas, and voting for Liberty and Free Soil in the 1840s, but not petitions on slavery in the district of Columbia or the Gag-Rule or high levels of subscription to the *Liberator*. Rather, the antislavery towns of the late 1830s seem to have shared an orientation toward certain religious variables – the Congregational revivals following the War of 1812 and during the early 1830s and the presence of Methodist and Baptist churches stand out. These patterns suggest – not surprisingly – that evangelical channels were more important than the small-shop economy or Antimasonry in spreading abolitionist sentiment through the county.

This aggregate picture is confirmed by a consideration of the prior experience of the men who joined antislavery societies in Worcester, Millbury, Leicester, and Brookfield, or who signed the early petitions from Millbury against slavery in the District of Columbia and the petitions against the Gag-Rule from Millbury and Worcester.[26] Antimasons certainly did not avoid the antislavery petitions. The first signature on the February 2, 1835, petition from Millbury was that of Ebenezer W. Goffe, Joseph's son, immediately followed by sixteen other die-hard

---

[26] Antislavery society membership from *Proceedings of the Massachusetts Antislavery Society, 1840* (Boston, 1840), xlix–lxiv; "Worcester County Anti-Slavery Society, South Division Record Book, 1840–1865," Worcester Historical Museum. Petitions of Ebenezer W. Goffe and 137 others of Millbury, February 2, 1835 (LC/HR Col. Box 48 originally in HR23A-G4.3) and John Morse and 152 others of Millbury, January 12, 1836 (HR24A-H1.3), for the abolition of slavery and the slave trade in the District of Columbia. Petitions of Elias Forbes and 244 others of Millbury, February 5, 1838 (HR25A-H1.7), Calvin Barker and 135 others of Millbury, undated, Stephan Blanchard and 60 others of West Millbury, undated, (both in LC/HR Col. Box 133, originally in HR25A-H1.7), and Austin Coltin and 95 others of Worcester, undated (HR25A-H1.7) against the Gag-Rule, to the Massachusetts Senate and House, House Docs., Unpassed Legislation, 788, 1840.

Antimasons who signed the last Antimasonic petition later that year. But a year later, after 230 men in Millbury had signed this and another petition regarding the District of Columbia, the signers of the 1835 temperance petition had edged out the Antimasons as the leading antislavery constituency. (See Appendix 3, Table 3a.) More specifically, antislavery sentiment was most strongly situated among a group who can be best described as the moral Whigs, men who signed both the Second Bank and temperance petitions; in this group Antimasons were virtually indistinguishable from non-Antimasons. Most importantly, Antimasons who avoided both the Second Bank and the temperance petitions were unlikely to sign these petitions. Precisely the same picture emerges from an analysis of the signers of five petitions against the Gag-Rule sent from Millbury and Worcester in 1838 and 1840. (See Appendix 3, Tables 2e and 3b.) In both towns temperance men outdid Antimasons in signing the Gag-Rule protests, and again the center of gravity lay among the moral Whigs – the Second Bank and temperance signers – whether or not they had Antimasonic inclinations. Even more strikingly, former Antimasons were far outnumbered by Second Bank and temperance petitioners among the signers of a petition to the Twenty-Fifth Congress from Millbury opposing the admission of Florida as a slave state.[27] (See Appendix 3, Table 3c.) Although Antimasons were clearly predominant among the male membership of the antislavery societies in Worcester, Leicester, and Millbury, these men had also declared their allegiance to moral Whiggery in signing the Second Bank and temperance petitions in large numbers. The antislavery societies also attracted Freemasons, which suggests the coalitions of the early 1830s were not critical to the new organizations. (Appendix 3, Tables 1g, 2f.) On the other hand, although these antislavery men came from the broader evangelical insurgency within the Whig ranks, they were not Log Cabin men. In Worcester, the Gag-Rule petitioners included an important selection of the Whigs newly mobilized for the 1837 campaign, but they did not contribute in significant numbers to the Log Cabin crusade.

Overall, the evidence suggests that the political landscape on which antislavery emerged can be divided into three fields. First there were the major party activists who spurned both Antimasonry and the antislavery appeal – Nationals, Democrats, and early Whigs. These men were associated with Masonry and the Worcester Agricultural Society, and, in the town of Worcester, opposed temperance legislation. Beyond these activists, of course, lay the larger Democratic and Whig constituencies historically accessible only in aggregate. Second, there was a sequence of groups that can be called the moral Whigs, spanning a spectrum from the Log Cabin Whigs – many of whom were members of the Agricultural Society – to the signers of Gag-Rule and slavery in the District petitions to the members of

---

[27] Petition of Samuel Waters and 184 others, undated, against the admission of Florida (LC/HR Col. Box 131, original in HR 25A-H1.8).

antislavery societies – often advocates of a Garrisonian antipartyism, all of
whom shared a similar background at the *intersection* of Whiggery, temperance,
and Antimasonry. And third, there was the Antimasonic majority who had
neglected to sign the Second Bank petition. Cool to Whiggery and temperance,
they were not drawn to antislavery societies or much of the early petitioning. In
the longer run, however, they were not immune to the broader antislavery
impulse.

Liberty and Free Soil

The spread of antislavery sentiment around Worcester and along the central
corridor would have important consequences for the shape of the county's politics
over the coming years. From these origins, Worcester County's central corridor
would develop into one of the most militant Free Soil–Republican regions in the
entire North. But this outcome was not yet evident in 1840. The year of the Log
Cabin found the broad spectrum of moral Whig activists sorely divided. At one
extreme, the Worcester South Antislavery Society was adamantly opposed to
involvement in party politics. For an abolitionist to vote for either of the
presidential candidates in 1840 would involve "a sacrifice of his abolitionist to
other views and principles," and the establishment of a political party devoted to the
abolition of slavery was "calculated to produce disastrous effects to the abolition
enterprise." The Gag-Rule protesters from Worcester, a middling element,
steered clear of the Log Cabin Whig demonstrations, but they did not yet have the
momentum to enter partisan politics. That October an antislavery convention met
in Worcester, and although there was sentiment to form an antislavery party, its
proponents were outnumbered by the Garrison forces. Liberty Party candidates
drew only about a thousand votes across the state that November.[28] Within two
years, however, this new party would be playing a central role in both state and
county electoral politics. In 1841 its votes tripled, and doubled again in 1842 to a
total of just over six thousand. These votes were drawn from potential Whig voters
and, with the Democrats benefiting from sympathy for the Dorr Rebellion in
Rhode Island, the result was to tip the balance against the Whigs for the second
time in four years. Although the Liberty vote was roughly 5 percent of the
statewide total, it constituted 7 percent of the total in Worcester County.
Worcester County would lead the state in votes for the Liberty Party between 1841
and 1847, reaching 14 percent of the total vote.[29]

[28] Quoted in Mooney, "Antislavery," 71–3; on the convention and the Liberty vote total, see
Mooney, 74–5, and Darling *Political Changes*, 268–71.
[29] Formisano, *The Transformation*, 351; Returns for Governor, Massachusetts Archives.

Clearly, the Liberty constituency was drawn from a segment of the broader moral Whig spectrum. The 1844 and 1847 elections produced a sample of twelve leading Liberty towns, in which Liberty votes were strong enough to come in second behind the Whigs. (See Figure 7b.) These Liberty towns were oriented toward the central corridor, and inclined to be places where there had been evidence of Antimasonic sentiment and Congregational revivalism in the early 1830s, and were likely to have Baptist churches. But rather than the shoe-and-shop economy that characterized Antimasonry, the Liberty towns had a slight tendency toward the textile economy. Within the antislavery coalition, they were typically places that had sent petitions opposing the Gag-Rule and slavery in the District of Columbia and in which there were at least ten subscriptions to the *Liberator*; on the other hand, they were not associated with towns with antislavery societies, a suggestion of the continuing division between Garrisonians and anti-Garrisonians. The Liberty towns shared with the Gag-Rule towns a strong relationship with 1838 votes for Temperance Whig representatives, suggesting a common theme of coercive, political pietism. Within these towns, it seems reasonable to suggest that the Liberty voters were men of moral Whig origins, of a profile not unlike the Worcester and Millbury Gag-Rule protesters, situated somewhere within the same intersection of Antimasonry, Whiggery, and temperance that characterized the leading elements of the antislavery coalition of the late 1830s.

There was, of course, one other important manifestation of the broader antislavery movement. Twenty-six towns sent Twenty-Fifth Congress thirty-seven petitions protesting the annexation of Texas. In aggregate, these Texas petition towns lay just outside the mainstream of the antislavery coalition. (See Figures 7a and 7b.) They were not associated with the triad of the Gag-Rule, Liberty, and 1838 Temperance towns, nor were they places with concentrations of *Liberator* subscriptions; rather, they were places with a background of Congregational revivalism and Antimasonry, and places where antislavery societies were being organized and where petitions against slavery in the District were being circulated. Oriented toward the central corridor, the economies of these anti-Texas towns tended to focus on farming rather than shoework or textiles.

Two anti-Texas petitions signed by 162 men in the south and east villages in Brookfield provide a window onto this corner of the antislavery constituency.[30] Just as the anti-Texas towns were quite distinct from the antislavery mainstream, so too were the Brookfield petitioners. (See Appendix 2, Table 4a.) Antimasons who avoided signing the Second Bank petition appeared among these anti-Texas

[30] Petitions of Rufus Harrington and 29 others of East Brookfield, September 19, 1837, John Hobbs and 134 others of Brookfield, September 25, 1837, against the annexation of Texas (HR25A-H1.1), and of Seth Field and 83 others of West Brookfield, January 31, 1839; against the admission of Florida (HR25A-H1.8).

petitioners in significant numbers, and these non-Whig Antimasons also made up an important segment of the signers of an anti-Florida petition that circulated in the west village in 1838–9. (See Appendix 3, Table 4b.) In sharp contrast, such Antimasons who sidestepped moral Whiggery made a poor showing among the Nationals and Whig activists, temperance men, antislavery society members, and Gag-Rule and slavery in the District petitioners. The only other group to draw on these non-Whig Antimasons were the Democratic activists from the six towns; suggestively, there was also a connection between Democratic affiliation and the Brookfield anti-Texas petitioners. None of the Brookfield anti-Texas petitioners were members of the Worcester South Antislavery Society, which drew its primary following in the west village. At least in Brookfield, the issue of Texas – and more broadly the expansion of the slave South – attracted the attention of men of Antimasonic inclinations who were situated outside the moral Whig mainstream of the antislavery coalition.

In aggregate, the anti-Texas towns did not bear a strong relationship to the Free Soil towns of 1848, perhaps because many of these petitions were drawn up by nonvoting women.[31] But the Brookfield anti-Texas petitioners did count in their ranks a significant number of men who would be Free Soil activists in 1848. And equally importantly, the language of the Brookfield petition – a printed form widely distributed in Massachusetts – anticipated that of Free Soil. The women's petitions – such as those from Worcester and Leicester – spoke briefly of "the sinfulness of Slavery" in protesting the annexation of Texas "with all our souls." For contrast, the Brookfield Texas petition avoided any moral appeal. The statement that these petitioners signed was divided into three heads. First, Mexico did not recognize the independence of Texas: Annexation would provoke war. Second, Congress did not have "the power to *abolish* slavery in the Several States," but it ought to stand in the way of its "*further extension.*" Third, Texas might be divided into six slave states, which would "give predominant power, in our national councils, to the slaveholding interest, and . . . reduce to complete subjugation, *the interests of the free States*, and especially, the interests of FREE LABOR, which is the foundation of their wealth and property." The result would be "A DISSOLUTION OF THE UNION."[32] These sentiments, focusing on the livelihood of laboring men hopeful of a propertied independence, had a long history in Worcester County, and would centrally shape the Free Soil–Republican appeal.

[31] The sample of petitions examined (see above, note 24) suggests that women signed Texas petitions in larger numbers than the petitions against slavery in the District or against the Gag-Rule: 16 out of 21 Texas petitions were signed by women, as against 18 out of 35 slavery in the District petitions and 18 out of 54 Gag-Rule petitions.

[32] Petitions of Lucy Earle and 165 women of Leicester, September 21, 1837, and Anne E. Colton and 169 women of Worcester, September 18, 1837, against the annexation of Texas (HR25A-H1.1), and the Brookfield Texas petitions noted above.

The Texas question grew more heated over the early 1840s, and appears to have worked to broaden the antislavery constituency. Preparing the way for Free Soil, a nonpartisan county convention met in May 1844 in Worcester to condemn the annexation of Texas. The opportunity for a fundamental break came in 1848, when the county was swept by Free Soil. Twenty-nine towns voted Free Soil in 1848, and with 43 percent of the vote, Worcester was the only Free Soil county in Massachusetts and one of only three Free Soil counties east of the Burned-Over District. After a close election, Worcester Congressional district elected Charles Allen – who had emerged as a leading antislavery figure in the 1844 convention on Texas – the only declared Free Soil congressman from Massachusetts to go to Washington.[33]

The Free Soil coalition was broad and inclusive and was ultimately much more than simply an evangelical middle-class movement. But it is also clear that it had its origins in the urban, moral intersection of Antimasonry and temperance Whiggery in which Liberty support had developed. This intersection had long been most pronounced in the growing city of Worcester.

The emergence of Free Soil in Worcester was preceded by a series of local dramas, as the rising evangelical machinist class challenged the old elite for control of the town. In November 1847 a committee had been formed to seek a city charter. The ten men chosen were the core of the old guard in Worcester; led by former Governor Levi Lincoln, nine were members of the Worcester Agricultural Society, seven were lawyers, and nine were either Whig or Democratic Party men. Only iron manufacturer Edward Earle had signed the Antimasonic petition. By the following spring the charter had been granted, but the first signs of an insurgency came when one-third of the voters refused to accept the charter. In the April elections for mayor the men in the mechanics' shops began to grumble against the nomination of Levi Lincoln. Running an opposing temperance ticket, they almost elected their candidate with 44 percent of the vote.[34] Two months later the split took on wider connotations. In early June the Whig elite, including three of the charter committeemen, announced the nomination of Zachary Taylor at the national convention in Philadelphia, and began planning for the fall election. But on the 21st, Charles Allen, as a dissident antislavery Whig delegate, attacked the Taylor nomination in a two-hour speech closely followed by "the men from the shops." A resolution written by his brother George Allen was "adopted with shouts," declaring that "Massachusetts wears no chains and spurns all bribes;

[33] Hurd, *Worcester County*, 2:1660; Joseph G. Rayback, *Free Soil: The Election of 1848* (Lexington, Ky., 1970), endpaper map; Frederick J. Blue, *The Free Soilers: Third Party Politics, 1848–1854* (Chicago, 1973), 302.

[34] Joshua S. Chasan, "Civilizing Worcester: The Creation of Institutional and Cultural Order, Worcester, Massachusetts, 1848–1876," Ph.D. dissertation, University of Pittsburgh, 1974, 25–7. Doherty, *Society and Power*, 92, argues that with establishment of the city and ward elections, skilled artisans expanded their participation in local government.

Massachusetts goes now, and will go forever, for free Soil and Free Men, Free Lips and a Free Press, for a free land and a free world." With the *Spy* as a party paper, the Free Soil movement thus got off to an early start in Worcester, with local meetings spreading the organization throughout the county by the middle of September.[35]

That September brought an important symbolic challenge to the old elite. The Mechanics Association, which had been established in Worcester in 1842 by a number of master machinists, put on its own fair and exhibition in September 1848, thereby removing itself from the auspices of the Worcester Agricultural Society. Of the judges serving in this and subsequent fairs, nine were Free Soil activists and none had served on the city charter committee.[36] The following November over 1,200 voters cast Free Soil ballots to give Martin Van Buren an overwhelming 57 percent of the presidential vote in Worcester. Antislavery politics in Worcester would be overturned only once in the years before the Civil War.

With the Free Soil explosion of 1848, antislavery politics reached far beyond the orbit of the Liberty Party, in the first of a series of surges that by 1860 would have drawn every town in the county into a Republican consensus. A broad political disquiet paved the way for Free Soil. Just as Antimasonry had mobilized older voters dissatisfied with the National Republican synthesis, Free Soil was grounded to some degree in a growing general disillusionment with party politics. An aggregate view of voting in the county and the state between 1844 and 1848 suggests that hostility to Zachary Taylor was particularly important in building the Free Soil vote in Worcester County. Where the Whig vote across the state rose by 8,000 votes between the governor's election of 1847 and the presidential vote of 1848, it dropped in Worcester County by 2,000. Even among those voting for the Whig candidate for governor in 1848, roughly 7 percent failed to vote for Taylor, in sharp contrast to the rest of the state. An equally important factor in the 1848 election was the significant drop in turnout since 1844; although participation was up from the governor's election of 1847. Both parties lost the support of significant numbers of voters after 1844, as a growing hostility toward the structure and content of party politics began to take hold. The exact origins of the Free Soil vote are difficult to determine, but if these discouraged voters dropping out of electoral politics between 1844 and 1847 are taken into account, it seems likely that Free Soil drew on a potential pool of once-active voters made up of roughly 40 percent former Whigs, 30 percent former Democrats, and 30 percent Liberty men. Of course there were new voters brought into this election – and they may have

---

[35] Mooney, "Antislavery," 152–6; *Spy*, June 21, 28, through September 20, 1848.
[36] Chasan, "Civilizing Worcester," 164–9, biographical data, 452–88; Free Soil activists from *Spy*, June 28, September 6, 1848.

been relatively important in the county – but their numbers are impossible to determine.[37]

A tinge of Democratic experience is evident in the profile of the Free Soil activists from Worcester and some of the surrounding towns,[38] but if former Democrats made up as much as 30 percent of the Free Soil vote in 1848, their impact was certainly not decisive in the traditionally Democratic towns. The twenty-nine towns that voted Free Soil in 1848 had a familiar profile. (See Figures 7 and 8.) All but five had been Federalist in the early 1820s, all but eight had harbored Antimasonic sentiment of varying intensity in the early 1830s; they included most of the temperance towns and the towns in the broader antislavery coalition of the late 1830s, as well as the Liberty towns. But, unlike the temperance, antislavery, and Liberty towns, they showed no particular religious orientation, other than toward the presence of Baptists.

As much as any other factor, Free Soil voting was associated with the small-shop economy and shoemaking of the central corridor towns, another point of commonality with the Antimasonic towns and a point of difference with the temperance, antislavery, and Liberty towns. All but two of the seventeen central corridor towns, all but two of the twelve 1820 small-shop towns, and all but two of the twelve 1837 shoe towns voted Free Soil in 1848. Agricultural and textile towns, north county and south county towns, all fell far behind, leaning toward their

---

[37] *The possible sources of the Free Soil vote: 1844–8*

	County		State	
	Number	Percent	Number	Percent
Whig dropouts, 1844–7	1,172	*14*	13,267	*32*
Whig dropouts, 1847–8	2,191	*27*	0	
Dem dropouts, 1844–7	1,880	*23*	13,641	*33*
Dem dropouts, 1847–8	579	*7*	4,117	*10*
Maximum Liberty vote	2,253	*28*	10,830	*26*
"Available" for Free Soil	8,075	*100*	41,855	*100*
Other voters	576		?	
Free Soil, 1848	8,651		38,307	

Note: The voters who "dropped out" of party politics are estimated from the decline in votes cast in 1844, 1847, and 1848. This method can only be impressionistic at best. For the problems of voter turnover inherent in this analysis, see Kenneth J. Winkle, "A Social Analysis of Voter Turnout in Ohio, 1850–1860," *Journal of Interdisciplinary History*, 13 (1983), 411–35.
Source: Darling, *Political Changes*, 319, 345, 354; *Aegis*, November 13, 1844; *Spy*, November 15, 1844; Returns for Governor, MA.
[38] Free Soil activists in towns throughout Worcester County are listed in the *Spy*, June 14, 21, 28, July 5, 26, August 2, 16, 23, September 6, 13, 20, 1848.

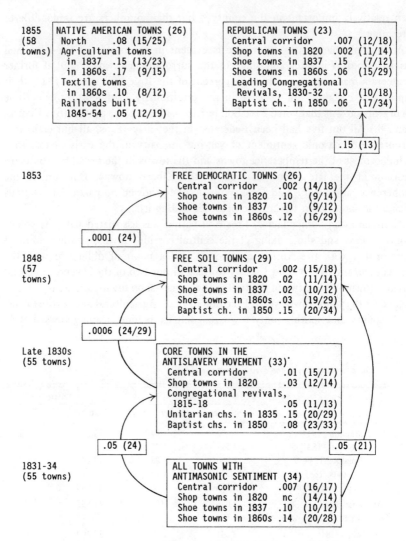

1855
(58
towns)

NATIVE AMERICAN TOWNS (26)
North   .08 (15/25)
Agricultural towns
  in 1837 .15 (13/23)
  in 1860s .17 (9/15)
Textile towns
  in 1860s .10 (8/12)
Railroads built
  1845-54 .05 (12/19)

REPUBLICAN TOWNS (23)
Central corridor   .007 (12/18)
Shop towns in 1820   .002 (11/14)
Shoe towns in 1837   .15 (7/12)
Shoe towns in 1860s   .06 (15/29)
Leading Congregational
  Revivals, 1830-32   .10 (10/18)
Baptist ch. in 1850   .06 (17/34)

.15 (13)

1853

FREE DEMOCRATIC TOWNS (26)
Central corridor   .002 (14/18)
Shop towns in 1820   .10 (9/14)
Shoe towns in 1837   .10 (9/12)
Shoe towns in 1860s   .12 (16/29)

.0001 (24)

1848
(57
towns)

FREE SOIL TOWNS (29)
Central corridor   .002 (15/18)
Shop towns in 1820   .02 (11/14)
Shoe towns in 1837   .02 (10/12)
Shoe towns in 1860s   .03 (19/29)
Baptist ch. in 1850   .15 (20/34)

.0006 (24/29)

Late 1830s
(55 towns)

CORE TOWNS IN THE
ANTISLAVERY MOVEMENT (33)*
Central corridor   .01 (15/17)
Shop towns in 1820   .03 (12/14)
Congregational revivals,
  1815-18   .05 (11/13)
Unitarian chs. in 1835   .15 (20/29)
Baptist chs. in 1850   .08 (23/33)

.05 (24)   .05 (21)

1831-34
(55 towns)

ALL TOWNS WITH
ANTIMASONIC SENTIMENT (34)
Central corridor   .007 (16/17)
Shop towns in 1820   nc   (14/14)
Shoe towns in 1837   .10 (10/12)
Shoe towns in 1860s   .14 (20/28)

*Towns with any two of the following: antislavery societies, at least ten subscriptions to the _Liberator_, or petitions against slavery in the District of Columbia, the Gag-Rule, or the annexation of Texas.

nc=noncalculable. Sources: see Appendix 2.

Figure 8. Antimasonry, antislavery, and the Free Soil–Republican insurgency.

traditional affiliations in Whiggery and Democracy. If the connection between the small-shop economy and Antimasonry was reasonably strong, its connection with Free Soil was overwhelming. Particularly interestingly, none of the initiatives within the antislavery coalition, nor a core group of thirty-three antislavery towns, showed the consistent orientation toward the shop and shoe economy that was so evident in Antimasonry and Free Soil, as well as the subsequent coalitions making up the Free Democrats and early Republican Party. The few Free Soil activists who can be identified also seem to have been inclined toward Antimasonry and the shoe economy. Twelve of the twenty-seven Free Soil leaders in Brookfield had signed an 1843 petition calling for tariffs on imported boots and shoes. The petition was clearly rooted in the Whig orbit in Brookfield, but it was couched in terms of a defense of labor; such a tariff would enable the shoe industry "to compete with the manufactures of Foreign Countries, without resorting to the low-wages system, which has crushed the laboring classes of Europe to the dust." And a minimal showing by the non-Whig Antimasons among the Free Soil activists from the six towns examined here in detail suggests – as do the voting aggregates – that Free Soil had a broader constituency than simply the moral Whiggery that had lain behind the abolitionist and Liberty sentiment of the preceding decade.[39] (See Appendix 3, Tables 1h, 2g, 3c, 4d.)

Once again, an insurgent politics surged through the strategic center of the county's politics and economy, in a distant echo of the provincial tradition of Popular orthodoxy. Within this center, Free Soil was compounded of at least two major strands, one responding to the evangelical imperatives of abolition and the second particularly shaped by the circumstances of the shop and shoe economy, and by the insurgent impulses rooted in that world.

Constrasting visions: "Hired laborers" or "a portion of the soil"

The Republican ideology of the 1850s would bring a broad summation, deriving its strength from themes and experiences from across the spectrum of political culture and action in the county, the commonwealth, and across the entire north.

---

[39] *Liberator* subscriptions from Mooney, "Antislavery," 280–1; broadly similar antislavery profiles have been established by Goodman, "The Politics of Industrialism"; Edward Magdol, "A Window on the Abolitionist Constituency: Antislavery Petitions, 1836–1839," in Kraut, ed., *Crusaders and Compromisers*, 45–70; and *The Antislavery Rank and File: A Social Profile of the Abolitionists' Constituency* (New York, 1986), 61–97; and Baum, *The Civil War Party System*, 73–100. The thirty-three "core antislavery towns" were defined as those towns which were characterized by any two of the following: antislavery societies in 1838, submitted three slavery in the District petitions, one Texas petition, or one Gag-Rule petition, or where there were ten or more subscriptions to the *Liberator*.

This summation would fuse themes of Lockean voluntarism and Harringtonian independence, priorities that had been in subtle competition for dominance within the county's political culture since the era of the Land Bank and the Great Awakening. But this summation would only come under the hand of Abraham Lincoln in the ensuing years of crisis and war, and in the preceding years these competing visions lay behind the deep fissures within the broader antislavery movement.[40]

Most fundamentally, abolitionism was grounded in an extreme Lockean worldview: individuals were to be freed from all constraints to act as rational, autonomous beings. The essential goals of abolition lay in the immediate liberation of blacks from slavery, and in the achievement of equality under the law for all citizens. With roots in part in the Finneyite revivals, which announced that the responsibility of moral beings was to act to perfect the world, abolitionism was powerfully informed by an aspiration that the human condition might be freed of restrictions of any sort, becoming a utopian state of nature in which individuals would be free to act on moral and rational grounds. Most basically, abolitionists saw slavery as merely the most extreme of a host of contemporary irrational interventions against human freedom.[41]

The abolitionist mentality had a deep-running anti-institutional strain, which had an immediate local impact. Not since the separations of the 1740s were there such wrenching assaults on the county's churches, as abolitionists condemned the conservatism of their ministers and fellow church members, and were condemned in turn. Deacon Josiah Henshaw, a prominent abolitionist in West Brookfield, was accused of belonging to "a society, whose apparent object is to strip the Church, the Clergy, and the Sabbath of their sanctity; a society whose members profess to believe the Church, the Clergy and the Sabbath are all of the Devil."[42] The Baptist Church in Southbridge, itself a lineal descendent of the Sturbridge Separates, was divided when abolitionists forced a vote on slavery in 1842; here the new Lockean thrust of abolitionism collided with the old. In an echo of the events

[40] The following discussion is particularly indebted to Eric Foner, "Abolitionism and the Labor Movement in Antebellum America," in *Politics and Ideology in the Age of the Civil War* (New York, 1980), 57–76; David B. Davis, *The Problem of Slavery in the Age of Revolution* (Ithaca, 1975), 347ff.; and Alan Dawley, *Class and Community: The Industrial Revolution in Lynn* (Harvard, 1976), 238–9; Lawrence Friedman, "'Pious Fellowship' and Modernity: A Psychosocial Interpretation," in Kraut, ed., *Crusaders and Compromisers*, 235–61; and Victor Turner, *The Ritual Process: Structure and Anti-Structure* (Ithaca, 1969).
[41] Ronald G. Walters, *The Antislavery Appeal: American Abolition after 1830* (Baltimore, 1976), 12–17, 54ff., 70ff., 111–28; Lewis Perry, *Radical Abolitionism: Anarchy and the Government of God in Antislavery Thought* (Ithaca, 1973), 15–16; Friedman, *Gregarious Saints,* 230–2; David B. Davis, "The Rise of Immediatism in British and American Antislavery Thought," *Mississippi Valley Historical Review* 49 (1962), 209–30; John L. Thomas, "Romantic Reform in America," *AQ* 17 (1965), 656–81.
[42] Walters, *Antislavery Appeal,* 6–9; Quarterly Meeting, June 28, 1842, Worcester County Antislavery Society, South Division, Record Book, 1840–65, WHM.

of a century before, the antiabolitionist separatists were led out by Deacon Henry Fisk, a grandson of the Henry Fisk who had led the separates out of the orthodox church in 1747. In North Brookfield abolitionists withdrew from their churches to form a nondenominational Union Society of likeminded comeouters.[43]

Among the Garrisonians, restrictions on the legal rights of women were natural targets for immediatist assault. If Abigail Kelley was the most prominent of the women's rights advocates in the county's abolitionist circle,[44] she was closely followed by Lucy Stone of North Brookfield. The granddaughter of Francis Stone, a leading Regulator, Lucy Stone's feminism took her far beyond the corporate world of her origins into a firm conviction of the Lockean state of nature. In 1853 she confronted William Greene, delegate to the constitutional convention for Brookfield. Greene told the assembled delegates that he had no argument when Lucy Stone demanded the natural right to vote on the constitutional amendments, since the preamble to the state constitution described it as a "covenant," a "social compact," mutually entered into by the "whole people." "She will say that she wants to enter into that covenant; and how can any men vote to refuse the privilege to women of entering into this compact, and at the same time affirm that the social compact is formed by a voluntary association or agreement of the whole people?"[45] Women were expressing their demands in the Lockean language forged by dissenters a century before, and taken up by abolitionists in the 1830s.

But Lockean individual autonomy provided a decidedly limited program for abolitionists' prescriptions for the end of slavery. The county's ministers in their 1837 "Declaration of Sentiments" had placed a premium on the means of a moral individualism when they stipulated that "Emancipation, to be of any value to the Slave, must be the free voluntary act of the Master, performed from a conviction of its propriety." The articles adopted by the Leicester Anti-Slavery Society, a printed form distributed by the New England Anti-Slavery Society, enumerated the limited set of "motives" for their single "object" of "the extinction of slavery." Most broadly, slaves were denied their natural rights of "life, liberty, and the pursuit of happiness"; they were unjustly and criminally reduced to property, and they were "compelled to labor without reward." In a final passage these articles invoked the central theme of Lockean voluntarism: "We would plead with the slave-holder to liberate his slaves, and to treat them as rational beings, with justice

[43] Mooney, "Antislavery," 106; *History of the Division of the First Baptist Church in Southbridge, Mass., Which Took Place in September 1842* (Worcester, 1842), 18; Temple, *North Brookfield*, 285; see Perry, *Radical Abolitionism*, 92–128; Glenn C. Altschuler and Jan M. Saltsgaber, *Revivalism, Social Conscience, and Community in the Burned-Over District: The Trial of Rhoda Bement* (Ithaca, 1983).

[44] Friedman, *Gregarious Saints*, 45.

[45] *Official Report of the Debates and Proceedings in the State Convention assembled May 4th, 1853, to Revise and Amend the Constitution* . . . (Boston, 1853), 1:47; Temple, *North Brookfield*, 746–8.

and humanity." But another passage suggests how such "rational beings" were to be "treated," in an argument for "the good of both masters and slaves" in emancipation. "[W]e have facts enough to prove that the interests of the masters will rather be promoted than made to suffer by the immediate, simultaneous emancipation, with a view to their employment as *hired laborers*, of all the slaves in the Union."[46] The history of reconstruction would prove that freed slaves had very different aspirations, aspirations that were not fundamentally different from those of northern whites. While abolitionists promised the fruits of their labor, freed slaves would be more interested in the means to their independence. Nowhere in the abolitionist ideology was there a place for property and economic independence for freed men and women: simple legal freedom was sufficient to meet the demands of conscience. Meeting these demands of conscience was as much as the women of Leicester seem to have hoped for when they signed a petition for the abolition of slavery and the slave trade in the District of Columbia. Their petition would "at least be a 'memorial of us,' that in the holy cause of Human Freedom, 'We have done what we could.'"[47]

   Whereas the antislavery society members and the petitioners against slavery in the District of Columbia can be termed immediatist abolitionists, the Gag-Rule petitioners and Liberty Party voters cannot; they were concerned primarily with the political rights of northern whites. But these activists shared the Lockean imperative that drove abolitionist sentiment. The Gag-Rule petitions were couched in terms of the language of rights and contract: the Gag-Rule was "a violation of the Federal Constitution, and an outrage on the rights of the people," it was a threat "to the fundamental principles of republican government, to the rights of minorities, to the sovereignty of the People, and TO THE UNION OF THESE UNITED STATES."[48] The common background in moral Whiggery that Gag-Rule petitioners shared with the District petitioners was equally significant. The combination of moral individualism and capitalist inclination manifested in support for temperance and the Second Bank was certainly compatible with the abolitionist position that freed blacks would become "hired laborers." Again, it is important that – in Brookfield at least – the Antimasons who avoided the Second Bank petition did not respond to the Lockean language of those abolitionist and Liberty initiatives. They did respond when the issue was couched in rather different terms.

   Free Soil would present a fundamentally different set of priorities, defined not

[46] Constitution of the Antislavery Society of Leicester, in Leicester, Mass., Papers, AAS (emphasis in original).

[47] Petition of Lucy Earle and 177 women of Leicester, January 3, 1838, against slavery in the District of Columbia (HR25A H1.8). For an analysis of the aspirations of the freedmen, and their conflict with abolitionist assumptions about emancipation, see Eric Foner, *Nothing But Freedom: Emancipation and Its Legacy* (Baton Rouge, 1983), esp. 55–6, 82–6, 107–8.

[48] Petitions of Elias Forbes et al. and Calvin Barker et al., of Millbury, against the Gag-Rule.

by Lockean voluntarism, but from the conservative, Harringtonian assumptions about property and independence, with their calculus of personal advantage and the public good. In its platform crafted at Buffalo in August 1848, the Free Soilers abandoned abolitionist demands for full legal equality for black Americans and explicitly disavowed direct interference with slavery in the states where it existed. It made no reference to slaves beng denied the rewards of their labor. Rather, it called broadly for "Free soil, free speech, free labor and free men." The extension of slavery into the western territories posed a threat to the aspirations of laboring men throughout the north. And, in violation of the laissez-faire beliefs of both southern Democrats and northern abolitionists, the Free Soilers advocated an activist role for the federal government, supporting both tariffs and internal improvements. But its most fundamental appeal was bound up in the slogan of "Free Soil." Here there was a powerful summation, a double meaning: Slavery was to be kept out of the territories, and the government was to make a "Free Grant" of land to "Actual Settlers, in consideration of the expenses they incur in making settlements in the wilderness." Four years later, the Free Democratic Party elaborated upon this language, resolving that "all men have a natural right to a portion of the soil; and that, as the use of the soil is indispensible to life, the right of all men to the soil is as sacred as their right to life itself." The public lands were "not to be sold to individuals nor granted to corporations, but should be held as a sacred trust . . ., and should be granted in limited quantities, free of cost, to landless settlers."[49]

The Free Soil and Free Democratic resolutions on the free distribution of land to settlers was borrowed from the Land Reform program of the National Reform Association, and here there were direct links with the Harringtonian tradition. Organized by George Henry Evans in New York City in 1844, the National Reform Association was one expression of the defensive stance of the American labor movement in the wake of the destruction of unions and economic hard times of the late 1830s. Based on the English agrarianism of Thomas Spence, whose proposals for the nationalization of land in Great Britain were drawn directly from his reading of Harrington's *Oceana*, the Land Reformers proposed the establishment of "Rural Republican Townships" in the west, where unemployed eastern mechanics and laborers would be given free grants of land, grants that were to be strictly limited in size and to be inalienable and exempt from seizure for debt. Rather than liberalism's simple compensation for labor, Evans and the Land Reformers proposed republican independence in the ownership of the means of subsistence and production. Even the Regulators of 1786 had failed to espouse the Harringtonian agrarian law of a limitation of property holdings, but the Land

---

[49] Free Soil and Free Democratic platforms, in Blue, *The Free Soilers*, 295–6, 299; for a recent assessment of Free Soil, see Richard H. Sewell, "Slavery, Race, and the Free Soil Party, 1848–1854," in Kraut, ed., *Crusaders and Compromisers*, 101–24.

Reformers made it a central part of their plan to restore the rough equality among households that had been destroyed in the process of industrial development.[50]

This nostalgic vision of a utopian republican society of equal and independent farming households had a counterpart in the Land League of disappointed English Chartists, and was espoused by New York City's most radical labor organizer, "shirtless" Mike Walsh. Popular with the transcendental communitarians at Brook Farm, the National Reform Association struck deeper roots when in 1845 it combined with the New England Workingmen's Association, and in 1846 undertook a national effort to encourage landless laborers to "Vote Yourself a Farm." In the fall of 1845 producers' and consumers' cooperative unions were founded in the same workingmen's circles, and rapidly spread across Massachusetts, only to collapse in the early 1850s.[51]

There are indications that cooperation took hold in parts of Worcester County. Such sentiments could be found among scattered families of English immigrants, such as the woolworking Hollingworths, as early as the 1820s. John Hollingworth wrote to his uncle from south Leicester in 1827, urging him to "fall in cooperative with us" in taking up land in western New York, which included a water privilege fit for a small mill.

> [I]t is our firm opinion that it will be best to form ourselves into a system after the manner of Robert Owen's plan, that is to form ourselves into a society in common to help and assist each other and to have one common stock, for it is the unnatural ideas of thine and mine that produces all the evils of tyranny, slavery, poverty, and oppression of the present day.[52]

The Hollingworths never did move to the west, but they were immersed in a world where "cooperative" – and Harringtonian – ideals flourished. John's brother Joseph posted up his Antimasonic doggerel before leaving south Leicester in 1831, but three years later he had returned, and with his father George signed 1834 Antimasonic petition. Four years later they were in Brookfield, and were among the signers of the petition against the annexation of Texas.[53] Here they were moving in an orbit at the intersection of Antimasonry and the Democratic

---

[50] On Spence and Harrington, see Olive D. Rudkin, *Thomas Spence and His Connections* (New York, 1966), 19–20, 115, 163; on Evans and Land Reform, see Norman Ware, *The Industrial Worker, 1840–1860: The Reaction of American Industrial Society to the Advance of the Industrial Revolution* (Boston, 1924), 180–4; and Wilentz, *Chants Democratic*, 335, 356–7, 384. On the connections between Land Reform and Free Soil see Rayback, *Free Soil*, 220–2, 264–6; and Foner, "Abolitionism and the Labor Movement," 61–2, 69–70, 72, 73; Foner, "Causes," 28.
[51] Wilentz, *Chants Democratic*, 330–6; Ware, *The Industrial Worker*, 177–8, 185–193; Rayback, *Free Soil*, 220.
[52] Leavitt, ed., *The Hollingworth Letters*, 5–6, see also 57–8.
[53] Leavitt, ed., *The Hollingworth Letters*, 74–6; Leicester Antimasonic Petition, 1834, House Unpassed, 13904A, Petition of Rufus Harrington et al. of East Brookfield, against the annexation of Texas.

Workingmen where cooperatism took root in the late 1840s. In 1850 there was a cooperative paper mill operating in nearby Hardwick, where Antimasonry swept all four governor's elections between 1831 and 1834, the Workingmen's candidate got a small minority in 1834, and Democrats did well during the 1840s. Two men involved in the mill in the 1830s, William Dickinson and William Mixter, signed the 1834 Antimasonic petition.[54] But cooperatism was also firmly rooted in Brookfield, where Antimasons had gravitated toward the Bancroft and Working-men's wing of the Democratic Party. In 1852 there were three cooperative New England Protective Union stores in Brookfield and West Brookfield. John P. Robinson, a partner in the largest central shoe shop in Brookfield, had been an Antimason and an agent for the Millbury *Plebian and Workingmen's Advocate*, as was an Antimasonic merchant in West Brookfield. The agent of the Protective Union store in Brookfield, Frederick Brigham, had signed the 1843 shoe tariff petition; he was the son of another Antimasonic merchant (and the grandson of a signer of the progovernment protest of January, 1787). In 1851 he, with his brother Charles, signed a petition requesting a charter for a bank in Brookfield; believing "the present organization of the currency to be unjust and oppressive," the petitioners moved to establish a bank, "the capital of which shall consist of *real estate*." In joining in this petition, with its echoes of the Land Bank of 1740, the Brigham brothers were in the company of three survivors of the Antimasonic crusade, five anti-Texas petitioners, two other shoe tariff petitioners, and at least two of the town's leading Free Soil activists.[55]

Thus there seems to have been a broad affinity among earlier traditions of Antimasonic and Workingmen's activism, the land reform and cooperative movements, and the rise of Free Soil antislavery politics. Although his first concern was the northern workingman, George Henry Evans favored the elimination of slavery, and there were strong suggestions of land reform impulses when Alexander DeWitt of Oxford, once a Democrat, now a Free Soiler, pressed for the rights of free blacks to homestead land in the west, and when Eli Thayer of Worcester organized the New England Emigrant Aid Company to help poor Yankee farmers settle in Kansas to directly confront the slave power.[56] There

---

[54] Paige, *Hardwick*, 310; Ware, *The Industrial Worker*, 187; Hardwick Antimasonic Petition, 1834, House Unpassed 13904A, MA.

[55] Massachusetts Register, 1852, 226; *Plebian and Advocate*, March 23, 1831; Brookfield Antimasonic Petitions, 1833, 1834, House Unpassed 12324 and 13904A; Brookfield Bank Petition, April 6, 1851, Senate Unpassed 12244 (emphasis in original); see also Brookfield Bank Petition, February, 1851, Senate Unpassed 13242/1. Free Soil Association and Delegates, Massachusetts *Spy*, September 6, 1848. On the basis of last names, at least three other Free Soil activists had connections with bank petitioners.

[56] Sewell, "Slavery, Race, and the Free Soil Party," in Kraut, *Crusaders and Compromisers*, 114; Mooney, "Antislavery," 214, 218, 229; Samuel A. Johnson, "The Genesis of the New England Aid Company," *NEQ* 3 (1930), 95–122; Hurd, *Worcester County*, 2:1669–72.

were also important connections with the critique of the industrial corporate capitalism that had underlain the more radical Antimasonry of men like Amasa Walker. Addressing the North Brookfield Lyceum in January 1848, Reubin Robinson listed among the "present organizations of society" that violated human freedom, slavery, serfdom, and the "system of oppression ... which gives to capital the exclusive command and control of labor." Robinson played on the Lockean assumptions that distinguished free-labor capitalism from slavery. Industrial capitalism "asserts no absurd right of property in man. It admits and insists upon the equality of all men; taunts and condemns those who deny it; but at the same time exalts the few and tramples upon the many."[57]

The state constitutional convention of 1853 was the occasion for a concerted effort to contain the power of corporations. Isaac Davis of Worcester and Alexander DeWitt both advocated a general law of incorporation on Jacksonian lines, but Amasa Walker delivered the most detailed attack on corporate power. Walker remained a Democrat from the breakup of Antimasonry until the fall of 1848, when he joined the Free Soil leadership. Representing North Brookfield in the 1853 convention, he condemned the entire system of incorporation for manufacturing in language that echoed that of Amos Singletary of Sutton at the ratifying convention six decades before. Fully half the wealth of the commonwealth was "embarked in enterprises of a corporate character," and this concentration gave undue power to a few well-placed individuals. Incorporation also destroyed "the natural relation between capital and labor," which were bound together as "natural copartners in production, and natural competitors for profits." Since society would not incorporate laborers, it should not incorporate capital. In the final analysis, Walker declared, [t]his system of corporations is nothing more than a moneyed feudalism; ... It concentrates vast masses of wealth, it places immense power in a few hands, and gives to both a permanent existence." Where Amos Singletary had seen the "great Leviathan" in a centralized national government, Amasa Walker saw it in incorporated capital.[58]

In the course of this speech, Amasa Walker pointed to the city of Worcester as the epitome of the social order that he espoused. Worcester had "not a single corporation there for any industrial purpose, and yet it is the most flourishing city in the Commonwealth." In language taken straight from the Harringtonian tradition, Walker argued that although towns dominated by industrial corporations were inhabited by tenants, Worcester was a city of "freeholders." Its most numerous citizens were "mechanics who do business on their own account, and who, when they acquire wealth, but a piece of land and build a house upon it. They are independent men, and act as they choose, and vote as they please."[59]

[57] Reubin T. Robinson, *The Development of the Idea of Human Freedom: A Lecture before the North Brookfield Lyseum, Delivered January 5, 1848* (Boston, 1848), 13–16.
[58] *Official Report ... 1853*, 3:59–62. See commentary in Eric Foner, *Free Soil, Free Labor, Free Men: the Ideology of the Republican Party before the Civil War* (New York, 1970), 22.
[59] *Official Report ... 1853*, 3:61.

Such a decentralized shop economy, with no corporations, had been evident since 1820 both in Worcester and along the central corridor; the 1843 shoe tariff petition had focused on this condition in noting that the 50,000 people working in the shoe trade in Massachusetts "are connected with no corporations, the business being sustained entirely by individual enterprise." These circumstances gave Worcester the qualities that drew George Frisbie Hoar to the Worcester bar and Thomas Wentworth Higginson to the pulpit of Worcester Free Church. Hoar extolled the "unsurpassed ingenuity" of Worcester's mechanics, and described the city and county as "the spot on the face of the earth where labor got the largest proportion of the joint production of labor and capital." Higginson called Worcester a "new cradle of liberty," and the members of his congregation "Jerusalem wild cats," "intelligent mechanics, a special breed . . . with keen eyes for machinery and reform." There was in Worcester "as much radicalism . . . as in Lynn, but more varied, more cultivated, and more balanced by an opposing force."[60] In the Free Soil insurgency the mechanics of Worcester rose up against this "opposing force," the old Nationals and party men of the Jeffersonian tradition. Firmly rooted in the networks of shoe production and shopwork along the central corridor, where the typical work experience was industrial, but still had qualities of the old agricultural household, and in the antimonopolist sentiment nurtured by Antimasonry, Free Soil voiced the old Harringtonian priorities of property, independence, and commonwealth. Here, rooted in traditional structures but not confined by them, the antislavery insurgency took a strong and deep grip.

The "subsoil plow": Nativism and the rise of the Republican Party

In 1850 Free Soil, now known as the Free Democratic Party, would again win in Worcester County, when Daniel Webster made allegiance to the Compromise of 1850, particularly its fugitive slave provisions, a condition of Whig loyalty. Throughout Massachusetts, Whig support for the compromise was seen as a conspiracy by the wealthy cotton-manufacturing Boston Whig elite, and Democrats and Free Soilers established a coalition that lasted for two years, based on a common agenda of opposition to the slave power and reform of the state laws.[61]

Again in 1852, when the Whigs regained control of the state, Worcester was the only county in the state to cast a majority for Horace Mann, the Free Democratic candidate for governor. The county was also the leading advocate of constitutional reform, and its six thousand vote margin was critical in the passage of a referendum calling for a constitution convention to consider issues ranging from

---

[60] Hoar, *Autobiography*, 1:159; Mooney, "Antislavery," 192, 196, 202.

[61] Formisano, *Transformation*, 330–1; Goodman, "The Politics of Industrialism"; Blue, *The Free Soilers*, 212–31; Kevin Sweeney, "Rum, Romanism, Representation, and Reform: Coalition Politics in Massachusetts, 1847–1853," *Civil War History* 12 (1976), 116–37.

the structure of the legislation, qualifications for the franchise, and a general law of incorporation. The next year, although the county voted almost 2 to 1 in favor of the various amendments, the constitutional revisions were rejected by voters across the state; in the fall election, Free Democratic candidate Henry Wilson received his only county majority from Worcester.[62]

The Free Democratic constituency was virtually the same as Free Soil. Free Democratic voting again was strongest in the central corridor and in the shoe towns, with Antimasonic and more especially antislavery roots. The central corridor towns overwhelmingly supported calling the constitutional convention in 1853, two-thirds voting in favor by a 2-to-1 margin. In a distant echo of the constitutional politics of the 1770s, the weight of the opposition to the convention came from northern towns of Whig politics and an agricultural economy. Again, northern Whig towns were the most likely to oppose the proposed constitutional amendments when they were put to a ratifying vote the next year.

But it is also clear that the voters in the central corridor and Free Democratic towns were distinctly less enthusiastic about ratifying the new constitution than they had been in calling for the convention to meet. Exactly which provisions of the proposed constitution alienated which part of the Worcester County electorate is difficult to say. The convention proposed amendments abolishing imprisonment for debt, and restricting the powers of corporations and banks. But most importantly, the convention was a symptom of fundamental changes taking place in the economic and demographic structure of the commonwealth. Fueled by the spread of railroads, industry and population were rapidly concentrating in urban places, and the small towns across the state were beginning to fall into a long decline. The 1850 census had recorded these changes, which had accelerated in the preceding decade, and Article 13 of the existing constitution required that as soon as population reached 770,000 representation was to be redistributed on a sliding scale. The result was that the declining or slow-growing smaller towns were threatened with the losses of their ancient right of annual representation in the General Court.

The call for a constitution to defend the rights of the small towns took on a double-edged quality. In part it had much of the old animus against the "money power," the wealthy interests – particularly those of Boston – which seemed to control the large, growing cities and towns. But there was also a strong current of moralistic nativism running through the proconvention rhetoric; the cities and industrial towns were home to the growing immigrant population who had different political priorities than the native-born, particularly on the issue of slavery. The convention's plan to protest the corporate representation of the small towns was couched in terms that conflated ethnicity and virtue, turn-

---

[62] *Official Report . . . 1853*, 1:736, 768.

ing the commonwealth's republican tradition to the uses of xenophobic nativism.[63]

The year following the defeat of the new constitution the Kansas–Nebraska Act and the Fugitive Slave Law brought violent demonstrations of antislavery sentiment. The arrest of escaped slave Anthony Burns in Boston enraged people throughout the state, and a band of fifty men from Worcester went down to Boston to participate in the unsuccessful attempt to free him. That fall, when Burn's captor, Federal Marshal Asa Butman, arrived in Worcester on the trail of another escaped slave, he barely survived the rage of a large crowd of black and white rioters.[64] But in 1854 the tidal wave of Nativism also swept across Massachusetts. Organizing in secret "Know-Nothing" Lodges, the Native American party took control of both the county and the state with 62 percent of the vote. Although some of the votes were close, the Nativist candidate for governor, Henry Gardner, won in every single town in Worcester County. The question of who the Nativist voters were – and where they went – is particularly controversial, and on this question hinges the definition of the Republican Party as motivated primarily by antislavery or xenophobia.[65] In Massachusetts the issue is compounded by the fact that the 1854 election saw a drop in turnout, and that the Know-Nothings seem to have drawn previously inactive men into electoral politics. In Worcester, the records of several Know-Nothing lodges suggest that the majority were young men of relatively little property, living in boardinghouses and employed in manufacturing. Most of these must have been recent migrants, many from small towns throughout the county. Many antislavery voters must have turned to the Native American Party; in Worcester County the Free Democratic vote of 1854 was only 27 percent of its 1853 total, while both Whigs and Democrats managed to hold onto 45 percent.[66] But, if many Free Democrats voted Nativist in 1854, they moved on to the Republicans in 1855. Although the state remained in the hands of the Nativists through 1856, the Native Americans' vote in the county dropped from 62 percent in 1854 to 3 percent in 1855, with the Republicans winning in a four-way election. The next year, when the State Republicans formed a coalition

[63] "Rum, Romanism, and Reform"; Shapiro, "The Conservative Dilemma: The Massachussests Constitutional Convention of 1853," *NEQ* 33 (1960), 216–17; Oscar Handlin, *Boston's Immigrants, 1790–1860*, revised ed. (New York, 1974), 178–206; *A Few Facts and Reasons Why a Convention Should Be Called to Revise the Constitution* (Boston, 1852), 4–5, 21–4.

[64] Mooney, "Antislavery," 218–21, 229–31; Hoar, *Autobiography*, 182–5.

[65] Baum, *The Civil War Party System*, 24–54, argues that Nativists did not make up a significant part of the Republican coalition in Massachusetts, but it seems clear that many indeed did join the party in the late 1850s. See William E. Gienap's critique of Baum in "Nativism and the Creation of a Republican Majority in the North before the Civil War," *JAH* 72 (1985), 556–8.

[66] Baum, *Civil War Party System*, 33; George H. Haynes, "A Chapter from the Local History of Knownothingism," *New England Magazine* N.S. 15 (1896), 82–96; *Massachusetts Register* (1855); Votes for Governor MA.

with the Nativists, a disproportionate number of Worcester County Republicans –
while voting for Fremont for president – boycotted the Nativist-Republican
candidate for governor. In 1857 the county vote again led the state with
neighboring Franklin and Hampshire, as the Republicans won the governorship
for the first time.[67] (See Appendix 1c.)

The 1855 election provides a window onto leading tendencies that the Nativist
landslide of 1854 obscured, suggesting the bases of the new Republican party and
the contexts where Nativism persisted most strongly. (See Figure 8.)

Once again, following the established Free Soil–Free Democrat pattern, the
Republicans did particularly well in the central corridor, in old Federalist,
Antimasonic, and antislavery towns, and in the small shop and shoe towns. The
Republicans also did reasonably well in towns where Congregational revivalism
had been pronounced in the early 1830s and in towns with Baptist churches.

Rather than simply a hostility to the presence of immigrants, Nativist politics
seems to have been rooted in a broad reaction to rapid change among people
bearing a particularly inflexible and conservative political tradition.[68] Voting for
Nativists was the most persistent in the north county towns, and particularly in
those towns along the Nashua River where there had been rapid development of
textile mills and railroads within the previous decade. These were traditionally
Whig towns, some of which had joined the anti–Fifteen Gallon surge to the
Democrats in the 1839 election. In a series of towns in the orbit of the old center of
Lancaster, Nativist voting was associated with opposition to the 1853 constitution,
and had its roots in the 1840s when these towns had cast strong minority votes for
early Nativist candidates Henry Shaw and Francis Baylies. A number of the textile
towns in the Blackstone Valley with large foreign-born populations also voted
Nativist in 1855. But across the entire county Nativist voting was not particularly
evident in towns with relatively large foreign-born populations, many of which
were located in the central corridor. It was in the central corridor towns, with their
long involvement in small shop industry and volatile insurgent politics, that
antislavery overrode the strident allure of nativism. In 1859, when the state ratified
a nativist proposal extending the naturalization period of immigrant aliens for an
additional two years, the towns of the central corridor stood out as opposing the

[67] In 1856, there were 10,231 fewer votes across the state for Henry Gardner, the Nativist-
Republican candidate for governor, than there were for John Fremont, the Republican
candidate for president. In Worcester County the gap between the two votes was 4,212, or 41%
of the state total, a disproportionate figure given that the county only made up 13% of the
state's population. *Massachusetts Register* (Boston, 1857), 227–8.
[68] Michael F. Holt, "The Politics of Impatience: The Origins of Know Nothingism," *JAH* 60
(1973), 309–31; a membership list of Association 49 is among the "Worcester, Mass., Native
American Party, Records, 1854–5, AAS. No attempt was made to analyze the entire list, but
among the fifteen men from Leicester and Millbury, none were linked with the Antimasons,
while three were Masons and one the son of a Mason.

measure. It was here that, as George F. Hoar put it, that antislavery men may typically have

> joined the movement simply in order that they might get rid of the old parties, and prepare the State as with a subsoil plow. They had no belief in proscriptive doctrines, and were willing that men of foreign birth and Catholics should have their just rights, and expected to destroy the Know Nothing Party in its turn when it had destroyed Whiggery and Democracy."[69]

Over the next five years Republicanism spread to dominate the entire county. Although roughly a third of the county's Republicans protested the Nativist-Republican candidate for governor in 1856, it is difficult to escape the conclusion that numbers of Nativists began to vote Republican in the following years. In 1857 the Republicans carried all but five of the county's fifty-eight towns. Although William Seward – a radical Republican of Antimasonic origins – was favored in the county for the presidential nomination in 1860, Abraham Lincoln carried all but two towns in 1860. But within this broad Republican support across the

[69] Hoar, *Autobiography*, 189.

Region, foreign-born population, and the 1855 election [towns voting]

	Democratic	Native American	Republican
North			
HiFB	0	1	0
Other	3	14	8
Central			
HiFB	0	0	6
Other	1	5	6
South			
HiFB	3	4	1
Other	2	2	2

Note: HiFB-high foreign born (above 20%/county level).
Source: Return for Governor, MA; Francis DeWitt, ed., *Abstract of the Census of the Commonwealth of Massachusetts ... 1855 ...* (Boston, 1857), 127–31. The regional breakdown of the towns opposing the 1859 amendment was as follows: North, 26.9% (7/26); Central Corridor, 55.5% (10/18); South, 35.7% (5/14). The county turnout for this issue was roughly 40% of the vote in the governor's election, and was higher than the state turnout, apparently a result of the relative strength of the county's opposition to the measure. *Acts and Resolves, 1860*, 235–7.

county, the towns of the central corridor stood out as the party's central constituency, leading the county in both the vote for Lincoln and in the overall turnout.[70]

A powerful chain of continuity thus continued to inform the antislavery impulse, even as an insurgency was transmuted into a county – and sectional – consensus. The antislavery insurgency culminating in the election of 1860 was firmly grounded in an orbit shaped in the first decades of the century by the fusion of commerce and shop production and more indirectly by the ancient center of the county's provincial politics, the tradition of Popular orthodoxy. This was a region in which competitive politics and the persistence and revival of old religious institutions had also worked to shape a series of political challenges to a social and economic elite, an elite similarly formed in the transformative decades that followed the establishment of the new nation.

[70] On Seward, *Dictionary of American Biography*, 18: 403; and Foner, *Free Soil*, 64–5.

County vote for Lincoln, 1860

	North		Central		South	
Total towns	26		18		14	
Towns with greater than county average:						
Republican vote (above 70%)	15	*58*	12	*67*	5	*36*
Turnout (above 84%)	9	*35*	11	*62*	3	*27*

Note: Figures in italics are percentages.
Source: Votes for Presidential Electors, 1860, MA.

Epilogue: Into the Civil War

When Amasa Walker, Thomas W. Higginson, and George F. Hoar celebrated the independent mechanics and farmers of the city and county of Worcester in the early 1850s, they evoked the essence of the Harringtonian vision. They depicted a society of rough equality, where independent heads of households were free to act on a strong sense of public purpose, not far from the world described by Timothy Dwight in the 1790s, and not incompatible with the aspirations of the Brookfield petitioners of a century before, who were "called of God" to settle in a dangerous land "capable of affording a comfortable subsistence to many families."[1]

But ever since the turn of the nineteenth century, when Thomas Denny commissioned Ralph Earle to paint the bucolic scene east from Denny Hill, as he moved to Leicester center to engage in commerce and the production of machine cards, the Harringtonian social landscape had been more dream than reality. By the 1850s the days of even a relative equality were long past, as were those of a modicum of household independence. The men who responded to the Kansas–Nebraska act in 1854 in Walker's Worcester were by no means independent in the traditional definition: almost two-thirds were without real property.[2] By the 1820s a complex web of private institutions had shouldered aside the eighteenth-century triad of household, town, and county court, and the stratification of wealth already evident in the 1820s and 1830s was intensified by the violent movements of the business cycle in the twenty years between 1837 and 1857, as the economy recovered from one crisis to surge and crash again.

With the transformation of the county's economy, the spread of the railroad brought a fundamental restructuring of the county, with a division between the city and the country towns progressively becoming the critical feature of the social landscape. Once a mosaic of towns of roughly equal size had characterized the county. The 1840s and 1850s brought a rapid differentiation of scale, as the population of Worcester surged from 7,500 to 25,000 in twenty years, and smaller outlying towns increasingly lost numbers. With those numbers they lost a certain vitality.

The progressive collapse of the country towns was particularly evident in political culture. During the 1830s, they had been the source of dozens of petitions to the legislature; by the 1850s petitions from the smaller towns were restricted to

---

[1] Dwight, *Travels* 1:265–74; Temple, *North Brookfield*, 15.
[2] Magdol, *The Antislavery Rank and File*, 129.

389

a few in favor of temperance, and a few in opposition to the proposal to limit industrial work to ten hours a day, petitions drawn up by mill agents to be signed by operatives who seemingly had little choice in the matter. In contrast, urban places were bubbling with political activity. Laboring people in Worcester, as in the other booming industrial cities, signed petitions for the ten-hour day in the thousands. Some, like "T. Proudman and 40 other Mechanics in the Worcester Railroad Repair Shop," seem to have defiantly circulated their petitions on the shop floor.[3] Similarly, leading men who previously found a living in the country towns, and represented their interests in the General Court and even in Congress, were gravitating toward Worcester and Boston along with the stream of young men seeking employment. In his history of Leicester published on the eve of the Civil War, Emory Washburn noted that there had "been – especially of late years, and since the opening of so many railroads – a tendency to *centralization*, drawing men of capital and enterprise to the focal points of business." The accelerating movements between city and country of an entire generation of men had profound political consequences. Outsiders to the established urban political structures, such men maintained their contacts and influence in their home towns, moving with unprecedented speed between city and town on the railroads, which were rapidly reconfiguring the ancient middle landscape. It was along these lines of recent emigration that the Republican coalition spread, as men like Amasa Walker, Alexander DeWitt, George Hoar, and Eli Thayer, with connections in both city and countryside, led the assault on "the Lords of the Loom and Lash."[4]

These rural-urban connections, and the very pace of change, worked to reinforce the nostalgic qualities of Republican rhetoric in the 1850s. But Republican ideology was not simply a restatement of the diffuse Harringtonian formula of independence and common purpose that had found such a receptive audience along the central corridor, among a people whose Federalist and Calvinist traditions and artisan economy underlay a persistent insurgent politics. If the Lockean qualities of the Popular tradition were tempered by a corporate, Harringtonian language to forge a consensus in the revolutionary crisis, so, too, the Harringtonian cast of the antebellum insurgencies was tamed in the years before the Civil War by a fusion with Locke. The middle-class Republican leadership moved the insurgent ideology into Lockean waters uncharted by Antimasonry and Free Soil, but well mapped by radical abolition. In this free-labor synthesis, Harringtonian and Lockean social visions were woven into a single fabric, far more successfully than they had been been by the Popular orthodoxy of the Revolutionary generation. During and after the Civil War, leading men from the Radical Republican circle, among them George F. Hoar, Amasa Walker, and his son

---

[3] See Ten-Hour Petitions, 1851–5, House Unpassed, 2708 3237a, 3757; Senate Unpassed, 18354.

[4] Washburn, Leicester, 339–40; on the disruptive change of the 1850s, see Holt, "The Politics of Impatience."

Francis Amasa, would attempt to maintain the coalition forged in the 1850s allying middle-class reformers with laboring men in an effort to improve the conditions of labor on the ancient dream of independence in commonwealth, and the harmony of interests. Their efforts would founder on late-nineteenth-century realities. Commonwealth and independence were hopelessly outmoded categories of political economy when wage labor confronted organized capital. The failure of the postwar reformers also rested in the powerful ideological synthesis that they had subscribed to – and helped to craft – on the eve of the Civil War. For if they had expectations of independence and commonwealth, the reformers held rigidly to the dogma of individual contract, unimpeded by the organization of labor and capital. The free-labor ideal was a powerfully multivocal summation that would drive the North to war when the South seceded from the Union. In turn, the experience of total war would finally destroy the innocent world that the free-labor ideology was articulated to defend.[5]

This fusion of Harrington and Locke was most publicly established in the Republican party platform adopted at the Chicago convention in May 1860. After bitter debate, the platform included a resolution declaring the party's commitment to the core values of the Declaration of Independence – "that all men are created equal; that they are endowed by their Creator with certain inalienable rights." This resolution was drawn directly from the Lockean priorities of abolitionism; it had been a central feature of the Liberty Party platform in the 1840s, but was abandoned by the Free Soilers and Free Democrats in 1848 and 1852. Conversely, the 1856 Republican platform – while including the Liberty plank on "inalienable rights," had neglected the Free Soil demands for free and equal access to public land; this Harringtonian inheritance from Land Reform was included without great controversy in the 1860 platform. In 1860, for the first time, the two antagonistic postures within the broader antislavery movement were brought together in Republican doctrine; these planks were only the most obvious symptoms of a fusion developing since the mid-1850s.[6]

In Worcester County, as probably throughout the north, the fusion of Lockean and Harringtonian themes seems to have been accelerated by the increasing cosmopolitan affiliations and detachment from locality of the reformer intellectuals who dominated public discourse. These men blurred the line between once distinct ideological positions, drawing on the full range of ideological rhetoric available variously from the print revolution, a wider education, and the lyceum

[5] David Montgomery, *Beyond Equality: Labor and the Radical Republicans, 1862–1872* (Urbana, 1981), esp. 72ff., 114ff., 446–7. Morton Keller, *Affairs of State: Public Life in Late Nineteenth Century America* (Cambridge, 1977), 164, 182, 192–3. See also, Foner, *Free Soil*, chap. 1; Foner, "Causes," 24; "Abolitionism and the Labor Movement"; Wilentz, *Chants Democratic*; Dawley, *Class and Community*.
[6] Kirk R. Proter, *National Party Platforms* (New York, 1924), 7–15, 47–50, 55–8; Blue, *Freesoilers* 293–301; Foner, *Free Soil*, 132–3; Kenneth Stampp, *The Imperiled Union: Essays on the Background of the Civil War* (New York, 1980), 153–4.

lectures and discussions. Such qualities of an elite intellectual eclecticism were particularly apparent in men such as Thomas W. Higginson and Amasa Walker. In the aftermath of the capture and deportation of Anthony Burns, Higginson preached in strikingly classical language on the death of "disinterested love of freedom" to the Worcester Free Church. In the most consistent classical critique of the corrupting qualities of commerce heard since the Revolution, Higginson warned that "our material prosperity, and our career of foreign conquest, and our acquisition of gold mines ... [were] precisely the symptoms which have prophesied the decline of every powerful commercial state." With the defeat of Fremont in 1856, Higginson decided that there was no future in the Union, and organized a secession convention in Worcester in 1857 with William Lloyd Garrison and the Worcester immediatists. Amasa Walker, whose celebration of household independence combined with an intensely laissez-faire economics in an eclecticism that defies simple categories, praised the convention. Walker was "sick of so much cant about 'the Union'," which should survive only "*provided the great ideas of the Declaration of Independence can be fully realized by it, but certainly not otherwise.*" Classical and liberal categories followed one on another in a bewildering sequence in the antislavery rhetoric of the mid-1850s.[7]

Most importantly, the free-labor ideology increasingly equated the Harringtonian expectation of independence with the Lockean right to freely enter into individual contract. Here the need to isolate the fundamental differences between North and South brought out the Lockean qualities of the free-labor argument. Economic independence certainly remained a central icon in the Republican worldview, but increasingly it shared the stage with wage labor. Lincoln's words were the definitive Republican paradigm. Keeping the fruits of his labor, the free workingman could progress to independence: "The man who labored for another last year, this year labors for himself, and next year he will hire others to work for him."[8]

Henry Wilson, the voice of Massachusetts labor, who began his working life as an apprentice shoemaker, was a prime architect of the economic rhetoric of Republicanism. The polar opposite of the immediatists within the broader antislavery coalition, Wilson condemned Higginson's disunion convention as an abandonment of the national collectivity and the antislavery cause. But even Wilson grew noticeably restrained in the language he used to define the con-

[7] Foner, *Free Soil*, 140–1; Thomas W. Higginson, *Massachusetts in Mourning. A Sermon Preached in Worcester, on Sunday, June 4, 1854* (Boston, 1854), 3, 7, 9; *Proceedings of the State Disunion Convention, Held at Worcester, Massachusetts, January 15, 1857* (Boston, 1857), Appendix 1–3; Mooney, "Antislavery," 245–6, 267, on the conflict between Foster and Higginson.

[8] Quoted in Foner, *Free Soil*, 29–30; on Lincoln, see Howe, *Political Culture of the American Whigs*, 290–1; John P. Diggins, *The Lost Soul of American Politics: Virtue, Self-Interest, and the Foundations of Liberalism* (New York, 1984), 312–33; Jean Baker, "From Belief into Culture: Republicanism in the Antebellum North," *AQ* 37 (1985), esp. 532–5.

trast between the free-labor and slave-labor economies. In 1846, addressing the Massachusetts House on the issue of the admission of Texas, Wilson described the Northern economy in Harringtonian terms. In contrast to the South, where "the soil is cut up into vast estates, owned by a few aristocrats who distain labor, and despise the laborer," across New England" our soil is divided into small estates . . ., and its cultivators stand upon their own acres, which they till." In this putative distribution of property Wilson saw the realization of the Roman plan to create "an independent yeomanry that should preserve and perpetuate the liberties of the commonwealth." But in October 1860, facing a more challenging audience in the workingmen of East Boston, Wilson was notably more reticent about independence. Urging them to vote Republican in November, he urged upon them that slavery was "the unappeasable enemy of the free laboring-men of America": it cast "baleful shadows over the homes, the fields, and the workshops, of the laboring-men of the North." The slave system was a threat to the dignity of Northern men who worked for wages. "The slavery of the black man has degraded labor and the white laboring-man of the south, and dishonored the white laboring-man of the North . . . [it] puts the brand of degradation on the brow of manual labor, free as well as slave." Wilson urged the "Working-men of Massachusetts" to make the "self-evident truths" of the Declaration of Independence "the active truth of America" by voting for Abraham Lincoln, who was "true to the rights, the interests, and the dignities of the working-men of the republic."[9]

Increasingly, the universal abstractions of the Declaration of Independence dominated the discourse of leading Republicans in Massachusetts, but over the late 1850s the voters of the Worcester congressional district were of a different mind. In a district noted for its distinguished and idealistic Republican leadership, Eli Thayer, the organizer of the New England Emigrant Aid Society, was elected in 1856 and 1858 to a seat in the United States Congress. Herein lay an instructive story, almost a comic tragedy. Thayer was a maverick within the district's Republican inner circle, perhaps something of a charlatan, and his election speaks to the persisting power of the Harringtonian vision.

Born in Mendon in a family and a town that a century before had been deeply involved in the Land Bank, Thayer settled in Worcester in 1845, marrying the daughter of Quaker abolitionists in Uxbridge and opening a seminary for young women. Elected to the General Court in 1853 as a Free Soiler, Thayer sponsored a bill to establish a bank of mutual redemption, which would allow the country banks to bypass the Suffolk system, a consortium of Boston banks that maintained a strict control over the state's currency. Similarly, when he organized the Emigrant Aid Society, he proposed that it be associated with a speculative land bank, allowing people to invest in Kansas lands. This entrepreneurial scheme would be only the first of his affronts to the dignity of the county's Republican

[9] Elias Nason and Thomas Russell, *The Life and Public Services of Henry Wilson* . . . (Boston, 1876), 71–2, 276–84; Friedman, *Gregarious Saints*, 230–1.

leadership. Elected to Congress in 1856 despite his known involvement in Nativism, Thayer was convinced that emigration companies from the North could flood the territories with settlers. He publicly rejected the Wilmot Proviso, espoused Douglas's "squatter sovereignty," and advocated free-state filibustering in Central America. Reelected by the Worcester District voters in 1858, Thayer led a small group of Republicans who voted for the admission of Oregon, in the face of the proposed state's constitution's proscription of free blacks.[10]

Finally, at the Republican convention in 1860, representing Oregon while still a congressman from Worcester, Thayer rose to speak against Joshua Giddings's demand that the platform include the "inalienable rights" clause from the Declaration of Independence. His defeat for the Worcester congressional seat in 1860 was led by George Allen, who, twenty-three years before, had explicitly made the Declaration the touchstone of the *Declaration of Sentiments* published by the Worcester County ministers' antislavery convention. Signing his "Address" to the voters as "Heart of the Commonwealth," Allen was outraged that the Worcester district, "everywhere honored by freedom and hated by slavery," could elect and then reelect such a self-interested traitor. Thayer's popularity was indeed an anomaly in a district encompassing much of the central corridor, where Nativism made only brief inroads on a strong tradition of Free Soil–Republicanism. Thayer was a showman, a booster whose promise of free land in the territories outweighed his Nativism and his rejection of the Wilmot Proviso. His popularity was testimony to the continuing power of the dream of Harringtonian independence for the electorate in Worcester County.[11]

The late 1850s brought new economic pressures that might well have provided the ground for Harringtonian fantasies, particularly among workers in the vast boot and shoe industry. The shoe trade employed by far the largest number of men and women in the county, roughly 13,000 in 1855, as against roughly 8,500 in textiles. Over the 1850s the industry went through a fundamental transformation, as a formerly decentralized system of outwork articulated in a network of central shops and domestic households was rapidly consolidated "under the roof" of new factory buildings, just as the outwork system of handweaving had been abandoned in textile manufacturing during the 1820s. The expansive economy of the early 1850s brought large orders to be filled for export to California and Australia in addition to the traditional southern and midwestern markets, and the shipping schedules required greater speed and regularity of delivery. Over the decade a trend toward centralization already evident was greatly accelerated, with the

---

[10] *Dictionary of American Biography*, 18:402–4; Broadside from the Worcester *Daily Spy*, October 25, 1860; Mooney, "Antislavery," 213–18, 244, 268–9; Hurd, *Worcester County*, 2:669–1672; Foner, *Free Soil*, 288–90.
[11] [George Allen,] *An Address to the Electors of the Ninth Congressional District of Massachusetts* [Worcester, 1860]; "Speech of P. Emory Aldrich, at Mechanics Hall in Worcester, August 6th, 1860, in Defense of Republican Principles," Worcester *Palladium* Extra.

application of new machinery for sewing the soft upper shoes, the close supervision under regular hours of the handwork of crimping and treeing, and in some places of the bottoming process, which would be mechanized in the 1860s with the development of the McKay stitcher. The 1857 depression and subsequent recovery only accelerated the movement from household to the factory.[12]

Responses to centralization varied across Worcester County. In Spencer, the average investment among a half dozen boot manufacturers rose from $8,750 to $19,000, as they began to put up factory structures. In Brookfield, the firm of John P. Robinson, once a Workingman and Antimason, delayed the introduction of centralized factory procedures until the early 1860s in part because – as an early historian put it – "they were public spirited and had a strong paternal feeling for the old shoe workers in their village[,] who would lose work by the introduction of new methods and new machinery in vogue in other factories and other towns." In Sutton a number of small shops had opened in the 1830s, three run by Free Soil activists, but after 1855 the trade – as the town historians wrote in the 1870 – "began to decline in consequence of the tendency to concentrate in large places and in the hands of large capitalists." The onset of these profound changes worked to undermine labor militance; as the great shoe strike of 1860 spread from Lynn and Natick west into Worcester County. Rather than expressing an unequivocal opposition to the local shoe bosses, strike meetings in the larger centers of Milford and Grafton were divided, with some – as the *Spy* reported – proposing a "plan of fixing a tariff of prices, and striking with the manufacturers for better pay." In both towns, hard-pressed manufacturers expressed sympathy for the strikers, but by the early spring all thoughts of a strike had faded, as an oversupply of shoes and surplus labor undermined the position of all involved in the shoe works.[13]

The challenges of factory production to the small-shop economy and the aborted shoe strike constituted the immediate background to the 1860 election and the Civil War crisis. They were also reflected in the patterns of military enlistment in the spring and summer of 1861. The *Spy* reported that the news of Fort Sumter's surrender and Lincoln's call for volunteers was greeted in North Brookfield with "intense excitement" and cheers of "Good for old Abe" and "Harrah for the Jacksonian spirit of 1832." It was reported that "laborers leave their work and talk of war." That June a company was enlisted in the Brookfields to serve in the 15th Regiment of Massachusetts Three Years Volunteers, recruited from towns across the county. Among the men from North Brookfield who joined

[12] DeWitt, ed., *Industry in Massachusetts . . . 1855*, 571, 575, 606; Hazard, *Boot and Shoe Industry*, 93–4, 97–112; Dawley, *Class and Community*, 73–96.

[13] Draper, *Spencer*, 112–23, *Plebian and Workingmen's Advocate*, March 23, 1831; Hazard, *Boot and Shoe Industry*, 115–16; Benedict and Tracy, *Sutton*, 530–1. For the 1860 strike in Worcester County, see the *Massachusetts Weekly Spy*, February 15, 22, 29, March 7, March 21, and April 4, 1860. See also Dawley, *Class and Community*, 78–89; and Mary H. Blewett, *Men, Women, and Work: Class, Gender, and Protest in the New England Shoe Industry, 1780–1910* (Urbana and Chicago, 1988), 97–141.

the 15th, shoemakers outnumbered farmers and farm laborers by a ratio of 6 to 1, and skilled artisans outnumbered agricultural workers by better than 7 to 1. The enlistment of shoeworkers was vastly disproportionate to their numbers, as the 1860 census put the ratio for the town as a whole at slightly better than 2 to 1. Similarly, among those men joining another company of the 15th raised in Oxford, the ratio was three shoemakers to each farm worker, in a town where the general ratio was probably only slightly better than 1 to 1.[14]

The disruption of the southern trade, especially important in North Brookfield, in part accounted for the disproportionate number of shoemaker volunteers, but elsewhere in Massachusetts skilled workers also led the early response to Lincoln's call for volunteers.[15] It is difficult not to see Harringtonian impulses, concerns about independence in an age of economic turmoil, in the mustering of companies of artisans and mechanics in the early, innocent months of the Civil War. The confrontation with the South was in an important sense the culmination of their long tradition of insurgent politics, running from Antimasonry to Free Soil and the early years of the Republican challenge. Poised on the edge of independence in the household system of shoe manufacture, the shoemakers' position between traditional and modern forms had critically shaped these insurgencies. The 1850s saw the accelerating intrusion of the factory and the wage-labor system, and the collapse of their balance between past and future. In the early spring and summer of 1861, army enlistment resolved a broad sense of frustration, as contemporary realities veered sharply away from ancient expectations.

The men of the 15th Massachusetts certainly did not carry copies of *Oceana* or *An Essay Concerning Human Understanding* in their packs as they marched off to confront the forces of secessionist slave power, but Harrington and Locke were certainly in their cultural baggage. In the spring and early summer months of 1861 these young artisans, apprehensive about the direction of change in the now old and deeply rooted shoe networks, channeled their hopes and expectations of a middling Harringtonian independence into a defense of the common good, of their individual and collective rights in the national constitutional social compact. Committed abolitionists saw the coming of war as the fulfillment of their long-held determination to restore natural and civil rights to black Americans in involuntary servitude; the motivations of the majority of the Worcester District voters and the shoemaker volunteers in the 15th Massachusetts were not quite so noble. But the very multivocality of the free-labor ideology would draw them into the abolition-

[14] Worcester *Daily Spy*, April 19, 1861. Sources for analysis of occupations of 1861 volunteers: Daniels, *Oxford*, 170–7; Temple, *North Brookfield*, 300–45; *The Massachusetts Register, 1862* (Boston, 1862), 310–11; G. W. Chase, comp., *Abstract of the Census of Massachusetts, 1860, from Eighth U. S. Census, with Remarks on the Same* (Boston, 1863), 354–5.
[15] Temple, *North Brookfield*, 272; William J. Rorabaugh, "Who Fought for the North in the Civil War? Concord, Massachusetts, Enlistments," *JAH* 73 (1986), 695–701.

ists' universal Lockean agenda. Just as eighteenth-century yeomen entered the Revolution with conservative, Harringtonian intentions, only to be dragged into Lockean constitutionalism by religious dissenters who had ventured "on upon a naked promise" in the Great Awakening, so, too, the Republican voters and volunteers of 1860 and 1861 would be the agents of a Lockean emancipation doggedly pursued by a determined band of abolitionists since the early 1830s. The sheer drama of this destruction of both slavery and the slave power would fix the free-labor ideology in the popular mind, and would make all the more problematic the late-nineteenth-century engagement of labor, capital, and the state.[16]

[16] Quotation from Fisk, "Testimony," BPAN. On the political economy of the immediate postwar era, see Montgomery, *Beyond Equality.*

Appendix 1.
Votes for governor in
Worcester County,
1780–1860

Appendix 1a. *Votes for governor, Worcester County, 1780–1800*

Year	For Federalist	For Antifederalist or Democratic Republican	Total vote	Percentage Federalist	Estimated electorate	Estimated turnout	Federalist vote as percentage of estimated electorate
1780	117	1,976	2,109	*5.5*	8,784	24.0	*1.3*
1781	84	1,491	1,575	*5.3*	9,074	17.4	*0.9*
1782	338	719	1,378	*24.5*	9,365	14.7	*3.6*
1783	—	—	—	—	—	—	—
1784	—	—	—	—	—	—	—
1785	509	476	1,338	*38.0*	10,238	13.1	*5.0*
1786	1,024	163	1,365	*75.0*	10,528	13.0	*9.7*
1787	557	3,472	4,113	*13.5*	10,819	38.0	*5.1*
1788	734	2,866	3,600	*20.4*	11,110	32.4	*6.6*
1789	399	3,876	3,477	*11.5*	11,401	30.5	*3.5*
1790	332	2,224	2,556	*13.0*	11,692	21.9	*2.8*
1791	197	2,244	2,441	*8.1*	11,803	20.7	*1.7*
1792	1,173	1,730	2,907	*40.4*	11,914	24.4	*9.8*
1793	279	2,249	2,528	*11.0*	12,065	21.0	*2.3*
1794	1,158	1,613	3,104	*37.3*	12,136	25.6	*9.5*
1795	456	2,084	2,540	*18.0*	12,247	20.7	*3.7*
1796	2,024	1,232	3,520	*57.5*	12,359	28.5	*16.4*
1787	2,431	697	3,479	*69.9*	12,470	27.9	*19.5*
1798	2,272	153	2,474	*91.8*	12,581	19.7	*18.1*
1799	2,933	294	3,272	*89.6*	12,692	25.8	*23.1*
1800	2,126	2,063	4,415	*48.2*	12,803	34.0	*16.6*

Note: No returns surviving for 1783 and 1784. Federalist vote 1788–93: scattered candidates other than Hancock. Percentages are in italics.
Source: "Returns for Governor," MA: U.S. and state censuses. On estimated electorate, see Chapter 7, note 53.

Appendix 1b. *Votes for governor in Worcester County, 1801–27*

Year	For Federalist or National Republican[a]	For Democratic Republican	Total vote	Percentage Federalist or National Republican	Estimated electorate	Estimated turnout	Federalist and National Republican votes as percentage of estimated electorate
1801	3,279	1,722	5,015	65.4	12,911	38.8	25.4
1802	4,189	1,854	6,064	69.1	13,020	46.6	32.2
1803	3,918	1,699	5,641	69.5	13,129	43.0	29.8
1804	4,169	1,728	5,920	70.4	13,239	44.7	31.5
1805	4,771	3,263	8,124	58.7	13,348	60.9	35.7
1806	5,196	3,341	8,560	60.7	13,457	63.6	38.6
1807	5,416	3,731	9,189	58.9	13,566	67.7	39.9
1808	5,029	3,394	8,464	59.4	13,674	61.9	36.8
1809	6,089	3,986	10,135	60.1	13,783	73.5	44.2
1810	5,502	4,054	9,579	57.4	13,892	69.0	39.6
1811	5,046	3,998	9,168	55.0	14,117	64.9	35.7
1812	6,457	4,334	10,801	59.8	14,342	75.3	45.0

1813	6,935	3,851	10,806	*64.2*	14,567	*74.2*	*47.6*
1814	7,121	4,174	11,321	*62.9*	14,792	*76.5*	*48.1*
1815	6,906	4,135	11,054	*62.5*	15,017	*73.6*	*46.0*
1816	6,738	4,178	10,978	*61.4*	15,242	*72.0*	*44.2*
1817	6,346	3,667	10,021	*63.3*	15,467	*64.8*	*41.0*
1818	5,776	3,125	8,918	*64.8*	15,692	*56.8*	*36.8*
1819	6,009	3,286	9,671	*62.1*	15,917	*60.8*	*37.8*
1820	5,519	3,390	9,086	*60.7*	16,141	*56.3*	*34.2*
1821	5,420	3,297	8,752	*61.9*	16,596	*52.7*	*32.7*
1822	5,380	3,416	8,821	*61.0*	17,051	*51.7*	*31.6*
1823	5,573	4,733	10,362	*53.8*	17,506	*59.2*	*31.8*
1824	6,393	5,206	11,616	*55.0*	17,961	*64.7*	*35.6*
1825	4,793		5,491	*87.3*	18,416	*29.8*	*26.0*
1826	2,912		6,423	*45.3*	18,871	*34.0*	*15.4*
1827	4,371		5,816	*75.2*	19,326	*30.1*	*22.6*

Note: Percentages are in italics.

[a] Federalist 1800–24, National Republican, 1825–7.

Source: "Returns for Governor," MA; U.S. and state censuses. On estimated electorate, see Chapter 7, note 53.

Appendix 1c. *Votes For governor, Worcester County, 1828–60*

Year	For National Republicans or Whig[a]	For Democrat	For Antimason, Liberty, Free Soil, Free Democrat, or Republican[b]	For Workingmen or Native American[c]	Total vote	Percentage National Republicans or Whig[a]	Percentage Antimason, Liberty, Free Soil, Free Democrat, or Republican[b]	Estimated electorate	Estimated turnout	National Republican, Whig, and post-1855 Republican as percentage of estimated electorate
1828	3,878	1,052			4,928	78.7		19,781	24.9	19.6
1829	2,851	2,173			5,943	48.0		20,236	29.4	14.1
1830	5,088	3,244			8,332	61.1		20,690	40.3	24.6
1831	4,508	2,219			6,727	67.0		21,092	31.9	21.4
1831[d]	4,313	2,322	1,831		8,466	50.9	21.6	21,092	40.1	20.4
1832	6,334	2,661	2,208		11,203	56.5	19.7	21,494	52.1	29.5
1833	6,170	2,701	2,356	132	11,227	55.0	21.0	21,897	51.3	28.2
1834	8,200	2,646	950	251	11,796	69.5	8.1	22,299	52.9	36.8
1835	6,771	3,407			10,178	66.5		22,701	44.8	29.8
1836	7,589	4,429			11,584	65.5		23,104	50.1	32.8
1837	8,526	4,145			12,671	67.3		23,506	53.9	36.3
1838	8,552	5,918			14,470	59.1		23,909	60.5	35.8
1839	8,214	7,647			15,861	51.8		24,311	65.2	33.8
1840	11,199	7,303	134		18,660	60.0	0.7	24,714	75.5	45.3
1841	9,395	6,783	582		16,793	55.9	3.5	25,787	65.1	36.4
1842	9,078	7,988	1,200		18,271	49.7	6.6	26,860	68.0	33.8

Year									
1843	8,920	7,956	1,671		18,601	*48.0*	*9.0*	27,933	*66.6*	*31.9*
1844	9,875	7,796	1,798		19,581	*50.4*	*9.2*	29,006	*67.5*	*34.0*
1845	8,032	5,998	1,925		16,709	*48.1*	*11.5*	30,079	*55.6*	*26.7*
1846	8,121	5,103	2,215		16,066	*50.5*	*13.8*	31,152	*51.6*	*26.1*
1847	8,187	5,682	2,253		16,467	*49.7*	*13.7*	32,225	*51.1*	*25.4*
1848	6,445	4,053	7,908		18,485	*34.9*	*42.8*	33,298	*55.5*	*19.4*
1849	6,600	4,751	6,460		17,816	*37.0*	*36.3*	34,371	*51.8*	*19.2*
1850	6,517	5,046	7,240		18,949	*34.4*	*38.2*	35,444	*53.5*	*18.4*
1851	7,817	5,675	7,397		20,952	*37.3*	*35.3*	36,632	*57.2*	*21.3*
1852	7,409	6,024	8,143		21,593	*34.3*	*37.7*	37,821	*57.1*	*19.6*
1853	7,281	5,607	7,424		20,683	*35.2*	*35.9*	39,009	*53.0*	*18.7*
1854	3,316	2,612	1,586	12,308	19,949	*16.6*	*8.0*	40,198	*49.6*	*8.2*
1855	1,360	5,932	7,453	6,706	21,462	*6.3*	*34.7*	41,386	*51.9*	*3.3*
1856		5,062	11,899		19,523		*60.9*	42,118	*46.4*	*28.3*
1857		4,370	10,708	4,525	19,684		*54.4*	42,850	*45.9*	*25.0*
1858		4,432	10,526	1,256	16,250		*64.8*	43,583	*37.3*	*24.2*
1859		4,999	9,605		15,825		*60.7*	44,315	*35.7*	*21.7*
1860		5,299	16,868		24,601		*68.6*	45,047	*54.6*	*37.4*

Note: Percentages are in italics.

[a] National Republican 1827–33, Whig 1834–55.

[b] Antimason 1831–4, Liberty 1840–7, Free Soil/Free Democrat 1848–54, Republican 1855–60.

[c] Workingmen 1833–4, Native American 1854–5, 1857–8.

[d] The electoral calendar changed in 1831, and there were two state elections in that year, in April and in November.

Source: "Returns for Governor," MA; U.S. and state censuses. On estimated electorate, see Chapter 7, note 53.

Appendix 2.
Town-level data: Methods and sources

The interpretations of this book are based in part on an aggregate analysis of political, religious, and economic information regarding the towns in Worcester County between the 1740s and the 1850s. This research is summarized in Figures 1–8, which indicate the most significant relationships that this research generated. These relationships were established using a logistic regression procedure.

Initially this information was summarized in multidimensional tables, which compared the presence of certain conditions (dissenting societies, strong involvement in the Land Bank, etc.) in a given group of towns (for example, towns voting with the Popular coalition between 1726 and 1764) with the presence of these conditions across the towns of the entire county. This method made it possible to display all of the information, but was extremely cumbersome, as the reader had to search through large tabular arrays for those relationships that seemed to be positive: that is, where the percentage of towns in a given category having a certain condition was substantially larger than similar towns in the county as a whole. This method did not indicate the strength of a relationship in a manner that allowed for a comparison of the results or that provided a strict guideline for accepting or rejecting the significance of a relationship between two variables.

On the advice of a reader, I reanalyzed the data using a logistic regression program (the CATMOD procedure within the SAS package). Logistic regression – or categorical modeling – programs allow one to test the relationship between variables that are qualitative rather than quantitative, where the information is in the form of presence or absence of a condition, rather than a numerical response. Given that much of the information involved was qualitative rather than quantitative, I have reduced all of the quantitative data to qualitative categories. Thus a town that cast 400 votes for the Federalists and 100 votes for the Republicans in the 1824 governors' election is categorized as a Federalist town for some purposes, and a town with a high Federalist vote (greater than 2 to 1) for other purposes. Although the logistic regression procedure is designed to allow the simultaneous analysis of more than two variables, the overall size of the universe (the number of towns in the county) was so small (between 24 and 58) that I only compared two variables at a time, and only of a positive or a negative response for each of these variables. Thus the results summarized on Figures 1–8 are the product of hundreds of separate, one-on-one analyses of dichotomous variables, not the result of a large-scale simultaneous modeling procedure, which might take into account the affects of a number of variables in a single run.

The logistic regression procedure provides a measure of the strength of a relationship of two variables, assessing the population under question–those cases in which both conditions are present. The resulting "analysis of variance" computes a chi-square and a P value in testing the null hypothesis that the independent variable has no effect upon the dependent variable. High chi-square and low P-value results are evidence for rejecting the null hypothesis of no effect, and for assigning significance to the tested relationship. Figures 1–8 provide the P-value results for the strongest (or most important) relationships. On Figures 1–5, 7, and 8 all results lower than .2 are reported; in a few cases I have included some of the weaker results to highlight the importance of the stronger relationships. On Figure 6 I have included all results lower than .3. (The three sections of Figure 6 should be viewed as a unit in which all significant results are shown.) Conventionally, .05 is the largest P value accepted for a significant relationship. However, given the small sample size involved in this aggregate analysis, any P-value result less than .1 can be considered a good relationship.

In each figure the key variables – usually political – are indicated in boldface. The number of towns where a "key variable" was present is indicated in parentheses after the variable name; the P value of the relationship with another "key variable" is associated with a pointing arrow, as well as the number of towns (in parentheses) where both conditions were in effect. Thus, on Figure 1, seven of the nine leading Land Bank towns were among the eight towns with orthodox churches that turned New Light during the Great Awakening and were listed on the 1743 valuation, producing a strong P-value result of .003. (In a few cases the changing number of towns in a given category requires that the size of the larger population be indicated. Thus two parishes with orthodox New Light churches were incorporated after 1743 as towns or districts, and they are included in the comparison of New Light orthodoxy and Popular voting, but are not included in the comparison of Land Bank and New Light towns.) The significant regional, economic, and religious circumstances of the "key variables" are listed below each entry, with the P-value result followed by the number of towns in which both conditions were fulfilled and (after a slash) the total number of towns in a given regional, economic, or religious category. Thus six of the nine leading Land Bank towns were among the seven towns in the southeast corner of the county, for a P-value result of .01; the Land Bank towns typically ranked in the wealthiest one-third of the towns listed on the 1761 valuation but they had not been disproportionately represented in the top third of the 1743 valuation. (*Note:* the logistic regression procedure cannot commute a result in situations where all of a given variable falls within another. These cases of a "100 percent relationship" are indicated by "nc," standing for noncalculable. For example, all four of the towns voting with the Court party before 1764 were places that had been Old Light during the Awakening.)

With a few exceptions, all of the significant relationships for all variables listed on a given figure are indicated. The exceptions are on Figures 6a–c, where the contribution of variables dating before 1820 are not estimated for the variables dating after 1820, and on Figure 8, where – for the sake of simplicity – the relationships of "key variables" dating before 1848 to Free Democratic and Republican voting of 1853 and 1855 are not indicated. The universes used in these calculations – the number of towns in the county at a given date – are important to the assessment of these results. They are listed below. 1743: 24; 1761: 35; 1775–80: 42; 1786–1800: 49; 1812: 52; 1820–32: 54; 1832–45: 55; 1848: 57; 1853–5: 58.

Guide to sources:

LAND BANK TOWNS: See Map 1, and Chapter 2, note 24.

OLD LIGHT AND NEW LIGHT TOWNS: See Map 1, and Chapter 3, note 5.

DISSENTING SOCIETIES AND NINETEENTH-CENTURY DENOMINATIONS: Pre-1786, see Chapter 4, note 38; otherwise see the *Massachusetts Register* for 1786, 1808, 1825, 1835.

1743 AND 1761 VALUATIONS: *JHRM*, 20:152–3, 38(Pt. 1): 104.

VOTING IN GENERAL COURT, 1726–64: From *JHRM*, see Chapter 4, notes 25, 39.

HALL CLASSIFICATION OF COMPLEXITY FOR THE 1780s (A, B, C), used on Figures 2 and 3: A measure of commercial development established by Van Beck Hall. A = most complex; C = least complex. See Van Beck Hall, *Politics without Parties*, 3–22, and the typescript appendixes available from Hall.

EIGHTEENTH-CENTURY REGIONS (Southeast, Southwest, Northeast, Northwest), used on Figures 1–5: See Maps 1 and 2, and Chapter 4, note 36.

NINETEENTH-CENTURY REGIONS (South, Central Corridor, North), used on Figures 6–8: See Map 3, Chapter 9, note 51.

1774 WORCESTER COUNTY CONVENTION: Lincoln, ed., *Journals of Each Provincial Congress*, 627–52.

CONSTITUTIONALIST POLITICS: From Handlin and Handlin, eds., *The Popular Sources of Political Authority*, 164–6, 201–401, 807–901; see also Patterson, *Political Parties*, 272–4.

1777 FISCAL PROTEST: *Acts and Resolves, Public and Private of the Province of Massachusetts Bay* ... (Boston, 1869–1922), 5: 516–18.

TOWNS WITH RIOTERS, 1781–3: SJC Docket Books, see Chapter 7, note 26.

PETITIONING, EXCISE REFUSALS, 1781–6: See Chapter 7, note 31.

REGULATOR AND CONFLICTED TOWNS, 1786–7: see Chapter 7, notes 35 and 39.

ELECTIONS: All from "Returns of Votes for Governor," Massachusetts Archives.

MASONIC LODGES AND CHAPTERS: See Chapter 10, note 29 and *Massachusetts Register for 1815, 1828.*

ANTIMASONIC SENTIMENT (34 towns): Towns with Antimasonic majorities or second-place minority votes; towns sending petitions (see Chapter 10, note 25).

ANTISLAVERY PETITIONING, LIBERATOR SUBSCRIPTIONS: See Chapter 11, notes 24 and 25.

ECONOMY IN 1820:

"Textile towns": towns with textile corporations capitalized at $100,000 or more by 1820 (13 towns).

"Small-shop towns": towns reporting 28% to 50% of their working population employed in manufacturing in 1820 and *without* corporations valued at $100,000 or more by 1820 (14 towns).

"Agricultural towns": all other towns (27 towns).

See Chapter 9, note 51.

ECONOMY IN 1837:

Statistics on employment in chairwork, shoes, and textiles from John P. Bigelow, ed., *Statistical Tables: Exhibiting the Condition and Products of Certain Branches of Industry in Massachusetts* ... (Boston, 1838), 42–73; agricultural employment from *Sixth Census or Enumeration of the Inhabitants of the United States, as Corrected at the Department of State, in 1840. Book 1* (Washington, D.C., 1841), 40–43. The following categories were determined by the relationship of the percentage of males aged 21 and over in 1840 employed in shoes and textiles in 1837 and in agriculture in 1840, relative to the county figure.

Agricultural: agricultural employment above county figure of 58%, employment in shoes and textiles below county figure (23 towns).

Chairs: employment in chair work between 18% and 99% of 1840 adult males, shoe and textile employment well below average (3 towns).

Shoes: employment in shoework above county figure of 17%, agricultural and textile employment below county figure; also includes Grafton (shoe employment 129%, textile employment 24%) (12 towns).

Textile/Agriculture: textile and agricultural employment both above county figures, shoe employment below county figures (5 towns);

Textile/Worcester: Worcester plus towns with textile employment above county figure of 11%, shoe and agricultural employment below county figure; also includes Millbury (Textile, 27%, shoe 24%) and Northbridge (textile 36%, shoe 21%) (12 towns).

1860s ECONOMY:

Statistics on employment in shoes, textiles, and agriculture in George W. Chase, comp., *Abstract of the Census of Massachusetts, 1860, from the Eighth United States Census, with remarks on the Same* (Boston, 1863), 354–5; *Abstract of the Census of the Commonwealth of Massachusetts Taken with Reference to Facts Existing on the First Day of June, 1865* (Boston, 1867), 146–7; 161–3.

Shoes in 1860: ratio of shoemakers to farmers and farm laborers in 1860 *greater that 1/5, and shoemakers greater than "laborers" (29 towns)*.

Textiles in 1860: ratio of "laborers" to farmers and farm laborers in 1860 greater than 3/10 (plus Webster and Dudley). The category of "laborers" reflects the presence of extensive textile or chair industries, because towns with large numbers of "laborers" in 1860 were typically important textile or chair centers in 1865. The only exceptions seem to be the towns of Dudley and Webster, which had relatively low numbers of "laborers" in 1860, although they were listed as textile centers in 1865 (12 towns).

Chairs in 1860: Ashburnham and Gardner. Agricultural in 1860: all other towns (23).

Appendix 3.
Individual-level data for the 1830: Method and tables

This book also rests in great part on quantitative analyses of data relating to individual political behavior. For the most part, the results of these analyses are summarized in the notes, and have not been explored with any sophisticated computer-aided procedures. However, the data on petitioning in the 1830s was so extensive that the logistic regression procedure was used to test the relationships between different groups in the activist population. The results are summarized in the following tables.

Six towns – Worcester, Leicester, Millbury, North Brookfield, Brookfield, and Southbridge – were selected for detailed analysis because the variety of petitions on different issues sent from these towns allows a comparative analysis impossible for towns that only petitioned on one issue. Antimasonic petitions sent to the General Court between 1831 and 1835 and the county's remonstrance against Jackson's policies toward the Second Bank of the United States identify the political allegiances of 2,013 men in these six towns, essentially the entire population of Antimasonic and National Republican (or Whig) voters. With the temperance, disestablishment, and antislavery petitions, they allow us sketch a reasonably precise picture of public opinion among non-Democrats. Lists from various sources identify proliquor advocates, Freemasons, the membership of the Worcester Agricultural Society, and the major party activists.

Again, the logistic regression procedure was run on pairs of variables to define the significance of relationships, and the P-value results are displayed in the following tables. Here the critical problem was defining a "universe" – an inclusive population that shaped the outer boundaries of the analysis. In each analysis the "universe" is made up of the total number of individuals involved in the associations and initiatives being tested against another variable. Thus Table 1a examines the relative likelihood of members of the Worcester Agricultural Society between 1819 and 1840 from six towns to have signed the Antimasonic or Second Bank petitions, to have been Freemasons, or National Republican, Whig, or Democratic activists. In each analysis the compared groups are the sum total of the members of these groups in the six towns (here 2,310 people) and the "linked subtotal" (here the 179 members of the WAS who signed these petitions or were

409

Freemasons or major party activists). The unlinked group, the 116 WAS members
who did not also fall into one of these other groupings, was eliminated from the
analysis. (In most of these analyses, if the unlinked group was include in an
analysis, none of the other groups showed significant relationships. Thus implicit
in what follows is the point that the largest group in most of these initiatives were
those people who could not be linked to another association or initiative.)

The petitions are not, however, exactly comparable. The Antimasonic, disestablishment, temperance, and antislavery petitions were signed within identified
towns, and the original manuscripts are located in the Massachusetts Archives and
the National Archives. The Second Bank Petition survives as a printed list of
roughly 6,180 names from all over Worcester County, without any indication of
the petitioners' towns. Upon a careful examination of this list, in conjunction with
the Index of the 1830 U.S. Census, the other petitions, and lists of occupations and
church members, blocks of names that clearly came from particular towns can be
identified. (This county petition probably combined a series of petitions signed
within the various towns before being collected and sent to Washington.) In the
interest of obtaining the most complete list possible, uncertain names were
included rather than *excluded*. The result has been that the Second Bank lists seem
significantly inflated when compared with the number of Antimasonic petitioners
and the Antimasonic and National vote totals. Since the Antimasonic vote dropped
significantly in 1834, with votes going to both the Whigs and the Democrats, *the
highest Antimasonic and National Republican vote totals between 1831 and 1833* were
taken so as to establish a comparative benchmark in these six towns.

Votes vs. petitions in six towns

	Total high vote	Total petitioners	Difference	
Antimasons	664	704	40	5.7
Nationals or non-Antimasonic Second Bank	1,042	1,284	242	19.5

If all voters signed the petitions, there were, by this measure, almost four times as
many unaccounted for National petitioners as Antimasons. This inflation most
likely stems from the procedure outlined above, which includes numbers of
questionable names. (These extra Second Bank signers were not Democrats. A
comparison of 187 National/Whig and Democratic committeemen in Southbridge
and Worcester shows that Whigs were ten times more likely to sign the Second
Bank petition (NR/W:76/123; DEM:4/64).

There was thus a possibility that the inflated group of Second Bank signers
would skew the analysis. To test for this problem I did a parallel analysis of the
Antimasonic and Second Bank signers, divided in "AM only," "AM and 2BUS,"
and "2BUS only" groups, in comparison with the highest votes in each of these

towns for the Antimasons and Nationals or Whigs in the years between 1831 and 1833. In general, the results were essentially the same as those obtained by using the petitioners as a universe. However, in six situations, the analysis using the highest votes as a comparative group showed a *positive* relationship between an initiative or group and the "Second Bank only" grouping, where the formal analysis showed a *negative* relationship. As these involve simple percentages, they are positive relationships, but not necessarily statistically significant. To save space I simply list these six groups here: Worcester Agricultural Society members (1a), Millbury slavery in D.C. petitioners (3a), Millbury Gag-Rule petitioners (3b), Millbury Florida petitioners (3c), and the "manufacturing only" and "agricultural only" groups on the 1840 Brookfield census (4d and 4f).

Table 1a. *Worcester Agricultural Society members in six towns, 1819–40*

	Sample			Universe	
	Number	Percent	P-value	Number	Percent
Total members	295				
Linked subtotal	179	*100*		2,310	*100*
Antimasonic petitioners, 1831–5	41	*23*	—	706	*31*
Second Bank of the U.S. petitioners	117	*65*	—	1,624	*70*
Freemasons to 1830	36	*20*	.0001	134	*6*
National Republican activists	35	*20*	.0001	122	*5*
Whig activists	83	*46*	.0001	333	*14*
Democratic activists	17	*9*	.0005	98	*4*
Antimasonic petitioners only (not 2BUS)	11	*6*	—	389	*17*
Both Antimasonic and Second Bank petitioners	30	*17*	.2200	317	*14*
Second Bank petitioners only (not Antimasonic)	87	*49[a]*	—	1,307	*57*

Note: The six towns are Worcester, Southbridge, Leicester, Millbury, Brookfield, and North Brookfield.
[a] Positive result when compared with high votes; see above.

Appendix 3

Table 1b. *Disestablishment petitioners in three towns, 1830–2*

| | Sample | | | Universe | |
	Number	Percent	P-value	Number	Percent
Total petitioners	258				
Linked subtotal	157	*100*		792	*100*
Antimasonic petitioners, 1831–5	68	*43*	.0365	286	*36*
Second Bank of the U.S. petitioners	110	*70*	.3315	529	*67*
Freemasons to 1830	11	*7*	.1820	39	*5*
Worcester Agricultural Society members	6	*4*	.3128	21	*3*
National Republican activists	18	*11*	.0146	55	*7*
Whig activists	25	*16*	.0001	54	*7*
Democratic activists	10	*6*	.3062	38	*5*
Antimasonic petitioners only (not 2BUS)	31	*20*	—	175	*22*
Both Antimasonic and Second Bank petitioners	37	*24*	.0002	111	*14*
Second Bank petitioners only (not Antimasonic)	73	*46*	—	418	*53*

Note: The three towns are Brookfield, North Brookfield, and Southbridge.

Table 1c. *Temperance petitioners and delegates in five towns, 1835–6*

| | Sample | | | Universe | |
	Number	Percent	P-value	Number	Percent
Total petitioners and delegates	960				
Linked subtotal	551	*100*		2,047	*100*
Antimasonic petitioners, 1831–5	204	*37*	.0001	562	*27*
Second Bank of the U.S. petitioners	421	*76*	.0001	1,348	*66*
Freemasons to 1830	32	*6*	—	117	*6*
Worcester Agricultural Society members	79	*14*	—	280	*14*
National Republican activists	36	*7*	—	120	*6*
Whig activists	126	*23*	.0001	312	*15*
Democratic activists	15	*3*	—	89	*4*
Antimasonic petitioners only (not 2BUS)	71	*13*	—	309	*15*
Both Antimasonic and Second Bank petitioners	133	*24*	.0001	253	*12*
Second Bank petitioners only (not Antimasonic)	288	*52*	.5004	1,059	*52*

Note: The five towns are Worcester, Southbridge, Leicester, Millbury, and North Brookfield.

Table 1d. *Democratic activists in five towns, 1829–40*

	Sample			Universe	
	Number	Percent	P-value	Number	Percent
Total	89				
Linked subtotal	47	*100*		2,305	*100*
Antimasonic petitioners, 1831–5	14	*30*	.3847	562	*24*
Second Bank of the U.S. petitioners	17	*36*	—	1,348	*58*
Temperance petitioners and delegates, 1835–6	15	*32*	—	960	*42*
Freemasons to 1830	10	*21*	.0001	117	*5*
Worcester Agricultural Society members	17	*36*	.0001	280	*12*
Antimasonic petitioners only (not 2BUS)	7	*15*	.7624	309	*13*
Antimasonic and Second Bank petitioners	7	*15*	.3878	253	*11*
Second Bank petitioners only (not Antimasonic)	10	*21*	—	1,095	*48*
Antimasonic and Second Bank petitioners (not Temperance)	6	*13*	.0237	120	*5*
Antimasonic, 2BUS, and Temperance	1	*2*	—	133	*6*
Second Bank and Temperance petitioners (not Antimasonic)	1	*2*	—	288	*12*

Note: The five towns are Worcester, Southbridge, North Brookfield, Leicester, and Millbury.

Appendix 3

Table 1e. *National Republican activists in three towns, 1832–3*

	Sample			Universe	
	Number	Percent	P-value	Number	Percent
Total	120				
Linked subtotal	94	*100*		1,572	*100*
Antimasonic petitioners, 1831–5	14	*15*	—	298	*19*
Second Bank of the U.S. petitioners	78	*83*	.0001	906	*58*
Temperance petitioners and delegates, 1835–6	36	*38*	—	629	*40*
Freemasons to 1830	9	*10*	.0821	87	*6*
Worcester Agricultural Society members	34	*36*	.0001	250	*16*
Antimasonic petitioners only (not 2BUS)	5	*5*	—	176	*11*
Antimasonic and Second Bank petitioners	9	*10*	.4989	122	*8*
Second Bank petitioners only (not Antimasonic)	69	*73*	.0001	784	*50*
Antimasonic, 2BUS, and Temperance petitioners	3	*3*	—	61	*4*
Second Bank and Temperance petitioners (not Antimasonic)	28	*30*	.0001	201	*13*
Second Bank petitioners (not Antimasonic or Temperance)	41	*44*	.1777	583	*37*

Note: The three towns are Worcester, Southbridge, and Leicester.

Table 1f. *Whig activists in five towns, 1834–40*

	Sample			Universe	
	Number	Percent	P-value	Number	Percent
Total	312				
Linked subtotal	223	*100*		2,305	*100*
Antimasonic petitioners, 1831–5	56	*25*	.7893	562	*24*
Second Bank of the U.S. petitioners	163	*73*	.0001	1,348	*58*
Temperance petitioners and delegates, 1835–6	126	*57*	.0001	960	*42*
Freemasons to 1830	23	*10*	.0003	117	*5*
Worcester Agricultural Society members	81	*36*	.0001	280	*12*
Antimasonic petitioners only (not 2BUS)	14	*6*	—	309	*13*
Antimasonic and Second Bank petitioners	42	*19*	.0001	253	*11*
Second Bank petitioners only (not Antimasonic)	121	*54*	.0341	1,095	*48*
Antimasonic, 2BUS, and Temperance	28	*13*	.0001	133	*6*
Second Bank and Temperance petitioners (not Antimasonic)	62	*28*	.0001	288	*12*

Note: The five towns are Worcester, Southbridge, North Brookfield, Leicester, and Millbury.

Table 1g. *Antislavery Society members in three towns, 1838–40*

	Sample			Universe	
	Number	Percent	P-value	Number	Percent
Total	139				
Linked subtotal	67	100		1,846	100
Antimasonic petitioners, 1831–5	32	48	.0001	420	23
Second Bank of the U.S. petitioners	46	69	.1153	1,095	59
Temperance petitioners and delegates, 1835–6	46	69	.0001	769	42
Freemasons to 1830	7	10	.0512	95	5
Worcester Agricultural Society members	13	19	.2870	274	15
Antimasonic petitioners only (not 2BUS)	8	12	—	214	12
Antimasonic and Second Bank petitioners	24	36	.0001	206	11
Second Bank petitioners only (not Antimasonic)	22	33	—	889	48
Antimasonic and 2BUS petitioners (not Temperance)	9	13	.0067	104	6
Antimasonic and Temperance petitioners (not 2BUS)	6	9	.0059	55	3
Antimasonic 2BUS, and Temperance	15	22	.0001	102	6
Second Bank and Temperance petitioners (not Antimasonic)	13	19	.1123	239	13

Note: The three towns are Worcester, Leicester, and Millbury.

Table 1h. *Free Soil activists in five towns, 1848*

	Sample			Universe	
	Number	Percent	P-value	Number	Percent
Total	96				
Linked subtotal	45	*100*		2,305	*100*
Antimasonic petitioners, 1831–5	12	*27*	.7186	562	*24*
Second Bank of the U.S. petitioners	26	*58*	—	1,348	*58*
Temperance petitioners and delegates, 1835–6	29	*64*	.0025	960	*42*
Freemasons to 1830	5	*11*	.0709	117	*5*
Worcester Agricultural Society members	10	*22*	.0410	280	*12*
Antimasonic petitioners only (not 2BUS)	7	*16*	.6694	309	*13*
Antimasonic and Second Bank petitioners	5	*11*	—	253	*11*
Second Bank petitioners only (not Antimasonic)	21	*47*	—	1,095	*48*
Antimasonic and Temperance petitioners (not 2BUS)	3	*7*	.1717	71	*3*
Antimasonic, 2BUS, and Temperance	3	*7*	.7947	133	*6*
Second Bank and Temperance petitioners (not Antimasonic)	13	*29*	.0013	288	*12*

Note: The five towns are Worcester, Southbridge, North Brookfield, Leicester, and Millbury.

Table 2a. *Worcester town: Democratic activists, 1832–40*

	Sample			Universe	
	Number	Percent	P-value	Number	Percent
Total	44				
Linked subtotal	29	*100*		1,031	*100*
Antimasonic petitioners, 1833	7	*24*	.1032	141	*14*
Second Bank of the U.S. petitioners	7	*24*	—	531	*52*
Freemasons to 1830	6	*21*	.0001	42	*4*
Worcester Agricultural Society members	13	*45*	.0037	225	*22*
Temperance petitioners and delegates 1835–6	9	*31*	—	464	*45*
Prolicense activists, 1838	11	*38*	.0001	78	*8*
Antimasonic petitioners only (not 2BUS)	3	*10*	.5835	79	*8*
Both Antimasonic and Second Bank petitioners	4	*14*	.0847	62	*6*
Second Bank petitioners only (not Antimasonic)	3	*10*	—	469	*45*
Antimasonic and 2BUS (not Temperance)	4	*14*	.0001	18	*2*
Antimasonic, 2BUS, and Temperance	0	—	—	44	*4*
2BUS and Temperance (not Antimasonic)	0	—	—	127	*12*

Table 2b. *Worcester town: National Republican and Whig activists, 1832–6*

	Sample			Universe	
	Number	Percent	P-value	Number	Percent
Total	76				
Linked subtotal	71	*100*		1,031	*100*
Antimasonic petitioners, 1833	12	*17*	.4136	141	*14*
Second Bank of the U.S. petitioners	57	*80*	.0001	531	*52*
Freemasons to 1830	7	*10*	.0144	42	*4*
Worcester Agricultural Society members	38	*54*	.0001	225	*22*
Temperance petitioners and delegates, 1835–6	32	*45*	—	464	*45*
Prolicense activists, 1838	19	*27*	.0001	78	*8*
Antimasonic petitioners only (not 2BUS)	0	—	—	79	*8*
Both Antimasonic and Second Bank petitioners	12	*17*	.0002	62	*6*
Second Bank petitioners only (not Antimasonic)	45	*63*	.0021	469	*45*
Antimasonic and 2BUS (not Temperance)	6	*8*	.0001	18	*2*
Antimasonic, 2BUS, and Temperance	21	*30*	.0781	44	*4*
2BUS and Temperance (not Antimasonic)	24	*34*	.0001	127	*12*

Table 2c. *Worcester town: New Whig activists in 1837*

	Sample			Universe	
	Number	Percent	P-value	Number	Percent
Total	71				
Linked subtotal	55	*100*		1,031	*100*
Antimasonic petitioners, 1833	8	*15*	.8471	141	*14*
Second Bank of the U.S. petitioners	36	*65*	.0358	531	*52*
Freemasons to 1830	0	—	—	42	*4*
Worcester Agricultural Society members	19	*35*	.0209	225	*22*
Temperance petitioners and delegates, 1835–6	30	*55*	.1461	464	*45*
Prolicense activists, 1838	15	*27*	.0001	78	*8*
Antimasonic petitioners only (not 2BUS)	3	*5*	—	79	*8*
Both Antimasonic and Second Bank petitioners	5	*9*	.3282	62	*6*
Second Bank petitioners only (not Antimasonic)	31	*56*	.0985	469	*45*
Antimasonic and Temperance (not 2BUS)	3	*5*	.1667	26	*3*
Antimasonic, 2BUS, and Temperance	5	*9*	.0776	44	*4*
2BUS and Temperance (not Antimasonic)	15	*27*	.0009	127	*12*

Table 2d. *Worcester town: New Whig activists in 1840 (Log Cabin Whigs)*

	Sample			Universe	
	Number	Percent	P-value	Number	Percent
Total	114				
Linked subtotal	62	*100*		1,031	*100*
Antimasonic petitioners, 1833	15	*24*	.0149	141	*14*
Second Bank of the U.S. petitioners	35	*56*	.4220	531	*52*
Freemasons to 1830	4	*6*	.3339	42	*4*
Worcester Agricultural Society members	22	*35*	.0084	225	*22*
Temperance petitioners and delegates, 1835–6	34	*55*	.1106	464	*45*
Prolicense activists, 1838	5	*8*	—	78	*8*
Antimasonic petitioners only (not 2BUS)	6	*10*	.5396	79	*8*
Both Antimasonic and Second Bank petitioners	9	*15*	.0054	62	*6*
Second Bank petitioners only (not Antimasonic)	26	*42*	—	469	*45*
Antimasonic, 2BUS, and Temperance	7	*11*	.0859	44	*4*
2BUS and Temperance (not Antimasonic)	12	*19*	.0809	127	*12*

Table 2e. *Worcester town: Gag-Rule petitioners, 1838 and 1840*

	Sample			Universe	
	Number	Percent	P-value	Number	Percent
Total	148				
Linked subtotal	61	*100*		1,130	*100*
Antimasonic petitioners, 1833	17	*28*	.0003	141	*12*
Second Bank of the U.S. petitioners	36	*59*	.0552	531	*47*
Freemasons to 1830	1	*2*	—	42	*4*
Worcester Agricultural Society members	5	*8*	—	225	*20*
Temperance petitioners and delegates, 1835–6	46	*75*	.0001	464	*41*
Prolicense activists, 1838	0	—	—	78	*7*
Democratic activists	0	—	—	44	*4*
National Republican/Whig activists, 1832–6	5	*8*	.6379	76	*7*
New Whig activists in 1837	7	*11*	.0920	71	*6*
New Whig activists in 1840	8	*13*	.4215	114	*10*
Antislavery society members, 1838–40	11	*18*	.0001	40	*4*
Antimasonic petitioners only (not 2BUS)	3	*5*	—	79	*7*
Both Antimasonic and Second Bank petitioners	14	*23*	.0001	62	*5*
Second Bank petitioners only (not Antimasonic)	22	*36*	—	469	*42*
Antimasonic, 2BUS, and Temperance	14	*23*	.0001	44	*4*
2BUS and Temperance (not Antimasonic)	16	*26*	.0003	127	*11*

Table 2f. *Worcester town: Antislavery Society members, 1838–40*

	Sample			Universe	
	Number	Percent	P-value	Number	Percent
Total	40				
Linked subtotal	17	*100*		1,107	*100*
Antimasonic petitioners, 1833	7	*41*	.0013	141	*13*
Second Bank of the U.S. petitioners	8	*47*	—	531	*48*
Freemasons to 1830	2	*12*	.1037	42	*4*
Worcester Agricultural Society members	4	*24*	.7411	225	*20*
Temperance petitioners and delegate, 1835–6	15	*88*	.0017	464	*42*
Prolicense activists, 1838	0	—	—	78	*7*
Democratic activists	0	—	—	44	*4*
National Republican/Whig activists, 1832–6	1	*6*	—	76	*7*
New Whig activists in 1837	2	*12*	.3731	71	*6*
New Whig activists in 1840	6	*35*	.0020	114	*10*
Antimasonic petitioners only (not 2BUS)	2	*12*	.4608	79	*7*
Both Antimasonic and Second Bank petitioners	5	*29*	.0002	62	*6*
Second Bank petitioners only (not Antimasonic)	3	*18*	—	469	*42*
Antimasonic and Temperance (not 2BUS)	2	*12*	.0235	26	*2*
Antimasonic, 2BUS, and Temperance	5	*29*	.0001	44	*4*

Table 2g. *Worcester town: Free Soil activists, 1848*

	Sample			Universe	
	Number	Percent	P-value	Number	Percent
Total	41				
Linked subtotal	23	*100*		1,217	*100*
Antimasonic petitioners, 1833	6	*26*	.0352	141	*12*
Second Bank of the U.S. petitioners	9	*39*	—	531	*44*
Freemasons to 1830	2	*9*	.1820	42	*3*
Worcester Agricultural Society members	6	*26*	.3472	225	*18*
Temperance petitioners and delegates, 1835–6	12	*52*	.1670	464	*38*
Prolicense activists, 1838	0	—	—	78	*6*
Democratic activists	3	*13*	.0243	44	*4*
National Republic/Whig activists, 1832–6	6	*26*	.0004	76	*6*
New Whigs in 1837	3	*13*	.1497	71	*6*
New Whig activists in 1840	5	*22*	.0485	114	*9*
Antislavery Society members, 1838–40	2	*9*	.1606	40	*3*
Gag-Rule petitioners, 1838, 1840	7	*30*	.0104	148	*12*
Antimasonic petitioners only (not 2BUS)	3	*13*	.2093	79	*6*
Both Antimasonic and Second Bank petitioners	3	*13*	.0943	62	*5*
Second Bank petitioners only (not Antimasonic)	6	*26*	—	469	*39*

Table 3a. *Millbury: Petitions for the abolition of slavery in the District of Columbia, 1835–6*

	Sample			Universe	
	Number	Percent	P-value	Number	Percent
Total petitioners	230				
Linked subtotal	164	*100*		526	*100*
Antimasonic petitioners, 1831–5	75	*46*	.0001	171	*33*
Second Bank of the U.S. petitioners	118	*72*	.0035	330	*63*
Temperance petitioners and delegates, 1835–6	*103*	63	.0001	185	*35*
Freemasons to 1830	9	*5*	—	29	*6*
Worcester Agricultural Society members	7	*4*	—	26	*5*
Whig activists	11	*7*	.0840	23	*4*
Democratic activists	2	*1*	—	9	*2*
Antislavery society members	28	*17*	.0068	60	*11*
Free Soil activists, 1848	3	*2*	.5064	7	*1*
Antimasonic petitioners only (not 2BUS)	22	*13*	—	78	*15*
Antimasonic and Second Bank petitioners	53	*32*	.0001	93	*18*
Second Bank petitioners only (not Antimasonic)	65	*40*[a]	—	237	*45*
Antimasonic and Temperance petitioners (not 2BUS)	11	*7*	.0241	20	*4*
Antimasonic, 2BUS, and Temperance petitioners	33	*20*	.0001	42	*8*
Second Bank and Temperance petitioners (not Antimasonic)	39	*24*	.0001	59	*11*

[a] Positive result when compared with high votes; see p. 411.

Table 3b. *Millbury: Petitions for rescinding the Gag-Rule, 1838–9*

	Sample			Universe	
	Number	Percent	P-value	Number	Percent
Total petitioners	344				
Linked subtotal	162	*100*		592	*100*
Antimasonic petitioners, 1831–5	62	*38*	.0021	171	*29*
Second Bank of the U.S. petitioners	102	*63*	.0304	330	*56*
Temperance petitioners and delegates, 1835–6	80	*49*	.0001	185	*31*
Freemasons to 1830	7	*4*	—	29	*5*
Worcester Agricultural Society members	5	*3*	—	26	*4*
Whig activists	14	*9*	.0007	23	*4*
Democratic activists	2	*1*	—	9	*2*
Antislavery society members	34	*21*	.0001	60	*10*
Slavery in D.C. petitioners	94	*58*	.0001	230	*39*
Free Soil activists, 1848	3	*2*	.3644	7	*1*
Antimasonic petitioners only (not 2BUS)	22	*14*	.8582	78	*13*
Antimasonic and Second Bank petitioners	40	*25*	.0003	93	*16*
Second Bank petitioners only (not Antimasonic)	62	*38*[a]	—	237	*40*
Antimasonic and 2BUS petitioners (not Temperance)	19	*12*	.1002	51	*9*
Antimasonic and Temperance petitioners (not 2BUS)	9	*6*	.0790	20	*3*
Antimasonic, 2BUS, and Temperance petitioners	21	*13*	.0010	42	*7*
Second Bank and Temperance petitioners (not Antimasonic)	34	*21*	.0001	59	*10*

[a] Positive result when compared with high votes; see p. 411.

Table 3c. *Millbury: Petition opposing the admission of Florida, 1839*

	Sample			Universe	
	Number	Percent	P-value	Number	Percent
Total petitioners	185				
Linked subtotal	128	*100*		774	*100*
Antimasonic petitioners, 1831–5	23	*18*	—	171	*22*
Second Bank of the U.S. petitioners	61	*48*	.2093	330	*43*
Temperance petitioners and delegates, 1835–6	52	*41*	.0001	185	*24*
Freemasons to 1830	9	*7*	.0372	29	*4*
Worcester Agricultural Society members	3	*2*	.4881	26	*3*
Whig activists	9	*7*	.0051	23	*3*
Democratic activists	2	*2*	.6461	9	*1*
Antislavery society members	15	*12*	.6930	60	*8*
Slavery in D.C. petitioners	59	*46*	.0001	230	*30*
Gag-Rule petitioners	108	*84*	.0001	344	*44*
Free Soil activists, 1848	2	*2*	—	7	*1*
Antimasonic petitioners only (not 2BUS)	5	*4*	—	78	*10*
Antimasonic and Second Bank petitioners	18	*14*	.4363	93	*12*
Second Bank petitioners only (not Antimasonic)	43	*34[a]*	.4246	237	*31*
Antimasonic, 2BUS, and Temperance petitioners	12	*9*	.0345	42	*5*
Second Bank and Temperance petitioners (not Antimasonic)	28	*22*	.0001	59	*8*

[a] Positive result when compared with high votes; see p. 411.

Table 4a. *East and South Brookfield: Two petitions against the annexation of Texas, 1837*

	Sample			Universe	
	Number	Percent	P-value	Number	Percent
Total petitioners	162				
Linked subtotal	55	*100*		406	*100*
Antimasonic petitioners, 1833, 1834	31	*56*	.0009	146	*36*
Second Bank of the U.S. petitioners	37	*67*	—	277	*68*
Freemasons to 1830	0	—	—	16	*4*
Worcester Agricultural Society members	0	—	—	14	*3*
Whig activists	3	*5*	—	21	*5*
Democratic activists	4	*7*	.0139	9	*2*
Antislavery society members	0	—	—	17	*4*
Free Soil activists, 1848	7	*13*	.0584	27	*7*
Antimasonic petitioners only (not 2BUS)	16	*29*	.0710	81	*20*
Antimasonic and Second Bank petitioners	15	*27*	.0163	65	*16*
Second Bank petitioners only (not Antimasonic)	22	*40*	—	212	*52*

Table 4b. *West Brookfield: Petition against the admission of Florida, 1839*

	Sample			Universe	
	Number	Percent	P-value	Number	Percent
Total petitioners	84				
Linked subtotal	38	*100*		406	*100*
Antimasonic petitioners, 1833, 1834	23	*61*	.0014	146	*36*
Second Bank of the U.S. petitioners	24	*63*	—	277	*68*
Freemasons to 1830	1	*3*	—	16	*4*
Worcester Agricultural Society members	1	*3*	—	14	*3*
Whig activists	3	*8*	.4307	21	*5*
Democratic activists	0	—	—	9	*2*
Antislavery society members	5	*13*	.0075	17	*4*
Free Soil activists, 1848	3	*8*	—	27	*7*
Antimasonic petitioners only (not 2BUS)	11	*29*	.1490	81	*20*
Antimasonic and Second Bank petitioners	12	*32*	.0078	65	*16*
Second Bank petitioners only (not Antimasonic)	12	*32*	—	212	*52*

Table 4c. *Brookfield petition for tariff on boots and shoes, 1843*

	Sample			Universe	
	Number	Percent	P-value	Number	Percent
Total petitioners	202				
Linked subtotal	98	*100*		559	*100*
Antimasonic petitioners, 1833–4	38	*39*	.0019	146	*26*
Second Bank of the U.S. petitioners	50	*51*	.7490	277	*50*
Freemasons to 1830	3	*3*	—	16	*3*
Worcester Agricultural Society members	5	*5*	.0810	14	*3*
Whig activists	14	*14*	.0001	21	*4*
Democratic activists	3	*3*	.2226	9	*2*
Antislavery society members	6	*6*	.5930	17	*3*
Anti-Texas petitioners, 1837	25	*26*	—	162	*29*
Anti-Florida petitioners, 1839	29	*30*	.0001	84	*15*
Free Soil activists, 1848	13	*13*	.0001	27	*5*
Antimasonic petitioners only (not 2BUS)	15	*15*	.8005	81	*14*
Antimasonic and Second Bank petitioners	23	*23*	.0001	65	*12*
Second Bank petitioners only (not Antimasonic)	27	*28*	—	212	*38*

Table 4d. *Brookfield households on the 1840 U.S. Census with persons employed only in manufacturing*

	Sample			Universe	
	Number	Percent	P-value	Number	Percent
Total	151				
Linked subtotal	83	*100*		663	*100*
Antimasonic petitioners, 1833, 1834	18	*22*	—	146	*22*
Second Bank of the U.S. petitioners	28	*34*	—	277	*42*
Freemasons to 1830	0	—	—	16	*2*
Worcester Agricultural Society members	1	*1*	—	14	*2*
Whig activists	5	*6*	.1215	21	*3*
Democratic activists	1	*1*	—	9	*1*
Antislavery society members	3	*4*	.5203	17	*3*
Anti-Texas petitioners, 1837	27	*33*	.0682	162	*24*
Anti-Florida petitioners, 1839	20	*24*	.0011	84	*13*
Shoe tariff petitioners, 1843	40	*48*	.0002	202	*30*
Free Soil activists, 1848	9	*11*	.0018	27	*4*
Antimasonic petitioners only (not 2BUS)	8	*10*	—	81	*12*
Antimasonic and Second Bank petitioners	10	*12*	.4634	65	*10*
Second Bank petitioners only (not Antimasonic)	18	*22*[a]	—	212	*32*

[a] Positive result when compared with high votes; see p. 411.

Table 4e. *Brookfield households on the 1840 U.S. Census with persons employed in both manufacturing and agriculture*

	Sample			Universe	
	Number	Percent	P-value	Number	Percent
Total	39				
Linked subtotal	22	100		663	100
Antimasonic petitioners, 1833, 1834	12	55	.0006	146	22
Second Bank of the U.S. petitioners	8	36	—	277	42
Freemasons to 1830	0	—	—	16	2
Worcester Agricultural Society members	0	—	—	14	2
Whig activists	0	—	—	21	3
Democratic activists	1	5	.2209	9	1
Antislavery Society members	0	—	—	17	3
Anti-Texas petitioners, 1837	8	36	.1912	162	24
Anti-Florida petitioners, 1839	5	23	.1579	84	13
Shoe tariff petitioners, 1843	8	36	.5423	202	30
Free Soil activists, 1848	1	5	—	27	4
Antimasonic petitioners only (not 2BUS)	8	36	.0012	81	12
Antimasonic and Second Bank petitioners	4	18	.1885	65	10
Second Bank petitioners only (not Antimasonic)	4	18	—	212	32

Table 4f. *Brookfield households on the 1840 U.S. Census with persons employed only in agriculture*

	Sample			Universe	
	Number	Percent	P-value	Number	Percent
Total	260				
Linked subtotal	146	*100*		663	*100*
Antimasonic petitioners, 1833, 1834	44	*30*	.0078	146	*22*
Second Bank of the U.S. petitioners	65	*45*	.4472	277	*42*
Freemasons to 1830	2	*1*	—	16	*2*
Worcester Agricultural Society members	1	*1*	—	14	*2*
Whig activists	9	*6*	.0243	21	*3*
Democratic activists	7	*5*	.0015	9	*1*
Antislavery society members	6	*4*	.1887	17	*3*
Anti-Texas petitioners, 1837	44	*30*	.0703	162	*24*
Anti-Florida petitioners, 1839	30	*21*	.0013	84	*13*
Shoe tariff petitioners, 1843	45	*31*	—	202	*30*
Free Soil activists, 1848	2	*1*	—	27	*4*
Antimasonic petitioners only (not 2BUS)	22	*15*	.2350	81	*12*
Antimasonic and Second Bank petitioners	22	*15*	.0169	65	*10*
Second Bank petitioners only (not Antimasonic)	43	*29[a]*	—	212	*32*

[a] Positive result when compared with high votes; see p. 411.

Index

Baptists (*cont.*)
  petition to king, 80–1; as artisans, 88–90;
  wealth, 90–2; ambitions, 90–2; ritual
  practice, 93–6; and military service, 111,
  116–17; and Revolutionary crisis, 156,
  160–5; and Constitutionalism, 159–88;
  challenge to orthodoxy, 159–60; and rioting
  in early 1780s, 201–4; class division in
  Regulation, 219–22; and textile
  manufacturing, 286–91; and Antimasonry,
  326, 345; and antislavery petitioning, 365–6;
  and Liberty voting, 369; and Free Soil-
  Republican voting, 373–4, 386
Barre, 303; core Regulator town, 213n;
  Federalist convention in 1808, 250, 283
Batchellor family (North Brookfield), 300, 324,
  334
Belcher, Governor Jonathan, and the Land
  Bank, 57, 61, 102–6, 113, 121, 237; and the
  Great Awakening, 66–67, 70
Berkshire Country, Constitutionalists in, 159n;
  indifference to price regulation, 194; woolen
  production, 276
Bernard, Francis, Gov., 156, patronage and
  voting, 132–3
Bigelow family (Worcester), 136, 137, 143, 155,
  195, 214, 268
black Americans, 45, 255, 312, 378, 385, 396
Blackstone Canal, 5, 306–7, 308, 339
Blackstone Valley, xv, 25, 118; and Land Bank,
  57; in Great Awakening, 69, 75, in
  Revolutionary crisis, 149; manufacturing in,
  271, 275, 292, 294; *see also* southeast towns
Blake, Francis, 263, 283
Blanchard family (Millbury), 338, 343
Blunt, John, Rev., 77, 80
boot and shoe manufacturing, concentrated in
  the central corridor, 294; organization and
  sociology of, 294–9; as an "adaptive
  traditionalism," 299, 396; Democratic-
  Republicans, 299–300; and 1816 direct tax,
  300; and Land Bank tradition, 302; and
  Antimasonry, 321, 332–5; 1843 tariff petition
  and Free Soil, 375, 381, 383, 427;
  centralization in 1850s, 394–5; strike in 1860,
  395, and Civil War crisis, 395–7
boot and shoe towns (1830–1860), wealth in,
  296n; persistence in, 299n; and Antimasonry,
  295, 329, 365–6; vs. antislavery petitioning,
  365–6; and Free Soil-Republican voting,
  365–6, 373–5; 384; *see* central corridor, shop
  production
Boston, 26, 28, 32, 49, 97, 153, 192, 211–12,
  317, 320–1, 323, Stamp act riot, 134–5,
  connections with Leicester and Worcester,
  135, 154, 317–18; committee of
  Correspondence, 142–3, 145, Tea Party,

143–4; Antimasonic leadership, 311, 327–9,
  340, 353
Boston Baptist Church, 75, 84, 87–8, 174
Boston Post Road, 27, 30, 38, 39–40, 292, 329
Bowdoin, James, Gov., 209, 225
Brazier, Samuel, Jr., 264, 266, 284
Brookfield, 27, 35, 49, 74, 118n, 241, 273–4;
  represented, 31, 97, 103, 107, 115, 117, 245;
  early settlement, 7–13, 21, 25; incorporation,
  17, 19, 24; South Parish, 38, 93, 240–1, 271;
  east neighborhood, 84; North Parish, 34–5,
  52, 84, 93, 110, 132, 146, 177; West Parish,
  156, 233, 240; and Land Bank, 61, 107, 136,
  195; Whitefield at, 67, 73; Hall at, 73;
  revolutionary politics in, 136, 143, 146;
  Congregational church admissions,
  1774–1782, 152, 177; support for Article III,
  184–5; debtors and creditors, 1785–6,
  210–13; Regulators and Friends of
  Government, 215–21, 245; Regulator
  petition, 223; Pro-Government Protest 223,
  241, 242n, 381; Federalists in 245, 263;
  Democratic-Republicans in, 254; Antimasons
  in, 324, 329–30; shoemaking and
  Antimasonary, 334–5, 342, 395, 428–30;
  Unitarian controversy and disestablishment,
  348–9; 1840 Census of, 334–5, 428–430;
  Democratic Antimasons in, 355, 380–1, 395;
  temperance and revivals, 244–5, 356–7;
  anti-Texas and anti-Florida petitioners in,
  369–70, 426; Free Soil, 380–1; cooperative
  store, 381; 1851 "land bank" petition, 381;
  see also North Brookfield, West Brookfield
Brookfield Association, 93, 118n
Brookfield Baptist Church and Society, 84,
  185–6, 300
Brown, John, Capt. (1703–1791), Land Banker
  at Louisburg, 111; Popular partisan, 114,
  116n, 117; Whig leader, 134–8; involved in
  economic politics of 1770s, 170; brother
  Samuel, 60, 61, 137; son Benjamin, 194; son
  John, 221
Burbank family (Millbury), 272, 330
burials, 23, as Congregation ritual, 94–5,
  Bapist, 94
Burns, Anthony, 385, 392
Burroughs, Stephen, 219

Calvinism, moderate, 93, revived, 239, 260–1;
  challenged by Bangs, 265
Callender, Elisha, 84, 86
capitalism, and the post-Revolutionary
  transformation of the economy, 307–9
card-manufacturing, *see* machine-card
  manufacturing
Central Bank, Worcester, 306, 318, 341
central corridor (1820–1861), defined, 118n,

Republican coalition, 252–3, 257–9, 267; and "cotton mill fever," 286–91; *see* Baptists, disestablishment of religion, Methodists, Quakers, Separate Congregationalists, Shakers, Universalists

Dorr, Joseph, Rev., as New Light, 69, opposes itinerancy, 74

Douglass, Universalists in, 184, riot in, 204, 291; Antifederalism, 228, 234

Dudley, 20, 36, 48, 56, 69, 110–11, 116n, 118n; represented, 117; Constitutionalism in, 171; de facto pluralism in, 181, 183; Universalists in, 184, 203–4; and rioting, 203–4, 206; Masons in, 248; textile manufacturing in, 285, 291, 304; Whigs in, 316; Workingmen's vote, 320

Dudley Baptist Church and Society, 171, revival, 177

Dudley Congregational Church and Society, 183

Dudley Woolen Manufacturing Company, 316

Dudley, Jospeph, Gov., 56–7, 98

Dudley, Paul, 57, 64–5

Dudley, Samuel, 72, 90, 102, 104, 126, dwelling house, dimensions, 38–39, 240

Dwight, Joseph, as Brookfield magnate, 30–1, 39, 50, 125; opposed to Land Bank, 62, 103, 107; and Great Awakening, 67, 73, 120; at Louisburg, 109–110

Dwight, Timothy, Rev., 1–2, 11, 389

Earle family (Leicester and Worcester), 1, 275–7, 337, 338n, 371

Eaton, Joshua, Rev., 21, 79–80, 93

economic politics, Land Bank, 55–65, 102–8, 121–4; and Revolutionary crisis, 136–42; 1776–1779, 168–71, 192–6; 1781–1787, 196–209, 291, 361; and First Party system, 278–911; and Second Party System, 313–19; and Antimasonry, 327–344, 252

economy, provincial, 31–65; role of dissenters, 83–92; economy, 1789–1830, 269–309; 1830–1834, 331–44; 1834–1840, 354, 356, education, Federalist view of, 260–1; Republican view of, 266; Workingmen's argument about, 310–11; Whig views, 310–11

Edwards, Johnatan, Rev., 66, 69, 74

elections, federal, 1788–1789, 234–6; 1790, 235–7; 1796, 237; 1800, 247–8, 262; 1840, 359–60; 1844–1848, 372–5; 1856, 386; 1860, 387–8

elections, gubernatorial, 1780–1786, 224, 244; 1787, 225; 1788–1796, 236–7, 244, 273; 1798–1815, 247–8, 251–3, 257–9; 1823–1825, 303; 1826, 329; 1825–1834, 323–5; 1831–1834, 325n, 329; 1835–1836,

355; 1838–1840, 248, 358–60; 1850–1856, 383–7

Embargo of 1807, 262, 273, 277, 283

emigration, 5, 238, 274, 302

estimated electorate, 224–5n, 399–403

Evans, George Henry, 379, 381

Ewing, John Rev., 77–8

exchange, among orthodox yeoman households, 51–3, among Baptist household, 88–90

Excise of 1754, 113

Excise of 1785, 208, 208n, 213,

Explanatory Charter of 1726, 101–2

Fayette Lodge (Charlton), 245, 248–9

Federalists, xvii, 216, 233–4, 270; 1788–1796, 234–8; and voluntary associations, 242–7, party organization, 250–1; unopposed in north after 1800, 252–3, 257–9, 262–3, 293, 301; and courts, 255–6; and Popular orthodoxy, 258–9, Harringtonian rhetoric in 1812, 262–3, 358; 1808 and 1812 conventions, 250, 262–3, 283; popular, 54, 262–3, 271, 323, 352; and commerce and domestic manufacturing, 273–8, 299, 329, 335, 344; and turnpikes and banks, 278–83; and woolen textiles, 288–90; contested towns and Antimasonry, 323–7

Fifteen Gallon Law, 356–60

Finneyite Congregational revivals (1827–1834), and temperance, 344–6, 356–60; and antislavery petitioning, 365–6, 369; and Liberty voting, 365, 369; and abolition, 376; and Republican voting, 374, 386; *see also* Congregational orthodoxy, New Divinity Revivals

First Massachusetts Turnpike Corporation, 279–80

First Party System, xvii, 247–59, 26–3, 269–70; collapse, 267–8; and politics of development and independence, 270, 279–83, 270, 283–91

Fiscal Protest, 1777, 167, 171, 193, 202, 252; and Popular tradition, 167, 169–71, 204–6, 206n; vs. Regulation, 206–7, 214

Fish, Elisha, Rev., 150–1, 160

Fisk, Daniel, Deacon, as Separate Baptist, 78, 80, 91, gravestone, 127n; as Constitutionalist, 166, 290; as representative, 168; grandson Moses Fisk, Henry, Lt., as Separate Baptist, 78, 80, 91, 377; as representative, 117, 168; gravestone, 127n; as Constitutionalist, 166, 290; protests approval of Art. III, 181; grandson Henry, 377

Fiske, Nathan, Rev., 24, 38, 93, in Revolutionary crisis, 149–51, 160, 240, 241, 242n, 246, 261

Fiske, Oliver, Dr., 261, 268, 280

economic politics, 194; and Antifederalism, 235; and Antimasonry in Leicester, 342–3

Separate Congregationalists, 76–83

Shakers, 185

Shay's Rebellion, *see* Regulation

Shirley, William, Gov., xvii, 68, 101, 156; Plan of Civil Government, 99; retires Land Bank, 106–8, 113; as governor, 108–14, 121, 124, 133; resumption of hard currency, 169, 192

shoe manufacturing, *see* boot and shoe manufacturing

Shoe Tariff petition of 1843, 375, 381, 383, 427

shop production, xvii-xviii; as middle ground between agriculture and factory labor, 270–1, 294–9, 334–5, 352, 394–7

shop towns of 1820, and central corridor, 292–9; and Land Bank and Popular orthodoxy, 139, 302–3, and Antimasonry, 295, 329, 352, 365–6, 383; vs. antislavery petitioning, 365–6, and Free Soil voting, 365–6; *see also* boot and shoe manufacturing, central corridor

Shrewsbury, 118n, 136, 189, 234, 323

Sibley, Jonas L., 316, 318, 342

Silver Bank of 1740, 57, 103, 106, 109

Singletary, Amos, Deacon, involved in Popular economic politics, 169, 229, 235, 291; mediator for Regulators, 226; as Antifederalist, 169, 226, 228–9, 237–8, 263, 382

Sixth Principle (Baptist) Association, 77–8, 96

Slater, George, as cultural Antimason, 336

Slater, Samuel, 5, 275–6, 304, 315, 336; and Oxford Bank, 305, 342

slave trade in Washington, D.C., petitions against, 360–1, 378, 423; petitioners and Moral Whiggery, 363–8

slavery, 45, 1767 Worcester instructions against, 140; abolition in Massachusetts, 255; abolitionists vs., 376–8

social libraries, 246

Society for the Encouragement of American Industry, 304

Southbridge Bank, 305, 342

Southbridge, Democratic-Republicans in, 284, Federalists in, 258n, 324–5; Nationals and Democrats in, 315; Antimasons in, 324–5, 330, 334, 336; textile manufacturing in, 272, 285, 291, 304, 315n, 334; abolitionist controversy, 376–7

Southbridge Manfacturing Company, 288, 315

South Brimfield, 77, 78, 80, 181, 184

Southborough, 30, 133

south county towns (1820–1861), textile industry, 290, 297; Democratic-Republicans in, 297, 302; Nationals in, 329; Democrats in, 297, 302, 373–5; *see also* central corridor, north county towns

Southgate family (Leicester), 78, 86, 212, 222

southeast region (1740–1820), defined, 118n; as Land Bank and Popular stronghold, 119, 121–4, 126–8; economic and constitutional politics in 1770s, 171, 208, opposition to Article III, 180, 185, conflicted in Regulation, 202, 213–15, Antifederalist voting, 1788–1789, 235, and First Party politics, 252–3, 257–8; *see also* Blackstone Valley, northeast region, northwest region

southwest region (1740–1820) defined, 118n; provincial politics, 121; Constitutional politics, 171, 204–8, opposition to Article III, 180, 185; and rioting of the early 1780s, 201–7; conflicted in Regulation, 202, 213–15; Federalist voting, 1788–9, 234–5; and Democratic-Republicans, 253, 257–9

Spencer, 6, 21, 22, 52–3, 89, 118n, 135; represented, 136, 246; Land Bank subscribers in, 135–7, 195, 214; separates and Baptists in 78–80, 116, in Revolutionary crisis, 135, 143, 151; economic politics 195, 214; protests Excise, proposes bank of paper money, 207, 279; calls convention, 209; debtors and creditors, 1785–1786, 210–13; core Regulator town, 213n; Regulators, 214–21, 243; Federalists, 245, 282; Democratic-Republicans, 282; bank petitioners, 282

Spencer Congregational Church and Society, 53, 79, 111, adopts Halfway Convenant, 93, admissions, 1774–1780, 151, 177

Spence, Thomas, 379

Sprague, Asa, and Leicester Academy, 186–7, debtor, surety, 221, dissenter-Regulator, 221–2

Spurr, John, 254–5, 282, 288

Stamp Act, 131, 133–5, 137–8, 144

State Bank, 282

Status rankings, 45–6; and debt, 49–50; and Land Bank subscribers, 58

Stephens family (Brookfield), 84, 88

Stoddard, Solomon, Rev., 24

Stone, Lucy, 377

Sturbridge, 19, 22, 88, 116n, 118n, 194, 325; represented, 117, 134, 168, 286, 323; Marcy family, 36–7, debtors, 49, and the Great Awakening, 76–8, in Revolution, 143, 148, 162; Constitutionalists in, 166–8, 171; approval of Article III protested, 181; pluralism accepted, 181–2; Universalists in, 184; Methodists in, 185; riot in, 204; debtors and creditors, 1785–1786, 210–13, Regulators and Friends of Government, 215–21, Democratic-Republicans in, 250, 254–5; textile manufacturing in, 285–6